Joint Ventures and Shareholders' Agreements

Joint Ventures and Shareholders' Agreements

Sixth Edition

Susan Singleton, LL B, Solicitor
Singletons
www.singlelaw.com

Bloomsbury Professional

LONDON · DUBLIN · EDINBURGH · NEW YORK · NEW DELHI · SYDNEY

BLOOMSBURY PROFESSIONAL
Bloomsbury Publishing Plc
50 Bedford Square, London, WC1B 3DP
1385 Broadway, New York, NY 10018, USA
29 Earlsfort Terrace, Dublin 2, Ireland

BLOOMSBURY and the Diana logo are trademarks of Bloomsbury Publishing Plc

British Library Cataloguing-in-Publication Data

A catalogue record for this book is available from the British Library.

ISBN:	Paper:	978 1 52651 608 4
	ePDF:	978 1 52651 610 7
	ePub:	978 1 52651 609 1

Typeset by Evolution Design & Digital Ltd, Kent
Printed and bound by CPI Group (UK) Ltd, Croydon, CR0 4YY

To find out more about our authors and books visit
www.bloomsburyprofessional.com. Here you will find extracts, author information,
details of forthcoming events and the option to sign up for our newsletters

Dedication

To my solicitor daughters, Rachel, Head of Banking and Finance Policy at Macfarlanes and Rebecca, ex Head of Legal at M&C Saatchi and now a freelance solicitor. To my twin sons Joe and Sam who started the Legal Practice Course this year – 2021. May you all continue to have as much fun in the law as I continue to do.

To my oldest son Ben who works for Ocado and whose academic path was ancient history rather than law.

To my grandchildren Rose and Frederick and the new baby, their cousin, due in December 2021. You have it all before you.

Preface to the sixth edition

I have now produced the fourth, fifth and sixth editions of this book. In the eight years since I took over the book the essence of joint ventures has remained the same. The challenges and the market for joint ventures varies, but the essential common law which applies to them and the Companies Acts over the years are remarkably similar in good times and bad, as much during the 2020 and 2021 Covid-19 (coronavirus) pandemic as in other times.

The UK left the EU on 31 January 2020 and this sixth edition is published as the post-Brexit transitional period is over and as the world remains paralysed by the global pandemic. However, joint venture activity continues as it always does in economically difficult times when entities often need to merge or collaborate with others to survive. Although in 2021 there was a reduction in mergers activity compared with pre-pandemic days joint venture activity has continued.

Part A of the book, the first 12 chapters, covers introductory and important issues such as contributions of the parties to a joint venture, employment and pensions issues, share incentive schemes, tax and the like as well as competition law.

From 1 January 2021 the EU Merger Regulation 139/2004 has not applied in the UK as the Brexit transitional period ended on 31 December 2020 following the UK's departure from the EU (and EEA) on 31 January 2020. In December 2020 the EU and UK agreed the EU-UK Trade and Co-operation Agreement. Yet where a UK merger involves EU companies the EU merger legislation remains relevant and is still included in this book. In any event the UK Enterprise Act 2002 (as amended) continues to set out the law on UK mergers. The UK has issued at least 1000 Statutory Instruments, in addition to the European Union (Withdrawal Agreement) Act 2020, to ensure existing UK legislation based on EU law in most areas continues unaffected by the 2021 changed relationship with the EU. Nevertheless readers should check on a case-by-case basis the Brexit implications of particular transactions and legislation as the position can be complex in some areas.

The fact some mergers will be examined by both EU and UK regulatory authorities will add to costs in the very few mergers which fall within the EU Merger Regulation. Brexit may lead to fewer mergers notified to the EU as UK turnover of a business or group is now excluded from calculations under the EU Merger Regulation. Chapter 9 covers EC competition law (Application of EC competition law to joint ventures) and Chapter 10 the UK position (UK competition law applying to joint ventures). Other regulatory matters are covered in Chapter 11.

Part B of the book covers key issues in structuring and drafting UK corporate joint venture documentation and shareholders' agreements. Part B also includes Chapter 13 on deadlock, Chapter 14 on minority protection, and Chapter 15 about typical minority vetoes. Put and call options, pre-emption rights on share transfers also have their own chapters. Chapter 22 covers share valuation and Chapter 23 dispute resolution.

Part C of the book (Chapters 24–28) addresses joint ventures and shareholders' agreements in practice and covers a wide range of topics including due diligence, warranties and indemnities and international joint ventures.

Part D ends the book with three case studies and then the seven precedents appear including a Shareholders' Agreement and Heads of Agreement.

Changes in taxation rates and tax law where relevant are included in this sixth edition of Joint Ventures and Shareholders' Agreements in particular in Chapter 7 (Tax considerations for UK joint ventures).

As with the fifth edition, the seven precedents, which are an important part of this book, are available to download, rather than being issued on a CD Rom.

Company law develops over the decades, the Companies Act 2006 being the current principal statue as most readers will know, following on from the Companies Act 1985 and before that the Companies Act 1948. English company law may well become longer and longer and develops both by statute and case law, but the essence of the private limited company remains the same as when it was set up largely by our Victorian ancestors.

By the 1400s English law was giving limited liability status to monasteries and trade guilds which held property in common. In 1600 the East India Company was given its Royal Charter, that company having been formed in 1599. The USA permitted limited liability companies in 1811. This was before the UK did so in 1855, and was less than 30 years after the USA won the war of independence from the UK. In the UK during the Victorian age there were concerns about allowing investors to walk away from insolvent companies which indeed is one reason many merchant banks remained as partnerships with full personal liability to investors until at least the 1990s with some firms, such as the writer's firm of solicitors Singletons in 2021, remaining subject to unlimited liability to this day. In the UK the Joint Stock Companies Act 1844 permitted a form of company under statute, but it was the Limited Liability Act 1855 which brought the modern form of limited liability company to the UK over 40 years after the USA had done so.

Not all joint ventures involve limited companies, although this book is about those which do. Plenty of collaboration agreements and profit sharing arrangements are set up without even a limited company held in common. The variety of joint venture is wide. It is always worth discussing the various kinds with the client before it decides what form of collaboration it needs. Sometimes a simple arrangement where the parties share commission or profits is possible instead of a new company.

Thanks continue to be due to Simmons and Simmons, as without their hard work on the first three editions of the book, this new 6th edition would not have come about. Again I thank the publishers at Bloomsbury, particularly Ellie Coull and Andy Hill and also my clients and family for their support.

Finally, a word of warning, repeated from the last edition but always worth remembering – solicitors must be sure in giving advice on joint ventures whether they are acting for one joint venture party only or the joint venture company as their professional duty will be to that person or entity only. Also make this clear in writing to the client and advise the other parties to take their own separate independent legal advice.

Elizabeth Susan Singleton

September 2021

susan@singlelaw.com
Singletons, Solicitors
www.singlelaw.com
twitter: @singlelaw

Preface to the fifth edition

I have had the privilege of producing the fourth and now the fifth edition of this work. The challenges of forming successful joint ventures and reaching amicable agreement between shareholders whilst complying with a vast array of laws from company law to contract law, competition law to rules on intellectual property always continue. As a practising solicitor with a wide range of work in this field I see both the setting up of such arrangements but also handle many a dispute between shareholders, often between those who have no written agreement and who usually later regret that fact.

The aim of the book continues to be to guide the reader in all relevant areas of law in this field. It is unlikely that 2019 Brexit will change some of the law described herein, although it may become necessary for the very rare larger mergers to obtain competition law clearance in both the EU and UK and some of the relevant legislation might ultimately end up slightly different from current harmonised EU legislation. However most of the issues relevant to joint ventures will be unchanged when the UK leaves the EU.

Thanks continue to be due to Simmons and Simmons, as without their hard work on the first three editions of the book, this new 5th edition would not have come about. Again I thank the publishers at Bloomsbury, particularly Andy Hill, and also to my clients whose many and varied joint venture agreements and disputes teach me on a continuous basis how better to draft agreements and anticipate problems. It is an advantage to come from a family of psychiatrists in dealing with joint ventures and negotiations of disputes in this field and readers should bear in mind that the aim of these agreements is not to hammer the collaborating partner into submission and a deal they will resent from day two, but to set up workable relatively fair arrangements which protect the parties appropriately. A 1% shareholder of course should not expect the protection of a 40% minority shareholder and common sense needs to be applied in achieving a suitable agreement.

Finally, a word of warning – solicitors must be sure in giving advice on joint ventures whether they are acting for one joint venture party only or the joint venture company as their professional duty will be to that person or entity only. Also make this clear in writing to the client and advise the other parties to take their own separate independent legal advice.

Elizabeth Susan Singleton

August 2017

susan@singlelaw.com
Singletons, Solicitors
www.singlelaw.com
twitter: @singlelaw

Preface to the fourth edition

This fourth edition includes all changes since the Companies Act 2006 came into force, including merger law changes in the Enterprise and Regulatory Reform Act 2013 which are likely to come into force in 2014 and the Financial Services Act 2012 which abolished the FSA and replaced it with the Financial Conduct Authority (FCA) and Prudential Regulation Authority.

However the principal legal rules relating to joint ventures are materially unchanged, and even the Companies Act 2006 did not make major changes to the structure or law surrounding such agreements. Tax rate changes are noted in the new edition as are other competition law changes although the EU and UK merger threshold levels are unchanged.

The economic climate has resulted in more 'fire sale' joint ventures, those borne of administration and those set up by individuals who have suffered redundancy from their previous employer. The original authors who deserve most credit for the work 13 years ago were correct to make the book 'a one-stop general guide to the issues relevant in structuring and negotiating agreements between two or more shareholders in any type of private company, be they corporates, individuals, institutional investors or a combination of these'. The fourth edition in 2013 continues that tradition. There is no legal definition of a joint venture and in my practice at Slaughter and May, Bristows and more recently at my own solicitor's firm (Singletons) joint ventures take many forms. However, what they have in common is that they are a contract setting out how two or more people will operate a business. This book seeks to provide an update and thorough grounding in such agreements.

Any mistakes are mine. Thanks are, of course, due to Simmons and Simmons, as without their hard work on the first three editions of the book, this new 4th edition would not have come about. I would also like to thank the publishers at Bloomsbury, particularly Andy Hill, and also to my clients whose vast array of joint venture agreements and complex competition and intellectual property queries relating to them over the years regularly add to my understanding and knowledge.

Susan Singleton

September 2013

susan@singlelaw.com
Singletons, Solicitors
www.singlelaw.com
twitter: @singlelaw

Preface to the third edition

The third edition of this book is timed to coincide with the passing into law of the final provisions of the Companies Act 2006 on 1 October 2009. This legislation has been long in the making. It stems originally from an independent steering group who were commissioned by the DTI in 1998 to consider how company law could be modernised to provide 'a simple, efficient and cost effective framework for British business in the twenty-first century'. Whether it has succeeded in this objective or produced more uncertainty through a series of arguably unnecessary, inconsistent and, in some cases, ill thought out changes I will leave for others to judge!

Certainly, in the context of joint ventures many of the changes are more of form than substance although the introduction of a new derivative claim procedure extends considerably the statutory rights of minority shareholders in joint venture companies and the new Model Articles, which replace Table A, introduce a number of important changes.

This new edition has also been fully updated to reflect other changes in English law, particularly tax law, some of which have been quite substantial.

As ever, the production of this new edition has required assistance from numerous contributors, both within the various legal departments of Simmons & Simmons and from outside firms. I am particularly grateful to my partner Jo Weston, who is Head of our Professional Support team, for her patience and hard work in coordinating our collective efforts and applying a fine legal eye to the final results. My grateful thanks are also due to everyone who has helped in this collective effort.

Chris Wilkinson

July 2009

Preface to the second edition

The second edition of this book was meant to coincide with the passing into law of the Companies Bill, proposals for which were outlined in 'Modernising Company Law', published in July 2002. However, the bill has suffered various delays and no timetable for it is as yet forthcoming. It appears possible that the legislation will be introduced on a piecemeal basis.

Even though it has not been possible fully to reflect this proposed legislation, there have been sufficient other developments in the four years since the first edition was published to warrant a second. Both UK and European Union Competition laws have been overhauled by the Enterprise Act 2002 and the EC Merger Regulation 2004. There have been numerous tax changes which have necessitated much rewriting throughout the text. Various regulatory changes and the implementation of the Financial Services and Markets Act 2000 (which had not been achieved at the time of the first edition) have led to considerable amendment to the UK regulatory chapter. Limited Liability Partnerships have become available in the UK, which appear to be promising vehicles for joint ventures, and a new chapter has been added about them, together with a precedent for an LLP agreement. Numerous overseas developments have necessitated changes to Table 8. The introduction of international accounting standards has led to considerable additions to the accounting chapter. Pensions law has been overhauled by the Pensions Act 2004.

The proposals contained in the White Paper have been noted at the appropriate points in the text, and whilst they are far-reaching they are not likely to make very much difference to the methods and concepts employed in structuring joint ventures; the changes are more technical than substantive.

The law is stated by reference to the materials available to the authors on 19 November 2004. The Gambling Bill failed to reach the statute book by the end of the 2003/04 session of parliament; the information given about it is based on the latest available published version of the bill and may be subject to change before it is enacted. The Pensions Act 2004 received the Royal Assent at the very end of the session, but had not been published in its final form at the time this edition went to press and the information given about it must be regarded as rather provisional. The information given about international accounting standards should be similarly regarded; although the statutory instrument to bring in the new standards had just been made at the time of gong to press, the full implications of them will only become apparent as they are applied in practice.

Developments will doubtless continue apace. The Listing Rules are due to be overhauled and, whilst one important proposed change of importance to joint ventures has been noted, others may emerge. In the light of the

Lenz and *Manninen* decisions of the European Court of Justice (15 July and 7 September 2004 respectively) the UK tax system is in danger of being held to be discriminatory as between UK-resident and non-resident EU sources of income, contrary to the EU Treaty, which could lead to some far- reaching tax changes. The Chancellor has, as usual, announced a large number of tax avoidance measures in his pre-budget statement of 2 December 2004, which it has not been possible to reflect in this edition. These include measures relating to employee held shares (Chapter 27), controlled foreign companies and double taxation relief (Chapter 29) and options (Chapter 18). Whilst these measures are designed to attack deliberate tax avoidance, those chapters will need to be read with due regard to them.

As ever, the authors remain solely responsible for any errors or omissions.

As with the first edition, the second could not have been produced without a small army of contributors from both inside and outside Simmons & Simmons. Our grateful thanks is due to all of them.

Andrew Comben

Chris Wilkinson

December 2004

Preface to the first edition

This book originated with a request from the publishers for a practice manual on joint ventures which have become an increasingly sophisticated and widely used business medium in many industries and activities. The principal author immediately realised that since a joint venture is only a specialised form of a shareholders agreement and the issues which tend to arise between shareholders or intending shareholders are always essentially the same, the book might usefully be expanded to cover shareholders' agreements generally. The result is a book which, whilst mainly concentrating on joint venture companies established by two or more corporates (which is what is generally meant by a joint venture), is also offered as a one-stop general guide to the issues relevant in structuring and negotiating agreements between two or more shareholders in any type of private company, be they corporates, individuals, institutional investors or a combination of these.

Although concentrating on corporate vehicles, coverage is also given to certain aspects of non-corporate joint ventures, with a comparison between various different types of venture included in Chapter 1. We have concentrated on the issues which we believe most commonly arise in practice, including some which are not generally dealt with in other books, and we have tried to adopt a practical approach to each of them. The case law relating specifically to shareholders' agreements and articles of association is scanty, and we have endeavoured to suggest solutions to some of the difficulties which the law has not yet entirely resolved.

As with all authors of legal textbooks, we are greatly indebted to those who have gone before us. We have consulted much previously published material. In particular, we would like to mention Shareholders' Agreements by Graham Steadman and Janet Jones, which contains useful material on the enforcement of shareholders' agreements and articles of association, and minority protection generally. The various PLC publications contain some useful material and the established general works on company law, such as Gore Browne and Tolley, have been freely consulted. The principal source for this book is, however, the accumulated practical experience of the authors, gained over many years of acting in joint ventures and arrangements between shareholders of every kind, during the course of which we have been influenced by many ideas and solutions suggested by other practitioners, both in collaboration and opposition. Grateful acknowledgment is made to all of them, but the authors of course remain solely responsibility for any errors or omissions.

Andrew Comben
Chris Wilkinson
October 2000

About the author

Susan Singleton is a solicitor with her own London firm of solicitors, Singletons, which specialises in business law including corporate law, competition law, intellectual property law, IT/ecommerce and general commercial law. She advises on shareholders' agreements and joint ventures on a regular basis. Trained at Nabarro (now CMS), she joined Slaughter and May's EC/Competition Law Department on qualifying as a solicitor, moving to Bristows, where she remained until founding her own firm. Since then she has advised well over 1000 clients from all over the world. She has acted in a range of major competition cases including in the Court of Appeal in relation to internet selling policies and EU competition law and in the first UK damages action for breach of competition law to reach an English court (*Arkin v Borchard and Others*). She often advises in merger notification cases and also advises agents and principals in litigation relating to agency law under the Commercial Agents (Council Directive) Regulation 1993. Her clients range from major plcs and institutions to small start up businesses and are from all over the world. In 2015–2016 she acted from the tipping paper claimants in judicial review proceedings in two cases in the tobacco sector relating to EU and national packaging law in the High Court, Court of Appeal and CJEU.

She regularly advises on business sales, whether sale of a business or sale of shares, and has a network of contacts which can be used for bigger acquisitions.

She is author of over 30 law books on topics such as internet and e-commerce law, competition law, commercial agency law, data protection legislation and intellectual property. In 2010 she acquired IT Law Today, Corporate Briefing (both of which she also edits), Finance and Credit Law and International Trade Finance subscription journals from Informa. Several years later she acquired Farm Law, Housing Law Monitor, Education Law Monitor, Environmental Law Monthly, Food & Drink Law Monthly, and Pensions Today from Informa. All ten subscription journals are sold to subscribers in the UK and abroad. She is author of *Beswick and Wine: Buying and Selling Private Companies and Businesses* (10th edn, Bloomsbury Professional, 2018) and co-author of *Buying and Selling Insolvent Companies and Businesses* (Bloomsbury Professional). Three times a year she updates her book *Business the Internet and the Law* and is a contributing author and regular updater of *EContracts*, both of which books are now part of *Intellectual Property and IT* (both published by Bloomsbury). In 2020 and 2021 she updated the data protection and freedom of information law volume of LexisNexis' *Encyclopaedia of Forms and Precedents* to reflect new data protection legislation, most notably the Data Protection Act 2018, GDPR (and 'UKGDPR' from 1 January 2021) and Brexit. She wrote the 5th edition of Bloomsbury's *E-Commerce and Convergence – A Guide to the Law of Digital Media* (published 2021). For about 20 years she edited Kluwer's three volume looseleaf *Comparative Law of Monopolies* until it ceased publication in 2020. Her first book was published in 1992 – *Introduction to Competition Law.*

She has spoken over the years at about 1700 legal conferences around the world in areas such as contract law, data protection and intellectual property, competition and commercial law fields having spoken in Iran, Dubai, Trinidad, Nigeria and extensively around the EU/UK.

Until 2016 she was Vice Chairman of the Competition Law Association and is on the EC/Laws Committee of the Licensing Executives Society (EC/Laws Committee). Until 2012 for five years she sat as an independent member/ Director on the Direct Marketing Commission. She has five adult children and lives in London (Pinner Hill). Her hobbies include gardening, playing the piano and singing.

E. Susan Singleton
Singletons
Solicitors

Tel: 020 8866 1934

www.singlelaw.com
Email: susan@singlelaw.com
Twitter: @singlelaw

About Singletons, Solicitors

Singletons is a London firm of commercial law solicitors which provides advice to clients from all over the UK and abroad, from large plcs to small start up businesses, in the area covered by this book including the following:

– joint venture and partnership agreements

– commercial litigation/disputes

– competition law – advisory and guidance, litigation, CMA, EU

– intellectual property

– IT/e-commerce law particularly data protection law

– commercial agency regulations and claims

– agency and distribution agreements

Contents

Contents

Contents

Contents

Contents

Contents

Part C Joint ventures and shareholders' agreements in practice

Contents

Part D Case studies and precedents

Table of statutes

Table of statutory instruments

Table of cases

Table of cases

Table of cases

Table of European material

DECISIONS

Part A

Preliminary considerations

Chapter 1

Introduction

Summary

This chapter defines the nature of a joint venture and deals with some reasons and motivations for establishing them. It provides outline guidance on the main forms of joint venture, the special features of each and illustrates the importance of ensuring that a joint venture is adequately documented. Although this chapter is written from a mainly UK viewpoint, international joint ventures are considered.

1 What is a joint venture?

1.1   'Joint venture' is a term without any precise legal definition under English law, but may be described as an arrangement between two or more parties who pool their resources and collaborate in carrying on a business activity with a view to mutual profit. The parties may also agree to share the risks involved, but the degree to which they do so will vary depending upon the particular structure for the venture which they have chosen.

1.2   The term 'joint venture' is most commonly applied to an arrangement whereby two or more parties each provide capital, assets or other resources to a joint venture limited liability company in exchange for shares in that company, with the view to its carrying on a business, commonly involving expertise provided by each of them. This type of joint venture is generally referred to as a 'corporate' joint venture and this book will concentrate on these. However, there are many other possible types of structure which will be discussed in outline in section 3 of this chapter.

1.3   The main documents involved in a corporate joint venture are a shareholders' agreement and the articles of association of the joint company. Shareholders in any private company are likely to find themselves facing many of the same issues which arise in relation to a corporate joint venture, even though they have not labelled their relationship as such, and the considerations facing such shareholders can therefore be conveniently dealt with alongside joint ventures. Shareholders of a private company will also usually document their relationship by means of a shareholders' agreement and provisions in the company's articles.

1.4   Common situations other than corporate joint ventures in which shareholders' agreements and special provisions in the articles are required may be:

● where two or more individuals decide to go into business together and do so through the medium of a limited liability company in which they are all shareholders;

● where all or most of the shares in a private company are held by one or more families and they wish to enter into a shareholders' agreement to formalise their relationship; or

● where a business angel or venture capitalist/provider of private equity is providing capital for the establishment or development of a company, or to enable it to fund a buyout in return for shares in that company, and desires a shareholders' agreement (sometimes in this case referred to as an 'investment agreement') to protect its investment.

Indeed, the need for a shareholders' agreement and/or special articles may arise in any situation where a private company has more than one shareholder with a significant stake in the company.

1.5   Joint ventures between individuals give rise to some additional considerations (discussed in Chapter 26), as do venture capital and private equity transactions (the subject of Chapter 27). Participants in agreements between shareholders which are not in the strict sense joint ventures are likely to find matters of interest in almost every chapter of this book (all the chapters in Part B will be particularly relevant, as will Chapter 24 and possibly Chapter 25 in Part C). Where a chapter refers specifically to joint ventures it should not necessarily be assumed that it contains nothing relevant to a shareholders' agreement which the parties have not categorised as a joint venture.

2   Reasons and motivations for establishing a joint venture

1.6   The reasons and motivations for establishing a joint venture will of course differ in each individual case. However, generally speaking, a joint venture will be established between companies or individuals who each lack one or more of the resources necessary to establish and carry on a new business, or develop an existing business, but which by pooling their resources are able to do so. They may also wish to establish a joint venture in order to share risks, or to combine existing businesses to increase market power.

1.7   Examples could include the following:

● One party is able to make a product but lacks the contacts and/or expertise to market it, either at all, or in a new market which it wishes to exploit, and therefore combines with another party who has the necessary contacts and/or expertise.

- One party is able to establish a fully-effective business except that it lacks the financial resources to do so. It cannot borrow because the business is too risky or there is not enough initial cashflow to meet the interest and/or loan repayments. It therefore seeks a 'sleeping partner' who will subscribe for share capital and be compensated for the risk it is taking by reaping greater rewards for success than would be available to a lender at a fixed return.

- An inventor has devised a new product, but cannot proceed with it because he lacks some or all of the necessary design, production, marketing, financial or management expertise. He could employ people with the appropriate expertise, but finds that he cannot lure people of sufficient calibre unless he is prepared to offer them a stake in the business, so that they are more highly rewarded for success than by drawing only a salary.

- Each party has an established business involved in a particular product or service, but by bringing their expertise together the parties can create a new product or service which combines features of the existing ones.

- Both parties are already involved in the same business, but agree to combine their resources in order to share the cost of financing new products, to increase their market power, or to gain the additional financial strength to tender for larger contracts, or a combination of these. These advantages might be achieved by a full merger, but this may not be appropriate where the parties are both involved in other businesses or there are legal or financial considerations which preclude it, such as in the Reed/Elsevier joint arrangement.

- Two parties wish to tender for a major capital project. This involves a combination of skills which they possess together, but not individually; or perhaps neither of them is of sufficient financial standing to carry out the project alone, but together they could do so. By forming a joint vehicle which tenders for the project, they may be able to share in a profit that neither of them could otherwise have obtained. This, unlike all the others, is an example of a short-term joint venture or 'consortium' arrangement, which would not normally be continued after the contract has been performed.

1.8   In each of these typical examples, the needs and concerns of the parties will be different and will influence the structure of the venture, the safeguards desired by each party, the degree of risk and reward each is prepared to accept, and the assurances that each party will require from the others as to their ability to provide the particular ingredients required for success. Part of the art of advising on a joint venture is to appreciate these needs and concerns and to devise appropriate structures and documentation to meet them.

3   Alternative forms of joint venture

Introduction

1.9   A number of alternative forms of joint venture are now discussed, but these are by no means exhaustive. Some practitioners would dispute that some of these are joint ventures in the strictest sense; and would instead consider them to be alternatives to a joint venture. Nevertheless, they are all 'joint ventures' in the very broadest sense of that term, in that they all involve some form of collaboration and sharing of the resulting profits (in accordance with the definition in para 1.1). One of these forms may be more suited to the particular needs of the parties than a joint venture in its strictest sense, which is usually taken to mean either a 'contractual' joint venture within paras 1.22 to 1.28 or a partnership or corporate joint venture within paras 1.29 to 1.48. In paras 1.10 to 1.53 some forms of joint venture available under English law are considered, and a brief look is then taken at some available in other jurisdictions. Further information about joint venture vehicles established in overseas jurisdictions is contained in Chapter 29.

Agency agreement

1.10   An established manufacturer who wishes to exploit a new market may appoint an agent who has contacts in that particular market to sell the manufacturer's products on its behalf. In the most common form of such an arrangement the agent is remunerated entirely by a commission on the sales it achieves. All contracts of sale are in the name of the manufacturer, who retains most of the risk and reward of the business. The manufacturer supplies the products to the customers and is entitled to the entire price, less the commission due to the agent. The responsibility for any claims for defects or delivery delays will be with the manufacturer.

1.11   The agent's financial commitment is confined to the provision of one or more sales offices with all necessary staff and facilities, and taking financial responsibility for claims against the manufacturer which have arisen through some breach by the agent of the terms of the agency, such as a misrepresentation made by the agent giving rise to a claim. The agent is not normally responsible, beyond the loss of its commission, should any customers default, although some agents do assume this responsibility. On the other hand, the agent's return is limited to the agreed commission on sales; the agent can earn more profit by generating a greater level of sales in relation to its overheads, and the commission may be made more enticing by an agreement to pay bonuses or special rates for an especially high level of sales, but essentially the agent will, in general, only be able to retain a fairly small proportion of the margin made by the manufacturer. At least its return will bear a constant relationship to the sales turnover achieved, whereas the margin of the manufacturer may fluctuate. In good times the agent will do less well; in bad times it may have an advantage; but in really bad times when prices have to be cut, its commission will generally suffer accordingly.

1.12   The agent will not generally have a business which it can sell, since it acts only as the agent for the principal and the terms of the agency agreement will generally prohibit the transfer of the agency. The agreement may be terminable by the principal on notice, although in the case of an agency in the UK the Commercial Agents (Council Directive) Regulations 1993 (SI 1993/3053) (and for those in the UK similar regulations of the EU member states) may entitle the agent to compensation for termination, even where it was given the proper notice. Outside the UK and the European Union, local laws may well determine whether the principal can terminate the agency, the length of notice and whether any compensation will be payable.

Distribution agreement

1.13   In the same situation as that given in the previous paragraphs, the parties may instead decide to enter into a distribution agreement. As such an arrangement is most commonly understood, it transfers more of the risk and reward to the distributor than would be the case for someone acting as an agent. Instead of the distributor merely acting as agent of the manufacturer, the distributor buys the product from the manufacturer at a price governed by the terms of the agreement. Subject to any terms there may be concerning the prices to be charged by the distributor (and UK competition law restricts the ability to enforce such terms) the distributor is free, within market constraints, to charge what it likes for the products and to retain the entire profit thereby made.

1.14   The financial risks assumed by the distributor are greater, however. If it buys more products than it can sell, or buys them at too high a price in relation to the sale price, it suffers the resulting loss. It is the distributor, not the manufacturer, which is responsible to the customers for defects and delivery delays, subject to any claim the distributor may have against the manufacturer. To the costs of maintaining sales offices will generally be added the costs of maintaining a stock of the products, and usually of delivering the products to the customers. The entire cost of any customer defaults will lie with the distributor.

1.15   The manufacturer will only achieve the same selling price from the distributor no matter what profit is made by the distributor, but on the other hand its risk is less; if it distributes all its products through independent distributors it has only a few customers, the financial standing of which will generally be known to it.

1.16   Although the distributor trades as principal, and possesses a separate business, which may have considerable assets employed in it, it may nevertheless have the same difficulty in disposing of the goodwill of that business as is encountered by the agent. The distributorship is often not transferable without the consent of the manufacturer, who may also be able to terminate the agreement on notice. If termination is in accordance with the terms of the agreement, no compensation is payable to a distributor within the UK – the Commercial Agents (Council Directive) Regulations 1993 (and equivalent legislation in the EU) do not apply to distributors, although some local law such as that in Belgium does provide compensation on termination of distribution agreements. In the EU however strict competition rules under Article 101 of the TFEU and in particular as set out in the Vertical Block Exemption Regulation (330/2010) (VBER) and accompanying Guidelines on Vertical Restraints need to be considered in drafting such agreements and in the UK Competition (Amendment etc) (EU Exit) Regulations 2019 (SI 2019/93), as amended, have the effect that the VBER continues to provide exemption in the UK from UK competition law (here being that in the Competition Act 1998) after the end of the post-Brexit transition period ie from 1 January 2021. The VBER expires on 31 May 2022 but will be replaced by a similar regulation in the EU. Price fixing, export bans and some lengthy non-competition restrictions are prohibited in such agreements. Outside the European Union, local laws differ widely. In the UK the Competition Act 1998 applies but is along similar lines. UK distribution agreements which have an effect on trade in EU member states continue to be subject to EU competition law. Specialist advice should be taken on exports and imports and exhaustion of intellectual property rights in imports and exports under the new system in place from 1 January 2021.

Intellectual property licence

1.17   Where a party has the intellectual property rights to an invention or some proprietary know-how, it may, instead of assuming the financial burden of exploiting the invention or know-how for itself, decide to licence it to another. The licensee assumes the whole risk and reward of exploitation, subject to the payment to the licensor of a royalty on sales (as set out in the licence). The licensor therefore only reaps a fixed return on sales, but on the other hand its financial commitment is limited to its development costs and any fees involved in maintaining the intellectual property in existence.

1.18   The licence will not usually be transferable by the licensee without the licensor's consent, so the licensee may have difficulty in realising the goodwill it has built up. The licensor could, however, sell the intellectual property subject to the licence.

Franchise

1.19   A provider of services requiring a branch network to achieve adequate market penetration may seek to avoid most of the financial costs and risks of setting up the network by appointing franchisees to do so.

1.20   In a typical franchise arrangement, the franchisee assumes all the costs of establishing its branch and carries on the branch business on its own account, retaining any profit and assuming responsibility for all liabilities and losses, but receives considerable advice and assistance from the franchisor, who lends its brand name to the venture. The franchisee is normally required to purchase all consumables required by the business from the franchisor, and to follow business practices laid down by it. The franchisor's return is made from sales to the franchisee, and various fees and commissions it levies on the franchisee's gross income.

1.21   Although the franchisee may build up a profitable business with substantial assets, it may be difficult to realise the value in that business without the co-operation of the franchisor, whose consent will generally be required to transfer the franchise and, since the business is conducted under the franchisor's brand name, the franchisor effectively retains the goodwill. Franchisors, however, are now becoming sensitive to the need for the franchisee to be able to sell its business, and the agreement may provide that consent to transfer the franchise is not to be unreasonably withheld. Again, in the EU the EU Vertical Block Exemption Regulation (330/2010) must be considered – this sets out which clauses are void and prohibited under EU competition law in franchise agreements where the EU is involved. The Guidelines on Vertical Restraints 2010 provide useful guidance in relation to franchise agreements under competition law in the EU. The UK Competition Act 1998 as with distribution agreements also applies in the UK and the said block exemption as stated above at para 1.16 continues to apply to give exemption in the UK from the Competition Act 1998's provisions in this area, despite the end of the post-Brexit transition period and is an exemption of what is known as 'retained EU law.'.

Collaboration agreement

1.22   Under this arrangement the parties collaborate in a business enterprise, without becoming either partners or shareholders in a joint company. Such an arrangement is an example of what is generally referred to as a 'contractual' joint venture.

1.23   An example of such an arrangement is where one party (the 'producer') has developed a new product, but lacks the expertise to manufacture it, and turns to a manufacturer to do this. Instead of the parties forming a joint venture company to undertake the entire business of manufacturing and selling the product, the manufacturer agrees to manufacture the product exclusively for the producer, who resells and reaps whatever profit or loss results. The manufacturer receives from the producer a price for the products which is intended to cover its costs and provide a mark-up.

1.24   Arrangements differ as to the ownership of the tooling and the intellectual property. Sometimes the tooling is paid for by the producer, who will retain the ownership of it; sometimes the parties share its cost and own it jointly, in which case the manufacturer may often be allowed to manufacture the product for other parties in return for the payment of a royalty on such sales to the producer. Sometimes each party retains its own intellectual property, so that the producer owns that which relates to the design of the product, and the manufacturer owns any that relates to the process of manufacture. Sometimes the intellectual property is jointly owned.

1.25   An advantage of this type of arrangement is that it can be easily dismantled; each venturer retains its own assets and liabilities (other than any assets jointly owned) and neither is normally responsible for the debts and liabilities of the other in relation to the venture, since even if there are jointly owned assets this will not of itself make the parties partners (see the Partnership Act 1890, s 2(1)). Subject to the terms of the manufacturing agreement, the producer could, by assigning the benefit of that agreement to a purchaser, sell the business with its goodwill. The manufacturer, on the other hand, has none of the goodwill, except such as it may acquire through permitted direct sales. Another possible advantage of a contractual joint venture such as this is that since each venturer is separately taxed, each may be able to obtain relief for any losses which it makes against its other income.

Consortium agreement

1.26   A consortium agreement is another variety of contractual joint venture and is usually established to carry out a short-term project. An example of this is where two or more parties collaborate to carry out a contract for a third party, eg for a large construction project. Typically, the arrangement will only last for the performance of the contract. Each party is responsible for a defined part of the contract and for providing the materials, labour and plant to perform that part, and each party is remunerated by an agreed proportion of the contract price.

1.27   Each party alone will normally be responsible for the debts and liabilities it incurs during the course of the contract, since the sharing of gross returns does not of itself make the parties partners (see the Partnership

Act 1890, s 2(2)), except that all of them will be liable on the contract itself, and the insolvency of one of them could result in the insolvency of the others. This type of venture therefore involves more risk than the manufacturing arrangement discussed above, and it is usual to have provisions known as 'step in' rights under which, if one party is not able to perform its portion of the obligations under the contract, the others may take over that portion with a view to avoiding liability for non-performance.

Strategic alliance

1.28   Another variety of contractual joint venture is the strategic alliance, which has been particularly popular on the European continent. This can vary in its objects and structure; the parties may, for example, agree to collaborate on research, enter into cross-supply agreements, exchange staff or take cross-shareholdings in each other. Where a cross-shareholding is to be taken, minority protection and/or board representation may be conferred and a 'standstill' agreement, under which each party agrees not to bid for control of the other during the period of the alliance may also be entered into. What each party expects to gain from the venture is often left rather vague and a more formal structure is normally advisable if either party is expected to commit substantial resources; such an alliance may, however, be valuable in forging a relationship which may lead to something more concrete.

Partnership

1.29   Partnership is the first structure to be discussed which is an example of what might be termed a *'full-function'* joint venture, where the parties pool their resources for the long term in a jointly-owned business. A full-function joint venture which employs a joint venture vehicle other than a company is generally referred to as a non-corporate joint venture. Partnership is defined by the Partnership Act 1890, s 1(1) as 'carrying on a business in common with a view to profit'. Unlike partnerships in Scotland and in many continental countries, an English partnership is not a legal entity apart from its members. The joint venturers together own all the assets, including the goodwill of the joint venture, and are all responsible, jointly and sometimes severally, for all its liabilities.

1.30   Limited liability partnerships (LLPs) are common, particularly in areas such as financial services, law and accountancy – see para 1.40 for more detail on LLPs. However the tightening of the tax rules in relation to LLPs led many LLPs to convert to ordinary limited companies and/or to ensure all 'members' of the LLP were true partners, not quasi or actual employees.

Members of an LLP enjoy limited liability which is not the case for partners in a standard partnership nor for sole traders.

1.31 Between the partners in a traditional partnership (not an LLP nor a limited liability partnership), there will normally be a sharing of risks and rewards which reflects their respective capital contributions, although the precise distribution of risks and rewards will depend upon the agreement between them. As regards the outside world, however, each partner is liable for the whole of the liabilities of the partnership to its creditors, not only to the extent of its interest in the assets of the partnership, but also to almost the entire extent of its individual assets, and if made to pay more than his agreed proportion of such liabilities he can only rely on an indemnity from the other partners. This, however, is of little use against partners who have become insolvent. This is the great weakness of partnership, and explains why it has not generally been a usual structure for the carrying on of a business, and its use has mainly been confined to professional firms where they have been required by the rules of their professional bodies to assume unlimited liability. The advent of the limited liability partnership overcomes this weakness – see para 1.40.

1.32 One possible advantage of partnership, as compared with conducting a joint venture through a company, is fiscal transparency; generally speaking, each partner will be responsible for the tax arising on its share of the profits and gains, and this is sometimes attractive to corporate venturers. This might be particularly the case where the venture will be loss-making in the early years and the joint venturers wish to have the benefit of the losses themselves (with immediate set-off against their own profits, subject to certain anti-avoidance rules) rather than them accruing to a company which might not be able to utilise them against profits for many years. However, in a UK context, the consortium relief provisions enable a similar result to be achieved when a company is owned by corporate shareholders. Where the partners themselves have limited liability naturally the risk of failure will be reduced, but corporate venturers who wish to avoid any liability for the debts of a partnership could always interpose a subsidiary limited company between themselves and the partnership to assume any liability. This will not be effective to the extent that the joint venturers are required to guarantee the liabilities of the partnership, or may find themselves under a moral obligation or business pressure to discharge them. As regards the venturer interposing a company between itself and the partnership, tax transparency would extend only as far as the interposed company unless the interposed company is fiscally transparent.

1.33 The partners will each have a proportionate interest in the goodwill of the business of the joint venture, but they will need to act together to realise it. An assignee of a partnership share does not thereby become a partner in the place of the assignor, unless the partnership agreement provides otherwise, which is highly unlikely. It is therefore, in practice, likely to be impossible for a partner to sell his interest to an outsider not approved for admission as a partner by the other partners.

1.34   Partnership is a specialist topic and is not generally further dealt with in this book. Those needing further information should consult the established textbooks (eg Blackett-Ord, *Partnership Law,* 6th edn, 2020). Plenty of new businesses are formed, with or without a written agreement, as partnerships. The Partnership Act 1890 and any written agreement between them will govern their relationship. They are joint ventures of sorts but outside the scope of this book.

Limited partnership

1.35   The absence of the protection of limited liability made it difficult to attract 'sleeping partners' to invest in partnerships, and in 1907 the Limited Partnerships Act (LPA 1907) was passed which was intended to overcome this problem. Under this Act, a limited partnership must have at least one general partner who manages the partnership business and has unlimited liability for its debts. The remaining partners are the limited partners who are not able to intervene in the management of the business and are only liable up to the amount of the capital they have contributed to it. However, if they do intervene in the management, this protection is immediately lost.

1.36   Such partnerships have never become popular and generally are not an appropriate vehicle for conducting a joint venture – for the very reason that all the joint venturers normally wish to participate in management. They are, however, widely used as investment vehicles, particularly in the field of private equity. The investment manager becomes the general partner, and the investors become the limited partners. The attraction of this arrangement is the fiscal transparency of a partnership.

1.37   In 2017 the Government began consulting on the law in relation to limited partnerships (not to be confused with limited liability partnerships) – see https://www.gov.uk/government/consultations/review-of-limited-partnership-law-call-for-evidence particularly as it found that limited partnerships were being used for criminal activities after a surge in applications for limited partnerships in Scotland including one small house being the registered address of a Lithuanian man in Scotland being used for over 400 Scottish limited partnerships (which were not obliged to publish accounts) connected to a $1bn Moldovan bank fraud. However, numbers dropped after it became necessary to register details of the person controlling such partnerships ('persons of significant control' (PSCs)) for Scottish limited partnerships from 2017.

1.38   Limited partnerships have primarily been used by private equity and venture capital firms. The Legislative Reform (Private Fund Limited Partnerships) Order 2017 (SI 2017/514) amended the LPA 1907 as regards 'private fund limited partnerships (PFLPs)' making changes such as removing the requirement for limited partners to contribute capital to a PFLP and inserting in the LPA 1907 a list of actions which limited partners in a PFLP may take without being regarded as taking part in the management of the limited partnership and thus losing their limited liability status. The Explanatory Notes make it clear that:

> 'This is not an exhaustive list of actions which do not amount to taking part in management, and it does not affect the position for other actions or other limited partnerships; neither does it give limited partners an entitlement to take actions in the list if they would not otherwise be permitted to do so within the terms of the partnership agreement'.

The order in art 3 amended the Financial Services and Markets Act 2000 such that a PFLP cannot also be a contractual scheme eligible for authorisation under Part 17 of that Act. This was followed by a consultation in 2019 on 'limited partnerships' under the LPA 1907 – see https://www.gov.uk/government/consultations/limited-partnerships-reform-of-limited-partnership-law.

1.39   For transparency, always consider PSCs, the Trust Registration Service, the new PSCOC register and draft Registration of Overseas Entities Bill (the latter still a draft at July 2021) see paras 7.89 and 7.90. It can be vital for many clients to be advised at a very early stage as to the likely registrations that may need to be made and what information will be available on public registers once their new arrangements have been put into effect in the UK.

Limited liability partnerships

1.40   The Limited Liability Partnership (LLP) is a form of business entity which is the subject of the Limited Liability Partnerships Act 2000. LLPs were introduced as a result of the agitation by professional firms (particularly the accountants) for a form of business entity which would combine the protection of limited liability for all the partners, whether they participate in management or not, with the fiscal transparency of a partnership. Although they were originally to have been confined to professional firms, LLPs are available for the carrying on of any business. Ironically, some professional firms have been slow to take up LLPs, because the government has imposed virtually the same disclosure requirements (including the filing of accounts) as apply to limited companies, whereas professional partnerships have otherwise been able to keep their financial affairs secret. Certain overseas jurisdictions also do not allow a limited liability partnership to enjoy fiscal transparency and tax it as if it was a company; this has caused difficulties for international firms although these are slowly being overcome. The use of LLPs for professional purposes is now increasing and they are being used as vehicles for investment management firms, and also as vehicles for private equity funds in preference to limited partnerships formed under the LPA 1907. The fiscal transparency they enjoy in the UK together with their flexibility and absence of many of the restrictions that apply to companies make them attractive for many types of joint venture. An LLP is, unlike an ordinary partnership, a body corporate and a separate legal entity apart from its members. LLPs are discussed in more detail in Chapter 12.

1.41   In 2014 some changes were made to the taxation of LLPs under which some LLP members who have been taxed as self-employed are now taxed as if they are employees. Both the affected LLPs and their members now have to pay national insurance as if the affected members were employed by the LLPs. Under the provisions, any member who meets all three of the following conditions, is regarded as an employee (for tax purposes):

- *Condition A:* It is reasonable to expect that at least 80% of the member's pay is fixed, or if variable, then without reference to, or in practice unaffected by, the LLP's overall profit or loss;

- *Condition B:* The member has no significant influence over the affairs of the LLP;

- *Condition C:* The member's contribution to the LLP is less than 25% of the disguised salary.

Since the change came into effect some LLPs have changed their arrangements. A Law Society practice note on the changes is at http://www.lawsociety.org.uk/support-services/advice/practice-notes/llp-tax-changes/#llp2.

Limited company

1.42   The private limited company is by far the most popular form of joint venture vehicle in the UK. With the exception of different taxation treatment its economic effect is very similar to that of a partnership, with the addition of limited liability which means that the shareholders are, upon liquidation of the company, only liable up to any amount remaining unpaid by them on their shares. Once they have paid the whole of the agreed subscription price of their shares, the shareholders have no legal liability for the company's debts.

1.43   In practice, full limited liability is not often achieved. The joint venture company may not, especially in its early stages, have a balance sheet which is likely to impress creditors, and to the extent that it needs to borrow money this may very well not be possible unless the shareholders provide guarantees or security. The shareholders may also be required to guarantee large trading contracts undertaken by the joint venture company. Should the company fail, the shareholders, particularly if they are large corporations, may very well find themselves under considerable pressure to pay off the company's debts, even if they have not provided guarantees, since there may otherwise be considerable damage to their goodwill and reputation.

1.44   One advantage of a company is often stated to be the flexibility of its capital structure. Each participant holds a number of shares in the company to which may be attached rights of infinite variety as regards voting, participation in profits, and return of capital, such as will enable the draftsman to meet the special requirements of each venturer. Shares may be made convertible into shares of another class in defined circumstances and may be transferred (subject to the provisions of the company's articles and/ or the joint venture agreement) by the completion, signing and registration of a simple stock transfer form. However, a partnership or limited liability partnership may in practice be found to be even more flexible as regards profit distribution, especially as they have no share capital and the capital maintenance and distribution rules do not apply to them. Corporate joint venturers have usually preferred to be shareholders in a company, because this is a form of business organisation with which they are familiar and therefore understand. The LLP may, however, come to challenge the limited liability company in popularity as a joint venture vehicle, since it combines the flexibility and fiscal transparency of a partnership with limited liability.

1.45   Unlike a partnership, but similarly to an LLP, a company is a separate legal entity distinct from its shareholders. All the joint venture property will belong to the company, rather than being the joint property of the partners, except where one or more of the shareholders decides to keep certain assets outside the company, eg where a shareholder owns the freehold of the business premises, but only grants the company a lease or licence to occupy it. In a limited company all profits accrue to the company rather than the partners and the consequence of this is that the fiscal transparency of a partnership is lost. The company will be liable for corporation tax on its profits and gains, and these will form part of the income of the shareholders when distributed to them by way of dividend or otherwise. This is not necessarily a disadvantage, however, since under the current system of corporation tax there is no further tax to pay by a UK resident corporate recipient of a dividend from a UK resident company. Previously an individual recipient received a tax credit which he set against his own income tax liability when a dividend were paid, although he could have suffered an element of double taxation since the credit might have fallen short of his total income tax liability on the dividend. However, the current new regime is described in the box below:

Tax on dividends from April 2016

Since 6 April 2016 taxpayers did not had to pay tax on the first £5,000 of dividends per tax year. This reduced to £2000 in 2017.

Above this figure of £2000 the tax the taxpayer pays depends on the income tax band in which the taxpayer falls. The dividends are added to other taxable income in calculating what is due. There may be various rates of tax paid:

Tax band	Tax rate on dividends over £5,000
Basic rate	7.5%
Higher rate	32.5%
Additional rate	38.1%

HMRC gives the following example in 2020 (see https://www.gov.uk/tax-on-dividends) (and from 1 April 2022 rates increase by 1.25%):

'To work out your tax band, add your total dividend income to your other income. You may pay tax at more than one rate.

Example

You get £3,000 in dividends and earn £29,500 in wages in the 2020 to 2021 tax year.

This gives you a total income of £32,500.

You have a Personal Allowance of £12,500. Take this off your total income to leave a taxable income of £20,000.

This is in the basic rate tax band, so you would pay:

20% tax on £17,000 of wages

no tax on £2,000 of dividends, because of the dividend allowance

7.5% tax on £1,000 of dividends.'

The dividend taxation changes made many limited companies run by one person change to sole traders, although they then lose limited liability and may have more national insurance contributions to pay.

Individuals engaged in business may need to consider carefully whether a company or a partnership would be best for them in relation to taxation of profits (see para 26.19ff); if a partnership would be preferable, they may consider forming an LLP in order to secure limited liability. As regards capital gains, a double tax liability may arise if the joint venture company sells its undertaking and assets and distributes the gain to its shareholders in its subsequent liquidation. The shareholders will therefore be likely to prefer to exit from their investment by selling their shares in the joint venture, which does not involve a disposal of the underlying assets. Any gain made on the sale of the shares will be fully taxable in the hands of the shareholder (usually at 10% of the gain under business asset disposal relief (BADR) (previously called entrepreneurs' relief) by way of capital gains tax after deduction of the annual tax free CGT allowance) unless relief, such as the sustainable shareholder exemption, applies. In 2020 BADR was capped at a lifetime allowance of £1m per person. Again, an LLP avoids this disadvantage of potential double taxation.

1.46 The goodwill of the joint venture company will belong to the company and each joint venturer's interest in it may be realised by transferring its shares. In practice, its ability to do so is likely to depend on the co-operation of the other joint venturers. The articles of association will almost invariably contain restrictions on share transfers. Most commonly there will be a 'pre-emption' article under which shares may not be transferred to an outsider unless they are first offered for sale to all the other existing shareholders. To the extent that no existing shareholder will buy them, the articles usually provide that they may then be sold to any outsider. However, in the case of a minority shareholder, this is almost certainly a forlorn hope, since there is virtually no market for minority shareholdings in unquoted companies.

1.47 A limited company does, however, offer greater scope for the realisation of the interest of an outgoing venturer. It may be possible, subject to certain requirements being met for the protection of creditors, for the company itself to buy its shares. Subject to similar safeguards, shares may also be issued on terms that they are redeemable, providing another route whereby an outgoing venturer may realise its interest. If a sale of the whole undertaking is desired, this may be effected by a transfer of all the shares in the company to the purchaser, whereas realising a business owned by a partnership entails the partners conveying its assets to the purchaser, accepting indemnities in respect of their liabilities from the purchaser (or paying them off out of the sale proceeds), and then winding up the partnership and distributing the net proceeds to the partners – altogether a much more cumbersome procedure. It should, however, be pointed out that the disposal of the undertaking of an LLP presents fewer difficulties, since it is a legal entity separate from its members.

Publicity issues and persons of significant control

1.48 A disadvantage of a UK limited company compared with a partnership is that a company must make its affairs public to some extent. The constitution of a UK company is a public document, accessible to anyone upon the payment of a small fee, as are the various returns which a UK company must place on its public file which give details of its registered shareholders, copies of its accounts, and certain other information about its affairs. Parties who desire secrecy may therefore prefer a partnership (or to use a company incorporated in an overseas jurisdiction) to provide greater privacy for its affairs, although such public access has not in practice proved a significant disincentive to UK incorporation, particularly where the joint venturers are themselves companies subject to the same, or more onerous, requirements. In addition it is also necessary for limited companies to publish the 'persons of significant control' of their company (usually those with more than 25% of the shares or voting rights or who controls the company). See Government guidance on the PSC rules at https://www.gov.uk/government/uploads/system/uploads/attachment_data/file/555657/PSC_register_summary_guidance.pdf.

1.49   The PSC rules are in the Small Business, Enterprise and Employment Act 2015 and regulations made thereunder. The 4th Anti-Money Laundering Directive (EU) 2015/849 required similar rules to be brought in throughout the EU by 26 June 2017. Sole traders are not obliged to disclose who controls nor owns them and there is no public register of them. The PSC rules also apply to LLPs as well as limited companies. There are also other transparency rules particularly for property purchases and those with foreign owners and a new obligation to register even many bare trusts. This is a fast moving area on which specialist advice should be sought. Alert particularly foreign clients early on in a transaction about all possible UK transparency requirements. Below is a short summary of recent changes/proposed changes.

PROPOSED REGISTER OF BENEFICIAL OWNERSHIP OF REAL PROPERTY BY OVERSEAS ENTITIES

1.50   Overseas entities which own UK real property under proposed changes in the law planned for 2021 will be required to give details of beneficial ownership of the property (this does not so far apply to shares) – see www.gov.uk/government/publications/a-register-of-beneficial-owners-of-overseas-companies-and-other-legal-entities-potential-impacts. The aim is to ensure enforcement through 'novel land registration requirements' and criminal penalties including large fines and up to five years in jail. Those land registration requirements will consist of the addition of a restriction on the registered title of property owned by an overseas entity and preventing registration of transactions where an overseas entity has not complied with the rules. The proposals led to a draft Registration of Overseas Entities Bill, but in 2021 this had still not been enacted despite an obligation to report on progress about this to Parliament under the Sanctions and Anti-Money Laundering Act 2018, s 50.

REGISTRATION OF TRUSTS AND THEIR BENEFICIAL OWNERS

1.51   In 2017 the UK changed its trusts regime following the EU's 4th Anti-Money Laundering Directive (EU) 2015/849 and established the UK's Trust

Registration Service. The register was private and was only compulsory for trusts liable to pay tax. In a major change following the 5th Anti-Money Laundering Directive (EU) 2018/843 (even simple 'bare' trusts with no tax liability are since October 2020 obliged to register. People with a 'legitimate interest' will be allowed to search the register by virtue of Money Laundering and Terrorist Financing (Amendment) (EU Exit) Regulations 2020 (SI 2020/991) which amended existing legislation. There is an exception where life insurance proceeds or a pension are put in trust for the benefit of heirs in the event of death and also the automatic 'trust' arising under English law from simply owning a bank account in joint names. The obligation on trustees to collect information about beneficial owners of the trust begins on 20 March 2022.

UNEXPLAINED WEALTH ORDERS

1.52   The Criminal Finances Act 2017 introduced the UK unexplained wealth orders (UWOs). The order is a court order and can require an individual to explain their wealth and may result in assets being seized by the state if a satisfactory explanation is not given as to how the individual came to own the assets. Government guidance on UWOs is at www.gov.uk/government/publications/circular-0032018-criminal-finances-act-unexplained-wealth-orders/circular-0032018-unexplained-wealth-orders. The first three UWOs in the UK occurred between July 2019 and April 2020. Two related to property funded by criminal activity and one UWO was overturned by the High Court in April 2020. All the above PSC and other measures to ensure more transparency are relevant to the issue of ownership of a company and its shares.

1.53   Table 1 sets out some of the chief features of the four main forms of English full-function joint venture for comparison.

Table 1
Comparison between English partnerships, limited partnerships and private companies

	Partnership	Limited partnership	Private limited company	LLP
Public incorporation procedure	No	Yes	Yes	Yes
Limited liability	No	Only for the limited partners	Yes	Yes
Accounts publicly available	No	No	Yes	Yes
Fiscal transparency	Yes	Yes	No	Yes
Separate legal entity	No	No	Yes	Yes

UK European Economic Interest Groupings, Community Interest Companies and companies limited by guarantee

1.54   European Economic Interest Groupings (EEIGs) are creations of the European Union, and are of no use at all for carrying on a business, since their objects or purpose must be to facilitate or develop the economic activities of its members or increase the results of those activities, and not to make profits for themselves. They might be employed where a number of parties wish to collaborate in research and development for the advantage of each of their businesses, or to conduct some other form of co-operation for their common advantage. Very few of them have been formed. By 2021 only about 260 had been formed. One reason for this is that they do not confer limited liability, the members being jointly and severally responsible for their liabilities[1]. They must be in the EU and from 1 January 2021, unless they have before then changed their status, they were automatically converted to a United Kingdom Economic Interest Grouping (UKEIG) to ensure they continue to have legal status. The legislative changes for EEIGs are in the European Economic Interest Grouping (Amendment) (EU Exit) Regulations 2018 (SI 2018/1299).

Community Interest Companies are for those who want to engage in not for profit work. They are limited companies with extra features. The Department for Business states that they are 'created for the use of people who want to conduct a business or other activity for community benefit, and not purely for private advantage'. This is achieved by a 'community interest test' and 'asset lock', which ensure that the CIC is established for community purposes and the assets and profits are dedicated to these purposes. Registration of a company as a CIC has to be approved by the Regulator, who also has a continuing monitoring and enforcement role. See https://www.gov.uk/government/organisations/office-of-the-regulator-of-community-interest-companies.

Clients proposing a joint venture for a charitable venture may also like to consider a company limited by guarantee – perhaps the most common structure for that kind of venture. They may also wish to obtain charitable status under the Charities Act 2011 and other legislation. See the Charities Commission website at https://www.gov.uk/government/organisations/charity-commission.

Unincorporated associations and sole traders

1.55   Finally, some individuals decide to start a venture without any legal entity and form an 'unincorporated association'. They need to be

---

1   Further information about EEIGs may be obtained from Volume 19(2) of LexisNexis Butterworths *Encyclopaedia of Forms and Precedents* at p 615.

warned that each collaborative partner will be personally liable for the debts. This book does not cover unincorporated associations, although they are a form of joint venture. Textbooks such as *The Law of Unincorporated Associations* by Nicholas Stewart QC, Natalie Campbell and Simon Baughen; and *Unincorporated Associations* by Warburton set out the law in this field. Sometimes a new venture will be operated as a sole trader, as is the author's solicitor's firm. However this book concentrates on ventures involving several individuals, usually through a corporate structure, and of course those operating entirely alone hardly need an agreement with themselves as to how they will operate. On the other hand those setting up a tennis club, railway enthusiasts' association, rambling association, book club or play group etc do need careful legal advice, otherwise they will by accident more than design they will have formed an unincorporated association with unlimited liability for the participants, which may not have been their intention. Some form of company limited by guarantee, perhaps also registered as a charity (or possibly CIC as described above), may be a better option for them.

Overseas entities

1.56   The joint venturers need not confine their choice of vehicle to those available in the UK. They may wish to consider the entities available overseas, and this is likely to be particularly so where one or more of the joint venturers are overseas entities or multinational corporations. They need not confine their choice of the jurisdiction of the business operations, since it may be quite convenient to use an entity established under the law of another jurisdiction.

1.57   Virtually every jurisdiction is able to provide one or more forms of limited liability company, although these vary widely in their structure, and some may be found more suitable than others. Outside the UK, the United States and the other common law jurisdictions, local draftsmen may not find it easy to accommodate the requirements of the joint venturers within the constraints of local law; the difficulty is that, whilst in the common law jurisdictions the relationship between the parties is largely governed by contract, and considerable freedom is allowed to the parties as to the terms they may include, in civil law countries the content of each structure is usually regulated by the relevant civil code.

1.58   Where a merger involves a civil law jurisdiction or indeed any foreign law issue always take local advice.

1.59   Another consideration which may be relevant in choosing the jurisdiction in which to incorporate a limited company is the amount of information about the company and its shareholders which is required to be publicly disclosed. This ranges from the very full disclosure required in European and North American jurisdictions down to the minimal information required in most tax havens.

1.60   A key factor is the taxation position of the company. Taxes vary both in scope and rate, the highest rates generally being found in continental Europe. Incorporation within a tax haven jurisdiction may be attractive in that in most tax havens a company under foreign ownership pays little or no tax, but very few business operations can conveniently be located in tax havens, and there are also the taxes arising in the country of operation to be considered. A key factor involved in selecting the jurisdiction of incorporation, and possibly of operation (if there is a choice), is the availability of double tax treaties between that jurisdiction and that of the participants, the existence of which may avoid the profits being taxed twice.

1.61   A European company may in the future be found to be a suitable vehicle for a joint venture for those in the EU (but not the UK which left the EU on 31 January 2020). European Council Regulation (EC) 2157/2001 on the Statute for a European Company, which came into force on 8 October 2004, creates a new type of company, independent of national law, known as a '*societas europaea*' or 'SE'. However, this falls short of a pan-European solution since such companies are to a large extent governed by the laws of the EU state in which they are registered, including, for example, tax treatment, and directors' duties and liabilities. The tax treatment of such a company will therefore still be an important factor in determining the jurisdiction of registration. A truly pan-European solution could only come about by tax harmonisation, and the SE is unlikely to be a practical choice for some time. Employee participation is an important feature of an SE which may detract from its suitability as a joint venture vehicle. It is not possible to incorporate an SE completely from scratch, but only by derivation from one or more existing companies incorporated within the EU. The aim was to facilitate cross-border mergers and joint ventures by a merger of existing companies, the formation of a holding or subsidiary company, or conversion of an existing company. Companies House guidance on the 'SE' is at https://www.gov.uk/government/publications/european-companies-in-the-uk-registration-and-administration which includes the statement that:

> 'It is expected that the UK will no longer be able to participate in the SE framework after the end of the transition period. So our guidance on changes to company registration will apply for SEs from 1 January 2021'.

Any SE still registered in the UK from 1 January 2021 is automatically converted to a 'UK Societas'. It can remain as a UK Societas, be wound up or converted to a PLC. From 1 January 2021, no SEs can be formed in, or transferred in or out of the UK. UK branches of SEs registered in an EU member state will have to comply with the Overseas Companies Regulations 2009, SI 2009/1801 from 1 January 2021. The legislative changes for SEs are within:

- the European Public Limited-Liability Company (Amendment etc) (EU Exit) Regulations 2018 (SI 2018/1298);

- the International Accounting Standards and European Public Limited-Liability Company (Amendment etc) (EU Exit) Regulations 2019 (SI 2019/685).

The EU's general guidance on SEs is at https://europa.eu/youreurope/business/running-business/developing-business/setting-up-european-company/index_en.htm.

1.62   Most jurisdictions recognise the concept of partnership, but whereas in most common law jurisdictions the law relating to them is generally not dissimilar to English law, civil law jurisdictions typically impose restrictions on the parties. For example, the fiscal transparency associated with an English partnership is not necessarily available in other jurisdictions, some of which tax a partnership as if it was a corporation.

1.63   Many jurisdictions offer limited partnerships of various kinds. In this context, particular mention should be made of the limited partnerships available in the United States. A Delaware limited partnership offers a separate legal personality, fiscal transparency and limited liability for the limited partners. These features have made them particularly popular as vehicles for investment funds. A Delaware limited liability partnership goes one better by extending limited liability to the general partner whilst retaining the other attributes, and is therefore the equivalent of the UK LLP. Mention should be made of the Limited Liability Companies (LLCs) now available throughout the US which may elect to be taxed either as corporations or as partnerships; if the latter election is made, fiscal transparency is combined with limited liability. However, such structures are not necessarily tax efficient for UK investors; for example, investments in US LLCs often lead to unrelieved double taxation. Careful consideration is required into this aspect. It is wise to take legal and tax advice on the best jurisdiction for the venture. For example some jurisdictions such as the UK allow internet gambling companies, which some US states prohibit. Forum shopping both in relation to tax rates and to ascertain a jurisdiction where the proposed activity is lawful is crucial.

1.64   More detailed guidance on the choice of vehicle for cross-border joint ventures will be found at para 28.5ff.

'Dual headed' structure

1.65   A 'dual headed' structure is sometimes employed in international joint ventures. It is used where the joint venturers wish to operate the venture as a single entity for management purposes, but for tax or other reasons the venturers wish to retain their existing corporate structures. This can be achieved by means of contractual relationships between the venturers whereby they share profits or equalise dividends and agree to submit to a common management, although it has to be said these tend to result in fairly complex arrangements in practice.

4   The importance of adequate documentation

1.66   Having decided to embark on a joint venture, the parties would be advised to spend some time, money and effort on ensuring that it is adequately documented. Failure to do so may result in some expensive misunderstandings and, in an extreme case, may result in the premature termination of the venture.

1.67   A non-exhaustive summary of reasons for insisting on adequate documentation is as follows:

- to ensure that the parties' obligations to each other and to the joint venture vehicle are clear;

- to ensure, as far as possible, that the parties are clear as to their respective aspirations and objectives in relation to the joint venture;

- to provide protection for minorities and to attempt to avoid deadlock;

- to define in what circumstances the venture may be terminated, and as far as practicable to provide an exit route for the parties;

- to ensure the chosen structure works.

Clarity of obligations

1.68   The failure to set out the obligations of each party clearly and precisely may result in a misunderstanding about what one or more parties have agreed to do. It may also result in the other parties failing to receive from the joint venture that which they expected, and may mean a party may be unable successfully to sue an alleged defaulter (through ambiguity or uncertainty as to what it was to do).

1.69   For example, an understanding that one joint venturer will grant a licence of some important intellectual property to the joint venture vehicle lacks clarity unless at least the following questions are answered:

- What precisely is the intellectual property covered by the licence?

- What is the royalty rate and how is it to be calculated?

- What territory is covered by it?

- What precise acts of exploitation are permitted by it?

- Is it exclusive or non-exclusive?

- Does it cover improvements devised by the licensor?

- Who owns the licensee's improvements?

- How long does the licence go on for, and does it automatically end if the joint venture ends?

A lack of certainty in relation to any of the above points, or their complete omission from the parties' understanding, could prove very damaging, even fatal, to the joint venture, especially if the exploitation of the intellectual property is the central purpose of the venture. The only way of achieving a sufficient level of certainty is to draw up the licence at the same time as the rest of the documentation is drawn up and to insist that the proposed licensor enters into it as a pre-condition of the injection of any funds by the other parties. Otherwise, when the lawyers for the licensor get around to drafting the licence, perhaps some months after the joint venture has been commenced, it may turn out to be a rather different document from that expected by the other parties.

1.70   Allied to documenting obligations are assurances to the other parties that those undertaking the obligations are likely to be able to honour them. When the parties to the venture do not know each other well, or are not public corporations about which much information is publicly available, each party may be required to give warranties to the others concerning its financial standing. Further, when an asset is to be transferred or licensed to the joint venture, warranties as to the quality of the asset will be appropriate. For example, in the case of an intellectual property licence, it would be appropriate to take warranties that (inter alia) all patents comprised in it have actually been granted, that no person is trying to challenge the grants or alleging that they infringe its own rights, and that all sums required to keep the patents in force have been paid. Warranties are discussed in more detail in Chapter 26.

Aspirations and objectives

1.71   It is equally vital to a proposed venture that the parties should agree their aspirations and objectives. By setting down the parties' entire understanding in writing, any misunderstandings should become clear and be the subject of further negotiation until agreement on the final documents is achieved. Furthermore, any omissions in the parties' understanding can be addressed.

1.72   Unfortunately, this does not always produce the desired result, since lawyers are generally trained to consider the legal rather than all the commercial points. In one joint venture between Japanese and French corporations it became clear some time after the documents had been signed that the parties had different ideas on the return on capital. Initial losses had been expected, but the Japanese corporation was in for the long haul and was quite prepared to wait for many years for a return, as long as the market share of the joint venture kept on increasing; it wanted the prices of the products kept as low as possible so as to achieve maximum market penetration. The French corporation, on the other hand, had envisaged an earlier return of capital; it wanted to set higher prices to achieve early profitability and was not so concerned about market share. The French corporation was appalled at the mounting losses and the frequency with which calls for further capital were being made. The problem was only solved by the French buying out the Japanese. It was perhaps not surprising that there was nothing in the legal documents concerning this issue, and it appeared that neither side's lawyers had considered it. For this reason, the parties sometimes draw up a memorandum of understanding on commercial issues and attach it as an exhibit to the joint venture agreement; there was one in this case, but unfortunately the parties had failed to address this particular issue.

1.73   It is good practice for the parties to draw up a business plan dealing with at least the first year's operations, and preferably for a longer period. This should include a cashflow forecast, with an estimate of the working capital required, a projected profit and loss account and balance sheet, an operating budget (including an estimate of capital expenditure), a review of the projected business and a summary of business objectives. The early preparation of such a plan should reveal any disagreements.

Minority protection

1.74   In every joint venture which is a company or partnership (other than one which has only two participants with equal voting power) one or more parties will be in an actual or potential minority, and therefore capable of being outvoted on any occasion.

1.75   Although the parties may not address this issue in their initial discussions, it will almost invariably be appropriate for the minority to be afforded some protection from their interests being prejudiced by the actions of the majority except in cases where a very small minority of shares is given to minor employees, perhaps even just non-voting shares. In both partnerships and companies, the general rule is that the majority rules, and although the law does provide some protection to company shareholders, it is somewhat inadequate (see para 14.1ff). The protection will normally take the form of a series of acts which it is agreed are not to be carried out without unanimous consent, or the consent of a particular minority.

1.76 Such vetoes or blocking powers are, of course, entirely negative in character. They do not usually enable the minority to force any change of policy, and the majority could not be expected to agree to this, although through the minority's ability to refuse consent to a particular transaction it may, in practice, be able to insist on the adoption of an alternative.

1.77 The minority may, however, desire to have some positive rights which may be attached to their participation. In a company, for example, such rights may include the ability to appoint a director, or the right to a minimum return on their investment by way of interest and/or dividends. Since, in the absence of contrary agreement, the majority would appoint all the directors, without such agreement the minority cannot even be sure of a voice in the boardroom. Minority protection is further considered at para 14.28ff and in Chapter 15.

Deadlock

1.78 Where the participations of the parties to a two-party venture are equal, and neither party is prepared to concede control, the parties could find themselves in a deadlock since, in theory, no decisions can be made unless they both agree. Joint ventures are quite often established on this basis, but it is desirable to have some mechanism in place for resolving any deadlock when it arises, although the reality is that if the parties are perpetually in disagreement the joint venture is effectively doomed. Deadlock can also arise, but is less common, in a multi-party joint venture, where two combinations of parties with the same aggregate voting power continually oppose one another. It can also arise where a minority participant has been granted a veto over certain transactions, and persists in using it. The resolution of a deadlock is considered in Chapter 13.

Termination and exit routes

1.79 It may seem odd to suggest to parties who are about to embark on a joint venture, full of hope and expectation, that one of the vital issues that they need to address is what will happen if (or, more likely, when) one or more of them wishes to end it. However, it is a fact that few joint ventures endure for a long period of time, and the issue is therefore a very important one.

1.80 Factors which were unforeseen at the time the venture was entered into may lead to one or more of the parties seeking for it to be ended. The commercial policy of a party may change so that it no longer wishes to continue with the venture, the venture may be less profitable than was hoped, or the technology that it was established to exploit may become obsolete. The control of one party may change so that its commercial policy changes, or perhaps the new controller is a business rival of one of the other parties who wishes to bring it to an end. The parties may simply fall out, or one of them may breach the agreement, or become insolvent. In practice, the circumstances which might lead to one or more of the parties seeking to end the joint venture are too numerous to contemplate. Therefore, no party should enter into a joint venture without some method of extracting itself being built into the documentation.

1.81   Termination events require careful consideration. It needs to be clear whether the parties are committed for a fixed or minimum period or whether it can be terminated following the giving of notice. Another point to be addressed is what should happen if a third party makes an offer for the entire venture or an important licence or concession is lost by the joint venture or comes to an end. It may be desirable for there to be provisions to end the venture if the parties are in deadlock. A breach by a party of the agreement or the insolvency or change of control of a party are often made termination events. In a multi-party venture it needs to be considered whether a termination event affecting one party ends the whole venture, or only as to the party who wishes to leave or which is affected by the termination event. Termination events are discussed in detail in Chapter 17.

1.82   Another important factor requiring consideration is the realisation of the interests of the parties following termination. Is the joint venture to be liquidated, is one party entitled or required to buy out the other and, if so, at what price? Participation in a joint venture may become a valuable asset and without any special provisions its realisation may be frustrated, especially where the participation is a minority one.

1.83   Although provisions for realisation of interests on termination are highly desirable, it is difficult to obtain something which is fully effective, at least for the minority. The reality is that unless a minority holder has an agreement under which the majority can be compelled to buy its participation, it is generally locked into its participation unless or until another party to the venture agrees to buy it out, or agreement is reached for a third party to acquire the entire venture. It may be possible for the minority to negotiate a call option, so that if its participation is not purchased by the others, it may acquire their participations in order to be able to sell the entire venture. But this, in some cases, may not be a commercially viable or desirable option.

1.84   In the case of a company, three other routes may be open: it could purchase the shares of the minority holder, redeem redeemable shares held by it or, exceptionally, it may be floated so that the minority holder acquires shares which may be easily sold. Liquidation or dissolution may, in very limited circumstances, be capable of being forced through by the minority (see para 14.6ff), but might result in realisation at an unfavourable price. In the case of a UK company, a shareholder who can show 'unfair prejudice' may be able to obtain a court order requiring the majority to purchase its shares (see para 14.19ff).

1.85   Whilst the right to sell the minority interest to a third party may be catered for in the documentation, whether after a pre-emption process is followed or not, it is rarely achieved in practice. Nevertheless, some valuable provisions can be included, although these tend to be more in the nature of facilitating the realisation process rather than providing magic solutions whereby a minority interest can always be realised. Exit mechanisms are discussed further in Chapters 17 to 21.

1.86   Furthermore, the majority participant should not assume that its interest will always be saleable without assistance from the documentation. It may not be able to sell to a purchaser unless it can deliver 100% of the venture, since potential purchasers are usually unwilling to purchase with the minority still in place, given the rights which the documentation may confer upon it. Mechanisms designed to facilitate a sale by the majority are discussed at para 21.13ff.

Ensuring the structure works

1.87   Another reason for insisting upon full documentation is that the parties may otherwise overlook something in the proposed structure which may mean that it is not as effective as was intended.

1.88   This is particularly true of a venture which involves a large number of parties or which crosses borders, or involves more than one joint venture vehicle. Unless all important issues are properly addressed, and reflected appropriately in the documentation, difficulties may ensue. The parties may find that in their transmission from the jurisdiction of the joint venture to one of the participants in another jurisdiction, the profits become depleted by some tax or other imposition not foreseen. The parties may have overlooked the provisions of some local law which has a serious impact on the venture or may not have realised that a governmental consent was needed for a particular feature of the venture. Given that the parties may have invested heavily in establishing the joint venture, this could have expensive consequences. Such pitfalls can usually be avoided if appropriate local legal advice is taken, which is acted upon in the documents, especially as sometimes even a small change in the drafting can avoid a potential pitfall.

1.89   Where there are to be a large number of agreements, it is particularly important that their provisions interlock, and that they do not contain provisions which are in conflict. Alternatively, it may be laid down which document prevails should there be a conflict.

Chapter 2

Matching the aims and expectations of the parties

Summary

This chapter discusses the need to ascertain the aims and expectations of the parties and how a structure may be devised to meet them. It goes on to provide suggestions as to how, where the aims and expectations of the parties differ, they may all be accommodated by modifying the structure appropriately. This chapter is written from a UK viewpoint, but all the issues, if not the methods of addressing them, will arise internationally.

1 Introduction

2.1   No joint venture is likely to succeed if its structure fails to match the aims and, as far as possible, the expectations of the parties. One of the most important tasks of an adviser is to ascertain what these are, and then to devise a structure which is likely to give effect to them. The parties are often unlikely to have exactly the same aims and expectations, even at the outset.

2.2   For example, joint venturers who are companies will have differing cultures and business philosophies, which will guide the policies of their respective boards and of the executives to whom they delegate the supervision of their company's interest in the joint venture.

2.3   Directors of a company must also look to the interests of their shareholders, so that each corporate participant will be concerned to achieve a result which they can justify to their shareholders as being in accordance with previously declared aims, which represents a good deal for the company and which is likely to show a good return for many years.

2.4   The interests of an individual joint venturer who is working in the joint venture business are unlikely to be the same as those of the corporate joint venturer. His concern will be to ensure adequate return is received for his labours which would provide some wealth upon which he may retire.

2.5   Different again will be the interests of a venturer which is participating purely for a return on capital to be provided by it (such as a provider of private equity) and which will be less concerned with the long-term interests of the joint venture business. It will be more concerned with obtaining the highest return on capital it can over the shortest period possible.

2.6 Another illustration of the need to reconcile differing requirements would be a joint venture between a developer and a construction company. The construction company is likely to need a quick exit route in order to have capital available for its next project, whereas the developer may desire the long-term reward available from leasing the completed development. Private Finance Initiative projects involved the reconciliation of the need of the provider of the finance for a commercial return with that of the public authority desiring value for money and often a structure which enabled it to pay according to use. In 2012 the Government began a review of the PFI which resulted in a new system known as PF2. This was followed in 2018 by an announcement that the government would no longer use private finance (PF2), the then current model of PFI, for new government projects. Existing PFI and PF2 contracts, however, did not end and continue to be run as legacy arrangements.

2.7 The parties will need to strike a balance between conflicting requirements; if they cannot be reconciled, the structure of the venture will need to recognise the differences.

2 Long-term and short-term investors

2.8 A key factor is to determine whether the parties are long-term or short-term investors, or a mixture of the two.

2.9 Many corporate venturers are long-term investors. Their primary concern is to establish a profitable venture which will, for many years, add to the bottom line of the profit-and-loss account and will provide an acceptable return on the capital they have invested. Even if they or their lawyers have inserted appropriate realisation provisions into the documents, they may operate the venture in such a way that it is not independent of the joint venturers and therefore a sale will prove difficult, although to do this is usually misguided because there may be a time when it is found that the capital locked up in the venture could be invested more profitably elsewhere.

2.10 On the other hand, some corporates and most outside equity investors are short-term investors, although their horizons may differ considerably. Their primary concern may be to achieve capital growth which can be realised by sale, flotation or some other method. Such investors may be prepared to sacrifice early profit for growth, in the belief that this will ultimately result in a higher value for their investment. Others will require the combination of an income stream with capital growth. Other outside capital providers may desire a reasonable commercial income on their money but expect medium-term repayment.

2.11 As with corporates, so with working individuals. Long-term investors may see the establishment of the joint venture as a new career which they wish to see provide them with a high income until realisation on retirement. Other individuals are short-term investors, whose desire is for the business to grow with a view to sale or flotation within a few years, so as to produce a capital profit.

2.12   In some joint ventures it is appreciated from the outset that the dominant venturer views the establishment of the joint venture as a stepping stone to full control and will be looking to the others to exit early. The other parties will therefore be keen to maximise their return on early exit.

3 Achieving early exits

2.13   It may not be easy to structure a venture to cater for the needs of a party who desires a realisation earlier than the other venturers, without putting the other parties in the position that they may also have to exit early.

2.14   One solution is for one or more of the other parties to grant the party desiring an early exit a put option, whereby it is able to sell its participation to the others after an agreed period, at a price which recognises its proportion of the market value of the venture at that time, as determined by agreement or valuation (see Chapter 22).

2.15   Where the joint venture vehicle is a company, another possible route is for the company itself to buy or redeem the outgoing party's shares (see Chapter 20), but this depends upon the company having sufficient distributable profits to pay the required amount, or being able to issue further shares to fund it. Although in the case of a private company redemption out of capital is permitted, the capital will often be fully employed, so that the directors will be unable to make the required declaration that the company will be able to meet its liabilities after making the payment (see para 20.3). Provisions for the redemption of share capital will rarely give the redeeming shareholder the ability to realise the full commercial value of its shares, since usually redemption is at par or a small premium over par. In practice, redemption is usually a route by which a shareholder may secure the return of its capital invested in a venture which has not been a success.

2.16   Both these routes may be unattractive to the continuing shareholders in that they involve a direct or indirect cost to them. However, since they acquire the profit share of the departing participant, the cost may be justifiable. The departing participant may be concerned that a valuation of his interest, rather than an actual disposal to a third party, may undervalue its true worth in the market.

2.17   Another possible method of achieving an early exit for an individual participant in a venture including one or more listed or other quoted companies is for the individual to be granted options to subscribe for shares in those companies, which, on exercise, will give him shares he can sell in the market. This may not satisfy his aspirations, since the value of the joint venture will only partially be reflected in the share price, which may be dragged down by poor performance elsewhere. The legal and tax consequences would also need to be carefully considered.

2.18 Other methods of guaranteeing an early exit for a participant will put the others in the position of having to purchase the participation of the party wishing to leave (if they do not want to be forced to exit also). For example, the party wishing to exit early might be granted a call option so that if its participation is not bought by the others, it can call upon the others to sell their participations to it, so that it may acquire the whole venture and then exit by selling it to a third party (see para 17.9ff). Another route may be the use of 'drag along' provisions (see para 21.13ff), under which a participant could try to force an early exit by finding a third-party purchaser willing to make an offer for the participations of all the other parties (or making an offer itself). Such provisions provide that if the offer is approved by the requisite majority of the parties, all the parties are obliged to accept it, but, generally, this is only a certain route for majority holders who are able to secure approval of the offer. Other exit routes, such as the ability to insist on a sale or flotation, would not normally be negotiable unless all parties envisage an exit at the same time, and in any case depend upon the ability to find a purchaser, or on market conditions being favourable for a flotation.

2.19 A participant requiring income before the other participants receive income could be issued with some preference shares carrying a fixed or participating return, ranking ahead of the ordinary shares, perhaps taking a lower number of ordinary shares to compensate. If the dividend is made cumulative, those dividends which cannot be paid due to the insufficiency of distributable profits will be carried to later years and fall to be paid as soon as sufficient profits become available.

2.20 Other ways of achieving earlier or additional income include the payment of interest on loan capital, management fees, royalties and payments for services rendered. These may be more attractive than dividends in that, provided they are genuine and are not in excess of the market rate (and, in the case of interest, to the worldwide debt cap rules) and subject to any particular tax rules (eg 'thin capitalisation' issues), they should be deductible from profits for corporation tax purposes, and, unlike dividends, the ability to pay them depends only on the available cashflow and not on the existence of sufficient distributable profits. If they are unpaid and the venture enters liquidation, they rank ahead of the shareholders on a winding up.

2.21 Working individual participants can be given additional income by means of bonuses or commission dependent upon results, which may also serve as an additional motivation to achieve success. They may also be given additional capital growth by receiving options to subscribe for further shares in the venture by reference to a formula based on results, although the legal and tax consequences will need careful consideration (see Chapter 5). Options will only be attractive if there is some realisation mechanism for the acquired shares. Another alternative may be a 'ratchet' or equity kicker (see para 27.25) where the equity interest of the relevant individuals increases in proportion to the equity interests of the other participants according to a formula geared to results, although, again, the tax consequences of such a ratchet or equity kicker will need to be carefully considered. All these methods will involve a reduction of the proportionate shareholdings of the other participants who, on the other hand, may hope to be compensated by the increased value of the whole entity resulting from the additional motivation afforded to the option holders or those benefiting from the ratchet or equity kicker. They also all impact in one way or another on the availability or the extent of consortium relief (see para 7.41ff).

4 Different classes of shares

2.22   In the case of a corporate joint venture, one of the chief tools in meeting any differing requirements of the parties is to issue them with shares of different classes. Table 2 lists the types of share in common use with the different attributes of each, but the variety of rights which may be attached to a share is virtually infinite, although subject to the requirements of capital maintenance.

2.23   As well as the attributes listed in the table, shares may be issued with different minority protection rights attached to them as class rights (for example, rights to appoint directors and vetoes on specified transactions or matters) so there is generally sufficient flexibility to cater for a wide variety of different requirements. Similar rights may also be conferred by contractual provisions in the shareholders' agreement. These aspects are dealt with in more detail in Chapter 14.

5 Dealing with other expectations and requirements

2.24   Various other expectations and requirements of the parties are likely to need to be addressed in the documents.

● One of the most important concerns of a joint venturer is that the other joint venturers should be fully committed to the venture and will not compete with it. This will often be best achieved where their financial commitment is large, or where they are required to transfer existing goodwill into the venture, since the size and nature of the investment will mean that they will need to strive for its success, or face a large write-off in their accounts. A more direct method will be to obtain non-competition covenants from each venturer not to compete with the venture whilst they are engaged in it and for a period of years afterwards. The feasibility of this is discussed at para 10.58ff, but EU and UK competition law has an impact on such covenants. They need to be of limited scope to be enforceable in most cases.

● Venturers in a minority position will often want to ensure that they have a right to be consulted on important decisions of policy and that they will be able to veto certain transactions which they may consider detrimental to their interests. Minority protection is discussed in detail in Chapters 14 and 15.

● Venturers who are required to provide goods or services to the venture will be concerned to ensure that they receive a proper price for them and that the venture does not buy the product or service from elsewhere. Such concerns may be addressed by appropriate supply agreements, subject again to limitations imposed under EU laws (see para 3.15ff).

● Participants entering into full-time employment within the venture will be keen to ensure that they are guaranteed such employment for a minimum period and that their salary and benefits are clearly defined, which can be dealt with by the negotiation of a suitable service agreement.

Case studies showing the matching of aims and expectations

2.25   A US corporation owned the rights to some new technology. It was not able to obtain conventional loan finance to develop this into a viable product. Instead, it formed a new company into which the rights were transferred, and invited a consortium of venture capitalists to subscribe for shares in it. In order to meet their expectations of an exit and an adequate rate of return, the US corporation provided them with a put option under which, during a short period some years ahead, they were able to require the US corporation to purchase their shares at a price which would provide the venture capitalists with an internal rate of return of 30% compound per annum. By that time the product was expected to be fully developed and it was likely that alternative finance would be available to the US corporation. The price paid by the US corporation probably bore no relation to the market value of the shares at that time, but it did not mind paying over the odds if by doing so it could secure a 100% interest in the new product, which was expected to be highly profitable in the future and return the cost of acquisition many times over; the US corporation simply regarded the price as its cost of capital for the product. The venture capitalists secured a rate of return equivalent to the industry target without very much risk. Note how the structure of the deal was arranged so as to suit the requirements of the venture capitalists; they were not asked to make conventional loans at an exceptionally high rate of interest, since this would not have been in accordance with their usual investment criteria; they were asked to subscribe for equity because venture capitalists normally make their profit through investing in and disposing of equity.

2.26   A three party joint venture was established to open and run a nightclub. The participants consisted of an individual experienced in the management of nightclubs who was expected to provide the management, a bank who was to put up most of the money and a drinks firm who would supply drinks to the club. Each party took an equal share of the equity, and paid an equal amount for their shares, although this was only a very small proportion of the capital required. It was hoped that the company would eventually own a chain of nightclubs and that the parties would eventually realise their shareholdings by means of a flotation or trade sale of the company. Thus far their interests were identical, but the aims and expectations of the parties also reflected the different roles which they would have in the venture. In the case of the individual, the other parties expected him to devote himself full-time to the venture for a minimum period of years, and he expected to receive an appropriate salary for his services. He therefore entered into a service agreement. It was expected that the drinks company would supply drinks at a competitive price, and it expected to derive a profit from such sales. This need was met by a long-term supply agreement. The bank was to provide nearly all the money required by means of loan finance, and it obtained a debenture over the assets and undertaking of the joint company. When the venture failed, the interests of the joint venturers became radically different. The only party who was able to make any material recovery was the bank as secured creditor.

Table 2
Classes of shares in common use

Class	Dividends	Return of capital on liquidation	Voting rights	Others
Ordinary	Shareholders are entitled to all the distributed profits, once all preference dividends (if applicable) have been paid.	Are entitled to all the assets remaining after liabilities and all claims for return of capital to preference shareholders (if applicable) have been met.	Yes.	
Preference	Shareholders are entitled to a fixed dividend in priority to the ordinary shareholders.	Are entitled to the return of their capital in priority to the ordinary shares.	Not usually, but may vote if their dividend has not been paid.	
Cumulative preference	As for preference, except that if the dividend for any period is not paid in full, the unpaid amount is carried forward to the next year and ranks in front of the ordinary shareholders.	As for preference, except that they receive all arrears of dividends in priority to their capital.	As for preference.	
Participating preference	As for preference, except that once the ordinary shareholders have received a dividend equal to the fixed preference dividend, any remaining distributed profits are divided between participating preference and ordinary shareholders in accordance with their specific rights; the fixed dividend may be cumulative.	As for preference or cumulative preference, except that once the ordinary shareholders have received capital equivalent to the amount payable in respect of the participating preference shares any remaining assets are divided pari passu between the participating preference and ordinary shareholders.	Generally yes.	

Class	Dividends	Return of capital on liquidation	Voting rights	Others
Convertible preference	As for preference, but could be cumulative and/or participating.	As for preference, but could be cumulative and/or participating.	Generally yes – may vote as if they had converted.	Convertible into ordinary shares on a 1:1 basis or on a formula.
Redeemable preference	As for preference, but could be cumulative and/or participating.	As for preference but could be cumulative and/or participating.	Not usually, but may be entitled to vote if dividend is in arrears or redemption refused; sometimes obtain enhanced voting power on these events.	Capital and any arrears of any cumulative dividends are repayable by the company on a fixed date, or when required by the company or the shareholder.
Convertible redeemable preference	As for preference, but could be cumulative and/or participating.	As for preference but could be cumulative and/or participating.	Generally yes; may vote as if they had converted.	Convertible as for convertible preference shares, but if not converted by a fixed date capital is immediately repayable.
Deferred	No dividend until all dividends payable in priority have reached a specified amount.	No return of capital until all preference shareholders have received their capital, and all ordinary shareholders have received a specified amount.	Not usually.	

Chapter 3

The contributions of the parties to the joint venture

Summary

This chapter deals with the various contributions which each party may be required to make to the joint venture and appropriate methods of dealing with each. The subjects discussed include the advantages and disadvantages of establishing the joint venture as a self-contained entity, with appropriate transfers of physical assets and staff into it or on the basis that the joint venturers will supply it with all the services it requires. This chapter then discusses transfers of assets and undertakings, the advantages and disadvantages of a licence to use intellectual property compared with its outright transfer and the provision of supplies of goods and management and other services by the joint venturers, including the important issue of monitoring and enforcement. Transfers and secondments of employees are dealt with in Chapter 4, along with various other issues concerning employment law and pensions. This chapter assumes that the joint venture and its participants are located in the UK, although many of the same considerations, if not the same law, will arise in international joint ventures.

1 General

3.1   One of the chief matters to be decided in planning any joint venture is the contribution to be made by each participant. This is usually a key issue because such contributions are likely to form the whole foundation of the joint venture, with the expected contributions of the parties being the reason why the parties decided to get together in the first place. All parties will therefore be keen to tie the others down to detail in relation to the contributions each is contracted to make. Three main types of contribution may be relevant: the transfer of physical assets and associated intangibles, such as goodwill; transfers or licences of intellectual property; and the supply of manufactured articles, management and/or other services or finance. All these have their own considerations, but the most difficult relate to the provision of services where the level of performance required may be difficult to define and effective sanctions for non-performance will take some care to achieve.

3.2   There will often be a choice between transferring the actual assets needed for the venture to the joint venture vehicle or retaining them and contracting with the vehicle for the provision of the services carried out with those assets, or a licence to use them. Many joint ventures have been established on the basis that few or any physical assets are actually transferred. The joint venture vehicle may, for example, have a board of directors, a chief executive and some sales staff who obtain orders, but the goods ordered are then manufactured under contracts with the participating joint venturers, who retain all the plant, machinery and intellectual property necessary for that purpose, and deliver the goods to the customers. The joint venture company receives the price of the goods sold, pays the joint venturers for the services they have each provided, and periodically distributes the profits as dividends. The premises of the joint venture may be a few rooms in the premises of one of the joint venturers. Even the employees may be seconded from one or more of the joint venturers. Sometimes, there may not even be a sales staff, and those of the joint venturers canvass for their own employer as well as for the joint venture.

3.3   The advantage of few assets being transferred is that the joint venture is easy to dismantle, should that ever be necessary, as well as being likely to have fewer tax implications. However, it is unlikely to suit joint venturers who envisage a capital profit by the sale of the joint enterprise to a third party or by flotation. This will especially be the case where its name is a combination of the names of the joint venturers, and therefore it has no goodwill in its own right. An enterprise which is to be sold off or floated needs to be as free-standing as possible.

3.4   Another possible disadvantage of this structure is that if all services are provided by the joint venturers, there may be conflicts with their own requirements and the joint venture business may suffer as a result. Consideration should also be given to the risk of damage to the joint venture if a service provider gets into financial difficulty. Another point is that if some parties are reluctant to commit assets, others (eg financiers) may be concerned that they lack real commitment to the venture and that the venture may have insufficient assets to effectively secure borrowings. In practical terms, however, the venture may be so small to start with that it would not be economic for it to be self-standing, and the business plan may need to provide for a phased acquisition of its own facilities. If the venture is successful, this may be necessary in any case in order to avoid those of the joint venturers being overburdened. However, if a sale is envisaged, the venture should at least start with its own brand name.

2   Physical assets and undertakings

3.5   Where joint venturers are to contribute physical assets or an existing business undertaking to the venture, the same considerations will arise as on any such transfer. It is desirable that a proper agreement for the transfer is drawn up, together with the provision of appropriate warranties (see Chapter 25), just as in a transfer by a party at arm's length. All appropriate due diligence should be undertaken. The entire legal as well as the beneficial interest in the assets to be sold should be transferred (as far as practicable).

3.6   Where an existing business undertaking is being transferred, this may involve a transfer of all the shares in a subsidiary company of one of the participants, or a transfer of the assets and liabilities which comprise the business. In the latter case it is desirable that the joint venture vehicle should not be overburdened by existing liabilities. As far as is practicable, only those assets and liabilities which are actually necessary to the continuing undertaking should be transferred: the fixed assets, the stocks, the work in progress and the liabilities on uncompleted contracts. Book debts and undischarged liabilities relating to the period prior to transfer should generally stay with the seller. Employees of the undertaking will automatically transfer under TUPE[1].

3.7   The price to be paid will obviously be a matter for negotiation, but market value will generally be appropriate; there is no good reason why the joint venture vehicle should be made to pay a book value which is higher than market value, which would be unfair for the other participants. Another point to consider is that if the asset is to be transferred in exchange for shares and it has been overvalued, this could potentially result in an unlawful issue of shares at a discount. A sale at a book value lower than market value may be attractive to the other parties and is possible provided that a transferor which is a company has positive distributable profits. There may well be tax considerations for the seller in respect of any sale of assets.

3.8   Stamp duty will be payable on the transfer of shares, other marketable securities and partnership interests where the partnership does not hold land at a rate of 0.5% of the consideration unless the joint venture company is being established as at least a 75% subsidiary of the transferring venturer (allowing relief under the Finance Act 1930, s 42 – see para 7.32[2]). Stamp duty land tax ('SDLT') is payable in England and Northern Ireland on transfers of chargeable interests in land and on the grant of leases of land, at rates

---

1   SI 2006/246. See para 4.13ff. TUPE continues from 1 January 2021 despite the end of the post-Brexit transition period. Although the Government has stated it will consider changing employment law no Employment Bill has been produced by the date of this 6th edition and no mention was made of it in the 2021 Queen's Speech. It is possible new legislation may make it easier to harmonise TUPE transferred staff's employment terms to those of the buyer's existing employees, or to dismiss employees and possibly service provision changes may be removed from TUPE, but none of these changes has yet occurred.

2   For guidance on s 42 including SDLT procedural changes introduced due to the Covid-19 pandemic in 2020, see https://www.gov.uk/government/publications/relief-from-sd-when-documents-effect-intra-group-transfers-of-stock-or-marketable-securities/relief-from-stamp-duty-in-respect-of-documents-effecting-intra-group-transfers-of-stock-or-marketable-securities.

reaching to 5% of the consideration for commercial property freeholds, but again relief is available for a transfer into a subsidiary in which the transferor holds 75% or more. There are likely to be higher rates (an additional 2%) in England and Northern Ireland when the draft Finance Bill receives royal assent in 2021 in cases where the buyer of real property is a foreign buyer. Stamp duty land tax is payable on the transfer of partnership interests where the partnership owns land. SDLT is discussed in more detail at para 7.33. No other transfers of assets are liable to stamp duty or SDLT. VAT will also be payable on the transfer of those assets which attract it, unless they are transferred 'as a going concern' (essentially, they represent a business in their own right, in which case relief is available), or unless the transferor and the transferee are part of the same VAT group – see para 7.30ff. It may be possible to defer payment of these taxes if payment of the consideration is deferred. Stamp duty is also payable on top of any VAT. HMRC SDLT calculator is set out at https://www.tax.service.gov.uk/calculate-stamp-duty-land-tax/#/intro. Scotland has Land and Buildings Transaction Tax instead of SDLT with different rates and with a calculator being set out at https://www.revenue.scot/land-buildings-transaction-tax/tax-calculators. Wales has a land transaction tax with a rate of up to 6% for non-residential property – see https://gov.wales/land-transaction-tax-calculator.

3.9   The joint venture vehicle will need to be funded so as to be able to pay the price for the assets to be transferred to it. In the case of a company, the joint venturers may make cash subscriptions for shares or loans out of which the purchase price may be paid. Alternatively, if the purchase price does not exceed the transferor's participation, the assets may be transferred in exchange for an issue of shares credited as fully-paid to the transferor, or the price may be left outstanding on loan account. An issue of shares in exchange for assets is an issue otherwise than for cash, but the Companies Act 2006 (unlike the CA 1985) does not require the duly stamped transfer agreement or a statement of its terms to be placed on the public file of the joint venture company.

3   Intellectual property

3.10   Intellectual property (IP), if required by the joint venture, is normally licensed by its owner to the joint venture vehicle rather than transferred outright, so that it is still available to the owner if the venture fails.

3.11   The disadvantage of this arrangement is the lack of security for the joint venture vehicle, especially if the intellectual property is vital to the venture. Licences are invariably subject to termination in various circumstances, and a business in its early stages can easily fall into technical default. This may give the licensor very considerable additional bargaining power, or may result in the termination of the venture. Beware of conflicts of interest. If advising the new company, it may be in its interests to require the owner of such rights to assign them to the JV company, and indeed some financial investors may require this before they are prepared to invest in the company. If advising the individual IP owner it will be in his or her interests to retain the IP in their name in case the JV company later goes out of business.

3.12   The other venturers may therefore insist, where possible, that the proposed licensor transfers the whole of the intellectual property to the joint venture vehicle. Where the proposed licensor also needs to use it in its own business, this will not generally be practicable, but if this other use is relatively small, a possible solution is to transfer the intellectual property to the joint venture company which can then grant the transferor a non-exclusive royalty-free perpetual worldwide licence, limited to exploitation in any area outside the scope of the joint venture. It may be that it is possible to divide up the property: certain patents or other rights may only be of value to the joint venture and these can be transferred, with the joint venture vehicle accepting only a licence in respect of the other rights. An acceptable alternative to an outright transfer might be a perpetual licence to the joint venture. Take tax advice too as there may be some advantage in a UK subsidiary paying royalties to a parent company based in a tax haven (see A Fairpo, *Taxation of Intellectual Property*, 4th edn, 2016).

3.13   If a licence, perpetual or not, is to be employed, special care needs to be taken in drafting details of the events upon which it may be terminated. Generous periods for remedying breaches, particularly payments of royalties, may be appropriate. If a sale of the whole venture to a third party is envisaged, the licence ought to continue even if the joint venture terminates or the joint administration is likely to prevent a satisfactory realisation of the business in those events, and it may be appropriate to include a standstill period, during which the licence continues, so as to allow the administrator or liquidator to assign it with the business. This also involves the licensor accepting the assignment; a formula under which the licensor's consent is required but cannot be unreasonably withheld may be appropriate. Insolvency by itself should not be a termination event. It may well be difficult to persuade the licensor to agree to these points, but on the other hand they are desirable to protect the investments of the other parties, and may also turn out to benefit the licensor.

3.14   Royalties are obviously a matter for negotiation: in the early stages of the venture there may be a case for them being rolled up and paid later. Where the intellectual property is of no practical value without further development funded by the joint venturers, there is certainly a case for the licence being royalty free. There is no justification for a minimum royalty during a period in which no sales can be expected because the product is not yet ready for sale.

4 Supply of goods and management and other services

3.15   A joint venture will often be dependent upon the supply of goods, management and other services by one or more of the joint venturers, particularly in the early stages of a venture. Agreements under which such goods or services are supplied are referred to in this book as 'support agreements'.

3.16   A support agreement may be a vital ingredient for the success of the venture, and indeed the expectation of its availability may have led to the decision to establish the joint venture in the first place. These agreements involve particular difficulties because of their ongoing nature. An agreement to transfer specific assets or to license specific intellectual property will normally be performed at the joint venture completion meeting, and the other parties can simply refuse to complete and therefore refuse to inject their subscription monies if the necessary assignments or licences are not completed. However, an agreement to provide goods or services after completion requires subsequent monitoring and adequate sanctions to ensure performance. More fundamentally, the agreement will require very careful drafting in order to ensure that the precise specification, quality and timely delivery of the goods or services are adequately specified.

3.17   The need for adequate specifications in the agreement is, of course, not confined to joint ventures, but enforcement is a particular problem within them. The support agreement will invariably be made with the joint venture vehicle and therefore, in the absence of any special provisions, minority participants will have no ability to enforce the agreement against the contracting joint venturer. The minority participants may argue that the joint venture directors are under a statutory duty to see that the contract is enforced, but, in practice, if the board is dominated by the appointees of the contracting joint venturer such appointees may be able to find some reason as to why they do not think it is in the interests of the joint company to take any action.

3.18   Ways of addressing the issue could include:

(1) providing that the contracting joint venturers' board representatives may not vote on any matter concerning the support agreement or that the supervision of the support agreement shall be delegated to a committee of the board, which does not include any representatives of the contracting joint venturer, with authority for that committee to terminate the agreement and/or to institute legal proceedings if they are considered by it to be necessary (these may not be very effective sanctions, since litigation would be likely to be a drain on the resources of the joint venture and would distract it from the development of its business, and it may be impossible to obtain a substitute contractor);

(2)   laying down detailed milestones with target dates for their achievement
       in the support agreement and imposing sanctions if they are not met –
       these could potentially take the form of 'step in' rights or just agreed
       liquidated damages or, more drastically, the downward adjustment of
       the contracting joint venturer's participation in the venture by means of
       some kind of reverse ratchet mechanism, often referred to as a 'squeeze
       down' (see para 27.25);

(3)   making a material breach of the support agreement a ground for the
       termination of the joint venture agreement, and thereby triggering
       mechanisms which could result in the defaulting joint venturer being
       required to sell its shares or to buy those of the others (see para 17.15ff).
       Although there could be an argument as to whether a particular breach is
       sufficiently material; this would, in the absence of a negotiated solution,
       have to be resolved by the courts, or under the procedure in a dispute
       resolution agreement (see Chapter 23). A share purchase or sale in those
       circumstances should be at the request of the non-defaulting venturers –
       if this is automatic or at the option of the defaulter it could engineer its
       own exit by defaulting; the other venturers may prefer a minority joint
       venturer in breach to continue to hold its shares, but with the provision
       that its minority protections or even voting rights terminate on breach.

3.19   Particular care should be taken to ensure that if any joint venturer
is given a veto on the institution of legal proceedings by the joint venture
vehicle, the veto does not extend to the institution of proceedings against
that joint venturer itself.

3.20   Otherwise, the normal principles for drafting any such agreement
will apply. Generally speaking, the joint venture vehicle should pay the
proper market price for the services of one of its participants – if it pays less
than the full price, HMRC may adjust the transaction under the transfer
pricing legislation, and the directors of the supplier who approved the receipt
of a lower price may be in breach of their statutory duties. Quite apart from
this, if the joint venture pays less than the full price an element of unreality is
introduced into its accounts and there could be a sudden drop in profitability
if it has to employ another contractor.

3.21   What was said in para 3.11ff about events entitling intellectual
property licences to be terminated is also of relevance to a contract to
provide goods and services. In some cases it may be less crucial, in that the
joint venture vehicle could obtain another contractor to provide the goods
or service, but there are clearly circumstances in which this will not be the
case, such as where the provider owns the intellectual property involved, or
is possessed of unique know-how or resources, in which case arrangements
of the kind mentioned in para 3.13 will be relevant. In any event, it will often
be inappropriate to provide that the agreement ends automatically, or may
be terminated by the service provider, immediately its participation in the

joint venture ceases; a grace period should be considered to give time to obtain another provider. Apart from this, there is a case for including only one other termination event on the part of the joint venture vehicle, namely breach of the agreement (with a generous period for remedying breaches) and excluding any events related to insolvency.

3.22   The following points require particular attention:

- If the provider will be making use of its own intellectual property when providing the goods or services, the joint venture vehicle may subsequently need to use it for its own products or services; it may therefore be appropriate for it to receive a non-exclusive royalty-free perpetual worldwide licence to do so, with the power to grant sub-licences.

- Provisions under which the provider agrees to keep confidential specified information relating to the joint venture vehicle. A reverse undertaking may also be appropriate.

- Where employees of the provider will work on any premises of a joint venture vehicle, it will need to be clear who is responsible for health and safety matters. It is suggested that the joint venture vehicle should be responsible for ensuring a safe system of work on its premises, but that the provider should ensure it only uses properly trained staff who have their own safety equipment, and that any plant they bring with them is safe. This division of responsibility will only be effective as between the parties themselves, so mutual indemnities will need to be drawn up in order to distribute the liability between them in the agreed way, but each may still of course be liable to criminal prosecution if they have failed to carry out their legal responsibilities, even if this arises through default of the other party.

- Where managerial or advisory services are involved, it will generally be appropriate to state that the provider is not liable for any act, omission or error of judgment except where it arises through negligence, dishonesty or wilful default.

- Whether there should be agreed liquidated damages in relation to particular kinds of breach, or an overall limit on the provider's liability (excluding liability for death or personal injury caused by negligence or any loss caused by fraud). This is a particularly important issue in relation to a joint venture, because if the liability of the contracting joint venturer is to be limited in some way it may throw a disproportionate loss on the other joint venturers, who will sustain the whole loss of the value of their participations resulting from the breach by the provider.

- Force majeure.

- Where the joint venture company and any joint venturer are not in the same VAT group, VAT will be payable on the charges, which should therefore be expressed to be exclusive of VAT.

Note that the Unfair Contracts Terms Act 1977 will need to be taken into account when drafting any limitations of liability. Where an investor is an individual and not dealing as a consumer the Consumer Rights Act 2015 provisions on unfair terms may also be relevant.

5 Termination and exit provisions

3.23   Where licences of intellectual property or support agreements contain a right to terminate if the licensor or contractor ceases to be a participant in the venture, this can have significant implications in the exit provisions available to the outgoing participant. For example, the joint venture agreement may provide an exit for the outgoing shareholder by reference to valuation provisions which assume continuation of the joint venture and provide for the outgoing shareholder's participation to be valued accordingly. This is inappropriate if the outgoing participant can terminate the licence or support agreement immediately afterwards.

Chapter 4

Employment and pensions issues in UK based joint ventures

Summary

This chapter discusses the transfer and seconding of employees to a joint venture, with particular reference to the impact of TUPE. Pensions issues are then also discussed, including the types of scheme available and the advantages and disadvantages of the joint venture establishing its own scheme or participating in one established by one of the joint venturers. The practical consequences of each route are considered, together with the position should the joint venture vehicle take over the whole of an existing pension scheme from one of the joint venturers. This chapter assumes that the joint venture has its operations in the UK.

1 Transfer of employees

Transfer without an undertaking

4.1   Where it is proposed that employees of one or more joint venturers are to be transferred to the joint venture vehicle, it is important to establish whether they are being transferred with an 'undertaking'. If so, the Transfer of Undertakings (Protection of Employment) Regulations 2006 (as amended by Collective Redundancies and Transfer of Undertakings (Protection of Employment) (Amendment) Regulations 2014) ('TUPE')[1] will apply, and the relevant employees will transfer to the joint venture vehicle on their existing employment contracts and with their continuous service recognised. The impact of TUPE is discussed in para 4.13ff, together with guidance on what constitutes an 'undertaking' under TUPE. TUPE's predecessor regulations implemented the 1977 acquired rights EU directive into English law. TUPE continues to apply from 1 January 2021 when the post-Brexit transition period ended, although it is possible in due course the UK may choose to make some changes to TUPE.

4.2   Where there is no transfer of an 'undertaking' to the joint venture vehicle, a transfer of employees can only be achieved with the employees' consent to a change in the identity of the employer. This will essentially

---

1   SI 2006/246.

be a new offer of employment with a new employer. If more than one joint venturer is contributing employees and/or the joint venture vehicle is also recruiting employees from outside, the employer will want to harmonise terms and conditions as much as possible, so as to avoid future difficulties in employment relations and to ensure that the joint venture workforce is employed on the most competitive and effective terms.

4.3   There are two possible approaches to transferring employees to a new joint venture. The less aggressive approach is a two-stage process, whereby the employees concerned initially consent to the change in the identity of the employer and thereafter terms of employment are gradually harmonised over a period of time. The advantages of this route are its simplicity, the avoidance of unnecessary documentation and, possibly, more harmonious long-term working relations. The joint venture company will notify the affected employees of the necessary changes and request the employee sign a document, indicating their acceptance. This may not always work: there may be difficulty in persuading employees to consent to the change in the identity of the employer and they may seek consideration for the changes. Further, the employees may perform the new terms of employment under protest and subsequently challenge the transfer of employment, either by claiming damages for breach of contract or by resigning and claiming constructive dismissal.

4.4   A more robust approach is to make the necessary changes in one step by the termination of existing employment contracts by way of redundancy, ie because there is a diminished requirement for employees to do work of that particular kind, and the offering of new ones by the joint venture vehicle. Any redundancy process requires appropriate warning, consultation and careful selection of employees, and should comply with ACAS guidelines. The employee will be entitled to receive a statutory redundancy payment, their notice and any enhanced redundancy payments. An employer choosing this route does so on the basis that, since any employee refusing the new offer of employment will be redundant, most can be expected to accept the new offer, as long as it is on reasonable terms. The advantage of this approach is that the new contracts can offer completely new terms and conditions appropriate to the joint venture. If employees are transferring from more than one joint venturer, it is possible to achieve standard terms for all of them immediately, rather than an assortment of different existing terms which are likely to cause friction.

4.5   In the case of collective redundancies regard should be given to the Trade Union and Labour Relations (Consolidation) Act 1992, as amended most recently by Trade Union and Labour Relations (Consolidation) Act 1992 (Amendment) Order 2013[2] ('the Regulations'), which requires the employing

---

2   SI 2013/763.

joint venturer to consult with appropriate representatives and not to dismiss any employees during the 30 day consultation period (where it is proposed to dismiss between 20 and 99 employees) or 45 (previously 90) days (where it is proposed to dismiss 100 or more employees). This duty is separate from (and therefore may arise alongside) the obligations to inform and consult considered at para 4.17. The maximum penalty (called a 'protective award') for failure to inform and consult on collective redundancies is now 13 weeks' pay for each dismissed employee.

Under Collective Redundancies and Transfer of Undertakings (Protection of Employment) (Amendment) Regulations 2014 microbusinesses can consult direct with workers where there are no representatives. For these Government guidance states:

'You're entitled to a consultation with your employer if you're being made redundant. This involves speaking to them about:

- why you are being made redundant

- any alternatives to redundancy

If your employer is making up to 19 redundancies, there are no rules about how they should carry out the consultation. If they're making 20 or more redundancies at the same time, the collective redundancy rules apply. You can make a claim to an employment tribunal if your employer does not consult properly, for example if they start late, or do not consult at all.'

4.6   If the existing employer does not terminate on the basis of redundancy or fails to follow a proper dismissal process, employees with more than two years of service can claim unfair dismissal. An employee would be entitled to receive the following awards on the finding of unfair dismissal (as well as notice): any statutory redundancy entitlement, which is a fixed amount, depending on the level of pay, length of continuous employment and age of the employee (subject to a maximum £16,320), and a compensatory award for any loss sustained by the individual in consequence of the dismissal, which is an additional award of between 26 and 52 weeks' pay if the employer fails to comply with an order to re-instate or re-engage the employee (subject to a maximum of £89,493). The figures in this paragraph were current as at July 2021.

4.7   In practice, in order to avoid difficulties with the employees or their representatives, the joint venture company may have to offer terms to its 'new' employees which are equivalent to the best of the existing terms offered by the joint venturers, or are as favourable overall.

4.8   Where the joint venture company is an 'associated employer' of the previous employer (see para 4.11) the previous employer will be in a better position, because employees dismissed for redundancy will lose their right to redundancy pay if they unreasonably refuse an offer of suitable alternative employment (on the same terms with continuous service recognised and where the employment is suitable in relation to the employee). If the new terms differ from the previous employment contract, employees have a statutory trial period (of four weeks) in the new employment during which, if they reasonably decline to accept the new terms and conditions with the joint venture company, statutory redundancy payments will be due; but none will be due if they accept the new terms or unreasonably decline them.

4.9   Employees who are requested to transfer to a joint venture vehicle will often be concerned about the termination of their existing employment. They may request assurances that their return is possible at the grade at which they left, or any enhanced grade they may achieve whilst employed by the joint venture vehicle. Employees who have pension rights will generally wish to ensure that these are safeguarded. There will often also be concerns about job security, particularly as there may be a loss of continuity of employment for the purposes of minimum notice periods (in some situations), redundancy and protection against unfair dismissal, and there may be an added risk that the joint venture could fail.

4.10   Affected employees, particularly senior ones, may prefer to be seconded to the joint venture vehicle for a defined period, at least initially. Secondment would only be appropriate where an employee is only to work for the joint venture for a short period and TUPE does not apply. Secondment is dealt with in para 4.31ff.

4.11   Where employees enter into new contracts with the joint venture (after their existing contracts have terminated), their periods of continuous employment for the purpose of certain employment protection rights will be broken unless the joint venture vehicle is an 'associated employer' of the previous employer as provided by the Employment Rights Act 1996, s 218(6). Two employers are associated for this purpose where one company has direct or indirect control over the other (ie where the previous employer or its holding company holds more than half the voting rights in the joint venture company), or both are companies of which a third person has control directly or indirectly so that continuity will be preserved. In a 50:50 company, neither of the joint venturers is an associated employer of the joint venture company. Where the joint venture is a partnership, it will not be an associated employer, unless the former employer has control over the other joint venture partners. In practice, the offer of employment with the joint venture may need to provide for employment to be treated as continuous as an inducement for employees to accept it, and will be relevant for the accrual of statutory employment protection rights.

4.12   Where TUPE does not apply, collective bargaining agreements with trade unions will not transfer to the joint venture automatically. However in practice the relevant trade unions may press for recognition, which could result in employees of the joint venture transferring from different joint venturers being represented by different trade unions. It is worth nothing in this regard that there is a statutory procedure for compulsory recognition. These provisions provide that a union will be recognised where, via the statutory process, it is established that a majority of the workers in the section of the workforce that the union wants to represent support union recognition. This mandate for union recognition can be established either by reference to the number of union members in the section of the workforce the union wants to represent or, where a ballot is held, the union receiving sufficient votes in favour of recognition.

Transfer with an undertaking

4.13   Where the transfer of a business (or part thereof) of the joint venturers to the joint venture vehicle by means of a transfer of assets (rather than the transfer of its share capital) involves the transfer of an 'undertaking' (ie a discrete economic entity), the employees assigned to that undertaking will automatically transfer to the joint venture vehicle on their current terms and conditions, and with their continuous employment recognised. This includes any accrued rights relating to minimum notice periods, redundancy and unfair dismissal (on the basis that there is no termination of employment, so that periods of service with the transferor are continuous and count as service with the transferee) and terms as to pay and benefits. It is important to note that an employee's terms and conditions cannot be amended by reason of the transfer alone. This means that even consensual variations (before or after the transfer) are ineffective. However, there can be a valid variation for a reason other than because of the transfer.

4.14   Currently, the provisions of occupational pension schemes, in so far as they relate to retirement, invalidity or survivor's benefits, will not transfer. However, obligations in respect of early retirement and redundancy terms aligned to an occupational scheme may in fact transfer automatically. Much will depend on the structure of the occupational pension scheme in determining what aspects, if any, of the scheme will have to be replicated after the transfer. Furthermore, the law is being amended to oblige the new employer to provide certain specified minimum benefits in place of those provided under the old employer's scheme. This issue is discussed in para 4.103ff.

4.15   Any collective agreement made by the transferor with a recognised trade union will also transfer and will apply as if originally made with the transferee and that trade union.

4.16   An 'undertaking' is a discrete economic entity consisting of an organised group of persons (which may only consist of one person) and assets which are dedicated to the attainment of a specific objective. The economic entity must retain its identity after the transfer, evidenced, for example, by the same work being done by the same employees in the same place. Relevant factors include: the type of undertaking concerned; whether tangible assets are transferred; the value of the intangible assets; whether the majority of employees are taken over by the new employer; whether customers transfer; the degree of similarity between the activities carried on before and after the transfer; and any period of suspension of those activities. A separate profit centre with its goodwill, whether or not including all of its assets, is likely to be an undertaking, but a collection of assets not by themselves forming a separate profit centre will not be. An undertaking need not be in the nature of a commercial venture or necessarily have significant tangible or intangible assets, in particular where the activity is essentially based on manpower. A transfer of a staff canteen to a joint venture vehicle is likely to constitute a transfer of an undertaking, with the consequence that all employees assigned to the canteen will automatically transfer. The same is likely to apply to the transfer of any other service function of the transferor, such as an accounting or computer department. An undertaking includes part of an undertaking as long as it is a separate and self-contained part.

4.17   The Regulations requires the transferor to inform and consult with relevant trade unions and employee representatives on any proposed transfer of employment to be made under the regulations. TUPE also requires that certain information must be made available to those employees 'affected' by the transfer (not just those who will transfer). There are no specific time limits to consult under TUPE (unlike the Regulations), but information must be provided within a sufficient period to enable consultation to take place. Employers who recognise a trade union must consult that union as well as any other relevant representatives of the employees. Specific requirements are laid down for electing employee representatives who are to be consulted. If an employer invites affected employees to elect representatives but elections are not held within a reasonable time, the employer must give to each affected employee the information that would have been provided to the elected representatives. Representatives of all employees who may be affected need to be consulted. As stated above microbusinesses where there are no representatives may consult the employees direct.

4.18   The maximum penalty for failure to inform and consult under TUPE is 13 weeks' gross pay for each affected employee. The current position is that the transferor and transferee are jointly and severally liable for failure to consult in relation to TUPE.

4.19   An employee will be treated as having been automatically unfairly dismissed if the transfer or a reason connected with it is the reason or the principal reason for their dismissal, unless the dismissal is for an 'economic, technical or organisational reason entailing changes in the workforce' ('an

ETO reason') and a fair process has been followed. This is the case whether the dismissal takes place before or after the transfer. Where an employee establishes that they have been unfairly dismissed (whether automatically or by reason of a failure to follow a fair process), they will be entitled to recover compensation subject to the statutory cap applicable from time to time (see para 4.6).

4.20   In the context of a joint venture, a redundancy dismissal may be justified where the joint venture vehicle does not require as many employees to carry out the work that is transferring and the transferor/transferee does not have alternative work available. However, it is worth noting that in order to avoid liability under general unfair dismissal principles the redundancy would have to be based on a fair selection process and implemented in accordance with accepted good practice. If this is done, the employee will, on the face of it, only be entitled to a statutory redundancy payment and any contractual compensation which is due (eg contractual notice, accrued holiday pay etc).

4.21   In terms of liability for dismissals in the context of a TUPE transfer, currently the general principles are:

- pre-transfer dismissals which are not connected with the transfer remain the responsibility of the transferor;

- pre-transfer dismissals connected with the transfer but justified on an ETO basis remain the responsibility of the transferor;

- pre-transfer dismissals by reason of the transfer but where there is no ETO will result in liability for the dismissal transferring to the transferee (but see below); and

- post-transfer dismissals by reason of the transfer or otherwise will be the responsibility of the transferee.

4.22   TUPE allows for employees to object to the transfer. However, such a decision carries serious consequences for the employee. Where an employee exercises the right of statutory objection, his employment automatically terminates on completion of the transfer. The individual is not treated as having been dismissed (either by the transferor or by the transferee) and is not entitled to notice, a statutory redundancy or to pursue a claim of unfair dismissal. Accordingly, the statutory right to object is seldom used by employees.

4.23   Where a relevant transfer involves or would involve a substantial change in working conditions to the material detriment of the employee, the employee may treat the contract as having been terminated and claim constructive dismissal. Unlike other pre-transfer TUPE-related dismissals, liability for such a dismissal remains with the transferor. If after the transfer has taken place the transferee introduces such a change, the law may also regard such a variation as a constructive dismissal, but in this case the transferee remains liable for the dismissal. Where the changes introduced or proposed are connected with a TUPE transfer, such a constructive dismissal will be automatically unfair. The changes brought in by Collective Redundancies and Transfer of Undertakings (Protection of Employment) (Amendment) Regulations 2014 allow contractual changes for economic, technical or organisational reasons with the agreement of the employee and/ or where a contractual right of variation exists.

4.24   Until 2014 the previous law provided that changes to terms and conditions of employment by reason of a TUPE transfer were void, even if agreed to by the employees concerned. Despite the 2014 changes mentioned above it remains sensible to delay any proposed changes until some time after the transfer, and implement them in a subsequent reorganisation. When changes are made, they should be attributed to a reason other than the transfer[3], and they may be effected by either of the methods discussed in paras 4.3–4.6. The 2014 changes provide that businesses may now renegotiate terms and conditions in collective agreements one year after a transfer has taken place, provided that the overall change is no less favourable.

4.25   Alternatively, instead of transferring an 'undertaking' to the joint venture, a transferor may effect an internal reorganisation, hive down the relevant employees to a new subsidiary company and then sell the shares in the new company to the joint venture. Subsequently, harmonisation of employees' terms by the joint venture having purchased the company's shares may have nothing to do with the transfer. However, there is a risk that the hive down and share sale could be considered as a series of transactions which together constitute a transfer and therefore will attract the operation of TUPE.

4.26   The parties to a transfer may not contract out of TUPE, although it is possible to allocate responsibility for the financial consequences of a transfer by means of appropriately worded indemnities and warranties.

Restrictive covenants

4.27   One feature requiring attention is the position under confidentiality agreements and/or restrictive covenants which the employees have entered into with the transferor. The basic position is that the restrictive covenants contained in the transferring employee's contract are potentially capable of enforcement. However, with regard to matters such as non-solicitation, non-competition and non-dealing provisions, which restrict an employee's

---

3   For a case illustrating the difficulties involved in aligning terms and conditions, see *Martin v South Bank University* [2004] IRLR 74.

activities when their employment ends, these will be interpreted at the point the covenants were entered into. This means that, for example, non-solicitation of client provisions will be based on the clients of the transferor and not the transferee. In all likelihood, therefore, restrictive covenants may have limited effect where the transferee has acquired assets but applies those to a different client base or a more mixed client base using different personnel.

4.28   The obvious solution to this problem, to ask the employee to enter into new restrictive covenants following the transfer, whilst attractive, may not in many cases provide an effective answer. Any contractual changes introduced by the transferee by reason of the transfer will be unenforceable. It may therefore be better for the transferee to look to introduce changes in the contractual terms based on other matters such as the promotion of a transferred employee or through incentive programmes, eg the introduction of new bonus structures which are tied to certain conditions having been satisfied, which could include restrictive covenants. However, it must be clear that these initiatives are not connected with the transfer – and are therefore not a 'smoke screen' behind which the transferee hopes to introduce unlawful amendments to the contracts of employment. In some cases this may be a difficult burden of proof to satisfy.

4.29   Reference should be made to TUPE and to the established textbooks for further guidance on the effect of TUPE[4].

In January 2013 the Department for Business published a consultation on proposed changes to TUPE regulations. This consultation followed the Government's review of TUPE conducted under the Red Tape Challenge and BIS' Call for Evidence on the Effectiveness of the TUPE Regulations 2006. The government was concerned that TUPE may go further than the EU Acquired Rights Directive which TUPE implements and is bureaucratic. The government concluded that there was scope to amend the regulations by removing provisions which go further than the Acquired Rights Directive requires and generally improve how the regulations operate. This led to the amendments mentioned above with effect from 1 January 2014. Those changes do not apply to Northern Ireland.

Transfers of subsidiary companies

4.30   Where the business undertaking to be transferred is that of a subsidiary company of one of the joint venturers, and it is decided to transfer the shares of that subsidiary to the joint venture vehicle, rather than its assets

---

4   For example, McMullen, *Business Transfers and Employee Rights* (Lexis Nexis, 2020); Wynn-Evans, *The Law of TUPE Transfers* (2016); and Upex and Ryley, *TUPE: Law and Practice* (2014).

and liabilities, TUPE will not apply (but see para 4.25). The employment contracts of the employees are not affected by the transaction (subject to any change of control provisions providing for an ability by the employee to terminate on a change of control of the employing company) and they remain employees of the subsidiary on the same terms as before, including pension rights. This may of itself cause difficulty if their terms are different from those generally intended to apply to the employees of the joint venture vehicle and their contract terms may need to be renegotiated, in so far as this is practicable.

2   Secondment of employees

4.31   Where employees are reluctant to transfer to the joint venture vehicle, or an employer is unwilling to make a particular employee available to it, other than on a temporary basis, an employee may be seconded to the joint venture vehicle. However it is important to note that there may be a risk of the employee claiming that TUPE applies to the joint venture in any event.

4.32   The effect of a secondment is that the original employment contract continues in force and, subject to the employee's consent, his or her services are provided to a third party – in this case the joint venture vehicle – and generally for a fixed period. Typically, the joint venture vehicle will pay the employer a fee for the services of the employee equal to the total cost to the employer of employing the person concerned. VAT will have to be charged unless the employer joint venturer is grouped with the joint venture for VAT purposes.

4.33   Even if the employment contract of the employee to be seconded contains a 'mobility clause', entitling the employer to request the employee to work anywhere, it is unlikely that this will be sufficient to compel the employee to work for a joint venture vehicle. In any event, such a clause should only be applied in a reasonable manner.

4.34   Therefore, in most cases, it will not be possible to second an employee without his or her consent.

Employees will generally be concerned that they do not suffer any financial penalty or loss of status as a result of a secondment and, in particular, that they will continue to receive normal salary reviews and that their promotion prospects will not be affected.

4.35   A secondment normally involves two legal agreements: an agreement between the employer and the joint venture vehicle, and an agreement between the employer and each employee to be seconded.

4.36   The first of these agreements will generally deal with the following matters:

- Details of the employees to be seconded and for how long, and whether the employer is bound to provide substitutes for those who are unavailable, or who have resigned.

- A statement that the employees remain the employees of the employer, but whilst seconded will act on the instructions of the joint venture vehicle.

- An undertaking by the employer to procure that where such employees act as officers (eg directors or secretary) of the joint venture vehicle they will resign upon completion of their secondment.

- An undertaking by the employer that it will not, and that it will procure that the employees will not, disclose any confidential information relating to the joint venture or any other joint venturer.

- An undertaking by the joint venture vehicle that it will not disclose any confidential information relating to the employer.

- Undertakings by the joint venture vehicle to observe the terms of the employment of the employees, other than the payment of remuneration.

- An undertaking by the joint venture vehicle to keep the employer informed about the conduct and progress of the employees, and the discipline of the employees remaining with the employer.

- An undertaking by the joint venture vehicle to comply with health and safety requirements in respect of the employees. This arrangement will not necessarily shift the legal responsibility for health and safety matters, so it will need to be supported by an indemnity from the joint venture vehicle in respect of any health and safety liabilities the employer may incur, but this still leaves the employer exposed to the risk of prosecution.

- The fees to be paid by the joint venture vehicle, normally equal to the full employment costs of the employees (inclusive of bonus, benefits, tax and National Insurance contributions) plus VAT.

- Reimbursement of employees (and the employer) for expenses incurred in connection with the provision of the employees' services to the joint venture vehicle.

- The ability for the joint venture vehicle to request the removal of a secondee where he or she commits an act in breach of the contract of employment, or conducts himself or herself in a manner prejudicial to the joint venture business, or is guilty of dishonesty.

- An agreement that all intellectual property which arises during the course of the secondment will belong to the joint venture vehicle.

- An indemnity by the joint venture vehicle in favour of the employer in respect of any vicarious liability the employer may incur in consequence of actions of the employees whilst they are under the instructions of the joint venture vehicle.

- Possibly, an undertaking by the joint venture vehicle not to seek to employ the seconded employees after the secondment, and possibly also provisions whereby the employer agrees to use all reasonable endeavours to procure that the employees enter into direct covenants with the joint venture vehicle not to compete with it after their employment with the employer has terminated.

- The circumstances in which either party may terminate the agreement before expiry of the fixed term.

4.37   The agreements between the employer and the seconded employees will mirror the terms of the secondment agreement. Provisions which are appropriate include the following:

- Confirmation that the employment with the employer continues and that, save as set out in the agreement, its terms are unchanged.

- Provisions for the employee's title and location of work.

- An obligation to work for the joint venture vehicle and act under its instructions.

- Confirmation that salary and benefits will continue to be paid by the employer.

- Provisions for the term of secondment and for earlier termination, mirroring the right of the joint venture vehicle to request the removal of the secondee and any right of the employer to terminate the secondment.

- An undertaking to observe confidentiality in respect of the confidential information of the joint venture vehicle.

- An undertaking to resign from any offices held with the joint venture vehicle upon termination of the secondment.

- Confirmation that all intellectual property arising out of the employee's work during the secondment will belong to the joint venture vehicle.

- In some cases, a restrictive covenant not to compete with the joint venture company. This needs to be in favour of the joint venture company and would be best dealt with by the employee signing a separate deed of undertaking in favour of the joint venture company.

4.38   Where an employee is being seconded outside the UK for more than one month, it is a requirement under the Employment Rights Act 1996 that the agreement must state:

- the period for which the employee is to work outside the UK;

- the currency in which remuneration is to be paid while working outside the UK;

- any additional remuneration payable or additional benefits to be provided by reason of working outside the UK; and

- any terms and conditions relating to return to the UK.

3   Pension issues

4.39   Pensions may represent a significant element of payroll costs and the liabilities for past service benefits may be substantial. They also tend to be a sensitive subject with the employees. Therefore, it is important that they are addressed at an early stage. Consideration needs to be given to the pension arrangements to be made on the establishment of the joint venture, during its continuance and on its termination. Consideration also needs to be given to any exposure of the venturers to the pension liabilities of the joint venture vehicle (and vice versa).

4.40   The law relating to pensions has gone through a period of extensive reform with a then new tax regime introduced, with effect from 6 April 2006, by the Finance Act 2004 as amended (the 'FA 2004'). The Pensions Act 2004 as amended (the 'PA 2004') also introduced extensive reform for safeguarding the non-tax aspects of pensions provision and provided, amongst other things, for the establishment of the Pensions Regulator and the Pension Protection Fund. The scene changed again with the advent of the personal accounts regime. This entails a requirement automatically to enrol all eligible employees into a system of personal accounts set up by the Secretary of State for Work and Pensions, and operated by an independent trust corporation, or an alternative scheme that fulfils specified minimum requirements from the day they become eligible. This was phased in from October 2012 to 2018 and was called 'automatic enrolment'. Employees may opt out, and for some lower earners, given the charges applied to the pensions and the low sums they will accrue, it may be in their best interests to opt out. Enrolment need not be in an employer scheme and many employers have no pension scheme for staff. It can be through a general scheme such as NEST – see https://www.nestpensions.org.uk/schemeweb/nest.html. Where the employee does not opt out, the employer must pay 3% of pay into the scheme up to certain limits. See also https://www.thepensionsregulator.gov.uk/employers.

Some workers have 'stakeholder' workplace pensions. Since 1 October 2012 for new employees there is no longer a requirement to offer these – although by 2018 all employers of employees (but not self-employed workers) were already caught by automatic enrolment in workplace pensions.

4.41   The Pensions Regulator is particularly important in the context of joint venture transactions, having wide-reaching powers which enable it, in certain circumstances, to require parties connected or associated with the sponsoring employer of a pension scheme to make good any funding deficit in the scheme.

Type of schemes

4.42   A pension scheme may be either an occupational or personal pension scheme. Most of the complications arise in relation to occupational schemes, of which there are broadly two types.

4.43   The first is a defined benefit scheme which provides for a specified level of pension on retirement. The most common kind of defined benefit scheme is a final salary scheme which provides a pension based on a fraction of final pensionable salary at retirement (eg one-sixtieth of final pensionable salary for each year of pensionable service). Where the employee makes contributions, these are normally a fixed percentage of pensionable salary and it is then left to the employer to make whatever level of contributions is necessary to fund the required pensions. The employer, rather than the employee, bears the risk that the investment return on the contributions paid will not be sufficient to meet the promised level of benefits.

4.44   Many final salary schemes including newer NHS schemes have been converted to CARE schemes (career average revalued earnings schemes). These are still defined benefit schemes. A CARE scheme will, instead of providing a pension based on final salary at retirement, provide for each year of pensionable service completed a pension based on a fraction of the member's pensionable salary for that year, revalued up to retirement in line with price inflation, usually up to a specified limit (eg 2.5% a year). Less common are cash balance schemes which operate in a broadly similar way to a CARE scheme but just provide a cash sum at retirement, which the employee must use to provide retirement benefits. Both these types of schemes carry less risk for the employer than final salary schemes, as accrued benefits are not affected by future salary increases. With a cash balance scheme, the risk that annuity rates may change is transferred to the employee.

4.45   The second type of occupational scheme is a defined contribution or money purchase scheme. Under this type of scheme, the employer's contributions (and those of the employees, where they are required to contribute) are normally fixed percentages of salary, and on retirement the employee is entitled to such pension as can then be purchased out of the accumulated fund, represented by the contributions and the investment returns on them. The employee, and not the employer, therefore, takes the investment and annuity risks. Hybrid schemes are a combination of defined contribution and defined benefit.

4.46   There is a continuing shift from the provision of defined benefit to defined contribution schemes. The chief reasons are:

- cost-cutting (ie employers seeking to pay lower contributions than required under their final salary schemes);

- controlling future pension costs by putting the investment and annuity rate risks on the employees;

- concerns over the requirements for valuing defined benefit liabilities both in the employer's accounts and on the occurrence of certain types of corporate activity, which can result in such liabilities being valued on a basis which is more conservative than typically used for funding purposes and, as it is market related, is volatile in nature; and

- money-purchase benefits are considered more suited to today's workforce, which increasingly needs to be more mobile.

Save in the event of underfunding that might be caused by an employer's potential future insolvency it is, however, unlikely that defined contribution schemes will deliver the same level of benefits as defined benefit schemes, and they certainly will not do so if less is paid in. Underfunded pension schemes are a massive problem and prevent many business acquisitions proceeding.

4.47   As an alternative to occupational pension schemes, contributions (employer and employee) may be paid to personal pension schemes. Typically, these take the form of policies issued by an insurance company to the employees concerned. A group personal pension scheme is simply a series of personal schemes under an umbrella arrangement, although a more favourable charging structure usually applies than can be secured on an individual basis. Benefits accrue on a money-purchase basis. If, as is typical, the employer provides separate life cover, this will normally be arranged on a group basis through a trust arrangement.

4.48   The advantage of personal pension schemes over occupational schemes for pension provision is that, as they are essentially contractual arrangements between the employee and the insurance company, they relieve the employer of much of the increasing risks and compliance burden associated with occupational schemes.

4.49   The older stakeholder pensions were invariably personal pension schemes but can be occupational schemes. Whichever form they take, they were required to comply with certain additional requirements including, in particular, a strict limit on charges. Employers with a staff of five or more have been required to provide access to a stakeholder scheme unless all employees (with certain limited exceptions) are able to join an occupational scheme or the employers offer a group personal scheme to which they contribute at least 3% of earnings and which meets certain other requirements. Providing 'access' to a stakeholder scheme is not burdensome. Broadly the employer is required to do no more than designate a stakeholder scheme and for any employee who wishes to contribute to it deduct his contributions from his salary and pay them to the stakeholder scheme provider. For stakeholder pensions see https://www.gov.uk/personal-pensions-your-rights/stakeholder-pensions.

However, since 1 October 2012 for new employees there is no obligation on an employer to provide a stakeholder pension, although between 2012 and 2018 employer-provided work place pensions became compulsory (see 4.40 above) with 3% employer contribution, although employees who are auto enrolled are allowed to opt out if they choose.

Registered pension schemes

4.50   The FA 2004 introduced with effect from 6 April 2006 a unified tax regime which applies to all types of tax advantaged pension schemes, which are now known as registered pension schemes. Previously different tax rules applied depending on the type of scheme.

4.51   The unified tax regime is built around a lifetime allowance which caps the value of tax advantaged pension benefits. Everyone has a lifetime allowance. Broadly, this is the aggregate value of pension benefits which a person may build up under registered pension schemes over their lifetime on a tax-advantaged basis. The lifetime allowance amount for the 2020/21 tax year is £1,073,100 although some employees were able to register protection for bigger pension pots before that date.

4.52   On a member becoming entitled to a pension, the capital value of the benefits being crystallised is determined for the purposes of ascertaining the portion of the lifetime allowance being used. Under a defined benefit arrangement, the value crystallised on the pension becoming payable is normally taken to be 20 times the annual rate of that pension. Under a defined contribution arrangement, the value taken is the actual cost of buying the pension. To the extent that the aggregate value of benefits from all sources exceeds the lifetime allowance, a lifetime allowance charge is payable on the excess benefits. The charge is at the rate of 55% (2020/21 rate) on any lump sum benefit and 25% of the value crystallised on the pension becoming payable (on which income tax will also be payable).

4.53   Alongside the lifetime allowance, an annual allowance operates. Originally, under the FA 2004 regime, everyone could build up pension savings in any tax year up to the annual allowance. This is now being restricted for high earners (see para 4.54). Broadly, pension savings in any tax year are taken to be, for a defined benefit arrangement, the amount by which the value of the benefits increases over that year and, for a defined contribution arrangement, the sum of any relievable contributions (employer and/or employee) paid during that year. Pension savings under an arrangement in the tax year in which all the benefits under that arrangement become payable do not count towards the annual allowance, and so effectively in that year there is no limit apart from the lifetime allowance and any restrictions applicable to high earners. The annual allowance for the tax year 2020/21 is £40,000 for lower earners and down to only £10,000 for those with high incomes on a tapered sliding scale. For those who have already taken their pension pot as cash at age 55 their annual allowance then reduces to about £4000 thereafter in certain cases. It is vital to take specialist advice on pensions which is a quickly moving field. Any pension input in excess of the annual allowance in any tax year is subject to an annual allowance tax charge (currently, at the individual's marginal rate of tax, eg 45%). HMRC provides an online tool to check annual pension allowance which is at https://www.tax.service.gov.uk/pension-annual-allowance-calculator.

4.54   Generally, individuals under the age of 75 receive tax relief on their pension contributions as described above and subject to the limitations mentioned above, and are not assessed to tax on any employer contributions. Government guidance describes this age limitation as follows (see https://www.gov.uk/hmrc-internal-manuals/pensions-tax-manual/ptm044100):

'Contributions after age 75; Section 188(3)(a) Finance Act 2004.

Although contributions can be paid after a member has reached the age of 75, they are not relievable pension contributions and cannot qualify for tax relief.'

4.55   Under the FA 2004, and subject to transitional arrangements (see para 4.56), 25% of the value of the benefits under a registered pension scheme may be taken as a tax-free cash lump sum in most cases at the earliest currently at age 55 (due to rise to age 57 by 2028) when the pension is all taken as a cash lump sum or an annuity is bought. If the pension is cashed in stages eg as to a quarter of the pot every five years then 25% of each of those quarters would be tax free. For a defined benefit arrangement, the maximum tax-free lump sum is a quarter of the total value of the benefits using a factor for converting pension into lump sum no more generous than 20:1. For a defined contribution arrangement, the maximum tax-free lump sum is a quarter of the total value of the individual account at retirement.

4.56   With a view to ensuring the pension savings which individuals had built up prior to 6 April 2006 were not adversely affected, the FA 2004 contains various transitional arrangements provisions, the principal two being:

(1)   Primary protection – the lifetime allowance of the individual is increased by the percentage of £1.5m by which the value of the pre-6 April 2006 rights on 5 April 2006 exceeded £1.5m. For example, if the pre-6 April 2006 rights on 5 April 2006 are valued at £2.25m, the percentage increase is 50%. Therefore, if benefits crystallise in 2010 when the standard lifetime allowance is £1.8m, the individual's lifetime allowance will be

£2.7m. Whilst additional benefits may be accrued after 5 April 2006, the scope for doing so without incurring the lifetime allowance charge is limited, as on that date the value of the accrued benefits will already be equal in value to the individual's lifetime allowance. But there may be some scope: for instance, if the standard lifetime allowance increases faster than, in the case of defined benefits, earnings or, in the case of money purchase benefits, the money purchase funds. In 2021/22 the annual allowance is £1,073,100 although as stated earlier in this chapter some have been able to register to protect their higher value fund from the adverse tax consequences of exceeding this figure.

(2)   Enhanced protection – this exempts all benefits from the lifetime allowance charge. In order to qualify there are various restrictions. In particular, in a money-purchase arrangement no contributions may be paid after 5 April 2006 except minimum contributions for contracting-out of the state second pension and contributions for death benefits under an insurance contract, provided the contract complies with certain requirements[5].

(3)   For defined benefits, the benefits accrued prior to 6 April 2006 may be increased in one of two ways, whichever is the more favourable:

(a)   by the greatest of 5% per annum, the rise in the retail price index and the annual percentage prescribed by regulations[6];

(b)   in line with pensionable earnings, provided the emerging benefit must not be calculated by reference to an earnings figure exceeding, if the individual was subject to the earnings cap under the old tax regime, the lesser of the highest 12 months' earnings out of the last three years and 7.5% of the standard lifetime allowance or, if he was not subject to the earnings cap, the highest 12 months' earnings out of the last three years or, if that exceeds 7.5% of the standard lifetime allowance, the average annual earnings in the last three years. Most people were subject to the earnings cap under the old tax regime, the principal exception being those people who had been in continuous pensionable service under the same occupational pension scheme since before 1 June 1989.

Primary and enhanced protection must have been registered with HMRC on an individual basis by 5 April 2009.

4.57   In addition to primary and enhanced protections, there are other transitional arrangements to protect pre-6 April 2006 rights in relation to tax-free lump sums and certain rights to retire at age 50 (the FA 2004 increased

---

5   FA 2004, Sch 36, para 14(3).
6   Registered Pension Schemes (Uprating Percentages for Defined Benefits Arrangements and Enhanced Protection Limits) Regulations 2006 (SI 2006/130).

the minimum normal pension age from 50 to 55 on 6 April 2010, although retirement before that age on incapacity grounds will still be permitted and as stated above the age 55 limit is being raised to age 57 years by 2028 (see para 4.55 above).

Potential liability for underfunded defined benefits

4.58   Whether the joint venture makes pension provision through one or more existing schemes, or through a new scheme, the following considerations are of major importance in any transaction involving a defined benefit scheme.

4.59   Where a defined benefit scheme is wound-up, the amount of any deficit on a buy-out basis (ie the amount required to secure the accrued benefits with an insurance company) becomes a debt due to the trustees from the employer or employers (s 75 of the Pensions Act 1995 (the 'PA 1995')).

4.60   Sections 75 and 75A of the PA 1995 and the regulations thereunder (see para 4.61) provide that when an employer withdraws from an ongoing multi-employer scheme which is in deficit on a buy-out basis (eg on a business reorganisation or on the sale of the company, although at the time of writing the Government is considering the position in relation to corporate restructuring) a liability arises in respect of that employer's share of the pension deficit, which the employer is required to make good.

4.61   The Occupational Pension Schemes (Employer Debt) Regulations 2005 as amended (the 'Employer Debt Regulations')[7] come into operation where there is an 'employer cessation event'. Such an event occurs when an employer ceases to employ at least one active member in the scheme, while at least one other employer in the scheme, which is not a 'defined contribution employer' (ie which does not solely operate a money purchase arrangement), employs at least one active member. (The trigger can, however, be deferred if the employer gives the trustees notice within one month of the employer cessation event that it intends to employ at least one active member within 12 months, and does so.)

4.62   The employer's share of the deficit (the 'liability share') on exiting a multi-employer scheme is calculated on a buy-out basis. The liability share is that proportion of the total buy-out deficit in the scheme which the value of the scheme benefits for employees and former employees of the exiting employer bears to the aggregate value of the scheme benefits for employees and former employees of the exiting employer and of the continuing employer(s). In this way any deficit in respect of orphan liabilities (ie liabilities in respect of

---

7   SI 2005/678.

employees and former employees of employers who have already exited the scheme) is apportioned between the exiting employer and the continuing employer(s).

4.63   Where an employer notifies the trustees that a relevant transfer deduction is to apply to the exiting employer's liability share, the liability share of the exiting employer is calculated after any relevant transfers-out in the period ending not later than 12 months after the exiting employer last employs any active members of the scheme. Therefore, if a transfer were to be made for all employees and former employees of the exiting employer, the liability share of the exiting employer may be reduced to its share of the orphan liabilities, if any, but whether this is the case or not would depend on how the transfers-out were calculated.

4.64   If the trustees are agreeable and, if necessary, the Pensions Regulator's approval is obtained, the payment of the liability share can, at least in part, be deferred by entering into a withdrawal arrangement or, more commonly, a scheme apportionment arrangement. The decision whether or not to enter into such an arrangement is often not straightforward for the trustees having regard to the fiduciary responsibilities to the members. Their acquiescence should not, therefore, be taken for granted. They will need to be independently advised. Moreover, although in most cases it is not necessary to obtain the Pensions Regulator's approval to enter into such an arrangement, depending on the circumstances it may be advisable to obtain clearance from the Pensions Regulator (see paras 4.94 to 4.100).

4.65   'Withdrawal arrangements' are arrangements which meet certain prescribed requirements pursuant to which only part of the liability share is payable immediately and the balance (the 'balancing payment') is payable in the event of, amongst other things, the scheme going into wind-up, the last participating employer becoming insolvent, the occurrence of any event agreed between the guarantor and the trustees or, but only in the case of an approved withdrawal arrangement, the Pensions Regulator issuing a relevant notice. There is no limitation on who may be the guarantor other than that the trustees must be satisfied that the guarantor has the wherewithal to meet the liabilities under the guarantee. Therefore, it may be the exiting employer or a continuing employer or some other company. Unless it assumes the role of guarantor, the exiting employer has no liability for the balancing payment.

4.66   A withdrawal arrangement may be entered into without the Pensions Regulator's approval where all of the following occur.

(1)   A funding test is met. Under this when the arrangement takes effect the trustees must be reasonably satisfied that remaining employers will be reasonably likely to be able to fund the scheme going forward so that it has sufficient and appropriate assets to cover its technical provisions (broadly, the scheme's on-going funding basis, but taking account of any

changes which in the trustees' opinion are necessary on account of the withdrawal arrangement). The trustees may regard this test as having been met if they are of the opinion that the remaining employers are able to meet payments as they fall due under a schedule of contributions.

(2) The exiting employer agrees, instead of paying its liability share, to pay at least the amount equal to its share of any deficit in the scheme's on-going funding basis, which will usually be lower than the full buy-out basis – the 'withdrawal arrangement share'.

(3) A guarantor (or guarantors) approved by the trustees undertakes to pay the balancing payment (see para 4.65). The trustees are required to be satisfied that at the date the withdrawal arrangement is entered into the guarantors would have sufficient financial resources to be likely to be able to meet the balancing payment if such payment were at that date to become due.

4.67   Where the exiting employer proposes to pay less than the withdrawal arrangement share (see para 4.66), a withdrawal arrangement may be entered into only with the approval of the Pensions Regulator. It will still be necessary for the funding test to be met and the Pensions Regulator is permitted to give its approval only if it is satisfied that it is reasonable to do so having regard to, amongst other things, the effect of the proposed arrangements on the security of members' benefits.

4.68   A 'scheme apportionment arrangement' is an agreement entered into under the scheme rules that the exiting employer will pay less than its liability share on the basis that the balance will be apportioned to one or more of the remaining employers in the scheme, and it will usually specify when the balance will become payable.

4.69   Before entering into a scheme apportionment arrangement, the scheme trustees are required to apply a funding test (see para 4.66), but in addition they must be reasonably satisfied that the arrangement will not adversely affect the security of members' benefits as a result of (a) any material change in circumstances that would justify a change to the method or assumptions used in the last calculation of the scheme's technical provisions, or (b) any material revision to any existing recovery plan in place to address the scheme's deficit. Moreover, if the amount to be paid by an exiting employer is less than the amount of its liability share, the consent of any other employers to whom part or all of the exiting employer's liability share is apportioned will also be required.

4.70   A 'regulated apportionment arrangement' is only available in the limited circumstances where there is already employer insolvency or the likelihood of insolvency and is therefore of limited relevance for present purposes.

4.71   The provisions of the PA 1995 et al which require an employer to stand behind its pension promises may not from a social viewpoint be considered unreasonable. They do, however, bring home the exposure which an employer has to its defined benefit obligations. The real problem is the huge disparity which has emerged between the on-going and buy-out funding levels. Whereas once the difference was not of concern, it is now often the case that a scheme which is reasonably funded on an on-going basis is heavily in deficit on a buy-out basis and, as some schemes are relatively large when compared with the capitalised value of the employer, the contingent liability can be very significant.

4.72   Also far-reaching are the provisions relating to financial support directions and contribution notices contained in ss 38–51 of the PA 2004, which can expose the venturers directly to the pension liabilities of the joint venture vehicle (and vice versa) and even possibly their respective directors and employees. These 'anti-avoidance' powers, conferred under the PA 2004, were extended by the Pensions Act 2008 (the 'PA 2008'). Although in force as from November 2008 (apart from the provisions relating to the new 'material detriment' test applying to contribution notices (see para 4.79)), the amendments apply retrospectively to 14 April 2008.

Period of grace and deferred debt arrangements

4.73   Since 2018 it has become possible that where an employer ceases to employ active members of a scheme for a temporary period the employees may be able to delay their departure from the scheme by providing the trustees with a 'period of grace' notice.

Another mechanism which allows for the triggering of a section 75 debt to be suspended is a deferred debt arrangement (DDA). A DDA allows an employer participating in a multi-employer occupational pension scheme to defer the triggering of a section 75 debt, providing certain requirements are satisfied. On entering a DDA the deferred employer will remain responsible for its share of the scheme's liabilities, but its liability to pay the debt will be deferred.

Further information is on the Pensions Regulator's website at https://www.thepensionsregulator.gov.uk/en/document-library/regulatory-guidance/multi-employer-schemes-and-employer-departures.

Contribution notice where avoidance of section 75 debt

4.74   Pursuant to ss 38–42 of the PA 2004 (as amended by the PA 2008) the Pensions Regulator may serve a contribution notice requiring the recipient to pay an amount to a defined benefit scheme in respect of the amount due, or contingently due, from the employer under s 75 of the PA 1995 (the 'section 75 debt').

4.75　A contribution notice may be served on any person who at the time of the relevant act, or thereafter, is an employer in relation to the scheme or any person connected with, or an associate of, the employer[8]. A venturer will be an associate if, for example, it is able to exercise or control the exercise of one-third or more of the voting power at general meetings of the joint venture company. Care will therefore need to be taken if the degree of control of the joint venture vehicle is likely to increase in the future bringing it within the definition of associate, particularly as the Pensions Regulator can issue a contribution notice up to six years after the act.

4.76　The Pensions Regulator can issue a contribution notice following a bulk transfer into another scheme requiring payment to be made to that scheme, provided a contribution notice could have been issued requiring payment to the transferor scheme or if the bulk transfer itself is materially detrimental.

4.77　A contribution notice can essentially be issued on one of two bases. The first is that the Pensions Regulator is of the opinion that the person was a party to, or knowingly assisted in, an act (which for this purpose includes a deliberate failure to act) or series of acts, the main purpose, or one of the main purposes, of which was to avoid or reduce, or otherwise compromise or settle a section 75 debt which was or might become due from the employer.

4.78　The Pensions Regulator must be of the opinion that it is reasonable to impose the liability on the person to pay the sum specified in the notice. For these purposes the Pensions Regulator is required to consider, amongst other things, the degree of involvement of the person in the matter, his relationship with the employer and all the purposes of the act or failure to act (including whether a purpose was to prevent or limit loss of employment).

4.79　Such an event might occur after the joint venture is established, if, for example, it were to be restructured, and this resulted in a reduction in the net asset value of the employing company if the main purpose, or one

---

8　Connected' has the meaning given to it by s 249 of the Insolvency Act 1986 and 'associate' has the meaning given to it by s 435 of that Act and s 74 of the Bankruptcy (Scotland) Act 1985 – PA 2004, s 38(10). A person is connected with a company if:
　1　he is a director or shadow director of the company or an associate of such a director or shadow director, or
　2　he is an associate of the company.
　'Associate' is widely drawn and includes corporate bodies and private individuals such as husbands, wives and relatives. The definition could potentially catch a number of individuals or companies within a group structure – even unrelated companies could be treated as associated with each other and potentially brought into the scope of the Regulator's powers.

of them, was to protect assets from creditors of the joint venture vehicle of which the trustees would be one.

4.80   The second, and potentially far-reaching, extension of the Pensions Regulator's original power is contained in the PA 2008. It came into effect on 29 June 2009 but is retrospective to 14 April 2008. Under this provision the Pensions Regulator is able to issue a contribution notice if it considers that an act (which includes a failure to act) is 'materially detrimental' to the likelihood of a person receiving their accrued scheme benefits. For example in 2016 the Pensions Regulator confirmed that, following an investigation, it had begun enforcement action to seek redress on behalf of the BHS pension schemes (with 20,000 members). It sent 'Warning Notices' with alleged evidence to support the use of both its Contribution Notice (CN) and Financial Support Direction (FSD) powers (see 4.86 below). A CN demands a specified sum of money and an FSD requires respondents to put on-going support in place for a pension scheme, which must first be agreed with the Regulator. In 2017 one of those sent the notice agreed to pay £363m into the scheme.

4.81   In order to issue a contribution notice by reference to the material detriment test the Pensions Regulator must be of the opinion that:

- the act is materially detrimental to the likelihood of the accrued scheme benefits being received (whether as benefits under the scheme or otherwise);

- the available statutory defence (see para 4.82) is not met in relation to the act; and

- it is reasonable to impose liability on the person to pay the sum specified in the contribution notice, having regard to the extent to which in all the circumstances it was reasonable for the person to act in the way they did and such other matters as the Pensions Regulator considers relevant.

4.82   There is a statutory defence available to a target for the contribution notice if it can show it gave reasonable consideration to any potential detrimental impact, and having done so either concluded that there was no such impact, or took steps to minimise or eliminate it[9].

CONTRIBUTIONS NOTICE – CASE EXAMPLE

4.83   An example was published in 2012 relating to the Desmond and Sons Limited 1975 Pension and Life Assurance Scheme ('the Scheme'). Contribution notices (CNs) in the sums of £900,000 were issued in 2010 to Denis Desmond and £100,000 to Donal Gordon. This was appealed in 2011 and in 2012 an embargo on publication of the decision was lifted – see http://www.tribunals.gov.uk/financeandtax/Decisions.htm#pen.

---

9   PA 2004, s 38A. The Pensions Act 2021 inserted a new s 42A which makes it a criminal offence not to pay a contribution notice.

The Pensions Regulator's Determinations Panel, which issued its reasons for its determination in April 2010, found that Mr Desmond and Mr Gordon had been party to the act of placing the employer company in relation to the Scheme, Desmond & Sons Limited (a clothing manufacturer in Northern Ireland), into a Members' Voluntary Liquidation (MVL) in June 2004. The Pensions Regulator said in a press release at the time that:

> 'The use of the MVL allowed the employer to be treated as an insolvent company for the purposes of calculating the debt due to the pension scheme from the employer on the winding up of Desmond & Sons Limited. This was despite it being fully solvent. The debt to the Scheme was calculated using the "Minimum Funding Requirement" basis applicable to insolvent companies, rather than the buy-out basis applicable to solvent companies. The regulator argued that the use of an MVL had resulted in a shortfall to the scheme estimated at £10.9 million and allowed shareholders in Desmond, including Mr Desmond and Mr Gordon, to take distributions totaling some £26m'.

4.84   On 29 June 2009 the Pensions Regulator published high-level Guidance for employers considering corporate transactions[10], and its code of practice[11] setting out the circumstances in which it would expect to issue a contribution notice in relation to the material detriment test was formally adopted. The circumstances are:

● the transfer of the scheme out of the UK;

● the transfer of the sponsoring employer out of the UK or the replacement of the sponsoring employer with an entity outside the UK;

● where sponsor support is removed, substantially reduced or becomes nominal;

● the transfer of liabilities of the scheme to another pension scheme or arrangement, which leads to a significant reduction of the sponsor support in respect of these liabilities, or funding to cover these liabilities;

● a business model or the operation of the scheme which creates or is designed to create from the scheme a financial benefit for the employer or another person, where proper account has not been taken of the interests of the members of the scheme.

4.85   The Guidance explains that while some steps may be detrimental to the scheme, in the 'vast majority' of transactions this will not be the case and it would not be 'necessary or proportionate' for the Pensions Regulator to

---

10   Guidance – corporate transactions.
11   Code of Practice No 12 Circumstances in relation to the material detriment test, May 2009, to be read in conjunction with PA 2004, Part 1 as amended. This is on line at http://www.thepensionsregulator.gov.uk/codes/code-material-detriment-test.aspx.

intervene. It emphasises the importance of dialogue between employers and trustees, of managing any conflicts of interest and of proper record-keeping (particularly in the context of a future statutory defence). How this will work in practice is yet to be seen. While the material detriment test was introduced primarily to prevent companies attempting to divest themselves of pension liabilities by entering into bulk buy-outs of the scheme membership with non-regulated companies, and the perceived risks to members associated with this, the provisions have been drafted far more widely, and care will be needed when considering joint venture commercial activity.

Financial support direction

4.86   The Pensions Regulator may issue a financial support direction ('FSD') in relation to a defined benefit scheme where an employer is, or was, at any time during a look-back period of (as from 6 April 2010) the previous 24 months[12]:

(1)   a service company, being a company within a group of companies whose turnover is solely, or principally, derived from amounts charged for the providing services to other group members; or

(2)   insufficiently resourced. A company is insufficiently resourced if:

   (a)   the value of its resources is less than 50% of the employer debt (the difference being the 'relevant deficit') as decided by the Pensions Regulator, and

   (b)   the value of the aggregate resources with persons who are connected or associated with the employer (and with each other) is at least sufficient to make up the relevant deficit.

4.87   The Pensions Regulator is required to consider several factors to decide whether it is reasonable to impose an FSD on a target, which include the relationship of that person with the employer; the value of any benefits received, any connection or involvement with the scheme and its financial circumstances.

4.88   An FSD will require the recipient, amongst other things, to ensure financial support arrangements approved by the Pensions Regulator are put in place within the period specified in the direction.

4.89   An FSD may be issued to a current or former employer in relation to the scheme at the time or during the look-back period, or to a company who is

---

12   Under the Pensions Regulator (Miscellaneous Amendment) Regulations 2009 (SI 2009/617) this period gradually increased during the period from 6 April 2009 to 6 April 2010, from 12 months to 24 months.

connected with, or an associate of[13], the employer, but not to their respective directors and employees or other individuals. This is an important difference between FSDs and the contribution notices discussed above. (There is an exception to this where the employer is an individual but, in context, this is not relevant.)

4.90   In the event of non-compliance with an FSD the Pensions Regulator may issue a contribution notice on any person to whom the FSD was issued requiring that person to pay an amount specified in the notice to the scheme trustees, but the Pensions Regulator may do so only if it is of the opinion that it is reasonable to impose a liability on that person to pay that amount. In deciding whether it is reasonable the Pensions Regulator may have regard to such matters as it considers relevant including whether the person had taken reasonable steps to secure compliance with the FSD.

4.91   Again, the Pensions Regulator will be able to issue an FSD in relation to a receiving scheme following a bulk transfer.

CASE EXAMPLE – BOX CLEVER

4.92   In 2012, the Pensions Regulator published the Determinations Panel's determination notice and reasons relating to its decision to issue Financial Support Directions (FSDs) against five companies that form part of the ITV group. It held that it was reasonable for Granada UK Rental & Retail Limited, Granada Media Limited, Granada Group Limited, Granada Limited and ITV plc to provide financial support for the Box Clever Group Pension Scheme. The Box Clever group became insolvent in 2003, leaving the pension scheme with a deficit of approximately £62m at the end of 2009, on the section 75 'buy-out' basis.

The Regulator said 'Under UK pensions law, an FSD requires the recipient to secure that reasonable financial support is put in place for a particular pension scheme. The precise form of that support is not prescribed and in practice there is significant flexibility for FSD recipients. The "target" companies in this case have referred the decision to the Upper Tribunal. The regulator cannot issue FSDs whilst appeal proceedings are pending'.

The regulator's executive director for defined benefit regulation, Stephen Soper, said in a press release at the time:

'The Panel found that the target companies received valuable financial benefits from the creation and structure of the Box Clever joint venture. A highly leveraged structure was used, leaving the sponsoring employers in a weak position.

---

13 'Connected' and 'associated' have the same definitions as for a contribution notice – see n 8 at para 4.75.

The decision is potentially good news for the three thousand members of the scheme, but the case is still at an early stage. The target companies have referred the decision to the Upper Tribunal, meaning that the case is likely to continue for several more months.

We will continue to work closely with pension scheme trustees to protect members' benefits and to limit the risk of schemes entering the Pension Protection Fund.'

The Panel concluded that the scheme's principal employer, Box Clever Technology Ltd ('BCT'), was set up by the Granada and Thorn groups as part of a highly leveraged transaction that effectively extracted value from the consumer rentals businesses of those groups, whilst leaving the possibility for Granada and Thorn to share in any future profit of BCT. A requirement of the transaction was that a pension scheme was set up for transferring employees. The ITV group received cash proceeds of approximately £500m as a result of the Box Clever transaction, which was paid from total debt of £860m raised by the BCT group. That borrowing was secured on all the assets of BCT and the other sponsoring employers of the scheme, but not the Granada or Thorn group companies, thereby insulating them from any downside. The burden of servicing this debt was a major factor in the insolvency of BCT group, including the sponsoring employers of the scheme, in 2003.

The Panel did not find any misconduct on the part of the target companies, but considered FSDs to be an appropriate and reasonable response to these events. The case led to four years of litigation with the tribunal ruling in 2016[14] that the regulator had acted correctly.

Applying for clearance

4.93   Where there is a concern that the Pensions Regulator might issue a contribution notice or an FSD, a person who could be a target can make an application to the Pensions Regulator for clearance in relation to a transaction. A clearance statement gives assurance to the applicant that the Pensions Regulator will not use its powers in relation to the circumstances described in the application. Such a statement, if issued, will be binding on the Pensions Regulator unless the circumstances in which the act occurs are different to those described in the application and that difference is material to the exercise by the Pensions Regulator of its powers. In 2008 the Pensions Regulator published revised Clearance Guidance[15] which sets out an indicator of the circumstances that it would (and some that it might not) consider appropriate for clearance to be sought.

---

14   [2016] UKUT 0492 (TCC).
15   'Clearance Guidance' December 2008.

4.94   The Pensions Regulator summarises the issue of clearance as follows[16]:

- '● Clearance is the voluntary process for obtaining a clearance statement from the regulator.

- ● A clearance statement is not approval of a transaction such as an acquisition or merger; rather it gives assurance that we will not use our anti-avoidance powers in relation to that transaction.

- ● Clearance is relevant for those considering corporate transactions or scheme-related events which are materially detrimental to a defined benefit pension scheme and its members (known as "type A events")'.

The Pensions Regulator's detailed guidance is at https://www.thepensionsregulator.gov.uk/en/document-library/regulatory-guidance/clearance.

4.95   The Pensions Regulator expects clearance to be applied for in relation to a 'Type A event'. This is 'an event that is materially detrimental to the ability of the scheme to meet its pension liabilities'.

4.96   An event is detrimental to the scheme if it immediately or in the future stops the recovery of or reduces any part of the section 75 debt, otherwise compromises it or stops it becoming due, weakens the employer covenant, or reduces the dividend that the scheme would pay should the employers become insolvent. The emphasis is thus on the potential effect of a proposed transaction (or series of transactions). If an event is considered detrimental, employers and trustees then need to consider whether it is a Type A event.

4.97   Events that are detrimental to the scheme can be employer-related or scheme-related (or both). An employer-related event relates to corporate activity which has an impact on the employer group. Employer-related events include a change to group structure, a change of control or partial change of control of an employer, a change to the employer in relation to the scheme (including replacing a participating employer or merging employers, business and asset sales and purchases). However, an employer-related event will only be a Type A event in any transaction where the scheme has a relevant deficit. The Clearance Guidance indicates that employers and trustees should compare the strength of the employer pre- and post-event, and consider any change or effect on the wider employer group's financial strength.

4.98   Scheme-related events are events impacting directly on the scheme, and are Type A events irrespective of the level of funding of the scheme. A scheme apportionment arrangement is likely to by a Type A event where certain circumstances apply (eg broadly that the apportionment increases

---

16   See Key Points at https://www.thepensionsregulator.gov.uk/en/document-library/regulatory-guidance/clearance.

the section 75 debt that is immediately payable by another employer who can afford the increased debt and there is no net reduction in the employer covenant). Withdrawal arrangements may also be Type A events if a transaction is detrimental to the ability of the scheme to meet its liabilities and the trustees will particularly be wary of the terms of any guarantees.

4.99   The issue of a clearance statement will be of considerable comfort to the parties involved, particularly in the case of contribution notices, which may be issued against individuals. The price for clearance from the Pensions Regulator may be a cash payment or other arrangement eliminating all or part of a deficit. However, the clearance process is voluntary and if the venturer does not think it likely that the Pensions Regulator will issue a contribution notice or an FSD it may not wish to involve the Pensions Regulator by applying for clearance.

4.100   It must be remembered that trustees have a significant role to play, whether or not clearance is being sought. In this context it is important to ascertain what their powers are under the scheme documents. They are expected to assess the impact of an event and seek appropriate 'mitigation' for their agreement to any course of action. Where trustees become aware of a potential Type A event, they should discuss this with the employer. If no or inadequate mitigation is forthcoming they may consider contacting the Pensions Regulator themselves, although the Pensions Regulator will not have a formal role unless and until approached for clearance.

Notification

4.101   There are separate obligations on both employers and trustees to notify the Pensions Regulator if certain prescribed events occur[17]. The employer obligation arises, among other things, when a controlling employer decides to relinquish control of a subsidiary, unless the scheme is both fully funded on an ongoing basis and in the last 12 months the trustees have not had a duty to report a failure to meet the contributions schedule that they believe is materially significant to the Pensions Regulator. When a withdrawal arrangement or approved withdrawal arrangement is in force there are certain further employer-related notifiable events under PA 2004, s 69 and regulations made thereunder[18].

Transfers of pensionable employees

4.102   Where the joint venture vehicle is to take over the employment of pensionable employees from more than one of its joint venturers, the benefits

---

17   PA 2004, s 69.
18   Pensions Regulator (Notifiable Events) Regulations 2005 (SI 2005/900).

provided under their existing schemes are likely to differ, so the joint venture could end up with employees of similar status having different pension rights. The joint venture vehicle may, either immediately or at some later stage, recruit further employees to whom it may wish to offer pension benefits on other, different terms. Whilst it is not unusual to have different benefit structures for different groups of employees, it is generally perceived as undesirable from the point of view of employee relations. Harmonisation of benefits is, however, difficult and potentially expensive as it involves changing employees' pension rights and expectations – and not infrequently moving to the better benefits. It can usually be best achieved by the joint venture vehicle establishing its own pension scheme, although the administrative cost involved may be regarded as too high if there are only a small number of pensionable employees, and complete harmonisation may not be possible in any event if TUPE is applicable (see para 4.104).

4.103   If the shares in the company in which the employees are employed are being transferred to the joint venture, the creation of the joint venture will not result in any change in the identity of the employees' employer nor in the terms of their employment contracts. The scope for varying pension benefits in these circumstances is as discussed at para 4.124ff.

4.104   TUPE generally applies when there is a transfer of an undertaking or economic entity to the joint venture vehicle from one of the venturers. TUPE is intended to give effect to the European Acquired Rights Directive ('ARD') and, accordingly, is to be interpreted in line with the purposes of that Directive so far as possible. Broadly, TUPE provides for the transfer, by operation of law, of existing employment contracts from the venturer to the joint venture vehicle. However, there is an important exemption under TUPE to the employment rights which transfer: any rights relating to old-age, invalidity or survivors' benefits under an occupational scheme are exempt from being automatically transferred, but are dealt with in PA 2004 (see para 4.111). The exemption applies only to occupational schemes – any contractual obligation to contribute to an individual or group personal pension scheme will transfer. Similarly, the right to life cover under a standalone life cover only scheme will transfer. Despite the end of the post-Brexit transitional period on 31 December 2020 TUPE remains in force and there have been suggestions it will be amended or abolished. Under the EU-UK Trade and Cooperation Agreement (December 2020) the UK may, if it chooses, depart from EU law in the area of employment rights in due course, although the UK is committed to maintaining a level playing field with the EU including in relation to the restructuring of undertakings – see Title XI (Level Playing Field), Article 6.1.1(e)) of the said Trade Agreement. Title XI Article 6.2.2 provides that neither the EU nor UK shall 'weaken or reduce, in a manner affecting trade or investment between the Parties, its labour and social levels of protection below the levels in place at the end of the transition period [ie as at 31 December 2020], including by failing effectively [to] enforce its law and standards'.

4.105 The European Court of Justice ('ECJ') has given guidance on the extent of the 'old-age, invalidity and survivors' benefits' exemption in the decisions in *Beckmann v Dynamco Whicheloe Macfarlane*[19] and *Martin v South Bank University*[20]. To the extent that any benefits under an occupational scheme are not old-age, invalidity or survivors' benefits they would, it seems, have to be provided in addition.

4.106 The key question in the *Beckmann* case was whether certain early retirement benefits payable under an occupational scheme on dismissal from employment by reason of redundancy qualified as old-age benefits. The ECJ held that it was only those benefits paid to an employee from the 'end of [his] normal working life' that could be classified as old-age benefits. Consequently, it held 'early retirement benefits and any benefits intended to enhance the conditions of such early retirement paid in the event of dismissal to employees who have reached a certain age' were not within the 'old-age' exemption, and the obligation to provide such benefits transferred to a transferee under TUPE. In the *Martin* case the ECJ considered whether contractual rights to a lump sum and pension either in the event of redundancy or premature early retirement by agreement with the employer were within the old-age exemption. The ECJ construed the exemption narrowly and held that any rights 'contingent on dismissal or the grant of early retirement by agreement with the employer' were not old-age benefits for the purposes of the ARD and so were not included within the exemption. Therefore, the obligation to provide any such benefit transfers to the transferee. The suggestion in the *Martin* case is that all early retirement benefit entitlements (other than those relating to invalidity or ill health) would transfer under TUPE (but see para 4.108). In this context, it will be important to see if any rights to early retirement and enhanced benefits on redundancy have previously been transferred into a scheme with employees who are to transfer under TUPE.

4.107 Early retirement rights which transfer under TUPE are payable under the same terms and conditions as applied under the original employer's scheme and any relevant contractual provisions or collective agreement. It would appear that where a benefit is discretionary it remains discretionary and, where it is subject to actuarial reduction, it may be reduced. It is not clear how powers and discretions exercisable by the trustees under the original arrangements are to be given effect to and what the effect of any funding conditions is. Also, discretions exercisable by the employer (such as a requirement for company consent for early retirement) will be subject to any restrictions arising from custom and practice which also transfer.

---

19 C-164/00 [2002] ECR I-4893, ECJ.
20 C-4/01 [2004] 1 CMLR 472, ECJ.

4.108   The *Beckmann* and *Martin* cases deal with benefits payable on redundancy or on retirement 'in the interests of efficiency' respectively and, despite some of the sweeping statements made by the ECJ in these decisions, arguably normal early retirement pensions payable to employees who opt for early retirement still come within the old-age exemption to TUPE and, therefore, do not transfer to the transferee. To reason otherwise would significantly undermine the old-age exemption. A possible argument may be that if an employee, without any prompting from the employer, decides to take early retirement, then, by doing so, he has chosen to end his normal working life and therefore any benefits to which he becomes entitled are, in fact, related to old-age, and as such fall within the TUPE exemption. Other possible interpretations of the ECJ's judgments include that it is only the pension payable before normal retirement date which is not an old-age benefit and so the rights which transfer would be to a pension between the date of early retirement and normal retirement date but not to a pension for life. Alternatively, it can be argued that it is only to the extent that the early retirement terms exceed the pension which would have been payable to the employee had he left service with a deferred pension payable from normal retirement date which transfers. Further guidance from the ECJ is required to clarify these issues. In the meantime, it can only be safely said that a pension payable on retirement at normal retirement date, incapacity pensions and survivors' benefits are within the TUPE exemption.

4.109   It is, however, fairly clear that the fact that the pension was not payable by the employer but rather by the pension scheme would be rejected by the ECJ as an objection to the transfer of the obligation to pay the pension, since it rejected that argument in the *Beckmann* case, which concerned the NHS Superannuation Scheme (albeit that that scheme is set up under statute and not under trust). It would therefore appear that the transferee has an obligation to pay the pension or procure its provision even though the transferor's obligation was limited to funding benefits in accordance with the provisions of the trust deed of its scheme and subject to the power of amendment and any rights to terminate contributions. However, since the *Beckmann* and *Martin* cases both concerned a statutory scheme, there are still arguments to be run on these issues.

4.110   Sections 257 and 258 of the PA 2004 contain provisions which require the joint venture vehicle to provide certain specified minimum benefits following a TUPE transfer in the place of the old-age, invalidity and survivors' benefits which were provided for the employees under the venturer's occupational scheme.

4.111   The protection under the PA 2004 will apply only if:

(A)   the employee is, or is eligible to be, an active member of the transferor's occupational scheme or would have become so eligible had they been employed for a longer period; and

(B) if the scheme provides money purchase benefits, the transferor is required, or if the employee had become an active member would have been required, to pay contributions (other than minimum payments for the purposes of contracting-out of the state second pension) in respect of him or, if the employee is an active member, the transferor, or any associate of the transferor, has paid any such contributions in the past.

These conditions will be regarded as having been satisfied in any case where they would be satisfied but for any action taken by the transferor by reason of the transfer (eg the transferor terminating the scheme prior to the transfer).

4.112   Section 258 and the regulations made thereunder[21] provide that following such a transfer (and save to the extent that the employee and the transferee otherwise agree at any time after the transfer has taken place) it will be a condition of the contract of employment with the transferee that one or other of the following are complied with:

(1) occupational pension scheme option – the employee becomes, or is eligible to become, a member of an occupational scheme and:

    (a) if the transferee's scheme is a money purchase scheme, relevant contributions (see para 4.113) are payable by the transferee;

    (b) if the transferee's scheme is a defined benefit scheme, either it satisfies the statutory reference scheme test for contracting-out purposes, or the value of the benefits provided are at least 6% of pensionable pay (as defined in the scheme) for each year of service (this is additional to the value of the benefits provided by the member's contributions. The member must not be required to contribute more than 6% of pensionable pay).

(2) stakeholder pension scheme option (for those with stakeholder schemes – no longer compulsory) – the transferee makes relevant contributions to a stakeholder pension scheme (or has offered, and not withdrawn the offer, to do so).

There is thus a degree of choice as to the form of benefits to be provided.

4.113   'Relevant contributions' were contributions which matched the employee's contributions up to 6% of basic pay. This was so even where the transferor was not paying as much as 6%. In these circumstances, the transferee was saddled with higher pension costs than the transferor. Conversely, the requirements provided limited protection for those employees for whom the transferor provided a good final salary scheme or was contributing at a higher rate to a money purchase scheme. However, in 2014 the rules were slightly changed such that the 'transferee employer' meets the requirements under the amended regulations if:

---

21   Transfer of Employment (Pension Protection) Regulations 2005 (SI 2005/649).

(1)   where the transferring employee previously paid less than 6% employee contributions, the transferee employer matches that amount. Where the transferring employee paid contributions of 6% or more, the transferee employer needs only to contribute 6%; or

(2)   where, prior to the TUPE transfer, the transferring employer was required to make contributions to an occupational money purchase arrangement (and this was solely for producing money purchase benefits) then following the TUPE transfer the transferee employer simply has to match the transferor employer contributions.

Commenting on the change Richard Woodburn of Royds solicitors, writing about the issue at the time, stated:

'Point two highlights the update to the regulations. The reason for this change is to avoid employees, after a TUPE transfer, being placed into a more favourable position than they were previously and in particular, where the transferor employer was previously providing only the statutory minimum contribution requirements for auto-enrolment purposes. Previously the obligation on the transferee employer was to match employee contributions up to 6%. So if the transferor employer only paid 1% employer contributions but the employee paid, say, 6%, the transferee employer would have to match that – and provide the transferring employee with something of a windfall. The change enables the transferee employer to simply pay the same contributions as pre-transfer'.

'It is important to note that, where transferring employees previously participated in a personal pension scheme, the law remains unchanged and the transferee employer will still have to ensure that it pays employer contributions which the transferring employees were contractually entitled to under their previous contracts of employment'.

4.114   In the case of an employee who was only prospectively eligible for membership of the transferor's scheme, the transferee need only provide a scheme from when the employee would, apart from the transfer, have been able to join the transferor's scheme.

Joint venture vehicle participating in existing scheme

4.115   It may be possible for the joint venture vehicle to participate in one or more of the existing defined benefit schemes. Whether it can do so or not will turn on the scheme rules, which will need to be examined.

4.116   Where joint venture employees are to participate in an existing defined benefit scheme, the joint venture vehicle should obtain appropriate warranties as to the status and funding of the scheme. It will also be necessary to agree the rate of contributions which the joint venture vehicle will pay, and the position in relation to any surplus or deficiency which may now or in the future arise. Where there are two or more schemes available, consideration should be given as to which scheme or schemes should be used (and whether having employees in different schemes might lead to sex or age discrimination), and where new recruits will be placed.

4.117   There are various ways in which the question of contributions by the joint venture vehicle can be approached:

(1)   The joint venture vehicle could pay the same contributions as the other employers participating in the scheme. This has the advantage of simplicity. Leaving aside any surplus or deficiency, the contribution rate will depend on such factors as average ages, salary increases and staff turnover, and so, unless the joint venture employees are typical of other employees participating in the scheme, the joint venture vehicle may be paying more or less than the true cost of funding their benefits. If the scheme is in surplus and this is being used to reduce the employer contribution rate, the joint venturer whose scheme it is may, in any event, object, as it would be providing a benefit to the joint venture without receiving any corresponding benefit from it. Similarly if, which is perhaps more likely, the scheme is in deficit, the other venturers are likely to object.

(2)   The joint venture vehicle could pay a contribution rate calculated in relation to its own employees only, disregarding any surplus or deficiency in the scheme. This avoids some of the problems associated with the joint venture vehicle paying the same rate as the other participating employers. It does, however, mean that the joint venturer whose scheme it is will be assuming the risk as to the adequacy of the contribution rate.

(3)   A notional fund could be established within the scheme for the joint venture vehicle. Contributions of the joint venture vehicle and any of its employees would be paid into this fund and benefits for the joint venture employees paid out, with the intent that the fund would be operated so far as possible as if it were entirely separate from the rest of the scheme.

Alternatively the scheme can effectively be segregated (see para 4.121).

4.118   When establishing the joint venture, the terms upon which the joint venture vehicle may withdraw from the scheme should be considered, even if it is proposed that it should participate in the scheme on a long-term basis. The importance of this cannot be over-emphasised. The general intention, in the normal course, should be that the joint venture vehicle's share of the funding of the scheme would be made available for transfer to a successor scheme so that the same level of pension benefits can continue to be provided for the employees at approximately the same cost. This may not happen under the normal operation of the scheme rules, which may provide employees with no more than the minimum leaving service benefits.

4.119   More importantly, the joint venture vehicle may be faced with having to make a substantial funding deficiency payment when it withdraws from the scheme (as discussed at para 4.58ff). As the initial calculation of liability will normally exceed the amount required on the scheme on-going funding basis by a significant margin, any excess payment will usually result in a reduction in the future contribution liability of the venturer who sponsors the scheme. How equitable this is as between the venturers is debatable, but it needs to be borne in mind that the venturer sponsoring the scheme will have ultimate liability for the funding of that scheme.

4.120   The doomsday scenario for any employer participating in another company's scheme is that the other company becomes insolvent and, as a result, the employer becomes liable for a disproportionate amount of any funding deficiency.

4.121   An alternative approach would be to set up a segregated section under the scheme for the joint venture vehicle employees. Broadly, if the assets and liabilities of the section are held completely separate from the other assets and liabilities of the scheme and there can be no cross subsidiary, the section will for funding purposes and for the purposes of s 75 of the PA 1995 be treated as if it were a separate scheme. The joint venture vehicle's liabilities would therefore be similar to those which it would have if it were to establish its own scheme.

Consultations

4.122   A change of scheme or benefits may give rise to an obligation to consult. If the change coincides with a TUPE transfer, the consultations will be under TUPE. In other cases the obligation may arise under the regulations made pursuant to ss 259 to 261 of the PA 2004. These regulations apply to employers with at least 50 employees (whether or not they are members of the pension scheme).

4.123   The regulations require the employers to consult 'affected members' or their representatives in advance of making any 'listed changes'. These changes include, in relation to occupational schemes: (i) increasing normal pension age; (ii) preventing existing employees from joining; (iii) preventing or reducing future benefit accrual; and (iv) introducing or increasing member contributions and, in relation to personal pension schemes, reducing or stopping employer contributions or increasing member contributions[22]. Failure to comply with the regulations may result in action by the Pensions

---

22   Occupational and Personal Pension Schemes (Consultation by Employer and Miscellaneous Amendment) Regulations 2006 (SI 2006/349) and see also The Pensions Regulator's 2015 guidance consultation which is at http://www.thepensionsregulator.gov.uk/docs/employer-duty-to-consult-on-scheme-changes.pdf.

Regulator who can impose a fine (maximum £5,000 for individuals, or £50,000 for companies). Non-compliance will not, however, alter or affect the validity of a change.

Varying pension benefits

4.124   There is a strong trend nowadays to control costs and limit risks by converting final salary type benefits to money purchase benefits, and the opportunity of establishing new pension arrangements for the joint venture vehicle is sometimes seized on to effect such a conversion where employee relations and other considerations permit. (It should be noted that for any employee with enhanced protection under the FA 2004 such protection would be lost automatically if any contributions (employer or employee) are paid to provide money purchase benefits for them, other than minimum contributions for the purposes of contracting-out of the state second pension.)

4.125   Where such a switch is not being made, and costs considerations permit, the approach is likely to be to provide benefits at least as good as those available to the transferring employees under their existing schemes; and, where employees are being transferred to the joint venture from more than one venturer, to harmonise them. This may, however, be difficult to achieve without conferring some enhanced benefits on some of them. Where this is not acceptable from a cost point of view, the alternatives are to maintain the different benefit structure for different employees (see para 4.102) or, for future service benefits at least, harmonise on a basis which does not increase the overall costs which inevitably will mean reducing some employees' pension expectations.

4.126   When considering any variation in benefits the importance of employee relations cannot be over-emphasised (the provision of rights under an occupational scheme, especially a final salary scheme, is likely to be of great importance to the employees). Where the employees are transferred to the joint venture vehicle pursuant to TUPE, a key limitation on varying occupational scheme benefits would appear to be the extent to which rights to early retirement benefits are transferred in light of the *Beckmann* and *Martin* decisions. It was confirmed in the *Martin* case that on public policy grounds such rights cannot be changed, even with the employee's consent, for any reason connected with the transfer. However, subject to that limitation, a TUPE transfer affords an ideal opportunity from a legal viewpoint to vary benefits, given the limited obligations imposed by law on the joint venture vehicle with regard to future service benefits (which may be defined contributions even if the employees were previously provided with final salary pensions), and the employees do not appear to have any right of redress against the venturer from whom they are transferred. Regulation 10(3) of TUPE provides that employees cannot claim breach of contract or constructive unfair dismissal against the transferring employer arising out of a loss or reduction in their rights under an occupational scheme as a consequence of a TUPE transfer for an act taking place on or after that date.

4.127   If the shares of the company in which the employees are employed are transferred to the joint venture so that there is no change in the identity of their employer, the ability to change benefits will turn on the terms of the employment contract as well as employee relations considerations. Normally, the employment contract will simply enable the employee to be a member of the scheme, subject to its terms and conditions (which would include the powers of amendment and discontinuance). In such circumstances, and provided that the changes can be made without contravening the terms of the scheme, the making of them will not, it is thought, constitute a breach of the express terms of the contract (although it will still be necessary for the employer to act in a manner consistent with its implied duty of trust and confidence). Where consent is required, it should preferably be obtained. As an alternative to obtaining consent, consideration could be given to terminating the existing contracts and offering new ones. Before doing so, it would be necessary to consult with the trade unions or employees' representatives. There would be a risk that the termination of the original contract would be regarded as unfair. An employment tribunal is likely to consider the commercial need to make the changes (eg unifying benefits) and procedural issues (such as the manner of consultations) to be of paramount importance.

4.128   If a new scheme is to be established, and unless advantage is to be taken of the TUPE exemption, it may be desirable to have an interim period of, say, six months whilst the employees remain members of existing schemes but employer's pension contributions are made by the joint venture vehicle. Such an interim period is particularly useful if it is proposed to vary benefits, as it gives time in which to conduct a proper communications programme. In respect of any interim period, the same considerations apply as in paras 4.115–4.121.

Transfer of past service benefits

4.129   Where a new defined benefit scheme is being established into which existing pensionable employees of the joint venturers will transfer, consideration needs to be given to whether the past service benefits should be transferred to the new scheme and, if so, the respective amounts to be transferred from the joint venturers' schemes to fund such benefits.

4.130   Whilst previously past service benefits were routinely transferred, this is no longer the case. The risks attached to assuming the liability for such benefits is often of concern, even if a reasonable transfer payment is offered: the investments may fail to perform, the actuarial assumptions by reference to which the amount of the transfer is determined may understate the value of the liabilities (eg as a result of a further improvement in life expectancy) and the acceptance of the transfer may have negative accounting implications because the transfer payment is calculated on a basis which is not as conservative as that used for accounting purposes. Moreover, there are the issues concerning s 75 of the PA 1995 and FSDs as discussed in paras 4.58–4.101. On the other hand the ventures under whose scheme the past service liabilities have accrued may be concerned to be relieved from all liability relating to the business being transferred to the joint venture vehicle, and this will only be achieved on the pension front if the past service defined benefits of the current and former employees of the business are transferred to a new scheme.

4.131   Where a transfer payment is to be made, the joint venture agreement, or a separate agreement entered into at the same time, will need to provide for such payment and the precise method of calculating the amount thereof, as agreed between the parties' actuaries. While the trustees to the transferring schemes are not normally parties to the agreement, usually under the scheme rules, they will have the right to final approval of the transfer payment. This poses a dilemma. Either:

(A)   the venturer whose scheme it is only undertakes to use its reasonable endeavours to procure the payment of the agreed transfer value (which leaves the joint venture vehicle exposed to the risk that for some reason the trustees fail to deliver); or

(B)   the venturer undertakes to make good any shortfall in the amount paid (which means the venturer assumes the risk).

Usually, the venturer is prepared to take on the risk as, although it does not control the trustees, it will, generally, hold not insignificant influence over them and, in any event, to the extent that the agreed transfer value is not paid, the funds will remain in its scheme and so will be available to reduce future employer contributions.

4.132   A safer approach which avoids any risk is to agree the transfer basis at the outset with the transferring scheme trustees and then amend their scheme rules so that they become legally bound to make the transfer on that basis, subject to any considerations that may involve the Pensions Regulator.

4.133   Such a transfer will not normally upset the protection afforded to certain employees under the transitional provisions contained in the FA 2004 and indeed is required to extend such protection to future service benefits. In particular, if an employee has a right to take pension before the normal minimum pension age of 50 (or, on or after 6 April 2010, 55 and rising to age 57 by 2028) or to take more than 25% of uncrystallised rights as a lump sum, these will be preserved if there is a 'block transfer' (ie a transfer for the employee and at least one other employee) to the new scheme of all sums and assets representing their accrued rights, so long as such transfer is made within 12 months of the employees becoming members of the new scheme[23].

4.134   The position of employees who have enhanced protection under the FA 2004 needs to be considered. Such protection will be lost on a transfer to another arrangement unless the prescribed conditions are met. In particular, a transfer to another defined benefit arrangement will result in the protection being lost unless either the transfer occurs in connection with the winding-up of the transferring scheme and the new scheme relates to the same employment as the transferring scheme, or the transfer is a 'relevant business transfer' of at least 20 employees and relates to their current or former employment. This would cover a TUPE transfer between two parties that are not companies within the same group[24].

Taking over an existing pension scheme

4.135   Where all the working members of an existing pension scheme are to be taken over by the joint venture vehicle, it may be appropriate for it to take over the existing scheme. A supplemental trust deed will be drawn up under which the joint venture vehicle will become the principal employer under the scheme. Before taking over the scheme, the funding position should be investigated and, ideally, an undertaking obtained from the venturer whose scheme it is, to make good any existing deficit. Also, due diligence should be carried out to ensure, in particular, that the requisite approvals have been obtained and that there are no unrecognised liabilities (eg for sex equality). Compliance and funding warranties will also be appropriate. Even if the scheme is fully funded on an ongoing concern basis, it may have a significant deficit on a wind up basis because of the high cost of buying out benefits with an insurance company.

Given that on the termination of the scheme the joint venture vehicle would be liable to make good that deficit if the scheme were transferred to it, the other venturers may be reluctant to agree to the scheme being so transferred, particularly if it has substantial liabilities for people who have already retired or left service.

CASE EXAMPLE – BRITISH HOME STORES – 2015–2020

4.136   An example of a takeover where pensions issues had substantial consequences including for 19,000 employees the Arcadia takeover is worth

---

23   Registered Pension Schemes (Block Transfers) (Permitted Membership Period) Regulations 2006 (SI 2006/498).
24   FA 2004, Sch 36, para 22, as amended by the Taxation of Pension Schemes (Transitional Provisions) Order 2006 as amended (SI 2006/572) and the Registered Pension Schemes (Block Transfers) (Permitted Membership Period) Regulations 2006 (SI 2006/498).

consideration. In 2020 the Pensions Regulator published its report[25] into the Arcadia group pension schemes following a complex series of events including the purchase of BHS (British Home Stores) for £1 by companies owned in whole or part by an individual who in December 2020 was jailed for six years for tax evasion and who had been ordered in January 2020 to make a £9.5m payment into the pension scheme but did not have the funds to do so.

A £300m+ pensions 'blackhole' had been found 13 months after the 2015 acquisition. Previous owners (Philip Green's family) agreed to pay a large sum on a voluntary basis to assist. Separately in 2020 the remaining group Arcadia collapsed into administration in part due to the Covid-19 (coronavirus) pandemic. In December 2020 the regulator stated that the defined benefit schemes were expected to enter Pension Protection Fund (PPF) assessment 'shortly'.

The Upper Tribunal's decision[26] is worth consideration by buyers of pension schemes. The buyer was criticised as it: 'did little to investigate the matter of pensions or retain an understanding of the pension situation before the Sale and agreed to limited disclosure being given in relation to the Schemes' and '… It must have been apparent to [the buyer's board and owner of the buyer] that the pension issues facing BHS shortly after the Sale had been completed' were serious. Buyers need to ensure they undertake sufficient due diligence and indeed refuse to continue with a purchase of a business where the pensions deficit or problems are so large the legal risks are too great.

4.137   More generally, the ability of the Pensions Regulator to issue contribution notices and FSDs against any of the venturers in respect of the scheme now or in the future should be considered and clearance sought, if appropriate. Moreover, indemnities as between the venturers may be appropriate with a view to ensuring that the economic effect of any such direction falls appropriately between them, having regard to their respective interests in the joint venture.

Establishing a new scheme without transfers of existing employees

4.138   Where the joint venture vehicle will not be employing anyone who is a member of an existing pension scheme of one of the joint venturers, it will have complete freedom as to whether the joint venture vehicle establishes a scheme or not and of what type, subject to the constraints of the employment market. In a 'greenfield' situation, a group personal pension or a stakeholder scheme is likely to be the most suitable kind of arrangement.

---

25   See https://www.thepensionsregulator.gov.uk/en/document-library/enforcement-activity/regulatory-intervention-reports/arcadia-group-limited-regulatory-intervention-report.

26   See [2019] UKUT 0209 (TCC).

Employer-financed retirement benefit schemes

4.139   Special considerations apply to benefits payable under retirement benefit schemes which are not registered schemes. These are now known as employer-financed retirement benefit schemes. Prior to 6 April 2006 they were known as unapproved schemes. They may be unfunded and, as such, simply comprise a contractual promise to provide the benefits which would invariably be final salary or they may be funded and, as such, involve a trust in which assets are held to provide the benefits which usually would be money purchase. Income and capital gains tax would be payable on the trust investments.

4.140   With an unfunded scheme there is no tax charge on the employee until the benefit is paid out, when the benefits are subject to income tax. The employer cannot claim tax relief until the benefit is paid out. With a funded scheme, the tax position changed on 6 April 2006. For contributions paid prior to that date, the employee was charged to tax on, and the employer could claim tax relief for, contributions when they were paid, and the benefits could normally be paid in their entirety as a tax-free lump sum. For contributions paid on or after 6 April 2006 the employee is not charged to tax, and the employer cannot claim tax relief, on contributions when they are paid, but all benefits when payable will be subject to income tax in the hands of the employee, and attract relief for the employer.

4.141   Where the scheme is unfunded, the joint venture vehicle could assume the liability for all the benefits and an appropriate adjustment be made between the venturer who previously employed the employee concerned and the joint venture vehicle. This should be made by way of adjustment to the consideration for the business acquired from the venturer by the joint venture vehicle. The employee's consent would have to be obtained, otherwise the venturer will not be discharged from its liability to him. Alternatively, the venturer could retain liability for the past service benefits and the joint venture vehicle would assume liability for the future service benefits. The only difficulty with this is that the venturer's liability for past service benefits would be based on salary at the date the employee transfers to the joint venture vehicle, whereas the employee would have been promised for his service up to that date a pension based on his final salary at retirement. If the employee is not to lose out, either:

(1)   the venturer would have to extend its commitment to the employee so as to provide him with a pension for his service with it but based on his final salary at retirement from the joint venture vehicle (although the venturer may not be entitled to tax relief on its contributions to fund the increased liability as the contributions would not be 'wholly and exclusively' for the purposes of its business); or

(2)   the joint venture vehicle would have to make good the promise (possibly with a cash adjustment being made by the venturer).

4.142   Where a funded scheme has been set up as an individual money-purchase arrangement, it should be relatively straightforward to transfer the scheme to the joint venture vehicle by changing the principal employer under the scheme documents. If it is a group money purchase scheme, however, the capital gains tax position should be considered before any funds are transferred to a joint venture vehicle's scheme. If such a transfer would trigger a capital gains tax liability (and whether it does or not would depend on the nature of the assets), it may be better to leave the accumulated funds in the venturer's scheme and set up a new scheme for future service benefits. Similar issues arise in relation to final salary schemes, but for these it will also be necessary to consider the adequacy of the funding of the accrued benefits.

Specialist advice

4.143   Pensions are a specialist topic and this book has only attempted to provide an outline. However, it is clear that pensions provide many traps and liabilities for the unwary, and new considerations (the increased powers of the Pensions Regulator and the potential for joint and several liability across groups of companies, and in some cases individuals, not only immediately, but in the future) need to be carefully considered when embarking on any joint venture transaction. Many acquisitions fail because of pensions liabilities. Pensions can be a primary consideration in many a merger/deal although start up joint ventures are usually unaffected, as there may well be no transfers of any business into the JV. The monthly newsletter *Pensions Today* contains regular updates of pensions law which is a fast moving field.

Chapter 5

Share incentive schemes in UK joint venture companies

Summary

This chapter discusses the various types of share incentive schemes which are available in the UK, and the consents and approvals required by a joint venture company in order to establish a share incentive scheme using its own shares. Consideration is then given to the issues which arise when a joint venture company participates in an existing scheme established by a joint venture partner, or establishes its own scheme, under which the shares of one or more of the joint venture partners are made available. The position of a participant in an existing scheme whose employment is transferred to a joint venture company is then considered. The assumption is made throughout that the company and the scheme participants are resident in the UK for tax and regulatory purposes.

1 Introduction

5.1   Share incentive schemes are a popular and successful method of incentivising employees. For a private company, share incentive schemes are useful where an exit by means of sale or flotation of the whole enterprise is envisaged. Where this is not the case, such schemes may be less successful because there is unlikely to be a market for the shares which the employee receives. In the case of a typical corporate joint venture, the sale or flotation of the joint venture is an unlikely prospect and the use of share incentive schemes is therefore not particularly common in such cases. Where a share incentive scheme is nevertheless thought worthwhile, other mechanisms will need to be employed to provide the participants with a method of realising the gain on their shares. Where the joint venture partners are listed or quoted entities, they could make their own shares available, but the value of these is unlikely to reflect the results of the joint venture and they are not necessarily an effective motivating tool. A potentially more effective solution where a sale or flotation of the joint venture is not envisaged is for one or more of the joint venture partners to agree to buy the scheme shares or to arrange for their purchase by an employee benefit trust.

Owner-employees

5.2   The Finance Act 2014, Sch 37 gave new tax reliefs to promote employee ownership where an Employee Ownership Trust (EOT), a form of employee benefit trust (EBT) is set up. The EOT brings with it both capital gains tax and also income tax advantages.

The EOT enables the company's shares to be held for the benefit of all the employees. The CGT advantage of this structure is that on sale the CGT rate is 0% rather than the more usual 10% rate on sale of shares in a person's own company where business asset disposal relief (previously called entrepreneurs' relief until 6 April 2020) applies.

See at: https://www.gov.uk/government/uploads/system/uploads/attachment_ data/file/264598/7._Employee_ownership.pdf.

An EBT provides a market for shares held by employees and directors of private companies.

The HMRC guidance for employee share trusts is at https://assets.publishing. service.gov.uk/government/uploads/system/uploads/attachment_data/ file/365375/est-intro.pdf.Gannons Solicitors explain the differences as follows[1]:

- 'An EBT acts as market or warehouse for shares held by employees and or directors in private companies. The trustees of the EBT are only responsible for the assets placed under their trust via the EBT. The trustees are not responsible for the management of the employer company. There is usually no change of control when shares change hands as the shareholdings placed in the EBT are normally small and [comprise] less than 51% of the issued share capital.

- An EOT acquires the entire business and acts as new owner of the shares. The EOT takes over management of the business which becomes employee controlled. The vendors are usually the founders of the company and retire upon sale of their shares to the EOT or at the least take a back seat role'.

Share incentive schemes

5.3   Share incentive schemes should generally be designed so that the benefits available to each employee are tied to the financial results achieved by the company. The existing shareholders in the company will hope that the incentive provided by the scheme will increase the ultimate value of the

---

1   See https://www.gannons.co.uk/insights/employee-benefit-trust-ebt/.

company by more than the amount represented by the reduction in their interest in its equity, and thereby achieve a more profitable realisation.

5.4   Shareholders contemplating the introduction of a share incentive scheme must bear in mind the consequences upon the voting control of the company of issuing additional shares. Since HMRC-approved schemes generally require the issue to employees of shares which are identical to all shares of the same class, they will carry votes. Normally, the percentage of the voting power which will be issued to employees will be so small that it will not make any significant difference to the voting power of the non-employee shareholders, but there may be circumstances in which the employee shareholders hold the balance of power. In a 50:50 deadlock joint venture, the issue of shares to employees will mean that the parties are no longer deadlocked and the venture partner which secures the most employee votes will win a vote on any issue before a general meeting which requires an ordinary resolution. The effect of this may be mitigated by provisions in a shareholders' agreement whereby the joint venture partners agree to exercise their votes in order to oppose any resolution which is not supported by both partners. Nevertheless, the opening up of the joint venture to employee scrutiny may not be acceptable to joint venture partners, in which case they will need to consider issuing employees with shares in one or more of the joint venture partners rather than in the joint venture itself (especially where they are listed or quoted) or issuing 'phantom awards' (see para 5.51ff).

General tax position

5.5   Share incentive schemes are closely linked to tax law because, subject to the various exemptions available, a benefit conferred upon an employee by means of the acquisition of shares is a taxable emolument. If, in return for services, an employee receives shares, income tax is chargeable on the excess of the market value of the shares over any amount which the employee paid for them (*Weight v Salmon* (1935) 19 TC 174).

5.6   Part 7 of the Income Tax (Earnings and Pensions) Act 2003 ('ITEPA 2003') governs the taxation of employee share schemes. Generally no income tax is chargeable on the *grant* of an option. Similarly, no national insurance contributions will be due on grant. Under ss 476–482 of ITEPA 2003, subject to various exemptions, where an employee, who is both UK resident and ordinarily resident on his acquisition of an option to acquire shares, exercises that option, income tax is chargeable on the difference between the price paid under the option, both for its grant and to acquire the shares, and the market value of the shares acquired, whether or not they are actually sold. Similarly, where an employee acquires shares other than by exercise of an option (eg by receiving a share award), income tax is chargeable on the difference between the price paid for the shares and the market value of the shares.

5.7   The income tax charge on the acquisition of shares/the exercise of an option will be collected via PAYE where the shares acquired are 'readily convertible assets'. The definition of 'readily convertible assets' is extremely wide and, in addition to including quoted shares, covers any situation where there is a prospect of selling the option or the shares as well as any shares which do not qualify for the statutory corporation tax relief in what was Sch 23 to the Finance Act 2003 and now the CTA 2009 (see para 5.55ff). Where the option or the shares acquired are not readily convertible assets, the income tax charge will be collected via self-assessment, usually with the individuals paying the relevant tax on 31 January following the tax year in which the tax charge arose. On the subsequent sale of the acquired shares, the charge to tax on the profit on sale will usually be subject only to capital gains tax, provided that shares are not subject to an income tax charge under the employee securities rules contained in Part 7, Chapters 2–4 of ITEPA 2003 (see para 26.28ff).

5.8   National insurance contributions are payable where an income tax charge arises on the exercise of an option/acquisition of shares if the shares acquired are readily convertible assets. The levying of employers' national insurance contributions on the acquisition of shares has generally proved onerous for companies. However, where share options are concerned, employers are allowed, by a joint election or by an agreement with the employees, to pass the liability to employees. Under the National Insurance Contributions and Statutory Payments Act 2004, employers also have the ability to do this in relation to other post-acquisition national insurance contributions which arise after exercise of the option, eg where there is an income tax charge under the restricted securities legislation (see para 26.36ff).

5.9   A charge to capital gains tax arises upon the disposal of the shares acquired, which is levied on the difference between the cost of the shares (including any sum paid for the award/option) and the disposal proceeds. The capital gains tax annual exempt amount and capital losses may reduce the tax chargeable. Any sum chargeable to income tax on receipt of the award/exercise of the option is considered allowable expenditure and is deductible when determining the gain made on the disposal of the shares.

Schemes fall into the following categories:

- Share Incentive Plans;

- Save As You Earn Schemes;

- Company Share Option Plans;

- Enterprise Management Incentive Schemes;

- Employee shareholder shares;

- Employee Ownership Trust (EOT) schemes.

Employee Shareholder Schemes above are a common means of giving shares to employees which bear a tax advantage (who in return will give up certainly employment rights and have shares handed to them free of any CGT on sale up to certain limits – see below).

For employee shareholder shares the capital gains tax position differs depending on the sale date as follows:

'Before 17 March 2016

You only pay Capital Gains Tax on shares that were worth over £50,000 when you got them.

From 17 March 2016

You only pay Capital Gains Tax on gains over £100,000 that you make during your lifetime. The 'gain' is the profit you make when you sell shares that have increased in value.'

See further at https://www.gov.uk/tax-employee-share-schemes/employee-shareholder-shares.

2 Types of scheme

Approved company share option schemes (CSOPs)

5.10   Approved company share option schemes offer employees the opportunity to acquire shares on a tax-advantaged basis. The employee receives an option over shares which is exercisable after three to ten years. Early exercise is permitted in a number of specified circumstances such as death and redundancy. These schemes are flexible and the exercise of options can be linked to performance targets. They do not require any cash contributions from employers, and employees need only make payments on the exercise of options, and if this is delayed until just before realisation there is only a transitory outlay by the employee. Options can be granted to subscribe for new shares or to acquire shares from an existing holder, such as an employee benefit trust. Scheme documentation must be approved by HMRC in advance.

5.11   Any full-time director or employee of the grantor company, or of another company covered by a group scheme who is selected to do so, is eligible to participate in the scheme provided that he or she does not have a 'material interest' (which means, broadly speaking, a 25% interest in the grantor company).

5.12   The shares over which options are granted must be ordinary shares in the grantor company (or certain of its controlling companies). The shares must be: (a) listed on a recognised stock exchange; (b) held in a company which is not under the control of another company; or (c) held in a company which is under the control of a listed company. A joint venture company will therefore be able to establish an approved company share option scheme so as long as it is not under the control of any of the joint venture partners (ie the joint venture partners are all in a minority) or, if one joint venture partner holds a controlling interest, that joint venture partner is a listed company.

5.13   The shares must not be subject to any special restrictions other than restrictions attaching to all shares in the same class and/or restrictions imposed by the company's articles of association which requires directors and employees of the company or its subsidiaries to dispose of any shares held on cessation of their employment, provided that such disposal is by way of sale for money on the same terms laid down by the articles for the disposal of all shares of the same class. Compulsory transfers on leaving are, in any case, normally desired so as to prevent an employee from receiving further value from his shares after ceasing to work for the company.

5.14   If the company has more than one class of share, the majority of the shares over which options are granted must either be 'employee-control shares' or they must not be beneficially owned by persons who acquired the shares pursuant to a right or opportunity conferred on them by virtue of their employment or (if the shares are not quoted) held by the controlling company (or its associated company). Shares in a company are employee-control shares if the persons holding those shares are, as a result of holding them, together able to control the company, and those persons are or have been employees or directors of the company or of a company under its control.

5.15   The price to be paid for the shares must be stated at the time the option is granted (but there may be provision for its later alteration following a variation in the share capital) and must not be manifestly less than the market value of the shares at that time. In this and all other cases in which market value is relevant, the market value of the shares must be agreed with HM Revenue & Customs Shares and Assets Valuation (see further para 5.68). The value of the shares over which each participant may hold unexercised options is limited to £30,000. This value is ascertained at the time of grant of the options.

5.16   Options must not be capable of transfer, but may be exercised by the personal representatives of a deceased option-holder within one year of the option-holder's death (subject to the overall ten year rule). It is possible to include provisions in the scheme whereby, if the grantor company is taken over, the option is exchanged for a new option for the acquisition of shares in the acquiring company (subject to the consent of the acquiring company and the option-holder).

5.17   Generally, no income tax charge arises on the grant of the option. In addition, no income tax charge arises upon exercise of the option, provided that exercise occurs not less than three and not more than ten years after grant. Early exercise will give rise to an income tax charge, unless it occurs in certain specified circumstances such as redundancy and death. Where an income tax charge arises, employee and employer national insurance contributions are also due. With the employee's consent, the employer can transfer liability for payment of the employer national insurance contributions to the employee.

5.18   Capital gains tax will be payable on any gain on subsequent disposal of the shares.

5.19   In the light of the 2020/21 Covid-19 pandemic HMRC confirmed it accepts that where employees and full-time directors are furloughed, options granted before the pandemic will remain qualifying on the basis they were full-time directors and qualifying employees at the time of grant of options.

Approved savings related share option schemes (SAYE)

5.20   Approved savings related share option schemes (also known as SAYE schemes) operate such that the employees agree to make monthly contributions to a certified contractual savings plan within s 703 of the Income Tax (Trading and Other Income) Act 2005 for three or five years, and are granted an option over shares. Upon maturity of the savings plan, the employee can choose either to use the contributions, together with a bonus (see para 5.22), to fund the exercise of the option or to receive the contributions and bonus in cash (in which case the option will lapse). The scheme documentation must be approved in advance by HMRC. Generally, the financial institution offering the savings plan will also carry out the administration of the scheme.

5.21   All UK resident and ordinarily resident employees and full-time directors with at least five years' service must be offered the opportunity to participate in the scheme. Other employees and directors may also be offered the opportunity to participate at the company's discretion, but persons with a material interest (see para 5.11) are excluded.

5.22   The employee's contributions to the savings contract may not exceed £500 per month (2020 figure) and are made from the employee's post-tax salary. A minimum contribution can be imposed by the company, but it may not be more than £10. On maturity of the savings plan, in addition to repayment of the contributions, a tax-free bonus is also payable. The bonus rate is set by HM Treasury from time to time by reference to market interest rates and depends on the length of the savings plan (in the case of five year savings plans, the employee can choose to leave the contributions in the plan for a further two years (although no additional contributions are made) in return for a higher bonus on maturity). The options cannot normally be exercised until the expiry of the period required to attract the bonus on maturity of the savings plan, and the total value of the shares as at the date the option is granted must not exceed the proceeds of the savings plan.

5.23   The shares over which the options are granted must satisfy the requirements in paras 5.12–5.14. The option price must be fixed at the date of grant of the option and may not be less than 80% of the market value of the shares at the date of grant. Again, if the shares are not listed on a recognised stock exchange, the market value must be agreed with HM Revenue & Customs Shares and Assets Valuation.

5.24   Generally, options cannot be exercised until maturity of the savings contract. Upon maturity, the participant has six months in which to exercise their option. In addition, options may be exercised prior to maturity of the savings contract in certain specified circumstances such as redundancy and retirement (but only to the extent of the savings accumulated at the time). As with company share option schemes ('CSOPs'), options must not be capable of transfer, but may be exercised by the personal representatives of a deceased option-holder within one year of the later of the option-holder's death or the bonus date. The participant is not required to exercise the option and can choose to simply receive the accumulated savings and bonus.

5.25   No income tax charge arises on the grant or exercise of the option (save where the option is exercised within three years of the date of grant following a change of control, scheme of arrangement, winding up or sale of the company employing the participant). The only charge is to capital gains tax on any gain made on the subsequent disposal of the shares. If a participant chooses not to exercise their option or to terminate the savings contract early, no income tax is payable on the accumulated savings and any bonus or interest paid out. Employee and employer national insurance contributions will also be due where there is an income tax charge. Liability for payment of the employer national insurance contributions can be transferred to the employee with the employee's consent.

5.26   Capital gains tax will be payable on any gain on subsequent disposal of the shares. However there is no CGT if the employee places their SAYE shares into their own ISA or pension as soon as they buy them.

5.27   In 2020 due to the Covid-19 pandemic HMRC updated its guidance to confirm that employees with a savings contract in place on 10 June 2020 might delay their monthly contributions if delay were due to the impact of the pandemic. Postponing contributions put back the year maturity date by the number of months missed. It remained possible to make SAYE contributions by way of deduction from payments received through the

Coronavirus Job Retention Scheme (CJRS). Those unable to make payments from salary might also temporarily pay by standing order. HMRC updated its Specimen SAYE Prospectus from 10 June 2020 and guidance in Employee Tax Advantaged Share Scheme User Manual at ETASSUM34140 to reflect the changes.

Share incentive plans

5.28   Share incentive plans (SIPs) operate such that a trust buys or subscribes for shares which are subsequently awarded to or acquired by employees. The scheme involves up to four types of shares:

(a)   free shares: employers can give up to £3,600 (2021 figure) worth of free shares to employees each year free of income tax and national insurance contributions;

(b)   partnership shares: employees can buy partnership shares worth up to £1,800 – 2021 figure – (or 10% of the employee's salary, if less) from their pre-tax earnings each year, free of income tax and national insurance contributions;

(c)   matching shares: employers can give up to two free matching shares for each partnership share bought by employees; and

(d)   dividend shares: up to £1,500 of dividends a year received on shares held by the trustees can be reinvested and used to acquire dividend shares. HMRC says 'You may be able to buy more shares with the dividends you get from free, partnership or matching shares (but only if your employer's scheme allows it). You will not pay income tax if you keep the dividend shares for at least 3 years.'

For those placing their shares into a pension (SIP) note that there is an obligation to pay income tax and national insurance on any shares taken out of a SIP early.

5.29   All UK resident and ordinarily resident employees with at least 18 months' service must be offered the opportunity to participate in the plan. Other employees may also be offered the opportunity to participate at the company's discretion but persons with a material interest (see para 5.11) are excluded. Scheme documentation must be approved in advance by HMRC.

5.30   The shares awarded or acquired must satisfy the requirements in paras 5.12 and 5.13 and in addition must not be shares in a service company or a company which is under the control of a service company. A 'service company' is a company whose business consists substantially in the provision of services to: (i) a person who has control of the company; (ii) two or more people who together have control of the company; or (iii) a company associated with the company.

5.31   Awards of free shares can be tied to achievement of performance targets (whether personal, divisional or corporate), provided the targets are objective and certain conditions are complied with. If awards are not tied to performance targets, they must be made on 'similar terms' to all participants. Participants are required to hold free shares awarded to them in the trust for a period specified by the company (which must be at least three but not more than five years). The scheme can (but does not have to) provide that free shares will be forfeited if the participant ceases employment within a period of up to three years of the award (save in certain specified circumstances such as death and redundancy) or if the participant attempts to withdraw the free shares from the trust at any time. If free shares are not forfeited upon cessation of employment, they must be taken out of the trust at that time.

5.32   As partnership shares are acquired with the participants' own money, they cannot be subject to forfeiture provisions and can therefore be withdrawn from the scheme at any time (although this may have adverse tax consequences – see para 5.35).

5.33   The matching of shares can be capped so that only partnership shares acquired up to a certain value are matched. As with free shares, participants are required to hold matching shares awarded to them in the trust for a period specified by the company (which similarly must be at least three but not more than five years). Matching shares may also be made subject to forfeiture on cessation of employment or withdrawal of the matching shares from the trust in the same way as free shares and, if not subject to forfeiture, must be withdrawn from the trust on cessation of employment. The forfeiture provisions may also apply where the partnership shares in respect of which the matching shares were awarded are withdrawn from the trust.

5.34   The scheme can provide for dividends on shares held in the trust to be paid out to participants or for them to be reinvested and used to acquire further shares (up to a limit of £1,500 per year). The scheme may provide for one or other option to apply or may allow the participant to elect between the two. Any dividend shares must be held in the trust for three years and must be withdrawn if the participant ceases employment or withdraws his or her other shares from the trust.

5.35   Generally, employees will not pay any income tax in respect of their free, matching and partnership shares if they keep such shares in the plan for five years. Generally, on withdrawal of any such shares before the expiration of five years, income tax will become payable. If the shares are withdrawn less than three years from the date of award/purchase, the participant will be liable to income tax on their value at the date of their withdrawal from the scheme. If the shares are withdrawn more than three years after the date of award/purchase, the income tax charge will be based only on the lesser of the value of the shares on the date of award/purchase and their value on the date of their withdrawal from the scheme. Participants will not pay any income tax in respect of dividend shares provided the shares are kept in the scheme for three years. If such shares are withdrawn from the scheme within three years of their acquisition, an income tax charge on the value of the dividend(s) used to purchase them will arise. Early withdrawal of shares from the scheme for certain specified reasons (eg redundancy and retirement) will not give rise to an income tax charge. Employee and employer national insurance contributions will be due where an income tax charge is payable, but the employer cannot transfer liability for the employer national insurance contributions to the employee.

5.36   Capital gains tax will be payable on any subsequent disposals of shares withdrawn from the scheme on any gain in value between the date of their withdrawal from the scheme and the date of their disposal.

5.37   In 2020 due to the Covid-19 pandemic HMRC updated its guidance in relation to these schemes to confirm that payments under the coronavirus job retention scheme (CJRS) to furloughed employees may amount to a salary and SIP contributions may continue to be deducted. SIP participants were already allowed to stop deductions from their salary, but are not be allowed to make up missed deductions if they stop payment by reason of the pandemic.

Enterprise Management Incentive Schemes

5.38   The Enterprise Management Incentive (EMI) Scheme is designed for small, higher-risk independent trading companies and allows such companies to grant options over shares in the company which are tax-advantaged but do not need to satisfy as stringent requirements as applicable to an approved company share option scheme. No prior HMRC approval of the scheme documentation is required, but the grant of an EMI option must be notified to HMRC within 92 days, and HMRC can, if it chooses to do so, investigate whether the option satisfies the legislative requirements.

5.39   A qualifying company is able to grant options to any number of employees, each of whom may hold options over shares which are worth up to £250,000 (2021 figure) at the time of grant (options granted under CSOPs are included in this limit). The total value of shares in the company in respect of which unexercised qualifying options exist must not exceed £3m from time to time. The option price can be less than the market value of the share (and can be nil if the shares over which the option is granted are not newly issued shares).

5.40   In order to be a qualifying company, the grantor must satisfy certain conditions:

(1)   it must be an independent company (ie it must not be a 51% subsidiary or otherwise under the control of another company) and it must only have 'qualifying subsidiaries' itself (ie subsidiaries which are 51% subsidiaries

and not under the control of any company other than the grantor or one of its subsidiaries) – this may exclude some joint venture companies which are 51% subsidiaries of one of the joint venture partners;

(2)   it must be a trading company carrying on a qualifying trade – certain trades such as financial services are excluded;

(3)   it must not have gross assets exceeding £30m at the date of grant; and

(4)   it must have fewer than 250 employees at the date of grant.

5.41   If certain 'disqualifying events' occur, the EMI option will cease to benefit from the EMI treatment and associated tax advantages unless the option is exercised within 40 days of the event occurring. Disqualifying events include:

(1)   the grantor becoming a subsidiary of, or otherwise under the control of, another company (the EMI option may be exchanged in such circumstances for a replacement option over shares in the new parent company and will retain the EMI treatment and associated tax advantages if the exchange occurs within six months of the change of control);

(2)   the grantor ceases to carry on a qualifying trade;

(3)   the employee ceases to be employed by the grantor or one of its subsidiaries; or

(4)   the £250,000 individual limit is breached.

5.42   Provided that the option price is set at the market value of the shares as at the date of grant, there will be no income tax when the options are granted or exercised. If, however, the option price is set at less than the market value of the shares at the date of grant, income tax will be payable on exercise of the option on the lesser of the market value at the date of grant and the market value at the date of exercise (less the sum of the exercise price and any money paid for the grant of the option). Income tax will also be payable if a disqualifying event (see para 5.41) occurs and the option is not exercised within 40 days of that event. Employee and employer national insurance contributions will be payable where an income tax charge arises. Liability for the employer national insurance contributions can be transferred by the employer to the employee with the employee's consent.

Companies involved in the following 'excluded' activities may not operate EMIs:

●   banking;

●   farming;

●   property development;

●   provision of legal services;

●   ship building.

5.43   Capital gains tax will be payable on any gain on subsequent disposal of the shares.

More information on EMI schemes is available at: https://www.gov.uk/tax-employee-share-schemes/enterprise-management-incentives-emis.

5.44   In August 2020 HMRC confirmed that EMI options granted both before and after 19 March 2020 (date of first UK Covid-19 lockdown) remain qualifying where the employee otherwise remains employed but for eg furlough during the pandemic. The employer and the employee are required to keep evidence that the employee qualified. Separately HMRC may accept some delays with EMI notifications where genuinely caused by the pandemic.

Unapproved share option schemes

5.45   Unapproved share option schemes are similar to approved company share option plans, but because they do not comply with the HMRC requirements they do not share the same tax advantages. The tax consequences are therefore as set out in para 5.5ff.

5.46   Unapproved option schemes are generally used to incentivise executives where greater flexibility is desired than is available with an approved scheme. In addition, companies may wish to award higher value options than is permitted under an approved scheme, particularly where it is felt that the additional incentive available to the employees outweighs the tax disadvantage. If an employee can obtain shares of high value at low cost, a worthwhile profit may be obtained even though income tax and national insurance contributions will be payable. Moreover, if the option price is set at the market value of the shares at the date of grant, no income tax charge or national insurance contributions liability will arise until exercise of the option and, if the option is exercised just before a sale of the shares (usually on an exit by way of flotation or the sale of the company), the income tax charge and national insurance contributions liability which arise on exercise can be funded out of the sale proceeds. Liability for employer national insurance contributions arising on exercise of the option can be transferred by the employer to the employee with the employee's consent.

5.47   Capital gains tax will be payable on any gain on subsequent disposal of shares acquired under an unapproved share option scheme.

Long-term incentive plans (LTIPs)

5.48   Like unapproved share option schemes, LTIPs are non-approved share incentive schemes and therefore do not attract any tax concessions – the tax consequences are therefore as set out in para 5.5ff – but on the other hand are not subject to any HMRC requirements. They are generally used to reward executives, and their flexibility (due to the lack of HMRC constraints) enables rewards to be more closely related to performance.

5.49   Because of this flexibility, the features of such a plan are almost infinite, but they generally have the following common themes:

- The employee is awarded shares on deferred terms.

- The shares are awarded free to the employees. The issuing company therefore funds the whole cost of the scheme but, unlike an option, the employee is able to realise the whole value of the shares and not only the difference between the exercise price and the sale price.

- The award is subject to conditions, such as the achievement of performance targets and the continued employment of the employee for a defined period.

5.50   The following are some common permutations:

- *Contingent award:* The employee receives an award of shares which is contingent on certain performance targets. If these are not met, the award will be scaled back, sometimes to nothing. The employee will normally have no dividend or voting rights until vesting. Vesting will then be dependent upon the employee remaining in employment with the company, unless he leaves as a 'good leaver', eg through ill-health, retirement at normal retirement age, or redundancy.

- *Vested award:* A number of the shares will be awarded based on past performance. They will be held in trust and not released for a period, typically three to five years, and will be forfeited if the employee leaves before that period expires – unless he is a 'good leaver'.

- *Deferred bonus:* Plans often contain a deferred bonus element. The employee is invited to convert his potential bonus into shares, which will be held in trust and not released for a specified period. The company matches the shares acquired with an award for further shares of equivalent value (or in whatever ratio which it considers appropriate) at no cost to the employee. If the employee leaves (otherwise than as a 'good leaver') during the specified period, the shares (or at least the matching element) are forfeit.

- *Restricted shares:* The employee acquires shares which are subject to restrictions (eg no dividend or voting rights) which reduce their value, but such restrictions fall away if performance targets are achieved. If the employee leaves in the meantime, he must sell the shares at the reduced value. Alternatively, the right to acquire the shares may itself be subject to performance targets, so two targets must be met before the full value can be obtained.

Phantom share options and awards

5.51   If the employees receiving the shares have no ready method of realising the value of those shares, share incentives may prove to be an ineffective incentive. Where it is not possible to devise an effective realisation mechanism, phantom share options and share awards can provide a solution.

5.52   Under a phantom share option, the employee is granted an option over a number of units whose value is tied to the value of a share in the grantor company at that time (ie a unit is effectively a notional share). As with a normal share option, the employee has the right during the exercise period (normally between three and ten years from the date of grant) to exercise the option and receive the value of the units as a cash payment. The amount payable per unit will equal the difference between the market value of a share in the grantor company at the date of grant and the market value at the date of exercise.

5.53   Under a phantom share award, the employee receives an award of units whose value is again tied to the grantor company's share value. Generally, the award will vest after a specified period has elapsed (some schemes provide for the award to vest in full on a specified date whilst others provide for the award to vest in tranches) and the value of the units will be paid to the employee as a cash payment. As with a phantom option, the amount payable per unit will equal the difference between the market value of a share in the grantor company at the date of grant and the market value at the date of vesting.

5.54   Such a scheme will not qualify for any form of HMRC approval and is entirely funded by the grantor company. Income tax and national insurance contributions will be payable on the cash payment made to the employee upon exercise of the phantom option/vesting of the phantom award. It is not possible to transfer liability for employer national insurance contributions to the employee.

Corporation tax relief for employee share acquisitions

5.55   Part 11 of the Corporation Tax Act 2009 ('CTA 2009') provides for corporation tax relief for a company in relation to the provision of shares to employees under a SIP. The following relief is available:

- where free or matching shares are provided, the amount of the relief will be equal to the market value of the shares at the time of their acquisition by the trustees of the SIP; and

- where partnership shares are acquired by an employee and their market value at the time of their acquisition by the trustees of the SIP was greater than the partnership share money used by the employee to acquire them, relief equal to the excess will be available.

No relief is available in relation to the provision of dividend shares (including in relation to expenses incurred in providing such shares).

5.56   Part 11 of the CTA 2009 also provides for corporation tax relief for a company in relation to the following expenses incurred in relation to employee share plans:

(a)   expenses incurred by the company in setting up a SIP, CSOP or SAYE scheme;

(b)   expenses incurred by a company in contributing to the expenses of the trustees in running a SIP; and

(c)   payments made by a company to the trustees of a SIP to enable the trustees to acquire shares in the company, provided certain conditions are satisfied.

5.57   The amount of the relief under Part 11 of the CTA 2009 is given as a deduction in computing for the purposes of corporation tax the profits of the trade or property business carried on by the company.

5.58   Part 12 of the CTA 2009 provides for corporation tax relief for a company on an award of shares to an employee or an employee's acquisition of shares pursuant to the grant of an option (notwithstanding that the company may not have borne an economic expense in relation to the award or option). This relief is available in respect of all qualifying share awards and regardless of whether the option is unapproved or granted pursuant to a CSOP, SAYE or EMI scheme. The following conditions must be met in order to obtain relief:

(a)   The award must be made or the option granted in relation to a business carried on by the employing company and the employing company must be within the charge to corporation tax.

(b)   The shares acquired must be ordinary shares that are fully paid up and not redeemable and they must be either:

(i)   shares of a class listed on a recognised stock exchange;

(ii)   shares in a company that is not under the control of another company; or

(iii) shares in a company that is under the control of a listed company.

(c)   The shares acquired must be shares in either:

(i)   the employing company;

(ii)   a parent company of the employing company;

(iii) a company which is a member of a consortium that owns the employing company or the parent company of the employing company; or

(iv) where the employing company or its parent company is a member of a consortium that owns another company ('C'), a company that is a member of the consortium and is also a member of the same commercial association of companies as C.

(d) The employee must be subject to income tax under ITEPA 2003 in respect of the shares or on exercise of the option. The relief is also available if the employee would have been so subject if the employee was resident and ordinarily resident in the UK and had performed the relevant employment duties in the UK.

5.59 Where the shares acquired are restricted or convertible shares, the amount of the relief is the amount on which the employee is charged to income tax (or, in the case of an approved option, would have been charged to income tax had the option not been an approved option). Where the shares acquired are not restricted or convertible shares, the amount of the relief is the market value of the shares less any consideration paid for them (employer national insurance contributions which are paid by the employee pursuant to an election and the performance of employment duties do not constitute consideration for these purposes).

5.60 The amount of the relief under Part 12 of the CTA 2009 is given as a deduction in computing for the purposes of corporation tax the profits of the business for the purpose of which the award was made or the option was granted. If the award was made or the option was granted for the purposes of more than one business within the charge to corporation tax, the relief must be apportioned between the two businesses on a just and reasonable basis. If the award was made or the option was granted for the purposes of more than one business but the second business is not within the charge to corporation tax, the amount of the deduction must be reduced by a just and reasonable amount. The relief is given for the accounting period in which the employee acquires the shares (ie when the recipient acquires a beneficial interest in the shares).

3 Establishing a new scheme for a joint venture vehicle

5.61 If the intention is that employees of a joint venture vehicle should be able to participate in a share incentive scheme, the scheme can be established by the joint venture vehicle itself, using either its own shares or the shares of one or more of the joint venture partners, or the employees can participate in a suitable scheme established by one of the joint venture partners. A joint venture vehicle will only be able to establish an approved scheme if none of the joint venture participants has control over it, or the venture participant having control has its shares listed on a recognised investment exchange.

5.62 Awards or options under a scheme established by the joint venture company can be tied to the results achieved by the joint venture, but the main difficulty with this may lie in providing a suitable mechanism by which employees may realise their shares.

Realisation mechanisms

5.63 Where a flotation or the sale of the whole enterprise is contemplated at the outset, and is achieved, there is no difficulty in the employees realising their shares. Otherwise, the available routes are:

● the joint venture vehicle buys the shares back for cancellation;

● one of more of the joint venture participants buys the shares; or

● the shares are bought by an employee benefit trust, for subsequent distribution to other employees.

5.64 Buying back shares for cancellation involves an indirect cost to the joint venture participants, but does have the merit of restoring their relative percentage shareholdings. Unless the share repurchase falls within the conditions for capital gains tax treatment under ss 1033–1045 of the Corporation Tax Act 2010, the excess of the repurchase price over the amount originally paid for the shares (ie the exercise price or the acquisition price) for the shares will be treated as a distribution and will therefore be subject to income tax in the hands of a UK individual shareholder. In addition, the sale of shares is a disposal for capital gains purposes and a capital gain or a capital loss might arise (after taking into account the amount taxed as income), depending on the relative values of the amount originally subscribed and the shareholder's capital gains base cost (and assuming that the shares are not subject to an additional income tax charge under Part 7, Chapters 2–4 of ITEPA 2003). See para 26.31ff.

5.65 The tax position will depend on the circumstances of the shareholder and whether or not an income tax charge arose on the exercise of the option. On a distribution individual taxpayers will pay income tax at an effective rate of: (i) for basic rate tax payers 7.5%; (ii) for higher rate tax payers 32.5%; and (iii) for additional rate tax payers 38.1% on dividends/distribution income over the £2000 a year tax free dividend allowance (see para 26.4 and note 1.25% increase 1 April 2022), whereas the rate of capital gains tax may be less for higher and additional rate tax payers. Should any capital gains arise, an annual exemption may be available to limit the amount subject to tax. Where an individual has paid income tax on the exercise of an option, an effective double charge to income tax may arise if the shares acquired are bought back. Although compensating relief should be available in the form of a capital loss, in practice such relief is unlikely to be useful for many individual shareholders and a buy-back will usually be less attractive than a purchase where there has been an income tax charge on exercise.

5.66   Purchases by the joint venture participants involve a direct cost to the purchasers, who would need to buy them in agreed proportions if their relative shareholdings are to be maintained. Since there is no distribution, the ordinary rules for tax on the sale of shares apply so that the proceeds will normally only be liable to capital gains tax. This could be more or less attractive to the participants than a distribution, depending upon the same factors as were discussed in para 5.65.

5.67   The employee benefit trust route is only likely to be effective where there is a constant flow of share sales and purchases. The tax position for participants is the same as described at para 5.66.

Valuations

5.68   In the case of approved schemes involving unquoted shares, the market value of the shares concerned will need to be agreed with HM Revenue & Customs Shares and Assets Valuation. It may insist on a pro rata market valuation (without discounts for minority interests) if there are pre-emption provisions in the company's articles whereby shares are to be transferred on the basis of such a valuation. The principles of share valuation are discussed in Chapter 22.

Consents and regulatory issues

5.69   Where the joint venture company is a subsidiary undertaking of a listed company and directors of either the listed company or the joint venture company or their associates are to participate in the scheme, consideration will need to be given as to whether such participation is a related party transaction within Chapter 11 of the Listing Rules of the United Kingdom Listing Authority (UKLA, a division of the Financial Conduct Authority), therefore requiring the consent in general meeting of the shareholders of the listed company. However, in view of the exemptions for employee share schemes and long-term incentive schemes contained in LR 11 Annex 1.1.3, such consent is unlikely to be required.

5.70   Where the making of a share award or the granting of an option constitute a public offering of transferable securities, a prospectus approved by the Financial Conduct Authority ('FCA') will be required by virtue of the FCA's Prospectus Rules (which implement the provisions of EC Directive

2003/71/EC (the 'Prospectus Directive')). 'Securities' include shares and securities giving a right to acquire shares such as an option. However, share options will not fall within the prospectus regime if they are non-assignable as they will not be 'transferable'. Approved options are always non-assignable, whilst most unapproved options are also non-assignable. As such, the granting of options to employees by a joint venture company (or one of the joint venture participants) is unlikely to require the publication of a prospectus. The FCA has confirmed this interpretation and also that exercise of options does not in its opinion give rise to a requirement to publish a prospectus.

5.71   Similarly, although phantom share awards and phantom options are likely to constitute securities (as securities giving rise to a cash settlement determined by reference to other securities), they are unlikely to be assignable and will not therefore be transferable securities.

5.72   Shares in a listed company will clearly be transferable securities whilst shares in a private company are likely to be transferable securities on the basis that they are capable of being traded on a regulated market even if they are not in fact so traded (unless there are significant restrictions in the company's articles of association preventing the transfer of the shares). As such, an award of shares by the joint venture company or the trustees of an employee share scheme to an employee of the company will prima facie be a public offer of transferable securities requiring the publication of a prospectus. However, a number of exemptions are available as follows:

(1)   A prospectus will not be required where the total consideration for the offer (when aggregated with the consideration for all other offers of the same securities by the offeror in the last 12 months throughout the EEA) is less than €2.5 million[2]. Awards of shares for nil consideration (such as awards of free and matching shares in SIPs and awards under non-approved plans where the employee is not required to pay for the shares) will not therefore require the publication of a prospectus.

(2)   A prospectus will not be required if the offer is made to fewer than 100 persons in each member state at any time (there is no aggregation with other offers of the same securities made over a period of time)[3]. This exemption may be of assistance in relation to share incentive schemes which are designed to benefit only senior executives, such as LTIPs.

(3)   A full prospectus will not be required where the company has shares listed on an EEA regulated market[4]. If this exemption applies, the company need only make a document available to employees setting out:

(a)   the number and nature of the securities offered; and

(b)   the reasons for and details of the offer.

---

2   See Article 1(2)(h) of the Prospectus Directive.
3   See Article 3(2)(b) of the Prospectus Directive.
4   See Article 4(1)(e) of the Prospectus Directive.

It is therefore unlikely that publication of a prospectus will be required in relation to an employee share scheme. However, where employees will be required to pay for shares awarded to them (other than upon exercise of an option), the joint venture company should seek advice with regard to the need for a prospectus.

The UK retained EU law after 31 December 2020 in a process known as 'on-shoring'. The EU Securitisation Regulation 2017/2402 may be relevant in some cases where there are pooled debts although most joint ventures are not within that regime. The UK has retained the regulation but amended it for the UK by the Securitisation (Amendment) (EU Exit) Regulations 2019. This EU regulation has been in force since 2019 as retained EU law applicable in the UK.

5.73   The operation of the scheme will not ordinarily be a 'regulated activity' for the purposes of the Financial Services and Markets Act 2000 ('FSMA 2000'), so that it will not be necessary to involve an authorised person under s 19 of that Act by reason of the exemption contained in art 71 of the Financial Services and Markets Act 2000 (Regulated Activities) Order 2001[5].

5.74   Any circulation of material to employees relating to a scheme could be unlawful under FSMA 2000, s 21 as a financial promotion, unless it is issued or approved by an authorised person. Fortunately there is an exemption which applies to the making of financial promotions to specified participants under employees' share schemes[6]. A scheme may constitute a 'collective investment scheme' as defined in s 235 of FSMA 2000 which would deny the availability of this exemption. However, there is a further exemption in para 8 of the Schedule to the Financial Services and Markets Act 2000 (Collective Investment Schemes) Order 2001[7] which is available in the case of employees' share schemes.

4 Joint venture employees participating in a scheme established by one of the joint venture participants under which the joint venture participant's shares are issued

5.75   Allowing employees of the joint venture vehicle to participate in a share incentive scheme established by one of the joint venture participants using the joint venture participant's shares may be attractive where one of the joint venture participants is a listed or quoted company and its shares are

5   SI 2001/544.
6   See art 60 of the Financial Services and Markets Act 2000 (Financial Promotion) Order 2005 (SI 2005/1529) as amended.
7   SI 2001/1062.

readily marketable and where there is unlikely ever to be a market, or any other form of exit route, in relation to the shares of the joint venture vehicle. This is particularly the case where the listed or quoted company controls the joint venture. A disadvantage, however, is that the results of the joint venture are unlikely to be wholly reflected in the share price of the listed or quoted company, so that the value of the scheme as an incentive may be blunted. However, the number of shares issued may be tied to the results of the joint venture.

5.76   Where the joint venture vehicle is a subsidiary of the joint venture partner whose scheme is to be used and whose shares are to be issued (the 'issuer') the consequences are as follows:

(1)   any HMRC approval will not be affected by the inclusion of employees of the joint venture in the scheme;

(2)   the scheme will be an employees' share scheme for the purposes of s 1166 of the Companies Act 2006 ('CA 2006') (which replaced s 743 of the Companies Act 1985 ('CA 1985') with effect from 1 October 2009) so that:

    (a)   a joint venture participant which is a public company or its subsidiaries may lawfully provide 'financial assistance' for the purposes of the scheme without a breach of the general prohibition contained in ss 678 and 679 of the CA 2006 (which replaced s 151 of the CA 1985 with effect from 1 October 2009);

    (b)   shares may be allotted to joint venture employees without the necessity to obtain any disapplication for shareholders' pre-emption rights under ss 560–577 of the CA 2006 (which replaced ss 89–95 of the CA 1985 with effect from 1 October 2009);

(3)   the existing scheme will normally allow employees of subsidiaries to participate, so that no shareholder's consent to its amendment should be required;

(4)   the prospectus, regulated activities, financial promotion and collective investment scheme exemptions should apply; and

(5)   the related party exemption should apply.

5.77   Where the joint venture company is not a subsidiary of the issuer the consequences are that:

(1)   only an unapproved scheme is possible, unless advantage can be taken of the provisions relating to jointly owned companies in Schs 2–4 to the ITEPA 2003, which are available where two persons between them control the joint venture company and one of them is the issuer, in which case employees of the joint venture company and its subsidiaries may participate in the scheme;

(2)   the scheme will not be an employees' share scheme within s 1166 of the CA 2006, so that:

(a)   any financial assistance provided by the joint venture vehicle will not fall into the prohibition on such assistance in ss 678 and 679 of the CA 2006 since the assistance will not be provided for the acquisition of shares in its holding company, but the issuer will not be able to provide any financial assistance; and

(b)   the issue of shares by the issuer will be subject to the provisions conferring pre-emptive rights in favour of existing shareholders contained in ss 560–577 of the CA 2006 (however, a listed company will usually have sufficient headroom within a general disapplication of pre-emptive rights granted at a previous annual meeting to be able to issue the shares);

(3)   the scheme may need to be amended to allow the joint venture employees to participate, which may require the consent of the shareholders of the issuer in general meeting;

(4)   the related party provisions in Chapter 11 of the Listing Rules will not apply if the joint venture company is not the subsidiary undertaking of the issuer within the meaning of s 1162 of the CA 2006;

(5)   the prospectus, regulated activity, financial promotion and collective investment scheme exemptions may not be available. However, it should be noted that the FSMA 2000 exemptions apply an extended definition of 'group' in relation to the issuer (s 421). In particular, a group is treated as including any body corporate in which a member of the group holds a participating interest. A 'participating interest' means an interest held by an undertaking in the shares of another undertaking which it holds on a long-term basis for the purposes of securing a contribution to its activities by the exercise of control or influence arising from or related to that interest (see para 11 of Sch 10 to the Large and Medium-sized Companies and Groups (Accounts and Reports) Regulations 2008[8]).

5   Joint venture employees participating in a new scheme using shares in one or more of the joint venture participants

5.78   It is possible for the joint venture vehicle to establish its own share incentive scheme under which shares in one or more of the joint venture participants are made available. Where the participants in the joint venture

---

8   SI 2008/410.

include more than one listed or quoted company, institutional shareholders prefer schemes for joint venture companies to involve shares in all of them, so that the cost is shared between them.

5.79   The following issues will arise:

- *Financial assistance:* Where this is provided by the joint venture vehicle to a public company which is its holding company, the exemption for employee share schemes will apply; otherwise there is no prohibited financial assistance. An issuer which is a public company or one of its subsidiaries will only be able to provide financial assistance where it is the holding company of the joint venture vehicle, because otherwise the exemption for employee share schemes will not apply. More generally note that the CA 2006 abolished the prohibition on private companies providing financial assistance for purchase of their own shares, but retained it for public companies.

- *Regulated activities, financial promotions and collective investment schemes:* Generally, the FSMA 2000 exemptions will be available to the company establishing or operating the scheme, provided it is within the same group or groups (applying the extended definition of 'group' in s 421) of the company or companies whose shares are made available under the scheme.

- *Shareholder approval:* Where the joint venture company is a subsidiary undertaking of a listed issuer, the approval of the scheme by the issuer's shareholders in general meeting will be required. Where the joint venture company is a subsidiary of the issuer, no pre-emption disapplication will be required for the issue of shares under the scheme, but otherwise this will be required, although a general disapplication may be utilised.

- *HMRC approval:* If the joint venture is a subsidiary of the issuer, HMRC approval is not a problem. Otherwise, as long as the issuers together hold at least 75% of the shares in the joint venture company, and each has at least 5%, HMRC approval will be available for a scheme meeting the requirements for such approval (Schs 2–4 to ITEPA 2003).

6   The effect on employees transferring to the joint venture who are members of existing schemes

5.80   Where an employee of a joint venture participant is to be transferred to a joint venture company and is already a member of a share scheme established by the joint venture participant, consideration will need to be given to the effect of the transfer on their participation in the joint venture participant's scheme. They will usually be treated as a leaver under the rules of the scheme unless, as is sometimes the case, this treatment is not triggered where the employee is transferred to another entity in which the employing joint venture party has a stake (usually set at 50% or 20%).

5.81 In the case of a CSOP, the leaving rules may result in the options remaining exercisable for a limited period or at the discretion of the board, or lapsing altogether. If the effect of the transfer on options under the CSOP is thought undesirable, alterations of the scheme rules and the extension of the scheme to the joint venture company may allow the options to be preserved[9]. Care has to be taken that the alterations do not amount to conferring a new right on existing option holders. Otherwise, HMRC approval may not be forthcoming[10]. An income tax charge and national insurance contributions liability will arise if the transfer causes the option to be exercised within three years of its date of grant (save in certain specified circumstances such as redundancy). No income tax or national insurance contributions will be payable if the option is exercised more than three years but less than ten years after its date of grant.

5.82 In the case of an SAYE scheme, preservation is only possible if a 50:50 joint venture company is established, in which case options will automatically be preserved by virtue of para 46 of Sch 3 to ITEPA 2003. However, para 46 will allow employees of the joint venture company, not previously employed by the relevant joint venture participant, to receive further options under the scheme, which may be unwelcome. If options under an SAYE scheme cannot be preserved, they may be exercisable for up to six months after the transfer under provisions for exercise on redundancy or a business transfer, or if the scheme includes provisions allowing options to be held for more than three years to be exercised by 'other leavers' (see paras 34–37 of Sch 3 to ITEPA 2003). An income tax charge will arise if the transfer causes an option to be exercised within three years of its date of grant but no national insurance contributions will be payable as the shares acquired will not be 'readily convertible assets'[11]. No income tax or national insurance contributions will be payable if the option is exercised more than three years but less than ten years from its date of grant.

5.83 In the case of a SIP, existing awards under the SIP will not be affected by the transfer of the employee to the joint venture vehicle as the joint venture vehicle will be deemed to be controlled by the joint venture participant which established the SIP by virtue of para 91 of Sch 2 to ITEPA 2003. If the joint venture participant ceases to control the joint venture vehicle, shares held by transferred employees will have to be withdrawn from the trust. No income

---

9   *IRC v Reed International plc* [1994] STC 396.
10   *IRC v Eurocopy plc* [1991] STC 707.
11   See ITEPA 2003, ss 701 and 702 and Social Security (Contributions) Regulations 2001 (SI 2001/1004), Sch 3, Pt IX, para 7A.

tax charge or national insurance contributions liability will arise as a result of the withdrawal of the shares in these circumstances[12].

5.84   In the case of EMI options, transfer to a 50:50 joint venture vehicle will not affect existing EMI options granted to transferring employees by one of the joint venture participants. It will, however, prevent the grant of further EMI options by either joint venture participant as the joint venture vehicle will not be a 'qualifying subsidiary' (see para 5.40). If the joint venture vehicle becomes controlled by a 51% subsidiary of the other joint venture participant, this will constitute a 'disqualifying event'[13]. If the EMI option were exercised within 40 days of the disqualifying event, no income tax charge or national insurance contributions liability will arise. However, if it were exercised more than 40 days after the disqualifying event occurred, income tax and national insurance contributions will be payable.

5.85   In the case of an unapproved share incentive scheme or phantom share incentive scheme, the effect of the transfer will depend on the rules of the scheme. The transfer may have no impact on options/awards; it may cause options/awards to become exercisable/vest or it may cause them to lapse. Exercise of an option or vesting of an award will cause an income tax charge and national insurance contributions liability to arise.

---

12   See ITEPA 2003, s 488 and the Social Security (Contributions) Regulations 2001 (SI 2001/1004), reg 22(4).
13   ITEPA 2003, s 534.

Chapter 6

Financing a corporate joint venture in the UK

Summary

This chapter deals with some considerations relating to the provision of finance for a corporate joint venture in the UK, including the proportions of debt to share capital, the structuring of loan finance from the joint venturers, the requirements of outside financiers, and matters to be borne in mind by joint venturers who are required to provide guarantees or security.

1 Introduction

6.1   Whether the joint venturers intend to fund the venture out of their own resources or to seek finance from outside, the manner of structuring the finance will require early consideration. The venturers need to consider what proportion of the funds they inject should be share capital and what proportion will be loans and, if they choose loans, on what terms they are to be advanced. If outside finance is to be sought, the requirements of the outside financier will have a large impact on the structure of the joint venture as a whole. Where it is envisaged that the joint venturers will or may need to provide finance at a later stage, it will be important to ensure that they have a contractual commitment to do so. The venturers will also need to provide for what will happen if one or more of them leave the joint venture.

2 Loan finance or share capital?

6.2   There are attractions for joint venturers in financing the joint venture with only a small amount of share capital, sufficient only to establish the proportions in which they are to share the fruits of the venture and their respective voting rights, and to inject the rest of the funds by way of loans.

6.3   The advantages are:

● subject to the rules summarised in para 6.29ff, loan interest is normally an expense which is deductible in computing the profits of the joint venture for corporation tax purposes, thus reducing the tax liabilities of the joint venture;

- subject to there being sufficient cashflow, a loan can be repaid by the joint venture without the legal restrictions applying to the return of share capital;

- in theory, unless the loans are subordinated (see para 6.4), loans from the joint venturers rank pari passu with the other ordinary creditors of the joint venture, whereas shareholders always rank behind the creditors. Therefore in the event of the joint venture becoming insolvent, the prospect of recovering at least part of the funds is improved: if the loans are secured they will rank ahead of ordinary creditors, further improving the prospects of recovery.

6.4   The last advantage may prove illusory in that commercial pressures on the joint venturers may compel them to procure the discharge of all outside creditors from their own resources should the venture fail. Such pressures may also compel them to subordinate their loans to the claims of ordinary creditors. Save to the extent that the joint venturers' loans are secured by fixed, rather than floating, mortgages or charges, preferential creditors will rank in front of them and they often account for a substantial proportion of the creditors in a liquidation, although this will be less true now that Crown Preference has been abolished.

6.5   A possible disadvantage of advancing a large amount of loan capital relative to the share capital is that the balance sheet of the joint venture vehicle appears weak in the eyes of potential creditors. This may not matter too much where the joint venturers are each corporations of considerable financial standing, since creditors may regard them as standing behind the venture's liabilities, even where this is not legally the case. Otherwise, there may be difficulties in the joint venture vehicle obtaining substantial contracts without the provision of performance guarantees by the joint venturers. The position may be improved by the joint venturers agreeing to subordinate their loans to the claims of outside creditors, but this makes little impact on the structure of the balance sheet itself. Another problem with a large amount of debt to equity is that interest on the debt may cease to be fully deductible from profits for UK tax purposes (see para 6.30ff), although such deductibility is now a function of the transfer pricing rules rather than thin capitalisation as was historically the case.

6.6   Another potential disadvantage of a large amount of loan capital is that the interest on loans is a debt, whereas dividends on shares are not usually a debt (except sometimes in the case of unpaid dividends on preference shares, but then only to the extent of the distributable profits), and no consequence for the balance sheet ensues if dividends are not paid. This may not matter where the loans are being provided by the joint venturers themselves, who will usually defer or write off interest should the joint venture be less successful than was hoped. However, where outside lenders are involved, they may be less sympathetic, and an increased liability for unpaid interest, especially if the loan agreement provides for it to be 'rolled up' and added to principal, can give rise to the possibility of insolvency. Even where all loans are provided by the joint venturers, they may fall out at the critical moment over whether the unpaid interest should be written off or deferred[1], and again the likelihood of insolvency could easily increase.

6.7   Where a commercial rate of interest on an outside loan is less than the return which the joint venture vehicle can generate on the loaned funds, there has, in the past, been a great attraction for the joint venturers in allowing the venture to 'gear up' with outside loans, even where the joint venturers could themselves have provided the funds required. In the past, such 'gearing up' has allowed the joint venturers to make an extra profit, whilst at the same time reducing the funds required of them. Such a course should be taken with caution: business history is littered with cases of overgearing which have resulted in insolvency and liquidation, and this has never proved more true than in the current 'post credit-crunch' recession.

Government guidance on loans from shareholder/directors to the company is at https://www.gov.uk/directors-loans/you-lend-your-company-money.

As for loans in the other direction, note that from 20 March 2013 tax rules provide that where a shareholder borrows more than £10,000 (previously £5,000) from a company with five or fewer shareholders (a close company) there is a 25% tax charge on the loan (even if paid off in nine months but then taken out again – a practice known as 'bed and breakfasting'). This reflects HMRC practice but enshrines it in law. For loans from a company to the directors see guidance at https://www.gov.uk/directors-loans/you-owe-your-company-money.

6.8   HMRC guidance summarises[2] the rules on loans from the company to a director as follows:

'If you owe your company money

You or your company may have to pay tax if you take a director's loan.

Your personal and company tax responsibilities depend on how the loan is settled. You also need to check if you have extra tax responsibilities if:

● the loan was more than £10,000 (£5,000 in 2013–14)

● you paid your company interest on the loan below the official rate

---

1   But see para 6.15 as to the means by which such decisions could be made subject to a majority decision of the lenders.
2   See https://www.gov.uk/directors-loans/you-owe-your-company-money.

	Your company's responsibilities if you're a shareholder and director	Your personal responsibilities when you receive a director's loan
You repay the loan within 9 months of the end of your Corporation Tax accounting period	Use form CT600A when you prepare your Company Tax Return to show the amount owed at the end of the accounting period. If the loan was more than £5,000 (and you took another loan of £5,000 or more up to 30 days before or after you repaid it) pay Corporation Tax at 32.5% of the original loan, or 25% if the loan was made before 6 April 2016. After you permanently repay the original loan, you can reclaim the Corporation Tax – but not interest. If the loan was more than £15,000 (and you arranged another loan when you repaid it) pay Corporation Tax at 32.5% of the original loan, or 25% if the loan was made before 6 April 2016. After you permanently repay the original loan, you can reclaim the Corporation Tax – but not interest.	No responsibilities
You do not repay the loan within 9 months of the end of your Corporation Tax accounting period	Use form CT600A when you prepare your Company Tax Return to show the amount owed at the end of the accounting period. Pay Corporation Tax at 32.5% of the outstanding amount, or 25% if the loan was made before 6 April 2016. Interest on this Corporation Tax will be added until the Corporation Tax is paid or the loan is repaid. You can reclaim the Corporation Tax – but not interest.	No responsibilities
The loan is "written off" or "released" (not repaid)	Deduct Class 1 National Insurance through the company's payroll.	Pay Income Tax on the loan through a Self Assessment tax return

If the loan was more than £10,000 (£5,000 in 2013–14)

If you're a shareholder and director and you owe your company more than £10,000 (£5,000 in 2013 to 2014) at any time in the year, your company must:

- treat the loan as a "benefit in kind"
- deduct Class 1 National Insurance

You must report the loan on a personal Self Assessment tax return. You may have to pay tax on the loan at the official rate of interest.

If you paid interest below the official rate

If you're a shareholder and director, your company must:

- record interest you pay below the official rate as company income
- treat the discounted interest as a "benefit in kind"

You must report the interest on a personal Self Assessment tax return. You may have to pay tax on the difference between the official rate and the rate you paid.

Reclaim Corporation Tax

Your company can reclaim the Corporation Tax it pays on a director's loan that's been repaid, written off or released. You cannot reclaim any interest paid on the Corporation Tax.

Claim after the relief is due – this is 9 months and 1 day after the end of the Corporation Tax accounting period when the loan was repaid, written off or released. You will not be repaid before this.

You must claim within 4 years (or 6 years if the loan was repaid on or before 31 March 2010).

Reclaiming within 2 years

If you're reclaiming within 2 years of the end of the accounting period when the loan was taken out, use form CT600A to claim when you prepare a Company Tax Return for that accounting period or amend it online.

Use form L2P with your Company Tax Return instead if either:

- your tax return is for a different accounting period than the one when the loan was taken out
- you're amending your tax return in writing

Tell HMRC how you want the repayment in your Company Tax Return.

Reclaiming after 2 years

If you're reclaiming 2 years or more after the end of the accounting period when the loan was taken out, fill in form L2P and either include it with your latest Company Tax Return or post it separately.

HMRC will repay your company by either:

- using the details you gave in your latest Company Tax Return
- sending a cheque to your company's registered office address'

3 Loan finance from the parties

Structuring

6.9   The structuring of loan finance from the parties can involve some difficult issues, and the terms are likely to differ somewhat from those which would attach to a commercial loan. The problems which can arise include:

- What right, if any, should any lender have to recover its loan in advance of the other(s)?

- What events of default are appropriate and, if such events occur, can any lender take separate action to recover its own loan or is the action to be taken to be decided by a majority of the lenders?

- If the loans are being advanced by the joint venturers in instalments, what happens if one of the lenders defaults in making any advance? Can the others make the advance instead? If so, should they obtain a higher proportion of the equity of the venture in compensation, or what other rights would be appropriate?

- Can the company repay the loans other than pro rata to all the lenders at the same time?

- Should loans be repayable if the lender ceases to participate in the joint venture?

- Should lenders be able to assign their loans?

6.10   Where the joint venturers are required to make loans to the joint venture, they will usually do so in amounts pro rata to their equity participations, and there will usually be a desire on the part of the lenders to ensure that they are all treated alike, especially if they wish to claim consortium relief[3] pro rata to shareholdings, since if they are not treated alike the ability to claim such relief will be distorted. It will usually be considered inappropriate that any lender should be repaid before the others and, if security is to be provided, the lenders will normally desire that the security of each ranks pari passu.

6.11   If the joint venture company is unable to pay the interest due to all the lenders in full, the lenders will normally wish the deficiency to be suffered by them pro rata.

6.12   The events of default will usually be more relaxed than those applying in the case of a commercial loan. Generous periods for making good arrears of interest and capital repayments may be appropriate, but liquidation or administration should be made events of default. It will usually be inappropriate for insolvency alone to be an event of default.

---

3   See para 7.41ff.

6.13   If an event of default should occur, the lenders will usually not want any one lender to take enforcement action independently of the others, which may effectively force the end of the joint venture. Neither will they normally wish recovery to become a free for all between the lenders, with any of them recovering proportionately more of its loan than the others.

6.14   In order to avoid these undesirable possibilities, the joint venturers may wish to agree that all decisions relating to the enforcement of their loans should be taken unanimously or, if there are more than two lenders, by a majority decision, probably by reference to the amount they have each advanced.

6.15   Although such a position might be reached by each lender advancing an entirely separate loan and by including appropriate provisions in the shareholders' agreement, a neater solution is to follow the structure employed in public offers of loan securities, and issue each lender with loan stock in registered form constituted by a loan stock instrument, with the difference that if the loan stock is unsecured it would not normally be thought necessary to appoint trustees. The loan stock effectively comprises a single loan, with each stockholder lending a proportion of it, in contrast to a series of loan notes or agreements each comprising a separate loan.

6.16   The terms of the loan stock would be such that certain matters would be required to be approved by a resolution of the desired majority of the stockholders, either at a stockholders' meeting or by written resolution. These include all matters regarding early repayment, whether the loan should be required to be repaid if there is an event of default, and indeed any alteration to the terms of the loan, or any compromise or arrangement between the stockholders and the joint venture company. It may well be sensible to structure the required majority so it is the same as that required to veto certain transactions under the terms of the shareholders' agreement, so that the joint venturers have generally the same proportionate influence in relation to both their share and loan participations.

6.17   The terms of the loan stock will normally provide that all the stock ranks pari passu, so that all monies received from the joint company by way of interest and repayments will be applied in proportion to the amounts outstanding.

6.18   If one of the joint venturers should default in providing any tranche of its loan, the same difficulties regarding enforcement arise as with agreements by joint venturers to provide goods and services (as noted at para 3.17ff). However, a potentially more serious concern is that if the failure is not remedied, the joint company will suffer a shortage of funds. In such a case it might be provided that any other joint venturer could advance the tranche instead, but in order to provide an incentive to do so and a sanction against a failure to advance, it could be arranged that the equity of the defaulting joint venturer should be 'squeezed down' in some way.

6.19 If loan stock is convertible into equity, 'squeeze down' would automatically be achieved by the reduction in the conversion rights of the defaulter resulting from the tranche for which it should have subscribed being taken by another joint venturer. If tranches of share capital are being provided alongside the loans, the defaulter could simply be deprived of the right to subscribe for that tranche of share capital, which would go instead to a replacement lender. If all the shares have already been issued, some other mechanism might be used to squeeze down the equity, such as a compulsory transfer of shares by the defaulter at the original subscription price, or an initial issue of worthless deferred shares which are only converted into ordinary shares as loan tranches are advanced.

6.20 Whether loans should be repaid on the lender ceasing to participate in the joint venture is a difficult issue, but will normally be strongly desired by the outgoing lender. It will, however, involve the remaining venturers seeking replacement finance as well as possibly having to find the funds to purchase the shares of the outgoing venturer, which might cause considerable difficulty. If repayment on leaving is to be agreed, the repayment date should be no earlier than the scheduled completion date for the purchase of the outgoing venturer's shares, to provide time for any necessary financing to be put in place. A longer period of grace may be desirable.

6.21 It is, however, possible to imagine that a joint venturer might engineer its own exit in order to secure early repayment of its loan, perhaps by a deliberate breach of the shareholders' agreement. It is therefore a matter for consideration whether a shareholder in breach should be required to leave its loan in the joint venture vehicle until its original maturity date, and if so on what terms (eg new or further security, if appropriate).

6.22 The transfer of a joint venturer's loan to an outsider will not normally be acceptable; at the very least, the others would be likely to require to approve the assignee. The joint venturers are quite likely to require that loans and shares should be 'stapled' together so that a loan can only be transferred with the shares of the lender. However, this can cause tax problems, since the interest on the loan may be treated as a distribution rather than a tax deductible expense of the paying company, especially where the share and loan holder is outside the scope of UK corporation tax (see Corporation Tax Act 2010, ss 99 and 1030 and 1032).

Other general considerations

6.23 The rate of interest and other commercial terms will be another area for discussion. If the loan has been made on terms other than commercial ones, the UK's transfer pricing rules will be in point, although there are exceptions for certain types of companies (see para 6.30ff).

6.24   The general terms of joint venturers' loans should be structured so that obligations to pay interest and make capital repayments are in line with the projected cashflow. It may be necessary for the loans to be interest-free during the early stages of a venture, or perhaps deferred until sufficient cashflow is likely to be available, subject to transfer pricing considerations.

6.25   Subject to constraints imposed by outside lenders and other creditors, the joint venturers' loans could be unsecured, and either rank pari passu with the claims of ordinary creditors or be subordinated to such claims, or may be secured on the assets of the joint venture vehicle.

6.26   If joint venturers who have advanced loans to the joint company without security subsequently wish to take it, perhaps because the financial position of the company has deteriorated, they must bear in mind the provisions about preferences contained in the Insolvency Act 1986, s 239ff. Under s 240(1)(a), security created up to two years before the 'onset of insolvency' may be set aside as a preference (instead of the usual period of six months) where the holder of the security is 'connected' with the company. A holder of more than one-third of the votes exercisable at a general meeting of the company will be connected with it. Normally, in order for the security to be set aside, it is necessary to prove that the company was insolvent at the time the security was given, but in the case of security to a connected party this is presumed, although the presumption can be rebutted by proving solvency. The same two-year period applies to s 245, which provides for the avoidance of floating charges, save to the extent of the monies advanced in consideration of the creation of the charge.

Tax considerations

WITHHOLDING TAX

6.27   A UK tax resident company may pay loan interest to any UK tax resident corporate shareholder without having to deduct income tax. The loan interest is part of the profits of a UK tax resident payee and as such liable to corporation tax. The position of a shareholder who is non-UK resident for tax purposes is discussed at para 28.33ff.

6.28   Where the loan is structured as a security issued at a discount and is redeemable at par, no withholding tax is payable on redemption.

DEDUCTIBILITY FROM PROFITS

6.29   Loan interest is generally deductible in computing the profits of the paying company for the purposes of corporation tax as a debit under the loan relationships legislation. The deduction will normally be given on an accruals basis unless, broadly, the interest is not paid within 12 months of the end of the accounting period or the loan is structured as a relevant discounted security. In certain circumstances a deduction for the discount element of a discounted security can only be taken on redemption of the security. There are, however, exceptions to the general principles of deductibility, which are dealt with immediately below.

THIN CAPITALISATION

6.30   The UK's transfer pricing rules, which originally applied only to transactions between UK residents and non-residents, have been extended by the Finance Act 2004 to include those between residents, and the rules applying to loans are generally referred to as the 'thin capitalisation' rules. The rules also apply to payments for 'any security', a term which is widely defined, and includes securities which do not create or evidence a charge on assets (see below). See https://www.gov.uk/guidance/transfer-pricing-transactions-between-connected-companies.

6.31   Excessive interest will be disallowed for tax deduction purposes. Interest is excessive for these purposes if the amount of the loan exceeds the amount a third party would lend, if the third party would not have made the loan at all, or if the rate of interest is above an arm's length rate. There will also be a compensating adjustment, so the lender will only be taxed as though it had received the arm's length amount of interest.

6.32   When considering the debt capacity position of a company, it is permissible to take into account its assets and income, and the assets and income of its direct or indirect subsidiaries (on a worldwide basis, rather than a UK basis) to the extent that an unconnected lender would recognise them.

6.33   Thin capitalisation may result from the existence of a security, such as a loan guarantee, if this has the effect of increasing the amount which is lent to the borrower. In these circumstances, the interest on the excessive part of the loan will again be disallowed, whether paid to a connected or to an independent lender. There will, however, also be a compensating adjustment for the benefit of the guarantor in these circumstances. Effectively, the guarantor will be treated for UK tax purposes as if it had taken the loan and paid the interest, instead of the actual borrower. The guarantor will deduct the interest for tax purposes provided it meets the usual conditions for an interest deduction – in particular, to qualify for a deduction, it must not be thinly capitalised itself (this is unlikely in practice, as in such circumstances its guarantee would not have offered real support for the loan). All other tax consequences of the loan will also fall to the guarantor rather than the borrower.

6.34   A payer of interest may be obliged to deduct tax at source under UK withholding tax rules.

However, if no tax deduction is available in respect of the interest as a result of the transfer pricing rules, the lender can claim a compensating adjustment to enable the payment to be made without deduction of tax.

6.35   The disallowance under the transfer pricing rules together with the compensating adjustment have the effect that both borrower and lender are taxed as if the excessive interest had not been paid or received. The excessive interest can be paid without deduction of tax.

6.36   There is no special form for such a claim, but it should be made on the basis that the interest that is the subject of the claim will not be claimed as a tax deduction for the borrower. The compensating adjustment claim may be made by the lender, or by the borrower acting on behalf of the lender. If a loan guarantor is treated as if it were the lender under the special rules for loan guarantors, that company may make the claim on behalf of the lender.

6.37   The above rules do not apply if, taken on a group basis, the group falls within the small or medium sized enterprise exemption (see para 7.62). HMRC states (see https://www.gov.uk/guidance/transfer-pricing-transactions-between-connected-companies):

'**Exemptions:** There's an exemption that will apply for most small and medium sized enterprises.

Your business is a "small" enterprise if it has no more than 50 staff and either an annual turnover or balance sheet total of less than €10 million.

Your business is a "medium sized" enterprise if it has no more than 250 staff and either an annual turnover of less than €50 million or a balance sheet total of less than €43 million.'

TAX DEDUCTIONS FOR INTEREST PAYMENTS

6.38   As part of the Government's reform of the taxation of the foreign profits of companies, the Finance Act 2009 introduced a worldwide debt cap which applied to interest payable in accounting periods beginning on or after 1 January 2010. The effect of the original worldwide debt cap was to restrict the amount of interest on intra-group debt that UK companies within a worldwide group could claim as a deduction against their taxable profits by reference to the group's non-UK external debt financing costs. Broadly, to the extent that the relevant company's interest on intra-group debt exceeded the group's interest on non-UK external debt, the excess will be disallowed. The rules were amended by the Tax Treatment of Financing Costs and Income (Change of Accounting Standards: Investment Entities) Regulations 2015 from 2 April 2015. These amendments to the worldwide debt cap (WWDC) provisions ensure changes to accounting standards do not create unintended additional corporation tax liabilities. See further at https://www.gov.uk/government/publications/corporation-tax-changes-to-the-worldwide-debt-cap-provisions.

6.39   However from 1 April 2017, the UK planned to introduce new rules to limit tax deductions for interest expense and other similar financing costs, with the aim of aligning such deductions with the economic activities undertaken in the UK. The then existing debt cap rules are to be repealed and replaced with new rules. The measure was announced as follows in the Government press release and see also at https://www.gov.uk/government/publications/spring-budget-2017-overview-of-tax-legislation-and-rates-ootlar/spring-budget-2017-overview-of-tax-legislation-and-rates-ootlar:

'As announced at Budget 2016 and following consultation, the government will introduce legislation with effect from 1 April 2017 to limit the tax deductions that companies can claim for their interest expenses. The new rules will restrict each group's net deductions for interest to 30% of the earnings before interest, tax, depreciation and amortisation (EBITDA) that is taxable in the UK. An optional group ratio rule, based on the net-interest to EBITDA ratio for the worldwide group, may permit a greater amount to be deducted in some cases. The legislation also provides for repeal of the existing debt cap legislation and its replacement by a modified debt cap which will ensure that the net UK interest deduction does not exceed the total net interest expense of the worldwide group.'

'All groups will be able to deduct up to £2 million of net interest expense per annum, so groups below this threshold will not need to apply the rules.'

This was then brought into force through what are known as the 'Corporate Interest Restriction' (CIR) rules. They apply to individual companies or groups of companies that may deduct over £2 million in a 12-month period.

HMRC's guidance says:

'If you'll deduct less than £2 million

Your company or group does not need to submit a Corporate Interest Restriction return. However, you must keep documents that show that your company or group will not deduct more than £2 million in net interest and financing costs in that period of account.

You can still appoint a reporting company, this company must then submit an abbreviated return. To reduce a future interest restriction, you can carry forward unused interest allowance for up to 5 years by replacing the abbreviated return with a full return for that period of account.

If you'll deduct more than £2 million

You must work out your company's or group's "interest allowance". This is the maximum amount of net interest and financing costs your company or group can deduct in a period of account.

You can use the "fixed ratio method" or the "group ratio method". Use the method that gives you the largest allowance.

You must keep records of your calculation.

If your company's or group's net interest and financing costs are restricted, you should normally appoint a reporting company within 12 months of the end of the period of account. You then need to submit a full Corporate Interest Restriction return.

Fixed ratio method

Using the fixed ratio method, the interest allowance is the lower of:

- 30% of the company's or group's UK taxable profits before interest, taxes, capital allowances and some other tax reliefs

- the company's or group's worldwide net interest expense

Group ratio method

To use this method, you must:

- appoint a reporting company

- elect to use the method in a Corporate Interest Restriction return

Using the group ratio method, the interest allowance is the lower of:

- the ratio of the company's or group's worldwide net interest expense owed to unrelated parties, to the company's or group's overall profit before tax, interest, depreciation and amortisation multiplied by the company's or group's taxable UK profits before interest and capital allowances

- the company's or group's worldwide net interest expense owed to unrelated parties

If your interest deductions are not restricted

You can appoint a reporting company, which must then submit an abbreviated return. If you replace the abbreviated return with a full return for that period of account, you can carry forward unused interest allowance for up to 5 years to reduce a future interest restriction.

Appoint a reporting company

Individual companies and groups can appoint a reporting company. Your reporting company will be responsible for submitting your company's or group's Corporate Interest Restriction return. The reporting company must be:

- liable to UK Corporation Tax

- non-dormant

- authorised by at least 50% of the group's non-dormant companies (which are liable for UK Corporation Tax) to be appointed as the reporting company

When you have appointed a reporting company, you must submit a Corporate Interest Restriction return for every period of account, including when there's no interest restriction. If you revoke the appointment of a reporting company and do not have an interest restriction, you will not have to submit a return.

If you do not appoint a reporting company, HMRC might appoint one for you.'

From https://www.gov.uk/guidance/corporate-interest-restriction-on-deductions-for-groups. The above guidance also links to the form which can be used to notify HMRC of a reporting company.

INTEREST FLUCTUATING WITH PROFITS

6.40   Where the interest rate on the loan varies with the profitability of the company, such a variable interest rate may in certain circumstances result in the interest being treated as a distribution for tax purposes, which will render the interest non-deductible.

CONVERTIBLE LOANS

6.41   In relation to loans convertible into equity in a company, payments of interest or redemption premium will be treated as a distribution and therefore not deductible from profits for corporation tax purposes, unless the loan takes the form of securities listed on a recognised stock exchange or the securities are issued on terms which are reasonably comparable with the terms of issue of securities so listed.

CAPITAL LOSSES

6.42   It used to be important to structure a loan from a UK joint venturer as a 'debt on a security'. This is because a simple debt is not a chargeable asset for capital gains tax purposes, and therefore no allowable loss is available if it proves to be irrecoverable, whereas, should the venture fail, each joint venturer would at least wish to have an allowable loss to set against any future gains.

6.43   Now, under the Taxation of Chargeable Gains Act 1992, s 253, a joint venturer can obtain an allowable loss in respect of any loan which is not a debt on a security and is used by the borrower wholly for the purposes of a trade carried on by it, where the borrower is resident in the UK, the loan is wholly or partially irrecoverable, the lender has not assigned his right to recover the irrecoverable amount, and the lender and borrower were not in the same group of companies at the time the loan was made or at any subsequent time. A corporate lender should in any case obtain a loss for the purposes of corporation tax under the loan relationship legislation.

6.44   The above provisions make it generally unnecessary for a loan to be a debt on a security, but this will still be necessary where the requirements of s 253 cannot be met or no loss is available under the loan relationship legislation. In *Tarmac Roadstone Holdings Ltd v Williams*[4] it was held that the distinguishing feature of a debt on a security is that it is the nature of an investment which can be transferred and otherwise dealt in as such: hence the use of loan stock or loan notes which are in registered form or can be transferred by a stock transfer form, even though there is in fact no market in the debt. Security, in the sense of a mortgage or charge, is not required. The loan should be repayable on the expiry of a fixed period and not on a demand by the lender, and neither should the joint venture company have an option to repay early (see *Taylor Clark International Ltd v Lewis*[5]).

4 Outside finance

6.45   Where the joint venture is to seek outside finance, the same considerations which relate to finance to be provided to any business will apply. Such finance may take the form of bank overdrafts, term loans, or forms of finance which are not legally debt, such as invoice discounting, finance leasing or hire purchase. To the extent that the joint venturers are required to give guarantees or provide security for such financing, careful consideration needs to be given as to what would happen if one or more of such parties were to leave the joint venture at some point in the future. It may not be possible to negotiate a release of such obligations from the bank but it may be possible to negotiate from the continuing shareholders some form of indemnity (if that was likely to be of value).

Equity finance

6.46   Outside finance may also take the form of share capital provided by a 'business angel', a venture capitalist or other similar institution, whether in conjunction with loan finance or not. The share capital will consist of an equity stake, in order to give the financier a proportion of the realised value of the venture, but may also include preference shares (which will quite often be participating) to give a running yield on the sum invested. Convertible redeemable shares are also sometimes employed, which can be converted

---

4   [1996] STC 409.
5   [1998] STC 1259.

into equity if the venture is a success, but otherwise are redeemable, generally at par, so as to provide a mechanism for the return of the original capital.

6.47   The introduction of an equity financier is tantamount to introducing a new partner into the joint venture. Such a financier will have a large number of requirements, which will have an extensive impact on the documents and indeed the structure of the whole transaction. The particular considerations which such an investor is likely to have in mind are discussed in Chapter 28, but the most important factor is likely to be the ability to achieve an exit in the fairly short term, usually by means of a flotation or sale, although there are some investors who will accept a longer holding period provided they will receive a commercial income return during that period.

Security and guarantees

6.48   Providers of loan finance to the venture may require additional reassurance in the form of security over the joint venture assets, possibly supported by guarantees from the joint venturers. Except where the joint venturers are listed or otherwise substantial companies, the guarantees may be required to be secured on the assets of the guarantors.

6.49   Security over the assets of a joint venture company will generally consist of a debenture containing fixed and floating charges over its entire assets and undertaking. Such security will invariably be required to rank ahead of any security for loans advanced by the joint venturers.

6.50   In addition, an outside provider of loan finance will generally require that joint venturers' loans are postponed to its own loans as to repayment. This is normally achieved by a deed under which the joint company agrees that it will not, without the consent of the outside lender, repay the joint venturers' loans before complete repayment of the outside loan, and the joint venturers agree not to require repayment of their loans prior to that event, without such consent.

6.51   Individual joint venturers are often required to support their guarantees by providing security over their personal assets, including any equity in their matrimonial homes, especially where the joint venture company has few assets. Individuals will give such guarantees and security only with reluctance, but the loan facility may simply not be available without them. Banks often consider that their provision is a desirable indication of commitment on the part of the individual venturer and an incentive to avoid failure (as far as possible).

6.52   Where the matrimonial home is in the joint names of the venturer and his or her spouse, the spouse will be required to join in the mortgage, and where it is in the sole name of the joint venturer, the spouse will normally be required to postpone his or her right of occupation to the rights of the lender as mortgagee. That will require independent legal advice from a different solicitor to ensure there is no duress or undue influence involved and to ensure the validity of any deed which is executed as a result of the transaction.

Contribution and subrogation

6.53   Where joint venturers provide their guarantees for the obligations of the joint venture company they will generally be required on a joint and several basis. This places the lender in the position of being able to recover the sum owing from the joint venturers in any proportions or to pursue one or more of them to the complete exclusion of one or more others.

6.54   A guarantor who pays more than his due proportion of the guaranteed debt has at common law a right of contribution from the others. However, especially in a complex joint venture, the courts may have difficulty in determining the relative contributions, and may not do so to the satisfaction of one or more parties. It will therefore be preferable for the guarantors to enter into a contribution agreement between themselves which defines their respective liabilities in respect of the debt, and which provides that any guarantor who is made to pay more than his due proportion may recover the excess from the others in such amounts as will give effect to the agreed proportions. Such agreement should provide for the possibility that full recovery may be impossible from one or more of them by reason of bankruptcy or liquidation and provide for the others to assume responsibility for the irrecoverable amount: logically, they should bear it in the same proportions as the proportions in which they have agreed to bear the whole debt in relation to one another.

6.55   Once the guarantors have discharged the guaranteed debt in full, they will have the right to be subrogated to any security which the lender holds over the assets of the joint venture company. This will provide no comfort to them if the lender had full recourse to such security before calling upon the guarantors in respect of that part of the debt which could not be recovered from the security, but otherwise this can be a valuable right for the guarantors. Their contribution agreement should provide for them to collaborate in the realisation of any such security, the proceeds of which should be applied in or towards satisfaction of amounts paid by guarantors which are more than their due proportions of the debt, so that only any further amounts owing to them which cannot be met from the proceeds of the security should be met by the other joint venturers. If there should be a surplus from the security after reimbursing all the guarantors who have paid more than their due proportions of the debt, this would be paid to the joint venturers in their due proportions.

Chapter 7

Tax considerations for UK joint ventures

Summary

This chapter deals with the main tax considerations relating to joint ventures where one or more companies investing in the joint venture are resident for tax purposes in the UK and the joint venture activities are in the UK. It mainly focuses on corporate joint ventures, but also briefly discusses partnerships between corporates and contractual joint ventures. The issues discussed in relation to corporate joint ventures include those arising on their establishment, the rules relating to groups and consortia, taxation on monies flowing from the joint venture company to the joint venturers, transactions at an undervalue and tax matters arising on termination. Many other tax issues are dealt with in other chapters and these are listed at the end.

1 Introduction

7.1   This chapter mainly concentrates on the tax considerations relating to a UK corporate joint venture where the joint venture company is tax resident in the UK and one or more of the investors is a UK tax resident company. It does not consider the position of non-UK joint venturers, which is discussed, together with some tax considerations relevant to cross-border joint ventures, in Chapter 28. It also does not consider the position of individual joint venturers. This is discussed in Chapter 26.

7.2   This chapter also takes a brief look at the tax considerations relevant to partnerships whose members are all companies incorporated and tax resident in the UK, and the tax position where the joint venture is purely contractual (see para 1.22ff).

7.3   Not all tax issues are dealt with in this chapter, since it is felt more convenient to deal with many of them at the same time as the circumstances giving rise to the issue. A list at the end of this chapter sets out the tax issues discussed in other chapters and where they may be found.

2 UK corporate joint ventures

7.4   Although all tax issues which can be foreseen should be considered when a joint venture is being planned and its structure adjusted accordingly, generally speaking the tax issues divide themselves into three groups – those that arise when the joint venturers contribute assets into the joint venture in order to get it established, those that arise during its operation, and those which arise when it is being dismantled.

Transfer of assets into the venture

7.5   Since a company is a legal entity apart from its shareholders, where its shareholders transfer assets into it a liability to tax on those transfers may arise, depending on the nature of the particular assets and the tax position of the transferor.

Assets subject to corporation tax on chargeable gains

7.6   Many capital assets are chargeable assets for the purposes of corporation tax on chargeable gains.

Such assets include land and buildings and shares in companies being transferred to the joint venture. Goodwill and intellectual property will generally be treated as capital assets unless they have previously been acquired from a third party on or after 1 April 2002 or, in the case of intellectual property, specifically created on or after 1 April 2002.

7.7   Subject to special rules which apply where the transferee company is in the same capital gains tax group of companies as the transferor (see para 7.17), every transfer of chargeable assets will be a disposal giving rise to either a gain or a loss for the purposes of corporation tax on chargeable gains. The chargeable gain or loss will be the difference between the cost of acquisition of the asset by the transferor (or whichever company in the transferor's group first acquired it from a third party), the 'base cost', and the price paid for it by the transferee, except that if the latter is less than market value, HMRC may substitute market value as the disposal proceeds and charge tax on the transferor accordingly. The amount of the realised gain or loss is the difference between the disposal proceeds (or market value substituted by HMRC) and the base cost.

7.8   There are many general reliefs available to reduce the amount of tax chargeable where the asset transfer will crystallise a realised gain. For example, sums spent on improving the asset can be added to base cost. Other reliefs should also be considered, such as roll-over relief and, where the assets being transferred consist of shares, the availability of the capital gains substantial shareholdings exemption for corporates. This relief applies where the transferor company owns at least 10% of the ordinary shares in the company whose shares are being transferred and reduces any gain to nil, but to qualify the transferor company must be a trading company or a member of a trading group which has held the shares for a continuous period of at least 12 months during the previous two years, and the company whose shares are being transferred must be a trading company or the holding company of a trading group or sub-group. Section 37 of the Finance Act 2012 gave the Government power to change the classes of assets available for roll-over relief by statutory instrument.

7.9   The transferor should consider whether any allowable losses crystallised on other asset disposals can be utilised to set against the gain. Such losses, if available, do not have to be available in the transferor company. Two members of a 75% UK group of companies can elect that the transfer by one of them of an asset outside the group will be treated as made by the other with the available carried forward capital loss, without any actual intra-group transfer of the asset taking place or being necessary. This simplification of the law avoids the administrative burden of effecting intra-group transfers prior to sale. It would be usual for the transferor to pay compensation to the 'capital loss company' for the use of its losses.

7.10   Accordingly, if company A has the asset desired to be transferred to the joint venture, and company B has sufficient losses to absorb the gain that will be realised on the transfer, it is possible to elect for company B to apply part of its capital loss to set against company A's gain. For this to be possible, the transferor (company A) must own at least 75% of the capital loss company (company B), or vice versa, or both must be either direct or indirect 75% subsidiaries of a third company.

7.11   The Government introduced provisions in the Finance Act 2009 further to simplify the law. The effect of the provisions is to transfer a gain or loss from the company making the disposal to one or more other specified companies within the group when they jointly elect instead of deeming a transfer of an asset from one group company to another before the disposal. The former restrictions on the type of asset and the circumstances under which the gain or loss arises also no longer apply.

7.12   As mentioned at para 7.8, the transferor can claim roll-over relief to reduce or eliminate any gain, provided it re-invests all the proceeds of disposal in qualifying assets during the period beginning one year before and ending three years after the disposal of the old asset. Examples of qualifying assets include land and buildings and fixed plant or machinery. See further on roll-over relief at https://www.gov.uk/business-asset-rollover-relief.

7.13   The relief allows the capital gain to be sheltered if an amount equivalent to the proceeds attributable to the sale (not the proceeds of sale equal to the capital gains, but the whole proceeds) are reinvested within the period commencing one year before the sale and ending three years after the sale in other assets which would qualify for roll-over relief on disposal.

7.14   Although the legislation (TCGA 1992, ss 152–159) refers to the proceeds of the original assets being applied in the acquisition of new assets, HMRC has confirmed that the relief is available where the original assets are transferred in exchange for shares in the joint venture company, provided that an amount equivalent to the value of the shares received is invested by the transferor in other assets which qualify for roll-over relief.

7.15   Where the transferor is part of a 75% group, relief can be claimed even though the transferor and acquirer of the new assets are different members of the group.

7.16   It may be possible to avoid an immediate liability to a chargeable gain by making use of CTA 2009, s 789 which gives relief in respect of certain mergers. This could be achieved by each joint venturer placing in a newly-formed subsidiary the assets to be contributed by it and transferring the shares of the subsidiary to the joint venture company in exchange for shares and other consideration issued by that company. At least 25% of the consideration would need to be in shares. The values of the interest acquired in each part of the transaction must be substantially equal, but there is no minimum value for the interest to be acquired. Where s 789 applies, no capital gains de-grouping charge under TCGA 1992, s 179 (see para 7.17) arises when the new subsidiaries leave their respective groups on their shares being transferred to the joint venture company. On a disposal by the new subsidiaries of the relevant assets, the original base costs of their respective original groups will apply.

7.17   If a transferor transfers an asset into a company of which it has at least 75% ownership there is no immediate liability to corporation tax on chargeable gains, since the companies are part of the same group for capital gains purposes, but on the other hand the transferee company is then treated as having acquired the asset at the transferor's capital gain base cost, with the possibility of a larger liability when the transferee company disposes of the asset, ie the tax will be due not only on any appreciation of the asset whilst in the transferee's ownership, but also on any appreciation whilst it was in the ownership of the transferor or any other member of its group. So, although it is possible for the majority shareholder to transfer chargeable assets into a 75%:25% joint venture company without a charge to tax, the minority shareholders must bear in mind the potential extra cost of disposal of the asset. It should also be mentioned that if the transferor's interest in the transferee company drops below 75% within six years of the transfer of the asset (perhaps on admission of another party to the joint venture) an immediate 'degrouping' tax charge is suffered by the transferee company under TCGA 1992, s 179. The charge is calculated on the basis that the transferee company has sold and immediately reacquired the asset at its market value at the date of the transfer of the asset to it, although there are now provisions (discussed in para 7.9) under which the transferor and the transferee company may jointly elect for the transferor to absorb the charge itself or pass it on to any of the companies grouped with it for capital gains tax purposes. The minority shareholders may wish to insist that the charge is absorbed in this way, whenever possible.

7.18   HMRC summarise the position in relation to transfers within a group as follows[1]:

'**TCGA92/S171(1)**

The no gain/no loss rule in TCGA92/S171(1) ensures that assets can generally be moved around a group of companies without any immediate capital gains consequences. This recognises that business activities carried on within the overall economic ownership of a corporate group, within the charge to corporation tax, should, in broad terms, be tax neutral. This is achieved by fixing both the consideration received for the asset by the transferor and the consideration given for the asset by the transferee. The transferor has neither chargeable gain nor allowable loss. The transferee effectively takes over the transferor's capital gains cost, augmented by indexation allowance as appropriate.

The transferor and transferee companies are referred to as companies A and B in the legislation" and the rule is subject to the conditions in TCGA92/S171(1A), see CG45410.

Therefore a chargeable gain or allowable loss will accrue only when an asset is disposed of outside the group (or the part of the group that is chargeable to corporation tax on chargeable gains) and that gain or loss will reflect the economic gain or loss throughout the group's period of ownership.

Corporation tax group relief does not apply to allowable losses so the ability to make no gain/no loss transfers allows groups to bring together gains and losses so that only the overall net gains of a group are taxed. An election under TCGA92/S171A achieves the same effect without the need for any actual transfer.

Note that where a company has changed groups it is possible for the use of allowable losses to be restricted under TCGA92/S184A – F (CG47000+) or TCGA92/SCH7A (CG47520+, or CG474000+ where a company joined a group on or after 19 July 2011.

Apart from the main no gain/no loss rule for intra-group disposals in TCGA92/S171(1), there are other no gain/no loss rules for companies in the provisions dealing with

---

1   See https://www.gov.uk/hmrc-internal-manuals/capital-gains-manual/cg45305 (updated October 2020).

- schemes of reconstruction or amalgamation, see CG45630

- EC Mergers Directive – transfer of a UK trade, see CG45705+

- Public sector transfer schemes, see CG45750.'

Transfer of stock in trade

7.19   Where a joint venturer is transferring to the joint venture company stock in trade relating to a business which the transferor is discontinuing on transfer to the joint venture company which will carry on the business in the UK, the amount realised for the stock is not treated for tax purposes as market value but, rather, is the amount of the consideration paid for the stock irrespective of the actual value of the assets passing. This is because whatever tax HMRC fails to receive from the vendor it should receive from the purchaser.

Assets upon which capital allowances have been claimed

7.20   Where the assets to be transferred include any in respect of which the transferor has claimed capital allowances (such as plant and machinery or industrial buildings) the transferor will incur a balancing charge if the assets are transferred at more than their tax written-down value, or a balancing allowance if they are sold for less. Please note that following changes announced in the 2007 Budget, capital allowances on industrial buildings were gradually withdrawn over a period to April 2011. There are provisions for substituting market value for the actual consideration where the parties are connected.

7.21   This charge will not, however, arise where the share capital of the company owning the assets concerned is transferred to the joint venture instead of the assets themselves, or where the assets are transferred with a trade to a new company[2] at least 75% owned by the transferor. In these circumstances the joint venture company will only be able to claim the residuary writing-down allowances available to the transferor, rather than being able to claim capital allowances based on its own acquisition cost.

Trading losses

7.22   Where a trade to be contributed to the joint venture has made losses, it may be of importance to the parties to structure the transaction so that the accrued losses can be passed to the joint venture.

---

2   See para 7.23.

7.23   In principle, it is possible to arrange this if the contributing company first transfers the trade into a new subsidiary owned as to at least 75% by the transferor, which subsequently becomes the joint venture vehicle when the other joint venturers obtain shares in it.

7.24   Such a scheme takes advantage of the Corporation Tax Act 2010, s 944 whereby the transferee of the trade is treated as succeeding to the trade of the transferor without any discontinuance of the trade, provided that a 75% interest in the trade is owned by the same persons as before the transfer at any time within a two-year period commencing with the date of the transfer. A transfer to a 75% subsidiary will obviously meet the requirements.

7.25   It should be noted, however, that the whole of the accrued trading losses are not necessarily available to the joint venture company. They may be reduced. This applies where the relevant liabilities of the trade which are being retained by the vendor exceed the relevant assets being transferred. In these circumstances the losses carried forward are reduced by the amount of the excess. Vesting all available tax losses in the joint venture company could result in it taking over some unwelcome liabilities.

7.26   If at the time the transfer is carried out there are already 'arrangements', albeit not legally binding, for the establishment of the joint venture, it is possible that the contributing joint venturer may be held to have surrendered beneficial ownership of the transferred trade prior to its transfer, in which case the relief will not be available[3].

7.27   If the transfer is effective for these purposes, the joint venture company will inherit the capital allowances position of the transferor (see para 7.21). As soon as the transferee company leaves the transferor's group, a possible liability to corporation tax on chargeable gains will arise (see para 7.17).

7.28   If the transfer of the trade to a new company is initially successful in transferring the tax losses with it, the anti-avoidance provisions of the legislation will result in the ability to carry them forward being lost if the incoming joint venturers then acquire more than 50% of the ordinary share capital of the joint venture company (either immediately or within three years of the transfer of the trade) *and* within the same period there is a major change in the nature or conduct of the trade in which the losses arose. Since an intentional or unintentional reorganisation of the trade may be quite likely to follow its transfer to the joint venture, and it may acquire new customers and trade in different products so as to constitute a change in the nature of the trade, the application of the section may be a real risk. It may prove difficult in practice to pass on the losses, because even if the parties initially

---

3   *Wood Preservation v Prior* [1969] 1 WCR 1077; *O'Connor v Sainsbury* [1991] STC 318.

intend to carry on the trade as before, circumstances may cause a change of policy.

7.29   Similar considerations will apply to the carrying forward of management expenses, charges on income, and non-trading deficits in respect of loan relationships.

Value added tax

7.30   The parties will need to consider whether any transfer of assets into the joint venture is a supply for VAT purposes and whether VAT is chargeable on such a supply. Value added tax on any transfer of assets can be avoided if the joint venture company is first 'grouped' with the transferor for VAT purposes. In practice, this will almost certainly be thought undesirable by the other joint venturers because the joint venture company would be jointly and severally liable for the whole of the transferor's VAT liabilities. For start up companies with no assets transferring in this will not however be an issue.

7.31   Where assets are transferred along with a trade, no VAT will be chargeable if, as usually should be the case, the 'going concern' exemption is available[4]. Otherwise, transfers of individual assets to a non-group transferee will result in a liability for VAT arising which, subject to any other agreement, will fall on the joint venture company.

Stamp duty, stamp duty land tax and ATED

7.32   Stamp duty is now only payable on transfers of shares, other marketable securities and partnership interests where the partnership does not hold land and thus is not likely to be relevant in the majority of cases, but if land is to be transferred this is now subject to stamp duty land tax in England and Northern Ireland (Scotland and Wales have their own similar but differently named such tax). The rate of stamp duty is 0.5% of the consideration for shares (where over £1000) and marketable securities and ad valorem duty at rates from 1 to 4% of the consideration for partnership interests. Where stamp duty does apply and the joint venture company is being established as the 75% subsidiary of the transferring joint venturer relief under the Finance Act 1930, s 42 may be available. The conditions for the relief are, broadly, the same 75% test as applies for the grouping of trading losses. Relief will be denied where, at the time of the transfer there was an intention that the transferor's interest in the joint venture company would reduce below 75%,

---

4   See art 5 of the Value Added Tax (Special Provisions) Order 1995 (SI 1995/1268).

either because beneficial ownership of the shares required to establish the 75% interest has already passed at the time of transfer or because there are 'arrangements' within Finance Act 1967, s 27(3).

7.33   Transfers of freehold and leasehold and other interests in land and partnership interests where the partnership owns land are now subject to stamp duty land tax at rates of up to 4% of the consideration (or market value, if the consideration is below market value). Schedule 7 of the Finance Act 2003 provides for relief where the land or partnership interest is transferred to a 75% subsidiary, but the relief may be clawed back if the transferee company ceases to be a 75% subsidiary within three years of the transfer. There is no clawback provision in the case of s 42 relief from stamp duty. SDLT is also payable on the grant of leases. Scotland and Wales have similar taxes to SDLT. There are plans in the Finance Bill 2021 to charge an additional 2% SDLT where a property has one or more foreign owners. These are not yet in force.

7.34   Where a *residential* property (dwelling) is transferred into or owned by a company an annual tax on the 'enveloped dwelling' is likely to be payable (known as 'ATED') provided the value of the flat or house is more than £500,000. As a result some buyers have therefore moved to purchase properties under that threshold (usually therefore being properties outside the South East of England) to avoid ATED in the case of joint ventures set up to acquire residential properties. This has the double benefit that SDLT will also be less. In 2020/21 there was a temporary change to SDLT in England and Northern Ireland due to the Covid-19 pandemic whereby the rate was zero (the stamp duty 'holiday') for the purchase or properties up to £500,000 where they were a main residence for the buyer whether a first time buyer or not and 3% for properties up to £500,000 which are a second home or 'buy to let' property. The following *are not* dwellings caught by ATED:

- hotels;

- guest houses;

- boarding school accommodation;

- hospitals;

- student halls of residence;

- military accommodation;

- care homes;

- prisons.

ATED rates are set out below (2020/21).

CHARGEABLE AMOUNTS FOR 1 APRIL 2020 TO 31 MARCH 2021

7.35

Property value	Annual charge
More than £500,000 but not more than £1 million	£3,700 (unless within the stamp duty 'holiday' arrangements)
More than £1 million but not more than £2 million	£7,500
More than £2 million but not more than £5 million	£25,200
More than £5 million but not more than £10 million	£58,850
More than £10 million but not more than £20 million	£118,050
More than £20 million	£236,250

7.36   HMRC has listed the following as exemptions from ATED:

'Reliefs you can claim

You may be able to claim relief for your property [from ATED] if it is:

- let to a third party on a commercial basis and is not, at any time, occupied (or available for occupation) by anyone connected with the owner

- open to the public for at least 28 days a year

- being developed for resale by a property developer

- owned by a property trader as the stock of the business for the sole purpose of resale

- repossessed by a financial institution as a result of its business of lending money

- acquired under a regulated "Home Reversion Plan"

- being used by a trading business to provide living accommodation to certain qualifying employees

- a farmhouse occupied by a farm worker or a former long-serving farm worker

- owned by a registered provider of social housing'.

Also charitable organisations using the property for charitable purposes are exempt as are exempt public bodies and bodies established for national purposes.

ATED is also payable by partnerships where one of the partners is a limited company.

7.37   Stamp duty land tax rates on residential property with a value over £500,000 are 15% where the property is purchased within a limited company (ie higher even than the upper 12% stamp duty band). The 15% rate also applies to partnerships buying residential properties if one of the partners is a company.

The 15% SDLT rate does not apply to property bought by a company that is acting as a trustee of a settlement or bought by a company to be used for:

●   a property rental business;

●   property developers and trader;

●   property made available to the public;

●   financial institutions acquiring property in the course of lending;

●   property occupied by employees;

●   farmhouses. In the above cases the standard SDLT residential rate will apply instead.

7.38   The ATED and SDLT rules are complex and regularly change so it is important to take up to date legal advice at the time and this section simply summarises the principal issues.

See HMRC technical guidance on ATED at https://www.gov.uk/government/publications/annual-tax-on-enveloped-dwellings-technical-guidance.

Operational tax issues

GROUPS AND CONSORTIA

Groups

7.39   Where there is at least 75% ownership by a UK tax resident joint venturer, it is possible for all trading losses of the joint venture to be surrendered by a UK joint venture company to the relevant UK joint venturer and to members of its UK group and vice versa. This ability is often of significance, as many joint venture companies make losses in their early years and without the ability to surrender them the joint venture company would only be able to carry them forward for set off against future taxable profits from the same trade when made, which may not be for many years. If the losses are instead surrendered to a 75% shareholder or member of its group, the recipient can set them against its own profits for the same year in which the loss was incurred, and thereby obtain an immediate reduction of its corporation tax liability. Similar surrenders are also possible in respect of losses that arise in whole or in part because of capital allowances, management expenses of investment companies, non-trading deficits in respect of loan relationships and excess charges on income. 100% of the losses of the joint venture company are available for surrender to a 75% shareholder, notwithstanding that it owns fewer than 100% of the shares. Any payment for losses surrendered not exceeding their amount is outside the scope of UK tax. The minority holders in a company controlled by a shareholder holding 75% or more will be concerned to ensure that the company receives adequate compensation for losses surrendered to the controlling shareholder.

7.40   Broadly speaking, 'ownership' in this context means beneficial ownership of at least 75% of the ordinary share capital of the company, including entitlement to the required percentage of dividends, assets on a winding up and votes. The ownership may be direct, or indirect, where the claimant and surrendering companies are both directly or indirectly at least 75% owned by a holding company. Since 31 March 2000, the parent company need not be UK tax resident, but claims and surrenders can only be made by a company so resident, or which trades in the UK.

Consortia

7.41   Consortium relief was introduced to allow the surrender of losses between a corporate joint venture and its corporate shareholders where none of those shareholders own 75% or more of the joint venture company and therefore group relief is not available. At its simplest, losses can be surrendered by the joint venture company to members of the consortium, or vice versa, subject to the rules discussed below.

7.42   A company is owned by a consortium if its ordinary share capital is directly and beneficially owned by the consortium members (Corporation Tax Act 2010, Pt 4, Ch 5). All claimant and surrendering companies must be resident in the UK for tax purposes, and each of them must own at least 5% and together at least 75% of the shares in the consortium company, but none of them must individually own 75% or more. Since 1 April 2000, it is no longer necessary that all the members of the consortium company must be UK tax resident, but non-UK tax resident members are not able to participate in the surrenders of losses by or to the consortium company, save to the extent they have a trade in the UK. The consortium company must either be a trading company or a holding company whose business consists wholly or mainly of the holding of shares in trading companies which are each at least 90% directly owned by it, not all of which need be resident in the UK.

7.43   Where there is a consortium, the UK consortium company and its 90% trading subsidiaries may surrender to each UK tax resident member (or to members of its group) the member's proportionate entitlement to trading losses, capital allowances, management expenses, non-trading deficits in respect of loan relationships, and excess charges on income originally just for that accounting period and since 1 April 2017 when losses are carried forward they can be surrendered as consortium relief. The members of the consortium may also each surrender to the consortium company an amount of their own trading losses equivalent to their proportionate entitlement.

7.44   The proportionate entitlement in any accounting period is limited to whichever is lowest in that period of:

- the percentage of the ordinary share capital of the company beneficially owned by that member;

- the percentage to which that member is beneficially entitled of any profits available for distribution to equity holders of the company; and

- the percentage to which that member would be entitled to the company's assets available for distribution to its equity holders on a winding up.

Accordingly, if at the end of the accounting period one of the consortium members has share or other rights different from the other members (eg priority as to dividends and/or return of capital), and/or has lent money to the joint venture company by way of a non-commercial loan (eg where interest depends on the results of the business) and other shareholders have not, the entitlement to consortium relief will be distorted and will not necessarily be available by reference to ordinary share capital owned. Apportionment issues arise if the consortium company's accounting reference date is different from that of any of its members. The economic interest of a joint venturer may differ significantly from its percentage of the ordinary share capital where, for example, dividend rights are capped or limited. In such cases reference to Corporation Tax Act 2010, Pt 5, Ch 6 is required to determine the joint venturer's lowest percentage interest.

7.45   Previously, if a non-UK (or EEA) resident company (referred to as a link company) existed between the consortium member and the consortium company, consortium loss relief would not be available. In 2015 it was announced that for groups with a financial year stating on or after 10 December 2014 the link company can be resident anywhere in the world and consortium relief will still be available between UK consortium members and UK consortium companies. For international groups this change may mean that loss relief is more widely available than before.

Agreements concerning consortium or group relief

7.46   Where consortium or group relief is available, the joint venture agreement should contain provisions for the regulation of surrenders and claims. It is usual for the joint venture company to surrender losses, etc, to its shareholders in return for the payment to it of the amount of tax saved by the surrender, so that the benefit of the tax saving arises in the joint venture company. This is particularly important where one joint venturer has 75% or more of the joint venture company, since the company may surrender to such a holder 100% of the company's losses. It is also sensible to provide some machinery for agreement as to whether, and to what extent, the company will itself utilise the losses, etc, or whether it will surrender them. It may, for example, be appropriate to provide that the company will utilise them if it is able to do so in the same accounting period in which they arise, but to the extent they can only be carried forward, they will be surrendered if the joint venturers or their respective groups have the capacity to utilise them.

Loss of consortium relief or group relief where there are 'arrangements'

7.47   Entitlement to consortium or group relief is lost from the outset of the joint venture if there are at that time 'arrangements' in place for the consortium to cease to exist and, in effect, for the joint venture company to be grouped with a shareholder. Since joint venture agreements commonly include termination, transfer and deadlock provisions, this is a potentially serious problem. The legislation operates so that the amounts of consortium relief which may be surrendered will be adjusted where there are option arrangements in place which, if implemented, would alter the shareholders' economic interests or shareholdings in the company. 'Option arrangements' mean arrangements by which there could, as a result of the exercise of a right to acquire shares or securities in the consortium company, be a variation in the percentages of the profits available to equity holders or the assets to which any of the equity holders is entitled on a winding up. However, there was an HMRC extra-statutory concession (C10) and a Statement of Practice (SP3/1993) which confirmed that 'option arrangements' are not treated as being in place until a relevant triggering event occurs, so that the consortium will not be broken until that time. C10 was then enacted by SI 2012/266 by addition of the Corporation Tax Act 2010, s 174A with the same effect.

7.48   The 'relevant' triggering events are:

● the voluntary departure of a member of the joint venture company (see para 17.9);

● the commencement of the liquidation, administration or receivership of a member (see para 17.24);

● a serious deterioration in the financial condition of a member (see para 17.24);

● a change in the control or ownership of a member (see para 17.19ff);

● a default by a member in performing its obligations under the terms of an agreement between the members or with the company, including its articles of association (see para 17.15ff);

- an external change in the commercial circumstances in which the company operates so that its viability is seriously threatened;

- an unresolved disagreement among the members, eg an unresolved deadlock (see Chapter 13); or

- any contingency of a similar kind provided against but not expected to happen when the agreement was entered into.

It will be seen that these triggering events accord with those commonly included as termination events in a joint venture agreement, as discussed in Chapter 17. The Finance Act 2015 made some changes in this area, but further changes proposed in the Finance Bill 2017 were dropped before the 2017 general election.

The 2015 changes included a targeted anti-avoidance rule (TAAR) to stop arrangements by which some carried forward losses are used to generate other losses or deductions which could be used with more flexibility – see FA 2015, Sch 3, which introduced a new Pt 14B into the Corporation Tax Act 2010.

7.49   The concessionary treatment will apply where the joint venture agreement provides for the remaining members to acquire the shares of a departing member, or for a departing member to transfer its shares to the remaining members, on the occurrence of a triggering event, on the basis of:

- an offer pro rata to the remaining members' shareholdings, with the price fixed by agreement or independent valuation (as under a pre-emption article (see Chapter 19));

- a competitive tender amongst the remaining members, eg a 'Texas shoot out' (see para 17.43);

- a reciprocal process whereby members have matching put and call options over each others' shares (see para 17.28); or

- any other arrangements designed to ensure that a price appropriate to the commercial circumstances is struck.

7.50   The concessionary treatment is technically not available where the termination arrangements are not as set out above. Where this is so, it is possible that HMRC may grant an ad hoc concession on application by the parties, provided that they can be convinced that the arrangements are not such that the joint venture company should be treated as being within the group of one of the joint venturers by reason of the arrangements. This would be best applied for at the outset of the joint venture rather than waiting until the settlement of its tax liabilities for its first accounting period. Note, however, that if the consequence of termination is a realisation process different from one of those referred to in the concession, such as the sale of the entire company or the purchase of an outgoing investor's shares by the company or liquidation, which is arrived at as a result of negotiations between the parties in contemplation of or following termination, rather than being ordained by prior agreement, the concession should in the author's view still be available. In particular it is considered that it will be available if the parties include in the shareholders' agreement the 'multi-choice' realisation procedure suggested in para 17.45ff, since the effect of this is merely to oblige the parties to negotiate the method of realisation, without binding them to anything other than liquidation, should no agreed strategy for realisation result.

TRANSFERS OF FUNDS

Dividends

7.51   Payment of dividends has been subject to frequent tax changes. Previously a UK tax resident company could pay dividends or other distributions to UK tax resident shareholders without deduction of tax. Such a dividend or distribution did not form part of the income of a UK resident recipient company for corporation tax purposes, so had no tax effect at all, unless the loan relationships regime or the disguised interest legislation applied. A company will pay corporation tax on all its profits, whether distributed or not. The currently £2000 (and previously £5000) tax free dividend amount replaced the previous 'dividend tax credit'. However, within an ISA or pension dividend income is tax free. The effect is that basic-rate taxpayers pay 7.5% tax on any additional dividend earnings and higher-rate taxpayers (40% tax band) 32.5%, and additional rate taxpayers (£150k earnings – 45% tax band) 38.1% (all rates however increase by 1.25% from 1 April 2022).

7.52   The amount of tax due depends on the amount of dividend income received in the tax year:

● **less than £2,000** – no action need be taken and no tax is due;

● **between £2,000 and £10,000** – individuals should tell HMRC by:

  – contacting their helpline;

  – asking HMRC to change the tax payer's tax code – the tax will be taken from wages or pension;

  – putting it on the self-assessment tax return, for those tax payer who complete one;

● **over £10,000** – individuals must fill in a self-assessment tax return. If they do not usually complete one they should register by 5 October following the tax year they had this dividend.

HMRC states at https://www.gov.uk/tax-on-dividends:

  'You do not pay tax on dividends from shares in an ISA.

Dividend allowance

Tax year	Dividend allowance
6 April 2021 to 5 April 2022	£2,000
6 April 2020 to 5 April 2021	£2,000
6 April 2019 to 5 April 2020	£2,000
6 April 2018 to 5 April 2019	£2,000
6 April 2017 to 5 April 2018	£5,000
6 April 2016 to 5 April 2017	£5,000

The rules are different for dividends before 6 April 2016.

Working out tax on dividends

How much tax you pay on dividends above the dividend allowance depends on your Income Tax band.

Tax band	Tax rate on dividends over the allowance
Basic rate	7.5% (8.75% from 1 April 2022)
Higher rate	32.5% (33.75% from 1 April 2022)
Additional rate	38.1% (39.35% from 1 April 2022)

To work out your tax band, add your total dividend income to your other income. You may pay tax at more than one rate.

Example

You get £3,000 in dividends and earn £29,500 in wages in the 2020 to 2021 tax year.

This gives you a total income of £32,500.

You have a Personal Allowance of £12,500. Take this off your total income to leave a taxable income of £20,000.

This is in the basic rate tax band, so you would pay:

● 20% tax on £17,000 of wages

● no tax on £2,000 of dividends, because of the dividend allowance

● 7.5% tax on £1,000 of dividends' [8.75% from 1 April 2022].

7.53 The position as regards joint venturers who are individuals is discussed at para 26.1ff and that regarding joint venturers who are non-resident for UK tax purposes is discussed at para 28.31ff.

Royalties

7.54 Payment of royalties can be made without deduction of income tax by a UK tax resident joint venture company to any UK tax resident joint venturer. The payment of royalties to a non-UK tax resident joint venturer is discussed at para 28.46ff. Recent rules changes as set out in 28.33ff.

7.55   The HMRC Technical Note on 2016 changes was summarised as follows by Mazars at https://blogs.mazars.com/letstalktax/deduction-of-income-tax-at-source-from-royalty-payments/:

- 'A targeted anti-avoidance rule denying treaty benefits for royalty payments between connected persons where there are "treaty shopping" arrangements in place so that royalties are routed via a conduit company so that the royalties are ultimately paid tax free to a tax haven company;

- Widening the definition of "royalties" so that the withholding tax obligation covers payments made in respect of intellectual property previously not caught unless they were "annual payments", such as tradenames and trademarks;

- Providing a statutory definition make clear that payments made in connection with a UK permanent establishment (PE) or "avoided PE" under the diverted profits tax rules will have a UK source (and hence a withholding obligation as a result'.

Loan interest

7.56   As between UK tax resident companies, the position is the same as for royalties. The payment of interest to non-residents is dealt with at para 28.33ff.

Payments for goods or services

7.57   Where the joint venture company is to pay for goods or services provided by any of the joint venturers who are in the UK, and the payer and payee are not in the same VAT group, the payee will, if it is registered for VAT, have to account for VAT to HMRC, generally at 20% of the value of the goods or services provided. The agreement for the provision of the goods or services should make it clear that the consideration due is exclusive of VAT, which is additionally payable by the payee. If the agreement is silent, the consideration will be deemed to be inclusive of VAT and the payee will have a liability to pay the VAT to HMRC out of its receipt, and if that does not include any amount in respect of the VAT, the payee will be out of pocket.

TRANSACTIONS AT LESS THAN MARKET VALUE

7.58   To the extent that a joint venture entity transacts with its participants at less than market value, this may trigger both direct and indirect tax adjustments to the contracted price and allow HMRC to tax one or both parties as if market value had been received. This is not just a tax point but is also likely to be relevant in the company law context (see para 3.7).

7.59   Following the changes introduced by the Finance Act 2004, the UK's transfer pricing rules, which previously only affected transactions between UK and non-UK residents, are extended to transactions between UK residents.

7.60   The transfer pricing rules apply where there is a provision (a term which embraces all the terms and conditions attaching to a transaction or series of transactions) between a body corporate or partnership and any person who is directly or indirectly participating in the management, control or capital of that body corporate or partnership. The rules will also apply if a third person or persons was or were directly or indirectly participating in the management, control or capital of both the body corporate or partnership and the person with whom a provision has been made or imposed. Control is determined not only by legal control but by the existence of 'major participants' in the relevant entity. In the context of a joint venture, A is a 'major participant' in B, if B is a body corporate or partnership and A and another person each have at least a 40% interest in B.

7.61   If any provision between those parties differs from what would have been made as between independent enterprises, and the provision confers a potential advantage in relation to UK taxation on one or on each person, the profits and losses of the person with the potential advantage will be computed for tax purposes as if the arms' length provision had been made or imposed instead of the actual provision.

7.62   There is, however, an exemption from transfer pricing obligations for 'small and medium sized enterprises' (the 'SME exemption'). To be classified as a small enterprise, an entity (or, if the entity is part of a group, the entire group) must have a maximum staff of 50, and either an annual turnover of no more than €10m or a balance sheet total of no more than €10m. To be classified as a medium enterprise, an entity/group must have a maximum staff of 250, and either an annual turnover of no more than €50m or a balance sheet total of no more than €43m. The SME exemption will not apply if the small or medium sized enterprise makes an irrevocable election not to take advantage of the legislation. It will also not apply if, at the time the provision was made, the other party to the transaction was resident in a non-qualifying territory (essentially a territory with which the UK does not have a double tax treaty with an appropriate non-discrimination article). It will also not apply if the enterprise is a medium sized enterprise and HMRC serves a transfer pricing notice on it requiring it to compute its profits and losses in accordance with transfer pricing regulations.

7.63   Where transactions are within the scope of the UK's transfer pricing legislation HMRC has set out the content and form of records and evidence which a business needs to make available to it in order to demonstrate that transactions which are subject to the transfer pricing regime are in accordance with the transfer pricing rules, particularly the arms' length principle. These records fall into four categories: primary accounting records; tax adjustment records; records of transactions with associated businesses; and evidence to demonstrate an arms' length result.

7.64 On transfer pricing see https://www.gov.uk/government/publications/taxing-multinationals-transfer-pricing-rules/taxing-multinationals-how-international-transfer-pricing-rules-work and HMRC guidance on transfer pricing between connected companies – https://www.gov.uk/guidance/transfer-pricing-transactions-between-connected-companies.

DIVERTED PROFITS TAX ('DPT')

7.65 Since 2015 the diverted profits tax (DPT) may apply to some international transactions within a large international group. It applies at a rate of 25%. The current UK corporation tax rate is 19% and the DPT is intended as a penal tax to encourage businesses to restructure relevant arrangements such that profits are not diverted from the UK and instead the arrangements are subject to the lower 19% rate of corporation tax. Proposals to drop the rate below 19% were dropped. See guidance at https://www.gov.uk/hmrc-internal-manuals/international-manual/intm489500.

TAX ISSUES ON THE TERMINATION OF A JOINT VENTURE

7.66 Various tax issues may arise on termination of a joint venture, depending on the consequences of termination.

7.67 The assets of the joint venture may be sold or they may be returned to one or more of the joint venturers, in which case the joint venture company will need to consider the same tax issues which were discussed in connection with the transfer of assets to the company (see para 7.5ff).

7.68 More commonly, the shares of one or more joint venturers in the joint venture will be acquired by one or more other joint venturers, or by a third party. This may have tax consequences for the joint venture company, in that any group or consortium arrangements may come to an end and may possibly be replaced by others. If the joint venture company ceases to be part of a 75% group, any assets chargeable to corporation tax on chargeable gains which it has acquired from its parent or another group company will be deemed to be disposed of and immediately re-acquired at market value as at the date of the initial group transfer, resulting in a capital gain degrouping charge. Such a charge is, in certain circumstances, capable of being rolled over into other assets of the group or reallocated to another member of the vendor's group by joint election, so that it does not arise in the joint venture company. Subject to the substantial shareholding exemption applying (see para 7.8), the joint venturers who are UK resident and are disposing of their shares will make a disposal for capital gains purposes and, if selling at a profit, will have a chargeable gain or, if at a loss, will have an allowable loss.

7.69   Loans advanced by joint venturers are often repayable on termination. So long as loans are repaid at par this should have no impact under the loan relationship legislation.

7.70   Where the whole joint venture enterprise is to be sold to a third party, it is normally highly desirable that the purchaser should buy the shares of the joint venture company, rather than its assets. If the shares are sold there is only one charge to corporation tax on chargeable gains when the joint venturers sell their shares, which may be exempt if the shareholding falls within the substantial shareholding exemption – see para 7.8ff.

7.71   If instead the joint venture company sells its assets, there will be two charges – one falling on the company on the disposal of its assets, which is not subject to any relief unless the joint venture company is in the same capital gains group as one of the joint venturers, and one on the joint venturers when the sale proceeds are distributed to them in a subsequent liquidation of the joint venture company. Consideration should be given as to whether the liquidation attracts the substantial shareholding exemption for the joint venturers.

7.72   If a sale of assets cannot be avoided and the substantial shareholding exemption is not available, any capital gain may be mitigated by the joint venture company declaring and paying the maximum dividend which its distributable reserves will permit prior to its entry into liquidation.

7.73   Again, assuming the substantial shareholding exemption is not available, the same technique can be used to mitigate the capital gain on a sale of shares in the joint venture company, provided that it has, or can be provided with, sufficient resources to pay the dividend. The dividend can be paid tax-free and the price of the shares reduced by the amount of the assets paid away in the dividend. The dividend would need to be declared and, preferably, paid before any contract is entered into for the sale of the company.

7.74   Pre-termination dividends can fall foul of the value-shifting provisions in s 30 of TCGA 1992, subject to the exclusions in s 31 and the 2011 changes set out below in this paragraph. These provisions will operate to deem the sale price of the shares to be increased by the value removed from the shares by way of dividend. Section 31 excludes certain pre-sale dividends paid by one company to another where both are part of the same 75%-group, but no such provision is available where the pre-sale dividend is paid by a company not 75%-owned by any of the joint venturers. However, in practice, HMRC apply the same exclusion to such dividends[5]. The payment of a dividend in either of the circumstances described in paras 7.71 and 7.72 might be subject to attack under the anti-avoidance rules as an abnormal dividend, although it is rare for HMRC to take the point. Consideration should therefore be given to these provisions, and it should be considered whether a clearance should be

---

5   See [1994] STI 1624.

obtained. The Finance Act 2011 made some changes to the 1992 legislation. An extract from HMRC guidance updated October 2020 is below[6]:

'Value shifting: Corporation Tax anti-avoidance rule for disposals of shares or securities from 19 July 2011: examples

The following examples illustrate situations where HMRC would, or would not, consider that the rule applies. The question of whether there is a main purpose of obtaining a tax advantage is not considered in detail; a real case will depend on its particular facts but it would be highly unlikely that there would be no such main purpose in a case corresponding to an example where HMRC consider that the rule would apply.

Example 1

The target company has issued share capital of 100,000 × £1 ordinary shares. A third party has offered to buy the target company for £1 million.

The vendor group parent subscribes for a further 900,000 ordinary shares in the target company so as to increase the capital gains base cost to £1 million. The target company reduces its share capital, by re-denominating the shares as 1p shares and credits the amount of reduction, £990,000, to distributable reserves and then pays this amount to the parent as a dividend. The company is now worth approximately same as the capital gains base cost and so only a nominal gain will arise on the subsequent disposal.

The subscription for further shares, the reduction in share capital and the payment of the dividend constitute arrangements and a tax advantage is obtained. The arrangements do not consist solely of the making of an exempt dividend. Therefore the sale consideration is adjusted to reflect the uplift in base cost.

Example 2

The vendor group undertakes the drain out dividend scheme described in CG48510. However, instead of selling the shares in the target company, Q, to the third party, the third party instead subscribes for new shares in the target. The issue of new shares does not cause any reduction in the value of the shares held by the vendor group. The vendor group has not actually disposed of any shares and TCGA92/S29 will only create a deemed disposal if value has moved out of the vendor group's shares.

TCGA92/S31(5) ensures that the effect of the value reduction is ignored in considering the application of TCGA92/S29 and so there is a deemed disposal of the shares in the new company.

---

6   See https://www.gov.uk/hmrc-internal-manuals/capital-gains-manual/cg48560.

Example 3

The vendor group undertakes the drain out dividend scheme described in CG48510. However, instead of selling the shares in the target company, Q, to the third party, it instead transfers those shares to a newly incorporated group company in exchange for an issue of shares. The third party acquires the shares in this new company, together with its subsidiaries.

The shares disposed of have not been subject to a reduction in value. However, the shares in the target company have been and they are a "relevant asset" in connection with the disposal.

Note that in this situation TCGA92/S179(9) would also allow the degrouping charge arising from the transfer of the target company to be increased by the rule. However, the effect of TCGA92/S31(2) is that only one adjustment will be made.

Example 4

A group seeking to expand its overseas operations subscribed for 500 1 Crown ordinary shares in a Ruritanian company in 2008. These shares cost £100 at the prevailing exchange rate. The company bought an investment for 500 Crowns. In 2013 the company sells the investment for 800 Crowns and pays the 300 Crown profit to the group parent.

The company is now worth 500 Crowns but in 2013 this is equivalent to £125 so the company also reduces its share capital by 100 Crowns, in accordance with Ruritanian company law, and then pays its parent company a further dividend of 100 Crowns. The company is then wound up and the parent receives consideration of 400 Crowns, equivalent to £100 so no gain arises.

Although there has been no disposal of shares outside the group, the arrangements do not consist solely of the payment of an exempt distribution and were undertaken in order to secure a tax advantage. TCGA92/S31 would apply and the parent company's disposal consideration should be increased by £25. It is just and reasonable to adjust the consideration to reflect the exchange gain made on the shares.

Examples of situations where HMRC considers that the rule would not apply

Example 5

The target company has a large cash balance which it pays up to its group parent as a dividend before being sold. The purchaser pays what it considers to be a fair value for the shares following the dividend payment. If no dividend had been paid then the consideration would have been greater and more tax would have been payable (the purchaser would be "paying cash for cash").

However, HMRC does not interpret the legislation as requiring the existence of a tax advantage to be judged according to a comparison with the tax result of a commercial disposal that did not take place. Here no tax advantage is obtained because the proceeds correspond to the value of the assets held by the company that that have been disposed of out of the group.

Furthermore, the only arrangement is the payment of an exempt dividend. The exception in TCGA92/S31(1)(c) means that the value shifting rule does not apply.

Example 6

The target company has distributable profit reserves but no cash. It borrows money from its parent (it could be from another person) and uses this to pay a dividend. It is then sold to the purchaser and afterwards repays the loan.

The payment of existing distributable reserves before the sale of a company is normal commercial practice and so is not regarded as being tax motivated.

Here the arrangements did not consist solely of the payment of an exempt dividend because the target company needed to borrow the funds to make the payment. So the question is whether the arrangements had a main purpose of obtaining a tax advantage.

Contrast this with the drain out dividend scheme described in CG48510 where a transaction takes place before the disposal in order to create a reserve of untaxed profits, with the purpose of obtaining a tax advantage.

Example 7

This example illustrates various methods by which assets that are not required by a purchaser may be moved out of the target company:

7(a) The target company has an asset that the purchaser does not want and the vendor group does not wish to retain. As part of the sale process the asset is sold for cash and the proceeds paid up as a pre-sale dividend.

7(b) This is similar to example 7(a) apart from the fact that the asset is purchased by a fellow group company at market value and so TCGA92/S171 applied to the disposal.

7(c) This is similar to example 7(b) but the asset is transferred under TCGA92/S171 at its book value which is nominal and there is therefore no dividend payment.

Each of these transactions represents a normal part of the process of preparing the target company for a commercial sale and will not, of themselves, constitute arrangements with a main purpose of obtaining a tax advantage.

Example 8

A company has a wholly owned subsidiary company that was acquired for £4 million. The subsidiary is no longer active and is to be wound up.

The subsidiary has £10 million of assets (cash and debts due from group companies) and issued share capital of £10 million, In order to reduce the subsidiary's share capital it undertakes a capital reduction of £9.9 million and takes the £9.9 million to distributable reserves. It then pays out an exempt dividend of that amount from that distributable reserve and its remaining assets distributed to its parent company. It is then struck off or formally liquidated.

The dividend has not been paid out of funds lent to the subsidiary and its assets remain in the group, both factors are in contrast with those in example 1.

Where a company is simply being wound up for commercial reasons, as opposed to being disposed of, the arrangements will not be undertaken with a main purpose of obtaining a tax advantage.

The dividends paid are depreciatory and so TCGA92/S176 will ensure that there is no net capital loss.

A similar analysis would apply to situations where the reduction of value arises through the transfer of assets, rather than the payment of a dividend. For example, where historically a trade has been conducted through a subsidiary but is hived up to a parent.

Note that it is possible that a disposal of shares denominated in a foreign currency would result in a chargeable gain as a result of changes in exchange rates. TCGA92/S31 would be applicable to arrangements with a purpose of mitigating such a gain. See example 4 above.

Example 9

The target company has a large cash balance which is to be stripped out before sale. It makes a capital contribution to another group company. The purchaser pays what it considers to be a fair value for the shares following the capital contribution. If no contribution had been made then the consideration would have been greater and more tax would have been payable.

Paying out the surplus cash by making a capital contribution rather than paying a dividend means that the exception for exempt distributions in TCGA92/S31(1)(c) will not apply. However, this is the same routine pre-sale commercial transaction but effected by slightly different means. Therefore it would not constitute an arrangement with a main purpose of obtaining a tax advantage.

Example 10

The target company has an outstanding debt due to another member of the vendor group at the time an approach is received from the purchaser. The loan was taken out to acquire fixed assets for use in its business. The sale takes place and the purchaser subsequently injects funds that allow the loan to be repaid.

Although the vendor group receives funds from the purchaser in addition to the disposal consideration there has been no reduction in value. Therefore the vendor group does not obtain a tax advantage.'

7.75   The rule, which replaced TCGA 1992, ss 31–34 is a widely drawn, motive-based test. See https://www.taxjournal.com/articles/chargeable-gains-and-value-shifting-30032 which states:

'It applies if there are arrangements whereby the value of the shares or securities, or of an underlying asset, is materially reduced with a main purpose of obtaining a tax advantage, unless the arrangements consist solely of making an exempt distribution (so that paying a normal pre-sale distribution is not caught by the new rule). It is important to remember that the value shifting rules will not apply to disposals to which the substantial shareholdings exemption applies, so in many cases the new rule will not need to be considered.'

7.76   Otherwise, the normal methods to defer tax on a corporate disposal may be appropriate in the context of a sale of a joint venture interest. For example, the consideration could be received as loan notes issued by the purchaser.

7.77   Should the joint venture company fail and go into insolvent liquidation, each shareholder resident in the UK should be able to obtain a capital loss, since the shares will be treated as disposed of once they become of 'negligible value'. No capital loss will be available where the substantial shareholdings relief is available.

3   Corporate partnerships

7.78   Where UK tax resident corporate joint venturers are partners in a partnership formed under the Partnership Act 1890 or the Limited Partnership Act 1907 rather than shareholders in a company, the partnership has no separate legal personality from its members. This results in a partnership being 'transparent' for tax purposes, ie all its gains, profits, and losses are those of the partners, rather than the partnership. The same transparency is generally afforded to a limited liability partnership formed under the Limited Liability Partnerships Act 2000, notwithstanding that it is a legal entity.

Contributions of assets

7.79   Where partners contribute assets liable to corporation tax on chargeable gains to the partnership there is a part disposal of the asset, with the disposal consideration being calculated by reference to the fractional proportion of the actual consideration (or market value). Historically HMRC allowed the same relief as it allows on a change in the profit sharing ratios of a partnership.

7.80   Charges to corporation tax may arise for the joint venturers on transfers of trading stock by a partner to the partnership, on transfers of assets on which capital allowances have been claimed, and on the contribution of certain intellectual property rights.

7.81   HMRC takes the view that where an incoming partner contributes assets to the partnership, the incoming partner is in effect disposing of those assets for no consideration and, if the incoming partner is registered for VAT, VAT may be chargeable by the incoming partner and therefore should be charged to the partnership under provisions which deem a supply to take place where business assets are disposed of for no consideration (unless the transfer is a transfer of a going concern and is therefore not liable to VAT). The partnership may be entitled to recover any VAT charged to it by the incoming partner.

Profits

7.82   A partnership is not liable to corporation tax on its trading profits, so instead each partner is liable for corporation tax on its share of the trading profits or losses of the partnership. Subject to some qualifications, such trading profit or loss is first ascertained as if the partnership was a separate company, and is then apportioned between the partners according to their respective interests.

Capital gains and losses

7.83   Each partner is treated as owning a share of each partnership asset corresponding to its interest in the partnership. Every disposal of such an asset involves a separate disposal by each partner in its share of the asset. Such disposal will be subject to tax or relieved according to the respective tax positions of each partner. Rules for this are set out in HMRC's Statement of Practice (SP D12). SP D12 was revised in 2015 to take account of limited liability partnerships. HMRC said at the time that[7]:

> 'The enactment of the Limited Liability Partnership Act 2000 created, from April 2001, the concept of limited liability partnerships (as bodies corporate) in UK law. In conjunction with this, new CGT provisions dealing with such partnerships were introduced through TCGA92/S59A. TCGA92/S59A(1) complements TCGA92/S59 in treating any dealings in chargeable assets by a limited liability partnership as dealings by the individual members, as partners, for CGT purposes. Each member of a limited liability partnership to which TCGA92/S59A(1) applies has therefore to be regarded, like a partner in any other (non-corporate) partnership, as owning a fractional share of each of the partnership assets and not an interest in the partnership itself. This statement of practice was therefore extended to limited liability partnerships which meet the requirements of TCGA92/S59A(1), so that capital gains of a limited liability partnership fall to be charged on its members as partners. Accordingly, in the text of the statement of practice, all references to a "partnership" or "firm" include reference to limited liability partnerships to which TCGA92/S59A(1) applies, and all references to "partner" include reference to a member of a limited liability partnership to which TCGA92/S59A(1) applies.'

7.84   A change in the profit sharing ratios results, in relation to each of the partnership assets, is a disposal or part disposal by each partner whose share is being reduced, and an acquisition by each whose share is being increased. However, subject to some exceptions, HMRC defers the gain until any ultimate disposal to a third party, but each partner will inherit the original base cost attributable to its revised interest in the asset.

Termination

7.85   On the dissolution of the partnership involving a sale of all the partnership assets to a third party, each partner will make a disposal of its proportionate share in the partnership assets liable to corporation tax on chargeable gains. Similar results flow for the purpose of capital allowances.

7.86   If instead, assets are distributed to the partners on dissolution or on a partner leaving, this results in a disposal by every partner whose share in an

---

7   See Statement of Practice D12 at https://www.gov.uk/government/publications/statement-of-practice-d12/statement-of-practice-d12.

asset is reduced, and an acquisition by every partner whose share in an asset is increased. However, as long as the gain on such a disposal is allocated to the partner receiving the relevant asset, HMRC will, in practice, defer the gain until the acquiring partner disposes of the asset to a third party; but on such disposal the gain made on the intermediate transfer will be deducted from the base cost of the asset, thus increasing the chargeable gain on the disposal to the third party.

7.87   HMRC take the view that if a partner leaves the partnership and partnership assets are paid out to that partner, this is a supply for no consideration for VAT purposes and the partnership, where registered for VAT, may be required to account for VAT which it should charge to the outgoing partner.

4 Contractual joint ventures

7.88   In this type of joint venture (briefly reviewed in para 1.22ff) the affairs of each participant generally remain entirely separate. Their entitlements are governed entirely by the terms of the agreement between them.

7.89   It follows that each UK tax resident participant is liable to tax on its own profits flowing from the venture. No assets will normally be held in common, so no assets are contributed or returned and none of the complications in relation to such transfers will normally arise. Assuming that the participants are required to register for VAT, each will be separately registered and charge and account for VAT accordingly, although HMRC will treat the participants in a contractual joint venture as a single registered person if asked to do so.

5 Tax transparency issues – PSCs, TRS, PSCOC registers and the draft Registration of Overseas Entities Bill

7.90   Before setting up a joint venture, as important as taking tax advice as to the potential structure, is considering the issues of what information will become public as also mentioned in Chapter 1.

Bear in mind that even for ordinary limited companies in the UK under the 'persons of significant control' (PSC) rules on the annual confirmation statement (which replaced the 'Annual Return') companies must now display their ultimate owner, so the hiding of ownership is no longer possible, or at least not as easy. In addition, in April 2017, the Government was consulting on bringing in a register of beneficial ownership of UK properties owned by foreign entities – see https://www.gov.uk/government/consultations/ property-ownership-and-public-contracting-by-overseas-companies-and-legal-entities-beneficial-ownership-register. The new register is likely to be brought in from late 2021 with a one year transitional period. The register will be known as the Register of People with Significant Control over Overseas Companies (the PSCOC Register). Earlier in 2017 a new Trust Registration Service (TRS) was brought in in the UK which is to be expanded to impose compulsory registration on bare trusts (but not a simple trust such as a life insurance or pension provided by an employer held in trust for relatives on death of the individual). A useful summary of this new regime by solicitors Farrer & Co as at October 2020 can be seen at https://www.farrer.co.uk/ news-and-insights/uk-trust-registration-developments-the-new-expanded-regime/#.

7.91 The measures are contained in Money Laundering and Terrorist Financing (Amendment) (EU Exit) Regulations 2020 (SI 2020/991) the guidance (see https://www.legislation.gov.uk/uksi/2020/991/memorandum/ contents at para 7.11ff) to which says as follows:

'From 10 March 2022, when entering into a new business relationship with a trust that is required to register under the above requirements, obliged entities must collect proof of registration. To facilitate this, trustees will be able to download a digital proof of registration from the register which they can then provide to the obliged entity. This process will be set out in future guidance.

The trust register can already be accessed by law enforcement agencies to aid their work in countering money laundering and terrorist financing, and this will continue (see regulation 45(12)). From 10 March 2022, new regulation 45ZB broadens access to third parties who have demonstrated a legitimate interest in the information held on the register. Following a process to be set out in future guidance, third parties will be able to make a request to HMRC for information on a particular trust. To ensure that the appropriate balance is struck between the right of privacy of information held on the register and the need for transparency of information to assist AML/CTF activities, these Regulations require HMRC to consider a number of factors before determining whether information held on the register should be provided to a third party. Each request will be considered on its own merits with the aim of ensuring that information is only provided in furtherance of genuine AML/CTF activities. If all or part of the information requested is withheld, these Regulations require HMRC to offer the requester a review of that decision.

Regulation 45ZB also provides that access to information held on the register will be granted to a third party where the relevant trust has a controlling interest in a non-EEA legal entity.

To correspond with changes planned to be introduced under the Registration of Overseas Entities Bill, any non-UK express trust (but not a trust excluded by Schedule 3A) that acquires land or property in the UK must register by 10 March 2022 or 30 days from the relevant land registration date. These trusts will be on the register but will not be subject to the regulation 45ZB third party data sharing provisions unless they have at least one trustee resident or established in the UK.'

The draft Registration of Overseas Entities Bill by 2021 had still not been enacted despite an obligation to report on progress about this to Parliament under the Sanctions and Anti-Money Laundering Act 2018, s 50.

6   Tax issues dealt with elsewhere

7.92   The following tax issues are dealt with elsewhere in this book, and are listed here for convenience:

Share options and incentive schemes	Chapter 5
Tax considerations relating to loan finance	6.27ff
Tax on grant and exercise of put and call options	18.17ff
Tax considerations on the purchase by a company of its own shares	20.7ff
Tax position regarding redeemable shares	20.28
Tax position of individual joint venturers	26.1ff
Close companies	26.10ff
Company or partnership?	26.23ff
Income tax charges on the acquisition of shares	26.31ff
Enterprise Investment Scheme	26.43ff
Venture capital trusts	26.46ff
Dividends or remuneration for individuals?	26.23ff
Tax considerations on realisation of shareholdings of individuals	26.59ff
Relief for interest on loans incurred by individual joint venturers	26.21ff
Dealing with the retirement or death of working individual shareholders	26.71ff
Choice of vehicle to conduct an international joint venture	28.5ff
Other tax planning issues affecting the structure and operation of international joint ventures	28.18ff
Controlled foreign companies	28.24ff
UK corporate joint ventures with non-resident participants	28.31ff

Chapter 8

Accounting considerations for UK corporate joint venturers

Summary

This chapter explains the various forms of accounting treatment which may be applicable under UK GAAP (Generally Accepted Accounting Practices) to the accounts of a UK corporate joint venturer in relation to its interest in the joint venture, which may, depending on the circumstances, consist of full consolidation or equity accounting or showing the interest as an investment. The circumstances in which each treatment is to be employed are explained, and each treatment is separately analysed. A comparison of the requirements of International Financial Reporting Standards (IFRS) with the existing UK standards is included in the final section. In recent years the UK standards have become much closer to IFRS.

1 Introduction

8.1   The purpose of this chapter is to provide a general introduction for the lay reader to the considerations which apply to the presentation in the accounts of a UK company of its interest in a joint venture under UK GAAP and under IFRS. The subject is of some complexity and in order to deal with it in a reasonable space it has been necessary to simplify it in some respects. Whilst the chapter covers the broad principles, detailed accountancy advice should always be taken as to the appropriate accounting treatment in any particular case.

8.2   This chapter involves a difficulty with terminology because, whilst this book uses the term 'joint venture' in its broadest sense, in the eyes of an accountant a 'joint venture' may be taken to mean one within the considerably narrower definition contained in FRS 102 sections 14 (associates) and 15 (joint ventures) (replacing FRS 9 which was a previous separate stand alone rule in the joint ventures area) and in many situations in which a participant might regard itself as an investor in a joint venture its interest must in fact appear in its accounts as an 'associate'. For this reason, a joint venture within the narrower FRS definition is referred to in this chapter as an 'FRS joint venture'.

8.3   This chapter does not concern itself with the manner in which the joint venture entity is to prepare its accounts, but suffice to say that it will need to comply with the requirements of the relevant local law. A UK incorporated joint venture company will need to comply with the requirements of the Companies Act 2006 ('CA 2006') for financial years commencing on or after 6 April 2008, and applicable accounting standards in the UK.

8.4   These same sources of law and accounting standards are relevant to the accounts of a UK incorporated joint venturer. The most relevant accounting standard is now FRS 102 sections 14 (associates) and 15 (joint ventures) (previously FRS 9 'Associates and Joint Ventures', which was issued in November 1997 and was mandatory for accounting periods ending on or after 23 June 1998). However, two other standards were then also relevant, FRS 2 'Accounting for Subsidiary Undertakings' and FRS 5 'Reporting the Substance of Transactions'. Further information on UK GAAP is available at http://www.icaew.com/en/technical/financial-reporting/uk-gaap.

8.5   The accounting treatment which will be required can influence the structuring of the joint venture. The classic example is probably where a joint venturer has 50% of the shares of a joint venture company, but also has the right to appoint the chairman who has a casting vote. The existence of the casting vote will give the joint venturer control of the joint venture company and thus compel its consolidation in the accounts of the joint venturer, so that 100% of the joint venture company's debts have to appear in the consolidated accounts (subject to subsequent adjustment for minority interests) which may be unattractive. If, however, the joint venturer was prepared to concede the chairman's casting vote, it would probably be able to account for its investment in the joint venture as an FRS joint venture, so that gross equity accounting would be required and only 50% of the joint venture company's debt need appear in the joint venturer's accounts. Whether the controlling joint venturer would be prepared to give up the casting vote is of course another matter; the commercial consequences of doing so might be thought to outweigh the different accounting treatment.

8.6   Another example of the structure of a joint venture being adjusted in the light of accounting requirements might arise where it is proposed to establish a contractual joint venture between (say) three parties, and the venture involves each party being responsible for a stage in a manufacturing process, with the goods in production being sold on from one joint venturer to another at each stage, and the third joint venturer selling the products to the customer. If one of the venturers requires to borrow a large sum of money to finance its stage (eg in order to purchase some expensive machinery), it would have to show the whole amount of that debt in its own balance sheet. That joint venturer might wish to persuade the others to establish a separate company to carry on the venture as a self-contained business with its own board of directors able to determine policy, and which borrows the money to acquire the machinery. If it is able to equity account in relation to the joint venture company, only the proportion of the loan corresponding to its interest need appear in its accounts. The joint venture company could be structured so that each joint venturer receives the same proportion of the profits as it would have received through the contractual joint venture.

2   Subsidiary undertakings

8.7   The first step to understanding the accounting requirements for joint ventures is the definition of a 'subsidiary undertaking'. A subsidiary undertaking will normally be accounted for on a consolidated basis in the accounts of the parent undertaking. This is consistent with the objective of FRS 2 (now FRS 102) that parent undertakings should prepare consolidated financial statements, including the parent undertaking and its subsidiary undertakings, that show the economic resources controlled by the group, the obligations of the group and the results the group achieves with its resources. Thus the definition of a subsidiary undertaking is particularly important for accounting purposes.

8.8   The concept of the subsidiary undertaking was introduced into UK law by the Companies Act 1989 in order to give effect to the Seventh Company Law Directive of the European Community and to prevent previous abuses whereby artificial capital structures were used to avoid consolidation as subsidiaries of entities over which the holding company had effective control. Previously, only subsidiaries (as then defined) had to be consolidated, which included companies over which the parent had legal control, but may have excluded from consolidation certain companies over which the parent did not necessarily have legal control, but was in fact able to exercise control. The intention of the Directive was to ensure that companies over which the parent had either legal or actual control would be subsidiary undertakings and would have to be consolidated, unless specifically excluded. The concept has been augmented by the accounting standards.

8.9   The definition of a subsidiary undertaking is now found in CA 2006, s 1162 (previously CA 1985, s 258).

An undertaking is a parent undertaking in relation to another undertaking, which is its subsidiary undertaking, if it:

● holds a majority of the voting rights in the undertaking;

● is a member of the undertaking and has the right to appoint or remove a majority of its board of directors;

● has the right to exercise a dominant influence over the undertaking:

    (i)   by virtue of provisions contained in the undertaking's articles; or

    (ii) by virtue of a control contract;

- is a member of the undertaking and controls alone, pursuant to an agreement with the other shareholders or members, a majority of the voting rights in the undertaking; or

- if:

    (i)   it has the power to exercise or actually exercises a dominant influence or control over it; or

    (ii) it and the subsidiary undertaking are managed on a unified basis.

8.10   The CA 2006 amends the previous definition of a subsidiary undertaking in CA 1985 by deleting the requirement that there be a participating interest, so that the parent undertaking will be required to consolidate an undertaking where it exercises a dominant influence over that undertaking, or the parent and the undertaking are managed on a unified basis, irrespective of the interest the parent holds in it. FRS 2 (and now FRS 102) has been amended to correspond.

8.11   The accounting standards provide some additional guidance on the meanings of some elements of the definition. FRS 102 defines control (at page 329) as 'the ability of an undertaking to direct the financial and operating policies of another undertaking with a view to gaining economic benefits from its activities'.

Control can also exist 'when the parent has the power to exercise, or actually exercises, dominant influence or control over the undertaking or it and the undertaking are managed on a unified basis' (see FRS 102).

'Dominant influence' means influence that can be exercised to achieve the operating and financial policies desired by the holder of the influence, notwithstanding the rights or influence of any other party. The actual exercise of a dominant influence is the exercise of an influence that achieves the result that the operating and financial policies of the undertaking influenced are set in accordance with the wishes of the holder of the influence and for the holder's benefit whether or not those wishes are explicit. The actual exercise of dominant influence is identified by its effect in practice rather than by the way it is exercised. Managed on a unified basis applies as a concept where the whole of the operations of the undertakings are integrated and they are managed as a single unit – see Amendments to FRS 2 'Accounting for Subsidiary Undertakings', FRS 6 'Acquisitions and Mergers' and FRS 28 'Corresponding Amounts' Legal Changes – Accounting Standards Board June 2009). 'Integrated means the acquired business has been restructured or dissolved into the reporting entity or other subsidiaries' (FRS 102, para 27.27).

This is unlikely to be so in the case of most joint ventures. FRS 102 can be accessed at https://www.frc.org.uk/getattachment/e1d6b167-6cdb-4550-bde3-f94484226fbd/FRS-102-WEB-Ready-2015.pdf.

8.12   A subsidiary undertaking need not necessarily be a company. By CA 2006, s 1161 (CA 1985, s 259) the term is extended to include a partnership or an unincorporated association carrying on a trade or business with or without a view to profit.

8.13   A parent undertaking with one or more subsidiaries or subsidiary undertakings has to prepare group accounts under CA 2006, s 399 (CA 1985, s 227) unless it is able to utilise one of the company law exemptions that permits certain small- and medium-sized entities and certain intermediate parent companies not to prepare group accounts at all. Assuming group accounts are required, consolidated financial statements should include the parent undertaking and all its subsidiary undertakings, with the only exceptions being in respect of any subsidiary undertakings that fall within one of the limited exceptions outlined in FRS 102 and the CA 2006, s 405(3). Section 405(3) provides that exceptionally a subsidiary undertaking should be excluded from consolidation where, inter alia, severe long-term restrictions substantially hinder the exercise of the rights of the parent undertaking over the assets or management of the subsidiary undertaking.

8.14   FRS 102 as to provisions previously in FRS 5 also requires the consolidation of 'quasi-subsidiaries' which are outside the definition of a subsidiary undertaking but are nevertheless directly or indirectly controlled by the company whose accounts are being prepared. This part of the standard was introduced because of a feeling that the CA 1985 (now CA 2006) definition of a 'subsidiary undertaking' would not catch every undertaking where consolidation ought to be required. Consistent with this objective, a quasi-subsidiary is a company, trust, partnership or other vehicle that is directly or indirectly controlled by the reporting entity and which gives rise to benefits for that entity that are in substance no different from those that would arise if the vehicle was a subsidiary. 'Control' in this context means the ability to direct the financial and operating policies of that entity with a view to gaining economic benefit from its activities. This may mean that where the shareholdings and share rights in the joint venture vehicle have been carefully arranged so as to avoid its being a subsidiary undertaking of any of the participants, if one of them is able to exercise control of it, it will still have to be consolidated in the accounts of that participant. CA 2006 (CA 1985) does not require a quasi-subsidiary to be consolidated (such a term is not found in the Act) but FRS 102 requires consolidation in the majority of cases. ICAEW has a help sheet about when a subsidiary may be excluded from consolidation – see https://www.icaew.com/technical/tas-helpsheets/law-and-regulation/when-can-a-subsidiary-be-excluded-from-consolidation-under-frs-102.

8.15   Thus, the question as to whether or not an undertaking is required to be consolidated as a subsidiary or is to be treated as a quasi-subsidiary depends not only upon the size of the interest, but also upon the nature of the agreements between the joint venturers themselves, whether contained in a shareholders' agreement, the articles of association or other document and the actual rights exercised. Arrangements where there appears to be joint control of voting power, but one party derives a benefit from the arrangement in excess of their equity share should be examined carefully to ascertain the true commercial substance. This may particularly be the case in circumstances where the vehicle is thinly capitalised but has a large amount of debt. In this case, the party who in reality has control may wish to dress up the structure in an attempt to equity account it instead of consolidating it, so that the whole amount of the debt need not be shown in its consolidated balance sheet.

8.16   Where a joint venturer holds a minority stake it is unlikely that its interest will need to be consolidated, since the joint venture vehicle is unlikely to be its subsidiary undertaking or quasi-subsidiary. It is not likely to have a majority of the voting rights (except, possibly, in very special situations which may be disregarded) and neither is it likely to be able to appoint or remove a majority of the directors or to be able to exercise a dominant influence. It may have the ability to veto certain important transactions, but these essentially negative rights will not amount to control.

8.17   Where three or more participants in a joint venture are all in a minority, the joint venture vehicle is unlikely to be the subsidiary undertaking or quasi-subsidiary of any of them, in the absence of unusual features.

8.18   A 50:50 deadlock joint venture is also not likely to be a subsidiary undertaking, because neither participant is likely to hold a majority of the voting power nor be able to appoint a majority of the directors, and neither is likely to have a dominant influence.

8.19   Where a participant in a joint venture vehicle has a majority interest in it, the vehicle is likely to be its subsidiary undertaking. Even if the minority participants have various vetoes, it is likely to have retained a majority of the voting rights and the ability to appoint a majority of the directors, and the joint venture will be a subsidiary undertaking on these grounds alone and therefore require consolidation under FRS 102.

8.20   An important exception to the normal consolidation is the long-term restriction exemption referred to in para 8.13. FRS 102 indicates that in some cases an investor may qualify as the parent of an entity under the definition of a subsidiary undertaking, but contractual arrangements with the other shareholder(s) mean that in practice the shareholders share control over the entity, with each venturer having a veto over the high level strategic decisions. For example, an investor might control over 50% of an entity's voting rights but the joint venture agreement might significantly restrict this control, perhaps by requiring the unanimous agreement of each of the joint venturers before the entity could change its business plan or business direction, pay a dividend, pay directors, issue shares, borrow money, incur capital expenditure over a specified level, or change other major operating and financial policies. FRS 102 indicates that under the CA 2006 the interests of the minority shareholder could then amount to 'severe long-term restrictions' such that the parent does not control its subsidiary, and therefore the subsidiary should not be consolidated but rather should be accounted for as an FRS 102 joint venture. It is considered that this type of situation is unlikely to arise frequently in practice, particularly as the entity remains one that is classified as a subsidiary undertaking under FRS rules.

3 Accounting for joint ventures which do not have to be consolidated

8.21   Assuming that an interest in a joint venture does not have to be consolidated, its presentation in the accounts of its participants is governed partly by Sch 6 of either the Large and Medium-sized Companies and Groups (Accounts and Reports) Regulations 2008 ('SI 2008/410') or the Small Companies and Groups (Accounts and Directors' Report) Regulations 2008 ('SI 2008/409') – formerly CA 1985, Sch 4A – and partly by FRS 102 (previously FRS 9).

8.22   Before the introduction of equity accounting, interests in entities not required to be consolidated were generally treated as investments in the accounts of their participants, which meant that they were carried at cost in the balance sheet and only dividends or other distributions actually received were included in the profit and loss account. No part of the net assets or undistributed profits of the entity would appear in the participant's accounts.

8.23   In the 1960s this was perceived as being inadequate and the practice grew up of applying equity accounting where the participant had a substantial minority stake in another entity and exercised significant influence, although falling short of control. In essence, equity accounting requires the inclusion in the participant's consolidated balance sheet of its share of the net assets of the entity and the inclusion at some levels of its consolidated profit and loss account of its share of the results of the entity, whether or not profits are actually distributed.

8.24   Another form of presentation was proportional consolidation. This involved bringing into the participant's consolidated balance sheet on a line-by-line basis the appropriate proportion of the participant's interest in all the assets and liabilities of the other entity, and including the appropriate proportion of its income, expenses and results in the participant's consolidated profit and loss account.

8.25   Equity accounting was given formal effect in SSAP 1 in 1971, and CA 1989 introduced what was Sch 4A to CA 1985 (which has now been replaced by SI 2008/410 or SI 2008/409, Sch 6 for financial years beginning on or after 6 April 2008), which also requires equity accounting in relation to 'associated undertakings' – previously it had been permitted but was not mandatory. This legislation is now supplemented by FRS 102.

8.26   FRS 102 in sections 14 (associates) and 15 (joint ventures) distinguishes between three classes of investment:

- associates; and

- joint ventures which are entities.

Associates

8.27   SI 2008/410 or SI 2008/409, Sch 6, para 19 (formerly CA 1985, Sch 4A, para 20) defines an 'associated undertaking' as an undertaking in which an undertaking included in the consolidation has a participating interest, over whose operating and financial policy it exercises a significant influence and which is not a subsidiary undertaking or a joint venture within para 18. If the undertaking holds 20% or more of the voting rights of the other undertaking, it is presumed to exercise an influence, unless the contrary is shown.

8.28   Paragraph 21 expressly requires the equity method of accounting to be used in relation to an associated undertaking.

8.29   The same definition is generally followed in FRS 102 and before it FRS 9, except that 'entity' replaces the term 'undertaking'. The terms can be taken to be the same as 'undertaking' for most purposes, so that if the joint venture is not an entity it will not be an associated undertaking. There is one other difference, in that FRS 102 requires that the entity must be carrying on a business of its own.

8.30   SI 2008/410 or SI 2008/409, Sch 6, para 19 provides that paras 5–11 of Sch 7 to the CA 2006 apply in determining whether a participating interest exists. Under CA 1985, s 260(1) a 'participating interest' was defined as an interest held in the share of another undertaking on a long-term basis (ie not for resale) for the purpose of securing a contribution to its activities by the exercise of control or influence arising from or related to that interest. This definition is largely followed by FRS 102 (para 4 of FRS 9). A 'participating interest' may include an option over shares or an interest convertible into shares, which will have relevance where there are pre-termination put or call options, or a participant in a joint venture holds some shares or loan stock which are convertible into equity shares. Again, there is a rebuttable presumption that a holding of 20% or more is a participating interest.

8.31   FRS 102, however, expands on the law by providing that the presumption of a participating interest is to be rebutted if the interest is not long-term or beneficial. The definition of 'long-term' is more restrictive, whilst 'beneficial' is to be interpreted in a broad sense. The beneficial interest need not be confined to dividends and could include eg management fees based on performance.

8.32   Unlike CA 2006, FRS 102 also includes a definition of 'exercise of significant influence'. This requires that the participant be actively involved in, and influential in, the direction of the associate through participation in policy decisions relevant to the participant, including decisions on strategic issues such as:

●   expansion or contraction of the business, investments in other entities, and changes in products, markets and activities; and

●   whether profits should be distributed by dividends or reinvested.

8.33   The concept of the actual exercise of a significant influence could cause difficulties where there is such an exercise initially, but this then ceases. FRS 102 avoids any immediate change in the accounting treatment in this situation by providing that it is the exercise of the significant influence which determines the initial accounting treatment and the ability to exercise it (whether or not actually exercised) maintains it. It is only when that ability is lost that the accounting treatment is to be changed.

8.34   It should be noted that while the focus of the definitions is such that an entity in which an investor holds an interest of 20% or more is likely to be its associate, it is entirely possible that:

●   a holding in excess of 20% will not be treated as an associate if the interest is not held for the long-term, is not beneficial, or does not involve the actual exercise of significant influence; or

●   a holding of less than 20% will be treated as an associate where the conditions relating to the long-term and beneficial nature of the investment and the actual exercise of significant influence are demonstrated by the way in which the entity is managed.

8.35   In summary, it is necessary that each investment be evaluated to determine whether or not the definition of an associate is satisfied based on the facts of the situation, rather than applying a formula relating to percentage shareholdings.

FRS 102 (s 14/15) joint ventures

8.36   FRS 102 as regards joint ventures when it came into force did make more changes than were made in relation to 'associates' as above. Under FRS 102, a joint venture exists when there is joint control, defined as 'the contractually agreed sharing of control over an economic activity'. This must be contractual which is the same as under the previous FRS 9.

8.37   A joint venture is classified as being of one of three types:

● a jointly controlled operation;

● jointly controlled asset;

● or jointly controlled entity.

The main difference between a jointly controlled operation and jointly controlled entity is that in a jointly controlled entity there is a separate legal entity in which the shared operations take place. An arrangement that had been, under FRS 9, classified as a JANE (joint arrangement that is not an entity) would usually be a jointly controlled operation or jointly controlled asset under FRS 102.

8.38   In June 2016 the IASB issued a draft 'Definition of a business and accounting for previously held interests'. PriceWaterhouse Coopers describes the arrangements as follows:

'A joint arrangement is a contractual arrangement where at least two parties agree to share control over the activities of the arrangement. Unanimous consent towards decisions about relevant activities between the parties sharing control is a requirement in order to meet the definition of joint control. Joint arrangements can be joint operations or joint ventures. The classification is principle based and depends on the parties' exposure in relation to the arrangement. When the parties' exposure to the arrangement only extends to the net assets of the arrangement, the arrangement is a joint venture. Joint operators have rights to assets and obligations for liabilities. Joint operations are often not structured through separate vehicles.'

See https://viewpoint.pwc.com/uk/en.html.

8.39   When a joint arrangement is included in a separate vehicle, it can be either a joint operation or a joint venture. In such cases, further analysis is required on the legal form of the separate vehicle, the terms and conditions included in the contractual agreement and sometimes, other facts and circumstances. This is because in practice, the latter two can override the principles derived from the legal form of the separate vehicle. Joint operators account for their rights to assets and obligations for liabilities. Joint ventures account for their interest by using the equity method of accounting. The previous rules referred to JANEs (joint arrangements which are not entities).

4 Accounting treatments compared

Consolidation

8.40   Some of the description below is based on the previous FRS 9 but is still of historical interest.

Where a joint venture is to be consolidated in the accounts of one of the joint venturers, as regards its own accounts that venturer will show its interest in its individual balance sheet as an investment at cost or valuation, less amounts written off, and any income received from the investment will be shown in its individual profit and loss account.

8.41   As regards its consolidated accounts, the joint venturer will aggregate the whole amount of the subsidiary's assets and liabilities (including debt) with its own in the consolidated balance sheet (notwithstanding that it has less than a 100% interest), adjusting for the minority interest by means of a one line item referred to as 'minority interests'. In the consolidated profit and loss account the turnover, operating profit, interest and tax of the subsidiary will be aggregated with the investor's own and the minority share of profits deducted from the profit after tax. Consolidation adjustments would be made in accordance with the relevant rules.

Equity accounting

8.42   Where an investor must account for its investment as an associate, and equity accounting therefore applies, the investor will include in its individual balance sheet its investment at cost or valuation, less amounts written off, and in its individual profit and loss account any income received from the investment.

8.43   As regards its consolidated accounts, the joint venturer's balance sheet should include as an investment its share of the net assets of its associate as a separate item. The carrying amount should also include any goodwill at its written down amount, but this should be disclosed separately. Any dividends received have no impact on the profit and loss account, but will affect the consolidated balance sheet, since its proportion of the net assets of the joint venture will be reduced to reflect the cash paid out by way of dividend. In the consolidated profit and loss account the investor's share of its associates' operating results should be included immediately after group operating results (but after the share of the other FRS 102 joint venturers, if any). Any goodwill amortisation or write down should be charged at this point.

8.44   In the investor's consolidated cashflow statement, dividends received from its associate should be shown as a separate item between operating activities and returns on investments and servicing of finance. Other cashflows between the investor and the associate are to be reflected under the appropriate heading. The internal cashflows of the associate should not appear in the consolidated cashflow statement.

8.45   If the associate is loss-making, the investor must continue to account for its share of the losses. Where this results in an interest in net liabilities, FRS102 requires this to be reflected in the balance sheet as a provision or liability.

8.46   Investors which do not prepare consolidated financial statements are required by FRS 102 to present the relevant amounts for associates by preparing a separate set of financial statements, or by showing the relevant amounts as additional information in their own financial statements. Investors that are exempt from preparing consolidated financial statements (under either CA 1985, s 228 or 248 (CA 2006, s 399ff)), or which would be exempt if they had subsidiaries, are exempt from this requirement.

8.47   The investor's share of the associate's exceptional items, interest payable and receivable, and tax are also included in the profit and loss account, with separate disclosure in the notes. Additionally, the share of turnover may be included with the joint venturer's turnover as a memorandum item on the face of the profit and loss account, but the investor's share of the associate's turnover has to be clearly distinguished from group turnover (ie that of the investor and its subsidiary undertakings).

Equity accounting – gross equity method (previous rules)

8.48   Where an investor prepares consolidated financial statements, investments in FRS 102 joint ventures previously they were accounted for using what was known as the gross equity method.

Nowadays this is, instead, done under the 'equity method' (rather than the gross equity method required by the old FRS 9). This change has had little impact, but the simplification was welcomed by accountants and meant that accounting for associates and joint ventures is now consistent in consolidated financial statements.

8.49   The gross equity method, no longer used, provided that the treatment is the same as the (net) equity method used for associates except that:

● in the consolidated profit and loss account, the investor's share of the joint venture turnover must be shown, but not as part of group turnover; and

- in the consolidated balance sheet the investor's share of the gross assets and liabilities underlying the (net) equity method must be shown in amplification of that net amount.

8.50   The accounting treatment for a loss-making joint venture before the change to the 'equity method' was the same as that for a loss-making associate, except that the investor's share of gross assets and liabilities of the joint venture had still to be shown (within the liabilities or provisions section of the balance sheet).

8.51   The requirement to show the gross assets and liabilities rather than netting them off in some cases made a considerable difference to the appearance of the investor's accounts.

A good summary of the changes in FRS 102 is at https://www.crowe.com/uk/croweuk/services/audit/financial-reporting-standards/frs-102-accounting-for-groups.

Consolidation and equity accounting compared

8.52   The crucial difference between the two methods is that consolidation always requires the whole amount of each item of the consolidated entity's assets and liabilities to appear on the consolidated balance sheet, even though the reporting entity does not own 100% of the subsidiary or subsidiary undertaking in which the assets and liabilities are recorded. The adjustment for the minority interests is made in a separate line of the balance sheet. Similarly, the whole amount of the profits and losses must appear in the consolidated profit and loss account, with subsequent adjustment for the minority interests. In contrast, equity accounting only records the group's share of the profits or losses and net assets or net liabilities (or, in the case of the gross equity method, the gross assets and gross liabilities), even though further sub-division and disclosure is made in the accounts.

8.53   Participants in a joint venture which has a particularly large amount of debt or other liabilities, or is making losses, may prefer to equity account rather than consolidate, if the venture can be structured in such a way that this is permitted. Although the difference is to some extent presentational, other differences are more significant. Consolidation can have the effect of some unpleasantly large negative numbers appearing in the consolidated accounts, to which the subsequent adjustment for minority interests is not directly referable on the face of the accounts. A majority shareholder who wishes to avoid consolidation might be tempted to put in place an arrangement with a friendly minority party such that the minority, although having various vetoes, will never exercise them in practice. Clearly such an arrangement is not a joint venture and should not be accounted for as such; it is substance, not form, which governs the correct method of accounting. The combination of what was FRS 2 and FRS 5 (and now FRS 102) has meant consolidation will be needed wherever an investor controls another entity in terms of those standards. In any cases of doubt, directors and auditors will also be mindful that there is an accounts enforcement regime whereby a company could be reported to the Financial Reporting Review Panel if its accounts failed to comply with those standards.

Accounting for the interest as an investment

8.54   Where an interest is to be accounted for as an investment, the treatment in the individual accounts is as set out in para 8.22. If the joint venturer also has subsidiary undertakings, and must therefore prepare consolidated accounts, the amounts shown in the individual accounts will be carried forward into the consolidation.

5   International Financial Reporting Standards

Introduction

8.55   Listed companies within the European Union are required to prepare their consolidated financial statements under International Financial Reporting Standards (IFRS). The UK dealt with the end of the post-Brexit transition period from 1 January 2021 and currently the UK and EU rules remain similar although there be divergence in due course. The FRC amendments relating to Brexit are summarised in 'Amendments to UK and Republic of Ireland accounting standards UK exit from the European Union' (December 2020) at https://www.frc.org.uk/getattachment/8214be0e-d10e-440c-9406-5be7d049aefb/Amendments-to-UK-and-RoI-accounting-standards-UK-exit-from-the-EU-(Dec-2020).pdf.

8.56   Listed companies do not include those which are admitted to AIM, but the London Stock Exchange also requires such companies to prepare their consolidated financial statements under IFRS. Non-listed UK companies currently have the option of preparing their accounts either under UK GAAP or under IFRS.

8.57   However, following the International Accounting Standards Board's launch of the International Financial Reporting Standard for Small and Medium-sized Entities (the IFRS for SMEs), it appears likely that the Accounting Standards Board will adopt this as a replacement for UK GAAP in the future. IFRS for SMEs is an IFRS based standard which is designed specifically for non-listed companies. The principles of accounting for subsidiaries, associates and joint ventures under IFRS for SMEs are not different to those in IFRS.

Flowchart 1

Joint venture accounting requirements under UK GAAP

This flowchart illustrates the considerations which govern how a joint venturer (ABC) should account for its interest in a joint venture (XYZ). This is somewhat simplified and is not intended to override the text; it is very difficult to illustrate the concepts diagramatically.

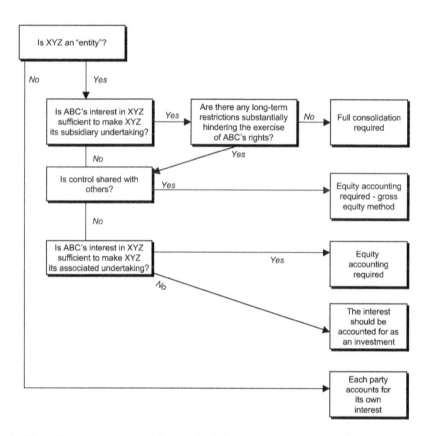

8.58   Since many participants in joint ventures are listed companies, they are currently required to account for their interests in them under IFRS, and in order to simplify this process they may require their joint venture companies to do so also. Quite apart from this, some joint venture companies will probably choose to do so, particularly those where the parties envisage that their exit will be achieved by means of a flotation, or where the joint venture company is very large and wishes to account under IFRS in order to maintain comparisons with its competitors.

8.59   Consolidation is dealt with under IFRS by International Accounting Standard IAS 27 'Consolidated and Separate Financial Statements' and associates by IAS 28 'Investments in Associates and Joint Ventures.

IFRS 11 Joint Arrangements 2016 Changes

8.60   In June 2016 the IASB issued a new 'Definition of a business and accounting for previously held interests'. See 8.38 above for further information.

When a joint arrangement is included in a separate vehicle, it can be either a joint operation or a joint venture. In such cases, further analysis is required on the legal form of the separate vehicle, the terms and conditions included in the contractual agreement and sometimes, other facts and circumstances. This is because in practice, the latter two can override the principles derived from the legal form of the separate vehicle. Joint operators account for their rights to assets and obligations for liabilities. Joint ventures account for their interest by using the equity method of accounting. The previous rules referred to JANEs (joint arrangements which are not entities).

Consolidation of subsidiaries

8.61   Under IAS 27 a parent must prepare consolidated accounts in which it consolidates its investments in its subsidiaries. IAS 27 defines a subsidiary as 'an entity, including an unincorporated entity such as a partnership, that is controlled by another entity (known as the parent)'. Control is defined as 'the power to govern the financial and operating policies of an entity so as to obtain benefits from its activities'.

8.62   Control is presumed to exist when the parent owns, directly or indirectly, more than half of the voting power of an entity unless, in exceptional circumstances, it can be clearly demonstrated that such ownership does not constitute control. Control also exists where the parent owns half or less of the voting power of an entity when there is:

(a)   power over more than half of the voting rights by virtue of an agreement with other investors;

(b)   power to govern the financial and operating policies of the entity under a statute or an agreement;

(c)   power to appoint or remove the majority of the members of the board of directors or equivalent governing body, and control of the entity is by that board or body; or

(d) power to cast the majority of the votes at meetings of the board of directors or equivalent governing body, and control of the entity is by that board or body.

This approach is very similar to the UK approach. IAS 27 does not deal specifically with the situation where a parent has a participating interest in the enterprise with dominant influence or unified management, but where this is the case the enterprise is likely to be controlled by the parent. The principles of consolidation are very similar to those under FRS 102.

Associates

8.63   The requirements of IAS 28 are, in broad terms, similar to the requirements of FRS 102. The definition of an associate under IFRS, however, does not require that the investor actually exercises significant influence, merely that it is in a position to do so.

8.64   In addition, IAS 28 provides specifically that an associate should not be included in the financial statements using the equity method when the investment is acquired and held exclusively with a view to its disposal within 12 months from acquisition and management is actively seeking a buyer, in which case the investment should be classified as held for sale in accordance with IFRS 5 'Non-current assets held for sale and discontinued operations' and measured at the lower of its carrying amount at the date of its classification of held for sale and its fair value less cost to sell. If a buyer is not found within that 12 month period, however, the standard requires that the financial statements are restated to include that associate under the equity method from the date of its acquisition.

Accounting for associates

8.65   FRS 102 is much more prescriptive than IFRS in terms of the presentation of associates in the financial statements, with IAS 28 requiring only that the investor's share of the profit or loss of the associate (post-tax) is recognised in the investor's income statement. The standard does not specify where in the income statement this should be included, nor does it include any of the requirements of FRS 102 with regard to operating profit and items below operating profit.

8.66   The requirements of IAS 28 apply to both consolidated and unconsolidated financial statements. A company which has no subsidiary undertakings, but which has associates, is therefore required to account for its associates under the equity method in its own financial statements, as opposed to presenting an additional set of financial statements, or providing additional disclosures under FRS 102. IAS 28 also contains a further detailed exemption from the requirement to equity account when the investor is a subsidiary of another entity.

8.67   Under IAS 28, where an associate is loss-making, an investor accounts for its share of the losses only until its investment (including long-term interests such as debt or preference shares) is reduced to zero. Beyond this point, additional losses are provided for, and a liability recognised, only to the extent that the investor has assumed either a legal or constructive obligation on behalf of the associate.

Jointly controlled entities

8.68   The definition of a joint venture in FRS 102 is similar to that of a jointly controlled entity under IAS 31. However, the definition in IFRS specifically requires the formation of an entity (in the legal sense), otherwise the joint venture arrangement falls to be treated as a jointly controlled operation or jointly controlled assets.

8.69   The definition under IAS 31 does not require the formation of a separate legal entity as the IAS 31 definition of joint venture refers to the undertaking of an 'economic activity'. This can take many different forms, including jointly controlled operation, jointly controlled assets and jointly controlled entities (IAS 31.7). IAS 31 prescribes different accounting treatment for each form of joint venture. It is the FRS 102 definition of a joint venture which refers specifically to 'an entity'.

8.70   A JANE under UK GAAP which involves the formation of an entity (in the legal sense) will fall to be treated as a jointly controlled entity under IAS 31.

8.71   IAS 31 allows two accounting treatments for jointly controlled entities: proportional consolidation and equity accounting, both of which are discussed further below. However, it should be noted that the standard specifically states that the use of the equity method is not recommended. This is therefore a reversal of UK policy, although proportional consolidation is currently prohibited under UK law (see the proposed change below).

8.72   As for associates (see para 8.64), IAS 31 provides that a jointly controlled entity should not be accounted for by either proportional consolidation or equity accounting where it is acquired and held exclusively with a view to subsequent disposal within 12 months from acquisition, and management is actively seeking a buyer. Instead they should be classified as held for sale in accordance with IFRS 5 and measured at the lower of its carrying amount at the date of its classification of held for sale and its fair value less cost to sell.

Changes to joint venture accounting

8.73   IAS 31 was withdrawn for periods starting on or after 1 January 2013 (1 January 2014 for EU preparers) and is now superseded by IAS 28 (2011) 'Investments in Associates and Joint Ventures', IFRS 11 'Joint Arrangements' and IFRS 12 'Disclosure of Interests in Other Entities'.

In July 2013 consideration was being given to additional guidance in Exposure Draft ED/2012/3 'Equity Method: Share of Other Net Asset Changes', which proposes limited scope amendments to IAS 28 to include guidance on how an investor accounts for its share of the changes in net assets of an associate or joint venture that are not recognised in profit or loss or other comprehensive income of the investee.

In meetings during 2013 and 2014, the IASB decided to proceed with the amendments on the basis set out in the Exposure Draft, but modified to reflect a decision that an investor should only reflect those changes in net assets which were attributable to it. This means that an investor would not recognise a change in net assets due to a share-based payment reserve or the issuance of a warrant. On 28 March 2014 EFRAG (European Financial Reporting Advisory Group) (an association) sent a letter to the IASB expressing concerns that the amendments were expected to be finalised on the basis set out in the draft. In particular, EFRAG reiterated its concerns that the changes would result in conflicts with existing IFRS, economically similar transactions being accounted for in a different way and deferred recognition of losses. The letter also set out an alternative model that is consistent with both current practice and existing IFRS. At its May 2014 meeting, the IASB decided to abandon the proposed amendments.

8.74   The legal form of an arrangement should not be the determining factor when selecting the appropriate accounting for the arrangement. This is a departure from the treatment prescribed in IAS 31, which was closely aligned to the legal structure of joint venture arrangements.

8.75   A joint venturer should recognise its interest in a joint venture using the equity method. Proportionate consolidation is not to be permitted.

8.76   Details of IAS 28 are online at http://www.icaew.com/en/library/subject-gateways/accounting-standards/ifrs/ias-28.

Accounting for jointly controlled entities

8.77   Should an investor choose to account for jointly controlled entities using the equity method, the application of this method is identical to that described for associates at para 8.63ff. Once again, the requirements under IFRS are much less detailed than those for joint ventures under FRS 102, although IAS 31 does require additional disclosures to be given in the notes, which in some cases will be in excess of those required by FRS 102.

8.78   Where an investor chooses to use proportional consolidation (see para 8.24 above), two reporting formats are permitted:

• the investor may combine its share of the assets, liabilities, income, expenses and cashflows on a line-to-line basis with similar items in its own financial statements; or

• separate items may be included.

8.79   Where a jointly controlled entity is loss-making, if applying the equity method the investor will stop recognising its share of losses when the investment (including long-term interests such as debt and preference shares) is reduced to zero, unless the joint venturer has assumed either a legal or constructive obligation on behalf of the joint venture. If applying proportional consolidation, the investor must continue to account for its share of the net liabilities of the jointly controlled entity.

8.80   Once again, investments in jointly controlled entities are excluded from equity accounting or proportional consolidation where they are held exclusively with a view to disposal, and should be accounted for in accordance with IFRS 5.

Jointly controlled operations and jointly controlled assets

8.81   A jointly controlled operation is one which involves the use of assets and other resources of the venturers rather than the establishment of a corporation, partnership, other entity or financial structure that is separate from the venturers themselves (eg a contractual joint venture within para 1.22 above).

8.82   Jointly controlled assets are assets subject to joint control (and often ownership) by venturers, and are contributed to, or acquired for the purpose of, the joint venture and dedicated to the purposes of the joint venture.

8.83   A venture involving jointly controlled assets is again one which does not involve the creation of an entity, and is common in certain types of industry, such as oil and gas.

8.84   It can be seen from the definitions that most, if not all, non-corporate JANEs will fall to be treated as either jointly controlled operations or a venture involving jointly controlled assets. In addition, some joint ventures within FRS 102 that do not involve the creation of an entity may well fall to be treated as jointly controlled operations or ventures involving jointly controlled assets under IAS 31.

Accounting considerations for UK corporate joint venturers   Chapter 8

8.85   The accounting of jointly controlled operations and jointly controlled assets is broadly similar to that for JANEs under FRS 102, with each investor accounting for its own assets, liabilities, income, expenses and cashflows according to the terms of the arrangement. These requirements will be followed in consolidated, unconsolidated and, if presented, separate financial statements.

Chapter 9

Application of EC competition law to joint ventures

Summary

This chapter discusses the main aspects of EC competition law as applied to joint ventures, in particular the potential application of the EC Merger Regulation and arts 101 and 102 of the EC Treaty. Although the EC merger laws ceased to apply in the UK from 1 January 2021 many UK joint ventures involve EU subsidiaries or parent companies. The effect of Brexit is that some mergers need to be examined by both the EU and UK merger authorities. UK Competition Law is addressed in the next chapter (Chapter 10). The procedures for making a merger notification to the European Commission and obtaining clearance are discussed, together with the criteria applied to the substantive assessment of a joint venture under the EC Merger Regulation and the art 101 and 102 prohibitions. The chapter does not extend to specific sectors where special rules apply under arts 101 and 102, such as insurance.

1 Introduction

9.1 There is no precise definition of a 'joint venture' for the purposes of EC competition law. The term is used in a very broad sense and covers a variety of different types of arrangement in which two or more separate enterprises pool or share their resources in some way. Joint ventures can take various forms, from contractual, collaborative arrangements, through to concentrative arrangements where the parties use a corporate vehicle to combine all or part of their activities or resources on a lasting basis.

9.2 The application of EC competition law to joint ventures and the inter-relationship with the national competition and merger laws of the EU Member States is complex. The different procedures that may apply have to be considered with care, particularly as they may affect the ability of the parties to complete the transaction to their preferred timetable. The European Commission is currently the principal enforcement authority and its decisions are subject to review by the European courts. However, following the 'modernisation' of the application of arts 101 and 102 of the EC Treaty[1], which took effect on 1 May 2004, the national competition

---

1   See Regulation (EC) 1/2003, OJ L1/1.

authorities ('NCAs') of the EU member states also have the power fully to apply and enforce these prohibitions, alongside the European Commission. The European Commission has issued detailed guidelines regarding the appropriate allocation of cases between itself and the NCAs, with a view to ensuring that each case is dealt with by the best placed authority. In the UK, the Competition and Markets Authority (the 'CMA') regulates mergers but due to Brexit is no longer an NCA. The various sectoral regulators with concurrent competition powers also have powers and there is a right of appeal against their decisions to the Competition Appeal Tribunal where UK merger law applies. Very few UK mergers are large enough to fall within the EU Merger Regulation and relate sufficiently to the EU after Brexit that the EU Merger Regulation applies. Therefore, it is the next chapter (Chapter 10) on UK merger control which is most likely to be relevant. The EU thresholds are at para 9.29 below. However, some mergers below those thresholds contain restrictions, or the fact the companies have merged is anti-competitive, so consideration of the other EU competition issues in this chapter is still relevant such as para 9.62 (ancillary restraints).

9.3   The CMA issued some guidance on competition law post-Brexit at   https://assets.publishing.service.gov.uk/government/uploads/system/ uploads/attachment_data/file/940943/Guidance_Document_for_End_of_ Transition_Period_--.pdf.

This chapter describes EU merger law. Where a merger has no effects in the EU then Chapter 10 should be considered instead. From 1 January 2021 however, even if a merger has to be notified to the EU it may still have to be considered under UK merger law in addition. Competition law and mergers is a complicated issue and it is best to take advice from competition law solicitors. This chapter simply provides a brief overview. A consultation of the EU closed in January 2017 on certain possible changes to the EU merger regulation. This looks at the effectiveness of purely turnover-based jurisdictional thresholds, specifically at whether they capture all transactions which can potentially have an impact in the internal market. The EU stated in the said consultation:

'This may be particularly significant in certain sectors, such as the digital and pharmaceutical industries, where the acquired company, while having generated little turnover as yet, may play a competitive role, hold commercially valuable data or have a considerable market potential for other reasons. Other technical aspects: recent experience in enforcing the EU Merger Regulation has shown the opportunity to evaluate certain technical aspects of the procedural and investigative framework for the assessment of mergers. Some of these aspects had already been identified in the 2014 Commission Staff Working Document accompanying the White Paper.'

However by late 2020 the EU had decided changes to the EU Merger Regulation were too politically difficult and instead it decided to concentrate on reforming other areas of EU competition law. In 2020 the EU proposed changes to its market definition notice for mergers, but in 2021 these are not yet in force nor agreed – see https://ec.europa.eu/info/law/better-regulation/have-your-say/initiatives/12325-EU-competition-law-market-definition-notice-evaluation-_en.

9.4   In addition to observing any future legislative change UK readers need to be aware, as mentioned above, that from 1 January 2021 due to the ending of the post-Brexit transitional period some very large EU mergers may need to be considered both under the EU Merger Regulation and also UK merger law. Similarly with joint ventures which do not amount to 'mergers' under merger law UK and EU competition law may both need to be considered. Even after Brexit if an agreement has effects in the EU then even though subject to English law EU competition law will apply.

9.5   As a basic principle, EC competition law is unlikely to be relevant where the joint venture and its participants are active in only one member state or outside the EU, provided that the activities of the joint venture are not likely to have an appreciable direct or indirect effect on trade between member states. The European Commission has issued detailed guidelines on the circumstances in which such an effect is likely to arise (see para 9.80 for more details). It is also fair to say that a joint venture formed to develop and market a new product or service is less likely to run into difficulties than one which is established to absorb existing activities of the joint venturers.

9.6   Similar rules, including merger control, apply in relation to joint ventures which may affect trade within the wider European Economic Area ('EEA'), ie including Norway, Iceland and Liechtenstein (but not the UK which is neither a member of the EEA nor EU). These are not considered further in this book, but the substantive analysis would be broadly similar. There are detailed rules for allocating jurisdiction in any given case, and for co-operation between the European Commission and the EFTA Surveillance Authority.

9.7   This book makes no attempt to deal with the competition and merger laws of individual EU/EEA countries other than the UK (in Chapter 10), nor of countries outside the EU. Where such laws may apply, appropriate local advice should be sought.

The circumstances in which EC competition law is relevant

9.8   European competition law prohibits:

- agreements between undertakings whose object or effect is appreciably to restrict, prevent or distort competition and which may appreciably affect inter-state trade (EC Treaty, art 101); and

- the abuse by an undertaking or undertakings of a dominant position in so far as it may affect trade between member states (EC Treaty, art 102).

9.9   The assessment of joint ventures depends very much upon their potential effect upon the behaviour of the parties, their likely exclusionary or foreclosure effect vis-à-vis third parties, and the extent to which a position of market power may be created or reinforced. The European Commission concluded that arts 101 and 102 were insufficient to deal with the concentration of market power through structural change (essentially mergers and acquisitions) and the EC Merger Regulation ('ECMR') was introduced in 1989 to remedy this. The ECMR, which has been amended twice[2] since its introduction, also covers certain types of joint venture.

9.10   In terms of the approach to the analysis and procedure, a fundamental distinction is drawn between a concentrative joint venture which brings about a lasting change in structure, and a joint venture which is not concentrative.

9.11   One of the key distinctions is in relation to process. In summary, a concentrative joint venture which satisfies the turnover thresholds under the ECMR will be dealt with under that procedure. As explained below, this has implications for the timing of completion of the transaction, given the ECMR's mandatory notification and suspension requirements. However, in principle, if the ECMR applies, the national merger control and competition law regimes of EU countries are then excluded (the 'one-stop shop' principle), although of course countries outside the EU may still have to be considered.

9.12   Non-concentrative joint ventures are subject to assessment under arts 101 and 102 of the EC Treaty and do not require pre-clearance. Indeed, following modernisation on 1 May 2004, the voluntary notification procedure for obtaining clearance of anti-competitive agreements from the European Commission was abolished (but not the notification process for mergers), with the result that the onus is now firmly on the parties to carry out a self-assessment of the competition law implications of their joint venture. However, the European Commission has published a number of detailed guidelines to assist with this assessment, which are based to a large extent on past case law and practice. Also, it remains possible to obtain informal, non-binding guidance from the European Commission or the CMA regarding the compatibility of non-concentrative joint ventures with arts 101 and 102 in cases which give rise to novel or unresolved questions about the applicability of the rules.

---

2   The current ECMR is Regulation (EC) 139/2004, OJ L24/1.

9.13   National competition law regimes may also apply to non-concentrative joint ventures. EU member states are able to apply their own domestic competition law in parallel with EC Treaty, arts 101 and 102, although this is subject to the fundamental principle of the primacy of Community law. Since 1 January 2021 the EU rules do not apply in the UK so there is no longer parallel application in relation to the UK. There is a specific requirement in Regulation (EC) 1/2003 that the parallel application of national competition law may not lead to the prohibition of an agreement which would not be prohibited under art 101[3]. As explained in Chapter 10, UK competition law is closely modelled on EC competition law and the substantive approach under the two regimes is broadly consistent.

2   Joint ventures within the EC Merger Regulation

9.14   For a joint venture to fall within the EC Merger Regulation (Council Regulation (EC) 139/2004 ('ECMR')) it must:

● be concentrative; and

● satisfy the relevant turnover thresholds.

The individual merger regulation/notices and guidelines etc are also online at https://ec.europa.eu/competition-policy/mergers/legislation_en.

Is the venture concentrative?

9.15   As explained in para 9.1, the term 'joint venture' can be used rather loosely, and so not all joint ventures will constitute a concentration for the purposes of the ECMR.

9.16   The ECMR provides that a concentration arises when there is an acquisition of 'control'. 'Control' in this context is defined as the possibility of exercising decisive influence over an undertaking (ECMR, art 3(2)). Specifically, a joint venture will constitute a concentration if two or more undertakings (or two or more persons already controlling one or more undertakings) acquire direct or indirect *joint control* over the business in question. The ECMR would not apply to the creation of a joint venture, therefore, where only one of the participants has control and the others have only a minority interest[4], or where no shareholder or group of shareholders is able to exercise control.

---

3   This limitation does not apply to EC Treaty, art 102 (EU member states may adopt stricter national laws which prohibit or sanction unilateral conduct), nor to the application of national merger control laws, subject to general principles and other provisions of EU law.
4   Unless this has involved a change in control.

Joint control

9.17   Control may be determined by both legal and factual considerations and it is not necessary to be able to demonstrate that control is actually exercised: the mere possibility of its exercise is sufficient (see Commission Consolidated Jurisdictional Notice[5]). The essence of control is the ability to determine the strategic commercial behaviour of the joint venture and is characterised by the possibility of a deadlock situation resulting from the power of two or more parent companies to reject proposed strategic decisions.

9.18   Joint control can arise though equality of shareholdings or voting rights, or equality in respect of appointments to the board, provided that the other terms of the arrangement are consistent with the principle of equality between the parent companies. The mere existence of a casting vote will not necessarily preclude joint control if it is available essentially only as a last resort[6].

9.19   It is irrelevant to the concept of joint control that one shareholder has more than a 50% interest in the share capital of the joint venture. Control may also arise through the ability to block strategic decisions by exercise of a right of veto. The types of veto rights which are commonly considered to give rise to joint control are in respect of:

● the budget;

● the appointment of key officers and management;

● the business plan; and

● control over major investments.

9.20   However, each case must be assessed on its facts and it may be a question of degree, eg the level of investment over which there is a right of veto or the amount of detail in the business plan. There are no hard and fast rules, and much will depend on the context. It is often difficult to distinguish veto rights which essentially exist to protect the financial interests of a minority or passive investor and those which, in the round, confer joint control. It is clear, however, that a veto right which does not relate to strategic commercial policy or which does not fall within any of the above categories cannot be regarded as giving joint control to its owner[7].

9.21   Joint control may be found even in the absence of specific veto rights, eg where minority shareholders act together in exercising their voting rights to give them a majority vote or exceptionally because there is such a strong

---

5   OJ [2008] C95/1.
6   See, for example, *British Telecom/Banco Santander* IV/M.425, *RTL/Veronica/Endemol*, IV/M.553 and *Pirelli/Edizione/Olivetti/Telecom Italia*, IV/M.2574.
7   *SITA-RPC/SCORI*, IV/M.295.

community of interest that the majority shareholder cannot act without regard to the interests of the minority.

Full-function

9.22   In addition, a joint venture will only give rise to a concentration if it is deemed to be *'full-function'*.

The ECMR sets out the concept of a 'full-function' joint venture in art 3(4), referring to a joint venture 'performing on a lasting basis all the functions of an autonomous economic entity'. What this means is further explained by the Commission Consolidated Jurisdictional Notice[8]. A joint venture will be full-function if it operates on a market, performing functions normally carried out by undertakings operating in the same market; it must have a management team dedicated to its day-to-day operations and access to sufficient resources, including finance, staff and tangible and intangible assets, in order to conduct its business activities on a lasting basis[9].

9.23   Most examples of full-function joint ventures falling within the ECMR have involved some structural change, ie the establishment of a joint venture company. However in *Alitalia/KLM*[10], the Commission examined a contractual joint venture under the ECMR for the first time.

9.24   A joint venture will not be full-function where it only takes over one specific function of the joint venturers, without separate access to the market (eg research and development, design, production or computer services), or where it only acts as an agent of the joint venturers when making sales. However, if the joint venture acts as principal, but makes sales through the distribution network of one of its parents, and in that context the latter acts as agent of the joint venture, this will not, of itself, result in loss of full-function status[11].

CASE EXAMPLE

9.25   In Case C-248/16 *Austria Asphalt GmbH & Co OG v Bundeskartellanwalt* the CJEU looked at this area and the decision is useful so is set out in large part:

'Consideration of the question referred

15   By its question, the referring court asks, in essence, whether Article 3(1)(b) and (4) of Regulation No 139/2004 must be

---

8   OJ [2008] C95/1.
9   See by contrast *RSB/Tenex/Fuel Logistic* IV/M.904, where no concentration was found to arise.
10   IV/JV.19.
11   *TNT/Canada Post* IV/M.102.

interpreted to the effect that a concentration is deemed to be created following a change in the form of control of an existing undertaking which, previously exclusive, becomes joint, only if the joint venture resulting from such a transaction performs on a lasting basis all the functions of an autonomous economic entity.

16   In order to answer that question, it should be noted that, according to Article 3(1)(b) of that regulation, a concentration is to be deemed to arise, inter alia, where a change of control on a lasting basis results from the acquisition, by one or more undertakings, of direct or indirect control of the whole or parts of one or more other undertakings.

17   However, according to Article 3(4) of the regulation, the creation of a joint venture is a concentration within the meaning Article 3(1)(b) thereof only where that undertaking performs on a lasting basis all of the functions of an autonomous economic entity.

18   Consequently, it cannot be determined from the wording of Article 3 of the regulation alone whether a concentration, within the meaning of that regulation, is deemed to arise as a result of a transaction by which the sole control of an existing undertaking becomes joint when the joint venture resulting from such a transaction does not perform all the functions of an autonomous economic entity.

19   Such a transaction, on the one hand, implies a change of control on a lasting basis of the undertaking forming the object of that transaction, thereby satisfying one of the criteria laid down in Article 3(1)(b) of that regulation and, on the other, may be regarded as creating a joint venture and thereby falling within the scope of Article 3(4) of that regulation, so that a concentration would be deemed to be created only if that undertaking performed on a lasting basis all the functions of an autonomous economic entity.

20   When a textual interpretation of a provision of EU law does not permit its precise scope to be assessed, the provision in question must be interpreted by reference to its purpose and general structure (see, to that effect, judgments of 31 March 1998, *France and Others v Commission*, C68/94 and C30/95, EU:C:1998:148, paragraph 168, and of 7 April 2016, *Marchon Germany*, C315/14, EU:C:2016:211, paragraphs 28 and 29).

21   As regards the objectives pursued by Regulation No 139/2004, it appears from recitals 5 and 6 thereof that the regulation seeks to ensure that the process of reorganisation of undertakings does not result in lasting damage to competition. According to those recitals, EU law must therefore include provisions governing those concentrations that may significantly impede effective competition

in the internal market or in a substantial part of it and permitting effective control of all concentrations in terms of their effect on the structure of competition in the European Union. Accordingly, that regulation should apply to significant structural changes the impact of which on the market goes beyond the national borders of any one Member State.

22   Therefore, as is apparent from recital 20 of the regulation, the concept of concentration must be defined in such a manner as to cover operations bringing about a lasting change in the control of the undertakings concerned and therefore in the structure of the market. Thus, as regards joint ventures, these must be included within the ambit of the regulation if they perform on a lasting basis all the functions of an autonomous economic entity.

23   In that regard, as the Advocate General stated in point 28 of her Opinion, Regulation No 139/2004 does not draw any distinction in its recitals between a newly created undertaking resulting from such a transaction and an existing undertaking hitherto subject to sole control by a group which passes to the joint control of several undertakings.

24   That lack of a distinction is entirely justified due to the fact that, although the creation of a joint venture must be assessed by the Commission as regards its effects on the structure of the market, the realisation of such effects depends on the actual emergence of a joint venture into the market, that is to say, of an undertaking performing on a lasting basis all the functions of an autonomous economic entity.

25   Article 3 of the regulation therefore concerns joint ventures only in so far as their creation provokes a lasting effect on the structure of the market.

26   Such an interpretation is supported by Article 3(1)(b) of the regulation which takes as the constituent element of the concept of concentration not the creation of an undertaking but a change in the control of an undertaking.

27   To follow the converse interpretation of Article 3 of Regulation No 139/2004, such as that espoused, inter alia, by the Commission, would lead to an unjustified difference in treatment between, on the one hand, undertakings newly created as a result of the transaction in question, which would be covered by the concept of concentration only if they performed on a lasting basis all the functions of autonomous economic entities, and, on the other, undertakings existing before such a transaction, which would be covered by that concept regardless of whether, once the transaction is completed, they performed those functions on a lasting basis.

28   It follows that, in the light of the objectives pursued by the regulation, Article 3(4) thereof must be interpreted as referring to the creation of a joint venture, that is to say to a transaction as a result of which an undertaking controlled jointly by at least two other undertakings emerges in the market, regardless of whether that undertaking, now jointly controlled, existed before the transaction in question.

29   Such an interpretation of Article 3 is also consonant with the general scheme of the regulation.

30   Although it is certainly true that, according to recital 6 of the regulation, the preventative control of all concentrations established under that regulation concerns concentrations having an effect on the structure of competition in the European Union, it does not follow that any action of undertakings not producing such effects escapes the control of the Commission or that of the competent national competition authorities.

31   That regulation, like, in particular, Regulation (EC) No 1/2003, forms part of a legislative whole intended to implement Articles 101 and 102 TFEU and to establish a system of control ensuring that competition is not distorted in the internal market of the European Union.

32   As follows from Article 21(1) of Regulation No 139/2004, that regulation alone is to apply to concentrations as defined in Article 3 of the regulation, to which Regulation No 1/2003 is not, in principle, applicable.

33   By contrast, Regulation No 1/2003 continues to apply to the actions of undertakings which, without constituting a concentration within the meaning of Regulation No 139/2004, are nevertheless capable of leading to coordination between undertakings in breach of Article 101 TFEU and which, for that reason, are subject to the control of the Commission or of the national competition authorities.

34   The Commission's interpretation of Article 3 of Regulation No 139/2004, according to which a change in the control of an undertaking which, previously exclusive, becomes joint is covered by the concept of concentration even if the undertaking does not perform on a lasting basis all the functions of an autonomous economic entity is not, therefore, consistent with Article 21(1) thereof. Such an interpretation would effectively extend the scope of the preventative control laid down in that regulation to transactions which are not capable of having an effect on the structure of the market in question and would, at the same time, limit the scope of Regulation No 1/2003, which would then no

longer be applicable to such transactions, even though they may lead to coordination between undertakings within the meaning of Article 101 TFEU.

35   Having regard to all of the foregoing considerations, the answer to the question referred is that Article 3 of Regulation No 139/2004 must be interpreted as meaning that a concentration is deemed to arise upon a change in the form of control of an existing undertaking which, previously exclusive, becomes joint, only if the joint venture created by such a transaction performs on a lasting basis all the functions of an autonomous economic entity'.

9.26   The presence of the joint venturers in upstream or downstream markets is a factor to be considered, particularly where this leads to substantial sales and purchases between the joint venture and the parent companies[12]: if trading with its parent companies is likely to comprise a significant proportion of its activities, the joint venture is unlikely to be full-function, although it may be if such trading is only expected to last for a short, initial period (normally not more than three years) in order to establish the joint venture on the market as an independent undertaking[13]. Another relevant factor is whether sales to the joint venturers are made on normal commercial terms – if not, this could indicate that the joint venture is not full-function.

9.27   Finally, in order to be full-function, the joint venture must be intended to operate on a lasting basis. The allocation of sufficient resources to enable it to operate on its own will normally demonstrate that this is the case. On the other hand, a joint venture established for a specific project of short, finite duration will not usually be regarded as full-function.

9.28   Nevertheless, the fact that the joint venture agreement contains provisions for its termination or the withdrawal of a joint venturer in certain circumstances, such as business failure or disagreement, will not necessarily prevent it from being regarded as existing on a lasting basis. Nor will the fact that the agreement specifies a fixed duration period for the joint venture in itself mean that it cannot be full-function, as long as the duration is sufficient to bring about a lasting change in the structure of the undertakings concerned. The Commission Notice does not specify any period, but seven years has been held to be long enough[14] and three years not enough[15].

---

12   *Preussag/Voest-Alpine* IV/M.979.

13   See, for example, *Mannesmann/RWE/Deutsche Bank* IV/M.394 and *Eastman Kodak/Sun Chemical* IV/M.1042.

14   *Go Ahead/VIA/Thameslink* IV/M.901

15   *BT/Banco Santander* IV/M.425, Lehman Brothers/Starwood/Le Meridien, COMP/M.3858.

9.29 A joint venture will be considered not to be full-function for as long as there remains outstanding decisions of third parties that are essential in order for the joint venture to start its business activity, for example in a tendering scenario where the final selection has not been made. However, once the outstanding decision is taken, full functionality arises.

Are the relevant thresholds exceeded?

9.30 A joint venture will fall within the ECMR if it has a 'Community dimension', ie if:

(a) the combined aggregate worldwide turnover of all the undertakings concerned is more than €5,000m; and

(b) the aggregate Community-wide turnover of each of at least two of the undertakings concerned is more than €250m,

unless each of the undertakings concerned achieves more than two-thirds of its aggregate Community-wide turnover in one and the same member state.

9.31 If this first set of thresholds is not met, a second set must be considered. These were first introduced in March 1998 in order to capture cross-border joint ventures which might otherwise have involved multiple national filings. They provide that there will also be a 'Community dimension' where:

(a) the combined aggregate worldwide turnover of all the undertakings concerned is more than €2,500m;

(b) in each of at least three member states, the combined aggregate turnover of all the undertakings concerned is more than €100m;

(c) in each of the same member states within (b), the aggregate turnover of each of at least two of the undertakings concerned is more than €25m; and

(d) the aggregate Community-wide turnover of each of at least two of the undertakings concerned is more than €100m,

unless each of the undertakings concerned achieves more than two-thirds of its aggregate Community-wide turnover within one and the same member state.

9.32 The calculation of 'turnover' for this purpose is a matter of some complexity, particularly in the case of joint ventures. The Commission Consolidated Jurisdictional Notice gives guidance on calculation of turnover and on the meaning of the term 'undertakings concerned'.

Undertakings concerned

9.33   Where joint control is acquired of a newly created joint venture company, the 'undertakings concerned' for the purposes of calculating the turnover thresholds are each of the companies acquiring joint control of the new company.

9.34   Where the joint venture entity already exists, and two or more companies acquire joint control over it, the 'undertakings concerned' are all the companies acquiring joint control, and the joint venture company itself. This situation would arise where joint venturers co-operate in acquiring control of an existing company in which neither previously had a controlling interest. If the acquisition of joint control is effected by means of an intermediate vehicle, effectively a shell company, the European Commission would look through the vehicle and treat each of its controlling shareholders as undertakings concerned for the purposes of assessing jurisdiction.

9.35   Where the joint venture vehicle is under the sole control of one of the participants, and one or more other shareholders acquires joint control alongside the original sole controller, the undertakings concerned are each of the joint controllers (including the original shareholder) but not the joint venture company itself, because its turnover is already taken into account as part of the turnover of the original sole controller. This includes where one undertaking contributes a pre-existing subsidiary or business to a newly created joint venture.

9.36   Where a company has a shareholding in the joint venture vehicle which carries rights falling short of joint control, it is not an 'undertaking concerned', but if it contributes assets, any turnover attributable to those assets should be taken into account. The retained businesses of the minority shareholder are disregarded in these circumstances (ECMR, art 5(2)).

9.37   Where interests in a joint venture are restructured, either through the exit or addition of a controlling shareholder, the key factor is whether there is consequently a change in the nature or quality of control. The entry or substitution of a controlling shareholder will normally be regarded as a significant change in the quality of control and constitute a concentration. Each of the controlling shareholders and the joint venture are undertakings concerned in such circumstances.

9.38   A concentration can arise where there is a change from joint control to sole control, such as where the joint venture is terminated and one shareholder buys out the other or others. In this case, the undertakings concerned are the remaining shareholder and the joint venture; the selling shareholders are excluded.

9.39   For the avoidance of doubt, it should be noted that the vendor of the whole or part of a business is not an undertaking concerned, save where it retains joint control.

Calculation of turnover

9.40   When assessing whether or not the turnover thresholds are met, it is necessary to include not only the turnover of the 'undertakings concerned', but also that of their broader groups, essentially any parent companies, all the subsidiaries of the parent(s), and of the undertaking concerned, and all companies controlled jointly by two or more of any of the above parties.

9.41   For this purpose, a subsidiary should be taken to include any entity in which the parent, directly or indirectly, has:

● ownership of more than half the capital or business assets;

● the power to exercise more than half the voting rights;

● the power to appoint more than half the directors; or

● the right to manage the entity's affairs.

9.42   'Turnover' means net external turnover derived from the ordinary operations of the relevant group (ie the sale of products and provision of services), net of sales rebates, value added tax and other taxes related to turnover. There are special rules for the calculation of turnover of credit and other financial institutions and insurance undertakings. There are special rules for the allocation of the external turnover of a jointly controlled undertaking; essentially, it is shared equally among the joint venturers.

9.43   The turnover to be taken in practice is that for the year covered by the latest available audited accounts, adjusted as may be necessary to reflect the turnover attributable to acquisitions and disposals since the date to which the accounts were prepared. If draft accounts are available for a subsequent year and those figures show a major divergence as to the amount of turnover, the draft figures may be taken into account. Temporary fluctuations in turnover (for example, due to market growth or decline) are ignored.

9.44   The geographical allocation of turnover in general depends on the location of the customer, because that is usually the place where competition for the goods or services occurs. However, again there are special rules for the calculation of turnover of credit and other financial institutions and insurance undertakings, and the Commission's Jurisdictional Notice highlights examples of other sectors where specific considerations may apply. A geographical breakdown of turnover in the various relevant EU member states will not often be found in a company's audited accounts and the Commission will then rely on the best available figures provided by the parties.

9.45   The ECMR also contains anti-avoidance provisions to capture staggered operations structured to try to circumvent the turnover thresholds (ECMR, art 5(2)). Turnover figures should be converted to euros at the average rate for the 12 months concerned (which can be obtained from the European Central Bank website at www.ecb.int).

Notification, implementation and penalties

9.46   Where the ECMR applies, the parties are obliged to notify the joint venture to the European Commission prior to its implementation. Notification may be made as soon as the undertakings concerned are able to demonstrate to the Commission a good faith intention to conclude an agreement, or alternatively following signature of the relevant agreements. The notification must be made jointly by the joint venturers.

9.47   The joint venture agreement may not be implemented before notification and thereafter until either the Commission clears it, or alternatively fails to make a decision within the time allowed (art 7(1)). In practice, this means that where it is thought that the ECMR will apply, the agreement should be made conditional on approval being obtained, and no steps should be taken to implement it (eg by issuing shares to the joint venturers or transferring assets to the joint venture) until it has been cleared. As a contractual matter, the parties may agree to use all reasonable endeavours to obtain clearance. The extent to which the parties should be free to walk away if the Commission raises serious concerns is a matter for negotiation between the parties. However, it is not uncommon for the parties to commit to accepting reasonable conditions which may be imposed in order to win approval.

9.48   A derogation from the suspension requirement may be sought, but it is rare for the Commission to grant such a request. In deciding whether or not to grant a derogation, the Commission takes into account the likely effects of the suspension on the parties and on third parties, and the threat to competition posed by the joint venture. A derogation may be made subject to conditions and obligations to ensure effective competition is maintained pending a final decision.

9.49   Notification is made on Form CO (concentration). This requires a great deal of information, so it is prudent to begin to prepare it substantially in advance of notification and also to discuss the likely key issues and information requirements with the Commission beforehand. The parties may decide to make a pre-notification request for referral of the merger to the national authorities of an EU member state (see paras 9.73ff, below), and informal discussions with the European Commission are likely to be advisable in these circumstances also. The Commission may be prepared to waive certain of the information requirements if they are not strictly necessary. A shorter version of Form CO may generally be used for joint ventures which satisfy the following criteria (a 'short-form' notification):

• the turnover of the joint venture and/or the contributed activities is less than €100m in the EEA territory and the total value of the assets transferred to the joint venture is less than €100m in the EEA territory;

• none of the parties to the joint venture is engaged in activities within the same product and geographic market (no 'horizontal' overlap) or in a market which is upstream or downstream of a market in which another party is engaged (no 'vertical' relationship);

• if there is a horizontal overlap, the combined market share of the parties to the joint venture is less than 15%, and/or to the extent that there is any vertical overlap the combined share of the parties at either level is less than 25%; or

• one of the parties to a joint venture acquires sole control over the undertaking.

In 2011 the EU issued its 'Best Practices for the submission of economic evidence and data collection in cases concerning the application of Articles 101 and 102 TFEU and in merger cases' (https://ec.europa.eu/competition/antitrust/legislation/best_practices_submission_en.pdf), which provides useful guidance for those submitting economic evidence on a merger notification.

9.50   Parties who intentionally or negligently fail to notify a concentration prior to its implementation may be fined up to 10% of their aggregate worldwide turnover. Fines may also be incurred if complete and correct information is not given to the Commission, either at the outset or in response to a request for further information, or in certain other cases if there is a lack of co-operation during the procedure. Periodic fines may also be imposed in certain circumstances.

Consideration by the Commission

9.51   After notification, the European Commission is required to examine the transaction to see if it is incompatible with the common market, essentially if it 'significantly impedes effective competition' ('SIEC'), in particular as a result of the creation or strengthening of a dominant position. If the answer to this is judged to be 'yes', it must be blocked (unless this can be remedied by commitments); if 'no', it must be cleared. The SIEC test was introduced in May 2004 as part of the EC merger reform package and replaces the 'pure' dominance test.

9.52   The ECMR states that the Commission must take into account:

(a)   the need to maintain and develop effective competition within the common market in view of, among other things, the structure of the relevant markets and actual or potential competition from undertakings within or outside the EU; and

(b)   the market position of the undertakings concerned and their economic and financial power, available alternative products or services, access of suppliers and users to supplies or markets, barriers to entry, supply and demand trends for the relevant goods and services, the interests of intermediate and ultimate consumers, and the development of technical and economic progress, provided this is to consumers' advantage and does not form an obstacle to competition.

9.53   The Commission has broadly followed the criteria applied under art 102 of the EC Treaty (prohibiting an abuse of dominant position) when assessing whether or not to allow a concentration. The Commission has confirmed that it will continue to apply the dominance principles that it and the European courts have developed over the years in assessing whether or not there is an SIEC, and has issued detailed guidelines on the assessment of horizontal mergers[16]. However, the new SIEC test expressly enables the Commission to intervene in relation to transactions which do not technically create or strengthen an individual or joint dominant position, but which nevertheless remove important competitive constraints that the parties previously exerted on one another and on other competitors (see *T-Mobile/ tele.ring*, COMP/M.3916).

9.54   A full-function joint venture within the ECMR may also be subject to scrutiny under art 101 criteria if its object or effect is the co-ordination of the competitive behaviour of the joint venturers as regards those aspects of their activities that are outside the joint venture.

9.55   The SIEC test is applied to the structural elements, to determine whether the creation of the particular full-function joint venture is compatible with the common market. The art 101 analysis is then applied to the co-operative elements to assess whether they will result in an appreciable restriction of competition (pursuant to ECMR, art 2(4)).

9.56   In making its appraisal of the co-ordination aspects, the Commission is particularly required to take into account (ECMR, art 2(5)):

---

16   OJ [2004] C31/5.

- whether the joint venturers retain to a significant extent activities in the same market as the joint venture or in an upstream or downstream market or in a closely related neighbouring market; and

- whether the co-ordination which is the direct consequence of the creation of the joint venture affords the undertakings concerned the possibility of eliminating competition in respect of a substantial part of the products or services in question.

9.57   The Commission is unlikely to invoke the art 2(4) analysis unless at least two parent companies are also active in the joint venture's market or where the 'spill-over effects' in upstream, downstream or neighbouring markets are likely to have a significant anti-competitive impact. Any potential co-ordination between one of the joint venturers and the venture itself is generally considered to be less important for ECMR purposes. The markets which are considered under ECMR, art 2(4) have been termed the 'candidate markets'.

9.58   In assessing the likelihood of co-ordination on the candidate markets, the Commission will consider, for example, the nature of the products/services concerned, the market position of the parties (generally a combined share below 10% will not create significant difficulties), the market structure and whether there are in reality any incentives for the parties to collude. There may be a greater likelihood of co-ordination if two or more parent companies retain significant activities in the joint venture's market. There must also be a degree of causality between the creation of the concentrative joint venture and the likely broader co-ordination between the parent companies.

9.59   The Commission will decide on an in-depth, 'second phase' investigation if it has serious doubts as to whether the joint venture is compatible with the common market. A second phase investigation can be avoided by the acceptance of undertakings from the parties during the initial investigation stage to allay the Commission's concerns. For example, in *Skandia/Storebrand/Pohjola*[17], a divestiture undertaking was agreed. In *Alitalia/KLM*[18] the parties agreed, among other things, to make airport slots available to new entrants, reduce frequencies on particular routes to facilitate successful entry, and to give up tying in certain markets. In *Fujitsu/Siemens*[19] Siemens agreed to divest its interest in an affiliate to address concerns about co-ordination in one of the candidate markets. Undertakings may also be proposed during a second phase investigation to deal with significant concerns. Commitments must be offered within a certain period and the Commission has published a Notice giving guidance on commitments that are likely to be acceptable

---

17   IV/JV.21.
18   IV/JV.19.
19   IV/JV.22.

(eg divestiture or behavioural undertakings) and on related procedural issues[20].

9.60   The Commission is given only a limited time to reach a decision, initially 25 working days from notification, although this may be extended to 35 working days in certain circumstances. If an in-depth investigation is necessary, a further 90 working days are allowed. This period can also be extended in certain circumstances by a maximum of 35 working days. If no decision is taken within the relevant periods, the concentration is deemed to be cleared (although the Commission has the power to suspend these time limits in exceptional circumstances). In addition to the parties, third parties showing a sufficient interest have a right to comment, and member states' competent authorities must also be consulted.

9.61   The Commission may attach conditions or obligations to a decision. Breach of an obligation may lead, in addition to fines, to revocation of a clearance decision, as may the provision of incorrect information in some instances.

9.62   A simplified procedure applies to certain concentrations that are likely to raise no substantive issues[21]. In such cases, a short-form clearance decision will usually be adopted within the initial 25 working day period and published in the usual way.

3 Ancillary restraints

9.63   A joint venture frequently contains restrictions on the activities of the parent companies in the field assigned to the joint venture and on the activities of the joint venture itself. These will not fall to be considered separately under EC Treaty, arts 101 and 102, and will be deemed to have been cleared by the ECMR procedure, if they are ancillary to the concentration, ie if they are directly related and necessary to its successful operation and go no further than necessary for such purpose.

9.64   It is up to the parties to assess whether the restrictions contained in the joint venture agreements are ancillary. However, the Commission has published a Notice which provides some guidance on the circumstances in which restrictions are likely to be deemed ancillary to a concentration[22]. This Notice deals with a number of restrictions common to joint ventures, such as non-compete covenants, licensing of intellectual property rights and sale and purchase arrangements, each of which is dealt with briefly below.

---

20 OJ [2008] C267/1.
21 Regulation (EC) 139/2004, [2005] C56/32.
22 'Commission notice on restrictions directly related and necessary to concentrations' [2005] C56/24.

Non-compete covenants

9.65   Covenants accepted by the parent companies (provided they have a controlling interest in the sense explained in para 9.17ff) not to compete with the joint venture for the lifetime of the venture are considered to be ancillary.

9.66   The covenant must also be appropriately limited in scope and in geographic terms. Essentially, it should cover only those products or services and the territory in which the joint venture is active at the outset, or where the joint venturers were active in relation to the relevant goods or services before establishing the joint venture. It is intended that non-solicitation and confidentiality clauses be treated in a similar way to non-compete covenants to the extent that they are designed to prevent competition between the parties. Such clauses should be more readily justifiable than non-compete restrictions, as they are usually narrower in scope.

CASE EXAMPLE

9.67   In *Telefónica* (2016) that company and PT (Portugal Telecom), the biggest telecoms operators in Spain and Portugal, jointly controlled Vivo, one of the largest telecoms operators in Brazil. In September 2010, Telefónica and PT agreed that Telefónica would buy out PT's stake in Vivo. The Share Purchase Agreement (SPA) included a non-compete clause which provided that, to the extent permitted by law, the parties would refrain from competing in the Spanish and Portuguese telecoms markets. The duration of the clause was from September 2010 to December 2011. In January 2011 the European Commission opened an investigation for breach of competition law, which prompted the parties to remove the clause in February 2011. The European Commission concluded its investigation in February 2013, deciding that the clause amounted to a market sharing agreement with the object of restricting competition in the internal market. It fined Telefónica and PT €67 million and €12 million respectively. The parties appealed the European Commission's decision to the General Court, but the General Court dismissed the appeal almost entirely.

Sheila Tormey of William Fry usefully summarised key issues in the case as follows:

'Whilst the full facts of the case are complex, two of the more important points are as follows:

- Under EU competition law, non-compete clauses in SPAs may be deemed compliant as long as they are directly related to, and necessary for, the implementation of the transaction. The European Commission found that a non-compete clause covering the Spanish and Portuguese markets could not be considered directly related to or necessary for Telefónica's buy-out of PT's stake in Vivo in Brazil, and this finding was upheld by the General Court.

• The parties argued that the clause did not constitute a restriction of competition by object, since the European Commission had not demonstrated that they were potential competitors and that the clause was therefore capable of restricting competition. The General Court held that the Commission was not obliged to carry out detailed analysis on this point, as the very existence of the clause was a strong indication of potential competition between Telefónica and PT'.

See also June 2016 CJEU press release at http://curia.europa.eu/jcms/upload/docs/application/pdf/2016-06/cp160068en.pdf. Cases T-208/13, *Portugal Telecom SGPS, SA v Commission*, and T-216/13, *Telefónica, SA v Commission*.

9.68 Suggestions on drafting a typical non-compete covenant are contained in Precedent 3, with an accompanying commentary set out in para 10.55ff.

Licensing of intellectual property rights

9.69 The licensing of intellectual property rights to a joint venture, even on an exclusive or perpetual basis, may be regarded as ancillary. Any limitation on field of use or territory would be acceptable, assuming it reflected the allocation of a specific function or territory to the joint venture. Licences granted by the joint venture to one of its parents, or cross-licence agreements, can be regarded as ancillary in similar circumstances. Licence agreements between parent companies will not, however, be considered ancillary.

9.70 Even if a patent or know-how licence would not be regarded as ancillary, it might nevertheless be possible to draft it to fall within the block exemption for technology transfer agreements (see para 9.119)[23]. That regulation is also 'retained EU law' following Brexit and applies to exempt the provisions within its terms from UK competition law in the Competition Act 1998 as well as under EU competition law.

Supply and purchase agreements

9.71 The existence of long-term purchase and supply commitments between a joint venture and its parents may undermine the full-function

---

23   Commission Regulation (EC) 316/2014 and see the accompanying IPR Guidelines of the EU (replacing Regulation 772/2004).

nature of the joint venture. Also, they are unlikely to be regarded as ancillary if they go further than merely safeguarding continuity of supplies for a transitional period (usually around five years)[24]. Agreements that provide for fixed quantities of supply will be ancillary, but agreements that grant exclusivity or preferred customer/supplier status are unlikely to be so. However, the block exemption for vertical agreements[25] and accompanying guidelines may provide some guidance in relation to whether supply agreements which are not ancillary would otherwise be compatible with art 101 of the EC Treaty.

4 Application of national merger and competition laws

9.72   In principle, the application of the ECMR excludes national competition laws of the EU member states, although member states can take measures to the extent necessary to safeguard other legitimate interests, eg their prudential rules, plurality of the media or certain aspects of sector specific regulation. It does not apply in the UK as the UK is not part of the EU. Any such action must still be compatible with Community law. For example, in 1999, the Commission ordered the suspension of measures Portugal had taken to block the acquisition by Banco Santander of joint control of the Champalimaud group of financial companies. It subsequently brought legal proceedings before the ECJ to compel compliance. These proceedings were subsequently withdrawn following completion of an acceptable transaction.

9.73   In certain circumstances, even if a concentration exceeds the jurisdictional thresholds of the ECMR, the parties to the concentration or a member state may ask that the whole or part of it be referred back to its own competent authorities for review. The parties may make such a request to the Commission prior to notification, but the Commission is not obliged to agree to such a request and may not do so if the member state to which the parties seek referral disagrees with the request. A referral back may also be requested by a member state (either on its own initiative or upon the invitation of the Commission) within 15 working days of receiving a copy of the Form CO notification from the Commission. Broadly, these referral provisions are applicable where a concentration affects competition on a distinct market within a member state.

9.74   If the European Commission were to decide that the concentration should be reviewed by a member state, that state's national merger control laws would apply.

---

24 Notice on restrictions directly related and necessary to concentrations [2005] C56/24.
25 Commission Regulation (EC) 330/2010 and accompanying Vertical Guidelines. This is due to be replaced by a similar regulation by 1 June 2022.

9.75   In addition, the parties to a concentration, or one or more member states, may request that a case which falls below the ECMR thresholds be dealt with by the European Commission under the ECMR in certain circumstances if trade between member states is affected. The parties may make such a request prior to making any national filings if the merger is capable of being reviewed by three or more member states. If at least one member state competent to examine the merger under its national legislation disagrees with the request, the Commission cannot grant the request. If, however, none of the competent member states disagrees, there is a deemed Community Dimension, and the Commission will review the merger under the ECMR.

9.76   One or more member states may also make such a request on their own initiative within 15 working days of receiving a national merger notification from the parties, or of being made aware of the concentration, if notification is not required. The Commission may also invite relevant member states to make such a request. Other member states are given the opportunity to join the request. Those that decline to do so can continue to apply their national merger control laws, if applicable. The European Commission has a discretion as to whether or not to accept the request and, if it does, it will review the merger under the ECMR, and those member states who made or joined in the request are obliged to disapply their national competition laws.

9.77   A concentrative joint venture which falls below the thresholds in the ECMR may be subject to review by the national authorities of the member states under their merger control or general competition laws. To the extent such a joint venture also involves co-operative elements, they may also be considered under art 101 of the EC Treaty.

5 Joint ventures within EC Treaty, art 101

When does art 101 apply?

9.78   As explained above, art 101 could apply in the EU to the co-operative elements of concentrative joint ventures falling outside the ECMR, as well as to restraints which are not ancillary to the concentration.

9.79   In addition, if a joint venture is not concentrative, so that it does not fall to be reviewed under the ECMR, it will fall within art 101(1) of the EC Treaty if:

- its object or effect is to prevent, restrict or distort competition within the common market; and

- it is capable of having an appreciable effect on trade between member states.

9.80   It is not just the terms of the agreement itself which are put under scrutiny, but also what the parties actually do in practice. Thus, even if a new joint venture agreement is outside art 101, it may later infringe the prohibition if the parties then pursue a course of conduct which has, or is intended to have, anti-competitive effects.

9.81   To be within art 101, the joint venture must appreciably affect trade between member states. The Commission has issued detailed guidance on the circumstances in which an agreement is likely to have an effect on trade between member states[26]. 'Trade between member states' is a broad concept, covering all cross-border economic activity, including establishment. Where the activities of a joint venture are confined to one, or part of one member state, it may nevertheless still have an effect on inter-state trade. For instance, it could possibly result in undertakings in other member states being cut off from an important channel of distribution or source of demand. The Commission gives the example of two or more distributors established within the same member state establishing a purchasing joint venture and combining their purchases of a product: assuming that the distributors account for a substantial share of imports of the products in question, the resulting reduction in the number of distribution channels could limit the possibility for suppliers from other member states to gain access to the national market in question and could, therefore, have an effect on inter-state trade.

9.82   If a joint venture agreement is prohibited under art 101, it is void and unenforceable. Generally this is interpreted to mean that only the particular provisions falling foul of art 101 are void. Nevertheless, there may be circumstances in which the business combination of itself may raise significant competition concerns and may not be permitted to proceed, either at all, or without compliance with stringent conditions.

9.83   Fines may also be imposed for infringement – up to 10% of a group's worldwide turnover in the last financial year – and third parties may seek injunctive relief and claim damages in respect of losses caused by any breach. Fines will reflect, among other things, the gravity and duration of the infringement.

9.84   However, the above consequences are avoided if the agreement satisfies the criteria set out in art 101(3). These criteria are that the joint venture agreement:

- contributes to improving the production or distribution of goods or to promoting technical or economic progress;

- allows consumers a fair share of the resulting benefit;

---

26   OJ [2004] C101/101.

- does not impose restrictions that are not indispensable; and

- does not eliminate competition in respect of a substantial part of the affected products or services.

9.85 Following modernisation of the application of EC competition law on 1 May 2004, the national competition authorities (NCAs) of the EU member states were given the power, and indeed have the obligation, to apply and enforce in full the art 101 and 102 prohibitions in parallel with the European Commission. As stated above, both NCAs and the national courts are required to interpret and apply arts 101 and 102 consistently with the European Commission and the European courts. A Network of Competition Authorities has been created, comprising the European Commission and the NCAs of the EU member states, and the European Commission has issued detailed guidelines explaining how, and on what grounds, cases should be allocated amongst the various authorities[27]. There is also a Notice setting out how the European Commission will co-operate with and assist the national courts in relation to the interpretation of arts 101 and 102 of the EC Treaty, where necessary[28].

9.86 Modernisation also resulted in the abolition of the notification system, with the result that it is now firmly the responsibility of the parties to a joint venture to assess whether their arrangements are compatible with art 101 as a whole, including the art 101(3) criteria referred to above. The Commission has enacted a number of block exemption regulations and Notices which help parties to assess whether or not their joint venture complies with art 101. If an agreement falls within the terms of a block exemption, the parties can be comfortable that it satisfies the art 101(3) criteria (subject to the possibility of withdrawal of the block exemption in certain limited circumstances).

Notice on the application of art 101(3)

9.87 The Commission's Notice on the application of art 101(3)[29] explains how the art 101(3) criteria should be applied. It provides a general analytical framework for the application of art 101(3), explaining, for example, how efficiencies are to be assessed and measured, and the extent to which the parties must be able to demonstrate in practice that these will be passed on to the consumer. It outlines and builds upon past case law and practice.

---

27   OJ [2004] C101/03.
28   OJ [2004] C101/04.
29   OJ [2004] C101/08.

Notice on agreements of minor importance

9.88   The Notice on agreements of minor importance[30] provides that a joint venture will fall outside the scope of art 101 if the combined share of the participating undertakings in any of the relevant markets does not exceed 10% in the case of a horizontal agreement (ie between companies operating at the same level of trade) or 15% in the case of a vertical agreement (where they are operating at different levels of trade for the purposes of the agreement).

9.89   The relevant markets comprise, first, the products or services dealt with by the participating undertakings and any others which are regarded as interchangeable or substitutable for them by reason of their characteristics, price and intended use and, second, the geographic area in which the participating undertakings are active and which can be distinguished from neighbouring areas because of different conditions of competition. Another Commission Notice provides guidance on the definition of relevant markets[31].

9.90   This 'safe harbour' does not apply to certain hardcore restrictions, such as price fixing, limitations on output or sales, market sharing, or provisions conferring absolute territorial protection. Where markets are characterised by networks of similar agreements which cumulatively have an appreciable anti-competitive effect, the safe harbour will only apply if the combined market share of the participating undertakings does not exceed 5%. Nor does it apply where the agreement contains 'restrictions by object' (which are per se illegal) such as was found in Case C-226/11 *Expedia Inc v Autorité de la concurrence*.

9.91   The Notice also states that agreements between small- and medium-sized enterprises (SMEs) will generally not fall within art 101, although again hardcore restrictions with an anti-competitive object, such as price fixing, would not be protected. SMEs are defined by reference to turnover (€50m or less) or assets (€43m or less) and number of employees (fewer than 250)[32].

9.92   Competition authorities are unlikely to investigate agreements covered by this Notice, either on their own initiative or in response to a complaint. Even in the case of agreements containing hardcore restrictions, the European Commission will only intervene if a particular Community interest demands, otherwise leaving enforcement primarily to the member states. In circumstances where the parties legitimately believe the Notice applies, but nevertheless an appreciable restriction on competition is found to exist, fines are unlikely to be imposed.

---

30   2014/C 291/01.
31   OJ [1997] C372/5.
32   See Commission Recommendation 2003/361/EC OJ [2003] L124/36 and see guidance on this at http://ec.europa.eu/growth/smes/business-friendly-environment/sme-definition_en.

Guidelines on horizontal co-operation agreements

9.93   The Commission's Guidelines on horizontal co-operation agreements[33] draws together current Commission practice and places a greater emphasis upon economic criteria. In 2019 the Commission began consulting on a possible replacement of the Guidelines (as at 2021 no replacement has yet been agreed). It is intended to give guidance on horizontal agreements, essentially agreements between two or more companies operating at the same level in the market place, ie agreements between actual or potential competitors. It covers research and development, production and specialisation, purchasing, commercialisation, information exchange (with effect from the 2011 version of the guidelines), standardisation and environmental agreements. It is not designed to cover complex arrangements which have no particular or obvious focus. Nor is it applicable where sector specific rules apply, eg in relation to agreements in the insurance sector. These Guidelines should be read in conjunction with the more general Notice on the application of the art 101(3) criteria, referred to above in para 9.87.

9.94   The Notice explains that if the object of a joint venture is to fix prices, limit output or share markets it will generally be presumed to have negative effects on competition unless such restrictions relate to the specific activities of the joint venture, for example controlling the capacity or production volumes of a joint venture, or where a joint venture sets the prices for products which it is responsible for distributing. Where there is no such object, any possible adverse impact on prices, innovation, variety, quality or output needs to be balanced against any pro-competitive effects of the joint venture.

9.95   The nature of the agreement will be important to the assessment, ie its objectives, the activities covered, the competitive relationship between the parties and the degree of collaboration. In principle, agreements on research and development and standardisation are less likely to have negative effects than collaboration on production or purchasing.

9.96   The following agreements are generally considered to fall outside art 101, subject to the degree of market power possessed by the parties or the extent of the potential for foreclosing opportunities to third parties:

- agreements between non-competitors;

- agreements between competitors if, objectively, the project could not be carried out independently (this might arise in particular if the parties individually did not have the necessary assets, know-how or other resources to engage in the activity[34]); and

---

33   OJ C 11 of 14.1.2011.
34   *Iridium* Decision 97/39/EC, OJ [1997] L16/87.

- co-operation concerning an activity which is sufficiently far removed from the market so as not to influence competition.

9.97 In balancing the pro- and anti-competitive effects of an agreement to assess whether art 101 applies in other circumstances, the following are relevant factors:

- the market power of the parties, both alone and in combination;

- the market structure and degree of market concentration;

- the stability of the market;

- barriers to entry and likelihood of entry;

- the countervailing power of buyers or sellers;

- the nature of the products and the maturity of the market;

- the proximity of the collaboration to the market;

- the scale and significance of the joint venture's activities as against the parents' activities.

9.98 The network effects of interlocking joint ventures will be an important factor also. The greater the links between competitors through joint ventures, particularly in a concentrated market, the more likely an agreement is to fall within art 101.

9.99 For example, the Commission considered that art 101 applied to the creation of 'Open' which was set up by BSkyB, BT, Midland Bank and Matsushita Electric to provide digital interactive television services, principally because of the significant market power of BT and BSkyB in related markets and because their participation eliminated them as potential competitors in the joint venture's market[35].

9.100 Assuming that the agreement falls within the scope of art 101, an assessment of the art 101(3) criteria will be necessary (as set out above in para 9.84). In general it is relatively straightforward to demonstrate economic benefits through, for example, the introduction of new or higher quality products. However, any efficiencies claimed have to be demonstrated and must not arise merely as a result of any restrictions of competition.

9.101 The degree to which consumers will benefit will depend upon the intensity of competition. In the 'Open' joint venture discussed above, the Commission took account of the consumer benefit in technical progress in these emerging media markets. Clearly it will be important to ensure the least restrictive form of collaboration is put in place. An exemption would be precluded where the collaboration amounted to an abuse of a dominant

---

35 Decision 99/781/EC, OJ [1999] L312/1.

position[36]. However, a collaboration involving a dominant player which may lead to the strengthening of its position in the relevant market would not of itself necessarily constitute such an abuse and could potentially merit exemption. For instance, where a dominant undertaking is party to a non-full function joint venture which is found to be restrictive of competition, but which does not risk eliminating competition altogether and is justifiable on the basis that it produces benefits for consumers in the form of reduced prices or greater innovation, an exemption might still be possible under art 101(3)[37].

9.102   The competition authorities may take the view that an agreement does not satisfy the art 101(3) criteria unless certain conditions or obligations are adhered to by the parties. In the past, the Commission has sought and obtained a variety of commitments to address competition concerns identified in the art 101 analysis, for example:

● in the Unisource and Uniworld decisions[38], undertakings were given to prevent discrimination by the parent companies in respect of leased lines and interconnection, to prevent misuse of confidential information, and to prevent cross-subsidies and tying or bundling;

● divestment or dissolution: the participants in 'UIP–Pay TV' were effectively required to dissolve their joint venture in relation to pay television[39]; BT agreed to sell its existing cable TV interests in the UK to win approval for 'Open'[40];

● open access to technology or services (Open).

Research and development agreements

9.103   Agreements on joint research and development, or joint development prior to commercialisation, generally do not fall within art 101 unless they have a significant impact on competition in innovation[41]. In 2019/20 the EU began consulting on revision of this regulation. The regulation exempts agreement not only from EU competition but also, as 'retained EU law' following Brexit from the provisions of the Competition Act 1998 Chapter I prohibition. Relevant considerations include:

● whether there is a potential negative impact on innovation (to ensure that sufficient independent poles of research remain);

---

36 Joined Cases T-191/98, T-212/98 and T-214/98, *Atlantic Container Line (TACA)* [2003] ECR II-3275.
37 OJ [2004] C101/97, paras 106, 107.
38 Commission Decisions 97/780/EC and 97/781/EC, OJ L318/1 and L318/24.
39 European Commission Press Release IP/97/227.
40 Decision 99/781/EC, OJ L312/1.
41 See, for example, *EUCAR* OJ [1997] C185/12 and IP/98/832.

- the extent to which the collaboration may lead to co-ordination of the behaviour of the joint venturers in the market for existing products;

- the degree of foreclosure of third parties, particularly if one of the joint venturers has a significant market position and/or access to key technology.

9.104   For example, the joint venture between Pratt & Whitney and General Electric Aircraft Engines Ltd was found to fall within art 101 on the basis that it would be feasible for both parties to develop the new product independently. Nevertheless, the Commission considered that art 101(3) would be satisfied if the agreements included obligations ensuring the parties' co-operation did not extend to other fields and preventing the exchange of competitively sensitive information (other than in relation to the functioning of the joint venture)[42]. Additional undertakings were agreed to limit the potential foreclosure effects of the co-operation.

9.105   Block Exemption Regulation (EC) 1217/2010 (the R&D block exemption) provides that certain joint ventures engaged in research and development of products or processes and/or the exploitation of the results of joint research and development will satisfy art 101(3) subject to a market share cap. Certain provisions are blacklisted (and prevent the entire arrangement from falling within the scope of the block exemption), such as restrictions on research and development in unrelated areas or on passive sales, active sales restrictions after a certain period, certain no challenge clauses and, with certain exceptions, restrictions on price, output or sales.

Production/specialisation agreements

9.106   Joint production or specialisation agreements will generally fall outside art 101 if, for example:

- they are between non-competitors;

- they simply involve outsourcing or sub-contracting;

- they are agreements between competitors if they compete on a related market but the co-operation is indispensable to enter a new market;

- the parties have a small proportion of their total costs in common.

9.107   The principal issue is the potential incentive for the parties to co-ordinate their competitive behaviour as suppliers. In addition to considering the market directly affected, the Commission will consider potential 'spill-over' effects on upstream, downstream or closely related neighbouring

---

42   Decision 00/182/EC, OJ [2000] L58/16.

markets. However, this will only be relevant if the co-operation in the primary market necessarily leads to co-ordination in the related market, ie if there are sufficient links between them and the parties have a strong market position in such markets.

9.108   Block Exemption Regulation (EC) 1218/2010 (the specialisation block exemption) provides that certain joint ventures in which the parties agree to manufacture certain products jointly, or agree unilaterally or reciprocally to cease production of a product and to purchase it from the other party or from the joint venture will satisfy art 101(3). The block exemption applies provided that the combined market share of the parties does not exceed 20%. Certain ancillary supply and purchase obligations are also covered by the block exemption. Various restrictions are blacklisted (taking the whole arrangement outside the scope of the block exemption), specifically, restrictions on price, market sharing and limitations on output or sales (with certain exceptions).

Joint purchasing

9.109   In this case, the parties would need to consider the potential impact of the joint venture on the purchasing market as well as on the downstream sales market if the parties are competitors in such markets also. The concern is that significant buyer power will lead to prices below competitive levels or significant foreclosure. Where buyers have substantial market power, it is less likely that reduced prices will be passed on to consumers, particularly if the buyers also have a strong position on the downstream market and a high degree of common costs. Joint buying may also increase costs for the group's competitors in certain circumstances.

9.110   Unless it is merely a disguised cartel, the Guidelines on Horizontal Co-operation Agreements suggest that a joint purchasing agreement is unlikely to give rise to significant difficulties if the combined market share of the parties on both the purchasing market and the downstream market is less than 15%.

Commercialisation agreements

9.111   This covers agreements whose focus is joint selling, distribution or promotion. These agreements are generally not within art 101 if they are between non-competitors or where they are objectively necessary to enter a new market. The latter may apply to consortium agreements where no party alone could put together a credible tender (see para 1.26ff).

9.112   The main concern in relation to joint selling is that it is likely to lead to co-ordination of pricing policy and output or market partitioning. While such arrangements are always likely to fall within art 101, they may be capable of exemption in limited circumstances[43].

9.113   The Commission would also be concerned that joint commercialisation arrangements do not lead to the exchange of commercially sensitive information or influence a significant element of the parties' final costs. The Guidelines on Horizontal Co-operation Agreements state that a combined market share of less than 15% may suggest that such an agreement is outside art 101.

Standardisation agreements

9.114   A standardisation agreement is likely to fall outside art 101 if, for example, participation in standard setting arrangements is unrestricted and transparent and there is no obligation on the parties to comply with the standard[44]. The agreement should also not be part of a wider anti-competitive agreement in relation to the affected products or services. There should generally be a clear distinction between the setting of the standard and related research and development or commercial exploitation.

9.115   Article 101 may apply, however, if the collaboration is used to foreclose the market to competitors or to limit the freedom of the participants to develop and sell non-standard models or to develop alternative standards.

9.116   Awarding exclusive rights to test for compliance may be restrictive, as may a restriction on who may apply conformity marking (unless this is imposed by regulatory provisions).

Environmental agreements

9.117   Agreements designed to achieve environmental objectives may fall within art 101 if the arrangement covers a major proportion of the industry and there is an appreciable restriction on the parties' ability to differentiate their products or processes, or if it has a substantial negative effect on the output of third parties[45]. However, the positive environmental impact of an agreement will be highly relevant to the application of art 101(3)[46].

---

43   See, for example, *UIP* Commission Press Release IP/99/681.
44   See, for example, *Stack* 1998 Competition Policy Report, p 153.
45   *Valpak* 1998 Competition Policy Report, p 152.
46   See, for example, *CECED*, Decision 2000/475/EC, OJ L187/47.

Other potentially relevant guidelines and block exemptions

9.118   It should be noted that, in addition to the above, there are a number of other guidelines and block exemptions in existence which may be relevant to joint ventures. This chapter has not gone into detail on all of these here, but mention two in particular for the sake of completeness.

9.119   First, the Technology Transfer Regulation[47], which came into force on 1 May 2014, exempts agreements which license, among other things, patents, know-how, software copyright (or a combination thereof), provided that the market share of the parties does not exceed the specified thresholds and the agreement does not contain any of the listed hardcore restrictions. This block exemption will be relevant where technology licences are required between the joint venture and its parents. As with other such exemptions it is also 'retained EU law' and therefore from 1 January 2021 provides post-Brexit exemption under UK competition law from the Chapter 1 prohibition in the Competition Act 1998 as well.

9.120   Second, the block exemption and guidelines relating to vertical agreements may also be relevant to certain joint ventures, eg where there are supply/purchase agreements or licences between a parent company and the joint venture (to the extent that they are not ancillary to a merger). 'Vertical' agreements are those entered into between two or more parties who operate at different levels of the distribution chain. The Vertical Agreements Block Exemption will not apply if the parties are actual or potential competitors in the manufacture or supply of the products/services in question, subject to limited exceptions. However, the principles set out in the block exemption and related guidelines may provide some guidance as to the types of restriction that may be acceptable in this context[48].

Additional restrictions

9.121   As well as considering the potential impact of the collaboration itself, it is necessary to assess any additional restrictions on competition.

9.122   Restrictions which are ancillary to the joint venture will stand or fall with it. If the joint venture falls outside art 101 altogether, so will the ancillary restrictions, and if it does not satisfy the art 101(3) criteria, neither can the restrictions.

---

47   Commission Regulation (EC) 316/2014 (which replaced regulation 772/2004) and accompanying Intellectual Property Guidelines (2014).
48   Regulation (EC) 330/2010 and accompanying Vertical Guidelines which is due to be replaced by a similar block exemption from 1 June 2022.

9.123   Non-ancillary restrictions on competition will be examined separately; in other words, the joint venture may be exempted and the restrictions may not be.

9.124   By analogy with the principles laid down in the Commission's Notice on ancillary restraints (see para 9.63ff), the following restrictions on the joint venture will normally be regarded as ancillary:

- Contract clauses specifying its product range or production location.

- Where the joint venture involves the creation of additional production capacity or the transfer of technology from one or more joint venturer, an undertaking by the joint venture not to manufacture or market products competing with the licensed products.

- Clauses limiting co-operation to a certain area or specific technical application of transferred technology.

- In the case of full-function joint ventures established to operate at an intermediary stage in the production process, obligations on the joint venture to purchase from or supply the joint venturers, at least during a start-up period.

6 Article 102

9.125   Article 102 prohibits the abuse by one or more undertakings of a dominant position within the common market, or a substantial part of it, in so far as it may affect trade between member states[49]. Examples of what may constitute an abuse are given in art 102:

- directly or indirectly imposing unfair purchase or selling prices or other unfair trading conditions;

- limiting production, markets or technical development to the prejudice of consumers;

- applying dissimilar conditions to equivalent transactions with other parties, so as to place them at a competitive disadvantage;

- making the conclusion of contracts subject to acceptance of supplementary unconnected obligations.

9.126   The mere existence of a dominant position is not prohibited under art 102, only its abuse. However, as discussed above in para 9.101, a joint venture which strengthened a dominant position would be unlikely to fulfil the art 101(3) criteria unless the parties could demonstrate that competition

---

49   For the effect on inter-state trade concept, see para 9.78.

would not be eliminated altogether and that the joint venture would create real benefits for consumers.

Flowchart 2

European Competition Law

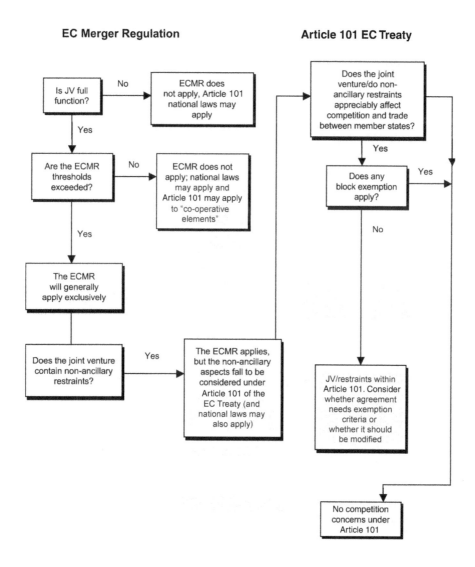

EC Merger Regulation

Article 101 EC Treaty

Chapter 10

UK competition law applying to joint ventures

Summary

This chapter considers the application of UK competition law to joint ventures, including the merger control provisions contained in the Enterprise Act 2002 as amended and the prohibitions on anti-competitive behaviour in the Competition Act 1998. These prohibitions are of similar effect to arts 101 and 102 of the EC Treaty. From 1 January 2021 the UK provisions apply in the UK and the EU merger rules discussed in Chapter 9 apply in the EU. National Security and Investment Act 2021 made the biggest change in 20 years in the field of UK mergers with national security implications.

1 Introduction

10.1 As under EC competition law, joint ventures may fall to be considered under the UK merger control regime (under the Enterprise Act 2002 ('EA 2002')) or under the Competition Act 1998 ('CA 1998'), which contains prohibitions on anti-competitive agreements and the abuse of a dominant position (respectively, the 'Chapter I' and 'Chapter II' prohibitions). The Chapter I and Chapter II prohibitions are closely modelled upon arts 101 and 102 of the EC Treaty, save that there is a requirement that there be an effect on competition and trade within the UK as opposed to an effect on trade between Member States. The Enterprise and Regulatory Reform Act 2013 made some procedural changes to UK merger law.

From April 2014 the Competition and Markets Authority (CMA) took over from its predecessor bodies the Competition Commission and Office of Fair Trading (OFT).

2 Relationship between UK and EC law

10.2 Since 1 January 2021 UK mergers are regulated under UK merger law. However where a merger affects EU states then it may be investigated both by EU and UK merger authorities. Until that date in the case of a full-function concentrative joint venture (as defined under the EC Merger Regulation ('ECMR') – see Chapter 9), UK competition law had to be considered where:

- the joint venture fell below the turnover thresholds set out in the ECMR, particularly where the parties achieved more than two-thirds of their EU turnover in the UK (see para 9.30ff);

- the ECMR applied, but the case was referred to the UK authorities under art 4 or 9 of the ECMR (see para 9.73ff);

- the ECMR applied, but the joint venture contained additional restrictions on competition which are not regarded as ancillary, in which case the UK regime in the CA 1998 could apply those terms, as well as art 101.

This is no longer the case and UK mergers may be subject to a dual regime where they also affect EU states. The CMA hired new staff and estimated that the 2021 changes mean it is likely to review an extra 30–50 transactions each year – a 50% increase.

In addition the National Security and Investment Act 2021 made some major changes to merger law to permit additional state involvement where national security issues arise (see para 10.33).

10.3   A joint venture may not be concentrative for the purposes of EC merger control law, and so fall outside the ECMR, but it may nevertheless constitute a relevant merger situation under the criteria laid down by the EA 2002. For example, there may be material influence for the purposes of UK merger control (see para 10.7 below), but this may fall short of the EC concept of control. If UK merger control does not apply, the CA 1998 and art 101 will nevertheless potentially apply as they regulate 'agreements' and plenty of co-operation agreements fall short of a full merger, but are still anti-competitive.

3 Merger control

When is a joint venture a relevant merger situation?

10.4   UK merger control is governed by the EA 2002. The UK authorities may investigate a joint venture where a 'relevant merger situation' is created. A relevant merger situation is created where:

- two or more enterprises cease to be distinct enterprises, or arrangements are in progress which will bring this about; and

- either:

  - this results in the creation or increase of a share of supply of goods or of services of 25% or more in the UK or a substantial part of it; or

  - the UK turnover of the enterprise being acquired exceeds £70m.

See para 10.34 below for lower thresholds (eg £1m turnover) in certain sensitive sectors which might affect national security.

10.5   An 'enterprise' means the whole or part of the activities of a business (EA 2002, s 129). The term 'business' is widely defined and will essentially embrace any form of business activity, including a professional practice, which is carried on for gain or reward. In making a judgment as to whether certain activities constitute an enterprise, the UK competition authorities will have regard to the substance of the arrangement under consideration rather than its legal form. The transfer of bare assets, such as plant or intellectual property rights, may not amount to an enterprise, but the surrounding circumstances are important, including whether turnover directly related to those assets is transferred. So, for example, if a company ceases to trade and sells the residual assets to a competitor, a merger situation may arise if this has the effect in practice (and taking into account the surrounding facts) of effectively transferring the activities of a business or part of a business to the acquirer (see, for example, the Monopolies and Mergers Commission (now the Competition Commission/Competition and Markets Authority) Report on *AAH Holdings plc/Medicopharma NV* (March 1992) and see also the Reports on *William Cook plc acquisitions* (August 1990) and *Stagecoach Holdings plc/Lancaster City Transport Limited* (December 1993)). In *Arcelor SA/Corus UK Limited* (February 2005), the Competition Commission/Competition and Markets Authority considered that the transfer of goodwill, employees, business information and business records was an enterprise despite there being no transfer of premises.

10.6   In *Société Coopérative de Production SeaFrance SA (Respondent) v The Competition and Markets Authority and another (Appellants)*[1] the UK Supreme Court held that the merger control provisions of the Enterprise Act 2002 are not limited to the acquisition of a business that is a 'going concern'. The possession of 'activities' is a descriptive characteristic of an enterprise under the Act. An enterprise is subject to merger control if the capacity to perform those activities as part of the same business subsists.

The court in its press summary said:

'The test is one of economic continuity. An Acquirer acquiring assets acquires an "enterprise" where (i) those assets give the Acquirer more than might have otherwise been acquired by going into the market and buying factors of production and (ii) the extra is attributable to the fact that the assets were previously employed in combination in the "activities" of the target enterprise. The period of time between cessation of trading and acquisition of control of the assets may be a relevant factor, but is not necessarily decisive.

1   [2015] UKSC 75, on appeal from [2015] EWCA Civ 487.

This was substantially the same principle set out by the Competition Appeal Tribunal in *Eurotunnel I*, which the Competition and Markets Authority applied in this case. The Court of Appeal's finding that the Authority's evaluation was irrational was unjustified. GET and SCOP acquired substantially all the assets of SeaFrance, including trademarks, goodwill, specialist vessels maintained in a serviceable condition, and substantially the same personnel. The Authority's conclusion that this demonstrated "considerable continuity and momentum" and "the embers of an enterprise", which could be passed to GET and SCOP, was unimpeachable. The order of the French Court of 9 January 2012 to dismiss the employees did not disrupt that continuity and momentum because the order was made on terms that the PS3 preserved the prospect of employment on the ships for the dismissed crew members.

The majority of the Court of Appeal was wrong to narrow the question of economic continuity to the legal effect of the decision of the French Court in January 2012 and whether this terminated the employment relationship between SeaFrance and its employees. The Competition and Markets Authority is not entitled to any special level of deference: the test for determining whether there is a "relevant merger situation" and relevant "activities" is a legal question. But the Authority undertook a broader economic analysis, concluding that there was economic continuity. That evaluation was complex and sensitive to a whole range of factors. It was not a purely legal enquiry. Its economic analysis should be respected.'

When do enterprises cease to be distinct?

10.7   Two or more enterprises cease to be distinct if they are brought under common ownership or control (EA 2002, s 26).

10.8   For these purposes, control may be acquired at three levels. Firstly, control is acquired when a person acquires the ability to 'materially influence' the policy of another undertaking. Material influence is likely to arise by virtue of a shareholding of more than 25% but may also be acquired through a shareholding as low as 15%, particularly in combination with other factors, such as presence on the board, other strong economic links or an otherwise fragmented shareholder base. For example, the acquisition by Vivendi SA of a 24.44% stake in BSkyB, together with the right to appoint a board director, against the background of the scope and incentives for co-operation between the two groups, were considered to confer this type of control (CC Report, April 2000). More recently, the acquisition by BSkyB of a 17.9% shareholding in ITV was found to give BSkyB material influence over ITV (*BSkyB/ITV,*

December 2007). BSkyB's shareholding, considered in both absolute and relative terms, was found by the then Competition Commission to be such that, on the basis of past voting patterns, BSkyB would be able to block special resolutions proposed by ITV's management and thereby to limit some of ITV's strategic options. The Competition Commission also considered that BSkyB's importance and stature as an industry player, together with its position as the largest shareholder, would mean that considerable weight would be given to BSkyB's views. In certain circumstances, control may arise in the absence of any equity interest at all (see *Stora Kopparbergs Bergslags AB/ Swedish Match*, March 1991).

10.9   Secondly, control will arise if a person has the ability to control the policy of an undertaking, for example through the ability in practice to control more than half the votes actually cast at shareholder meetings, even where it does not have a controlling interest (*de facto* control), or thirdly, if a person has a controlling interest (*de jure* control). Moving from one level of control to another, for example from having material influence to a position of *de facto* control, will give rise to a merger for EA 2002 purposes.

10.10   'Associated persons' (defined in EA 2002, s 127) and any companies which they control are treated as a single person for these purposes, so that separate interests may be aggregated if, for example, companies are acting together to secure or exercise control of another company or enterprise.

10.11   If two companies each transfer a business into a joint venture company, and each has a stake in it sufficient to give them material influence over its policy, a number of merger situations qualifying for investigation might arise:

● the joint venture company obtains control over the two businesses of the joint venturers, which are now under its ownership;

● each joint venturer obtains material influence over the affairs of the joint venture company, and thereby over the business of the other party which has now been transferred into the joint venture.

10.12   On the other hand, if two or more joint venturers establish a joint venture to enter a new market in the UK and they do not transfer any existing business to the joint venture, there is no merger. Rather than two or more enterprises ceasing to be distinct, a new enterprise has been created.

How are market shares to be calculated?

10.13   The market share test is met if a 25% share is created or enhanced in the supply of goods or services of any 'description'. First, the businesses of the parties must overlap. The test will not be satisfied unless there is an increase in one party's market share. Secondly, the authorities have a considerable degree of discretion in assessing the applicable description of goods or services involved (EA 2002, s 23(5)) and they need not necessarily equate to a market in economic terms, although the authorities will have regard to a reasonable description of a set of goods or services. There is also discretion in assessing the relevant share, eg by value or volume of sales, capacity, or number of employees. In joint venture situations, the share of supply is assessed by reference to the activities of the joint venture, although any share of the joint venture parents will be taken into account where they remain active in the same field as the joint venture.

What is the UK turnover of the enterprise taken over?

10.14   Pursuant to EA 2002, s 28, the value of turnover of the enterprise being taken over is determined by taking the total of the UK turnover of the enterprises which cease to be distinct, but not the turnover of:

●   any enterprise which remains under the same ownership and control; or

●   where none of the enterprises remain under the same ownership and control, the enterprise having the highest turnover.

10.15   The consequences of this in a joint venture scenario are not straightforward. The relevant UK competition authority has suggested the following in its jurisdictional and procedural guidance.

●   Where the joint venture is formed by two or more companies incorporating their assets and businesses in a particular area of activity, turnover should be calculated by adding together the turnover of each of the contributed enterprises. In such a case, each parent company ceases to be distinct from the contributed business of the other parent, but itself remains under the same ownership or control.

●   Where the joint venture is formed by two companies forming a joint venture incorporating all their assets and businesses, turnover would be calculated by adding together the UK turnover of the businesses contributed to the joint venture and deducting the higher of the two figures. In practice, this means in such cases that the turnover of both of the contributed businesses will need to be above £70m to fall within the jurisdiction of EA 2002.

10.16   The turnover test applies to the turnover of the acquired enterprise that was generated in relation to customers within the UK in the business year preceding the date of completion of the merger or, if the merger has not yet taken place, the date of reference to the Competition and Markets Authority. The figures in the relevant enterprise's latest published accounts will be sufficient unless there have been significant changes since the accounts were prepared, or the accounts do not provide a relevant figure because, for example, only part of the business is being transferred into the joint venture. In such a situation, the joint venture parties would need to work out as accurately as possible what they believe to be the value of UK turnover for merger control purposes.

Notification procedure

10.17   Notification of a proposed merger and prior clearance are not compulsory under EA 2002 (save in the case of mergers in the water sector, where a reference to the Competition and Markets Authority is compulsory in some circumstances) and the Enterprise and Regulatory Reform Act 2013, which made some merger law changes (in force April 2014), did not alter this. However, if the parties decide not to notify and if the merger meets the thresholds for investigation there is a risk of a reference being made to the Competition and Markets Authority for four months after completion of the transaction (or its becoming public, whichever is later), with the consequent risk that the parties may be ordered to unwind the venture or make substantial modifications if an adverse finding is made. As of March 2008, the CMA has a dedicated Mergers Intelligence Officer responsible for monitoring non-notified merger activity and liaising with other competition authorities. Therefore, if the joint venture is clearly, or may well be, referable, the prudent course is to notify it before completion. This is reinforced by the fact that the CMA is likely to seek undertakings (or impose an order) requiring the merging businesses to be 'held separate' (ie preventing the parties integrating, or further integrating, the merging businesses) until the transaction is cleared or remedial action is taken in all completed merger cases where it has reasonable grounds for suspecting that a merger is likely to raise competition concerns and that such steps are appropriate to prevent pre-emptive action. There are also provisions in EA 2002 to capture the acquisition of 'creeping' control, which might otherwise escape scrutiny by being time barred. As mentioned at para 10.34 below some national security mergers require prior clearance following the National Security and Investment Act 2021 once it is fully in force.

10.18   Notification is made to the CMA, whose function is to decide whether the merger should be referred to a Phase 2 investigation for detailed investigation. Two procedures may be used: informal submission or statutory notification. No matter which process is used, the CMA encourages the use of pre-notification discussions in advance of filing. There used to be a specific informal advice procedure/confidential guidance but that was abolished. However it remains possible to ask the CMA for guidance. For mergers which are confidential the CMA can be asked if the matter is likely to be referred to Phase 2 and a meeting arranged with the CMA which may give its advice at the end of the meeting and often within ten working days of the receipt of the application for informal advice. The advice is not binding.

10.19   The statutory procedure under EA 2002 and Enterprise and Regulatory Reform Act 2013 provides that the CMA has 40 working days to complete its initial review of a notified merger (this is known as Phase 1). If no reference is made within that period, no reference may be made (subject to certain exceptions). The Merger Notice procedure can only be used in the case of proposed, rather than completed mergers, which must already have been made public. Although there is nothing preventing this procedure applying to all anticipated merger cases that have been made public, in practice, the CMA regards this more as a fast track procedure appropriate for transactions that do not raise anti-competitive concerns.

From April 2014 the Enterprise and Regulatory Reform Act 2013 has the effect that the CMA has wider powers to require merging businesses to be operated independently during the CMA's review stage. It also gives powers to impose heavy penalties for breach. This increased merger costs for mergers with competition issues where the merger proceeds without advance merger clearance. Binding deadlines and information gathering powers were also brought in by this Act at Phase I stage. Companies were given under the Act a statutory window of 50–90 working days from announcement of a decision to open a Phase 2 investigation, during which period they may offer, negotiate and finalise remedies to avoid going into Phase 2.

The ERRA also provides (from 2014) for a 12 week statutory time limit from the date of the final report, which can be extended by six weeks for the CMA to implement remedies.

10.20   As stated above it is possible for the parties to seek 'informal advice' from the CMA in certain limited circumstances. Informal advice is available only for confidential transactions in relation to which there is a good faith intention to proceed where the CMA's duty to refer is a genuine issue. Informal advice comprises the view of the CMA staff in the Merger Group and cannot bind the CMA. The fact of seeking informal advice and the fact and content of the reply must remain confidential, even after the deal becomes public.

10.21   Where the CMA believes that a joint venture raises competition concerns, rather than referring it for Phase 2 consideration, it may instead accept undertakings in lieu of a reference. These undertakings may relate to structural matters, eg a commitment to divest part of the business, or behavioural issues, although the former are preferred. Third parties are given an opportunity to comment before the undertakings are accepted.

10.22   A fee is payable for making a merger filing when the formal Merger Notice procedure is used or when a controlling interest is to be acquired.

Merger fees

10.23   Most mergers which are investigated by the CMA and those which qualify for a reference to phase 2 are subject to a fee, irrespective of whether a reference is made.

Fees vary according to the value of the UK turnover of the business being acquired.

Fee	Charge Band
£40,000	Value of the UK turnover of the enterprises being acquired is £20 million or less
£80,000	Value of the UK turnover of the enterprises being acquired is over £20 million but not over £70 million
£120,000	Value of the UK turnover of the enterprises being acquired exceeds £70 million, but does not exceed £120 million
£160,000	Value of the UK turnover of the enterprises being acquired exceeds £120 million

The fee is payable when the CMA makes its phase 1 merger decision (2021 figures above). Companies with low turnover (about £10m and less) are usually exempt from fees. The fee is payable on filing the Merger Notice or, in other cases, on the date of the reference to the Competition and Markets Authority or clearance by the CMA (where no reference is made). Note that the fee is paid even if the parties choose not to notify a merger and the CMA then investigates after the merger has taken place of its own volition.

See further for merger fees at https://assets.publishing.service.gov.uk/government/uploads/system/uploads/attachment_data/file/821121/Merger_fees_information.pdf.

Phase 2 – Competition and Markets Authority

10.24   Except in certain narrowly defined circumstances, the CMA is obliged to refer a merger to Phase 2 if it believes that it is or may be the case that a relevant merger situation has been created or such arrangements are in progress or in contemplation, and that the creation of that situation has resulted, or might be expected to result, in a substantial lessening of competition within any market or markets in the UK.

10.25   The test which the CMA must apply in determining whether or not it is obliged to refer a merger to Phase 2 was the subject of clarification in the Court of Appeal case of *IBA Health Ltd v The Office of Fair Trading*[2]. In that

---

2   [2004] EWCA Civ 142.

case, the then CMA had previously decided not to refer the iSOFT/Torex merger to the Competition Commission and IBA Health Ltd, a competitor of the merging parties, appealed that decision. The Court of Appeal found that the CMA had no duty to seek to anticipate the view of the Competition Commission (as suggested by the Competition Appeal Tribunal) and was only required to make up its own mind on the basis of the test set down in EA 2002, s 33(1). The wording in s 33(1) was to be given its ordinary meaning, in other words the CMA was obliged to refer a merger where the probability that it would result in a substantial lessening of competition was: (a) more than 50%; or (b) less than 50% but more than fanciful, and in between these two points the CMA was required to exercise its discretion, which was subject to the ordinary administrative law principles on reasonableness. See also *Celesio AG v The Office of Fair Trading*[3] where the Competition Appeal Tribunal rejected the argument that the CMA is always under a duty to refer a merger where the prospect of there being a substantial lessening of competition is more than fanciful.

10.26   When making a reference to Phase 2, the CMA will investigate and report on whether a relevant merger situation has been created (or will be created if the proposed arrangements are carried into effect), and whether that merger would or may be expected to result in a substantial lessening of competition.

10.27   The investigation will normally take approximately four to five months. However, the statutory maximum is 24 weeks (approximately six months), with the possibility of an extension by a further eight weeks (EA 2002, s 39).

10.28   The Competition and Markets Authority has the power to make orders or obtain undertakings from the parties to a completed merger with a view to preventing 'pre-emptive action', ie action which might prejudice a reference or make it difficult to take action on the Competition and Markets Authority's findings in the event of an adverse report. Such orders or undertakings will normally require the joint venture not to take further steps to integrate the joint venture businesses or to implement the joint venture until the CMA has decided not to refer the matter to Phase 2 (with or without undertakings), or until the outcome of the Competition and Markets Authority's investigation is known. As indicated above, the CMA now routinely requires such orders or undertakings in completed mergers where it has reasonable grounds for suspecting that a merger is likely to raise competition concerns.

10.29   In addition to these powers, where the joint venture arrangements involve the acquisition of shares, and the transaction has been referred to the Competition and Markets Authority but has not yet been completed, EA 2002,

---

3   [2006] CAT 9.

s 78 prohibits the parties from acquiring further interests in the joint venture company's shares during the reference period without the Competition and Markets Authority's consent.

10.30 When assessing a merger, the Competition and Markets Authority will consult third parties who are likely to be affected by the joint venture as well as the parties. It will request further information by way of a detailed questionnaire and receive written submissions on the issues and also on possible remedies. The Competition and Markets Authority will also hold formal hearings and has the power to compel the attendance of witnesses and the production of documents.

10.31 If the Competition and Markets Authority considers that the joint venture may not be expected to result in a substantial lessening of competition, it can take no further action. However, if the Competition and Markets Authority concludes that the joint venture can be expected to substantially lessen competition in the whole or any part of the UK, it is required to implement appropriate remedies.

10.32 The Competition and Markets Authority is given extensive powers under Sch 8 of EA 2002, including the power to order the dismantling of the joint venture, but it may also accept undertakings from the parties as to divestment or their future conduct instead of making a formal order, and in practice most such cases are dealt with by undertakings.

Public interest intervention process

10.33 The EA 2002 took Ministers out of the decision-making process in most cases. However, it reserved the Secretary of State's ability to intervene in certain cases in order to protect certain public interest considerations. Currently, the Secretary of State has the power to intervene in cases involving national security[4] (including public security), newspapers, broadcast media and cross media interests[5] and to maintain the stability of the UK financial system[6]. The Secretary of State may also intervene in defence industry mergers which would not otherwise qualify for investigation under the general UK merger regime[7], and in mergers involving newspaper or broadcast media enterprises where one of the parties has a share of supply of newspapers or of broadcasting of 25% or more in the UK or in a substantial part of the UK

---

4   See for example, *Alvis plc/General Dynamics Corporation*, 2004; *Finmeccanica/Augusta Westland*, 2004; *Insys Group/Lockheed Martin*, 2005; *General Electric Company/Smiths Aerospace*, 2007.
5   See *BSkyB/ITV*, 2007/08.
6   See the decision by the Secretary of State, BERR not to refer to the Competition Commission the *Lloyds TSB/HBOS* merger under EA 2002, s 45, 31 October 2008.
7   A special intervention notice was given to the CMA on 15 May 2009 in relation to the anticipated acquisition of *QinetiQ's* underwater systems division by *Atlas Elektronik*.

(special public interest mergers) (see para 11.25ff). Unlike the share of supply test explained above in para 10.13, there is no requirement for an overlap in the activities of the parties in order for the special public interest merger regime to apply. Also, ministerial intervention is possible in cases falling for consideration under the ECMR which affect the legitimate interests of the UK (eg prudential rules, public security, plurality of the media, certain aspects of sector specific regulation etc).

The detailed procedure which the Secretary of State is required to follow and his or her powers are principally set out in EA 2002 and in the Enterprise Act 2002 (Protection of Legitimate Interests) Order 2003 (SI 2003/1592).

National Security and Investment Act 2021, the Investment Security Unit and earlier 2018 changes

10.34   Legislation from 2018 (mentioned below) allowed more state involvement where a merger involves: military or dual-use goods subject to export control; computer processing units; or quantum technology. This remains the case. This was followed in 2021 by the National Security and Investment Act 2021 (NSIA 2021). The provisions of all these pieces of legislation are detailed and complex and beyond the scope of this book. They do not affect most mergers, but in all cases solicitors should check if there are any risks the merger involves the kinds of technology or security issues or military use items that may be caught. Even batteries at times have caused problems under UK export control legislation. Consider these issues early on as the NSIA 2021 includes in some cases a compulsory prior notification period. In addition as can be seen below the thresholds for UK merger law to apply are as low as £1m turnover for many of these sensitive sectors. Foreign direct investment (FDI) via UK mergers from 4 January 2022 can be scrutinised more on national security grounds.

10.35   When the NSIA 2021 received Royal Assent the Government summarised it in its press release as follows:

'*   Biggest shake-up of UK's investment screening regime in 20 years confirmed today as National Security and Investment Bill receives Royal Assent

*   new Act will modernise government's powers to investigate and intervene in potentially hostile foreign direct investment, while advancing the UK's world-leading reputation as an attractive place to invest.'

The summary below shows the breadth of the NSIA 2021 (from the Government's press release):

'This Act means that:

- the government will be able to scrutinise, impose conditions on or, as a last resort, block a deal wherever there is an unacceptable risk to Britain's national security

- investors and businesses will have to notify a dedicated government unit – the Investment Security Unit – through a digital portal about certain types of transactions in designated sensitive sectors, such as artificial intelligence

- the UK's screening powers will also be extended to include assets like intellectual property as well as companies

- the vast majority of transactions will be able to proceed unhindered and investments will be screened much faster than the current regime

- transactions are expected to be assessed within 30 working days and often more quickly, with timelines set out in law for the very first time

- investors can also notify any transaction voluntarily if they believe it has implications for national security

- to ensure that no dangerous deal can slip through the net unchecked, in addition to mandatory notification for certain sectors, the Secretary of State will also have the power to "call in" acquisitions in the wider economy which were not notified to government but may raise national security concerns.'

The NSIA 2021 is in force from 4 January 2022 (with some rights to 'call in a merger' from 12 November 2020).

The Explanatory Notes with the NSIA 2021, which made some major changes for mergers affecting national security, include the following:

'**Public Interest Cases**

...

15 The Enterprise Act 2002 (Share of Supply Test) (Amendment) Order 2018 (SI 2018/578) and the Enterprise Act 2002 (Turnover Test) (Amendment) Order 2018 (SI 2018/593), both of which came into force on 11 June 2018, amended the share of supply test and the turnover test, respectively. The turnover threshold was lowered from £70 million to £1 million for takeovers of "relevant enterprises", ie those active in any of the following sectors: military or dual-use goods subject to export control; computer processing units; or quantum technology. The share of supply test was amended so that the test is additionally met if the takeover is of a "relevant enterprise" that already had at least a 25% share of supply or purchase in, or in a substantial part of, the UK of goods or services before the merger. The goods or services must be connected to the activities by virtue of which it qualifies as a "relevant enterprise". The Enterprise Act

2002 (Share of Supply Test) (Amendment) Order 2020 (SI 2020/748) and the Enterprise Act 2002 (Turnover Test) (Amendment) Order 2020 (SI 2020/763), both of which came into force on 21 July 2020, amended the list of "relevant enterprises" to include those active in any of the following sectors: artificial intelligence; cryptographic authentication technology; or advanced materials. These changes were made to enable the Secretary of State to intervene in additional mergers which might give rise to national security implications.'

'Special public interest cases

21 Section 59 of the Act allows the Secretary of State to intervene in a limited number of mergers of special public interest on the basis of the public interest considerations specified in section 58 of the Act (which, as already stated, include national security) where the standard jurisdictional thresholds relating to turnover and share of supply are not satisfied. These include for example, mergers involving Government defence contractors authorised to hold or receive confidential information. The subsequent process is similar to the public interest intervention procedure set out above, except that there is no competition assessment.'

10.36   The NSIA 2021 also includes a mandatory notification regime for certain mergers with national security implications. Again a summary in the Explanatory Notes with the NSIA 2021 states as follows:

'Mandatory notification

33 The Act provides for a mandatory notification requirement for acquisitions of certain shares or voting rights in the qualifying entities to be specified in regulations made by the Secretary of State, which are termed "notifiable acquisitions". Proposed acquirers must notify the Secretary of State of notifiable acquisitions before they take place in order to obtain clearance to go ahead.

34 A notifiable acquisition that is completed before being approved by the Secretary of State is void and of no legal effect. Additionally, the acquirer may be subject to criminal or civil penalties for completing the acquisition without clearance. The Secretary of State may retrospectively validate a notifiable acquisition. Regulations will specify how to notify the Secretary of State of notifiable acquisitions

35 The Act provides a power for the Secretary of State to amend the acquisitions which are notifiable through regulations. The Secretary of State may also make regulations exempting acquisitions from the mandatory notification regime on the basis of the characteristics of the acquirer. These powers collectively allow the regime to reflect changing national security risks.

Voluntary notification regime

36 Businesses and other entities who do not meet the criteria for mandatory notification may submit a notification to the Secretary of State if they consider that their trigger event could raise national security concerns. To help inform their assessment as to whether a voluntary notification should be issued, they make reference to the statutory statement about the exercise of the call-in power.'

10.37   The Explanatory Notes to the NSIA 2021 are 40 pages long and anyone with a merger which may fall within the national security provisions or even suspects it might do so should check the NSIA 2021 and the guidelines as the rules are complicated and build on earlier provisions relating to national security, technology and the like.

The Explanatory Notes which accompany the NSIA 2021 are online at https://www.legislation.gov.uk/ukpga/2021/25/pdfs/ukpgaen_20210025_en.pdf.

Special sectors

10.38   Special merger control rules apply to mergers in the water sector (see para 11.19).

4   Examination of joint ventures under CA 1998

10.39   As noted above, the prohibitions on anti-competitive agreements (the Chapter I prohibition) and abuse of a dominant position (the Chapter II prohibition) contained in CA 1998 closely follow arts 101 and 201 of the EC Treaty, but require the agreement or conduct to have as its object or effect an impact on competition and trade within the UK.

10.40   Until 1 January 2021 following Brexit on 31 January 2020 and also following the end of the post-Brexit transition period which expired on 31 December 2020, the general principle of the supremacy of EC law was restated in art 3 of Regulation (EC) 1/2003. Also, CA 1998, s 60 specifically provided that UK law must be interpreted in line with EC law (ie the principles laid down by the EC Treaty and the decisions and principles laid down by the European courts) as far as possible, having regard to any relevant statements (such as Notices and Guidelines) and decisions of the European Commission.

However, the Competition (Amendment etc) (EU Exit) Regulations 2019, SI 2019/93 removed the CA 1998, s 60 and in its place added s 60A which simply requires the CMA and courts to avoid inconsistency between UK decisions and EU law and the decisions of the European Court of Justice before 31 January 2020 (exit day).

So to an extent the principles set out in EC Block Exemptions, Commission notices and decisions continue to apply in the same way to Chapter I and Chapter II cases as they would if art 101 or art 102 of the EC Treaty applied (because the relevant agreement had an effect on trade between member states which now does not include the UK). For further guidance on the substantive assessment of a joint venture under the UK prohibitions, reference should be made to Chapter 9 above, and to the various Block Exemptions and European Commission notices referred to there. As at 2021 there are few major differences, but over time this may change. Developments will need to be watched closely to determine the future weight of CJEU decisions in relation to interpretation of UK legislation based on EU laws. It is likely that EU and UK competition law will develop along similar lines.

10.41   As with EC law, an infringement of the UK prohibitions will lead to the agreements or conduct in question being void and unenforceable, and third parties will be entitled to claim damages from the infringing parties. Also, an infringement can be punished by the imposition of financial penalties. The maximum financial penalty that can be imposed for intentional or negligent infringement of the UK prohibitions is the same as for infringement of EC Treaty, arts 101 and 102, ie a maximum of 10% of worldwide turnover. Unlike arts 101 and 102, however, CA 1998 provides that agreements or conduct involving undertakings with turnover falling below certain thresholds will be immune from financial penalties, save in relation to price-fixing agreements and subject to the CMA's right to withdraw the immunity in certain cases. This immunity will not protect parties from intervention by the authorities regarding their future conduct, third-party actions in damages, or the consequences of unenforceability. Where both the EC and UK prohibitions apply, the CMA will take into account any penalties imposed under the EC regime so as to avoid double jeopardy. This is likely even after the end of the post-Brexit transitional period which ended on 31 December 2020.

10.42   Interim measures may also be ordered (as under the EC system) where the CMA has a reasonable suspicion that an infringement has occurred, the matter is urgent, and serious, irreparable damage would otherwise result, or it is in the public interest to act.

10.43   In order to bring the UK competition regime into line with the EC position, on 1 May 2004 the system for notifying an agreement or conduct to the then CMA was abolished, and the onus is therefore now on the parties to satisfy themselves that their agreement or conduct complies with UK competition law, by reference to the various Block Exemptions and Notices published by the European Commission (as even from 2021 these remain 'retained EU law' and give block exemption provision from the CA 1998 in the UK) and the CMA. As with the EC position, the parties to an agreement or conduct may approach the CMA informally for their view where the case gives rise to novel or unresolved questions of law. A list of retained EU law block exemptions can be seen at https://www.gov.uk/government/publications/retained-block-exemptions/retained-block-exemptions and is as follows:

List of retained block exemptions and expiry dates	
Category of exemption	Expiry date
Vertical agreements	31 May 2022
Research and development agreements (horizontal cooperation)	31 December 2022
Specialisation agreements (horizontal cooperation)	31 December 2022
Motor Vehicle vertical agreements	31 May 2023
Liner shipping consortia agreements	25 April 2024
Technology transfer agreements	30 April 2026
Rail, road and inland waterways transport	No expiry date

See European Union (Withdrawal) Act 2018, ss 6 and 7, and the Competition (Amendment etc) (EU Exit) Regulations 2019, Sch 4, Pt 2 (amended by the Competition (Amendment etc) (EU Exit) Regulations 2020) and the Competition Act 1998, s 10A as inserted by the 2019 Regulations.

Types of co-operation, information exchange and case example

10.44   Sometimes a joint venture company or other collaboration if between competitors per se might have anti-competitive effects and the parties should not even form the venture. Always take competition law advice. This book merely touches on the complex issues involved.

In other cases the joint venture parties are not competitors and it will only be the detail of the specific restrictions in the agreement such as non-competition restrictions (see below) which need to be considered.

10.45   Where the parties are competitors or where disclosing information about the parties' prices or even costs could have anti-competitive effects it can sometimes be necessary to set up systems regarding access to information such as Chinese walls and other arrangements with the result that each of the competitor owners of the JV do not have full access to sensitive information eg the price at which JV partner A is selling products to JV Co and the price at which JV partner B is selling products to JV Co.

Sometimes large projects such as construction of a ready mixed concrete plant cannot easily be undertaken by one company alone so two or more competitors collaborate and need to be particularly careful not to breach competition law.

Exchange of sensitive information has led to competition law fines in several cases over the years and in the joint venture context this is an important area to consider.

CASE EXAMPLE – CLEANROOM LAUNDRY SERVICES AND PRODUCTS: ANTI-COMPETITIVE AGREEMENT (CASE 50283, 14 DECEMBER 2017)

10.46   £1.7m fine.

In 2017 the Competition and Markets Authority fined two companies which had operated a long standing joint venture in relation to cleaning services. The CMA summarised the case as follows (see https://www.gov.uk/cma-cases/cleaning-services-sector-suspected-anti-competitive-arrangement-s):

'The specialist laundry services they supply include the cleaning of garments worn by people working in "cleanrooms". These are highly sanitised environments used by businesses such as pharmaceutical and medical device manufacturers as well as NHS pharmacies. Both businesses had been trading under the "Micronclean" brand since the 1980s in a longstanding joint venture agreement. In May 2012 the companies entered into new, reciprocal trademark licence arrangements under which they agreed not to compete against each other. Under the agreement, Micronclean Limited served customers in an area north of a line drawn broadly between London and Anglesey, and Berendsen Cleanroom Services Limited served customers located south of that line. The companies also agreed not to compete for certain other customers, irrespective of their location.

Market-sharing arrangements like these are generally illegal under competition law. For customers, these arrangements prevented them from shopping around to get a better deal and that can lead to higher prices, less choice and less innovation in the market.

In reaching its decision, the CMA considered whether the wider joint venture between the companies, including any benefits which flowed from it, meant that these market-sharing arrangements were necessary or justified. The CMA concluded that they were not.

It said that in "reaching this Decision, the CMA has taken the wider context of the Joint Venture fully into account. In particular, the CMA finds that (i) the territorial and customer allocation was not objectively necessary for the operation of the Joint Ventureor the licensing of the shared Trade Marks, and (ii) the agreement did not benefit from an individual exemption under section 9 of the Act (or indeed a block exemption under section 10 of the [Competition Act 1998]). By the start of the Relevant Period, any significant investments had been made many years before, and any efficiencies or benefits had already been materially attained. The Relevant Markets were mature and each Party was well-established. There is no link between the territorial and customer allocation under the TMLAs [2012 trade mark licences which had been entered into] and any prior, contemporaneous or future investments, sharing of knowhow or benefits to customers".

Ann Pope, CMA Senior Director for Antitrust Enforcement, said: "Market-sharing agreements are well established and serious breaches of competition law. Organisations like the NHS rely on the cleanroom laundry services provided by these companies, but we have found the 2 biggest players were dividing customers between them, leaving those customers with very little choice in service provider. Companies must regularly check their trading arrangements, including long-running joint ventures and collaborative agreements, to make sure they're not breaking the law. The entry into new trade mark licence agreements in 2012 was an opportunity for the businesses to consider the competition law implications of their commercial arrangements".

The case came to the CMA's attention in the context of 2 related merger reviews. The CMA investigated and cleared a merger between the joint venture vehicle then jointly owned by Fenland and Berendsen Newbury, ie Micronclean Limited (since re-named, as of 1 July 2016, Fenland Laundries Limited), and Guardline Technology Limited. The CMA also investigated a proposed merger between Fenland and Fishers Cleanroom, which was ultimately abandoned.

The suppliers involved were:

●   Micronclean Limited, known prior to 1 July 2016 as Fenland Laundries Limited (Fenland); and

●   Berendsen Cleanroom Services Limited, known prior to 15 September 2015 as Micronclean (Newbury) Limited (Berendsen Newbury).

The total fine for Micronclean Limited was £510,118. The total fine for Berendsen Cleanroom Services Limited was £1,197,956. As the parent company of Berendsen Cleanroom Services Limited for the latter part of the period during which the law was broken, Berendsen plc was held by the CMA to be jointly and severally liable for £1,028,671 of Berendsen Cleanroom Services Limited's fine.'

The non-confidential version of the decision of the CMA (Cleanroom laundry services and products: anti-competitive agreement Case 50283, 14 December 2017) is 240 pages long and is online at https://assets.publishing.service.gov.uk/media/5a7c1830ed915d210ade18c9/case_50283_decision.pdf.

Exclusion of mergers

10.47   Until 1 January 2021 joint ventures which fell within the scope of the EC Merger Regulation were excluded from CA 1998[8]. Due to Brexit this is no longer the case.

10.48   Until that date mergers subject to the EA 2002 were also excluded from CA 1998, regardless of whether or not they qualified for investigation under the turnover or share of supply test. The exclusion applied both to the Chapter I and Chapter II prohibitions. It extended to any provisions directly related and necessary to the implementation of the merger, ie to the 'ancillary' restrictions. In its jurisdictional and procedural guidance the CMA cross-referred to the European Commission's notice on this issue, which is considered above in paras 9.62 to 9.69. However, now there is no such exclusion and the CMA expects its workload to double due to examining mergers which previously would only have been examined at EU level which, in addition, will now be examined in the UK. There were provisions about mergers in the process of consideration by the CMA or EU as at 1 January 2021 which should be considered for those affected.

10.49   This previous exclusion for mergers applied only to the extent a transaction amounted to a merger under the EA 2002. The exclusion from Chapter I (not Chapter II) can be withdrawn by the CMA in certain circumstances, but not with retrospective effect. In particular, the exclusion could have been subject to 'clawback' where a party failed to provide information in response to a formal written request without reasonable excuse, or where:

● the CMA considered that the agreement would, if not excluded, infringe Chapter I; and

● that it was not likely to grant an unconditional exemption; provided that

● the agreement was not a 'protected' agreement.

10.50   A 'protected agreement' is:

● one which has been cleared by the Secretary of State or CMA, or undertakings in lieu have been given;

● one which, following a reference to the Competition and Markets Authority, has been found to amount to a relevant merger situation or a special merger situation (under the special public interest regime);

● one which otherwise involves the acquisition of a controlling interest (rather than any lesser degree of control or influence); or

● one giving rise to a merger subject to mandatory investigation under the Water Industry Act 1991.

---

8   CA 1998, Sch 1, Pt II.

Other exclusions and exemptions

10.51   In addition to the exclusions for mergers, there are a number of other exclusions from the application of the UK competition prohibitions. For instance, conduct or agreements entered into in order to comply with a legal requirement, or which are necessary for compelling reasons of public policy, will not be caught by the UK competition prohibitions. The Competition Act 1998 (Land Agreements Exclusion and Revocation) Order 2004[9] used to provide that the Chapter I prohibition did not apply to certain land agreements. This latter provision however has now been abolished, and land agreements are fully subject to the UK competition rules. Of course, it should be remembered that these exclusions do not prevent the application of arts 101 and/or 102 of the EC Treaty if there is an effect on trade between member states: see para 9.80. Many UK companies engage in activities where eg they trade in France and export from there to Spain. It is possible that the UK may re-introduce some specific block exemption regulations in certain areas of competition law again. In 2021 the CMA began a review of the retained Vertical Block Exemption which expires in the EU and UK on 30 June 2022 – see https://www.gov.uk/government/consultations/retained-vertical-block-exemption-regulation. The CMA will be reviewing the other retained Block Exemption Regulations in due course in order to make a recommendation to the Secretary of State. However, it is very likely that similar exemption regulations to those in the EU will continue to apply in the UK.

10.52   The Secretary of State has the power, acting on the CMA's recommendation, to make block exemptions that exempt particular categories of agreement from the Chapter I prohibition. Only one has so far been issued (for public transport ticketing schemes – see the Competition Act 1998 (Public Transport Ticketing Schemes Block Exemption) Order 2001 (SI 2001/319) as amended by the Competition Act 1998 (Public Transport Ticketing Schemes Block Exemption) (Amendment) Order 2016 (SI 2016/126) which exemption is due to expire in 2026). Again, such UK block exemptions would not serve to exempt the agreement or conduct from the application of EC competition law.

Regulated sectors

10.53   It should be noted that most of the sectoral regulators (for example, for gas, electricity, water, railways and communications), but not all (such as

---

9   SI 2004/1260, revoked by the Competition Act 1998 (Land Agreements Exclusion Revocation) Order 2010 (SI 2010/1709), and see also CMA/OFT Land Agreements Guidance at http://www.oft.gov.uk/OFTwork/policy/land-agreements/#.Uc6KepyKLPQ.

Ofcom), have concurrent jurisdiction with the CMA to enforce CA 1998 and to act upon complaints.

Appeals

10.54   The CA 1998 also provides an appeal mechanism in respect of decisions of the CMA or other regulators to the Competition Appeal Tribunal. Appeals may be brought by the parties concerned, or by third parties. Broadly, the Tribunal may confirm, vary or set aside a decision, or remit the matter to the relevant authority.

5   Other provisions

10.55   The restraint of trade doctrine at common law should not be overlooked, although its importance is arguably substantially diminished now that the CA 1998 is in force and following the modernisation of competition law under Regulation 1/2003[10]. This doctrine seeks to ensure that covenants are not enforceable if they amount to an unreasonable restraint of trade. In the context of a joint venture, this may apply in particular to non-competition covenants or covenants against the solicitation of customers or employees.

10.56   Although only of residual application, it is worth noting the basic principles. First, it is necessary that the covenantee has a legitimate interest to protect. Even then, the covenant may go no further than is reasonable in terms of scope, duration and geographical extent. A court may nevertheless find that a covenant is not reasonable in the public interest and is therefore unenforceable.

10.57   What is reasonable will vary from case to case, but a restrictive covenant which complies with EC/UK guidelines on ancillary restraints[11] will almost certainly be considered to satisfy this criterion, even where the joint venture is below the merger control thresholds or does not give rise to a merger at all, as in the case of a start up or greenfield venture. The UK courts have condemned a broad employee non-solicitation covenant which did not distinguish between those employees who were valuable to the business and those who were not[12]. This underlines the importance of including appropriate severance wording in the joint venture agreement.

---

10   *Days Medical Aids v Pihsiang Machinery* [2004] 1 All ER (Comm) 991 where it was established that the application of this doctrine could not operate to invalidate an agreement that was legal under EC Treaty, art 101.

11   See paras 9.62ff and 10.40.

12   *Dawnay Day & Co Ltd v de Braconier d'Alphen* [1997] IRLR 285.

6 Typical restrictive covenants

10.58   An example of a suggested covenant is included at clause 10 of Precedent 3. It essentially provides that neither a joint venturer nor its group companies will:

- be engaged, concerned or interested in any business of the same kind as that conducted by the joint venture within the area of operation of the joint venture;

- solicit any current or recent customers of the joint venture in relation to goods or services of the same kind as those supplied by the joint venture; or

- solicit any senior employees of the joint venture with a view to seeking to employ them or to hire them as consultants.

10.59   For business sales in general competition law tends to conclude that a restriction of up to three years on competing with a company which has been sold is acceptable where knowhow and goodwill have been sold as long the product and geographical markets are reasonable and those in which the sold entity operated. Anyone trying a five year restriction should take specialist advice over the likely enforceability of such a long period. For joint ventures the position is more complicated as two companies might operate their venture over many years.

10.60   In *Guest Services Worldwide Ltd v Shelmerdine*[13] a non-competition covenant in a shareholders' agreement, which lasted for 12 months after the individual ceased to be an employee, was upheld. Even though this could have been some years after Mr Shelmerdine had ceased to be an employee it was reasonable it continued to run until the 12 months were over. He was a consultant under a consultancy agreement until 2017 but continued to provide consultancy services until February 2019 without entering into a new consultancy agreement. He was also party to the shareholders' agreement which included the relevant clause.

The court concluded at paras 41–44:

'There is no dispute that all covenants in restraint of trade are, prima facie, unenforceable at common law unless they are reasonable. The first issue in such circumstances is to determine the level of scrutiny which is appropriate. Mr Budworth says that the court is less vigilant where covenants of this kind are contained in a Shareholders' Agreement or an agreement akin to it, rather than in an employment contract. I agree. Mr Budworth took us to the judgment of Neuberger J (as he then was) in *Dyno-Rod & Anr v Reeve* [1999] FSR 148. That was a case

---

13   [2020] EWCA Civ 85.

in which the claimant organised its business on a franchise basis. The franchise agreement contained restrictive covenants. Injunctive relief was obtained on the strength of evidence that the franchisee who had received extensive training from the claimant company had covertly been running a parallel business in breach of the restrictive covenant. Neuberger J granted an injunction and noted at 152 the comments of Lord Denning in *Office Overload Ltd v Gunn* [1977] FSR 39 at [41], that where the agreement in question is a franchise agreement, it does not fall happily between employee/employer cases and vendor/purchaser cases. Having also noted that in *Scully UK Ltd v Lee* [1998] IRLR 259, the Court of Appeal decided that an employee restraint clause had to be subject to very rigorous and careful scrutiny and enforced only if it went no further than necessary to protect the trade secrets of the previous employer, he went on at 154 as follows:

> "That emphasises the extent to which the court is concerned that a restrictive covenant is reasonable before it will be enforced, but it is to be borne in mind that the court was there dealing with an employer/ employee covenant which – the passages to which I have referred in particular – the observations of Lord Denning indicate have to satisfy far more stringent tests before they are reasonable."

Indeed, he went on to state that he found it difficult to see how it could seriously be argued that a period of 12 months could not be reasonable, in the circumstances of that case.

In *Ideal Standard v Herbert* [2018] EWHC 3326 (Comm) the court was concerned with a non-competition clause in a shareholders' agreement. In considering this, Sir Ross Cranston noted at [28] as follows:

> "My reading of these authorities is that it is not simply a matter of categorization, non-compete clauses in employment agreements on one hand, non-compete clauses in shareholder agreements on the other. Non-compete clauses for the vendor of a partnership share or the shares in a business will generally be enforced as reasonable and enforceable. Apart from anything else, such clauses are negotiated in a commercial context and have the legitimate aim of preventing vendors from attacking the goodwill of the partnership or business which they have just transferred. Towards the other end of the spectrum are ordinary employees, who have a small shareholding in their employer-company as part of a share participation scheme."

Wyn Williams J also gave detailed consideration of the circumstances in which such clauses are enforceable where they arise in a shareholders' agreement and seek to bind employees in *Kynixa Ltd v Hynes & Ors* [2008] EWHC 1495 (QB). His explanation of the relevant analysis bears careful consideration. See, in particular, [130]–[132].

Taking all of this into account I do not accept that a period of 12 months is unreasonable in respect of the restraints specified in clause 5 and, in particular, in relation to clause 5.1. Firstly, it is clear that GSW has a legitimate interest in seeking to prevent Employee Shareholders from competing with the business and soliciting clients, given the particular nature of the business and the knowledge that such individuals are likely to have obtained. Secondly, the clause appears in a shareholders' agreement made between experienced commercial parties. Thirdly, in my judgment, a period of restraint lasting 12 months was entirely reasonable to protect that interest. It seems to me that that is the case even though the 12 month period under clause 5.1(b) runs from the date on which the individual ceases to be a Shareholder rather than the cessation of his employment, agency or directorship. As I have already mentioned, in all likelihood, the cessation of employment, agency or directorship and ceasing to be a Shareholder will be co-terminous or, at least, there will be only a limited lapse of time between the cessation of employment and the disposal of the individual's shares. Although I accept that delay in the process of relinquishing Shares in GSW is possible, I do not consider that the clause should be declared to be unreasonable on the basis of the relatively unlikely possibility that there may be considerable delay or the extreme and very unlikely possibility that a Shareholder may be locked in indefinitely.

It follows, therefore, that I would allow the appeal on both grounds. In the circumstances, the issues raised in the Respondent's Notice as to whether the restrictions in clauses 5.1 and 5.2 are unenforceable as a result of their area and scope become live. However, they are essentially questions of fact and it seems to me that we are not best placed to deal with them. Those matters should be remitted to be dealt with in the Business and Property Courts.'

10.61   As discussed above, restrictive covenants which are drafted to go no further than the European Commission's guidance on ancillary restraints (which remain relevant in the UK despite Brexit as 'retained EU law') are likely to be defensible under both EC and UK competition law. Covenants in a joint venture agreement are therefore only likely to be enforceable where the covenantor has a controlling interest in the wide sense explained in para 9.17ff, and may only continue for so long as the controlling interest subsists and not after the venture has terminated.

10.62   In light of UK case law (see para 10.57), it may also be advisable to limit the scope of the employee non-solicitation covenant to senior employees or those who have a particular skill which is valuable to the business.

10.63   It is not uncommon for key directors to give similar covenants in a joint venture or shareholders' agreement in circumstances where they also have a minority stake in the company rather than a controlling interest. As indicated above, such covenants may not be enforceable against them in their capacity as shareholders. The position is exacerbated if the director has left the employment of the company but for some reason is unable to sell his minority stake and the covenant is expressed to continue for as long as his shareholding continues. Practitioners should advise clients that such restrictions in the agreement may not be enforceable and a suitable covenant should be included in the director's service contract, although this will have the effect that the covenant will be enforceable only by the company and not by the shareholders party to the joint venture agreement. A minority shareholder may therefore have difficulty in procuring the company to enforce the covenant, unless special provision is made for this.

10.64   Non-compete covenants often contain carve-outs to permit the shareholders to hold very small stakes in competing companies. This can be made more elaborate to cater for circumstances where a parent company acquires independently an interest in a competing company, by requiring the relevant shareholder to sell on the interest either to the joint venture or to a third party within a certain period.

10.65   It is also important to include appropriate severance wording such that if any covenant were, for whatever reason, drafted too broadly, it would be possible to delete the offending elements of the covenant and to leave a core, enforceable restriction.

Flowchart 3

United Kingdom Competition Law

Enterprise Act 2002

Competition Act 1998

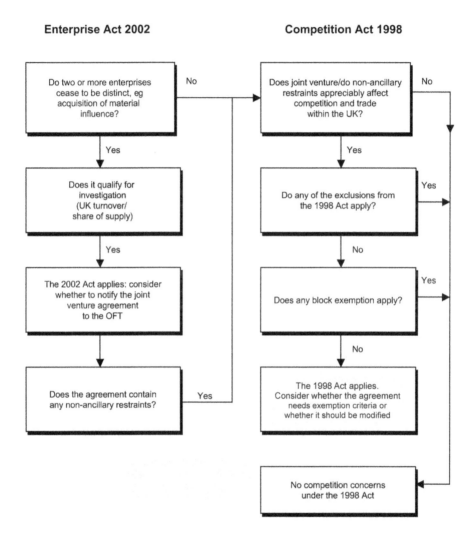

Do two or more enterprises cease to be distinct, eg acquisition of material influence? — No →

Does joint venture/do non-ancillary restraints appreciably affect competition and trade within the UK? — No →

Yes ↓

Yes ↓

Does it qualify for investigation (UK turnover/ share of supply)

Do any of the exclusions from the 1998 Act apply? — Yes →

Yes ↓

No ↓

The 2002 Act applies: consider whether to notify the joint venture agreement to the OFT

Does any block exemption apply? — Yes →

No ↓

Does the agreement contain any non-ancillary restraints? — Yes →

The 1998 Act applies. Consider whether the agreement needs exemption criteria or whether it should be modified

No competition concerns under the 1998 Act

Chapter 11

Other regulatory matters in the UK

Summary

This chapter considers various other regulatory matters applying in the UK, including those applicable to businesses which cannot be conducted without a licence or similar authorisation, various requirements which could affect a joint venture or shareholders' agreement including one or more listed public companies, the effect of the Takeover Code where the object of a joint venture is to obtain control of a UK public company, and the provisions of the Financial Services and Markets Act 2000 which affect the circulation of investment invitations by prospective joint venturers or other persons seeking capital. The circumstances in which a joint venture can be a collective investment scheme are also discussed.

1 Regulated businesses

11.1   Various kinds of business can only be carried on in the UK under a licence or similar authorisation from a government authority or other regulatory body. Where a company or joint venture is to be established to conduct any of these businesses, it will be important to ensure that the appropriate licence or authority (or a suitable exemption) is available. In a corporate or partnership joint venture, performing the full functions of the business concerned, it will be the joint venture company or partnership which normally requires the licence or authority. In some agency situations it may be possible for the joint venture to operate under its principal's licence, although this varies from sector to sector. In a contractual joint venture it may be possible to rely on a licence or authority (or exemption) available to one of the joint venturers if only that venturer is carrying on the activities for which the licence or authority is required, but careful investigation is required into this aspect.

11.2   The terms of the licence or authority may require a consent to be obtained prior to any change of control of the licensee, or make it prudent to seek advance clearance. This will have implications not only where a company or joint venture undergoes a change in control, for example where a new shareholder is admitted to a joint venture company, but also where the whole company or joint venture enterprise is being sold or where particular assets are transferred from the licensee on the termination of the venture, whether to one of the joint venturers or to a third party. Most licences and authorities are not assignable, which has implications where the undertaking of a joint venture business is to be sold. A consent may also be required in order to transfer an existing company, business or particular assets into a joint venture.

11.3   As well as ensuring that a licence or authority (or suitable exemption) is available, it will also be necessary to ensure that the company or joint venture is managed so as to comply with the appropriate requirements of the licence or authority as well as the appropriate statutory and regulatory requirements. Many businesses not requiring a licence will be subject to many government regulations, some of general application and some of which apply to particular businesses.

11.4   The loss of a relevant licence or authority may need to be made a ground for the termination of a joint venture or shareholders' agreement.

11.5   The following is a non-exhaustive list of businesses where a licence or other authority is or might be required.

Financial services (including investments, banking, mortgage business and insurance)

11.6   All these activities are now governed by the Financial Services and Markets Act 2000 ('FSMA 2000'). Under that Act no person may carry on a regulated activity in the United Kingdom or purport to do so unless he is individually authorised to do so by the Financial Conduct Authority ('FCA', previously the FSA) or is an exempt person. Further, no person may perform certain functions (called 'controlled functions') in relation to an authorised person's regulated activities unless approval is first obtained from the FCA. This means that certain key employees need to be approved by the FCA. The regulated activities are prescribed by the Financial Services and Markets Act 2000 (Regulated Activities) Order 2001[1] as amended. Under FSMA 2000, s 104 no insurance or banking business may be transferred without a court order, subject to certain exceptions. These provisions apply to the transfer of a business undertaking and not to the transfer of shares, and they provide an advantage in that the court order transfers the business by operation of law, without any need to obtain customer consents. The provisions relating to banks are not yet in force, so a court order for the transfer of a banking business remains voluntary. Under FSMA 2000, s 178 a person who decides to acquire or increase control over a UK authorised person must give the

---

1   SI 2001/544.

FCA notice in writing before making the acquisition. The FCA may approve or object to the acquisition. 'Control' is very widely defined, and a person holding 10% of the shares in an authorised person will control it, as will a person who is able to exercise significant influence over the authorised person irrespective of shareholding.

Telecommunications and broadcasting and IT

11.7   The Communications Act 2003 transferred the functions of the previous regulators for telecommunications and broadcasting to a new regulator, the Office of Communications or Ofcom, established by the Office of Communications Act 2002. However, much of the old law is retained and it is still necessary to consider each type of service separately.

TELECOMMUNICATIONS

11.8   Under the Communications Act 2003, it is, broadly speaking, unnecessary for a licence to be obtained or held by a provider of electronic communications networks (essentially relating to the transmission of electrical, magnetic or electro-magnetic energy) or electronic communications services. Instead, an 'authorisation regime' applies, whereby providers of such networks, services or associated facilities must comply with certain general, and in some cases, specific, conditions of entitlement. The applicable conditions will depend on the particular provider and activities involved. Although the 2003 Act envisages that providers will be required to notify Ofcom on commencing their services where Ofcom requires this, Ofcom has not so far laid down any such requirement. Certain conditions in licences granted prior to 25 July 2003 by the previous regulator, the Office of Telecommunications, were carried over by way of 'continuation notices' under the new regime pending completion of the market reviews required by EU legislation. Ofcom summarises the current regime as follows:

> **'The General Authorisation Regime**
>
> The telecommunications licensing regime has now been replaced by a general authorisation regime with the General Conditions of entitlement (that is, conditions which apply to all) and specific conditions (that is, conditions which apply to individuals). This area sets out the General and Specific conditions.' [There is then a link to those conditions on the Ofcom site: http://stakeholders.ofcom.org.uk/telecoms/]

11.9   Providers of mobile telephone services, using radio waves rather than wires for transmission, also come within the regime for regulation of wireless telegraphy. Under the Wireless Telegraphy Act 2006, it is a criminal offence to establish or use any station or apparatus for wireless telegraphy unless a licence from Ofcom is obtained and is in force, or unless certain exemptions laid down by Ofcom apply, which will depend on the particular person or activities involved. Licences already granted prior to 8 February 2007, when the new Act came into force, were carried over into the new regime.

INDEPENDENT TELEVISION (IE NON-BBC) AND VOICE ON DEMAND SERVICES

11.10   Licensing of independent television is regulated by the Broadcasting Acts 1990 and 1996, as amended and supplemented by the Communications Act 2003. Commercial television companies wishing to broadcast in and from the UK, by whatever method, must have an appropriate licence. Ofcom is responsible for granting licences. Ofcom may only grant a licence to a 'fit and proper' person and must do all that it can to ensure that a licensee does not remain the holder of a licence if it ceases to be such. Licences are not transferable without the consent of Ofcom. In certain circumstances, licences can be revoked on a change of control and therefore if it is possible such circumstances might apply, it may be advisable to give Ofcom advance notice of any such change of control with representations as to why the licence should not be revoked. Licences for Channel 3 services and Channel 5 contain specific conditions requiring advance notice to be given to Ofcom of any proposals that may result in a change of control of the licensee or of any connected person who is, or is likely to become, involved to a substantial extent in providing programming for the licensed service. Ofcom's broadcasting licensing regime is further described on its website at https://www.ofcom.org.uk/tv-radio-and-on-demand/broadcast-codes.

11.11   Licences for digital television programme services, digital television additional services (ie text services) and television licensable content services (ie cable and satellite services) are generally readily available subject to the overriding 'fit and proper person' test and in principle continue for an indefinite period. By contrast, licences for the mainstream public service terrestrial channels (Channel 3, Channel 5 or public teletext) had to be bid for in a competitive tender and in principle are for a fixed term, although they are renewable. Therefore access to such licences is limited in practice. The media ownership rules under the 1990 and 1996 Broadcasting Acts were considerably relaxed by the 2003 Act, both in terms of the disqualification rules and the restrictions on the accumulation of broadcasting interests and cross-media ownership. However, although a number of sector-specific ownership rules were abolished, under the Enterprise Act 2002 the Secretary of State for Business, Energy and Industrial Strategy may intervene in certain cases if wider public interest concerns are raised in the context of a change of control of media enterprises (see further paras 11.25 and 11.26 below).

11.12   Under the Audiovisual Media Services Regulations 2020 (SI 2020/1062) video on demand (VoD) provisions new notification obligations arose for VoD services. The Explanatory Notes with the 2020 Regulations state as follows:

> 'The appropriate regulatory authority will oversee a notification regime for VSP providers established or deemed to be established in the UK. This means that VSP providers will be required to notify the authority that they provide a service that meets the statutory definition of a VSP and pay an annual fee set by the authority.
>
> The Regulations include transitional provision, specifying that, in relation to VSPs which are already operating when the advance notification requirement comes into force on 6 April 2021, providers will be required to notify that they are already providing the service (rather than intending to do so) by 6 of May 2021. Once VSP providers have notified the authority in regard to the services they provide, Ofcom must establish and maintain a list of VSPs within UK jurisdiction.'

Further details of the regime for this sector is in the book *Ecommerce and Convergence – the Law of Digital Media* by Susan Singleton (5th edn 2021, published by Bloomsbury Professional).

ONLINE SAFETY BILL

11.13   In 2021 the UK was considering considerably more control over the internet including in its Online Safety Bill set out in the 2021 Queen's Speech. This followed a 2020 Online Harms White Paper. This may well lead to more regulation which, although not the same as an official regulator for particular sectors, could mean those involved with mergers and joint ventures need to consider new legislation in this field. For example companies such as Facebook and Google may be given active duties to attempt to prevent illegal and 'harmful' (however that is defined) content online. Regulation will be overseen by Ofcom, which will be granted powers to fine companies up to 10 per cent of annual turnover or £18m – whichever is greater.

INDEPENDENT RADIO

11.14   Ofcom is also responsible for regulating and licensing independent radio under the Broadcasting Acts 1990 and 1996, again as amended and supplemented by the Communications Act 2003. This legislation stipulates the categories of activities which cannot be undertaken without a licence. A licence under the Wireless Telegraphy Act 2006 is also required (also granted by Ofcom) – see para 11.9 above. Certain types of radio licences (eg local analogue commercial radio licences) are made available through a competitive tender process which differs depending on the nature of the licence available. Licences for other services are more readily available, subject only to limited statutory grounds for refusing the licence.

11.15 Again, radio licences under the Broadcasting Acts cannot be transferred without Ofcom's consent and there are circumstances in which they can be revoked on a change of control. Licences for local sound broadcasting services include a condition requiring Ofcom to be notified in advance of certain changes of control (as in the case of Channel 3, for example). The restrictions on ownership of radio licences have also been revised and broadly relaxed by the Communications Act 2003, but mergers involving independent radio broadcasting, including where they also involve television broadcasting or newspapers, are subject to the public interest regime discussed below (see further paras 11.25 and 11.26).

Railways

11.16 Railways are regulated principally under the Railways Act 1993 as amended ('RA 1993'). Any person who acts as the operator of railway assets (trains, stations, networks and light maintenance depots) in Great Britain is guilty of an offence unless he is authorised by a licence or is exempt from that requirement. Licences are granted mainly by the Office of Rail and Road (previously the Office of Rail Regulation) ('ORR') but may also be granted by the Secretary of State. Such licences may be assigned provided this is envisaged in the licence and with the consent of the Secretary of State (if so specified) or otherwise with the ORR's consent. Such consent may be given subject to conditions. ORR's website is https://www.orr.gov.uk/. In 2021 due in part to the Covid-19/coronavirus pandemic and changes to travel to work patterns as a result, proposals were issued for changes to the current regime. Great British Railways (GBR) would be set up which would set timetables and prices, sell tickets in England and manage rail infrastructure.

11.17 Operators of certain passenger and freight services had to have a European licence (which could be issued by the ORR) granting rights to operate such services across the EEA (under the Railway (Licensing of Railway Undertakings) Regulations 2005, SI 2005/3050). However the Railway (Licensing of Railway Undertakings) (Amendment etc) (EU Exit) Regulations 2019 (SI 2019/700) made some changes in this field due to Brexit. Such operators also needed from the ORR a Statement of National Regulatory Provisions. Even if a European licence is held, a licence under the RA 1993 is still required for any station, light maintenance depot, network or maintenance train operator running on the rail network in Great Britain. There are complex Brexit provisions affecting licences. Readers should examine the ORR guidance in detail – see https://www.orr.gov.uk/sites/default/files/2021-01/eu-passenger-and-freight-licences-and-snrps-from-2021-01-01.pdf.

11.18 Licences can be terminated on a change of control.

Water

11.19   Regulation of the water industry is governed by the Water Industry Act 1991 and the Water Act 2003. The Water Act 2014 expanded the licensing regime further. It is an offence for any person to supply water or sewerage services unless authorised to do so by licence (or exemption) under this legislation. The Water Services Regulation Authority (known as Ofwat) is the economic regulator of the water and sewerage industry in England and Wales. The conditions imposed on companies providing water and sewerage services are set out in a licence (called the Instrument of Appointment). Each Instrument of Appointment specifies the geographical area served by the Appointee. The principal conditions of appointment are common to all companies. They cover price control, ensuring that the supply and quality of service is maintained, and protecting the interests of customers. Charges for the provision of water supply or sewerage services are subject to limits set by the Water Services Regulation Authority and are subject to periodic review at five yearly intervals. Each Instrument of Appointment is for a term of at least 25 years. Appointments are not assignable and may be terminated by the Secretary of State for the Environment, Food and Rural Affairs or the National Assembly for Wales (in the case of a Welsh appointment) at any time on, or after, the expiry of that period, provided ten years' notice is given. If the Water Services Regulation Authority considers that the Appointee is carrying out its functions in a manner that operates against the public interest, it can require the Competition and Markets Authority to investigate whether any modifications to the licence are required. Ofwat's website is http://www.ofwat.gov.uk/.

11.20   Appointments are not by their terms terminable on a change of control of the Appointee, but the Water Services Regulation Authority could suggest amendments to the licence in such a case if it believed the change of control would affect its ability to perform its statutory duties, and it could refer the matter to the Competition and Markets Authority if they were not accepted. If a new controller is already a water enterprise (or is controlled by a water enterprise), the special merger rules under the Water Industry Act 1991 might be relevant. These require the Secretary of State to refer a merger of water enterprises to the Competition and Markets Authority if the gross assets of each of the water enterprises to be merged exceed £10m.

Electricity and gas

11.21   Electricity and gas are under the control of a single regulator, the Gas and Electricity Markets Authority (OFGEM) ('the Authority') which was created by the Utilities Act 2000. Ofgem's website is http://www.ofgem.gov.uk.

11.22   The supply of electricity is governed by the Electricity Act 1989, as amended. Any person who generates, transmits, distributes or supplies electricity to any premises is guilty of an offence unless he is authorised to do so by a licence granted by the Authority, or is exempted.

11.23   The supply of gas is regulated by the Gas Acts 1986 and 1995, as amended, and the Utilities Act 2000, and such a supply is unlawful unless authorised by a licence granted by the Authority. There are four types of licence: supply, shipper, transporter and interconnector. The holder of a transporter licence cannot hold a shipper or supply licence. Some licences contain a prohibition on the sale of the regulated assets without consent. Electricity and gas licences are assignable with the consent of the Authority, subject to any additional conditions contained in the licence.

Newspapers

11.24   No licence is required to publish a newspaper, but the printers and publishers of every newspaper used to have to make an annual return containing specified particulars, which was then entered in the register of newspaper proprietors (see the Newspaper Libel and Registration Act 1881). There was no obligation to register any change of ownership of a newspaper between annual returns, but anyone who ceased to be or became a newspaper proprietor had to make a return to that effect. However these requirements were removed now that most newspapers are owned by limited companies who have obligations under company law in general to file annual accounts and make a confirmation statement to Companies House. The Newspaper Libel and Registration Act 1881, s 4 – inquiry by court of a summary jurisdiction as to libel being for public benefit or being true – remains in place for Northern Ireland.

11.25   The Communications Act 2003 replaced previous restrictions on the transfer of the ownership in newspapers with an ability of the Secretary of State for Business, Energy and industrial Strategy to intervene in the case of changes of control of enterprises that own newspapers. These powers apply either where the transaction would satisfy the standard jurisdictional criteria described in Chapter 10 or where at least one of the parties controls a newspaper enterprise which has a share of supply of newspapers of at least 25% in the UK (or in a substantial part of the UK). The Secretary of State may require an investigation of whether or not the merger would raise public interest concerns relating to the need for accurate presentation of news or free expression of opinion in newspapers, or for a sufficient plurality of views in newspapers in each newspaper market in the UK or part of the UK. The Secretary of State will request that the Competition and Marketing Authority ('CMA') and Ofcom prepare reports on the competition/public interest issues raised, and if it appears that the acquisition raises public interest concerns, it may be referred to the CMA for further investigation on this basis also (in addition to any competition grounds for such a reference). The Secretary of State has the power to seek undertakings from the parties in lieu of a reference to the CMA or to seek undertakings (or impose remedies by order) following a CMA reference in order to address any public interest concerns arising from the merger (in addition to any competition concerns identified).

11.26   Similar provisions apply to transactions involving mergers involving broadcast media enterprises (television and radio), provided that either the standard jurisdictional criteria apply or that at least one of the parties has a share of supply of broadcasting of any description of at least 25% in the UK (or in a substantial part of the UK). Cross media mergers involving both newspapers and broadcast media are also subject to this public interest intervention process. Where broadcast media enterprises are involved, the public interest considerations taken into account are the need for a sufficient plurality of persons controlling media enterprises (in this case including newspapers) to serve a particular audience, the need for the availability throughout the UK of a wide range of broadcasting of high quality and appealing to a wide variety of tastes and interests, and the need for persons carrying on media enterprises to have a genuine commitment to specified broadcasting standards objectives.

11.27   These provisions must be borne in mind by joint venturers who wish to acquire control of an existing newspaper or broadcast media enterprise, and they can also be relevant where any joint venturer joins or leaves a venture involved in such activities, or if the control of the joint venture otherwise changes.

Ofcom in 2018 summarised the then media ownership rules as follows[2]:

> **'Parliament has put in place a number of restrictions in respect of the ownership of media enterprises and broadcast licences**
>
> 1.1 Parliament has put in place the following rules, collectively referred to as the "media ownership rules":
>
> i)   the national cross-media ownership rule, which (broadly) prevents large newspaper groups from owning a Channel 3 licence;
>
> ii)   the Channel 3 appointed news provider rule, which requires the regional Channel 3 licensees to appoint a single news provider;
>
> iii)   the Media Public Interest Test, which allows the Secretary of State to intervene in media mergers to determine whether the merger might result in harm to the public interest; and

---

2   See   https://www.ofcom.org.uk/__data/assets/pdf_file/0030/127929/Media-ownership-rules-report-2018.pdf.

iv)   the Disqualified Persons Restrictions, which prevent certain bodies or persons from holding broadcast licences generally, others from holding certain types of broadcasting licences and still others from holding broadcast licences unless Ofcom has determined that it is appropriate for them to do so.

1.2 Taken together, the rules are intended to protect the public interest by promoting plurality and preventing undue influence by any one, or certain types of, media owner.'

Consumer credit and consumer hire

11.28   The provision of loans, hire purchase, conditional sale or credit sale (consumer credit) or contracts of hire (consumer hire) to individuals (including sole traders and partnerships) is regulated by the Consumer Credit Act 1974, as amended by the Consumer Credit Act 2006. Prior to 6 April 2008, consumer credit agreements were only regulated if the credit was less than £25,000. Since 6 April 2008, all consumer credit agreements have been regulated save that the limit remains for any agreement which varies or supplements an agreement made before 6 April 2008 (where the credit exceeded £25,000) and which would not be treated as a regulated credit agreement if it was not varying or supplementing an existing one. A person must not engage in the business of providing consumer credit or consumer hire without a licence. Licences are not assignable. There is no provision under which licences automatically terminate on a change of control, but such an event has to be notified to the OFT/CMA. Such a change could result in revocation of the licence if the Office of Fair Trading is not satisfied that the new controller is a fit and proper person. The industry is heavily regulated. Banks often undertake consumer credit transactions and then require a licence both under the Financial Services and Markets Act 2000 and the Consumer Credit Act 1974, as amended.

From 1 April 2014, the Financial Conduct Authority ('FCA', previously FSA) replaced the then OFT as the consumer credit regulator. 50,000 licence-holders were licensed by the OFT and had to be processed under the new regime and applied for 'interim permission' from the FCA to continue via an on line application.

Prior clearance of mergers where there is a consumer credit licence – s 178 Notices

11.29   If the joint venture might amount to a merger it may be necessary to obtain prior clearance from the FCA where the entity being acquired holds consumer credit licences/FCA registered. Previously all that was needed was to notify the FCA so this did not hold up a merger. Now that clearance must be obtained it is vital to mention this to clients early on in the transaction and explain to them the implications for the timetable. Where a group of companies are acquired with different companies holding the licences it can be even more complicated and detailed application forms may need to be submitted to the FCA in relation to every company and certain shareholder individuals in addition – quite a substantial task. Not surprisingly as with merger clearances sometimes the sale and purchase agreement where a sale of a business is taking place will contain conditions around such FCA clearances.

11.30   It is a criminal offence under the FSMA 2000, s 191F to:

• acquire or increase control without notifying the FCA first;

• fail to obtain prior approval in such circumstances.

Dual-regulated firms (banks, building societies, credit unions etc) need to obtain approval from the Prudential Regulation Authority. A change in control can also take place when an existing controller of a firm decreases their control – see the FSMA 2000, s 191D or SUP 11 in the FCA Handbook for full details of the thresholds and requirements.

Obviously some joint ventures of FCA regulated entities may amount to one licensed party decreasing their control, so although joint ventures are less likely than sales of a business to result in a requirement to obtain FCA approval, it is not impossible.

11.31   The FCA states:

'Section 178

Notifications for changes in control are known as Section 178 notices – you should send us a notification as soon as you have made a decision to acquire a control in an authorised firm. Making a decision to acquire could for example include circumstances where a proposed controller decides not to take any action to prevent or reduce their increase in control to below the relevant threshold.

We have 60 working days (excluding any interruption period) to assess a change of control case. This period begins on the day we acknowledge receipt of a complete Section 178 notice.'

That is a very long period to wait for approval. The documents needed to be submitted to the FCA are substantial – see https://www.fca.org.uk/firms/change-control.

The FCA also says as follows for non-FSMA firms (see https://www.fca.org.uk/firms/change-control/change-control-requirements):

'In January 2018 PSD2 came into force, which means that the FSMA controllers' regime now also applies to Authorised Payment Institutions. See our Payment Services Directive (PSD2) pages [at https://www.fca. org.uk/firms/payment-services-regulations-e-money-regulations]   for information on change in control for PSD firms. Controllers of E-Money firms (registered under the EMD) are already subject to the FSMA controllers' regime.'

And for overseas firms:

'Overseas authorised firms do not require FCA approval for changes in control. However, you must inform us of details of any changes in control so we can assess the new controller(s) and update our records.'

The FSMA 2000, s 178 can be complicated in practice. Seek early advice from the FCA and/or experts in this field.

Non-UK ventures

11.32   Where a joint venture is being established to conduct a business outside the UK, enquiry should be made to ascertain whether there is any requirement to obtain a licence and what other regulatory requirements may apply. Many of the regulated businesses dealt with above will be found to be subject to regulation in overseas jurisdictions.

2   Requirements for UK listed companies

11.33   Companies whose shares have been granted a listing in the UK by the UK Listing Authority ('UKLA', part of the Financial Conduct Authority previously the FSA) will need to consider whether they are required under the UKLA's Listing Rules to make a public announcement or obtain an ordinary resolution of their shareholders to enter into a joint venture.

11.34   Chapter 10 of the Listing Rules governs transactions by a listed company, and will apply where a listed joint venturer, or a joint venturer which is a subsidiary of a listed company, is required to transfer business assets into the joint venture or to subscribe to its capital, including loan capital. References in this chapter to listed companies should be taken to include their subsidiary undertakings. It is perhaps unlikely that the establishment of a joint venture to conduct a new business will come within any of the thresholds set out in Chapter 10, let alone reach Class 1 where shareholders' consent is required, but the transfer of an existing business to a joint venture could well do so, as could the purchase by a listed joint venturer of the shares of another party to the venture, or a transfer of an undertaking or assets to a listed joint venturer on termination of the venture.

11.35   A transaction relating to the inception of a joint venture will not reach Class 1, unless it involves:

● the contribution to the joint venture of at least 25% of its gross assets or an amount representing at least 25% of its market capitalisation; or

● the transfer to the joint venture of an undertaking accounting for at least 25% of its profits or turnover.

In the case of an acquisition of shares, an undertaking or assets, the Class 1 thresholds will be reached where any one or more of the following calculations produces a percentage ratio of 25% or more:

● the gross assets the subject of the transaction divided by the gross assets of the listed company;

● the profits attributable to the assets the subject of the transaction divided by the profits of the listed company;

● the consideration for the transaction as a percentage of the aggregate market value of all the ordinary shares of the listed company; or

● the gross capital of the company or undertaking being acquired divided by the gross capital of the listed company.

11.36   Where the acquisition of the shares or undertaking will result in the results of the company or undertaking concerned being consolidated with those of the listed company[3], the calculation must be performed as if 100% of the shares or undertaking are being acquired; otherwise the profits may be prorated and the gross assets treated as equal to the consideration together with any liabilities assumed – see the class tests of the Listing Rules. In the case of assets not comprising an undertaking, the assets are treated as equal to the consideration, or their book value if higher. The same aggregation rule applies where a listed joint venturer has to consolidate the results of a joint venture and the joint venture makes an acquisition or disposal; the listed company is treated as if it owned 100% of what is acquired or disposed of. If a joint venturer has to consolidate the results of the joint venture and disposes of the whole or part of its interest so that it no longer has to consolidate, it will be treated as if it was disposing of 100% of the assets of the joint venture.

11.37   There is, however, a nasty trap to be found in Listing Rule 10.1.2 (as shown below), in that a 'transaction' includes the grant or acquisition of an option as if the option had been exercised, except that, if exercise is solely at the listed company's discretion, the transaction will be classified on exercise and only the consideration (if any) for the option will be classified on the grant or acquisition. For this purpose, 'option' is construed very widely, so it will cover many termination arrangements under which the listed company

---

3   See para 8.7ff.

has the right to purchase the shares of another party to the venture or might be required to buy or sell shares of another venturer (see para 17.28ff for details of some typical termination arrangements).

> '(2) includes the grant or acquisition of an option as if the option had been exercised except that, if exercise is solely at the listed company's or subsidiary undertaking's discretion, the transaction will be classified on exercise and only the consideration (if any) for the option will be classified on the grant or acquisition' – http://fshandbook.info/FS/html/handbook/LR/10/1.

The exit provisions in joint venture agreements typically give each shareholder a combination of rights and obligations to either sell their own holding or to acquire the other shareholder's holding if certain triggering events occur. If the consideration to be paid is to be determined by reference to future profitability of the joint venture or an independent valuation at the time of exercise, then the consideration will be treated as uncapped. The transaction will then be classified as a Class 1 transaction if the other class tests indicate that it is a Class 2 transaction. If the other class tests indicate that it is a Class 3 transaction, then it will be treated as a Class 2 transaction.

11.38   If the listed company retains sole discretion over the triggering event, for example if in the case of a call option (ie a right to buy shares or other assets) its exercise will be at the discretion of the listed company, this will be classified upon exercise, so that the listed company will need to consider whether to obtain its shareholders' consent before exercising it or to make its exercise conditional upon obtaining such consent if the terms of the option so allow. If it is possible that the exercise of a call option might involve a Class 1 transaction, care will need to be taken when drafting it to ensure that the exercise period is long enough to allow for the obtaining of shareholders' consent. Similarly if the listed company makes a choice to buy or sell following an event triggered by another shareholder, the purchase or sale will be classified when the choice is made.

11.39   If the listed company does not retain sole discretion over the triggering event, for example in the case of a put option (ie the right of another party to require the listed company to buy shares of that party), this is classified at the time it is agreed as though it had been exercised at the outset of the joint venture. This also applies to any terms within a joint venture agreement which may involve the listed company in purchasing the shares of another party or selling its shares to another party in circumstances beyond its control, such as under change of control provisions and Russian roulette arrangements (see para 17.19ff and 17.33ff).

11.40   Chapter 11 of the Listing Rules (online at https://www.handbook.fca.org.uk/handbook/LR/11/?view=chapter) deals with transactions with related parties (as therein defined). Chapter 11 could become relevant if a joint venture to which a listed company is to be party includes another party who is a substantial shareholder in the listed company (ie a shareholder who is, or within the 12 months before the date of the transaction was, entitled to exercise or to control the exercise of 10% or more of the votes exercisable in general meeting), or is, or was within the 12 months before the date of the transaction, a director or shadow director of the listed company. The definition of a related party also extends to include a substantial shareholder, director or shadow director of any of the subsidiary undertakings of the listed company or of its parent undertaking (if any) and subsidiary undertakings of such parent undertaking, and also the associates of the substantial shareholder, director or shadow director (widely defined). The UKLA treat joint venture shareholders as related parties of a listed joint venture company as they are persons who exercise significant influence (under LR 11.1.4(4) (R)). As such, all transactions between a listed joint venture company and any of its shareholders will potentially be within the Chapter 11 regime. If a joint venture is a subsidiary undertaking of a listed company, all its external transactions will need to be considered in relation to the Chapter 10 requirements, which may include the consent of the shareholders of the parent.

11.41 If Chapter 11 applies, subject to certain 'de minimis' thresholds (which are a lot lower than for Chapter 10), the listed company will have to convene a meeting of its shareholders to obtain an ordinary resolution to authorise the entry into the joint venture and any other transaction affecting it which involves the related party.

11.42 It should be noted that whenever a shareholder consent is required under Chapter 10 or Chapter 11, a circular must be despatched to the shareholders of the listed company which requires considerable information about the joint venture, as well as certain information about the listed company itself. In the case of a related party transaction where any percentage ratio is 25% or more, an independent valuation of the subject matter of the transaction is required unless appropriate financial information is available in respect of it, and in every case the independent directors must make a statement in the circular that the transaction is fair and reasonable so far as the shareholders of the listed company are concerned and that the directors have been so advised by an independent adviser acceptable to the UKLA. In any case requiring a circular, the joint venture agreement will have to be put on public display. The inclusion in the circular or the joint venture agreement of commercially sensitive material may therefore result in its becoming public knowledge, although it is possible to apply to the FCA for a modification or dispensation from the Listing Rules under Listing Rule 1.2, for example to allow such material to be excluded from the circular or to be withheld from display. However, some 2020 changes may affect this. The requirements in Listing Rule 13 regarding shareholder circulars and putting documents 'on display' was amended to clarify that on a class 1 transaction, a share purchase agreement does not have to be made available online. A copy of the share purchase agreement must be made available in hard copy for inspection and the issuer will need to specify where it can be found. Clearly makes it much less likely that it will be inspected.

3   Takeover code implications

11.43   Where a joint venture is being established to acquire control over a UK public company (or certain private companies whose shares have been publicly dealt with in the past) it will be necessary to bear in mind the provisions of the City Code on Takeovers and Mergers ('the Code'; a copy is available at http://www.thetakeoverpanel.org.uk/the-code/download-code) which is administered by the Panel on Takeover and Mergers ('the Panel'). The Panel and the Code now have legal effect in relation to all transactions which fall within the Code. Persons authorised by the FCA (who must either send out or approve the offer document) are required to comply with the Code under the rules applicable to them.

11.44   Effective control is not only obtained by making purchases in the market, since once the combined stakes of the joint venturers (who will all be regarded as 'acting in concert' under the Code) have reached 30% they will be required to offer for the remaining shares.

4   Financial promotions

11.45   Where persons are seeking others to subscribe for shares in a company, or make loans constituted as debenture stock, loan stock, bonds or by other similar instruments to any kind of vehicle, they must take care not to breach FSMA 2000, s 21. Any invitation to subscribe for shares or such loan capital is likely to be a financial promotion, which may not be issued unless it is either issued or approved by a person authorised under the Act.

11.46   Fortunately, there are a number of useful exemptions which are contained in the Financial Services and Markets Act 2000 (Financial Promotion) Order 2005 ('the Order'). In July 2020 HM Treasury began a consultation in this field – see the 'Regulatory Framework for Approval of Financial Promotions – Consultation'[4]. This may lead to changes in due course of the right of FCA authorised firms to approve promotions by non-authorised firms.

---

4   See https://www.gov.uk/government/consultations/regulatory-framework-for-approval-of-financial-promotions.

11.47   Probably the most useful exemption is in art 49 of the Order, which exempts financial promotions made to (inter alia) any body corporate which has a called up share capital or net assets of not less than £500,000 in the case of a body corporate which has more than 20 members, or is a subsidiary undertaking of a parent undertaking which has more than 20 members and not less than £5,000,000 in any other case. This is likely to apply to most invitations to potential joint venture partners. Note, however, that conditions attach to the exemption, which are designed to ensure that the financial promotion is not available to persons outside the exemption; in practice this is easily achieved by directing the invitation to a named person within the recipient's organisation marked 'private and confidential' and making it clear in the invitation that it is not available to anyone other than that organisation.

11.48   Persons seeking finance from private equity funds or any other institutional investors are likely to find that they are authorised persons under FSMA 2000, so that the financial promotion is exempt under art 19 of the Order. Business plans and financial information may therefore be sent to such potential investors without contravening the Order, although similar conditions attach to the exemption as apply to that contained in art 49. Even if the recipient is not such an authorised person, the promotion will still fall within the exemption if the recipient's ordinary activities include the making of investments for the purpose of a business carried on by him.

11.49   Although there are many other exemptions which could be relevant, mention should be made of those in arts 48, 50 and 50A of the Order, which were specifically introduced to aid the obtaining of finance from individuals prepared to act as 'business angels'. Article 48 exempts promotions made to 'Certified High Net Worth Individuals' who are those with an income of not less than £100,000 or net assets of not less than £250,000, excluding his or her home, rights under life insurance contracts and pension benefits, and who has signed a certificate to that effect; but again, conditions attach to the exemption. Article 50 exempts promotions relating to a particular class of investment made to 'Certified Sophisticated Investors' who are individuals who hold a certificate signed by a person who is authorised under FSMA 2000 confirming that the individual is sufficiently knowledgeable to understand the risks associated with that class of investment. Again, conditions attach to the exemption. Article 50A exempts promotions to 'self-certified sophisticated investors' who: (i) are individuals who have been members of a network or syndicate of business angels for at least the last six months; (ii) have made more than one investment in an unlisted company in the previous two years; (iii) are working, or had worked in the last two years, in a professional capacity in the private equity sector or providing finance for small and medium enterprises; or (iv) are currently, or have been in the last two years, a director of a company with an annual turnover of at least £1m, and in each case have signed a certificate to that effect.

11.50   Where an invitation to invest is circulated, it should not be described as a 'prospectus', because this implies that it has been approved as a prospectus by the FCA and complies with the requirements in the Prospectus Rules which apply to a prospectus. A prospectus would only be required in relation to a 'public offer' of shares or debentures, which may not be made by a private company. The dissemination of an investment invitation to only a few potential joint venture partners or investors will not amount to an offer to the 'public' as long as the invitation is not calculated to result, directly or indirectly, in the shares or debentures becoming available to persons other than those receiving the offer – see CA 2006, s 756.

FCI temporary product intervention powers – example

11.51   In November 2019, the FCA made rules under its temporary product intervention (TPI) powers which banned the promotion of high-risk speculative illiquid securities (such as mini-bonds) to most retail consumers (excluding sophisticated and high net worth retail investors) with effect from 1 January 2020.

The Government summarised this as follows in its press release:

> 'The ban applies to more complex and opaque securities issues where the funds raised by the issuer are used to lend to a third party, buy or acquire investments, or buy or fund the construction of property. The FCA consulted on permanent measures on 18 June 2020.

> The context for the FCA's intervention was the failure of the firm London Capital and Finance (LCF) in January 2019. LCF was an authorised firm that issued mini-bonds worth more than £230m to over 11,000 investors. Prior to the firm's failure, the FCA had intervened to ban misleading promotions issued by LCF. The Treasury subsequently directed the FCA to launch an independent investigation into the circumstances surrounding the collapse of LCF and the FCA's supervision of the firm.'

Alongside the independent investigation, the Treasury also announced a review to consider the wider regulatory arrangements currently in place for the issuance of non-transferable debt securities, such as some 'mini-bonds', including the financial promotions regime which governs the marketing of those products. Although LCF was an authorised firm, the case has prompted HMT to consider further measures to strengthen consumer protection across the financial promotions regime, including the proposals concerning unauthorised firms' promotions in this consultation. These proposals are not limited to the market for non-transferable securities. In June 2020 the FCA announced proposals to make permanent its ban on the mass-marketing of speculative illiquid securities, including speculative mini-bonds, to retail investors.

5 Collective investment schemes

11.52   Generally, bodies corporate (including companies incorporated under the Companies Act 1985 and the Companies Act 2006) will not be collective investment schemes (see para 21 of the Schedule to the Financial Services and Markets Act 2000 (Collective Investment Schemes) Order 2001[5]). However, 'open-ended investment companies' (see FSMA 2000, s 236) are collective investment schemes. A characteristic of an open-ended investment company is that its purpose is the investment of its funds with the aim of spreading investment risk. Therefore, companies formed for trading rather than investment purposes are unlikely to be collective investment schemes even if they have the other characteristics of an 'open-ended' company, but companies carrying on investment activities may well be collective investment schemes. Entities who operate or manage business-angel-led Enterprise Capital Funds, which are designed to enable small- and medium-sized enterprises to receive equity funding from a mixture of private and government capital, and which are clearly collective investment schemes, can also do so without needing FCA authorisation. For FCA 2016 Guidance on unregulated collective investment schemes in general see https://www.fca.org.uk/consumers/unregulated-collective-investment-schemes.

11.53   An English limited partnership established under the 1907 Act for investment purposes[6] will be a collective investment scheme under FSMA 2000, and the general partner must be a person authorised under that Act if it carries on the regulated activity of establishing or operating the collective investment scheme or any other regulated activity. In practice, the general partner will typically delegate the management to a person so authorised and thereby avoid carrying on any regulated activity, but the mere fact of delegation does not avoid the need for authorisation if the general partner nevertheless carries on a regulated activity.

11.54   A joint venture conducted through an ordinary partnership or limited liability partnership is unlikely to constitute a collective investment scheme, because FSMA 2000, s 235(2) only applies the collective investment scheme provisions to an arrangement under which all the participants (ie the investors) do not have day-to-day control over the management of the property of the partnership, whereas partners in such partnerships will generally have day-to-day control over management. In the context of property investment clubs, the FCA's Perimeter Guidance Manual (PERG, online at https://www.handbook.fca.org.uk/handbook/PERG/) states that 'day-to-day control'

---

5   SI 2001/1062. As amended by the Financial Services and Markets Act 2000 (Collective Investment Schemes) (Amendment) Order 2008 (SI 2008/1641) and the Financial Services and Markets Act 2000 (Collective Investment Schemes) (Amendment) (No 2) Order 2008 (SI 2008/1813).
6   See para 1.35 above.

should have its ordinary meaning: namely that a participant has the power, from day-to-day, to decide how the property owned by the club is managed and that whilst actual management can be delegated, the participant needs to retain day-to-day control for the collective investment scheme rules not to apply (see response to Q.6, PERG 11.2). Whilst the FCA guidance is provided in relation to property investment clubs, readers may find this a useful insight into how the FCA interprets s 235 generally.

11.55   In view of the above, where the joint venture involves one or more 'sleeping' or passive participants who delegate management of the joint venture to a board or other management structure, a careful analysis of the facts should be undertaken. Notwithstanding the lack of managerial involvement, further relief from the collective investment scheme rules may be obtained by virtue of para 9 of the Schedule to the Financial Services and Markets Act 2000 (Collective Investment Schemes) Order 2001 (as amended), which excludes any arrangement where each of the participants carries on a business other than investment business and enters into the arrangements for commercial purposes related to that business. This provision will exclude most joint ventures established for trading purposes, no matter through what kind of vehicle they are conducted.

Chapter 12

UK limited liability partnerships

Summary

This chapter discusses in broad outline the main features of a UK limited liability partnership and discusses its advantages and disadvantages over other UK constituted entities. The chapter assumes that the LLP is resident in the UK for tax purposes, and that, except where otherwise stated, the members are similarly resident.

1 Introduction

12.1 The limited liability partnership ('LLP') is a form of corporate entity introduced into English law by the Limited Liability Partnerships Act 2000.

12.2 An LLP combines features of both a UK partnership and a UK limited company. On the one hand, like a limited company, it is a legal entity apart from its members, and all its members have limited liability. On the other hand it is taxed in the UK as if it were a partnership and its constitution is, in practice, almost entirely governed by an agreement between its members which tends to look very like a partnership deed, and not by memorandum and articles of association. Companies House has information on LLPs at https://www.gov.uk/government/collections/companies-house-guidance-for-limited-companies-partnerships-and-other-company-types#limited-liability-partnerships-(llps).

12.3 LLPs were introduced in the UK as a result of pressure from professional bodies, particularly those representing accountants, for a form of organisation which would confer limited liability on its members, but would preserve the taxation regime enjoyed in the UK by professional and other partnerships. Ironically, the professions were initially slow to adopt LLPs because the government has imposed virtually the same filing and disclosure obligations on them as for companies, so that the greater privacy given to partnerships is not carried over to LLPs. Furthermore, tax difficulties have arisen in certain overseas jurisdictions which treat LLPs as if they were companies for tax purposes. However, the professions have now come around to the general consensus that the benefits of the LLP outweigh any other concerns (including those related to privacy) and it is now the vehicle of choice for most large legal, accountancy, consultancy and surveying firms.

12.4   LLPs have also become popular vehicles for investment management businesses, for which they are particularly suited and indeed many investment management firms have converted from limited companies and limited partnerships into LLPs. They are also coming into use for constituting venture capital funds as replacements for UK limited partnerships constituted under the Limited Partnerships Act 1907, the advantage of an LLP being that the investors can become involved in the management of the fund, as well as withdraw their capital, without losing the protection of limited liability. Although the LLP is a popular choice for certain situations, it has not yet made quite the same breakthrough as a vehicle for general business use, including joint ventures. Indeed disadvantageous tax changes led some LLPs to become limited companies (see para 12.7).

2   Advantages and disadvantages of LLPs compared with limited companies

Fiscal transparency

12.5   In the UK, LLPs are taxed like partnerships, so that each member is treated for tax purposes as being directly in receipt of the profits or losses of the LLP, be they income or capital gains.

12.6   A UK resident corporate member liable to UK corporation tax does not gain any tax advantage from being a member of an LLP compared with its being a shareholder of a UK tax resident company. A corporate member will be taxed currently on any profit of the LLP allocated to it.

12.7   From 6 April 2014, new taxation rules came into effect for LLP members under which some LLP members who had been taxed as self-employed are now taxed as if they are employees. Both the affected LLPs and their members have to pay national insurance contributions if the affected members were employed by the LLPs. Under the provisions, any member who meets all three of the following conditions is regarded as an employee:

- Condition A: It is reasonable to expect that at least 80% of the member's pay is fixed, or if variable, then without reference to, or in practice unaffected by, the LLP's overall profit or loss.

- Condition B: The member has no significant influence over the affairs of the LLP.

- Condition C: The member's contribution to the LLP is less than 25% of the disguised salary.

In most cases only senior members/partners will be regarded as having 'significant influence' over the affairs of the LLP. It is therefore important for everyone to be aware of these changes as it is likely to be conditions A and C that may be, or may become, not satisfied.

12.8   In many professional partnerships there are the newer members who are 'fixed-share LLP members'. These have tended to take out thousands of loans according to the major banks – ie they have made a large contribution to the firm which otherwise they would not have had to do, as they are keen not to be taxed as an employee. For smaller LLPs Condition B can be used – ensuring they have a significant influence over the affairs of the LLP, in order to avoid being classed as an employee.

12.9   In cases where the LLP member is not caught by the provisions at para 12.7 above and is not classed for tax purposes as an employee, a UK resident individual member of an LLP may, however, be better off from a tax point of view taking into account the reduced level of national insurance contribution. However, this advantage is lost to the extent that profits are not all paid out. A member of an LLP is taxed on the whole of his profit share, whether he receives it or not, whereas if he were a shareholder in a company he would pay no income tax on any retained profits, which would bear corporation tax at a maximum rate of 20% (2021/22 rates although rates are rising to 25% by 2023/24). The sale of a company with undistributed profits inside it normally only attracts capital gains tax at 10% where business asset disposal relief (BADR) (previously called entrepreneurs' relief) applies. Therefore, once profits have risen to a greater level than is required to be taken as salary, or profits have to be retained to build up working capital, membership of an LLP becomes disadvantageous for an individual, although this may be counteracted by introducing a UK resident company to the LLP as a corporate member and allocating such profits to it and subject always to the rules described at para 12.7 above.

12.10   Whether a non-UK resident investor is advantaged by being a member of a UK LLP will depend upon the circumstances. The use of an LLP may reduce double taxation which would otherwise be suffered if profits are received as dividends. If an LLP is not advantageous (eg for a non-resident investor subject to a lower rate of tax in its own jurisdiction) the investor might overcome the disadvantage by interposing a UK company through which it invests, which would replicate the position which would have obtained had the investor made a direct investment into such a company.

12.11   If an LLP makes a loss, the position may be more advantageous than that which would apply in the case of a company, in that the members of the LLP may be able to obtain relief for that loss against their other income in whatever way applies in relation to their particular tax positions without having to be sure to comply with the conditions for consortium relief which apply if a company makes a loss. Consortium relief is in any case not available to individuals or to non-resident companies without a trade in the UK. However, the losses available for set off are limited to the capital contribution to the LLP of the member concerned. Similarly, profits from LLPs allocated to members may be capable of being set against available tax losses of the member. Since joint ventures often make losses in the early years, the ability to obtain relief for them may make LLPs attractive, particularly where the members are a mixture of UK residents and non-residents.

12.12   Gains arising on the disposal of assets used in the business of an LLP are chargeable to UK capital gains tax rather than corporation tax at a maximum of 19% (up to 25% 2023/24). CGT is likely to be at a lower rate. However, there used to be a much bigger difference when corporation tax was higher. A disadvantage of an LLP is that, should its undertaking and assets be sold for a consideration consisting of shares or other securities, the gain made on the sale cannot be 'rolled over' into the consideration shares or securities. This is perhaps a more relevant consideration since the abolition of taper relief.

Greater flexibility of operation

12.13   An LLP is not required to file any constitutional documents, such as a memorandum and articles of association. The relationship between the members will usually, but does not have to be, governed by a deed made between them, which can be in any form and contain any provisions, subject to the constraints of the general law. If there is no deed, certain 'default' provisions automatically apply. LLPs have unlimited capacity, ie they may do anything which an individual may do, and are not constrained by a memorandum of association, but only by whatever contractual restrictions may be contained in the deed.

12.14   The admission or retirement of a member of an LLP is a tax neutral event as far as the other partners are concerned, unless a payment is made between members, or assets are revalued in the accounts.

12.15   The business of an LLP can be (provided it is with a view to profit), but does not have to be, in the hands of a board of directors. The members are free to make whatever arrangements they wish in relation to the decision-making process and the management of the business.

12.16   An LLP does not have a share capital. The share of the income and capital profits to which each member is entitled is regulated entirely by the agreement between them, and does not have to bear any fixed relationship to the capital they have each contributed.

12.17   Another key benefit of LLPs is the ability to separate legal, management and economic ownership easily. Whereas to achieve an equivalent effect using a company would likely require the company to have a complicated multiple share class structure, the effect can be achieved simply through the provisions of the LLP deed. This could be particularly attractive to joint venture participants where the participants might have different objectives arising out of their participation. There is also flexibility for interests to change over time and/or be subject to contingencies, such as milestones being achieved.

Reduced capital maintenance requirements

12.18   The capital maintenance provisions and provisions restricting dividend distributions applicable to limited companies do not apply to LLPs, although notwithstanding this there may be industry specific rules which require the LLP to maintain a particular level of capital.

12.19   The only restrictions on distribution of assets are the unfair and fraudulent trading rules and s 214A of the Insolvency Act 1986, which provides that, if within the two years prior to the liquidation of an LLP a member of the LLP withdraws any property from the LLP, and it is proved that at the time of the withdrawal the member knew or had reasonable grounds for believing that the LLP was unable to pay its debts within the meaning of s 123 of the Insolvency Act 1986, or would be so unable after the withdrawal and all other withdrawals made at the same time, and the member knew or ought to have concluded that there was no reasonable prospect that the LLP would avoid insolvent liquidation, the member is liable to make such contribution to the assets of the LLP as the court thinks proper, up to the amount of the withdrawal.

Members of an LLP are not employees

12.20   An individual member of an LLP, even if he works full time for the LLP, originally did not become an employee of the LLP. Even if the member is taxed as an employee (see 12.6ff above) they were still not necessarily an employee for other purposes, such as employment protection. (A member will be an employee only if, were the LLP a partnership, he would be regarded as an employee of the partnership – in effect, the position of a salaried partner.) Consequently, the drawings of a member were not liable to PAYE deductions, and his share of the profits of the LLP is taxed as trading income not as employment income. Class 2 and Class 4 national insurance contributions are payable, which are at a lower rate than employer's and employee's Class 1 contributions.

Furthermore, it may be possible to create option and incentive schemes, under which additional interests in the LLP may be acquired by a member without the member incurring an income tax charge. Gains made on the disposal of the interests would normally attract only capital gains tax. The fact that an LLP does not have share capital requires a different approach to the structuring of option and incentive schemes. The currency of the option or incentive schemes will be the right to receive a certain proportion of the profits, and possibly capital, of the LLP, rather than the right to receive shares. Given that an LLP could never be floated (at least, not without its first transferring its assets and undertaking to a company, which may be difficult to structure in a tax-efficient way, or by interposing a limited company between the LLP and its members), the incentivised member could in practice only cash in his rights on a repurchase by the LLP, a sale to another member, or on a sale of the whole of the undertaking and assets of the LLP to a trade or financial buyer.

However in 2014, as mentioned at para 12.7 above, this changed such that where all the conditions A–C in the legislation are met, the individual is now treated as an employee for tax purposes £80% of pay is fixed, the member has no significant influence over the affairs of the LLP and the member's contribution is less than 25% of the disguised salary. As the Law Society said at the time in a press release:

> 'It's likely that in most cases, only senior partners will be regarded as having "significant influence" over the affairs of the LLP. It is therefore important for everyone to be aware of these changes as it is likely to be conditions A and C that may be, or may become, not satisfied.'

Advantages of LLPs over partnerships

12.21   The chief advantage is limited liability. In an ordinary partnership, all the partners incur joint and several unlimited liability for the partnership's debts. In a limited partnership under the Limited Partnerships Act 1907 all partners other than the general partner have limited liability, but any limited partner who becomes involved in the management of the partnership business loses the protection of limited liability. An LLP enables all members to participate in management and retain limited liability (subject to the usual rules on assumption of personal responsibility[1]).

12.22   Another key advantage of an LLP is that, unlike a partnership, it may grant a floating charge over its assets. This is likely to make it easier for an LLP to raise loan finance and will tend to make it less likely that the members will be required to provide security over their personal assets in respect of such borrowings.

---

1   Individual members can be liable for their own negligence in certain circumstances (see Limited Liability Partnerships Act 2000, s 6(4) and *Williams v Natural Life Health Foods Ltd* [1998] BCLC 689).

12.23   The LLP also provides for a much easier exit of its members than would be the case with a partner leaving a partnership. In the latter case, a departing partner seeking to strengthen their bargaining position could seek an account of his legal (if any) and beneficial interest in the assets and liabilities of the partnership. This is a most costly and time-consuming exercise for the partnership if it is raised; some partnership accounts can take years to finalise. By contrast, because an LLP is a separate legal entity which holds, and is subject to, its own assets and liabilities, similar problems do not arise in the context of members departing from an LLP.

Collective investment schemes

12.24   When using an LLP as a joint venture vehicle, care needs to be taken to analyse the applicability of the collective investment scheme rules to the joint venture. See para 11.52 for further commentary on this point.

3   Statutory regime governing LLPs

12.25   It would be out of place here to go into great detail concerning the law governing LLPs. Various textbooks are available on the subject. The law is contained in the Limited Liability Partnerships Act 2000, supplemented by the Limited Liability Partnerships (Application of Companies Act 2006) Regulations 2009 (which replaced the Limited Liability Partnerships Regulations 2001), which import a great deal of UK company law into the law relating to LLPs, with appropriate modifications.

12.26   Incorporation of an LLP is extremely simple. Two or more persons associated for carrying on a lawful business with a view to profit subscribe their names to an incorporation document and complete a written statement, giving certain details of the LLP and its members. The incorporation document and statement are combined in Form LLP2, which is filed at the UK Companies Registration Office, which registers it and issues a certificate of incorporation. No other documentation is required by law, although in practice there will be a deed between the members setting out their rights and obligations, which is likely to be a lengthy document, requiring considerable negotiation.

12.27   An LLP must have at least two designated members, whose principal role is to perform administrative and filing duties and also to perform tasks on behalf of the other members, such as signing the LLP's accounts. A designated member should not be assumed to be the equivalent of a director of a company. All the members of an LLP may participate in management, subject to the terms of the agreement between them.

12.28   An LLP, like a limited company, must disclose its persons of significant control. Partnerships, unless they have a corporate member, do not have to do so and thus maintain more privacy. The Limited Liability Partnerships (Register of People with Significant Control) Regulations 2016 (SI 2016/340) set out the relevant law. The regulations were made under the Small Business, Enterprise and Employment Act 2015. LLPs must state who ultimately controls them or has more than 25% of voting power. See also paras 16.44–16.46 for the application of the PSC rules to limited companies and in particular the guidance relating to when particular control clauses in agreements may make even a smaller shareholder a PSC whose identity must be disclosed.

4 Conclusion

12.29   Given the flexibility and potential fiscal advantages, it is perhaps surprising that LLPs are still rarely used as commercial joint venture vehicles. This probably stems, in part at least, from the fact that commercial or industrial joint venturers are more familiar with the limited liability company entity whose structure (and limitations) are better known. It remains to be seen whether this will change in the years to come. A precedent for a limited liability partnership deed suitable for a joint venture between corporates for commercial purposes can be found in Precedent 7.

Part B

Key issues in structuring and drafting UK corporate joint venture documentation and shareholders' agreements

Chapter 13

Deadlock companies in English company law

Summary

This chapter deals with the issues which arise in structuring a 'deadlock 50:50' company, where both parties are equal shareholders and neither is willing to surrender control to the other. The mechanics of structuring a deadlock company are first discussed, and then consideration is given to methods by which deadlocks or failures to reach decisions may be avoided and resolved. Although this chapter concerns English company law only, the methods for resolving deadlock may be adaptable to the corporate law of other jurisdictions.

1 Structuring a deadlock company

13.1 Corporate joint ventures and shareholders' agreements tend to fall into one of two categories: those where equal parties are deadlocked, and those in which one or more, or perhaps all, the parties are in a minority. This chapter deals with only the first of these types.

13.2 A 'deadlock' company is a popular way of structuring a corporate joint venture or shareholders' agreement where there are two parties, each of whom is to hold one-half of the shares and neither of whom is willing to surrender control to the other. They will inevitably wish to have an equal number of directors, with a view to ensuring that neither can outvote the other at a board meeting.

13.3 The Companies Act 2006 provides for model articles for private companies limited by shares which can be adopted by any company from 1 October 2009 ('the Model Articles'). These are set out in Sch 1 to the Companies (Model Articles) Regulations 2008[1]. From 1 October 2009, if a private company limited by shares fails to register any articles of association on incorporation, the Model Articles will be its default articles, replacing Table A regulations, which applied under the Companies Act 1985.

---

1 SI 2008/3229.

13.4 If two shareholders each have equal voting rights in a company which has adopted articles of association in the form of the Model Articles, complete deadlock is not in fact achieved. First, art 13 of the Model Articles gives the chairman a casting vote at a board meeting. This means that board control is in the hands of whichever party a permanent chairman happens to represent, or will be held by the party who is represented by whoever is the chairman of the particular meeting. If this provision is removed, and it is expressly provided that the chairman shall not have a casting vote, then, since an equality of votes will negative the decision under discussion, nothing can be resolved upon unless both parties agree. Note that under the Companies Act 2006, a chairman's casting vote at a shareholders' meeting is no longer valid – unless such a right existed in the company's articles of association immediately before 1 October 2007. However, a later legislative amendment now allows non-traded companies only whose articles provided for a chairman's casting vote before 1 October 2007 to retain or reinstate such provisions – see Companies Act 2006 (Commencement No 5, Transitional Provisions and Savings) Order 2007 (SI 2007/3495).

13.5 Secondly, although initially each party may secure the appointment of an equal number of directors, this will cease to be so as directors resign or retire, and since under the Model Articles (art 17), a new director can be appointed by a decision of the board or by ordinary resolution in general meeting, neither party will have the ability to secure the appointment of the replacement directors necessary to re-establish equality. The articles or the shareholders' agreement will therefore need to be structured so that each has a right to appoint a given number of directors (and also to remove any director it has appointed and to appoint a replacement). The mechanics for achieving this are discussed at para 16.1ff. Model Article 17 will also have to be excluded so as to avoid additional directors being appointed during any period in which either party is temporarily in a minority on the board (which may occur because one of its board appointees has resigned and no replacement has, as yet, been appointed) and also to avoid any appointment of a director being made in general meeting where either party happens not to be fully represented.

13.6 In order further to reinforce the desired deadlock, the articles or shareholders' agreement will usually provide that there is no quorum at a board meeting unless both parties have an equal number of directors present, or in a case where each party is able to appoint more than one director, the articles may provide that if a party's appointed directors are not all present, those who are present can exercise the votes of those who are absent. Deadlock could also be preserved by each absent director appointing an alternate director to attend in his place, but it is not always possible to organise this, especially as a director may be unexpectedly unable to attend a meeting. In any event, the Model Articles do not make provision for the appointment of alternate directors. As such, any company wishing to allow for the appointment of alternates must include express provision in its articles of association. Note also that consideration should be given to whether the deadlock provisions in the articles relating to board meetings should also apply to decisions taken by a committee of the board. It is common to provide that a decision of any such committee should require at least one nominated director of each party, or possibly all directors who are present at the meeting must vote in its favour.

13.7 In order to avoid the directors of either party being taken by surprise, it is normal to provide that board meetings can only be held on notice of not less than a specified period (the Model Articles do not specify a minimum period of notice), and to provide that the notice must be accompanied by an agenda detailing the items to be discussed and a full set of the relevant papers. There is often an exemption to allow the holding of a board meeting on much shorter notice in the case of emergency, provided that the notice is sent to all directors or provided that at least one director from each class agrees in writing to the shorter notice.

13.8 Deadlock is enforced at general meetings by providing that there is no quorum unless an authorised representative of each corporate shareholder is present; or, in the case of an individual shareholder, unless he is present in person or has appointed a proxy to attend in his place. Detailed provisions about notices are unnecessary, since the Companies Act 2006 contains suitable periods of notice (normally 14 days), but the provisions of the Act as to the mechanics of giving notice may need to be modified, particularly in relation to deemed times of delivery (for example the 48 hours deemed delivery time for documents and information sent by electronic means may be too long).

13.9 A director must avoid a situation in which he has, or can have, a direct or indirect interest that conflicts, or possibly may conflict, with the interests of the company[2]. The duty will not be infringed if the matter is authorised by the board (though any interested director cannot participate in the authorisation process) or it cannot reasonably be regarded as likely to give rise to a conflict. In the context of a joint venture company, conflict situations are likely to arise where the director of the joint venture is also a director of the corporate shareholder that appointed him or a director/employee of other companies in the shareholder's group. For private companies incorporated on or after 1 October 2008, the directors may authorise conflicts where the constitution does not invalidate the authorisation (the Model Articles are silent on s 175 authorisation by the board). However, for a joint venture company, it may be that the shareholders do not want to permit the independent directors to authorise a director's conflict as this may cut across the purpose of the joint venture. An alternative is for the articles of association to require that a potential conflict situation be referred to the shareholders for authorisation.

---

2   CA 2006, s 175(1).

The articles could also set out some of the terms and conditions upon which the shareholders may grant such an authorisation.

Table 3
Provisions of the model articles likely to require amendment when structuring a deadlock company

Model Article	Amendment/Deletion likely to be required
6(2)	Rules for committee meetings of directors
7	Decision-making by directors
8	Unanimous decisions of directors
9	Calling a directors' meeting
11	Quorum for directors' meetings
12–13	Chairing of directors' meetings and casting vote
14	Conflicts of interest
16	Directors' discretion to make further rules
17	Methods of appointing directors
27–29	Rights of transmittees
36	Authority to capitalise and appropriation of capitalised sums
43	Errors and disputes
44(2)	Persons who may demand a poll
50	No right to inspect accounts and other records
51	Provision for employees on cessation of business
52–53	Indemnity and insurance

2   Avoiding and resolving deadlocks

Avoiding deadlock

13.10   In practice, there is of course no way of completely avoiding a deadlock (or failure to agree on an issue) arising, but in view of the paralysis such a situation would cause, the shareholders in a 'deadlock company' have to strive particularly hard to overcome any disagreements.

13.11   One way of minimising disagreements is to have particularly full documentation, setting out very detailed arrangements for the establishment, development and operation of the joint venture company. A detailed business plan (see para 1.73) is particularly desirable in a deadlock company. However, the world constantly changes and a carefully drawn up business plan setting out a strategy for some years ahead may become inappropriate through a change in the relevant market, the emergence of an unexpected competitor, or any number of other reasons. In revising the plan to meet these new contingencies, a disagreement may easily arise, and indeed a very detailed plan may prove counterproductive in that positions based on it may prove difficult to change.

Resolving deadlock

13.12   Recognising that disagreements cannot always be avoided, and that a deadlock may thereby arise, it is desirable for the documentation to include a procedure for their resolution, since the law provides for no effective solution other than the liquidation of the joint venture company. It has long been established that a deadlock in management can be a basis for a successful petition for compulsory winding up on the ground that it would be just and equitable to do so under s 122(1)(g) of the Insolvency Act 1986[3].

13.13   In *Chu v Lau*[4] following *Ebrahimi v Westbourne Galleries Ltd*[5], the Privy Council found that if a company is a quasi-partnership there are two 'related but distinct' grounds upon which it can be wound up:

● to resolve a functional deadlock; and

● as a response to an irretrievable breakdown in trust and confidence.

The court found the court below was wrong to suggest buying one shareholders' shares was a remedy as this was only available in an unfair prejudice case not a winding up case. Nor did a theoretical freedom of one party to sell his shares mean there were solutions other than winding up. No one might necessarily buy the shares. Nor did the principle of only coming to the court with 'clean hands' bar the party here from obtaining the winding up order. He was only partly to blame for the dispute. His fellow shareholder was just as much to blame.

13.14   Winding up would be unlikely to provide a very satisfactory solution for either party; the development of a promising enterprise may be cut short, its assets may have to be realised on otherwise than the best terms (especially if vital support agreements or intellectual property licences with either of the shareholders terminate on liquidation), and if the assets can be realised there is then the possibility of double taxation when the proceeds are distributed to the shareholders (see para 7.62).

13.15   One provision which is quite often seen is a so-called 'gin and tonic clause', where, if a deadlock arises, the chairmen of each party meet and attempt to resolve it in a face-to-face discussion. The theory is that these elder

---

3   See *Re Yenidje Tobacco Co* [1916] 2 Ch 426.
4   [2020] UKPC 24.
5   [1973] AC 360.

statesmen, who are removed from the detail at the operational level of the joint venture and perhaps can see beyond the cause of the conflict to the wider interests of the two companies, may be able to find a sensible solution where their respective executive teams cannot. It must be doubtful whether this will necessarily be the case, particularly where one or both chairmen are executive, and in any event such a provision provides no solution where the chairmen cannot agree. It does, however, at least buy time within which the parties may be able to resolve their differences.

13.16   Another approach is for one or other of the parties to agree to surrender control temporarily to the other. In this case the chairman's casting vote at board meetings is retained, on the basis that the parties will alternate in appointing the chairman, perhaps for a year at a time. As a chairman's casting vote is no longer valid for shareholders' meetings, any attempt to include a provision for a tie-breaker vote at a general meeting will have to be drafted as a class right – ie an additional vote attaching to a share held by a particular shareholder. This solution has been successfully employed in many 50:50 joint ventures, and provides a mechanism for ensuring that a deadlock can be overcome, and at the same time enables each party to have a decisive say in the decisions that have to be made during the times that it has control. The disadvantages of this method are that the policy of the joint venture company may be subject to considerable fluctuation, and a particularly crucial decision might have to be made during one party's period of control, which is made in a way which the other party finds unable to accept. However, in view of possible 'retaliatory' action when the other party is in control, in practice the parties have an incentive to behave sensibly and reach decisions by consensus.

13.17   If the parties are not able to accept the complete discretion of the other party when it is in control, this can be addressed by providing that both parties must approve certain major transactions. These could be similar to the vetoes commonly afforded to a minority (see Chapter 15). However, this of course may mean that there is then a deadlock over one of the relevant transactions, but at least most other matters could be dealt with without the danger of a deadlock.

13.18   Another approach is to place the balance of power in the hands of an independent party. This is often the best approach and is preferable to winding up the company. The chairman's casting vote at board meetings could be retained, and the parties would agree that the chairman shall be independent. However, it could be difficult to persuade someone to take on that role, and there is always the risk that he might resign at the very moment when the dispute between the shareholders becomes most heated and his services are most required: there may then be a dispute about the identity of his successor. A variation is to appoint an independent non-executive director, with the chairman having no casting vote. This could be a truly neutral third party both parties trust, set up when the joint venture is set up.

13.19   A further similar approach, which is often suggested by the parties, is for the company itself to be deadlocked, but in the event of a deadlock arising, the dispute is to be referred to an independent expert, whose decision is to be final. One difficulty with this is that business decisions are not issues which are readily solved by an expert, being matters of business judgment. Another point is that it must be questioned whether there are many appropriately qualified people who would be prepared to take on such a role and whether, in actuality, the parties would always be happy to accept his binding decision. In practice, there are few businessmen who would allow a third party not involved in the business to make crucial decisions for them if the parties themselves cannot agree. However again this may be preferable to a winding up of the company and also may be so unpopular with both 'sides' they force themselves to work out a compromise before the dispute goes to such expert.

13.20   Chapter 23, on dispute resolution, considers the various means by which the parties can look outside the company to resolve disagreements. These include mediation (which does not necessarily lead to a binding determination), as well as expert determination, arbitration and litigation (which do produce a binding outcome, but on a legal or technical basis and not necessarily one which is commercially desirable).

13.21   A further approach, which is really an extension of the concept of submission to a third party, is for the parties to accept that although the company is 50:50 owned, it is in fact inappropriate, and indeed may be stifling of corporate enterprise, for all decisions to be made by its founders alone, and that most decisions are best left to an independent board who can be expected to make their decisions in the best interests of the joint venture company, and ultimately of the joint venturers. Although the articles or shareholders' agreement may still provide for the appointment of a certain number of directors by each shareholder, there will also be scope for the appointment of a number of additional directors who will hold the balance of power. They will most likely have executive roles in the joint venture company, and will not be the 'yes men' of either party, and may indeed have been recruited from outside or, in time, to have grown up, in terms of experience, with the joint venture. This solution is particularly appropriate for a sizeable full-function joint venture which is intended to be long-term and, in time, to be operationally independent of its founders and it is suggested that this is often the most rational way of structuring such a venture.

Termination on unresolved deadlock

13.22   Not all the above methods provide a certain way of resolving a deadlock should it arise. Except where the parties are prepared in every situation to bind themselves to accept the decision of the other party, or of another party who is brought in to resolve the dispute, the parties may still find themselves with a deadlock which cannot be resolved.

13.23   The normal remedy provided for in this event is termination of the shareholders' agreement. This is a solution which is likely to be so unpalatable to the parties that it is included more in the hope that the parties will try to avoid it by making every effort to negotiate a solution to the deadlock. In practice, termination will only be resorted to when the business relationship of the parties has completely broken down. With a view to ensuring that this is in fact the last resort, the documents will quite often provide that the right of termination can only be exercised after the parties have taken some defined steps to resolve the dispute. A clause might not allow a termination notice to be served until the following have occurred:

• there has been an equality of votes on a matter which has been raised at a board or general meeting;

• either party has served on the other a notice requesting the convening of a special board or general meeting to consider the issue again, and which states that if an equality of votes again results (or the other party's representatives absent themselves from the meeting so that there is no quorum) a deadlock will exist;

• at the special meeting there is again an equality of votes or there is no quorum;

• the 'gin and tonic clause' is invoked; and

• the chairmen have failed to resolve the dispute within, say, 30 days.

13.24   There is invariably a time limit on serving a termination notice, so that an old unresolved dispute about which no action has been taken for a long time cannot be made a ground for termination.

13.25   Since the parties will probably by now be unable to agree on anything and they may both have an equal desire to acquire the others' shares, the consequences of termination typically consist of some rather pre-emptory and uncertain arrangements for the acquisition of one party's participation by the other, which neither party will be particularly keen to use in case it ends up on the losing side. Such arrangements might include a 'Russian roulette' (see para 17.33) or a 'Texas shoot out' clause (see para 17.38). If these arrangements fail, the usual consequence is liquidation of the company.

Chapter 14

Minority protection under English company law

Summary

This chapter considers the law relating to the protection of minority shareholders and illustrates why its inadequacy gives rise to the need to provide for minority protection in a shareholders' agreement or articles of association. The different types of minority protection are then discussed. The chapter then considers to what extent it is best to insert minority protection provisions in the articles or in a shareholders' agreement and reviews the law relating to the enforcement of each. This chapter deals with English company law only; although the need for minority protection may arise in any jurisdiction, but the mechanics of achieving this will vary in each jurisdiction.

1 Why minority protection is needed

14.1   This chapter deals with the other major type of joint venture and shareholders' arrangements; that is where one or more parties are in a minority, whether or not another party is in a majority.

Control by majority

14.2   The general principle of English company law is that decisions are made by the majority and the minority is afforded very few rights. For example, decisions as to whether another shareholder should be admitted by the issue of further shares, the appointment of directors, how much of the profits should be distributed or retained in the company's business, whether or not the company's undertaking or assets should be sold and for how much, whether the company should enter a new business and whether it should be wound up, are all decisions which are made by the majority in the absence of any special provisions in the company's constitution or any shareholders' agreement.

14.3   The extent of that majority varies from a simple majority of the votes cast in a general meeting of the shareholders to a majority of 75% of the votes cast to pass a special resolution. Of the examples given in the last paragraph, only a change in any restriction on the objects of the company in the articles of association (which *might* be required to enable the company to enter a new business) and the liquidation of the company when solvent require such a majority. It is true that if new shares are to be offered to shareholders otherwise than pro-rata to existing shareholdings, a special resolution would be required to obtain a disapplication of the statutory pre-emption rights contained in s 561 of the Companies Act 2006 ('CA 2006') (formerly s 89 of the Companies Act 1985 ('CA 1985')), assuming that the articles do not exclude these rights altogether, which is permitted in the case of a private company. (Under the CA 1985 the alteration of the objects was one of those rare cases in which there was provision for an application to the court by minority holders holding not less than a 15% interest to cancel the alteration. Such rights were, however, not resorted to very often, and there was little guidance as to the basis upon which the courts would have ordered a cancellation).

14.4   All the other examples require only the decision of a simple majority of the votes cast in a general meeting, or simply a decision of the directors, who reach their decisions by a simple majority vote and are themselves appointed by a simple majority vote of the shareholders, or by the directors themselves. The directors have most matters relating to the affairs of the company in their hands, and this is where the power to make decisions is concentrated; few matters require the shareholders' decision.

Minority protection given by law

14.5   English law does recognise that the minority is entitled to a certain degree of protection from the unfettered discretion of the majority.

LIQUIDATION

14.6   The Insolvency Act 1986 allows a court to make a winding-up order where it finds it is just and equitable to do so[1]. In a long line of decisions with their roots in partnership law and culminating with the decision of the House of Lords in *Re Westbourne Galleries*[2], it has become established that where a private company is a 'quasi-partnership', a winding-up order can be made on the just and equitable ground where the facts would enable the dissolution of a partnership.

14.7   In *Re Westbourne Galleries* the petitioner had been removed as a director by the majority shareholder in breach of an implied understanding

---

1   Insolvency Act 1986, s 122(1)(g).
2   [1973] AC 360.

that he would be able to participate in management, and winding up was ordered. See also *Chu v Lau*[3] at 13.12.

14.8   The principle is not, however, confined to exclusion from management; any conduct which has the effect of causing a breakdown in the mutual trust and confidence between the shareholders may successfully ground a petition. In *Loch v John Blackwood*[4] the managing director and majority shareholder was deliberately keeping the minority shareholders in ignorance of the company's financial position in order to acquire their shares at an undervalue. In *Re a Company, ex p Glossop*[5] the minority had been excluded from participation in profits by a board which had carried to reserves sums greatly in excess of those required to finance the business. In *Jesner v Jarrad Properties Ltd*[6] misconduct of the company's affairs led to a successful petition.

14.9   Although a joint venture may well have the characteristics of a 'quasi-partnership', the principle is not confined to these, and any relationship of a personal character which makes it unjust or inequitable to insist on legal rights will be sufficient[7]. Even if the shareholders' agreement declares that the parties are not partners (which is quite usual) a winding-up order may still be made[8]. It is, however, open to question whether the position is the same in a case where the complaining party is an investment institution which has no personal relationship with any of the other shareholders. It has now been held at first instance[9], following *O'Neill v Phillips*, that conduct which is not unfairly prejudicial (see para 14.19ff) cannot support a winding-up order on the just and equitable ground. This would mean that the jurisdiction to make such a winding-up order and one based on unfair prejudice is essentially the same, although it is questionable whether this is right; in the deadlock cases such as *Re Yenidje Tobacco Co*[10], winding up was granted without any proof of unfairness but merely because the shareholders could not resolve their deadlock. Current practice is to petition on both grounds in the hope that if the court will not grant a remedy for 'unfair prejudice' it will at least wind the company up instead, although a Practice Direction discourages applications for both remedies unless winding up is genuinely sought. Winding up need not be granted where there is an alternative remedy (such as a petition for unfair prejudice) which has not been pursued[11].

---

3   [2020] UKPC 24.
4   [1924] AC 783.
5   [1988] 1 WLR 1068.
6   [1993] BCLC 1032.
7   *Re Ringtower Holdings plc* (1989) 5 BCC 82.
8   *Re a Company* [1988] BCLC 282.
9   *Re Guidezone Ltd* [2002] 2 BCLC 321.
10   [1916] 2 Ch 426.
11   Insolvency Act 2006, s 125(2) and *In the matter of Woven Rugs Ltd* [2008] BCC 903.

14.10   Even where winding up is available, it is a blunt instrument and is not likely to provide a satisfactory solution for the aggrieved party, although the threat to petition for winding up is often a valuable bargaining counter, and has probably enabled many aggrieved minority holders to achieve a satisfactory settlement.

MINORITY SHAREHOLDERS' ACTIONS

14.11   The law does provide two alternatives to the rather unsatisfactory and limited remedy of winding up. First, there is the possibility of the minority shareholder bringing what is known as a 'derivative claim' to redress wrongs inflicted upon the company by the controlling majority, which have prejudiced the shareholding of the minority. Second, there is the possibility of being able to petition under CA 2006, s 994 for 'unfair prejudice' (which has replaced CA 1985, s 459 but is virtually identical). A derivative claim is so called because, on the basis that it is only the company who can sue for wrongs done to it, the rights of the minority shareholder are 'derived' from those of the company. Both the minority holder or holders and the company itself are made the claimants in the action. The rule that the company is the only proper claimant for a wrong done against it, and that shareholders cannot complain of irregularities in the conduct of its internal affairs, was laid down in *Foss v Harbottle*[12], and to mount a derivative action the minority shareholder had to show that its case came within one of its exceptions, and leave of the court was required.

14.12   The common law rules in *Foss v Harbottle* have now been replaced (with effect from 1 October 2007) by a new statutory derivative claim in Part 11 of the CA 2006. A derivative claim can now only be brought under CA 2006, Part 11 or by order of the court in proceedings under CA 2006, s 994 (see below).

14.13   The rules in Part 11 apply to all derivative claims brought on or after 1 October 2007. If, however, the act or omission in question occurred prior to that date, then the court should determine the outcome on the basis of the common law rules which applied at the time.

14.14   The circumstances in which a shareholder can bring a claim have been widened, but the CA 2006 also introduces additional procedural steps which have to be followed to avoid non-meritorious claims being brought.

14.15   Under the old common law a shareholder had to show that there had been a fraud on the minority (in that the director had committed a breach of duty) and that the directors concerned had control of the company and had used that control to prevent a claim being brought by the company itself.

---

12   (1843) 2 Hare 461.

14.16   Under the new statutory procedure, an action can be brought for any act or omission involving negligence, default, breach of duty or breach of trust by a director – so that negligence will be sufficient. The director no longer has to have benefitted personally from the breach.

14.17   An action can be brought against a director or another third party. However, the Explanatory Notes to the CA 2006 state that an action should only be brought against a third party in very narrow circumstances, where the damage suffered arose from an act involving a breach of duty by a director.

14.18   The procedural steps under the CA 2006 are as follows:

● Step 1 – the shareholder brings the claim but he also has to make an application to the court for permission to continue the claim. The shareholder has to make a prima facie case at this stage, based on evidence from the shareholder alone. If no prima facie case is made, the court has to dismiss the application.

● Step 2 – if the action passes, then the court decides whether to grant permission to continue the claim based on evidence provided by both parties. Only if the court gives permission to continue at Step 2, will the action proceed to a full hearing.

UNFAIR PREJUDICE

14.19   The second alternative to winding up is a statutory remedy contained in CA 2006, s 994 (formerly CA 1985, s 459).

14.20   If the court is satisfied that a shareholder has suffered 'unfair prejudice', it may make such order as it thinks fit for giving relief in respect of the matters complained of, which may include, but is not limited to:

● regulating the conduct of the company's affairs in the future;

● requiring the company to refrain from doing or continuing to do an act complained of by the petitioner, or to do an act that the petitioner has complained it has omitted to do;

● authorising civil proceedings to be brought in the name and on behalf of the company by such person or persons and on such terms as the court may direct; or

● providing for the purchase of the shares of any member of the company by other members or by the company itself and, in the case of a purchase by the company itself, the reduction of the company's capital accordingly.

14.21   The last of these remedies is the one almost always ordered, since it is recognised that if the relationship between the shareholders has broken down, the best solution is usually to bring it to an end. In fact, the Court of

Appeal has recently confirmed that a buy out should be the normal remedy[13]. Winding up cannot be ordered. Once unfair prejudice has been established, the court is given a wide discretion as to the relief to be granted – it is not limited merely to reversing or putting right the immediate conduct. The court is entitled to look at the reality and practicalities of the overall situation, past, present and future.

14.22   Any 'member' of the company may petition for an order on the ground that the company's affairs are being, or have been, conducted in a manner that is unfairly prejudicial to the interests of the company's members generally or of some part of its members (including at least the petitioner), or that an actual or proposed act or omission of the company (including an act or omission on its behalf) is or would be so prejudicial.

14.23   A 'member' includes not only an existing member but also a person to whom shares in the company have been transferred or transmitted by operation of law, so that a person who is refused registration as a member may apply.

14.24   A new provision introduced by the CA 2006 (s 994(1A)) is that the removal of a company's auditors from office on grounds of divergence of opinion on accounting treatments or audit procedures or any other improper grounds will be treated as unfair prejudice.

14.25   Cases on CA 2006, s 994 (predecessor s 459 of the CA 1985) provide that an order can be made if the petitioner can show that the course of conduct complained of is unfair and as a result the value of his shareholding has been seriously diminished or at least seriously jeopardised[14]. The test of unfairness is objective, not subjective, and there is no need to show any bad faith or lack of probity or that the conduct complained of was unlawful. Such conduct need not be sufficient to justify a winding-up order. Unfortunately the decision in *O'Neill v Phillips*[15] appears to have considerably restricted the availability of the remedy by holding that a member will not ordinarily be able to complain of unfairness unless there has been a breach of the terms or understanding on which it has been agreed that the affairs of the company should be conducted, whether written or oral, and whether contractually binding or not, although equitable considerations may also enable the court to hold that those terms are being performed in a manner which equity regards as a breach of good faith. The decision in *O'Neill v Phillips* emphasises the need for the parties to commit all their understandings to writing, since although the existence of an oral understanding might be established by the evidence, this is obviously much more uncertain than producing a written agreement.

---

13   *Grace v Biagoli & Ors* [2005] EWCA Civ 1222.
14   Slade J in *Re Bovey Hotel Ventures Ltd*, unreported and approved by Norse J in *Re R A Noble Clothing Ltd* (1983) BCLC 273.
15   [1999] 1 WLR 1092.

14.26 It will be seen that although the law does provide for a certain amount of minority protection, its effectiveness and scope is limited and uncertain. The minority shareholder is obviously much better off if he is given some express rights under the articles of association or in a shareholders' agreement which can be acted upon if breached, rather than having to prove the terms of an oral understanding or to rely on vague concepts such as unfairness, which might be interpreted differently by different judges.

14.27 An interesting question which arose in relation to the previous s 459 was whether a term in a shareholders' agreement excluding the operation of the section is enforceable. It may be thought that, after a long and hard negotiation to arrive at a shareholders' agreement, it would be inconvenient if a shareholder could have successfully petitioned under s 459 on the basis of some unfairness which was expressly permitted by, or at least was not a breach of, the terms of the agreement. Although it had been argued to the contrary, the better view would appear to be that such a provision is not effective, and was held to be so[16]. This would presumably also apply to CA 2006, s 994 although there is not as yet any authority on the point. In view of the approach taken in *O'Neill v Phillips*[17] the question may to a considerable extent be academic, in that the court's starting point will be to see whether the alleged unfairness is a breach of the shareholders' agreement and would be likely to refuse to grant any relief where it is not. The scope for arguments that there were informal understandings or implied terms not reflected in the shareholders' agreement must be very limited where it is very comprehensively drafted, especially if it contains an 'entire agreement' clause. The approach taken in *O'Neill v Phillips* was endorsed by the Company Law Steering Group.

2   Types of express minority protection

14.28 Minority protection can generally be divided into positive and negative rights and, typically, a minority shareholder will negotiate protection which is a combination of both.

Positive rights

RIGHT TO APPOINT DIRECTORS

14.29 One of the most important positive rights of a minority shareholder may be the ability to appoint one or more directors to the board of the

---

16   *Exeter City AFC Ltd v The Football Conference Ltd* [2004] 1 WLR 2911.
17   [1999] 1 WLR 1092.

company, albeit that such a right is of itself of limited value where the majority appoints a majority of the directors. This form of protection is dealt with in detail at para 16.1ff.

SHARE RIGHTS

14.30 The majority shareholder will, where its shares are ordinary voting shares, have the right to attend and vote at general meetings. The shareholders' agreement or the articles may provide that there is no quorum unless the minority shareholder is represented at a general meeting. However, in order to avoid a shareholder being able to block every resolution to which it is opposed by failing to attend or send a representative to the meeting at which the resolution is being proposed, there will usually be a provision to the effect that if there is no quorum the meeting is adjourned for a short period, say seven days, and if there is no quorum at the adjourned meeting the shareholders present will be a quorum, whether all shareholders (or classes of them) are represented or not. Sometimes the shareholder is given a further chance by means of a second adjournment and it is only on the third attempt to hold the meeting that the provisions for a reduced quorum come into operation. Apart from the elimination of casting votes, Table 3 (see Chapter 13, section 1) is equally relevant to companies which are not deadlocked. Where the minority holder holds a special class of shares, he may have other positive rights such as the right to a preferential fixed dividend or the right to priority on a return of capital on a winding up – such rights are referred to as 'class rights'.

DIVIDEND POLICY

14.31 A provision regarding the dividend policy of the company is often included in the shareholders' agreement. Commonly, this provides that it is the intention that the whole, or perhaps a percentage, of the profits earned and available for distribution in each financial year of the company will be paid out as dividends, except such part of them as the board reasonably believes should be retained to meet the future capital needs of the company. Such a provision (expressed only as an 'intention') suffers from the disadvantage that if the majority controls the board it could, by finding reasons to retain profits, deny dividends to the minority, or severely restrict their amount. If the minority has a right of veto in respect of the business plans of the company (see para 15.40), a better solution would be to require that dividend policy should be dealt with in each business plan, so giving the minority some control over it. If minority approval is required for capital expenditure (see para 15.28) this may be another way of indirectly controlling dividend policy, since if capital expenditure is restricted it will probably increase the amount of profits which could be distributed.

VISITATION RIGHTS AND PROVISION OF INFORMATION

14.32 Another positive right which is sometimes seen is the *visitation right* (an expression originating in the United States) under which the minority holder is given the right to visit the company's premises, inspect its books and records, and interview and obtain information from its directors and senior staff. This right adds little or nothing to those which are available to a director, but they could be useful to an investor without board representation and are quite often included in favour of a shareholder which is primarily providing finance, such as a venture capital investor. Visitation rights can be coupled with the right to receive information about the progress of the company at regular intervals, such as the right to receive monthly or quarterly internal management accounts, cashflow forecasts and sales figures which would ordinarily only be available to the directors. Those advising the company will wish to ensure that the information is provided under the protection of a confidentiality undertaking, and such provisions are usually contained in shareholders' agreements.

RIGHT TO APPOINT AN OBSERVER

14.33 A further positive right which is sometimes given is the ability to appoint an observer to attend board meetings. This will be included where the shareholder concerned either has been given no board representation, or is worried about using it because it is a passive investor whose representative will have only the knowledge gleaned from attending board meetings. If its representative was appointed a director he might incur personal liability if, unbeknown to him, the affairs of the company are unlawfully conducted, eg if it trades whilst insolvent. The observer may or may not be given the right to speak, but will not, of course, be entitled to vote.

RIGHT TO REQUIRE PROPER CONDUCT OF THE BUSINESS

14.34 Other positive rights which are sometimes included are those which are designed to ensure that the affairs of the company are properly conducted, and are to some extent statements of the obvious, or even statutory requirements. Those which are most often seen are that the company maintains proper insurance, prepares and maintains proper books of account and has them audited in accordance with the legal requirements, and that it conducts its business in accordance with all applicable laws. It is also common for there to be a time limit for the production and audit of the accounts for each year, and the identity of the auditors is sometimes a matter requiring minority approval. There may be issues of substance in the insurance provisions, since without an agreement there may be a dispute over the scope and amount of cover the company should obtain. Of particular relevance is product liability insurance, which is so expensive that it may be necessary to limit the cover as to amount or as to the jurisdictions to which it will apply. There are also sometimes provisions under which 'key man' insurance will be taken out in respect of certain executive directors or senior employees; this is often insisted upon by institutional providers of equity finance. In the case of a company which is to exploit an invention, there may be a positive obligation to pursue patent applications, either generally or in various agreed jurisdictions.

14.35   In addition to these provisions, there is often a provision in a shareholders' agreement under which each shareholder undertakes to the others to act with the utmost good faith (or some similar expression) towards the company, not to allow its own interests to conflict with the company and to join with the others in procuring that the business of the company is efficiently conducted and in accordance with best practice. Such vague statements of general principle may be difficult to enforce in practice, but they can be useful provisions for a minority shareholder to be able to highlight in a dispute. A point to watch is whether the good faith provisions can be effectively extended to other companies within a covenantor's group. The good faith provisions fall short of a positive obligation not to compete, so non-competition covenants should also be taken where appropriate (see para 10.57ff).

SHARE TRANSFERS

14.36   Other positive rights may be conferred in relation to share transfers, such as the right to transfer shares subject to any pre-emption provisions and the right to buy shares under such provisions (see Chapter 19). Various other share transfer rights may be granted, and are discussed at para 17.28ff (termination put and call options, Russian roulette, Texas shoot out and multi-choice realisation procedure) and para 21.13 ('tag along and drag along').

IMPOSITION OF TERMS IN EMPLOYMENT CONTRACTS

14.37   Minority shareholders will often be keen to ensure that all key employees enter into non-competition covenants, confidentiality agreements and, as far as the law allows, will wish to ensure that employment contracts provide that all intellectual property devised by employees belongs to the company. Positive obligations to this effect could be imposed in the shareholders' agreement but this may be of limited value unless the employees in question are contractually bound by it.

RIGHT TO ENFORCE ANCILLARY CONTRACTS

14.38   An important minority protection can be a right to enforce the company's rights under ancillary agreements which are made between the company and another shareholder, which would normally be entirely in the hands of the board. Methods of achieving this in relation to support agreements are discussed at para 3.15ff. The same principles could be applied in relation to other ancillary contracts, eg the breach of a patent licence by withholding improvements from the company or the breach of a warranty contained in an agreement for the transfer of business assets to the company.

NON-COMPETITION

14.39   A minority shareholder will usually have the benefit of a restrictive covenant in the shareholders' agreement under which all the shareholders agree with each other not to compete with the company, and it may possibly require shareholders to channel any business opportunity within the scope of the company's activities to the company rather than exploit it themselves, or through another member of their group[18].

TAX

14.40   Another positive right which may be afforded to a minority shareholder in a company which is a consortium for tax purposes is the ability to avail itself of consortium relief by surrendering the appropriate proportion of its trading losses to the company and receiving payment for them. Consortium relief is discussed at para 7.39ff.

Negative rights

14.41   It is common for minority shareholders to be provided with a large number of vetoes, ie the ability to require that particular transactions are not carried out unless one or more minority shareholders approve them first. Where such rights are available to more than one minority shareholder, the approval of all, or of a defined majority, of them may be required. Minority vetoes are discussed in more detail in the next chapter, but where they should be placed in the documentation is discussed in paras 14.42–14.88.

3   Should the minority protection rights be conferred by a shareholders' agreement or the articles of association?

14.42   Every joint venture or arrangement between shareholders where there is a written agreement is likely to involve both the articles of association and a shareholders' agreement. A company must have articles of association

---

18   Non-competition covenants are discussed in more detail at para 10.55ff.

and, although it is possible to adopt Model A in its entirety and include all minority protections in the shareholders' agreement, it is rare that the articles are not affected in some way by the agreement between the parties. Many provisions commonly required, such as the positive obligations discussed above, being personal in nature, do not conveniently fit into the articles (which generally only deal with the rights and restrictions attaching to shares), so a shareholders' agreement is more or less indispensable. Some minority protection provisions fit more conveniently into one than the other, and considerations of enforceability also affect the choice.

14.43   Issues of enforceability are best discussed first in relation to shareholders' vetoes, since these provisions can fit very easily into either document and there is often uncertainty, and indeed divergence between practitioners, as to where it is best to put them. As the discussion develops, it is possible to illustrate how the general principles can be applied to other types of minority right.

The enforcement of shareholders' agreements

14.44   A shareholders' agreement is a contract like any other and as long as it is supported by consideration (which it invariably will be) or signed as a deed and subject to the highly unlikely possibility that it may be void or voidable, any shareholder, who is party to the agreement and has the benefit of any of its provisions, may enforce them against any other shareholder, subject to the burden of those provisions. Damages for breach are available, subject to equitable considerations, rescission, injunctions and specific performance.

14.45   A shareholder's veto in a shareholders' agreement is structured as an undertaking by the shareholder or shareholders having the majority of the voting rights to exercise all the rights attaching to their shares in such a way as will give effect to the minority veto. In essence they agree not to propose, or to secure the defeat of, any transaction not approved by the minority.

14.46   This is workable where only one shareholder makes up the required majority, but where no shareholder has a majority the situation becomes more complicated because a minority veto may only be secured by the joint efforts of those shareholders having the veto and sufficient other minority holders to make up the required majority. In these circumstances, since none of the shareholders giving the undertaking to procure compliance with the veto can enforce the veto on their own, they are likely to be unwilling to undertake to do so, and will insist on undertaking to procure 'as far as they are able', which (since none of them are able to do so on their own) achieves nothing.

14.47   Whether this is a problem depends on how the veto is structured. Where the veto is available to all the minority shareholders, but is only exercisable by their majority decision, it may be that the majority has enough voting power to ensure that the veto can be enforced. For example, if there are three shareholders each with a third of the ordinary share capital and they agree that certain things shall not be done unless at least two out of three agree, then these two will have two-thirds of the voting power and therefore will be able to block the matter being vetoed, without any action being required from the third shareholder.

14.48   If, on the other hand, each of the three shareholders is given an individual veto, and one of them wishes to exercise it and the other two are opposed, the shareholder exercising the veto will need the support of at least one other in order to be able to block the proposal it wishes to veto, assuming the matter concerned requires an ordinary resolution. This is a less common situation, because individual vetoes are often undesirable, but if such a veto is agreed to, and is to be effective, an undertaking from other shareholders to procure the veto will become necessary.

14.49   To be effective, such an undertaking needs to be an undertaking by each minority holder to join with the others in procuring the enforcement of the veto, and to meet objections by minority holders who are not by themselves able to enforce the veto, a formula along the following lines is appropriate:

> 'Each of the Shareholders will join with each other Shareholder in exercising all voting and other rights as are from time to time respectively available to them in relation to the Company and their beneficial shareholdings in the Company under the Articles of Association of the Company for the time being in force, and will each take or refrain from taking all other appropriate action within their respective powers to procure [...] and they will also procure that their respective nominees and (subject to their fiduciary duties) the directors respectively appointed by them will also do so. The liability of each Shareholder will in each case be several, so that each Shareholder will only be liable for his own actions or failures to act, and no Shareholder will be liable for a failure to so procure where it is attributable to any action or failure to act by one or more other Shareholders, but without prejudice to the liability of such other Shareholder or Shareholders.'

This provision is designed to make it clear that a shareholder is not to be penalised where he did everything he could to enforce the veto, but could not do so because of the failures of others to act with him, who are alone to be responsible for the failure.

14.50   Even if this kind of provision is included, it is by no means entirely clear how far a shareholder is required to go to prevent the action which is the subject of the veto. The matter in question may be one for the board, and if the board proceeds to pass a resolution to approve a transaction which is not approved by the minority, then if that resolution is within the powers of the directors it will be perfectly lawful as far as the company is concerned. Are the appointors of those directors required to remove them, and appoint others more compliant who will reverse the decision? Arguably, yes, although there must be a doubt, because directors have statutory duties to their company which override any duties to their appointor (see para 16.14). Also, if the director concerned happens to be executive, his removal could be rather expensive. Removal of directors may be avoided by appointing additional directors if the articles allow that.

14.51   Although the orthodox solution to the board's failure to comply with a veto is to rearrange the board to secure that the action to be vetoed is not taken, a simpler solution for achieving this would be to pass a shareholders' resolution vetoing the proposed action, if the articles allow this. Although art 3 of the Model Articles gives the directors the management of the business and the ability to exercise all the powers of the company, the members can, by special resolution, direct the directors to take, or refrain from taking, specified action, so there seems no reason why the shareholders could not procure the passing of a special resolution directing the directors not to carry out the action to be vetoed. In order to avoid the delay involved in the shareholders using the statutory procedure for requisitioning the necessary shareholders' meeting (assuming the board will not convene the meeting), the articles could provide that any shareholder could convene a meeting and serve notice of the meeting under its own name. If those bound by the procuring obligation account for 90% or more of the nominal value of the voting shares, the meeting could then be held at short notice. Alternatively if shareholders who are bound account for 75% or more they could be required to sign a written resolution under the statutory procedure, so avoiding a meeting altogether. The statutory procedure is not, however, available for the removal of a director or the auditors.

14.52   In practice, little difficulty is normally experienced in enforcing shareholder vetoes, since the parties will normally operate on the basis that the company is unable to carry out the relevant acts without the required shareholder consent (even though this is not technically the case) and will instruct their appointed directors, who are usually their respective employees, accordingly.

14.53   The possibility of suing the company has not yet been mentioned, which would appear more effective than suing the other shareholders. However, an undertaking by the company itself not to carry out a transaction without minority consent may not be enforceable.

14.54   In *Russell v Northern Bank Development Corpn Ltd*[19] it was held that a company could not bind itself in favour of particular shareholders not to

---

19   [1992] BCLC 431, CA.

exercise powers which by statute are exercisable by a particular majority of shareholders. The particular issue was whether a company could bind itself not to create or issue any further share capital without the consent of all the shareholders, whereas CA 1985 allowed the company to increase its share capital by ordinary resolution. It was held that it could not do so, on the ground that it would mean that the company would not be able to increase its capital for so long as any of the parties to the agreement were shareholders, even after they had parted with control of the company to others. The basis of the decision is that a company should not bind itself to particular shareholders not to do something which the law allows its shareholders for the time being to require the company to do.

14.55   However, on appeal to the then House of Lords[20] it was held that a private agreement between the *shareholders* of a company to exercise their voting power in a particular way was valid, and this separate undertaking could on that occasion be severed from the invalid undertaking given by the company.

14.56   Although the House of Lords did not hold this, it is suggested that a veto on the exercise of a statutory power which is conferred on a particular class of members as a class right embodied in the articles would be valid, as would weighted voting rights. These rights would attach to the holders for the time being of the shares of the relevant class, and would not be rights only available to particular shareholders, and furthermore would not be the subject of an express undertaking by the company contained in a shareholders' agreement, thereby overcoming the basis of the *Russell* decision. Weighted voting rights were impliedly approved in *Russell* and in any case were held to be valid in the House of Lords decision in *Bushell v Faith*[21], in which it was held that if a shareholder was given extra votes on an ordinary resolution to remove a director this did not contravene the statutory provisions allowing a director to be removed by an ordinary resolution, normally passed by a simple majority vote.

14.57   In view of the decision in *Russell* it has become common not to include the company as a party to undertakings to enforce vetoes and, if this is possible, to avoid making the company a party to the shareholders' agreement at all. An alternative course of action is to join the company as a party but to omit it from any undertakings which may be caught by the rule in *Russell* and, for good measure, to expressly provide that the agreement is not to be read so that the company is bound to do any act which would infringe the rule in *Russell*, and that any such provision shall be severable from the procuring undertakings on the part of the shareholders.

---

20   [1992] BCLC 1016, HL.
21   [1970] AC 1099.

14.58   Another reason for excluding the company as a party to a shareholders' agreement was the concern that if the company was party to obligations contained in the agreement, it could be providing financial assistance for the purchase of its own shares in breach of CA 1985, s 151. However, CA 2006 abolished the prohibition on financial assistance for private companies but not for public companies. A positive or negative procuring obligation would only be likely to be 'other financial assistance' within the old s 152(1)(a)(iv) and, if so, would be lawful as long as it did not materially reduce the net assets. Although there is no authority, it is suggested that a commitment not to do something is not likely to contravene the section. A positive procuring obligation may or may not reduce the net assets. This is, however, no longer an issue as the financial assistance provisions for private companies in connection with a purchase of their own shares have now been abolished.

14.59   The decision in *Russell* has no bearing upon *positive* undertakings by a company, as long as it is empowered to deliver them without a decision of its shareholders. Thus, an agreement with a shareholder to take out product liability insurance, which is within the powers of the company and is duly authorised by a resolution of its directors, is valid. Such positive obligations do not easily fit into the articles, and would be better placed in the shareholders' agreement. *Russell* also does not apply to negative obligations which relate to matters reserved to the directors rather than the shareholders. For directors to cause the company to enter into such a negative obligation with a shareholder may be more difficult to justify, especially if the undertaking may apply in circumstances very different from those which applied when it was given. However, as long as the directors justifiably consider the undertaking to be in the interests of the company when it is given, it will still be enforceable if circumstances change (see the decision of the Court of Appeal in *Fulham Football Club v Cabra Estates Ltd*[22]). This will be especially so where the company receives substantial benefits (such as new funds) in return for the undertaking.

14.60   However, although such positive and negative obligations may be enforceable against the company by injunction or specific performance, damages may not be available from the company. This is not a serious issue, because a shareholder is unlikely to want these damages since this would reduce the value of its own investment in the company. Damages from the other shareholders for failure to procure the company to do the thing concerned would be a much more useful remedy, which leads to the conclusion that positive undertakings should take the form of procuring undertakings by shareholders, and that there is in fact no need or point in joining the company as a party at all.

---

22   [1994] 1 BCLC 363.

14.61   The possible non-availability of damages from the company stems from the decision in *Houldsworth v City of Glasgow Bank*[23] that a shareholder in a company could not claim damages against the company on the basis that he could not claim to be a creditor of a body of shareholders which included himself. CA 1985, s 111A (now replaced by CA 2006, s 655 which is identical) was intended to abolish this rule, but unfortunately the section did not specify how a shareholder creditor ranks in relation to other creditors. The decision in *Barclays Bank v British & Commonwealth Holdings Ltd*[24] indicates that if the company has insufficient distributable profits to fund the damages, payment of them may be an unauthorised return of capital and on a liquidation they will rank behind the claims of non-shareholder creditors. The subsequent decision in *Soden v British & Commonwealth Holdings Ltd*[25] is to the effect that a purchaser of existing shares ranks as an ordinary creditor for loss suffered other than as a shareholder. However, many claims under a shareholders' agreement are likely to be outside this decision, which in any case does not address the position of a subscriber for new shares who has a claim other than as a shareholder, although the position is likely to be the same. The effect of this case law is that damages are unlikely to be recoverable until all outside creditors have been satisfied, which, since many claims will be made against the background of a company in financial difficulty, is a considerable limitation in practice.

The enforcement of the articles of association

14.62   The enforcement of provisions in shareholders' agreements may therefore be subject to limitations, at least in theory. Is the position under the articles of association any better?

14.63   The technique which is generally used to confer vetoes on a particular shareholder or group of shareholders by means of the articles of association is to issue them with a separate class of shares. Vetoes can then be attached as class rights, so that the relevant acts cannot validly be carried out unless there is first compliance with the variation of rights clause, which generally requires that any variation or abrogation of the rights requires the sanction of a resolution of the class (75% of the votes cast) or the written consent of three quarters of the holders of the shares of the class. There is no need for the shares concerned to have any special rights apart from the class rights. They could be ordinary shares with the majority having 'A' shares and the minority 'B' shares: both classes could have exactly the same rights, except for the special class rights for the 'B' shares.

---

23   (1880) 5 App Cas 317.
24   [1995] BCC 19.
25   [1996] BCLC 207.

14.64   The ability of a shareholder to enforce the articles depends upon CA 2006, s 33(1) (which has replaced CA 1985, s 14(1)) which provides that:

'The provisions of a company's constitution bind the company and its members to the same extent as if there were covenants on the part of the company and of each member to observe these provisions.'

14.65   The CA 1985 section was defectively drafted as it did not refer to a covenant on the part of the company. Nevertheless, it had been held that a company was obliged as regards its members to comply with its articles to the extent that the articles affect the rights and obligations of the members in their capacity as such[26]. This is now expressly stated in CA 2006, s 33(1).

14.66   It has also been held that each member is bound to the company to comply with the articles, but only in his capacity as a member[27].

14.67   It has been held that the articles constitute a contract between the members, but it is uncertain whether they can enforce it directly or only through the company. The better view, however, is that the intervention of the company is not necessary[28].

14.68   The above propositions were subject to the rule in *Foss v Harbottle*[29], under which, in order to avoid endless disputes as to the precise conduct of the internal affairs of a company, the courts would not interfere where the act alleged to be irregular or unlawful could be ratified by a simple majority of the members, but an individual right of a member would be enforced. These common law principles are maintained in the derivative claim provisions in CA 2006 as the court must refuse permission to continue a claim if the act or omission giving rise to the claim has occurred and has subsequently been ratified. Where the act or omission has not yet occurred, the court has to take into account whether it could be, and the circumstances in which it is likely to be, ratified by the company.

14.69   It is submitted that class rights are capable of being enforced against the company. In *Quin & Axtens Ltd v Salmon*[30], a decision of the House of Lords, there was a provision in the articles of association which stated that no resolution of a meeting of the directors which was to consider the acquisition or letting of premises should be valid unless notice of the meeting was given to each of the two managing directors and neither of them dissented from the proposal. One of the managing directors was granted an injunction restraining the company from acting on such a resolution to which he had not assented. Although there appears to be no decision directly on the enforcement of a veto enshrined as a class right, it is submitted that the *Quin*

---

26   *Quin Axtens Ltd v Salmon* [1909] AC 442; and *Hickman v Kent or Romney Marsh Sheep Breeders Association* [1915] 1 Ch 881.
27   *Biggood v Henderson's Transvaal Estates Ltd* [1908] 1 Ch 743.
28   *Rayfield v Hands* [1960] Ch 1.
29   (1843) 2 Hare 461.
30   [1909] 1 Ch 311.

case dealt with what is in essence the same thing. This did not offend against the rule in *Foss v Harbottle* because a special majority is needed to carry out an act the subject of the veto. The courts will certainly enforce a positive class right, such as the right to a fixed dividend.

14.70   It is also clear that pre-emption rights on share transfers (being individual rights) will be enforced as between members. In *Rayfield v Hands*[31] the articles of a company stated that any member who proposed to transfer his shares should serve a transfer notice and the shares would then be purchased by the directors 'equally between them at fair value'. The directors contended they were not bound by the article, but it was held that it could be enforced against them, and without the intervention of the company.

14.71   Although an injunction may be available against the company, damages against the company may not be available; and there is in fact no authority to suggest that a member could claim damages against a company for breach of its articles. No doubt this is due to the decision in *Houldsworth*[32]. However, damages have to be distinguished from an action for a debt – a shareholder certainly can sue in debt for an unpaid dividend once it has become a debt. Damages may also be available against shareholders who are in breach of provisions in the articles which are enforceable against them by other shareholders, such as for failure to complete the sale of shares in the company under the provisions of a pre-emption article.

14.72   Where class rights are used, the problem of the recalcitrant board does not arise. The matters which are the subject of the veto are simply beyond the powers of the directors unless the requisite class consent is obtained. The threat to impose personal liability upon directors who try to defy the articles is normally sufficient to ensure their compliance, even where the directors are not party to any shareholders' agreement, and are therefore not bound by its provisions.

14.73   CA 2006, s 22 introduced (with effect from 1 October 2009) the ability for shareholders to entrench provisions in the articles of association. These provisions can only be made on formation of the company or with the consent of all members. This allows minority rights to be entrenched in articles without formally creating 'class rights'.

Dealing with enforcement by and against transferees and new shareholders

14.74   Where the original signatories to the shareholders' agreement remain the only shareholders, the enforcement of the shareholders' agreement may

---

31   [1960] Ch 1, [1958] 2 All ER 194.
32   See para 14.61.

be relatively straightforward, but the advantage still lies with a class right because of the possible weaknesses of a procuring obligation. When the position after a change of shareholders is considered, the advantage is even more with a class right.

14.75   The statutory contract in CA 2006, s 33(1) binds the members from time to time. Once a new member becomes a shareholder he is automatically bound by the articles, and if he is a holder of shares of the same class as those which have a class right attached to them, the same class right is automatically available to him.

14.76   In contrast, where a shareholders' agreement is to continue in being, notwithstanding that one or more signatories have ceased to be shareholders, the only effective way of ensuring that new shareholders are bound by and have the benefit of the agreement is to require each new shareholder to sign a deed adhering to the provisions of the agreement.

14.77   In order to ensure that each new shareholder must enter into a deed of adherence, it has become quite common to stipulate in the articles that no shares may be issued to a new member and no transfer to a new member may be registered unless and until he has executed a deed of adherence. Whilst this may be effective in theory, there is plenty of scope for accidental failure to obtain the deed before the new shareholder is registered.

14.78   The Contracts (Rights of Third Parties) Act 1999 is of no help in avoiding this cumbersome procedure, since although it allows a person who is not party to a contract to take a benefit under it, the burden cannot be transferred to him without his express agreement. It will normally be necessary for him to be bound by the procuring obligations and it may be desired to impose other positive obligations on him, such as confidentiality provisions.

14.79   Articles are also, arguably, more easily amended than shareholders' agreements. Whether this is to be considered as an advantage depends upon whether it is viewed from the perspective of a majority or a minority shareholder. Should the holder of a veto enshrined as a class right agree to give it up altogether, a special resolution can be passed to alter the articles, supported by the necessary class consent. In contrast, the alteration of a shareholders' agreement prima facie requires the agreement of all its signatories, even those who have ceased to be shareholders where they are still bound by provisions which apply after such cessation. In order to avoid this, shareholders' agreements sometimes provide that the agreement of an ex-shareholder is not required to any amendment, except that no additional liability shall be imposed on him without his consent. Even this would require the agreement of all current shareholders. A class consent or special resolution to alter the articles would only require a 75% majority. For this reason, a shareholders' agreement sometimes seeks to provide that its terms can be amended by a particular majority of the current shareholders.

14.80 Another matter which needs to be addressed in relation to shareholders' agreements is the release from liability of a signatory who has ceased to be a shareholder. The agreement should make it clear that once a party ceases to be a shareholder, having procured his transferee to enter into a deed of adherence, he is released from liability. Exceptions should, however, be made for provisions which continue to apply to him, such as restrictive covenants (where the law so permits), confidentiality undertakings, and warranties and indemnities where the time limit for making a claim has not expired.

Possible disadvantages of class rights

14.81 All things being equal, class rights have a clear advantage over vetoes in a shareholders' agreement. However, provisions in the articles will always become public by virtue of the need to file a copy with the Companies Registration Office, therefore confidential provisions should not go in the articles. On the other hand, the shareholders' agreement might also become public if it is a material contract of a listed company and has to be placed on public display (although such display will continue only for a limited period), and a certain degree of confidentiality could also be lost if it has to be produced to the Competition and Markets Authority or the European Commission. If at all possible, the shareholders' agreement ought not to be referred to in the articles because of the risk that the shareholders' agreement may have to be filed at the Companies Registration Office (see para 24.18), although sometimes this can be overcome obliquely by a provision in the articles to the effect that 'unless all the shareholders for the time being of the Company otherwise agree in writing'.

14.82 Some vetoes are not amenable to being made into class rights. Provisions which are personal to the original signatories or of a temporary character ought not, as a general rule, to be included in articles. The articles could conceivably survive the agreement and it is in any case good practice to draft them so that they will stand alone if the shareholders' agreement comes to an end. The articles will survive unless and until a resolution is passed to amend them or to adopt new articles. It should also be mentioned that in the *Russell*[33] decision there is a passage in the judgment of Lord Jauncey which suggests that a personal right embodied in articles would be invalid. However, it is difficult to reconcile this with the earlier decision in *Cumbrian Newspapers Group Ltd v Cumberland and Westmorland Herald Newspaper and Printing Co Ltd*[34] which decided that an individual right could take effect as a class right.

---

33 [1992] BCLC 1016, HL.
34 [1986] 1 WLR 26.

14.83   Technically, a class right which consists of the ability to veto a particular transaction cannot extend to subsidiaries, although class rights which purport to do so are frequently seen. A subsidiary cannot be bound by provisions in the articles of association of its parent, and it is doubtful whether an undertaking by the company to exercise its voting powers over the subsidiary to ensure it does not carry out the prohibited transactions can be inferred. In this respect, one falls back on the solution suggested in para 14.86 by including in the shareholders' agreement an undertaking by the shareholders to enforce the provisions in the articles restricting the activities of the subsidiaries. This issue is discussed further at para 15.7ff.

Suggested solutions

14.84   The positive rights of shareholders, not directly attaching to their shares, ought to appear in the shareholders' agreement. The obligations to enforce these positive rights attach to the parties undertaking those obligations, and not to their shares, and have no place in the articles.

14.85   Rights attaching to shares, such as dividend or voting rights, naturally fall into the articles. Rights relating to share transfers could go in either document, but pre-emption rights are generally placed in the articles, as are any other rights which are intended to benefit present and future holders of the shares. Rights relating to share transfers which are purely personal to particular shareholders such as options, 'Russian Roulette', or other realisation clauses should go into the shareholders' agreement.

14.86   Minority vetoes can go in either place, but are best placed in the articles if not of a personal nature, and they should be structured as class rights. However, possibly because of slight doubts over enforceability coupled with the undesirability of claiming damages against the company, even if they are available[35], they are often put in both places. If this is desired, it is suggested that it is generally unnecessary to repeat all the provisions in full. If the vetoes are structured as class rights, and a clause appears in the shareholders' agreement whereby the shareholders agree to observe and perform the articles and to procure that their appointed directors shall do so, the objective will be achieved. Damages are of course available against the shareholders. Such an undertaking is easier for the relevant shareholders to accept than an undertaking to procure that certain specific acts shall not be done. Any recalcitrant non-shareholder directors will be acting unlawfully and in breach of their statutory duties if they try to contravene the class rights, so that much greater pressure can be put on them; no such breach

---

35   See para 14.61ff.

of statutory duty arises if their actions cause a breach of a shareholders' agreement, especially if the company is not a party to it.

Self-help remedies

14.87   The enforcement of express minority shareholders' rights, whether included in the articles or in a shareholders' agreement, can be a difficult exercise. If the other shareholders are determined to breach the minority rights, it will be necessary for the minority to resort to litigation, with the expense this will involve, coupled with the possibility of long delays, although an injunction or other interlocutory relief can usually be obtained quickly. The minority may therefore wish to consider the introduction of a 'self-help' remedy whereby, if there is a breach, additional voting power is available to them so that they can take appropriate action to remedy the breach. It is occasionally provided in the rights attaching to preference shares that if the dividend goes into arrear or redemption is refused the preference shareholders are able to exercise 75% of the votes exercisable in a general meeting, usually with a view to their passing a winding-up resolution and obtaining their money in the subsequent liquidation. A similar provision might apply where there has been any breach of the shareholders' agreement or the articles. 'Voting switches' or 'disaster clauses' are beginning to be seen in private equity investment agreements and might, in appropriate cases, be employed in any joint venture or shareholders' agreement. A clause drafted by the author provides for the investor to obtain control at both board and general meeting level. Since it is designed for venture capital transactions, it is not primarily directed at breach but at situations likely to be prejudicial to the investment, and comes into operation not only on breach but on a failure to meet a forecast or projection made to the venture capital investor, deficiency in accounting systems, insolvency, a need for unanticipated further funding, suspected irregularities in the accounts and suspected fraud, dishonesty or serious mismanagement. There is no reversal of the voting switch should the relevant triggering event be remedied. This is capable of justification in a venture capital investment agreement where the triggering event might well be terminal without remedial action over an extended period and where the investor has a lot of money at stake. It is more difficult to justify it in a shareholders' agreement where the triggering event is a breach of the agreement. On the other hand, should a party protest against the clause in negotiations this might be taken by the other party to indicate an intention to breach the agreement, so it might in practice be accepted, subject to the breach being a material wilful breach.

14.88   In practice, although the minority might gain an initial advantage from exercising their enhanced voting rights, to do so would be likely to give rise to the very litigation which the use of the rights was intended to avoid.

The majority might dispute whether there was in fact a breach, or complain to the court that the minority had gone far further than was necessary merely to remedy the breach, and had thereby mismanaged the affairs of the company or themselves committed breaches of the shareholders' agreement. Actions to enforce shareholders' agreements and articles of association are in fact rare, so it may be correct to assume that deliberate breaches of them are in fact uncommon, and the need for self-help remedies does not normally arise. However, it is something which a minority holder may wish to consider.

Chapter 15

Typical minority vetoes

Summary

This chapter discusses those minority protections which take the form of vetoes over certain transactions. Some general points about structuring any such veto are outlined and then some typical vetoes are dealt with in detail, dividing them between the important fundamental vetoes, and the less important operational vetoes. Although this chapter is written from a UK perspective, the vetoes discussed are usually equally applicable in any other jurisdiction.

1 Introduction

15.1   This chapter deals with minority vetoes which are typically inserted into a shareholders' agreement or attached as class rights in the articles of association. These have been divided into those which are particularly important, the 'fundamental' vetoes which even a shareholder with a small stake ought to have, and the less important, 'operational', vetoes which only a shareholder with a large stake could be expected to have. The division is perhaps a little arbitrary, and not every practitioner will agree which vetoes should be within each category.

Individual or majority vetoes?

15.2   Where the vetoes are being taken for the protection of more than one minority shareholder, the question arises as to whether they should each have an individual veto or whether they should decide whether to exercise the veto by majority decision, and this will usually depend on the particular nature of the veto. It will usually be impossibly inconvenient for every shareholder to have an individual veto for every transaction requiring approval, especially if there are more than a few minority shareholders, since the chances of them all taking the same position on an issue are probably small, and the company could find itself paralysed if just one shareholder exercises its veto. There are many possible ways of resolving this problem, and which is selected will doubtless depend upon the circumstances and the negotiating power of particular parties. One solution would be to grant individual vetoes for the fundamental matters with a majority vote for the operational matters, or perhaps a 75% majority for the fundamental matters and a simple majority for the operational matters.

15.3   Care will need to be taken in defining 'the majority' for this purpose; it will almost certainly not be a majority in number, but by reference to the nominal value of the shares held, or the number of votes exercisable in general meeting, if this is different.

Over-regulation?

15.4   When drafting minority vetoes, there is often a temptation to include as many as can be thought of; however, it is suggested that this will often be counter-productive in that it will be difficult to conduct the company's affairs efficiently if the directors are frequently having to approach shareholders for consents. Many of the operational matters can be left to the common sense of the board; but of course if the board is controlled by a majority shareholder there may be a fear that it will make its decisions with too much regard for the interests of the majority. On the other hand, the vetoes can be tailored to catch most of the more likely serious abuses. Where no shareholder has a majority, the risk of abuse is obviously less.

15.5   Venture capitalists and other institutional investors are particularly keen on shareholder vetoes and it is usually difficult to negotiate any deletions; since they are generally putting up by far the largest proportion of the capital they will usually get their way. However, it may be possible to negotiate 'de minimis' provisions, which will reduce the need to seek consents.

Deemed consent

15.6   In order to avoid the possible need for frequent class meetings or consents, it is often provided that if a director appointed by a shareholder approves a transaction at a board meeting, or gives his written consent, the appointing shareholder is deemed to have approved it also. The company need then only minute the approval, or insert the written consent into the minute book.

Extension of vetoes to subsidiaries

15.7   When drafting shareholder vetoes it is sensible to extend them to cover transactions by subsidiaries, even if the company has no subsidiaries at the time the documentation is signed, since some could be formed in the future. If the vetoes are not so extended, it may be possible to evade them by carrying on all major aspects of the business through a subsidiary.

15.8   It has to be accepted that a veto which is so extended can become rather tenuous, especially if the subsidiaries themselves also have subsidiaries, since a company can only control a subsidiary through the exercise of its votes in its general meetings and by determining the composition of its board, which is in the latter case subject to the overriding fiduciary duties of its directors. The directors of a subsidiary are of course not automatically bound by the holding company's articles, and a class right contained in them could only be enforced by the holding company taking such steps as may be available to it to reverse the decision of the subsidiary board which led to the breach. Similarly, the board of the subsidiary is not bound by a provision in a shareholders' agreement relating to the holding company. As discussed in para 14.83, structuring a veto on the actions of a subsidiary as a class right in the parent's articles is likely to be ineffective. An undertaking from the shareholders of the parent to procure a subsidiary to refrain from the relevant transactions involves the shareholders exercising their voting rights in relation to the parent to secure the appointment of a parent board which, in turn, is prepared to procure the company to exercise its voting rights in the subsidiary to secure the appointment of a subsidiary board which is prepared to procure that the subsidiary does not undertake the prohibited transactions. Probably because of these difficulties, provisions are sometimes seen under which the establishment of a subsidiary requires shareholder consent. On the other hand, an undertaking by a company to procure its subsidiary to refrain from taking certain actions should not necessarily infringe the rule in *Russell*[1], since the exercise of control over the subsidiary is not a matter reserved to the shareholders of the parent, and neither does the giving of such an undertaking necessarily involve a breach of the fiduciary duties of the directors of the parent. Such an undertaking may itself become tenuous if the subsidiary has one or more subsidiaries and the undertaking is also extended to them. Certainly the proliferation of unnecessary subsidiaries is to be discouraged.

Vetoes applicable to a minimum shareholding

15.9   It may be that, originally, a shareholder has a substantial stake in the company which is later reduced to insignificance by reason of the issue of further shares (otherwise than pro rata to existing shareholdings), or the admission of a new shareholder. It is sensible to anticipate that possibility by providing that a shareholder ceases to be entitled to its vetoes if its holding

---

1   *Russell v Northern Bank Development Corpn Ltd* [1992] BCLC 1016, HL; see para 14.55ff.

drops below a specified level – 10% or 5% may be appropriate. Different percentages might apply to the fundamental and operational vetoes. Rights to appoint directors should similarly reduce as the shareholding reduces, and drop away when the chosen minimum level is reached.

2   Fundamental vetoes

Change in the nature of the business

15.10   There will invariably be a provision that the nature of the business of the company and its subsidiaries (which may be tightly defined) is not to be changed without shareholder consent. This should not be equated with a change to the objects clause of the company's memorandum of association. This is customarily drafted in a very wide way, so as to cover incidental activities, and a company could usually change its business completely without this being ultra vires the objects clause. These days, the company may have the objects of a 'general commercial company' and thereby be empowered to carry on any business at all, although the better practice for a joint venture company is to adopt appropriate specific objects. The veto may also extend to cover the commencement of additional activities where the general nature of the existing activities remains the same.

Changes in share capital

15.11   A primary concern of a minority holder is that its proportionate stake in the company should not be reduced without its consent. Such a reduction could arise through the issue of new shares (otherwise than pro rata to shareholdings) or the alteration in the rights attaching to certain shares and not others. It is then necessary for the veto to extend beyond the actual issue of shares to the grant of options, and subscription and conversion rights which will require shares to be issued in the future. The veto should also extend to other alterations of share capital, such as consolidations, subdivisions and reductions, and redemption or purchase of shares otherwise than in accordance with the articles, since this will have the effect of diverting monies which might have been distributed pro rata as dividends into the hands of those whose shares are being redeemed or purchased. The veto may also extend to the creation of any new equity interest for sharing income or profits, whether in the form of shares, rights to acquire shares, or otherwise.

15.12   It is, however, open to question whether any shareholder should have a complete veto on the issue of shares. Difficulties can arise where the company requires additional capital to expand and develop its business, or more acutely where it is insolvent and urgently needs to issue further shares, and all shareholders except one or two approve the transaction and the dissentients block it with a veto.

15.13   It is almost certainly preferable to provide instead that it is only the issue of new shares, otherwise than pursuant to provisions in the articles requiring all new shares to be offered to all the shareholders pro rata, which requires consent. A shareholder who is unable or unwilling to take up the shares offered to it will then simply suffer a reduction in its shareholding, and will not be able to block the transaction. Such a provision should expressly provide for excess applications by shareholders and should also expressly state that shares not taken up by existing shareholders may be offered to outsiders, provided that they enter into a deed of adherence.

15.14   Whilst this addresses the main difficulty, there is still room for abuse of the minority if the majority causes the shares to be issued at too low a price, since a minority holder not taking up the shares will then suffer an effective reduction in the value of its interest. A possible solution to this difficulty is to provide that the shares must be offered at a price approved by the company's auditors or an independent valuer as being fair. This will involve many of the considerations which arise in relation to share valuation provisions[2].

15.15   There is sometimes an exception to any restrictions on issues of new shares to allow the establishment of employee share schemes, but these will normally be limited to a defined number of shares, so as to limit the dilution suffered by other shareholders.

15.16   There should also be a veto on the ability of subsidiaries to issue share capital otherwise than to their immediate parents.

Liquidation

15.17   It will often be provided that a minority consent is required to the taking of any steps to wind up the company, but subject to an exception where the company is insolvent or unable to pay its debts within the meaning of the Insolvency Act 1986, s 123.

Sale of the business or material assets

15.18   There will invariably be a prohibition on the sale by the company and its subsidiaries of the whole or a material part of their combined undertakings or of a substantial part of their assets. 'Material' and 'substantial' should be defined, and how this is to be done will depend on the circumstances.

---

2   Discussed in Chapter 22.

It could be by reference to book values, profits or turnover, or some combination of these. An express sale prohibition might be placed on certain important individual assets such as specified intellectual property. Normally, the restriction should operate by reference to the combined undertakings and assets of the group, and should not apply to the individual companies, because otherwise sales by an insignificant subsidiary would be caught.

15.19　A related veto is a prohibition on the reduction of the interest in a subsidiary. This could occur without a disposal or a new issue of shares in the subsidiary if a partly-owned subsidiary was to change the rights attaching to the shares held by the outsider so as to increase its relative rights in the subsidiary, which is not covered by a veto on a subsidiary issuing shares otherwise than to its parent.

Acquisitions

15.20　There will often be a veto which applies to the acquisition of new businesses, either by the purchase of the shares of the company carrying on the business or by buying the assets and undertaking of that business. The veto will often extend to the purchase of major assets, by means of a limit on the purchase price, and the entry into partnerships, joint ventures, collaboration agreements and other arrangements for sharing profits.

Making of loans and the giving of guarantees

15.21　The assets of the company could be easily dissipated if it lent out money to third parties or gave guarantees for their liabilities, and as a result this will often be the subject of a veto. An exemption is usually made for loans and guarantees made in the ordinary course of business, because every company will need to grant a certain amount of credit to its customers, and will often need to make other small loans, such as season ticket loans to employees. Guarantees in relation to goods and services supplied by the company are inescapable.

Transactions with connected parties etc

15.22　This veto is directed at ensuring that the company does not enter into or vary a very favourable transaction with one of its shareholders or persons connected with a shareholder to the disadvantage of the other shareholders through the imposition of management charges, royalties etc, resulting in unfair leakages of shareholder value. The veto will generally presume that all such transactions, and perhaps the exercise of rights and discretions in relation to them, require examination and shareholder approval, whether they appear to be fair or not. Usually the veto extends to any transaction with any other party which is not dealing on arms' length terms.

Management contracts

15.23   This veto is directed at ensuring that the control exercised collectively by the shareholders is not negated by the company entering into a management contract under which the manager is given a wide discretion over matters which would normally be decided by the board.

Transfer of shares

15.24   In a closely held company, where the identity of the shareholders is an important factor, there may be a veto on the registration of a share transfer.

3   Operational vetoes

Borrowings

15.25   There will quite often be a veto on borrowings in excess of a stated limit, the purpose of which is to prevent the company becoming overgeared. The limit to be chosen is a matter for negotiation and will depend upon the likely availability of cashflow to pay the interest. A fixed limit is likely to be too constraining for a growing company, so the limit may be similar to the kind often seen in debenture stock trust deeds or public company articles of association, whereby borrowings are limited to a defined multiple of shareholders' funds (ie capital and reserves). Since these should increase as the company grows, the borrowing limit increases in step. A start-up or early stage company is unlikely to have any reserves, and so such a limit may not at first be appropriate; a solution is to limit borrowings to the greater of a fixed sum and the required multiple of shareholders' funds.

15.26   There are many transactions such as finance leases, hire purchase, and debt factoring which are effectively, although not technically, borrowings, so the definition of borrowings should be worded so as to extend to these.

15.27   The borrowing limit is often combined with another veto relating to the granting of mortgages, charges, and other security over the company's assets. Since decisions relating to guarantees and borrowing are usually already the subject of vetoes, this is arguably then unnecessary, but nevertheless is very commonly included.

Capital expenditure

15.28   Capital expenditure beyond a certain amount per annum is commonly made the subject of veto. This is sometimes done by automatically allowing any capital expenditure appearing in the current business plan, with allowance for a cost overrun of (say) 10%, with anything over that requiring approval.

Dividends

15.29   In order to prevent excessive dividends from depleting the working capital of the company, the declaration and payment of dividends may be made the subject of a veto. There will invariably be an exemption to cover the payment of any fixed dividends due on preference shares and for any dividend within the agreed dividend policy set out in the shareholders' agreement. The veto needs to be extended to cover any distribution of any kind, whether of a revenue or capital nature. Even bonus issues are likely to be covered by a veto if there are redeemable shares in issue, since a bonus issue will deplete the reserves available for the payment of the redemption monies. Payment of dividends must also be in accordance with the law. In 2017 ICAEW and ICAS published their guidance on realised and distributable profits which takes into account the introduction of the FRS 102 accounting rules.

Exclusive agency and distribution agreements

15.30   Where a company is expected to be particularly dependent on agency and distribution arrangements, there could be a veto on the entry into such agreements which give, or purport to give, the agent or distributor exclusivity, since if an unsatisfactory agent or distributor is appointed this could spoil the sales prospects of the company in the territory concerned for many years. In addition termination of agency agreements protected by the Commercial Agents (Council Directive) Regulations 1993, SI 1993/3053, can result in an obligation on the principal to pay substantial damages or an indemnity payment on termination of the agency agreement. An exclusive agreement on terms which are too generous to the agent or distributor would be likely to damage profitability. Non-exclusive agreements are not normally a problem, since another representative can be appointed to cover the area concerned.

Licences of intellectual property

15.31   There is a possibility that a company could effectively divest itself of its intellectual property if it granted an exclusive licence of it on unfavourable terms, so that where such a property is important to the business a veto on the grant of such licences is likely to be included. Some companies, such as software and publishing houses, cannot carry on business at all without granting licences all the time, so there will sometimes be an exemption to allow licences in the ordinary course of business, although what is thereby permitted might well be tightly defined.

Service agreements etc

15.32   A veto on the grant of service agreements longer than, say, six or 12 months is quite often seen, since terminating a long-term agreement could be very expensive, especially for a small company which cannot afford any strain on its resources.

15.33   In a small company there may be vetoes on recruiting new employees who are entitled to annual remuneration beyond a certain figure, or on increasing the remuneration of existing employees beyond a certain annual percentage (the RPI might be used as a baseline, but confining increases only to the RPI would probably be too restrictive). In such a case, 'remuneration' will need to be widely defined to include such extras as commissions, bonuses, and fringe benefits such as company cars, medical insurance, and pension contributions. A convenient way of dealing with this is to include anything which would be 'earnings' under the employment income rules (formerly Schedule E), although this would have to be expanded to cover pension contributions (if this coverage is desired).

15.34   In *(1) Donald Booth (2) Charles Robert Wilkinson (3) Jane Ann Compton v Clarence Kenneth Fredrick Booth and 9 Others*[3], the High Court held that the payment of excessive remuneration to directors amounted to unfairly prejudicial conduct where there was a policy of not paying dividends to shareholders (see *Corporate Briefing* journal May 2017 issue).

15.35   Even in a large company with a small number of shareholders, shareholder approval might be required of the identity of persons to fill certain key offices, such as managing director, finance director or marketing director.

15.36   The dismissal of certain key employees might be made the subject of a veto, as might the voluntary release of obligations on employees contained in their service agreements, particularly non-competition covenants.

---

3   [2017] EWHC 457 (Ch).

Consultancy, management and like agreements

15.37 Such agreements may be the subject of a veto if they are likely to be important to the business.

Leasing transactions

15.38 Operating leases might be the subject of a veto if they involve the payment of large amounts.

Finance leases will usually be treated as borrowings.

Auditors and accounts

15.39 Any change to the company's auditors, accounting year-end or accounting policies will quite often be the subject of a veto, as may a change in the authorised signatories to cheques and other instructions to banks.

Litigation

15.40 The institution of litigation may be made a matter requiring minority consent, but only where the amount involved is substantial. The veto should not extend to cover the institution of proceedings by the company against the holder of the veto, in respect of any claim under a contract made between the company and the veto holder (see para 3.19).

Business plan

15.41 This veto can be controversial. The minority shareholder will argue that it must be able to approve all business plans and modifications to them in order to have any degree of control over the way the company's business is conducted. A majority shareholder will argue that the direction of the business is a matter for the board and it is an unreasonable fetter on the board's ability to function properly if they have to get every plan approved by the minority. There is much merit in this argument and the effective management of the company may be impeded if every detail of a plan needs minority approval. The majority will also point out that they usually have more money invested in the company and their views should therefore receive proportionate weight. This might be coupled with the argument that the minority may have so many vetoes already that they do not need to approve the plan as well; for example, if the plan involves borrowing in excess of any agreed fixed limit, an approval has to be obtained in any case. As already pointed out, over-regulation may be counter-productive. However, the business plan may include fundamental matters of commercial policy as well as detailed plans for the period to which it relates, and the minority may well wish to be able to veto any change in the former. This might be achieved by employing two documents, a statement of fundamental business policy in addition to a detailed business plan, with minority vetoes attaching only to the former, although this arrangement is not generally seen in practice. Another solution might be to retain the minority veto, but limit the business plan to general policy and leave the detail to the board.

4 General conclusions

15.42   There are no hard and fast rules as to what the minority may expect by way of vetoes. Everything depends on the circumstances and the respective bargaining positions of the parties, and in any case what the minority regards as important will vary in different circumstances.

15.43   Where a minority shareholder is a frequent user of its vetoes, this may point to a lack of harmony within the venture and it may well be appropriate to include provisions for the minority to be removed in these circumstances (see para 17.14).

Chapter 16

Directors of UK companies

Summary

This chapter discusses the methods by which a minority shareholder may secure board representation. The position of a director appointed by a shareholder is then reviewed, particularly as to the situation where his duties to the company may conflict with his duties to his appointor, and practical guidance is given as to how such difficulties may be resolved. Shadow directors are then considered and the chapter highlights how a shareholder or employee may become a shadow director and be liable as if he were a director. This chapter is written from a UK standpoint, and discusses points arising under English company law. However, conflicts between a director's interests and his duty are liable to occur in any jurisdiction and what is said about these may be of wider application. The chapter also looks at when shareholder rights might make a shareholder a person of significant control (a PSC) under company law.

1 The structuring of board representation

Methods of securing board representation

16.1   As with vetoes, there are two methods which are generally used to confer a right on a minority to appoint a director. Firstly, the right may be contained in the shareholders' agreement, and will provide that each shareholder can nominate and remove its own appointees to the board by giving notice to the joint venture company and the other parties.

16.2   The second method is to entrench the right to appoint directors into the articles of association as a class right. The appointor is issued with a special class of share (which may be identical to all other shares apart from the right to appoint one or more directors). The class right gives the appointor the right to appoint one or more directors, up to the allowed number, by lodging a notice in writing at the registered office of the company or perhaps producing it at a board meeting. The person appointed then becomes a director. Removal is effected in a similar manner.

16.3   A drafting point in connection with such a right is to ensure that it is not worded as an ability to appoint a certain number of directors without qualification, since this might be construed to mean that the specified number of directors can be appointed on any one occasion, without limit on the cumulative number of directors appointed. It is far better to stipulate that the right is to appoint the specified number of directors 'holding office at any one time'.

16.4   A right structured as set out above will not be completely effective, since CA 2006, s 168 provides that a director may always be removed by ordinary resolution before the expiration of his period of office, notwithstanding anything in any agreement between the company and the director. This provision may be circumvented by employing weighted voting rights so that, on a resolution to remove a director, his appointor is given enough extra votes to be able to exercise a majority of the votes exercisable at that general meeting. It is advisable that the precise number of votes exercisable is stated rather than specifying that the relevant party has one more vote than those actually exercised in opposition. The appointor should be given enough votes to defeat removal irrespective of the number of votes cast in favour of removal, eg such number of votes as exceeds by one vote the number of votes exercisable by all other shareholders. The validity of weighted voting rights in this situation was upheld by the decision at the House of Lords in *Bushell v Faith*[1]. Another equally effective method is to provide that on a resolution to remove a director, all shareholders except the appointor have no right to vote. Many companies have different categories or classes of shares some with votes and some without votes (and indeed some dividend and non-dividend bearing).

16.5   Currently UK directors can be individuals or corporate directors (limited companies). Under the Small Business, Enterprise and Employment Act 2015 the Government planned to abolish corporate directors in October 2016 but this has been delayed (a consultation ended in 2021) and is not yet in force so always check the current position before appointing a company as a director. Corporate directors are notified to Companies House on form AP02.

Alternate directors and quora

16.6   A director will usually be given the right to appoint an alternate director to attend a board meeting in his place should he be unable to attend, and who is able to exercise the vote of his appointor. As the Model Articles do not include such a right, one will need to be included in the articles of

---

1   [1970] All ER 53. See para 14.56.

association. It is preferable for a director to have the ability to appoint anyone he likes to be an alternate. A compromise would provide for the approval of the appointee by the rest of the board not to be unreasonably withheld, but this provides opportunities for debate about what is unreasonable and may lead to consequent delay in implementing the appointment.

16.7   The points made in para 13.6 above concerning quora are just as important here as they are in relation to a deadlock company. However, in order that a minority holder does not have a perpetual block on the conduct of the affairs of the company, it is quite usual to provide in the articles of association that where a quorum of the board is to include a director representing a particular shareholder or class of shares, then if such a quorum is not present within a certain time after the time of the commencement of the meeting specified in the notice convening it the meeting is adjourned to another time, and if at the reconvened meeting a quorum is not present within a certain time, the directors present shall be a quorum. The appointor is therefore allowed one 'miss' and after that it must ensure either that its director attends in person or sends an alternate. For this to be fair there needs to be provision for adequate notice of board meetings so that the directors are not taken by surprise by a meeting being held at short notice. Short notice may, however, be permitted in an emergency. It is also desirable that it should be provided that all notices convening a board meeting should be accompanied by an agenda detailing all items to be discussed, together with all the appropriate background papers. Where the company is not a deadlock company it is optional whether the chairman has a casting vote, but this may be desirable to avoid a deadlock where the parties have cast an equal number of votes on a resolution, although this is only likely to occur where there are several parties to the joint venture, none of whom has a majority.

2 The position of an appointed director

16.8   When considering the position of a director appointed by a shareholder one is faced with a considerable divergence between the law and the practical reality. The appointed director owes to the company of which he is a director the same duties that are owed by any other director, and these take precedence over the duties which the director owes to his appointor, who should not therefore assume that his appointee will always be a mere 'yes man', always willing and able to conform to the appointor's directions as to how he will vote in a board meeting[2].

16.9   The practical reality is that in nearly all cases both appointor and appointee will assume that the appointee's function on the board is to represent

---

2   See, for example, *ESSO Petroleum Co Ltd v Texaco Ltd* PBD LTL [1999] All ER (D) 1122.

the appointor's interests in relation to the company and the appointee will normally follow the instructions of the appointor. Very often the appointee is the employee of the appointor and will regard himself as having no choice but to comply. Whether the appointee is an employee or not, an appointor who is dissatisfied with its appointee always has the ability to remove him from the board and appoint someone who is more compliant to its wishes.

16.10   In the vast majority of cases, this divergence of the law and practice has no practical implications. The interests of the appointor very often do have a strong correlation with those of the company. Where this is not so (such as where there is a conflict of interest, particularly concerning the enforcement or termination of support agreements between the company and a shareholder), the conduct of the appointee is not very often subjected to critical examination; there is in fact something of a dearth of legal authority on the position of an appointed director.

16.11   However, it may be dangerous in some circumstances to ignore the legal duties of the appointee. The company may be commercially unsuccessful and be placed in insolvent liquidation, in which case the liquidator may have reason to examine the past conduct of the directors, and hold them to account for any breach of their statutory duties. The company may be subject to a takeover, and the new owners, should they find that its affairs have not been conducted properly, may also inquire into the previous conduct of the directors. One or more of the other shareholders who are aggrieved by a decision of the board in which the appointee has participated may challenge it by bringing a derivative claim[3] – and expose the appointee to a possible liability for damages. Unfair pressure on an appointee to agree to a transaction which is manifestly not in the interests of the company thus exposes him to risk and may place him in an impossible position.

16.12   Directors may also now find themselves in breach of a statutory duty as the conflicts of interest duty (introduced by CA 2006, s 175) provides that a director must avoid a situation in which he has, or can have, a direct or indirect interest that conflicts, or may conflict, with the interests of the company. Where a director is also a director or employee of the shareholder appointing him, then he is likely to be in a potential conflict situation (the potential conflict being his obligations to the shareholder who has appointed him and his duties to the company). This potential conflict will put the director in breach of his duties unless it has been authorised and therefore the shareholders should authorise the potential conflict before he is appointed.

16.13   This chapter therefore examines the legal position of a director appointed by a shareholder, and suggests solutions to some of the practical difficulties which may arise.

---

3   Companies Act 2006, s 260.

The duties of a director to his company

16.14   A director owes various duties to the company of which he is a director. The CA 2006 introduced a statutory statement of these duties which has replaced the previous common law duties. The new statutory duties can be summarised as follows:

- To act within his powers – a director must act in accordance with the company's constitution and only exercise his powers for the purposes for which they are conferred.

- To promote the success of the company – a director has to act in a way he considers, in good faith, would be most likely to promote the success of the company for the benefit of its members as a whole. And, in doing so, has to have regard (amongst other matters) to six specific factors (see CA 2006, s 172).

- To exercise independent judgment – a director has to act independently. For example, a director cannot agree with his appointer to vote in a particular way at board meetings. The duty is not infringed, however, if he acts in accordance with an agreement that restricts his discretion or if he acts in a way authorised by the constitution. Therefore, if the joint venture company's articles of association or the shareholders' agreement authorises a director to act in accordance with the wishes of his appointer, he will not be in breach of this duty if he does.

- To exercise reasonable care, skill and diligence – a director has to exercise the care, skill and diligence of a reasonably diligent person with:

  (i)   the general knowledge, skill and experience that may reasonably be expected of a person carrying out his functions (an objective test); and

  (ii)   the general knowledge, skill and experience that the director actually has (a subjective test).

- To avoid conflicts of interest – a director must avoid a situation in which he has, or can have, a direct or indirect interest that conflicts, or possibly may conflict, with the interests of the company.

- Not to accept benefits from third parties – a director must not accept a benefit from a third party conferred by reason of his being a director or his doing (or not doing) anything as a director.

- To declare an interest in a proposed transaction – a director has to declare any direct or indirect interest in a proposed transaction or arrangement with the company – see para 16.18.

Directors also have to declare any interest in any transaction or arrangement that has been entered into by the company – see para 16.18.

16.15   Under the old common law rules, the company in this context generally meant, in the case of a solvent company, the company alone, whose affairs had to be conducted by the directors so as to promote the interests of all its shareholders present and future, and not only a particular group of them. An exception was the statutory duty owed to the company's employees which was only enforceable by the company. In very limited circumstances the duties could be extended to the members themselves. Where there was an offer for the company, the duties of the directors were to the then current shareholders[4]. See also *Platt v Platt*[5] as to the duties of a director to advise shareholders of matters material to the proposed transfer of their shares.

16.16   Although there is no definition in the CA 2006 of 'members as a whole', for the purposes of the duty to promote the success of the company the government always maintained that the new duty merely codified the previous law and that regard should be had to the corresponding common law rules and equitable principles when interpreting and applying the codified duties. Therefore, the duty is likely to be interpreted in the same way as the old common law duty. In addition, the directors will have to have regard to certain factors including the interests of the company's employees and the impact of the company's operations on the community and the environment.

16.17   Where a company is insolvent, or nearly insolvent, a director's duties are primarily to its creditors, with the risk of personal liability to them if the company carries on business whilst insolvent.

16.18   The conflicts of interest duty is not infringed if the matter has been authorised by the directors (although any interested director cannot participate in the authorisation process) or it cannot reasonably be regarded as likely to give rise to a conflict. Directors of a private company incorporated on or after 1 October 2008 can authorise conflicts unless the articles provide otherwise. (Directors of companies incorporated pre-1 October 2008 will not be able to authorise conflicts unless they have been given authority to do so.) Shareholders of a joint venture company will, however, usually want to provide that any potential or actual conflicts should only be approved by them and not by the directors and the articles of association will have to be amended to reflect this.

Directors voting on transactions in which they are interested

16.19   The duty to avoid conflicts of interest is reinforced by the duty to declare any interests in a proposed transaction or arrangement with the company and the requirement to declare any interest in a transaction or

---

4   *Heron International v Lord Grade* [1983] BCLC 244.
5   [1999] 2 BCLC 745.

arrangement that has been entered into by the company (CA 2006, s 182). The Model Articles and nearly all public company articles go further and prevent the director from voting on a contract in which he is interested, subject to certain exceptions, but in the case of a private company this article is normally excluded so that a director may, subject to the mandatory declaration of interest, vote on any contract in which he is interested and may be counted in the quorum at the relevant board meeting. This will also be subject to any restrictions on voting imposed by the shareholders if they approve a conflict of interest. However, this does not obviate the need for the director concerned to consider whether voting in favour of the contract will promote the success of the company.

Compulsion on director to vote in a particular way

16.20   Once appointed, a nominee director must exercise his best judgment in the interests of the company and ignore the interests and instructions of his appointor otherwise he will be in breach of the duty to exercise independent judgment. The duty will not, however, be infringed if the nominee director acts in accordance with an agreement properly entered into by the company that restricts the future exercise of the director's discretion or in a way authorised by the company's constitution. This new exception (which has been introduced by CA 2006), therefore, allows a nominee director to act in accordance with his appointor's instructions provided the joint venture agreement or articles of association reserve that right. A nominee would still, however, have to comply with all of his other duties.

Duties of confidentiality

16.21   A director owes a duty of confidentiality to the company of which he is a director.

16.22   This duty is owed to the company, and therefore a director who has confidential information about the company may not disclose it to his appointing shareholder, save to the extent that the company authorises this. Sometimes under competition law it is necessary also to maintain some kind of Chinese wall between the joint venture partner directors and the companies which appointed them in relation to disclosure of secret technical or financial/pricing information. The exchange of sensitive current price information for example between competitors who may have set up the joint venture could breach the Competition Act 1998 Chapter I prohibition (or Article 101 of TFEU). In such cases specialist competition law advice should be taken.

Dual directorships

16.23   The potential for a conflict of interest becomes all the greater where a director of a joint company is not only the appointee of one of its shareholders, but is also a director of that shareholder or of one or more companies in its group. Every time arrangements between the company and any one or more of the other companies are to be discussed by their respective boards he will have a conflict of interest and will either have to get the conflict authorised or have to make the appropriate declaration of his interest. Duties of confidentiality will flow both ways. Where the company is a subsidiary of another company, the position of a person who is a director of both is eased slightly, because it has been held that he may take into account the interests of the group as a whole, as long as he believes the transaction will not prejudice the subsidiary[6]. However, if there is a conflict between the interests of the subsidiary and the group he must act so as to protect the interests of the subsidiary, particularly having regard to the position of any minority shareholders. In some cases advice from competition law solicitors should also be sought as a flow of information between competitors which both own shares in a joint venture company may amount to an illegal sharing of confidential information, particularly about price, which could breach the Competition Act 1998. Chinese walls and other methods of restricting information of certain kinds between the joint venture company and its owners may be necessary. See para 10.46 for details of the *Cleanroom laundry services and products: anti-competitive agreement* (Case 50283, 14 December 2017), Competition and Markets Authority investigation into a co-operative market sharing joint venture which led to £1.7m fines under the Competition Act 1998.

Resolving conflicts in practice

VOTING

16.24   Undoubtedly, the proper course for a director is for him to declare his interest, leave the meeting and allow the matter to be resolved by the disinterested directors, even if the articles of association technically allow him to vote. Another solution is to delegate the matter to a committee of the directors, excluding all the interested directors. In practice, the directors concerned may well not recognise that they have a conflict of interest and they are likely to participate in the decision.

16.25   These solutions will only be workable where there is a sufficient number of disinterested directors. In a typical joint venture company all, or

---

6   *Charterbridge Corpn v Lloyds Bank Ltd* [1969] 2 All ER 1185.

nearly all, of the directors will be the appointees of the shareholders. Where the matter for consideration is a contract or other arrangement between the company and one of the joint venturers, it may be perfectly workable for the director concerned to withdraw from the meeting or for a committee to be appointed, but in many cases the matter before the board will involve a change of the position of all the shareholders, so that none of their appointees is without a possible conflict of interest. If, for example, a major refinancing is under discussion, this is likely to affect the financial position of all the shareholders as regards their participation in the joint company, which may bring their interests into conflict. Apart from highlighting the desirability of a joint company having some independent directors, it is obvious that the joint company will not be able to function if all interested directors abstain from discussions on all matters in which their appointors are interested.

16.26   Each director will then have to try to balance the conflict in his interests and duties. Fortunately, in many cases the interests of the company and his appointor will be the same, so that there may not be any great practical difficulty in the director coming to a decision. However, directors placing themselves in this position should take particular care to ensure the reasons for any affected board decision are minuted, and in particular that the contribution of each affected director to the meeting is minuted.

16.27   Where all, or most, of the directors have a conflict of interest, and the matter before them is of great importance, they may feel unable to make a decision, in which case an appeal to the shareholders to resolve the matter may be indicated. Sometimes the articles or shareholders' agreement will leave them no choice in the matter, because the matter is reserved for a shareholder decision under one or other of those documents. Where this is not the case, the directors may well be best advised to put the decision to a general meeting, or to seek a unanimous written resolution of the shareholders, although in practice this is rarely done.

16.28   Generally speaking, if the shareholders approved or ratified a transaction in general meeting or by written resolution and absolved the directors from liability, the directors were absolved from all concerns as to whether they had made the correct decision in relation to that transaction. This common law rule was subject to certain qualifications:

- There was arguably a duty upon the directors to ensure that they had given the shareholders all information material to making the decision.

- On the authority of *Rolled Steel Products (Holdings) Ltd v British Steel Corpn*[7] it was possible that where the transaction could be questioned as to whether the powers of the company had been used for proper purposes, for example regarding a transaction which particularly favoured the

---

7   [1986] 1 Ch 246.

interests of one or more of the shareholders to the exclusion of the company or the interests of a director or third party, the decision required the unanimous consent of the shareholders. In any case, the obtaining of such a consent was advisable if the directors wished to avoid a derivative claim against them under one of the exceptions to *Foss v Harbottle*[8], such as the fraud on a minority exception.

- Where the company was insolvent, the duty of a director to its creditors overrode the ability of the shareholders to ratify the transaction.

- There were further limits to ratification, although they were difficult to determine from the case law. A breach of company law such as an unlawful dividend or a breach of the financial assistance rules could never be ratified, but it would appear that dishonest, rather than unlawful, transactions could be unanimously ratified under the *Rolled Steel* principle. A transaction which was ultra vires but otherwise bona fide could be ratified by special resolution under CA 1985, s 35(3); a separate special resolution was required to absolve the directors from liability in relation to the ultra vires transaction. The ban on provision of financial assistance by a company for purchase of its own shares was removed by CA 2006 but remains in place for public companies.

16.29   CA 2006, s 239 now provides that shareholders can ratify, by ordinary resolution, a director's conduct amounting to negligence, default, breach of duty or breach of trust in relation to a company. However, any director whose conduct is being ratified (and any member connected with him) cannot vote on any ratification resolution. (This has replaced the common law rules on ratification (described above) which allowed shareholders to ratify a breach of directors' duties by ordinary resolution and all directors could vote on the resolution.) Shareholders can also still ratify acts of directors by unanimous consent.

16.30   The statutory ratification provision is in addition to any other limitations or restrictions imposed by the law as to what may or may not be ratified and when. A 2008 case[9] confirmed that it is still good law that a company cannot ratify breaches of duty by a director where the affirmation or adoption was brought about by unfair or improper means or was illegal, fraudulent or oppressive towards those shareholders who opposed it, nor can it ratify ultra vires acts.

16.31   In practice, the points made above are often ignored, and directors are apt to fail to recognise that they have a conflict of interest and continue to participate in decisions. To avoid this it is desirable that either the articles or the shareholders' agreement should expressly disenfranchise a director from voting on or in relation to any contract in which his appointor is interested.

---

8   (1843) 2 Hare 461; see para 14.11ff.
9   *Franbar Holdings Ltd v Patel and ors* [2008] EWHC 1534 (Ch).

16.32   Particular difficulties arise for appointed directors where the company is insolvent, and the appointors are urging them to allow the company to continue to trade, since such action could result in the appointees becoming personally liable for the company's debts under the Insolvency Act 1986, s 213 or s 214, and any subsequent winding up could also expose the appointees to investigation by the liquidator as to their conduct as directors. In these circumstances, the appointees should not hesitate to appoint an insolvency practitioner to advise them as to the financial position of the company and, if necessary, commence an insolvency procedure, unless of course the shareholders are willing to provide sufficient funds to enable the company to continue trading, or effective guarantees or indemnities in respect of its liabilities. Indemnities from the appointors to the directors purporting to cover their potential liability for trading whilst insolvent are useless, since they will be ineffective to cover liability for any illegal acts and cannot in any case absolve a director from any individual criminal prosecution. Subject to certain exceptions, an indemnity from the company (or another UK group company) against liability in respect of a director's negligence, default, breach of duty or breach of trust in relation to the company would be void under CA 2006, s 232; not that an indemnity from an insolvent company could ever be of any value. Similar considerations apply to an indemnity offered by a shareholder to an appointee as an incentive to agree to approve any transaction which is illegal or potentially illegal. An indemnity in respect of liability for wrongful or fraudulent trading will therefore still be void, being a liability to contribute to the company's assets made by the liquidator, albeit for the benefit of creditors.

CONFIDENTIALITY

16.33   It is clear that the affairs of a company are not likely to be effectively carried on if the directors appointed by the shareholders are unable to impart to them any confidential information. The shareholders will wish to have fully up-to-date information going far beyond the annual report and accounts, including sales statistics, management accounts, detailed cash flow forecasts and various other reports, all of which are confidential to the company. Without that information they will have insufficient knowledge about how their investment is performing and whether the latest business plan is being fulfilled.

16.34   The solution to this difficulty is for the company to authorise the disclosure of the information. Very often the shareholders' agreement will contain provisions to this effect, coupled with visitation rights (see para 14.27), and, if the company is a party to the agreement, that will be sufficient authority for the directors to release the information; if not, a board resolution can be passed in fulfilment of a procuring obligation contained in the shareholders' agreement.

16.35   Such disclosure should be subject to confidentiality undertakings by the shareholders to whom the information is to be imparted, which are also conveniently contained in the shareholders' agreement. Such undertakings should limit the persons within the recipient organisation to whom the information may be imparted and contain a prohibition on the recipient making use of the information for its own purposes.

16.36   Particular difficulties may arise if shareholders in a company are actual or potential competitors since, unless precautions are taken, they may become possessed of information which other shareholders do not want them to have. In such a case there is likely to be pressure for the exclusion of a director appointed by a shareholder from a board meeting at which a contract between the competitor shareholder and the company is being discussed, lest such director should become aware of confidential information about the competitor, even though the duty of confidentiality of the director prevents him from disclosing the information. Concerns over confidentiality are a good reason for not entering into a joint venture with a competitor (unless the whole of the competing businesses are merged in the joint venture), and are a reason why the transfer of the control of a joint venturer is often made a ground for terminating a joint venture.

16.37   Difficulties can also arise where, under the terms of the joint venture agreement, one joint venturer is required to impart to the joint venture company some highly confidential know-how, such as a secret formula, which it is anxious should not be disclosed to the other venturers. Special precautions may need to be taken to ensure that the information only reaches those within the joint venture company who need to have it and that they are all subject to confidentiality undertakings, whether they are directors or not.

3   Shadow directors

16.38   There is a risk that a joint venturer or other major shareholder in a company or any of their respective directors may become a 'shadow director' of the company, with the consequence that most of the potential liabilities of a director, including the duties of a director, the possible liability to creditors of an insolvent company and the possibility of becoming the subject of a disqualification order, will attach to him. Venture capital investors and their staffs, 'company doctors', management consultants, lenders to and creditors of the company all run the risk of becoming shadow directors.

16.39   CA 2006, s 251 defines a shadow director as 'a person in accordance with whose directions or instructions the directors are accustomed to act'.

16.40   Note that mere interference in the affairs of the company is not enough to make a person a shadow director. The definition requires that he should actually direct its affairs, ie 'call the shots', without actually being a director. Later changes to the legislation make it clear that giving guidance or advice to the company under a legislative requirement is not enough to make someone a shadow director. In a joint venture context it is easy to see how a shadow directorship might arise. If such a company should get into financial difficulty it is not uncommon for one of the shareholders to install one of its executives in the premises of the company to try and turn it round. If he merely advises the board, he will not be a shadow director, but if he dictates their decisions he will become one. The situation may easily arise where the board becomes afraid to go against his requests because of various commercial threats which may be made, such as to withdraw business or funding if the required actions are not carried out. The same situation can arise where an executive of a venture capital investor imposes certain requirements on the investee company with which its directors have no choice but to comply, given that such an investor is usually the largest provider of funds and often the only source of additional capital should this be required. An executive of a lending bank can easily put himself in the same position. A majority shareholder in a joint venture company who dictates its policy is always at risk of becoming a shadow director, although the CA 2006 makes it clear that a parent company will not be regarded as a shadow director of a subsidiary for the purposes of the general directors' duties by reason only that the directors of the subsidiary are accustomed to act in accordance with its directions.

16.41   Various precautions may be taken by such a person to try to avoid becoming a shadow director. He can try to ensure that all instructions he gives to the directors are approved by the board and minuted accordingly, although if it becomes apparent later that the 'decisions' were made in response to his directions, this tactic will not succeed. Where he is an employee of another company or organisation he can try to ensure that he merely relays its instructions, so that it, and not him, is to be regarded as the shadow director. Where a company is found to be a shadow director of another company it does not automatically mean that every director or employee of the first company is a shadow director of the second[10].

16.42   If a person finds himself in a position where he is liable to be held to be a shadow director, he should be careful to conduct himself so as to comply with all the duties and responsibilities of a director, failing which he should cease to act.

16.43   A shadow director should be distinguished from a 'de facto' or 'de jure' director. A shadow director does not hold himself out as a director, but nevertheless directs the company's operations. A de facto director is held out

10   *Re Hydrodam (Corby) Ltd* [1994] 2 BCLC 180; and *Secretary of State for Trade and Industry v Laing* [1996] 2 BCLC 324.

343

as being a director, although he is not in fact one. A de facto director incurs all the liabilities of a director, irrespective of the actual influence over policy which he has.

Small Business, Enterprise and Employment Act 2015 ('SBEE'), Shadow Directors and People of Significant Control Rules

16.44   The duties of directors set out in CA 2016 due to the Small Business, Enterprise and Employment Act 2015 now apply to shadow directors in the same way as other directors. The definition of 'shadow director' in the Companies Act 2006, the Insolvency Act 1986 and the Company Directors Disqualification Act 1986 were also changed at the same time to make the definition clearer. Advice, guidance, directions or instructions given in exercise of a function conferred by or under legislation is not sufficient to satisfy the definition of shadow director, nor is any advice or guidance issued by a Minister of the Crown. Solicitors Macfarlanes summarised this as follows:

> **'Shadow directors bound by same duties as appointed directors**
>
> Historically there has been some uncertainty about the extent to which directors' fiduciary duties applied to shadow directors. A shadow director is a person in accordance with whose directions or instructions the directors of the company are accustomed to act. The person is not held out to be a director and does not claim to be one. SBEE has now clarified this uncertainty amending the CA 2006 to state that directors' general duties apply to a shadow director of a company where and to the extent that they are capable of so applying.'

The above changes came into force on 26 May 2015. The definition of 'shadow director' in CA 2006, s 251 was thus amended by SBEEA 2015, s 89. The same legislation also abolished bearer shares. It is consistent with abolition of bearer shares that the regulations requiring disclosure of company control and 25%+ ownership (the PSC rules) came into force for companies and LLPs. It is hard for a company which is honest to hide its ownership of shares.

16.45   The PSC guidance is below and is very important in the joint venture context as often JV partners want to hide their activities in a similar way some will want to use 'shadow' directors. External solicitors need to be very careful indeed if clients want to engage in any conduct of this kind in case it is criminal and should take their own separate advice in cases of doubt. Below is an extract from the Government PSC guidance which helps to explain when someone may be a person of significant control whose control must be disclosed on the company's published Annual Confirmation Statement. In summary, if there are simply minority protection rights under a shareholders' agreement but that person has 25% or fewer of the shares, they are unlikely to be a PSC but other controlling factors may make them so.

EXTRACT FROM GUIDANCE

16.46   The following extract is from the PSC Guidance at: https://assets.
publishing.service.gov.uk/government/uploads/system/uploads/attachment
_data/file/621568/170622_NON-STAT_Summary_Guidance_4MLD_Final.
pdf.

	'Condition:	What you need to consider:
(i)	An individual who holds **more than 25% of shares** in the company.	Review your company's register of members and identify shareholdings of over 25%.
(ii)	An individual who holds **more than 25% of voting rights** in the company.	Review your company's register of members, articles of association, and identify people with voting rights (often attached to shares) over 25%.
(iii)	An individual who holds the right **to appoint or remove the majority of the board of directors** of the company.	Look at your company's constitution, including articles of association, and identify whether anyone has this right. If there is only one director and someone has the right to appoint them, then they would meet this condition.
The following conditions apply only in limited circumstances and are explained in Statutory Guidance.		
(iv)	An individual who has the right to exercise, or actually exercises, **significant influence or control** over the company.	You would consider this where an individual **does not meet one of conditions (i) to (iii)** but does exercise 'significant influence or control' over the company. The statutory guidance sets out principles and situations where an individual would be a PSC.
(v)	Where a **trust or firm** would satisfy one of the first four conditions if it were an individual. Any individual holding the right to exercise, or actually exercising, **significant influence or control over the activities of that trust or firm**.	If one of the above conditions is met by a trust or firm (without legal personality), read the relevant section in the statutory guidance to identify who should be included in the PSC register.'

16.47   One issue for those drafting shareholders' agreement is which elements of minority protection (or indeed other) clauses give someone 'control' under the PSC legislation. The guidance states as follows (see https://www.gov.uk/government/uploads/system/uploads/attachment_data/file/523120/PSC_statutory_guidance_companies.pdf):

'Examples

2.5.   Paragraphs 2.6–2.9 set out a number of examples of what might constitute a right to exercise significant influence or control, while paragraph 2.10 sets out a number of examples where rights relating to minority protection would not on their own constitute a right to exercise significant influence or control. The examples do not constitute an exhaustive list.

2.6.   Where a person has absolute decision rights over decisions related to the running of the business of the company, for example relating to:

   a)   Adopting or amending the company's business plan;

   b)   Changing the nature of the company's business;

   c)   Making any additional borrowing from lenders;

   d)   Appointment or removal of the CEO;

   e)   Establishing or amending any profit-sharing, bonus or other incentive scheme of any nature for directors or employees; or

   f)   The grant of options under a share option or other share based incentive scheme.

2.7.   Where a person has absolute veto rights over decisions related to the running of the business of the company, for example relating to:

   a)   Adopting or amending the company's business plan;

   b)   Making any additional borrowing from lenders (except as a minority protection as described in paragraph 2.8 below).

2.8.   However, if a person holds absolute veto rights in relation to certain fundamental matters for the purposes of protecting minority interests in the company then this is unlikely, on its own, to constitute "significant influence or control" over the company. When used for the purposes of protecting minority interests these veto rights could include (or relate to) the following:

   a)   Changing the company's constitution;

   b)   Dilution of shares or rights, including establishing a share option or other share based incentive scheme;

   c)   Making any additional borrowing from lenders, outside previously agreed lending thresholds;

   d)   Fundamental changes to the nature of the company's business; or

   e)   Winding up the company.

2.9. Where a person holds absolute veto rights over the appointment of the majority of directors, meaning those directors who hold a majority of the voting rights at meetings of the board on all or substantially all matters.

2.10. A person would not have "significant influence or control" where the absolute decision rights or veto derive solely from being a prospective purchaser in relation to the company, on a temporary basis, for example pending clearance by the Competition and Markets Authority.

2.11. In this guidance the term 'absolute' is used in relation to decision rights or a veto to mean that a person has the ability to make or veto a decision without reference to or collaboration with anyone else.

3.   Actually exercises significant influence or control over a company

3.1. Paragraphs 3.2 and 3.3 provide a list of situations which would be indicative of a person actually exercising significant influence or control.

3.2. All relationships that a person has with the company or other individuals who have responsibility for managing the company, should be taken into account, to identify whether the cumulative effect of those relationships places the individual in a position where they actually exercise significant influence or control. For example:

> A director who also owns important assets or has key relationships that are important to the running of the business (e.g. intellectual property rights), and uses this additional power to influence the outcome of decisions related to the running of the business of the company.

3.3. A person would exercise "significant influence or control" if:

a)   They are significantly involved in the management and direction of the company, for example:

> A person, who is not a member of the board of directors, but regularly or consistently directs or influences a significant section of the board, or is regularly consulted on board decisions and whose views influence decisions made by the board.

> This would include a person who falls within the definition of "shadow director" set out in section 251 of the Act, but the situation is not confined to shadow directors.

b)   Their recommendations are always or almost always followed by shareholders who hold the majority of the voting rights in the company, when they are deciding how to vote. For example:

A company founder who no longer has a significant shareholding in the company they started, but makes recommendations to the other shareholders on how to vote and those recommendations are always or almost always followed.

4.   Fourth condition: excepted roles with respect to companies

4.1. The following is a non-exhaustive list of roles and relationships which would not, on their own, result in that person being considered to be exercising significant influence or control for the purposes of the fourth condition.

4.2. Where the person provides advice or direction in a professional capacity, for example, as:

   a)   A Lawyer;

   b)   An Accountant;

   c)   A Management consultant;

   d)   An Investment manager

   e)   A Tax advisor; or

   f)   A Financial advisor.

4.3. Where the person deals with the company under a third party commercial or financial agreement, for example, as:

   a)   A Supplier;

   b)   A Customer; or

   c)   A Lender.

4.4. Where the person exercises a function under an enactment, for example, as:

   a)   A Regulator; or

   b)   A Liquidator or receiver.

4.5. Where the person is an employee acting in the course of their employment and nominee for their employer, including an employee, director or CEO of a third party (such as a corporate director company), which has significant influence or control over the company.

4.6. Where the person is a director of a company, including, as:

   a)   A Managing director;

   b)   A Sole director; or

   c)   A Non-executive or executive director who holds a casting vote.

4.7. A person who makes recommendations to shareholders on an issue, or set of issues, on a one-off occasion, which is subject to a shareholder vote.

4.8. Rights held by all or a group of employees, for the purpose of representing the employees interests in an employee-owned company.

4.9. Any person or entity in relation to any association, professional standards organisation or network of companies or firms which promulgates common rules, policies or standards to be adopted by the members of the network, but does not otherwise have control of members of the network.

4.10. A person who has a role or relationship of the kind listed above with the company may, however, be a person with significant influence over the company either:

a)   If the role or relationship differs in material respects or contains significantly different features from how the role or relationship is generally understood; or

b)   If the role or relationship forms one of several opportunities which that person has to exercise significant influence or control.'

16.48 The guidance then looks at trusts and firms but this is not reproduced here.

The PSC guidance is online at https://www.gov.uk/government/publications/guidance-to-the-people-with-significant-control-requirements-for-companies-and-limited-liability-partnerships.

The PSC rules are very complicated and all the guidance must be read. There are useful charts to help ascertain who is a PSC in the Government guidance at: https://assets.publishing.service.gov.uk/government/uploads/system/uploads/attachment_data/file/753027/170623_NONSTAT_GU__1_.pdf.

Chapter 17

Termination and its consequences

Summary

This chapter deals with the provisions for termination normally inserted in shareholders' agreements and their likely consequences, which usually consist of some machinery whereby one or more shareholders may purchase all the shares of the other or others or, failing that, liquidation of the company. The chapter discusses other methods of realisation which might be employed. Other matters requiring attention on termination are discussed, including its effects on ancillary agreements, together with the provisions of a shareholders' agreement which usually survive termination.

1 Introduction

17.1   One of the most important issues concerning any joint venture or shareholders' agreement is the circumstances in which it may be terminated. This issue is very much bound up with realisation and exit routes. There is little point in providing for termination without considering arrangements for the acquisition by one party of the shares of the others, or the sale or realisation of the whole venture, or perhaps liquidation. If no provision is made for such arrangements, termination is largely pointless because if the parties remain shareholders as before, but without a shareholders' agreement, the minority holders are put in a worse position, with only such rights as may be available in the articles of association or as are afforded by the law. The position of any majority holder will of course be enhanced.

17.2   This chapter deals with a selection of exit arrangements which may be brought into operation where the shareholders' agreement has been, or is to be, terminated.

17.3   However, there are other methods of exit which are discussed in the following chapters. Chapter 18 deals with pre-termination put and call options, which are sometimes included to provide an early exit for a party which may be independent of the termination of the shareholders' agreement as regards continuing shareholders. Chapter 19 deals with pre-emptive rights on share transfers, which again may provide another method of exit, without necessarily resulting in the termination of the shareholders' agreement. Chapter 20 deals with purchase and redemption of shares by the company; the purchase of shares will not normally be provided for in advance but may come about as an exit route agreed to by the parties following, or in contemplation of, termination, but the issue of any redeemable shares will take place at the outset of the arrangements because the terms of redemption must be set out in the share rights. Chapter 21 deals with exits by sale or flotation of the company. A sale may come about in consequence of termination, or may always have been contemplated by the parties and provided for in the shareholders' agreement, or it may come about through the making of a third-party offer.

17.4   When considering realisation resulting from termination, it needs to be considered whether a sale to an existing shareholder or to a third party is in fact a practical proposition. If the company is entirely the creation of its shareholders and the continued involvement of all of them is a vital ingredient for success, or if it is reliant on the know-how or intellectual property held on licence from one of them, which by its negotiated terms will not survive termination, then the shareholders should be providing for liquidation as the only termination consequence. However, it may be that if any shareholder has injected substantial assets into the company it may desire their return, either by means of a resale immediately before liquidation or as a distribution in specie in the liquidation.

17.5   Another important issue related to termination of an agreement between more than two shareholders is whether a shareholder is to be entitled to transfer its shares and leave the company without this affecting the continuance of the shareholders' agreement (to which any transferee of the outgoing shareholder may be required to adhere), or whether the decision to leave by one shareholder brings the agreement to an end for all of them, with a subsequent realisation or liquidation. With a company which is not dependent on any existing shareholder, as will be the case with many private companies which were not formed as joint ventures in the strict sense, the former will usually be desired. In a family controlled company, or one in which individuals (whether or not related) are the only, or major, shareholders, there will usually be a desire to allow transfers to other family members (particularly to the next generation) or to family trusts (see para 26.70ff). If, however, the company cannot continue without the active participation of one or more shareholders, the result is likely to be that the decision of any such shareholder to leave will result in termination of the shareholders' agreement and the discontinuance or sale of the business.

17.6   An equally important issue when considering the consequences of termination is its effect on agreements and arrangements ancillary to the shareholders' agreement, such as shareholders' loans and guarantees, intellectual property licences, support agreements and similar arrangements. These issues can present some intractable problems which may greatly affect the outcome of a termination, or even the decision to terminate in the first place, and for this reason they are best addressed at the outset[1].

2   Typical termination events and resulting exit provisions

17.7   Some typical termination events are now reviewed, together with the exit or realisation mechanism which the parties will generally wish to choose in each case; each such mechanism is then discussed.

Expiry

17.8   Although this is uncommon, the shareholders' agreement may provide for its automatic termination at the expiration of a fixed period. The resulting exit provisions provided for in the agreement may include any of those mentioned in this chapter but are most likely to consist of put and call options, or the 'multi-choice' realisation procedure suggested at para 17.39ff, with liquidation if all else fails. Less uncommon is the shareholders' agreement which terminates automatically on the happening of a specified event. If, for example, the joint venture company was established to carry out a particular project, it is likely that the shareholders' agreement will provide for termination at the end of the project. Here the only exit route is likely to be liquidation, since the joint venture company will have no ongoing business which will attract a purchaser.

Notice to terminate

17.9   The shareholders' agreement may provide that any shareholder may give notice to terminate it at any time after a fixed date, prior to which all shareholders are committed to the venture. It is a matter for negotiation whether the shareholders' agreement continues as regards the remaining shareholders or whether it comes to an end. Where the shares are held in large blocks and all shareholders are in a minority, the former arrangement is in fact only likely to be practicable if there is a legally certain arrangement for the purchase of the shares of the outgoing shareholder by the others. The outgoing shareholder will not wish to be 'locked in', and if no shareholder is

---

1   See Chapter 3.

prepared to buy its shares and no third party can be found to do so, and the company is unwilling or unable to purchase them, the likely consequence is an agreement to seek a purchaser for the whole issued share capital of the company or a right for the outgoing party to buy the shares of the others so that it may sell the whole company. In the case of a small shareholder giving notice to leave, it is unlikely to be realistic for it to insist on a sale of the whole share capital, should no other shareholder be willing to purchase its shares.

17.10 Subject to these considerations, the realisation route provided could be any of those dealt with in this chapter, but is most likely to consist of termination put and call options, or perhaps a 'multi-choice' realisation provision, with liquidation if all else fails.

17.11 A related situation is where the agreement simply provides that no shareholder is entitled to transfer its shares other than under the provisions of the articles of association. These then contain a pre-emption provision (discussed in detail in Chapter 19) under which the intending transferee is bound to offer its shares to the other shareholders, failing which it can, in theory, transfer its shares to an outsider, usually on condition that the transferee becomes bound by the shareholders' agreement, although in actuality an outside purchaser is most unlikely to be found. This is a kind of conditional termination event; if the intending transferee is successful in selling its shares, it ceases to be a shareholder and a well drafted shareholders' agreement will state that he ceases to be party to it (subject to certain reservations, as to which see para 17.63ff). If the intending transferee fails to do so, it remains a shareholder and party to the agreement, subject of course to its right to serve another transfer notice at a later time. A large minority shareholder will not be happy to rely on a pre-emption provision alone, because of the danger of being 'locked in' and will desire one of the other realisation procedures mentioned in this chapter.

Deadlock

17.12 Where there are two 50:50 shareholders in a deadlock company[2], an unresolved deadlock is usually made a ground for termination. Such a termination event is discussed in detail at para 13.22ff.

17.13 Although deadlock is most likely in a company which has been established as a 'deadlock company', it can of course occur in a company with more than two shareholders if opposing combinations of them have the same voting power and the chairman's casting vote has been removed. This could also be a ground for termination if the dispute cannot be resolved.

---

2   See Chapter 13.

Persistent use of vetoes

17.14   In a company with two or more shareholders a minority shareholder provided with a selection of vetoes (depending on that to which they related) could severely obstruct the business of the company if it uses them persistently, so there is a school of thought in those circumstances (mainly by the majority shareholder or its advisers it has to be said) that the persistent use of vetoes should be a termination event (at the option of the majority holder). Where there are more than two parties, it would almost certainly be thought unreasonable for this to be a termination event as regards all the parties, and it is unlikely that the other shareholders would be prepared to be obliged to buy out the disaffected shareholder, because it could then engineer an exit through deliberate non-co-operation. The probable solution for a company with two shareholders would be a call option in favour of the majority holder, and for a company with more than two shareholders it could be provided that the disaffected shareholder would be obliged to offer its shares for sale to the others, either through a share transfer pre-emption provision in the articles, if there is one, or otherwise under a clause to that effect in the shareholders' agreement. This would therefore be another 'conditional' termination, since if no internal purchaser could be found and no sale to a third party was possible under the pre-emption article (if available) the disaffected shareholder would presumably remain a shareholder with its vetoes intact, unless it was provided that the compulsory offer brought them to an end, which might be thought too draconian. There would, however, be a very strong incentive on the other shareholders to find a way of buying out the disaffected shareholder in order to avoid the disruption caused by continual use of its veto. There is obviously much room for negotiation on what constitutes the persistent use of a veto.

Breach

17.15   The shareholders' agreement will almost invariably provide that a breach is not a ground for termination unless it is 'material' and not until the defaulter has been served with a notice requiring it to remedy the breach (unless incapable of remedy) within a fixed period (usually 30 days). There may be endless arguments over what is a material breach, but attempts to define what it means are usually futile; it is something difficult to define but generally apparent when you see it. There is very little relevant case law on the subject. In *D B Rare Books Ltd v Antiqbooks*[3] it was decided, in relation to whether a breach of a partnership deed was material, that the word 'material' should be given its dictionary meaning as something of 'serious or

---

3   [1995] 2 BCLC 306.

substantial import, of such consequence, important'. This is not particularly helpful, but in the context of a shareholders' agreement it is suggested that a material breach will be something which is likely to prejudice the long-term relationship between the shareholders or will tend to produce a different commercial result from that intended when the agreement was entered into. There is sometimes an argument over whether a 'material' breach means a breach of a material term or a material breach of any term, and it is suggested that the latter is correct; materiality is to be judged by the likely consequences of the breach and a minor breach of a material term is not likely to have any material consequences.

17.16   Where the agreement contains warranties given by any shareholder, a material breach of these is likely to be a termination event, and where there are agreements ancillary to the shareholders' agreement it is for consideration whether a material breach or termination of one of these should also be a ground for termination of the shareholders' agreement.

17.17   If there is a breach of the agreement or of a warranty, then the preferred realisation mechanism is likely to be termination put and call options exercisable only by the non-defaulters or, for a small stake, a compulsory transfer notice under pre-emption provisions or liquidation at the option of the non-defaulters. The valuation formula could involve a reduction to reflect any damage done to the company by the breach; this would involve the valuer determining the value of the company with and without the breach, and then apportioning the whole of the reduction to the shareholder in breach. However, before incorporating this it would be best to check that the valuer considers the arrangement workable and is happy with the wording, because it may be thought difficult to value a company on the assumption that an event which has occurred has not occurred. It is thought that this is not likely to be an unenforceable penalty, because it will be regarded as a genuine pre-estimate of the loss suffered by the other shareholders – arguably all it does is to translate the damages which might have been claimed by the other shareholders into a reduction of the consideration for the defaulter's shares of the same amount, although it should be provided that, if the defaulter's shares are transferred, there is no other remedy available against it for the breach. This may work unfairly if the other shareholders do not acquire the defaulter's shares pro rata to their existing shareholdings, and it may be preferable simply to value the defaulter's shares by reference to the breach (so only the appropriate proportion of the loss falls on the defaulter) and preserve the remedies of the other shareholders for the breach.

17.18   A termination notice ought only to be capable of being served within a limited period after the breach has arisen or been discovered, so that breaches which appear to be acquiesced in cannot later become a ground for termination.

Change of control

17.19   A change of the control of a party is often made a ground for termination. This is because if the change of control is to a competitor of the joint venture company, or of one of the shareholders, the new controlling party could acquire useful information concerning its competitor and by the use of voting powers or veto seriously disrupt the business of the company to its advantage, or the identity of the new controller may simply be unacceptable to the other shareholders for other reasons. The consequent realisation mechanism could be any of those mentioned in this chapter, but termination put and call options are probably the most likely.

17.20   It is highly desirable to define what is meant by a change of control. If the expression 'control' or 'effective control' is used, its meaning may be uncertain. In *Sanofi-Synthelabo SPA v 3M Health Care*[4] Italian and US joint venturers had entered into a joint venture agreement governed by English law which included a right of termination should either party undergo a change in its 'effective control'. Laddie J interpreted this expression as meaning the ability of a shareholder to ensure that the relevant entity complied with its wishes. He rejected the submissions of two continental experts that 'control' could include 'joint control' by two or more shareholders. Indeed, as has been seen, EU competition law readily accepts the concept of joint control. Had the agreement been governed by Italian law, the result might well have been different, and now that EU law has been part of English law at least until 1 January 2021, the end of the post-Brexit transition period, but in practice even thereafter as it will take a while for divergence to occur, it is far from certain that in a future case an agreement governed by English law would be construed in the same way as it was in the cited case, especially if the agreement includes European partners who can produce evidence that another interpretation was intended. Note also that the agreement referred to 'effective' control; the result might have been different had it just said 'control'.

17.21   Some care needs to be taken over the definition of a change of control. The definitions in the Corporation Tax Act 2010 (previously the Income and Corporation Taxes Act 1988 ('ICTA 1988'), s 416, or s 840) are often used. The old definitions in ICTA 1988, ss 416 and 840 were re-enacted as the CTA 2010, ss 450, 451 and 1124 without change.

The definition in s 450 (previously s 416) is very wide and may result in more than one person having control of a company at the same time and, depending upon the terms of the termination provisions, could result in a termination event occurring as regards a particular party every time one of its controllers ceases to have control or an additional controller is added. It

---

4   [2002] All ER (D) 181 (Apr), [2003] ETMR 45.

defines control by virtue of the possession of specific rights, and also provides that a right to acquire control is 'control'. It may be more appropriate to use the narrower definition contained in s 1124 (previously s 840), which provides that a person has control of a company if he has the ability to ensure its affairs are conducted in accordance with his wishes, which should certainly meet the purpose for which the termination event is being included. Both definitions operate so that where a participant in a company holds its interest through a subsidiary in its group, both the participant and its subsidiary will be taken to have control of the company. It will usually not concern the other parties if the participant's interest is transferred to another subsidiary, and to avoid the possibility of a termination in this event it will usually be desirable to provide that termination is only possible where the control of the named parent company changes or the subsidiary ceases to be controlled by the named parent.

17.22 There is no particular reason to use either definition of 'control'. The parties may prefer to have the definition set out in the agreement, rather than defined by what may seem to them to be an obscure piece of legislation which may not be readily accessible to them. Certainly, this is often preferred in international joint ventures. A simple and readily understandable definition of control for a company would be the ability to exercise more than half the votes exercisable at a general meeting or the ability to appoint more than one-half of the directors, and a change of control would then occur if such control passes to one or more persons who do not currently have such control.

17.23 A change of control may be involuntary, eg if one of the parties is the subject of a hostile takeover bid, but the view will generally be taken that such a change of control should nevertheless be a termination event; it is the possible effect of the change of control and not its cause which matters. In *Dee Valley Group PLC*[5] – share splitting by target shareholder to defeat a scheme of arrangement in a hostile takeover failed. Care should be taken when seeking to challenge an unwelcome takeover bid of artificial attempts, to prevent it proceeding and detailed legal advice should always be taken. An obligation on a listed company to sell or buy shares of another party in consequence of the change of control of the listed company may cause problems under the Listing Rules (para 11.34ff).

Liquidation, bankruptcy or insolvency of a party

17.24 These events affecting a party are invariably a ground for termination. A typical clause will provide that the events leading to termination are liquidation, whether voluntary or compulsory (except for the purposes of

---

5   [2017] EWHC 184 (Ch).

a bona fide reconstruction or amalgamation with the consent of the other parties, not to be unreasonably withheld), the making of an administration order or the appointment of a receiver or administrative receiver or, in the case of an individual, his becoming bankrupt. It is for consideration whether a company or individual voluntary arrangement or an informal composition or arrangement with creditors should be a termination event. The usual realisation mechanism will be the sale of the shares of the affected party to the other parties under a termination call option, or a compulsory transfer notice under a pre-emption provision. No shareholder will wish to be bound to buy the shares of the insolvent shareholder, so a put option in favour of the liquidator, receiver or trustee in bankruptcy is not likely. However, at least if the stake is a minority one, the liquidator, receiver or trustee in bankruptcy will usually be very keen to effect a sale, since otherwise he may be unable to satisfactorily conclude the liquidation, receivership or bankruptcy. The same may apply to an administrator, unless it is expected that the company in administration will be able to survive.

17.25   It might be questioned whether a provision requiring a liquidator, administrator, receiver or trustee in bankruptcy of a shareholder to offer the shares of that shareholder for sale is enforceable, since such officers are not ordinarily bound by contracts entered into by the insolvent company or bankrupt individual. However, in *Borland's Trustee v Steel Brothers & Co Ltd*[6] the court had no difficulty in finding that a trustee in bankruptcy was bound by a pre-emption article containing a compulsory transfer provision, provided the price was fair. It would seem that this decision was made on the basis that such provision was in the interests of the bankrupt's creditors in providing a mechanism for realising the bankrupt's shares. The same principle can no doubt be extended to a liquidator, but there seems to be no authority as to whether the same applies to receivers or administrators. Likewise there is no authority on whether a provision for compulsory transfer upon insolvency which is contained in a shareholders' agreement rather than in the articles is valid. Logically, there seems no reason why a provision in a shareholders' agreement should be treated differently to one in the articles, but the *Borland* decision was clearly influenced by the fact that a provision in the articles binds all present and future shareholders alike, whereas a shareholders' agreement binds only the signatories to it and will not bind future shareholders unless provision is made for them to become bound to it by executing a deed of adherence. It may therefore be the case that a call option in a shareholders' agreement is not enforceable against a liquidator, receiver, administrator or trustee in bankruptcy, although such provisions are frequently seen and, in practice, as mentioned above, a liquidator, receiver or trustee may well wish to agree to the relevant sale, if satisfied the price is fair. However, it is for consideration whether

---

6   [1901] 1 Ch 279.

it would be preferable to rely on a compulsory transfer provision in the articles; certainly the articles should contain such a provision, so that it can be used as an alternative to the call option should it fail.

Liquidation of the company

17.26 The liquidation of the company itself is usually made an event which automatically terminates the shareholders' agreement, but in any event its operation thereafter (except in relation to the rights as between shareholders) will effectively be impossible, since the direction of the company will pass out of the hands of its directors and into the hands of the liquidator.

Continuance of minority protection after termination

17.27 A point generally overlooked is that the realisation process consequent upon termination can be a long, drawn-out affair, especially if the parties have agreed to seek a purchaser for the whole issued share capital. Most termination clauses terminate the agreement with immediate effect so that all minority protections therein immediately cease, but the company will still need to be run while realisation is being arranged, and if total discretion passes to the majority, a favourable realisation for the minority could be prejudiced. It may therefore be appropriate for the minority protections to continue up to realisation. Such a provision is unlikely to be necessary if the preferred realisation mechanism is a short procedure such as the exercise of termination put and call options or a 'Russian roulette' or 'Texas shoot out' provision, with liquidation should they fail. Such continuance provisions will probably also be thought inappropriate to benefit a minority party where termination has arisen through the breach or insolvency of that party, or perhaps where it has undergone a change of control.

3 Realisation mechanisms on termination

Termination put and call options

17.28 Under this arrangement the party or parties serving the termination notice (the 'terminator') may require the party or parties upon whom that notice was served (the 'terminatee') either:

● to purchase all of the shares of the terminator; or

● to sell to the terminator all the shares of the terminatee.

The terminatee then becomes bound to either buy or sell as required by the notice at a price fixed by valuation (as to which see Chapter 22).

17.29   If the terminator does not exercise its option, the terminatee may be given the right within, say, 30 days to serve a counter notice on the terminator requiring it to sell all its shares to the terminatee and the terminator then becomes bound to do so. This latter option will not usually be given to the terminatee where the original termination notice was served in consequence of a breach by the terminatee or of another termination event affecting the terminatee.

17.30   If neither the terminator nor the terminatee exercises their option, the agreement will often provide that the company shall be wound up. Even if the terminatee has no wish to retain an investment in the company, it may still wish to exercise its option in order to be able to acquire the whole of the share capital of the company for onward sale.

17.31   Under this arrangement, the terminatee can be faced with becoming bound to purchase all the shares of the terminator, which the terminatee is only likely to accept if it can expect to have the resources to do so. A variation on the above, involving call options only, enables the terminator to serve notice on the terminatee requesting it to purchase the shares of the terminator and, if the terminatee fails to serve a counter-notice agreeing to do so within a certain time, the terminator has the right to buy out the terminatee. This is suitable where the terminator is serving the notice because it simply wishes to withdraw from the venture under a clause giving it the right to do so after a certain number of years. In effect the terminator is saying: 'I want out, either buy my shares, or I will buy yours and sell the whole company'.

17.32   Put and call options work best where there are only two shareholders or, at most, three or four. If more than one party is to exercise a call option jointly or be faced with a put option exercised against them, they will first have to agree between themselves the proportions in which they will purchase the shares. The more shareholders there are the more difficult this is to achieve and the more unworkable the arrangements become, and in such a situation a compulsory transfer provision applying to the terminatee with a right of pre-emption for other shareholders is often a more practical arrangement. In relation to any termination arrangements involving the grant of options the tax considerations mentioned in the next chapter are relevant.

'Russian roulette'

17.33   This is generally only applicable to a two-party shareholders' agreement, and will usually only be employed where deadlock has given rise to termination. Since its results are highly unpredictable, it is not usually thought appropriate in other circumstances. It is best suited to a situation where the parties are of roughly equivalent economic strength.

17.34   Either party ('the server') may serve a notice on the other party ('the recipient') which may either require the recipient to sell its shares to the server or buy the server's shares – in either case at a price which is specified by the server. The recipient can either do nothing, in which case it is bound by the server's notice, or it may within, say, 30 days serve a counter-notice which, if the original notice required the recipient to sell its shares to the server, can require the server to sell its shares to the recipient, or if the original notice required the recipient to buy the shares of the server may require the server to purchase the shares of the recipient. The server then becomes bound by the counter-notice.

17.35   A variation is for the server to have the ability to give the recipient the choice of buying or selling at the same price, but if the recipient fails to elect within, say, 30 days, the server can make it either buy or sell.

17.36   If neither party serves a notice to start the procedure within a specified time after it has been triggered, the company is wound up.

17.37   One point possibly in favour of this procedure is that, unlike the put and call option, since there is no compulsion to serve a notice, neither party can be compelled to buy, only to sell (unless the recipient fails to serve a counter-notice in time), so, apart from this, there is no risk of a party finding itself bound to buy without the resources to do so. Another point in its favour is that because the server must name a price at which it is prepared to both buy and sell, the price is more likely to be a fair one. It also avoids a valuation, which involves the risk that the valuer will determine a price which the selling party finds unappealing. The stronger party will always win because it can serve a notice to buy knowing that the weaker party can only comply, not having the resources to buy itself. The weaker party will only be able to sell and therefore may not be prepared to serve a notice at all, lest it should be compelled to buy by a counter-notice. Assuming it has the resources, a party whose only desire is to realise its interest does not have to wait for the other party to serve a 'buy' notice; it can itself serve a 'buy' notice, and either accept a counter-notice to sell or acquire 100% of the company and then sell it on.

Flowchart 4
Termination put and call options

This flowchart shows the various possible permutations involved in put and call options

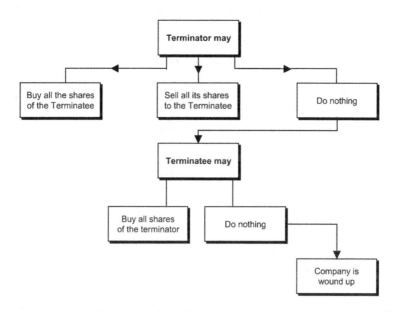

Variation with call options only:

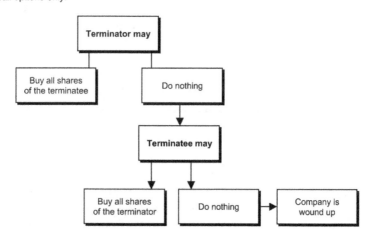

Flowchart 5
'Russian roulette' provision

This flowchart shows the operation of a typical Russian roulette clause

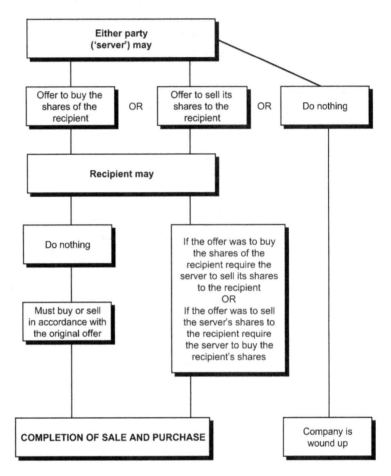

'Texas shoot out' – or 'Dutch auction'

17.38   On termination, each party has the right within, say, 30 days to submit a sealed bid, which, depending upon the wording of the clause, may contain an offer to purchase the shares of the outgoing party, or the shares of all the other parties, or perhaps an offer to acquire the business of the company, which is then wound up. The party submitting the highest bid is bound to buy in accordance with the bid. If nobody bids, liquidation ensues. Again, nobody is bound to buy, only to sell, but since none may bid it is not a reliable method for unlocking a minority. The price should be fair in that a shareholder who is really keen to buy will offer a very full price, so as not to risk being beaten by the others, and a valuation is avoided. Nevertheless, it is sensible to provide that an offer is to be made on a 'per share' basis, without any discount to reflect any minority interest, or indeed a control premium. A Texas shoot out is probably most appropriate for a company which has been formed to hold assets rather than conduct a business, such as one holding real or intellectual property. This type of company is more easily valued by the parties themselves, since its value will closely relate to the value of the underlying assets, and there is therefore less risk of the bidder subsequently discovering that it has paid too much by reason of some hidden liabilities of the company. However, its effectiveness does, to a large extent, depend on having parties of roughly similar economic worth and with similar or identically sized shareholdings.

'Multi-choice realisation procedure'

17.39   The realisation procedures so far discussed have been confined to the sale and purchase of shares between the parties or, failing that, liquidation. However, other possibilities may provide a more satisfactory realisation, such as the purchase of shares by the company, the purchase of an outgoing shareholder's stake by a third party, or the sale of the whole issued share capital or business of the company. The parties may wish these possibilities to be taken into consideration.

17.40   A clause which it is believed will be particularly appropriate in a case where termination does not flow from breach or insolvency, and the termination event affects the outgoing party only, is to provide that the parties will negotiate in good faith to achieve one of the following within a certain period of the termination notice being served:

- the purchase by the company of the outgoing party's shares, if lawful and practicable, including, if possible, a purchase out of capital;

- the purchase by one or more of the other parties of the outgoing party's shares;

- the purchase by one or more third parties of the outgoing party's shares; or

- the sale of the whole issued share capital of the company, including the outgoing party's shares, to a third party.

If none of these is achieved by the stated time, the parties will be obliged to place the company in liquidation.

17.41   The parties may be tempted to provide for a preferred order of preference and to include elaborate provisions for co-operation between the parties, but it is suggested that this is unlikely to be necessary. The prospect of liquidation if a negotiated solution cannot be achieved within the stated time should be a sufficient incentive to arrive at one.

17.42   As well as helping to ensure all the options are explored, such a clause is likely to promote a successful realisation. Nobody is put under any commitment to buy or sell, the possible trauma of a 'Russian roulette' or 'Texas shoot out' provision is avoided, and all the pressure is imposed by the liquidation deadline. Since liquidation is the solution least likely to suit any of the parties, they may each find it in their interests to act reasonably (thus avoiding liquidation). The shareholder who is leaving may be concerned that the sanction of liquidation will not be strong enough to provide it with a guaranteed exit, in which case a possible solution is to provide that if none of the prescribed realisation alternatives is achieved by the deadline, the outgoing shareholder may call for all other shares so as to achieve a realisation by the sale of the whole issued share capital of the company.

17.43   As to the third of the suggested choices, although there is generally no market for shares in private companies and even a majority stake may be difficult to sell if it is encumbered with minority rights in the articles of association or a shareholders' agreement, it may sometimes be possible for an outgoing shareholder to sell its stake to an outsider. There may be circumstances in which another party in the same or a related business to that carried on by the outgoing shareholder may be prepared to join an existing shareholders' or joint venture agreement in replacement of the outgoing shareholder. Such a party would obviously have to be acceptable to the shareholders who are remaining, who may well wish to be satisfied that the new shareholder is capable of contributing something to the venture, and any sale would result from tripartite negotiations between the outgoing shareholder, the prospective shareholder and the remaining shareholders, which may involve the negotiation of a completely new agreement. Similarly, institutional shareholders are sometimes able to sell their stakes to another institution.

17.44   Considerations relating to the purchase of the shares by the company are dealt with in Chapter 20.

17.45   Considerations relating to the sale of the whole issued share capital of the company are dealt with at para 21.1ff.

4   Completion of the sale

17.46   Where the chosen consequence of termination will or may be the purchase of shares in the company by one shareholder from another, the shareholders' agreement ought to contain provisions regulating the completion of the sale and purchase. The provisions will be similar to those in a share purchase agreement and will generally provide for the seller to deliver to the purchaser the share certificates for the shares to be sold, together with an executed stock transfer form in favour of the purchaser in exchange for the price, which may be paid by banker's draft or a bank transfer. It is important to set a time by when completion is to take place. Clearly, that cannot be earlier than the date on which the price is determined. Other matters to be dealt with on completion may be those referred to under 'Other termination consequences' below. In addition, the seller will normally be required to procure the resignations of the directors which it has appointed to the board of the company. If the registration of the share transfer cannot be achieved without the assistance of other shareholders, they may be obliged to provide such assistance by executing any necessary waivers of pre-emption rights or procuring their appointed directors to vote in favour of the registration of the transfer.

17.47   The seller may be required to sell the shares with full title guarantee, so as to oblige it to procure the release of the shares from all mortgages, charges and other encumbrances to which they may be subject, but the seller will not normally be asked to provide any other warranties.

5   Other termination consequences

17.48   Except in a case where the result of termination is to be liquidation, various other issues will arise on termination. If termination results in the shares of one or more of the shareholders being purchased by one or more others, the shareholders' agreement will normally provide for these matters to be dealt with at the same time as the completion of the purchase of the shares, but if termination results in the sale of the whole issued share capital, or the shares of one or more shareholders being purchased by an outsider, the matter will need to be resolved between the shareholders and the outsider. However, provisions in a shareholders' agreement which contemplate a sale to an outsider ought to address these issues. They will also need to be addressed where the shares of a shareholder are being purchased by the company.

Repayment of loans

17.49   The shareholders' agreement will often provide that an outgoing shareholder is entitled to the immediate repayment of any loans it has advanced to the company at the same time as the purchase of its shares is completed. Whether this is always appropriate is discussed at para 6.19ff, but complying with this requirement may mean that the continuing shareholders will need to advance loans to the company or to subscribe for additional share capital of equivalent amount to the loans to be repaid, or will have to arrange for the company to borrow an equivalent amount from outside, which may mean that the continuing shareholders have to provide guarantees.

Flowchart 6

Multi-choice realisation procedure

This flowchart illustrates the operation of the multi-choice realisation procedure - the precise order of events depends upon the priority which the parties decide to give to the various choices, and the order shown is purely illustrative. In practice, only one or some of the choices may be feasible. More than one choice might be pursued simultaneously.

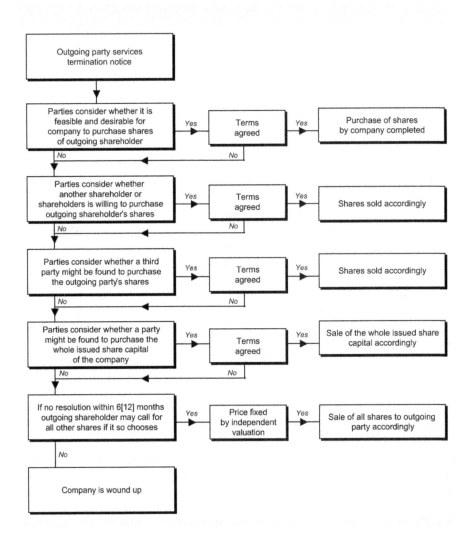

Release of guarantees

17.50   The shareholders' agreement will also usually provide that the outgoing shareholder is to be released from all guarantees, indemnities and similar obligations which it has given in respect of the liabilities and obligations of the company (in so far as this may be possible), which could include, for example, a guarantee of the company's bank overdraft. No shareholder would normally be expected to agree to the continuance of its guarantee or other similar obligation after it has sold its shares and lost any influence over the affairs of the company, including any influence over the amount and nature of the liabilities it is guaranteeing, or at least not without an effective counter-indemnity. A possible exception might be if it is that party's breach which has triggered termination. However, even in that case it would be normal for some safeguards or time limits to be introduced.

17.51   In order to secure the release of the relevant guarantees, the other shareholders may have to inject further sums into the company in order to discharge the guarantees or the liabilities in respect of which they were given, or provide their own guarantees in substitution.

17.52   Negotiations for the release and substitution of guarantees can take time, and the shareholders' agreement may contemplate that a release at the same time as the completion of the purchase of the shares of the outgoing shareholder may not be practicable, and will then include undertakings from the continuing shareholders to indemnify the outgoing shareholder against the guaranteed liabilities pending the release of its guarantees. This will only be acceptable to the outgoing shareholder if the continuing shareholders are of sufficient substance and, if not, the outgoing shareholder will insist on being released on the completion of the sale of its shares.

Ancillary agreements

17.53   Ancillary agreements, such as support agreements and intellectual property licences with the outgoing shareholder, may provide for their termination on the outgoing shareholder ceasing to hold any shares in the company. The issue is discussed at para 3.10ff and para 3.21.

17.54   It is more likely that the outgoing shareholder will be inclined to continue an intellectual property licence than a support agreement, since the former is more of a passive obligation, whereas the latter is a more onerous commitment. However, a support agreement ought at least to run for a short grace period after termination of the shareholders' agreement and preferably should continue for its whole contractual period notwithstanding termination of the shareholders' agreement.

17.55   The non-continuance of an important ancillary agreement which cannot easily be replaced by a new agreement entered into with an outsider may jeopardise the continuance of the business of the company. This is a very important point, not only to be considered by those desiring to terminate the shareholders' agreement but also in relation to the price to be paid for the outgoing shareholder's shares after termination. The price to be paid should reflect the loss of any agreement which is to be terminated on the completion of the sale or which could be terminated shortly thereafter. The avoidance of such a downward price adjustment may in fact be an incentive for the outgoing shareholder to continue the agreement, and there may be a case for making the purchase of the outgoing shareholder's shares conditional upon the agreements continuing for a minimum period.

Names

17.56   Where the name of the company, or one of its trading names, incorporates the whole or part of the name of the outgoing shareholder, it may insist that such names are changed shortly after the completion of the sale of its shares so as not to suggest any continuing connection with the outgoing shareholder. This may damage the goodwill of the company and so affect its valuation, and gives rise to the same kinds of considerations as apply to the termination of ancillary agreements. It is in fact better for a joint venture to avoid the use of such names where at all possible, although marketing considerations may require it to build on the established reputation of one or more of the joint venturers and compel a choice of name which suggests an association with them.

VAT

17.57   Where the company has been grouped with an outgoing shareholder for VAT purposes, separate registrations will need to be arranged.

Regulatory matters

17.58   As explained in para 11.2, in many cases regulatory consents, licences and authorisations held by a company may be subject to termination if control of the company changes without consent to the change, and in some cases this will be treated as occurring if only a minority shareholding changes hands. Where the company is wholly dependent upon such a regulatory consent, licence or authorisation, it will be necessary to make any obligation to buy or sell shares which arises following a termination conditional upon the obtaining of any necessary consent.

17.59   Just as seriously, the obligation on one shareholder to buy the shares of another may, if it would result in a change of the control of the company, trigger a merger situation under the UK or EC merger control regime or that of another jurisdiction. If this is likely, completion of the sale and purchase should be conditional on the necessary clearances being received, and the agreement may also include provisions for the shareholders to co-operate with one another in relation to the seeking of clearance.

Conclusion

17.60   In many cases of termination, the sale and purchase of the shares of the outgoing shareholder will be a minor issue when compared with the other consequences which will have to be dealt with by the surviving shareholders if they are to carry on the business of the company after the outgoing shareholder has left. Indeed, some businesses may not survive such a termination, which will mean that shareholders contemplating the purchase of the shares of the outgoing shareholder will need to consider very carefully whether this will ever be a realistic option. The position following such a termination really needs to be addressed when the shareholders' agreement is negotiated; it is likely to be too late when termination actually occurs. The surviving shareholders will bear in mind that if it is possible to negotiate the continuance after termination of ancillary agreements with the outgoing shareholder, the support of the outgoing shareholder may not be very effective after it has ceased to retain its investment in the company.

17.61   The potential difficulties flowing from termination highlight the desirability of a joint venture company being independent of the joint venturers, as far as this is possible.

17.62   Where a sale to an outsider is contemplated, the potential difficulties may be less; the desirability of achieving the best price will be an incentive to the parties to behave reasonably regarding the continuance of ancillary agreements. If the purchaser is a substantial corporation, it will have no difficulty in repaying loans, and its indemnities in respect of continuing guarantees will be perfectly acceptable. However, there is no doubt that a purchaser may be dubious about buying into a company reliant upon ancillary agreements with the sellers which require the sellers to take active steps to perform them. This again points to the desirability of avoiding reliance upon such agreements if such a sale is contemplated, or at least recognising that the achievable sale price may be adversely affected.

6   Provisions surviving termination

17.63   A shareholders' agreement will typically provide that certain of its provisions will survive termination. These are generally the following:

- Confidentiality provisions are normally expressed to continue without limit of time; as regards those provisions for the protection of the confidential information of the shareholders, rather than the company, they will continue to be of relevance even after all the shareholders have ceased to hold their shares in the company.

- It should be clearly established whether any undertaking by a party not to compete with the business of the joint venture should continue, at least for a short period after termination or transfer of the relevant party's shares. Note should be taken that competition laws may prevent any post-termination restraint in the case of ventures with appreciable market impact[7].

- It is normal to provide that termination will be without prejudice to the rights which any shareholder may have against any other which subsist at the time of termination.

- Any warranties given by any party to the shareholders' agreement to any other party will survive termination to the extent that the period for making claims under them has not expired by the time of termination; a breach of warranty could of course precipitate termination.

- Any indemnities in respect of guarantees of the liabilities of the company which are given to an outgoing shareholder will of course survive the sale of his shares and could continue to be relevant notwithstanding a subsequent termination of the agreement by the surviving shareholders, for so long as such liabilities remain undischarged.

---

7   Discussed at para 10.57ff.

Chapter 18

Pre-termination put and call options

Summary

This chapter deals with the legal and tax considerations which apply to put and call options which are included at the outset in the shareholders' agreement, rather than arising on termination. An option may be granted to provide a party with an early exit or to facilitate the acquisition of another party's shares on pre-agreed terms. Guidance on drafting such options is provided.

1 Introduction

18.1   Where it is agreed that one or more shareholders shall be entitled to exit before the others, it is sometimes provided at the outset that such a party shall have a put option, entitling it to require another party to purchase its shares after a certain period, or upon the happening of a particular future event. Such a right might, for example, be granted to an individual who is a minority shareholder in a joint venture with one or more corporations who envisage the venture continuing for many years, and where without a put option the individual would be 'locked in'. Such an option would be particularly appropriate where the individual will be making an important contribution to getting the venture started but whose services will not be required after a few years, since he will then wish to reap the reward for his efforts and move on to something else.

18.2   Sometimes a party will be granted a call option entitling it to require another party to sell its shares to it. This might be appropriate where it is envisaged that in time a joint venture shall become the wholly-owned subsidiary of the majority shareholder once certain other venturers have made their initial contributions and the controlling shareholder wishes to choose the time at which it will assume complete ownership, with the ability not to do so if the venture does not turn out as planned.

18.3   Mutual put and call options are sometimes seen. In the example given in para 18.1, as well as the individual choosing the time at which he will exit, the corporation may wish to have the ability to require him to sell out. There is a danger that such an arrangement could result in the immediate

373

disposal of the shares the subject of the option for capital gains purposes as soon as the options are granted. It is likely that the HMRC will not be able to treat such an arrangement as a disposal, especially if material terms of the options, such as the exercise period or exercise price, are not exactly the same, but it is possible they may be able to do so where the purpose of the options is only to delay the date of the disposal, where the circumstances are such that the exercise of one or other of the options is very likely, or there is no good commercial reason for the grant of the options.

18.4   The possible difficulty involved in a listed company entering into an option under which it may be bound to buy or sell shares was discussed at para 11.37ff.

18.5   To be effective, an option must specify the price at which the shares the subject of it will be bought and sold upon its exercise. If the earliest exercise may be some years in the future, it is unlikely to be a fixed price. If it is a fixed price, it will need to be made adjustable to take into account subsequent share issues and reorganisations, as referred to in para 18.9, with such adjustment being subject to expert determination if there is a failure to agree the adjustment. A formula price based on the profits or net assets shown by the last audited accounts at the time of exercise might be used, but will have to be carefully worded and is best avoided lest the formula turns out to be inappropriate in the light of the circumstances at the time of exercise. Where it is intended the price shall be equal to market or fair value at the time of exercise, it is usual to provide that the price shall be determined by a valuation made by the auditors or an independent accountant. A provision that the parties will first try to agree the price, with a valuation provision if they should fail to do so, is quite often seen. Share valuation provisions are dealt with in detail in Chapter 22.

2   Structuring an option

Avoiding conflict with other provisions

18.6   Care needs to be taken to ensure that an option is not contrary to other provisions of the documents, such as pre-emption provisions or restrictions on transfer in the articles of association. It will usually be necessary to provide that it takes precedence over such other provisions and that any necessary action will be taken to give effect to an exercise of the option, such as granting pre-emption waivers or procuring the registration of a transfer. Parties other than those to the option may need to be involved in this to ensure these provisions are effective, and it will therefore usually be convenient to incorporate the option in the shareholders' agreement.

Time of exercise

18.7   The terms of the option should define the period during which the option is exercisable and state whether the option may only be exercised once in respect of all the shares subject to it, or whether there may be more than one partial exercise. A provision that a partial exercise must relate to a minimum number of shares is desirable to avoid the seller being left with only a small number of shares, possibly without any minority protection if this falls away when a holding becomes minimal[1]. If there is to be a long delay between the grant and the earliest date of exercise of the option, it may be appropriate to allow for earlier exercise in certain events such as a change of control, an offer for the whole issued share capital of the company or its listing; here the option should be exercisable immediately before the event in question, so that the option holder may benefit from the sale or listing, a point which is sometimes overlooked. Exercise may be subject to the satisfaction of conditions set out in the agreement, and there could be undertakings on the part of the parties to the option or other shareholders to endeavour to procure that they are satisfied. The exercise period will then normally commence on satisfaction of the conditions and continue for a short period afterwards. Alternatively, it may be better to make the completion of the sale and purchase consequent upon exercise of the option subject to the required conditions. This avoids the grantor being involved in time and effort in satisfying the conditions without its knowing whether the grantee will exercise the option should they be satisfied. The choice of route will depend on the nature of the conditions and whether they are a necessary objective for the company, or something special to the transaction with the purchaser. If the conditions could be satisfied on more than one occasion, it should be specified whether the option can only be exercised by reference to the first occasion, or whether to the extent not then exercised it may be exercised on a subsequent occasion.

The shares the subject of the option

18.8   There will need to be provisions identifying the shares which form the subject of the option, which will not necessarily be simply all the shares held by the seller at the date of grant. The seller may subsequently be issued with further shares, or the identity of its shares may change as a result of reorganisation of the share capital, or could even become shares in a different company, and it will need to be clear whether the extra or substituted shares are included in the option. Where additional shares are issued to the seller without any consideration, such as a bonus issue, no difficulty results in

---

1   See para 15.9.

including these in the option. However, where the seller can only obtain the shares by subscribing for them, it needs to be agreed whether any such additional shares are included, and whether the seller is obliged to subscribe for them, which may be onerous. An alternative is for the seller to be obliged, if requested, to assign the right to subscribe for all such additional shares to the prospective purchaser, either altogether or to the extent that the seller does not take them up.

Adjustment of the consideration for the option shares

18.9   A related question is whether, assuming that the shares resulting from any such reorganisation are included in the option, the option price should be adjusted to reflect any such capital reorganisation. Where the price is to be fixed by valuation, no adjustment mechanism is necessary, since the valuer will simply value the shares which are the subject of the option at the time of exercise. Where, however, the initial price is fixed or is based on a formula, it may be necessary to adjust it to take account of subsequent reorganisations. The option agreement will usually leave such an adjustment to the expert determination of an independent accountant or the auditors, but this is not really adequate, and it would be preferable for the terms of the option to set out some guidelines for the valuer to follow. Where the number of shares changes due to a sub-division or consolidation, or there is a bonus issue of new shares or some other reorganisation not involving the introduction of new funds or the extraction of funds from the company, the overall consideration for the exercise of the option in full should not change, but the price per share will increase or reduce to reflect the lower or higher number of shares included in the option. Where the prospective seller has had to pay additional sums to secure additional shares, the overall price should normally be adjusted upwards to reflect the amount paid. On the other hand, if the prospective purchaser has received a capital sum from the company in respect of any of the shares or some of them have been purchased or redeemed, the overall price may be adjusted downwards to reflect the consequent outflow from the assets of the company.

Perpetuities

18.10   The rule against perpetuities may in theory apply to commercial contracts involving a contingent interest by the Perpetuities and Accumulations Act 1964, s 10, and this is most likely to arise in relation to options. Section 10 was not altered by the Perpetuities and Accumulations Act 2009. However, given that the perpetuity period is a life or lives in being at the date of grant plus 21 years thereafter, it is extremely unlikely that the rule will have any practical relevance, since most options between shareholders have a life far shorter than 21 years, and in any case it is possible, under s 3 of the above Act, to 'wait and see'; ie a disposition is not void for remoteness until such time as it becomes certain that the contingent interest cannot vest in the perpetuity period. Where there is any possibility that the rule might be infringed, the alternative 80-year limitation period permitted by the Act should be used.

Multi-party options

18.11   If the option extends over the shares held by more than one potential seller, or the shares are to be purchased by more than one party, provisions will need to be included for joint exercise and/or joint obligations as to the delivery of the shares. The proportions in which the shares are to be purchased will need to be specified, and a provision that neither the sellers nor the purchasers are obliged to complete unless all the shares are paid for and delivered at the same time will be desirable. It will need to be specified whether the exercise of the option is by agreement between the prospective purchasers (or sellers if it is a put option) or whether a majority may exercise it on behalf of all of them. If the latter is chosen, performance of the purchase obligation might be secured by the grant of power of attorney, possibly coupled with the right to recover from any parties who fail to provide their proportions of the purchase price in favour of those who provide such monies in their places.

Restrictions on disposal

18.12   The prospective purchaser will wish to include a restriction on the prospective seller from disposing of the shares the subject of the option to a third party at any time prior to the expiry of the exercise period, although such a term is implied anyway. This should not result in the immediate passing of beneficial ownership.

Voting rights and dividends

18.13   It will need to be agreed whether it is the prospective seller or the prospective purchaser who is to be entitled to exercise the voting rights and receive dividends and other distributions in respect of the shares the subject of the option down to the date of exercise or completion. Normally, the prospective seller will remain so entitled, since there is no reason why it should be deprived of its rights where it has not received the price of its shares or even a binding commitment for such purchase from the option holder;

indeed if it is not so entitled it may indicate possible loss of the beneficial ownership of the shares and this could result in the disposal for capital gains purposes of the shares at the time the option is granted. Also, there may be a loss of 'grouping' status. For example, if the prospective seller owns 80% of the shares of a company, it will be entitled to 'group' it for tax purposes (see para 7.39ff), but if it then grants an option over a 10% stake, and agrees that the prospective purchaser shall be entitled to the dividends and votes on those shares, it will only receive dividends and votes on a 70% stake and may lose its ability to 'group'. Although the voting rights may be retained by the prospective seller, the prospective purchaser may wish to make the ability to vote in respect of certain transactions subject to its approval, although this is rare. This could enable the prospective purchaser to obtain some minority protection in respect of the stake it would be acquiring. This could be particularly important if it is not already a shareholder or its existing stake does not carry sufficient, or any, minority protection. Such an arrangement should not cause any loss of beneficial ownership or the ability to 'group'.

Completion

18.14   The option will need to include provisions relating to the completion of the sale and purchase of the shares following exercise, which will basically oblige the seller to hand over an executed transfer and the share certificates and the purchaser to pay the price of the shares. These will be similar to the provisions contained in a share sale and purchase agreement, but other points may need to be dealt with, such as an obligation upon the seller to remove its board appointee or to procure registration of the transfer. If the agreement is silent on the latter point, the seller is not obliged to procure registration.

Warranties

18.15   Warranties will be taken by the prospective purchaser as to the prospective seller's title to the option shares and the seller will generally be required to sell with full title guarantee. If the prospective purchaser is not already a shareholder, it may also desire warranties concerning the affairs of the company. This is problematical – any warranties taken at the time of grant are not likely to remain true at the time of exercise. The purchaser will want assurances about the situation at the date of exercise and the seller will not be willing to warrant the future. A possible solution to this difficulty is for the seller to undertake to disclose everything contrary to the warranties (which are worded to refer to the position at the date of exercise) with the purchaser having the right to withdraw if it does not like the position revealed by the disclosure letter, without prejudice to a subsequent exercise of the option subject to any general time limit on exercise. No liability would fall on the seller if the option notice is withdrawn, but where the purchaser proceeds to completion the seller would be liable if it failed to make a true and complete disclosure so as to render any of the warranties untrue when read together with the disclosure letter. The timing would be that once the (conditional) notice exercising the option has been served, the seller would have an agreed period to prepare its disclosure letter and the purchaser would then have an agreed period to consider this and serve notice either affirming its exercise of the option or withdrawing. A difficulty may be that the seller does have access to sufficient information about the company to give the warranties, especially if it has no board representation. Warranties are discussed in more detail in Chapter 25.

Consideration for grant

18.16   To be enforceable, the grant of the option must be for consideration, or the option granted by deed. One pound is quite sufficient and there is not normally any reason for making it any higher. If the option is contained in a shareholders' agreement, other undertakings contained in it on the part of the grantee will normally provide sufficient consideration.

Tax position

18.17   If the consideration for the grant of an option is a monetary amount greater than a nominal sum or represents less than the market value of the option, it becomes necessary to consider the special rules which apply for capital gains purposes to the grant and exercise of options under s 144 of the Taxation of Chargeable Gains Act 1992 (TCGA 1992).

18.18   An option is treated as a separate asset for capital gains purposes. When an option is granted it is treated as a disposal of the option by the grantor for the consideration received for the grant, even though there was no acquisition of the option by the grantor, from which it follows that no acquisition cost can be deducted from the consideration received from the grant, except the legal and other expenses relating to such grant. A capital gains liability can therefore arise as soon as the option is granted.

18.19   When the option is exercised, the grant or acquisition of the option is treated as the same transaction as its exercise. In the case of the grantor:

- if the option is a call option under which it can be required to sell shares, the consideration it received for the grant of the option is added to the sale proceeds of the shares, so that a gain is made on the difference between the base cost of the shares and the aggregate of the sums received on grant and exercise; and

- if the option is a put option under which it can be required to buy shares, the consideration it received for the grant of the option is deducted from its acquisition cost of the shares, so that when it comes to sell the shares acquired under the option, the gain will be the difference between the price then received minus the sum paid for the acquired shares after deducting the sum received for the grant of the option.

18.20   The position of the grantee is as follows:

- if the option is a call option under which it may call for shares to be sold to it, the sum it paid to the grantor for the option is added to the base cost of the shares acquired; and

- if the option is a put option, under which it may require the grantor to buy its shares, the sum it paid to the grantor for the option is treated as an expense of the sale, so reducing the capital gain.

18.21   As a consequence of the option being exercised, the grant of the option ceases to be an occasion of charge. Accordingly, any capital gains tax paid by the grantor on any gain arising on the grant should be set off or repaid by HMRC (HMRC Capital Gains Manual: Shares and Securities: Quoted options to subscribe for shares, traded and financial options and see https://www.gov.uk/hmrc-internal-manuals/capital-gains-manual/cg55400p).

18.22   In certain circumstances (eg where the parties are connected), the market value rule in s 17(1) of the TCGA 1992 may apply to the grant of the option, the acquisition of the option by the person exercising it or the transaction resulting from its exercise. This would result in the position of the parties being different from their economic position.

18.23   In the case of mutual put and call options, the consideration for the grant of each option is the value of the option received in exchange. This can result in tax being payable without funds being received out of which it may be paid.

18.24   Since an option is a chargeable asset, the assignment of an option and the cancellation of an option can both be disposals. Virtually all private company options will have a life of less than 50 years and are 'wasting assets', which has the effect that the acquisition cost of the asset is to be written down on a straight line daily basis over the option period. This means that the base cost of the option will decline over its life, so on a disposal for a fixed amount the gain will increase the later the disposal takes place, but on the other hand one might expect the consideration for the disposal to be less as the available period for exercising the option shortens. The same principles are applied in relation to the release of an option; this is a disposal of the option for the sum paid for the release[2].

---

2   *Powlson v Welbeck Securities Ltd* [1987] STC 468.

18.25   If a share option is itself a marketable security (as defined for these purposes at s 122 of the Stamp Act 1891) the grant or transfer on sale of the option, if in writing, will be chargeable with stamp duty at the rate of 0.5% of the amount or value of the consideration. If the option is not itself a marketable security no stamp duty is payable on transfer or grant. If an option is listed, it will be a marketable security and a transfer in writing of such an option will be chargeable with stamp duty at 0.5%.

18.26   Whether or not they are marketable securities for stamp duty purposes, stamp duty reserve tax ('SDRT') is imposed at 0.5% on transfers of 'chargeable securities' which would include an agreement to transfer a call option. However, despite such a call option being a chargeable security for the purposes of SDRT, no SDRT will be due upon the grant of such an option, as the grant constitutes the creation of new rights rather than the transfer of existing rights. See also HMRC's webpage on SDRT at https://www.gov.uk/tax-buy-shares.

18.27   Generally speaking, put options are not marketable securities for stamp duty purposes, nor are they chargeable securities for SDRT purposes, and, as such, no stamp duty or SDRT will be chargeable on their grant or transfer.

18.28   Where an option is granted to a director or employee, the tax considerations referred to in Chapter 26 will apply.

Dangers of put options

18.29   Put options which may be exercisable a long time after they have been granted can be dangerous for the grantor. When the grantee puts the shares on the grantor, the circumstances then existing may be completely different from those that were envisaged when the option was granted. Although, if the price is to be fixed by valuation, a deterioration in the financial position of the company could be expected to be reflected in the valuation (although if this is to be based on the last audited accounts, there is always the possibility of a deterioration since they were prepared), there may be circumstances in which the grantor is not prepared to purchase at any price, and the grantor may wish to specify that the happening of certain future events, such as the loss of an important licence or concession, or other events likely to seriously disrupt the business, will release the option. Such a suggestion will probably be bitterly resisted by the grantee, who is relying on the option to ensure its exit. Formula prices are obviously especially dangerous.

Chapter 19

Pre-emption rights on share transfers

Summary

This chapter deals in detail with the pre-emption rights on share transfers which are commonly included in the articles of association of UK companies and deals with the various practical considerations involved in successfully drafting such provisions.

1 Introduction

19.1   Pre-emption rights on share transfers are very commonly seen in the articles of association of private companies and they are useful in many cases where there are more than two shareholders and it is intended that the withdrawal of one of them from the company shall not terminate the shareholders' or joint venture agreement as regards the other shareholders.

19.2   In essence, under a typical pre-emption provision, a shareholder wishing to sell all or some of its shares must serve a transfer notice on the directors of the company and, subject to certain specified exceptions, no transfer of shares may be registered unless a transfer notice is first served. The transfer notice specifies the number of shares which the would-be transferor wishes to sell, and authorises the directors to offer them for sale to the other shareholders. The directors offer the shares by means of a notice to the other shareholders. If there are more buyers than there are shares, they are allocated to the buyers pro rata to their existing shareholdings. Once the shares have been allocated, the directors will give notice of the allocation to the shareholders concerned, and the would-be transferor becomes bound to sell the shares specified in the transfer notice to the allocated buyers. If there are insufficient buyers to take all the shares, the would-be transferor may transfer the remainder to an outsider, but normally only within a limited period and at no lower price than they were offered to the other shareholders.

19.3   As a minority protection device, pre-emption rights are of very little use. If no existing shareholder will buy the shares, it is in fact very unlikely that a sale of a minority stake to a third party will be possible; there is simply no market for such stakes. Even where the stake appears attractive to an outsider, most likely to a competitor, an outsider will rarely intervene, since it will know that a sale to one of the existing shareholders is the most likely outcome. Therefore, in a two-shareholder company pre-emption rights are really no use at all; there is only one likely buyer, and whether it is prepared to buy and at what price can be established by negotiation. However, since a two-shareholder company may in the future have more than two shareholders, the inclusion of pre-emption provisions may come to have value. 'Tag along' and 'drag along' provisions (see para 21.13ff) are a much more effective minority protection device.

19.4   In a company with more than two shareholders, pre-emption rights can be useful in that they provide machinery for allocating the shares between competing shareholder purchasers, thus avoiding squabbles between them as to who is to have the shares. Even here, the complete use of the pre-emption machinery is rarely seen because, usually, if a shareholder wishes to sell, a negotiated deal is struck with the other shareholders, and the shares are transferred on the basis of a waiver of the pre-emption rights signed by all the shareholders other than the transferor. However, the machinery set out in the pre-emption article is often of use as a bargaining counter upon which the would-be transferor can negotiate.

19.5   Over the years, pre-emption rights have become more sophisticated, and the following paragraphs set out the most important considerations when drafting such provisions.

19.6   The CA 2006, s 561 by way of background gives a pre-emption right to existing shareholders in relation to allotment (not transfer) of shares:

'S 561 Existing shareholders' right of pre-emption

(1) A company must not allot equity securities to a person on any terms unless—

(a)   it has made an offer to each person who holds ordinary shares in the company to allot to him on the same or more favourable terms a proportion of those securities that is as nearly as practicable equal to the proportion in nominal value held by him of the ordinary share capital of the company, and

(b)   the period during which any such offer may be accepted has expired or the company has received notice of the acceptance or refusal of every offer so made.'

Private companies will often exclude this right in their articles and it relates to allotment of shares not the share transfer provisions considered in this chapter.

2 Key points in drafting pre-emption rights

Beneficial interests in shares and changes in control

19.7   A shareholder who wishes to effectively transfer his shares may decide not to execute a transfer requiring registration, but may simply declare himself trustee for the purchaser. That a shareholder should be acting on the instructions of a third party which may be hostile is obviously undesirable. A reasonably effective solution is to provide that a transfer notice must be served by a shareholder where it wishes to transfer the whole or any part of the beneficial interest in a share (and also to provide that a transfer notice has to be served if it wishes to mortgage or charge the share or any beneficial interest therein). Since the transfer of the beneficial interest in a share is likely to be covert, the articles of association should go on to provide that if the directors discover that any beneficial interest in any shares has been transferred, they may then require the shareholder concerned to give a transfer notice in respect of the shares and, if it fails to do so, one will be deemed to have been given. This can be coupled with powers for the directors to make enquiries as to whether any beneficial interest has been transferred and a shareholder failing to provide answers to the enquiries, or providing false ones, can be deemed to have given a transfer notice.

19.8   Where a shareholder has made its investment through a special purpose subsidiary, it might circumvent the above provisions by selling the share capital of the subsidiary, which does not involve any change in the beneficial interest in the shares themselves. To deal with this it could be provided that the change of the control of a shareholder gives rise to a compulsory transfer; the point is in fact more general than this and might be applied to any corporate shareholder.

Price determination

19.9   The price at which the shares are to be offered to the other shareholders will need to be established. There are two main variations. In the first, the price may be agreed between the intending transferor and the directors and, if they fail to agree, a price is determined by the auditors or an independent firm of accountants acting as experts. In the second, the intending transferor names its own price. The latter variation is often preferred by venture capitalists and other institutional investors who fear that the auditors or independent accountants will not have enough knowledge of the market to establish the true market value of the shares to be transferred. This will particularly apply to 'high-tech' companies which, in their early stages, may well have very little, or negative, net worth on their balance sheets, but have a new product which will be very attractive to a purchaser which might be prepared to pay a very high price for the shares. The proposing transferor is effectively restrained from asking for a price which is manifestly too high, because if it does so, no shareholder will be willing to buy, and a sale to a third party (should it be possible at all) will be frustrated by the common provision that the shares may not be offered to a third party at a price lower than they were offered to the shareholders. The over-ambitious proposed transferor will thus have to start all over again with a new transfer notice. Valuation of shares is dealt with in detail in Chapter 22.

Allocation of the shares

19.10   As mentioned in para 19.2, in the case of competition for the shares between existing shareholders, they will normally be allocated pro rata to existing shareholdings. Where there is more than one class of shares, it is often stipulated that a separate transfer notice must be given for the shares comprised in each class, and the shares are first to be offered to the holders of shares of the same class, and if there is competition they shall be allocated to the holders of that class pro rata to their holdings of the class. If all the shares cannot be sold to the holders of that class, the rest may be offered pro rata to the holders of the other class or classes, again with allocation pro rata to existing holdings in case of competition. Sometimes, where there are three or more classes of shares, there is a provision under which the shares are offered in turn to the other classes in a specified order. Where each investor in a company has holdings of shares in different classes, each holder having the same proportion of each class, the classes may be 'stapled' together, so that an intending transferor can only give a transfer notice consisting of a package of shares from all the classes in the same proportions as they are allocated to all shareholders, and the shareholders can only offer to buy all or a part of the package comprising shares of all the classes in those same proportions. The purpose of such a provision is to ensure that each shareholder has the same 'mix' of shareholding interests, and shares the same interests as all the other shareholders; if a shareholder only has, say, one class of shares, his interests will be different from the others, which could cause a strain in the relations between shareholders.

19.11   The transfer notice may have a 'total transfer condition', so that if shareholders are not found to purchase all the shares comprised in the transfer notice the transferor may withdraw the transfer notice and not sell any. Alternatively, the withdrawing transferor may be permitted to offer all the shares to outsiders, but often with a stipulation that all, and not some only, must be so transferred. A total transfer condition is designed to avoid the transferor being left with only a small rump of shares which it may not be able to sell easily on a subsequent occasion and may, if the valuers are able to apply a minority discount when valuing the shares, have a value much less than they would have if they were offered with the rest of the holding. For example, if a shareholder has a 26% stake, so that it can block a special resolution, it would not wish to sell if shares representing only a 2% stake are offered for by other shareholders, perhaps with the deliberate idea of depriving the intending transferor of its veto. The ability for the proposed transferor to include a total transfer condition is not usually made available where the transfer is compulsory[1].

19.12   The proposing transferor is quite often given the right to withdraw its transfer notice if it is dissatisfied with the decision of the expert valuer; again, this is not likely to be allowed where the transfer is compulsory.

19.13   Apart from these two instances, the transfer notice is usually made irrevocable, so that once the procedure has been started the intending transferor is bound to go through with it.

Completion

19.14   A pre-emption article will need to include machinery for the transfer of the shares. Normally, the transferor is required to hand over a duly executed transfer of the shares and the share certificate or other document of title against delivery by the buyer of the price. No warranties are ever included, but the article might specify that the transfer is to be made with 'full title guarantee', in which case the buyer will receive from the transferor the assurances regarding its title comprised in a full title guarantee contained in Part 1 of the Law of Property (Miscellaneous Provisions) Act 1994.

19.15   Where the transfer is compulsory, the transferor may be very unwilling to complete it, and even if it is voluntary, the transferor's dissatisfaction with the result of the sale may make it unwilling to complete. It is therefore invariably provided that, if the transferor fails to do so, the directors may appoint someone to execute the transfer on its behalf and the company may receive the sale proceeds and hold them in trust for the transferor. The directors will simply issue a new share certificate to the transferee and will record the original one as cancelled.

Ability to transfer to an outsider

19.16   Assuming that no existing shareholder is willing to buy all the shares offered, the would-be transferor is normally given a period, usually between three and six months, to sell the shares to an outsider at a price no lower

---

1   See para 19.24.

than that at which they were offered to the other shareholders. It needs to be considered whether the pre-emption article should provide that the directors must register a transfer to any third party, or whether they have a discretion to refuse to do so, being either an absolute discretion or subject to reasons. Where the directors refuse to register a transfer, the reasons for the refusal have to be given to the transferor, even if there is absolute discretion to do so. From a minority shareholders' point of view it can be argued that it is a case of 'put up, or shut up' and there should be no discretion not to register a transfer – if the existing shareholders are so concerned about a transfer to an outsider they ought to be prepared to find some way of purchasing the shares offered.

19.17   In the case of a minority stake being offered for sale, the point is in fact probably academic because of the lack of a market for minority holdings, but there may be occasions where a competitor of the company is willing to acquire a minority stake and thereby acquire a window on its affairs. No doubt it is this fear which inspires the insertion of a discretion for the directors to refuse to register a transfer to an outsider, but if the directors are given a complete discretion the proposing transferor may be 'locked in'. Wording allowing the directors to refuse to register a transfer to a competitor or any other person who they reasonably deem unsuitable to admit to membership may bridge the gap, although the minority are nearly always going to be 'locked in' anyway.

19.18   It may, however, be made a condition on registering a transfer to an outsider that it first enters into a deed of adherence in respect of any shareholders' agreement. Indeed, if this is desired, as it usually will be, the directors ought normally to have a positive obligation to refuse to register a transfer unless this is done.

19.19   A factor further limiting the effective ability to sell to an outsider is that the period of time allowed for such a sale is invariably limited, and sometimes the time given is not really long enough. For example, a period of three months is really too short; six months is much more realistic.

Waiver of pre-emption article

19.20   It is common to include a provision that the pre-emption provisions may be waived by all the shareholders (or even just a specified proportion of them) other than the proposing transferor, so as to allow a transfer which has the approval of all of them to go through without the need to go through the pre-emption procedure, or amend the articles by special resolution. An amendment to the articles to take out or amend the pre-emption rights might be successfully challenged by a minority shareholder.

Permitted transfers

19.21   It is usually found too restrictive to prevent any share transfer without a transfer notice first being given. In the case of a company with corporate shareholders, it is quite common to provide that shares may be transferred within the group to which such a shareholder belongs, as long as the transferee enters into a deed of adherence. There are usually transfer back provisions if the transferee ceases to be part of the group.

19.22   Where a company has individual shareholders, it is common for the articles of association to allow them to transfer their shares to their relatives or to trustees of family trusts. Such provisions are discussed at para 26.70ff.

19.23   Where the company has investment funds as shareholders, it is quite common to provide that their shares may be transferred to other funds under the same management.

Compulsory transfers

19.24   It has already been noted that a requirement for compulsory transfer can be imposed where a shareholder has gone into liquidation or is bankrupt[2] and also where the intending transferor has tried to evade the pre-emption article by transferring only the beneficial interest in its shares[3] or has suffered a change of control[4]. Other circumstances in which a compulsory transfer will often be required are where a shareholder has died, in which case his personal representatives may be required to give a transfer notice, or where an employee shareholder has ceased to be an employee. Issues relating to deceased and employee shareholders are discussed in more detail at para 26.71ff.

Last right of refusal

19.25   An alternative to pre-emption provisions which is sometimes found in shareholders' agreements is a 'last right of refusal', which means that if a shareholder desiring to leave negotiates a price with a third-party purchaser, it cannot complete it without first giving the other shareholder(s) the opportunity of improving upon that price. This makes it very difficult to obtain any interest from third-party purchasers, since they know that there is the risk that any offer they make will be improved on, and the time, effort and cost of their negotiations is likely to be wasted.

---

2   See para 17.24ff.
3   See para 19.7.
4   See para 19.8.

Flowchart 7

Pre-emption provisions in articles

This flowchart illustrates the steps involved in relation to a proposed transfer of shares under a typical pre-emption article.

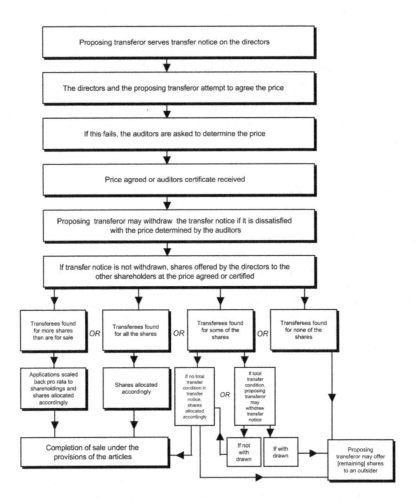

Chapter 20

Purchase and redemption of shares by a UK company

Summary

This chapter deals with the legal, tax and practical aspects relating to two further possible exit routes for a shareholder: the purchase or redemption of its shares by the company. It only considers the position under English law.

1 Purchase of shares

General

20.1   If no existing shareholder is willing to purchase the shares of a shareholder which wishes to transfer its shares, and the sale of the shares to a third party is not likely, a possible solution is for the company to purchase those shares. Due to the difficulty of being sure in advance whether the statutory requirements for such a purchase can be met, it is not likely this will be an exit route provided for in a shareholders' agreement. It is much more likely that it will be a realisation process which is agreed to in consequence of a termination notice and thus only available at the option of the remaining shareholders.

20.2   A purchase of shares by a company is only likely to be practicable where it has a mature business which has not only given rise to the accumulation of sufficient distributable profits, but has also generated cash surplus to immediate business requirements so as to be able to purchase the shares without damaging its business or leaving itself with liabilities it cannot discharge. However, it may be possible to make the purchase out of the proceeds of a new issue of shares if one can be arranged.

20.3   A private company may also purchase shares out of capital, but this will only be applicable where its capital is larger than is necessary to meet its obligations; the company could not pay away assets represented by capital so as to leave creditors unpaid. A company can only purchase its shares out of capital if its directors make a statement that, after having made full inquiry into the affairs and prospects of the company, they have formed the opinion that, immediately following the date upon which the payment out of capital is proposed to be made, there will be no grounds upon which the company could then be found unable to pay its debts, and that as regards its prospects for the year immediately following that date, having regard to their intentions with respect to the management of the company's business during that year and to the amount and character of the financial resources which will in their view be available to the company in that year, the company will be able to continue to carry on business as a going concern (and will accordingly be able to pay its debts as they fall due) throughout the year[1]. The CA 2006 provisions requiring a directors' statement apply where that statement is made on or after 1 October 2009. A directors' statement must be signed by each of the directors, but does not need to be sworn before a solicitor or Commissioner of Oaths. Prior to that date, the provisions of the CA 1985 were still applicable and these required the directors to swear a statutory declaration in relation to the company's financial position[2]. The CA 2006 also includes provisions for creditors and dissenting members to challenge payments for shares made out of capital[3].

20.4   The above requirements make it difficult for the company to contract to acquire its own shares in advance. CA 2006, s 694 allows for contingent purchase contracts, which will allow a company to grant to a shareholder the option of requiring the company to purchase its shares, but the availability of the necessary distributable profits, or the ability to make a payment of capital, is to be determined at the time the option is exercised, not when it is granted. If the requirements cannot be met at that time the option cannot be enforced[4]. The CA 2006 changes made it possible to enter into a contract for an off-market purchase before obtaining authorisation through a special resolution, if the contract provides that no shares may be bought under the contract until its terms have been authorised (s 694(2)(b)).

Procedure

20.5   Under the CA 2006, a company is permitted to purchase its own shares, whether it is an off-market purchase or a contingent purchase contract, unless there is a specific prohibition or restriction on such purchase in its articles of association[5]. Under the CA 1985, a company was required to have specific authorisation in its articles allowing it to do this[6]. The term 'contingent purchase contract' is not specifically used in the relevant provisions of the CA 2006 (it was in the CA 1985) but reference is still made

---

1   CA 2006, s 714(3).
2   CA 1985, s 173(3).
3   CA 2006, s 721.
4   See *Vision Express (UK) Ltd v Wilson* [1998] BCC 173.
5   CA 2006, s 690.
6   CA 1985, s 162.

to a contract 'that does not amount to a contract to purchase the shares but under which the company may (subject to any conditions) become entitled or obliged to purchase the shares'.

20.6   The contract must also be authorised by special resolution, which will be ineffective if any member holding shares which are to be purchased votes those shares on the resolution, and the resolution would not have been passed if he had not done so. Where the shares being purchased are those of a director, CA 2006, s 190 (substantial property transactions: requirement of members' approval) may apply, but the resolution authorising the contract may, if appropriately worded, double as the resolution required by s 190. The contract of purchase must be approved in advance of the making of the contract to purchase the shares, which cannot be made conditional upon shareholder approval. It may be necessary to obtain a waiver of pre-emptive rights on share transfers in order to enter into the contract, and it is possible that class consents or consents under any shareholders' agreement will also be necessary, since it is common for a minority shareholder to have a veto in respect of such a purchase.

Tax consequences

20.7   On the basis that the company whose shares are to be bought back is unquoted, any buy-back will be 'off market'.

20.8   A purchase by a company of its own shares may involve a qualifying distribution if the repurchase price is greater than the nominal value of the shares plus any premium for which the shares were issued, this excess amount being referred to below as the 'distribution element'. The nominal value and premium is referred to below as the 'capital element'.

20.9   Shareholders subject to corporation tax do not treat dividends from UK resident companies as taxable income. However, they will be liable to corporation tax on chargeable gains on any gain made, by reference to the full repurchase price.

20.10   This proposition is stated by HMRC in SP4/89, which provides that if the purchase of its own shares by a UK resident company gives rise to a distribution element, and a shareholder who receives that distribution is itself a company, the distribution will be included in the consideration for the disposal of the shares for the purposes of the charge to corporation tax on chargeable gains:

'If the purchase of its own shares by a company resident in the United Kingdom gives rise to a distribution, and a shareholder receiving such a distribution is itself a company, the distribution is included in the consideration for the disposal of the shares for the purposes of the charge to corporation tax on chargeable gains. In HM Revenue and Customs' view the effect of Sections 208 ICTA 1988 and Section 8(4) TCGA 1992 (formerly 345(3) ICTA 1988) is that the distribution does not suffer a tax charge as income within the terms of Section 37(1) TCGA 1992 (formerly Section 31(1) Capital Gains Tax Act 1979.) The Revenue will apply this Statement of Practice where a company purchases its own shares after 19 April 1989.' – see https://www.gov.uk/government/collections/statements-of-practice.

20.11   This interpretation was subject to some debate over the years; however, the Court of Appeal confirmed HMRC's position in *Strand Options and Futures Ltd v Vojak (Inspector of Taxes)*[7] in which they held that the distribution element will form part of the computation of the chargeable gain, notwithstanding the wording of ICTA 1988, s 208 as it was then (which the taxpayer claimed provided total relief from corporation tax on both income and chargeable gains in respect of the distribution element of the repurchase). From 1 July 2009 distributions are still not charged to corporation tax under the current legislation: CTA 2009, Pt 9A. POS gain exempt under SSE rules.

20.12   Current tax advice should always be considered as the rules regularly change. The Government states as follows in relation to changes from April 20017:

'The Substantial Shareholdings Exemption (SSE) exempts from the charge to tax gains or losses accruing on the disposal by companies of shares where certain conditions are met. The measure introduces changes to some of these qualifying conditions for the SSE for corporate capital gains.

The condition that the investing company is required to be a trading company or part of a trading group is being removed.

The condition that the investment must have been held for a continuous period, at minimum, of 12 months in the 2 years preceding the sale is being extended to a continuous period of 12 months in the 6 years preceding the sale. The condition that the company in which the shares are sold continues to be a qualifying company immediately after the sale is withdrawn, unless the sale is to a connected party.

For a class of investors defined as Qualifying Institutional Investors, the condition that the company in which the shares were sold is a trading company has also been removed. The legislation contains a list of Qualifying Institutional Investors.

The changes have effect for disposals on or after 1 April 2017.' See Policy paper 'Reform of Substantial Shareholding Exemption for qualifying

7   [2003] EWCA Civ 1457.

institutional investors'. Published 5 December 2016 at https://www.
gov.uk/government/publications/reform-of-substantial-shareholding-
exemption-for-qualifying-institutional-investors.

The SSE was introduced in 2002 with the aim of eliminating the potential
double taxation of trading profits in a company or sub-group being disposed
of when these are realised by the shareholder by way of a disposal of their
shareholding rather than, for example, by way of a dividend which would be
exempted from tax in the hands of a corporate shareholder, and to facilitate
the restructuring of groups without triggering a tax charge.

Pre April 2017 law

20.13   Finance Act 2002 introduced the SSE legislation. The SSE legislation
is set out as five distinct parts:

- Part 1 – the exemptions available. The main exemption applies where
  the conditions in Parts 2 and 3 are met. Two subsidiary exemptions apply
  in certain circumstances where these requirement are not fully met;

- Part 2 – the shareholding requirement. A company has a substantial
  shareholding in another company if it holds 10% or more of the ordinary
  share capital for a continuous period of 12 months beginning no more
  than two years before the date of a disposal;

- Part 3 – the conditions for both the company that makes the disposal
  and for the company, the shares in which have been disposed of. These
  are referred to as 'the investing company' and 'the company invested
  in' respectively. Generally these require that the two companies are
  members of a trading group (or a sole trading company) throughout
  the period mentioned in Part 2, and immediately after the disposal;

- Part 4 – interpretation;

- Part 5 – certain consequential matters.

2017 Changes

20.14   Legislation was introduced in the Finance Bill 2017 to amend the
following as described before the changes:

> 'Part 2 – the shareholding requirement – will be amended so that the
> substantial shareholding condition may be met where a substantial
> shareholding is held throughout a continuous 12-month period
> beginning not more than 6 years before the day on which the disposal

takes place. The shareholding requirement will be met in respect of qualifying shareholdings held up to four years earlier than at present.

Where the additional exemption relating to companies owned by qualifying institutional investors applies, the substantial shareholding condition may be met if the investing company's shareholding is below 10% of the ordinary share capital but cost more than £50 million.

Part 3 – the requirements for the investor company and the company invested in – the conditions set out in paragraph 18, specifying trading conditions which the investor company must satisfy, will be removed. There will be no requirement for the investor company to meet any trading requirement either individually or as part of a wider trading group.

The requirements for the company invested in, in paragraph 19, will be amended so that the requirement for the trading condition to be met immediately post-disposal will apply only in circumstances where the sale is to a person connected to the investing company. There will be no requirement for the company invested in to meet the trading conditions post-disposal where the sale is to an unconnected party.

For companies owned by a specific class of investors, defined as Qualifying Institutional Investors, the measure provides for a further exemption which only requires that the substantial shareholding condition is met, the requirements in Part 3 do not apply. If at least 80% of the ordinary share capital of that company is owned directly or indirectly by one or more qualifying investors, then gains and losses of a disposal of shares will be exempt in full. Where between 25% and 80% is so owned, then a proportionate exemption is available.' See https://www.gov.uk/government/publications/reform-of-substantial-shareholding-exemption-for-qualifying-institutional-investors.

As stated above the changes came into effect in April 2017.

20.15   An individual shareholder will be taxed in exactly the same way as if he had received a dividend equivalent to the distribution element of the sum paid for his shares. The tax position of an individual who receives a dividend or other qualifying distribution is discussed at para 7.51ff. The return of the capital element has no tax consequence for an individual shareholder, but if his shares are purchased at below this amount he will have a capital loss. The distribution element of the repurchase is ignored in calculating the individual's capital gains position (in contrast to the position for companies set out in paras 20.9–20.11 above).

20.16   The calculation of the capital element will be complicated if the company has made a bonus issue of shares or declared any scrip dividends, where the nominal value of those extra shares may be included in the distribution element. The purpose of this was to prevent the company capitalising distributable reserves by issuing bonus shares and then buying them back, so passing the distributable reserves to the shareholders without a distribution and therefore without any liability to account for Advance Corporation Tax ('ACT').

20.17   The company is treated as making a qualifying distribution of the distribution element. The payment is therefore not deductible in computing profits for corporation tax purposes. ACT has been abolished, but if the company had surplus ACT accumulated before 6 April 1999, the special rules regarding 'shadow ACT' will apply.

20.18   There is no distribution, either as regards the company or the selling individual shareholder, if the conditions set out in CTA 2010, s 1033 are fulfilled. If they are fulfilled, the selling individual shareholder is subject to tax as if he had sold shares to a third party purchaser and will therefore normally only be liable to capital gains tax. The main conditions include:

(1)   The company must be unquoted. An AIM company is unquoted for this purpose, but an unquoted 51% subsidiary of a quoted company is quoted.

(2)   The company must be a trading company or the holding company of a trading company.

(3)   The purpose of the purchase must be either:

–   wholly or mainly to benefit a trade carried on by the company or any of its 75% subsidiaries without forming part of a scheme to enable the owner of the shares to participate in profits without receiving a dividend or avoid tax (HMRC recognises that a purchase of the shares of a shareholder who is in dispute with the others or wishes to leave, can be for the benefit of the trade); or

–   to discharge an inheritance tax liability on death.

(4)   The seller (or any nominee through which the shares are held) must be resident and ordinarily resident in the UK in the year of assessment on which the purchase occurs.

(5)   The shares must have been owned by the selling shareholder for the five years before the purchase occurs; ownership by a spouse counts in the five years, and where the shares result from a reconstruction or reorganisation they are treated as having been acquired when the original holding was acquired. The minimum ownership period is reduced to three years where the shares were acquired under a will or intestacy.

(6)   The interest of the seller and his associates in the company must be substantially reduced by the sale; broadly speaking, his interest must be

reduced by at least one-quarter, taking into account that the shares sold will be cancelled. Therefore, selling 20% of an existing holding will not be enough.

20.19   Advance clearance from HMRC that CTA 2010, s 1033 will apply is normally sought in advance of the repurchase.

20.20   Generally it is advantageous for an individual selling shareholder to receive the proceeds of his shares with a liability to capital gains tax rather than income tax because capital gains tax would be chargeable at a rate of 18%, whereas the effective rate of income tax on the net amount received would be 25%, taking into account the availability of a tax credit on the distribution element.

20.21   The ITA 2007, s 682 allows HMRC to counteract a 'tax advantage' derived by a taxpayer through a transaction in securities. It would apply where a shareholder sells shares in circumstances where the shareholder could instead receive a dividend, including the distribution element of a share buyback. The provision does not apply where the transaction is undertaken for bona fide commercial reasons (or made in the ordinary course of making or managing investments) and without the obtaining of a tax advantage as its main, or one of the main, purposes. Clearance may be sought in advance.

20.22   Dividend tax changes in 2017 have an impact in this area – see http://www.taxadvisermagazine.com/article/transactions-securities-%E2%80%93-where-are-we-now which includes the following:

'Perhaps the most significant [2016] changes are the amendment of the counteraction procedures. These appear, in part, to attempt to align the counteraction process more closely with what would be expected with a self assessment enquiry but it still leave TIS outside of the self assessment framework. More wide reaching change was required here since there is now no specific reason why TIS should remain outside of self assessment. As proposed HMRC can open an enquiry in relation to a TIS up to six years after the year of assessment in which the TIS took place and once that enquiry is open it can go on forever unless HMRC give up or are told to give up by the Tribunal. It is not obvious why HMRC should be given this very generous leeway or in particular what policy justification allows taxpayers potentially impacted by them the same protections as are afforded by the discovery provisions and behaviour related time limits available in almost every other situation.'

20.23   The Chartered Institute of Taxation (CIOT) in 2017 expressed concerns that businesses undertaking commercial transactions face uncertainty because of a lack of clarity about the breadth of the then new targeted anti-avoidance tax rule (TAAR). Section 35 of the Finance Act 2016 introduced the rule for distributions of share capital made on winding up a company. The institute said the rule, which is widely drawn, could affect a range of legitimate commercial situations in which tax avoidance is not likely to be the motivating factor. Lack of a formal advance clearance procedure in the TAAR was adding to the uncertainty. Companies have to use the wording of the legislation and HMRC's guidance to decide whether the rule applies. Section 35 applies in winding up situations only.

20.24   Stamp duty is payable on the repurchase of shares at the rate of 0.5% of the consideration. Form SH03 (formerly Form 169) must be stamped accordingly, since there is no transfer which can be stamped, merely a cancellation, and no stock transfer form is required.

20.25   For sale of shares in general and taxation HMRC provides the following useful summary at https://www.gov.uk/tax-buy-shares:

'**Overview**

When you buy shares, you usually pay a tax or duty of 0.5% on the transaction.

If you buy:

- shares electronically, you'll pay Stamp Duty Reserve Tax (SDRT)

- shares using a stock transfer form, you'll pay Stamp Duty if the transaction is over £1,000

You'll have to pay tax at 1.5% if you transfer shares into some "depositary receipt schemes" or "clearance services".

You pay tax on the price you pay for the shares, even if their actual market value is much higher.

Transactions you pay tax on

You pay tax when you buy:

- existing shares in a company incorporated in the UK

- an option to buy shares

- an interest in shares, for example an interest in the money from selling them

- shares in a foreign company that has a share register in the UK

- rights arising from shares, for example rights you have when new shares are issued

When you do not pay tax

You do not have to pay tax if you:

- are given shares for nothing

- subscribe to a new issue of shares in a company

- buy shares in an 'open ended investment company' (OEIC) from the fund manager

- buy units in a unit trust from the fund manager

You do not normally have to pay Stamp Duty or SDRT if you buy foreign shares outside the UK. But you may have to pay other taxes.

When you sell the shares

You may need to pay Capital Gains Tax when you sell your shares.'

2 Redemption of shares

Introduction

20.26 Another method by which a shareholder may be given an exit is to issue him with shares which are redeemable by the company. This route would need to be arranged at the outset of the venture and could not be left until after a termination notice has been served. This is because existing shares cannot have their rights altered so as to become redeemable. The redemption date may be fixed, or may be at the option of the shareholder or the company, although in the latter case there is normally a long-stop date at which point the shares are automatically due for redemption without the need to serve a notice requiring this.

20.27 The considerations relating to the financing of the redemption of the shares are the same as those relating to a purchase of shares. The general rule is that the shares can only be redeemed out of distributable profits or a fresh issue of shares made for the purpose, but a private company can redeem the shares out of capital, subject to exactly the same conditions as apply to a share purchase out of capital. (Although the CA 2006 no longer includes a requirement that a private company's articles of association must authorise payments out of capital in connection with a redemption of shares, the shareholders may prohibit or restrict such a redemption by including a provision to this effect in the articles.)

20.28 Due to the restrictions on financing any redemption of shares, if the redemption date arrives and the company is not able to redeem the shares, the holder of the shares cannot compel redemption. For this reason it is quite often provided that, if the redemption on the due date would be illegal, the company is to redeem the shares as soon as possible thereafter, if necessary in a series of partial redemptions. A provision for interest on the redemption monies is sometimes seen, although since the interest must also come from distributable profits or the proceeds of a fresh issue of shares this will make it all the more difficult for the company to fund redemption.

20.29   Where a company has issued redeemable shares it is often appropriate for class rights to attach to them to the effect that the holders may veto transactions which will reduce the distributable profits and so make redemptions more difficult. A complete ban on bonus issues is appropriate, as are restrictions on the dividends payable on other classes of shares (beyond any fixed dividends payable) until redemption is achieved; although *Re Holders Investment Trust*[8] suggests that a holder of redeemable shares might be able to obtain an injunction to restrain the payment of dividends on other classes of shares until redemption has been achieved, it would be preferable to make this a class right. The company should also undertake to procure that its subsidiaries (if any) shall distribute all their available profits to the company by way of dividend, so as to boost the distributable profits of the company. Without such a provision the redeemable shareholders are powerless to prevent the accumulation or reinvestment by the subsidiaries of their profits.

The law regarding redeemable shares

20.30   Redeemable shares are regulated by CA 2006, ss 684–689. The most important points are:

- The issue of redeemable shares by a public company must be authorised by the articles; there is no such requirement for a private company although the articles of a private company may exclude or restrict the issue of redeemable shares. Under the CA 1985, all companies were required to have an authorising provision in their articles.

- Subject to being authorised to do so either by an ordinary resolution or by the articles of association, the directors of the company may determine the terms, conditions and manner of redemption of the shares. The directors must determine the terms of redemption prior to the issue of the shares.

- Redeemable shares cannot be issued at a time when there are no issued shares of the company which are not redeemable.

- Redeemable shares can only be redeemed if they are fully paid.

- The terms of redemption may provide that the amount payable on redemption may, by agreement between the company and the shareholder, be paid on a date later than the redemption date. (Under the CA 1985, the redemption amount was required to be paid on redemption.)

20.31   The only type of redeemable share which a company could issue prior to the Companies Act 1981 was a redeemable preference share, but

---

8   [1971] 2 All ER 289.

there is now no need for a redeemable share to carry any preferential rights as to dividend or return on capital.

20.32   The taxation position on the redemption of redeemable shares is very similar to that applying on a purchase of shares. Any part of the redemption monies which is in excess of the amount originally subscribed for the shares is a qualifying distribution, but the exemptions in CTA 2010, ss 1029–1048 (previously ICTA 1988, s 219) do not apply.

20.33   No stamp duty is payable on a redemption of redeemable shares.

General points

20.34   Due to the terms of redemption have to be established prior to the issue of the shares, redeemable shares do not provide a satisfactory exit route for a shareholder looking to realise a capital profit from its investment reflecting the increased value of the company, for which an equity share is a much more preferable proposition. They can provide an exit route for an investor who desires merely a running dividend yield on the amount invested and is content with the return of its capital on redemption or for the yield it requires to be rolled up in a redemption premium.

20.35   Investment institutions often subscribe for redeemable shares which are convertible into equity shares. The theory is that if the company does well, so that an exit route for the ordinary shareholders by way of a sale of the whole issued capital of the company or its flotation is likely, they can convert into ordinary shares and exit with the other ordinary shareholders at a profit. On the other hand, should the company not perform very well, so that such an exit route is unlikely, they can avoid being 'locked in' by not converting and waiting for the redemption date to arrive and at least get their money back, plus any yield available from any preference dividend or premium on redemption which may attach to the redeemable shares. The possible snag with this is that the company must have at least done well enough to have accrued distributable profits equivalent to the subscription monies paid for the shares plus any premium payable on redemption, after allowing for any dividends paid out prior to the redemption date, or must have sufficient surplus resources to pay that amount out of capital. It might, of course, be possible for the company to make a new issue of shares to fund the redemption monies, but this could not be relied upon.

20.36   The case of *Barclays Bank plc v British and Commonwealth Holdings plc*[9] involved a scheme designed to avoid the capital maintenance rules applying to redeemable shares, so that they could effectively be redeemed

---

9   [1996] 1 BCLC 1.

notwithstanding the non-availability of sufficient distributable profits. The redeemable shareholder in B&C was given an option, exercisable on a failure to redeem, to require another company (the 'purchaser') to buy the shares at a price equal to the redemption monies. A syndicate of banks had agreed to put the purchaser in funds to buy the shares. The loan agreement contained financial covenants by B&C in favour of the banks and the purchaser, which were designed to ensure that B&C would always be able to redeem the shares. These covenants having been breached, the banks and the purchaser sued B&C for damages for such breach, including the purchase price of the shares. The Court of Appeal upheld the claim, even though this meant that B&C was liable for a sum equal to the redemption monies which it could not pay due to lack of sufficient distributable profits.

20.37 However, there is considerable doubt as to whether the case was correctly decided and certainly it ought not to be relied upon. The circumstances were rather special in that the court had previously approved the scheme and the option under a scheme of arrangement pursuant to then CA 1985, s 425 and therefore the validity of the option and the covenants could not be called into question. Therefore, the judgments in both the High Court and the Court of Appeal were not based on the unauthorised return of capital to shareholders. The decision has not subsequently been followed in England and some commentators are of the view that it was incorrect; certainly if it were correct it would allow a substantial erosion of the established principles of capital maintenance.

Payment of break fee as 'financial assistance'

20.38 In *Paros Plc v Worldlink Group Plc*[10] the court thought an agreement providing for payment of a 'break fee' (paid where there was a failure to conclude a transaction) in the situation of a reverse takeover was 'financial assistance' given for the purchase by the company of its own shares. The courts said para 69:

'Even if ... [the break fee] is a flat fee (as I have held it is), the break fee is "other financial assistance" and has a material effect on the net assets of Worldlink. It is financial assistance because it is a proposed financial payment which "smooths the path" towards the acquisition of the shares. It is not clear whether a break fee is always financial assistance. It has been argued, based on dicta in *Barclays Bank plc v British & Commonwealth Holdings plc* [1995] BCC 1059 that in some circumstances a break fee could be characterised as an "inducement" rather than "assistance". However, in *Chaston*, Arden LJ indicated (at §44) that she

---

10   [2012] EWHC 394 (Comm).

did not consider *Barclays* to decide that an inducement was not financial assistance.'

Although CA 2006 abolished the prohibition on private companies providing financial assistance for purchase of their own shares there is still a prohibition for public companies in CA 2006, s 678.

Chapter 21

Sale or initial public offering of the company

Summary

This chapter deals with the legal and practical issues concerning two further important exit routes which may be available to shareholders, namely the sale of the whole issued share capital of the company to a third party or an initial public offering (IPO). The matters discussed are those issues which usually arise on the sale to a third party, including warranties and indemnities and non-competition covenants, offers from third parties, including 'tag along' and 'drag along' provisions, the issues which typically arise on an IPO, and the exit provisions generally required by institutional shareholders. The issues are discussed in a UK context, although the general principles have international application.

1 Sale of the entire issued share capital to a third party

Introduction

21.1   A sale of the entire issued share capital to a third party could come about in at least three different ways:

- where it was the pre-ordained policy, as enshrined in the shareholders' agreement, that the shareholders would all exit by means of such a sale at a future time;

- where a termination notice has been served, and such an exit results from subsequent negotiation, either because such an exit is then attractive to the other shareholders or because it is one of the alternatives to be explored by virtue of the termination provisions;

- where an offer for the entire share capital or a controlling interest is received from a third party, whether solicited by one or more of the shareholders or not.

21.2   In the first case, a sale will often be expressed as an alternative to an IPO and it is discussed below in conjunction with an IPO.

Sale following termination

21.3   In the second case the termination provisions in the shareholders' agreement may require the possibility of a sale of the whole issued share capital to be explored following the service of a termination notice, particularly because, if no other shareholder is willing to purchase the stake of the outgoing shareholder and its sale to the company cannot be arranged, the only other exit route for the outgoing shareholder will be to insist on liquidation, a probably unsatisfactory course of action for all parties. Although, of course, it is not possible to have any binding arrangements for such a sale, if the agreement provides that if it is not achieved within a certain time liquidation will ensue this is likely to be a powerful incentive for the shareholders to co-operate with one another to secure such a sale. Elaborate provisions regarding the instruction of outside advisers, the provision of information to prospective purchasers, and general co-operation between the shareholders to secure a sale are sometimes seen in agreements, but are probably not really necessary.

21.4   The most difficult issues to be confronted when considering a sale of the share capital to an outsider are securing a binding agreement for the sale and, related to that, the provision of warranties, indemnities and non-competition covenants to the purchaser.

21.5   As to the first issue, it is of course generally impossible to bind everyone in advance to a particular sale price or particular terms. These will only emerge once a prospective purchaser has been found. Every shareholder will normally need to approve the sale of its shares and sign the sale agreement, and it is often difficult for complete agreement to be reached even if there is a 'liquidation time bomb' ticking away. A possible solution is to provide in the articles or shareholders' agreement for compulsory transfers to the purchaser if a defined majority of all the shareholders approves the sale – the so called 'drag along' provisions. These are discussed in detail from para 21.20.

21.6   A purchaser will inevitably require the selling shareholders to provide warranties and indemnities in relation to the affairs of the company, which is a fruitful area for disagreement between the sellers. Institutional shareholders will usually refuse to provide any warranties or indemnities at all and where they are the majority shareholders may be prepared to accept a lower price rather than give them. Small shareholders may object to giving them on the normal joint and several basis alongside the other shareholders. If a shareholder has died, his personal representatives are unlikely to be willing to provide warranties or indemnities and, likewise, the trustees of a family trust. Shareholders who have no involvement in the business will argue that their ignorance of its affairs makes it unreasonable for them to provide warranties. It is in practice impossible for 'drag along' provisions to effectively bind selling shareholders to provide warranties and indemnities.

21.7   The precise warranties and indemnities will not be known until the draft sale and purchase agreement arrives (although their general content can certainly be predicted) and such a formula as binding shareholders to sign 'reasonable' warranties and indemnities will fail because there is no general agreement between lawyers as to what would be reasonable in a particular case. Simply relying on the approval of the majority of the warranties and indemnities under the 'drag along' provisions is unlikely to work, since the minority might successfully be able to challenge the clause as imposing unfair liabilities upon them.

21.8   In practice, the issue is usually dodged in the shareholders' agreement, with the result that the majority desiring a sale may in practice have to shoulder a greater warranty and indemnity burden than they would normally expect to bear in order to avoid imposing such liabilities on the minority. If the agreement says anything about the issue at all, this will usually be to the effect that certain parties, particularly institutional shareholders, are not to provide warranties and indemnities.

21.9   A possible solution to these difficulties is to provide in the agreement that the sellers will take out insurance to cover their liabilities under the warranties and indemnities. Whilst such insurance might well solve the impasse, it is not a magic solution to the problem, and has some drawbacks attached to it:

- subject to any other agreement, the sellers' sale proceeds will be reduced by the insurance premium, which varies according to the market but at the time of writing is usually around 1–2% of the sum to be insured;

- there will often be an excess under the policy;

- the following types of warranty may not be insurable:

    - the collectability of bad debts;

    - defects in products or services (but the company should have some insurance to cover these);

    - environmental liabilities;

    - adequacy of pension funding;

    - liabilities under warranties relating to future events (which the sellers should not give anyway);

    - liabilities under warranties that are incapable of verification (eg 'sweeper' warranties);

    - liabilities arising from warranties which directly underwrite the value of the company, eg as to net assets;

- in a seller's policy the fraud or dishonesty of the sellers will not be covered, but the purchaser may insure against this under a contingent policy, although the premium will be higher than for a seller's policy;

- there will be difficulty in recovering if the insured has given incorrect information in the proposal form, or has dishonestly withheld relevant information from the insurers.

It should be added that a seller's insurance policy will not directly benefit the purchaser, other than providing comfort that the sellers should have the money if a claim under the warranties and indemnities is made. The purchaser may take out insurance which provides cover, should it be unable to recover from the sellers, either because their policy has not responded (eg because of their fraud) or because they have not insured at all and cannot pay the claim. The proceeds of a seller's policy do not go to the purchaser unless it takes an assignment of the policy but, although the purchaser will then receive any proceeds, it will not have the conduct of the claim against the insurers. The purchaser is therefore better protected by taking out its own policy. 'Non-recourse' insurance whereby the purchaser became a loss payee under, or took on assignment of, the seller's policy, in exchange for agreeing with the sellers that the insurance policy would be its only recourse in respect of warranty and indemnity claims is now generally discredited.

21.10   In contrast to warranties concerning the affairs of the company, it may be perfectly reasonable to expect the minority to provide warranties concerning their title to their shares, even if they are unwilling sellers.

21.11   Non-competition covenants can also cause difficulties. Such covenants could not be imposed under a 'drag along' provision, so if a minority holder refuses to enter into the required covenants, and the lack of covenants from that particular shareholder is unacceptable to the prospective purchaser, the sale may grind to a halt.

21.12   Other matters requiring attention on the sale of the whole issued share capital are those referred to at para 17.48ff, although rather than these being matters for the continuing shareholders they will need to be dealt with by negotiation with the buyer.

2 Offer from a third party – 'tag along and drag along'

General

21.13   Possibly more likely than a sale of the whole issued share capital of the company following a termination notice is a sale in response to an offer received from a third party, whether unsolicited or engineered by a shareholder who wishes to sell.

21.14   Provisions dealing with such a sale strive to address two issues:

- the fear of the minority that the majority may sell their shares to an outsider, leaving the minority 'locked in' and not only deprived of any sale proceeds but also with a majority controller which they may not know; and

- the fear of the majority that the obstruction of the minority may block a sale where the prospective purchaser is unable to secure the signature of the sale agreement by all the shareholders and is unwilling to purchase with a 'rump' of them left behind.

21.15   The first issue is dealt with by 'tag along' provisions – ie the right of the minority to require the majority to allow the minority to tag along with them if a sale is in prospect. The second issue is dealt with by the 'drag along' provisions which are designed to bind a minority to accept an offer approved by the majority. Such provisions may be inserted into the shareholders' agreement or into the articles of association.

Provisions in shareholders' agreements

21.16   A provision in a shareholders' agreement would take the form of mutual undertakings between the shareholders that, should any shareholder or combination of shareholders receive an offer from a third party which they desire to accept, and which, if accepted, would result in a sale of a controlling interest, they will use all reasonable endeavours to extend it to all other shareholders. The minority would prefer that the majority agreed not to accept the offer unless it is so extended. The 'drag along' part of the provisions consists of an undertaking by the minority to accept the offer if it is so extended. It is a matter for negotiation whether the minority, or any proportion of it, is required to approve the offer before they all become bound to accept it and provisions defining the terms on which an offer must be made to bind all the shareholders (along the lines in para 21.18) may also be appropriate. Such mutual undertakings are suitable for use where there are only a few shareholders, and few, if any, transfers are envisaged, and so would be suitable for most joint venture companies. A provision outside the articles will require further undertakings to procure registration of the necessary share transfers, including the execution of any necessary waivers of pre-emption rights on share transfers.

Provisions in articles

21.17   For companies with more shareholders, or where more frequent transfers are envisaged, as with family-owned companies or companies whose shareholders include consortia of venture capital or other institutional investors, a provision in the articles is likely to be more appropriate. This can tie in the requirement to extend the offer with the ability to register a share transfer. The articles provide that no transfer of any shares conferring control shall be registered unless the prospective transferee ('the buyer') offers also to buy the shares of all the other shareholders on the same terms as those on which the controlling interest is sought to be acquired.

21.18   In practice, it is desirable to further elaborate the 'tag along' provisions as follows:

- The possibility that two or more buyers may together be seeking to acquire control can be addressed by defining 'buyer' to mean any one person or group of persons acting in concert (as defined by the City Code on Takeovers and Mergers) and providing that the right to tag along is triggered if transfers of shares are presented for registration which, taken together, amount to the transfer of a controlling interest in favour of such persons.

- A controlling interest should be defined, and a suitable definition might be shares conferring in aggregate more than half the votes exercisable at a general meeting of the company.

- The minimum price which has to be offered for all the minority's shares should be defined, which can be the higher of:

  (i)   the highest price per share at which the buyer shall have acquired any shares of the company during a period prior to the offer to the other shareholders (eg six months); and

  (ii)   the highest price per share offered by the buyer to any shareholder for any shares in the company during the same period, whether it was a binding offer or not.

- The highest price should be defined to include not only the price offered for the shares themselves, but also any additional consideration which can reasonably be regarded as an addition to the price (such as any 'sweeteners').

- The buyer should be required to make its offer to all shareholders on the same terms, but this should exclude any differences arising because some shareholders are to receive service and similar agreements and others will not, because shareholders may be providing warranties and indemnities or non-competition or confidentiality covenants on different terms, or sometimes not at all, or because only some of the shareholders are required to enter into lock up agreements (agreeing not to sell any consideration securities for a period after the sale), or irrevocable undertakings to accept the offer when made (applicable where the offer will be in a form of a takeover offering document rather than a private contract) and others are not, or they are doing so on different terms, or because it is necessary to make special arrangements as to the receipt of the documents and/or the consideration securities for some shareholders (because they are overseas and overseas securities laws may otherwise be infringed) and not for others.

• Where shareholders have advanced loans, it could be provided that the buyer must offer to procure their repayment or their assignment to the buyer on defined terms.

• Where there are outstanding options, the buyer should be obliged to extend its offer to include any shares issued on exercise of the options, on the same terms as apply to existing shareholders.

The articles will provide that only an offer by a third party for control which is capable of meeting these various requirements is an 'appropriate offer', which can lead to the registration of share transfers giving rise to a change of control; if the third party offer does not meet these minimum requirements it cannot proceed further.

21.19   There is no reason why the provision should not apply to an existing shareholder who is seeking to acquire control or already has control and is seeking to acquire further shares, in the same way as for third parties.

21.20   There are various methods of structuring 'drag along' provisions in the articles, but a convenient one is to provide for the convening of a general meeting to approve the offer. On the approval being obtained, all shareholders become bound to accept the offer and transfer their shares accordingly. Option holders who exercise their options should be similarly bound. The majority required to do so is a matter for negotiation, but a special resolution (75% of votes cast) or ordinary resolution (simple majority) could be appropriate. This provision pre-supposes that the 'buyer' has not already secured informal acceptance of its offer from a sufficient number of shareholders. Where this is so, the requirement for a special or any other resolution becomes a mere formality, but the requirement is included to define the level of acceptance required and, depending upon the acceptance level set, to provide some protection for the minority from being bought out at too low a price.

21.21   Such an article could provide for there to be circulated with the notice of the meeting a statement setting out the terms of the offer, together with copies of the sale and purchase agreement and all other documents required to be executed by the acceptors. It is a good idea to provide that short notice of the meeting is not to be given, to avoid any argument by holders of 10%[1] or less that they did not have the opportunity to consider the offer properly.

---

1   CA 2006, s 307(4)–(6) sets out the default short notice approval level for private companies as a majority of members together holding at least 90% of the shares giving the right to attend and vote at the meeting. The articles, however, can raise this to a maximum of 95%. The threshold for public companies is set at 95% for general meetings, but unanimity is required for an annual general meeting.

21.22   Should any shareholder be unwilling to accept an offer which has been approved, there could be provisions under which the directors may appoint a person to do so upon his behalf, with the purchase money being held on trust for him by the company.

21.23   If the resolution is passed, the article should provide that any pre-emption rights in the articles of association will not apply to any transfers made pursuant to acceptances of the offer and that, furthermore, the directors are bound to register every such transfer.

21.24   The article should make it clear that at the time the offer is put before the shareholders it may be subject to contract or be in some way conditional, and if it never becomes unconditional or ceases to be subject to contract, the resolution is a nullity and no shareholder is bound by it. This provision is designed to cover the point that a private contract for the acquisition of shares is usually subject to contract until the moment the purchaser executes and delivers it and may often be subject to conditions precedent which may not have been satisfied by the time the meeting is held.

21.25   A simpler course is to provide that the only approval required to trigger the 'drag along' provision is that received from the persons who have already signed transfers together amounting to the transfer of control, but such a provision offers less protection for the minority, especially as the transfer of a small stake to a shareholder which has already acquired an interest falling just short of control could trigger the 'drag along' provision.

21.26   In seeking to implement a 'drag along' provision the same difficulties as noted in para 21.6ff are likely to be encountered in relation to warranties, indemnities and non-competition covenants. It is therefore likely to be impossible to impose these upon an unwilling transferor.

3   Legality of 'drag along' provisions in articles

Legality of expropriation provisions

21.27   Although 'drag along' provisions contained in articles of association are in common use, there is no authority on their legal effectiveness and, in view of certain cases outlawing 'expropriation' provisions in articles, a slight doubt remains as to whether they are enforceable.

21.28   In *Re Bugle Press*[2] Harman LJ, in considering a case on what is now the Companies Act 2006, s 979, referred to the 'fundamental rule of company

---

2   [1961] 1 Ch 270.

law which forbids the majority of shareholders, unless the articles so provide, to expropriate a minority'. He did therefore accept that an expropriation article could be an exception to the general rule.

21.29   A number of old Chancery cases are relevant to the issue. In some of these cases expropriation clauses have been upheld and others not, but most of these cases dealt with attempts to expropriate the minority by means of the introduction of a new article for the purpose, and the cases all turned on whether the power of a company to alter its articles is entirely unfettered, or whether a new article can be challenged as not being in the interests of the company as a whole, and the courts have consistently held that they can be so challenged. However, it has been generally accepted that an expropriation provision in the company's original articles is good[3].

21.30   In *Phillips v Manufacturers Securities Ltd*[4], which was cited with approval in the *Sidebottom v Kershaw, Leese* case, the original articles included a provision that the company might, by resolution in general meeting, require that the shares of any member should be offered for sale by the company to the other members at a price fixed by the resolution, provided that the price was not less than one shilling per share, and if no price was fixed the price would be one shilling per share. It was held that the article was valid, although one can hardly imagine a more potentially unfair provision.

Conclusion and practical solutions

21.31   It is therefore submitted that, although an attempt to amend existing articles by including a 'drag along' provision might be subject to a successful challenge, one included in a shareholders' agreement executed by all the shareholders or in articles of association which have been approved by all the shareholders is fully enforceable against them. In order to be sure that all the shareholders are bound by a provision contained in the articles, it would be desirable, as is normal practice, to exhibit to the shareholders' agreement, or any other agreement under which they agree to subscribe for their shares, a copy of the agreed articles, with an obligation upon them to procure their adoption, and to include also an obligation on the subscribers to observe and perform the articles. This would make it perfectly clear that they all agreed to take their shares on the terms of the articles and would therefore avoid any argument that they are not bound by them. It would not be safe to rely entirely upon the adoption of the articles, since they may be those adopted on incorporation, or they may

---

3   See *Sidebottom v Kershaw, Leese & Co* [1920] 1 Ch 155 at 163; and *Brown v British Abrasive Wheel Ltd* [1919] 1 Ch 291 at 296.
4   (1917) 86 LJ Ch 305.

have been adopted by the subscribers to the memorandum, or only by some of the eventual signatories to the shareholders or subscription agreement; very often it will be the controllers of the company immediately before the main subscription who will adopt the articles. However, a written resolution adopting the articles signed by all the signatories to the agreement would be as good as a signed agreement to adopt them.

21.32   In view of the 'expropriation cases', some care needs to be taken to ensure that future shareholders are bound by a 'drag along' provision, whether it is contained in the articles or in a shareholders' agreement. In the case of such a provision in the shareholders' agreement, a deed of adherence should be executed by each new shareholder. In the case of such a provision in the articles, if the precaution is taken of expressing the obligation in the shareholders' agreement to observe the articles as extending to future shareholders and of requiring every new shareholder to sign a deed of adherence, this would make it very difficult for a new shareholder to argue that it was not bound by the articles, especially if it has subscribed for new shares rather than taking a transfer of existing shares and has signed the usual form of letter of application agreeing to take the shares subject to the articles.

Why not rely on CA 2006, s 979 instead of 'drag along' provisions?

21.33   The question may be asked as to why the majority could not rely on CA 2006, s 979, which allows the shares of the minority to be compulsorily acquired once the offeror has secured acceptance in respect of 90% of the shares included in the offer. There are three reasons why the insertion of a 'drag along' provision is preferable to relying on s 979:

(1)   the required majority to approve the sale may be lower;

(2)   the right of a dissentient to apply to the court is excluded; and

(3)   there is difficulty in applying s 979 to the acquisition of shares in a private company as normally conducted.

The reason for this last point is because the section requires an 'offer' to have been made for all the shares in a company, and this seems to require the circulation to all the shareholders of an offer document as in a public takeover bid, a procedure which many prospective purchasers would find burdensome and unfamiliar. If there is no 'drag along' provision, or there are doubts about its enforceability, the majority may very well try to bring the sale within s 979.

4 Sale or IPO

Impossibility of legal commitment

21.34   Quite often, all the shareholders are desirous from the beginning of achieving an exit through a trade sale or an IPO after a number of years and in such cases provisions to that effect are normally inserted in the shareholders' agreement; this is particularly the case where there is a substantial investment from a venture capitalist or other investment institution. Where a sale or IPO is intended, it is highly desirable to insert appropriate provisions in the shareholders' agreement in an effort to avoid some of the disagreements which might arise if matters are left for negotiation when steps are first taken to achieve such an exit.

21.35   It is quite impossible to structure a legally binding commitment to achieve such an exit; whether it will be possible, and within what timescale, will depend upon whether the company does well or badly and the state of the market at the time. Despite the great importance to institutional shareholders of achieving an exit (indeed, it is usually their sole reason for investing) it is usual for the shareholders' or investment agreement to include only vague provisions to the effect that it is the intention of the parties to work towards achieving an exit within, say, three to five years. Sometimes one sees provisions that the company will, within a certain timescale, appoint a financial adviser to give advice on the exit route and one may sometimes see obligations to follow the advice, although the effectiveness of such a provision is probably doubtful, and of itself will not necessarily result in a successful exit.

21.36   There are, however, a number of provisions which an institutional investor will typically seek to include with a view to facilitating its exit. These are discussed in more detail at para 21.41ff.

21.37   As far as a trade sale is concerned, the matters already discussed in paras 21.3–21.33 above in relation to a sale of the whole issued capital will be relevant. In particular, the 'tag along' and 'drag along' provisions are useful tools in engineering such an exit, as is warranty and indemnity insurance.

IPO

21.38   An important feature of an IPO is that it is unlikely to produce the whole value of the company in immediate cash, whereas a trade sale can be expected to do so – unless, of course, the consideration is in shares or loan paper, or is deferred. This is because the sponsor or nominated adviser to the IPO will usually insist that the principal shareholders enter into 'lock up' agreements under which there are limits on the number of shares they may sell for a period after the IPO. Such agreements are imposed to ensure an orderly market after the IPO by avoiding the steep drop in the post-IPO price which would occur if all the major shareholders attempted to sell their shares at once. Non-institutional shareholders may in fact not be too perturbed about entering into such agreements, in that they may well wish to stay in the company after an IPO in the hope of further capital appreciation or at least to spread the sale of their shares over a period of years in order to minimise their liability to capital gains taxation. In the case of a company to be floated on AIM, lock up agreements may be required by the AIM Rules.

21.39   Whilst a trade sale may result in the purchaser acquiring or procuring the payment of outstanding loans due to the shareholders, an IPO will not generally do so, since a listing or other quotation will not ordinarily be sought for loan capital, although such loans might be converted into shares immediately before the IPO. The company may not have a suitable capital structure for an IPO, in that it may have different classes of shares with associated rights of pre-emption and minority protections, whereas a company to be floated will generally be expected to have only one class of ordinary shares without any transfer restrictions. A capital reorganisation will therefore often be necessary prior to the IPO, and in order to avoid a disagreement concerning how this is to be done it is sensible to issue all shares other than ordinary shares on terms that they are convertible into ordinary shares on a defined basis and to make loan capital convertible on the same basis. As regards shares, it may be sensible to do the same if a trade sale is envisaged, so that each shareholder can be treated as owning a certain number of ordinary shares, so avoiding difficulties which might otherwise arise in agreeing the apportionment of the consideration between the different classes; although, if the total consideration which would be apportioned to ordinary shares arising from the conversion of preference shares is below the total amount paid by investors for such convertible preference shares, those investors will wish to retain their priority – see para 21.42.

21.40   The problems with warranties and indemnities noted at para 21.6 in relation to a sale of the whole issued share capital will also arise in relation to an IPO, where the sponsor or nominated adviser invariably requires warranties about the affairs of the company (which will usually be given by the company, the directors and the selling shareholders, if any), an indemnity in favour of itself to protect it from the consequences of misstatements in the prospectus or AIM admission document, and sometimes a tax indemnity. The directors of the company at the time of the issue of the prospectus or admission document will in any case assume personal liability to investors for the accuracy of their contents, and selling shareholders may also incur such liability.

Institutional protection

21.41   Institutional shareholders are particularly keen on provisions which will promote a satisfactory exit. The following are becoming common clauses in their investment agreements:

- A statement that they will not provide warranties and indemnities other than as to the title to their shares, the main justification for which is that the existence of the resulting contingent liability will impede the distribution of the proceeds of the sale to their investors – in practice, institutions are occasionally prepared to provide warranties and indemnities as long as their liability is strictly limited, perhaps to their proportion of a retention (which will not in any case be released to the sellers until some time after the sale), or by means of a warranty contribution agreement whereby the management bears the brunt of most of the potential claims.

- A commitment by the management shareholders that they will provide warranties and indemnities both in relation to a sale and an IPO, although it is accepted that this is probably unenforceable; those advising the managers will request that the warranties and indemnities be subject to the 'normal limitations', although there could be as much argument about what these are as there is concerning 'normal warranties'.

- An agreement that the management shareholders shall have the protection of warranty and indemnity insurance; such insurance has become so common that the management shareholders now quite often seek an undertaking from the institution to bear the cost of the policy.

- The 'drag along' provisions are often worded so that the conditions which an offer must fulfil to become an 'appropriate offer' must provide the institution with an exit in respect of all its shares and loans, which entails the purchaser offering to repay or purchase their loans as well as their shares.

- A requirement that where a sponsor to an IPO requires a 'lock up' period, the management shareholders will agree to this in the hope that this will satisfy the sponsor and leave the institution's shares outside the 'lock up'. If the management is prepared to do this, they may seek limitations on the proportion of their shareholdings which may be locked up and a maximum time period on the 'lock up', although it is not realistically possible to define this in advance.

- Provisions for the management shareholders to enter into new service agreements on exit, for periods of up to, say, 12 months, should this be required by a purchaser or sponsor, although this is not really possible to enforce.

- A provision for a warranty on exit by a sale that the purchase price receivable by the institution on exit is the same price management has received, after allowance for any bonuses or other 'sweeteners' which may be payable to the management either before or after the sale; an alternative is to require the purchaser to make appropriate payments to the institution where the company is on-sold by the purchaser at a higher price than it paid within a short time of the purchase or where it pays extra value to the managers after the purchase without proper performance criteria being applied.

- Adjustments to any ratchet (see para 27.25ff) so that the proportion of the consideration receivable by management goes down the longer an exit takes to achieve.

- A provision that in the case of an IPO the same proportion of the institution's shares will be marketed as for the manager's shares and, where the institution is selling shares, to provide that it may require the sponsor to purchase them and on-sell them to the public as principal, rather than as the institution's agent, so as to avoid liability in respect of misstatements in the prospectus or admission document falling upon the institution as a seller of shares (although the institution will normally be expected to bear any additional stamp duty or stamp duty reserve tax which arises in consequence).

- The price for a sale of the whole issued share capital under a 'drag along' provision often requires the approval of the institution instead of, or in addition to, a resolution of the shareholders, or if a shareholders' resolution is required and the institutions are in the majority, the percentage required to pass it is likely to be set at a level which ensures that management cannot block a sale.

21.42   An institutional holder having a mixture of shares of different classes, or of a different class to that held by management, is often concerned about the apportionment of the consideration on a sale of the whole issued share capital. For example, where the institution has subscribed for convertible preference shares and the price to be received is less than sufficient to recover the whole of the institution's investment, it will expect the whole of the price to go to it, in recognition of its preference on a return of capital in a winding up and for ordinary shareholders to receive only a nominal sum; in other words, it will wish the sale proceeds to be distributed as if they are proceeds in a winding up, notwithstanding that the sale price does not go to the company and its apportionment is a matter of negotiation between seller and purchaser. A solution is to word the 'drag along' provisions so that an offer for a controlling interest cannot be an 'appropriate offer' unless the offeror agrees to offer to acquire the entire share capital and apportion the consideration as if it was the proceeds of a liquidation.

Precedent

(Article requiring offers for control to be extended to all Shareholders and for Shareholders to be bound to accept such an offer if a certain percentage of the Shareholders does so: 'tag-along' and 'drag-along'.)

(A) Notwithstanding Article [...] (**pre-emption rights**) no Buyer (as defined below) shall be entitled or permitted to acquire a Controlling Interest and no Buyer who shall have a Controlling Interest shall acquire any additional shares in the Company and no transfers of shares conferring such a Controlling Interest or in respect of the acquisition of any additional shares as aforesaid shall be registered unless and until the Buyer shall have made an offer (the 'Offer') to all the holders of shares in the Company and all persons who are entitled by the exercise of any option, right of conversion or other right to acquire or have issued to them any shares in the Company at the relevant time or who would become so entitled on the implementation of the Offer after it is made (other than the Buyer if he is already a holder) to purchase from them for cash [or in exchange for readily marketable securities] their entire existing or prospective holdings of shares in the Company at the Total Price (as defined below) upon terms that the Total Price shall be apportioned between the existing and prospective holders of shares in the Company (other than the Buyer to the extent it is already a holder) in the same way as the Total Price would fall to be apportioned between such holders if the Total Price was the amount available for distribution between the Members on a winding up of the Company (on the basis that such distribution was not made in respect of any shares already held by the Buyer but that all such options, rights of conversion and other rights have been exercised in full and that all the shares falling to be issued on exercise thereof have been issued and are entitled to such distribution) and otherwise on the same terms.

(B) For the purposes of this Article [...]:

'**Buyer**' shall mean any one person or group of persons acting in concert (together with their respective subsidiaries and holding companies and all subsidiaries of any such holding company) and persons shall be deemed to be acting in concert if they would be regarded as so doing under the City Code on Takeovers and Mergers in force from time to time in relation to a public company;

the expression '**acquire**' shall mean being or becoming the beneficial owner of shares in the Company whether directly or indirectly (including the acquisition of shares or other rights of control over any body corporate or other entity which, directly or indirectly, holds shares in the Company) and whether by issue, transfer, renunciation or conversion of shares (or howsoever otherwise);

a '**Controlling Interest**' shall mean shares conferring in the aggregate more than half the votes exercisable at any general meeting of the Company [exclude any special voting rights exercisable in limited circumstances];

the '**Total Price**' shall mean the total consideration offered or paid or payable by the Buyer or his nominees for the entire issued and to be issued share capital of the Company (on the basis set out above) other than shares already held by the Buyer if applicable under the Offer but subject as set out below:

(1)   where any Member or person entitled to receive any shares in the Company (the 'recipient') has been, or is to be offered, or has received or may be entitled to receive any additional consideration (in cash or otherwise) which, having regard to the substance of the transaction as a whole, can reasonably be regarded as an addition to the price paid or payable for the shares of the recipient, such additional consideration shall be added to the Total Price and if it is not cash a cash equivalent shall be determined by the auditors to the Company (acting as experts and not as arbitrators) and there shall also be added thereto in respect of all the shares in the Company held or to be held otherwise than by the recipient, an additional sum per share which is equal to the sum per share represented by such additional consideration;

(2)   the Total Price, when apportioned as set out in paragraph (A) of this Article and expressed as an amount per share shall be not less than the higher of:

(i)   the highest price per share (after any additions as aforesaid) at which the Buyer shall have acquired any shares of the Company during the six months prior to the making of the Offer; and

(ii)   the highest price per share (after any additions as aforesaid) contained in any previous offer by the Buyer for the acquisition of any shares held by any Member made during the six months prior to the making of the Offer and for these purposes a price shall be treated as contained in an offer even if the offer was not legally binding or unconditional if it would be reasonable for the recipient to regard it as a proposal made with the intention to carry it into effect.

(C)   An Offer shall be communicated in writing to the Directors of the Company who shall as soon as practicable convene a General Meeting of the Company at which will be proposed a [Special Resolution] for the approval of the Offer by the Members. The Buyer (if a Member) shall not be entitled to vote in respect of any such resolution.

(D) If such a [Special Resolution] shall be passed every Member shall become bound to transfer all his shares in the Company to the Buyer (subject to the receipt of any regulatory approvals that may be required for such a transfer) for the consideration stated in and upon the other terms of the Offer. If any Member shall fail to so transfer all his shares the Directors may authorise some person to execute any transfers or other documents necessary to effect the transfer. The purchase money or other consideration due to such defaulting Member shall be received by the Company or by such person appointed by the Directors who shall hold the same in trust for the defaulting Member. The receipt by the Company or such authorised person for such purchase money or other consideration shall be a good discharge to the Buyer and after the name of the Buyer shall have been entered on the register in purported exercise of the said powers the validity of the proceedings shall not be questioned by any person.

(E) If such a [Special Resolution] shall be passed the restrictions on transfers of shares contained in Article [...] shall not apply in relation to the transfers of shares pursuant to the Offer and the Directors shall be bound to register every such transfer. [If such a Special Resolution shall not be passed then such restrictions shall continue to apply and no transfers of any shares pursuant to any acceptance of the Offer shall be registered unless and until each Member concerned shall have complied with Article [...] and the rights of pre-emption therein contained are exhausted.]

(F) For the avoidance of doubt an Offer may include one which is to be accepted by the making of a private contract as well as one made by general offer and may include one which is subject to contract or in some way conditional (and if the Offer does not become unconditional or the subject of a contract by reason of a withdrawal by the Buyer any [Special Resolution] passed as aforesaid shall be a nullity and no Member shall be bound to sell as aforesaid).

(G) No Member shall be bound to an Offer unless there is circulated to all Members with the notice convening the General Meeting convened under paragraph (C) of this Article a statement setting out the terms of the Offer together with copies of all documents required to be executed by acceptors of it, and notwithstanding any other provision of these Articles, 21 days' notice of the holding of such meeting shall be given.

(H) An Offer shall be regarded as made on the same terms to all Members notwithstanding that:

(i)   some Members and not others are to receive remuneration for services to be rendered by them provided that such remuneration represents an open market consideration for the provision of such services; and/or

(ii) some Members have agreed to provide warranties, indemnities or non-competition or confidentiality covenants more onerous than any contained or referred to in the Offer, or where no such provisions are mentioned in the Offer; and/or

(iii) special arrangements as to the receipt of documents [and/or consideration shares or securities] are made for overseas resident Members and not others; and/or

[(iv) some Members are required to undertake not to dispose of consideration shares or securities for a period after the sale, and others are not, or are required to do so on different terms; and/or]

(v) some Members are required to provide irrevocable undertakings to accept the Offer when made and others are not or are required to do so on different terms.

(I) If any person shall become a Member following the passing of a [Special Resolution] approving an Offer pursuant to any right to acquire any shares in the Company such Member shall be bound by the [Special Resolution] and shall be treated as a Member for all purposes of this Article [...] (except that he shall not be entitled to vote on the [Special Resolution]) and shall be bound to transfer all his shares in the Company as set out in Article [...] (D).

Chapter 22

Share valuation provisions

Summary

This chapter contains a brief summary of the principles of private company share valuation. It discusses the various methods which may be used to value a share and explains the concept of 'fair value' and how it differs from market value. It reaches the conclusion that many investors are likely to prefer the proportionate part of the market value of the company represented by their shares rather than the market value of their shares as such. Guidance is then given on appropriate wording for valuation clauses.

1 Introduction

22.1   Many exit provisions under which one shareholder sells shares to another provide for the price to be determined by valuation (as opposed to a price which is fixed or reached by application of a mathematical formula). A common example is the provision in a pre-emption right on share transfers that the shares to be transferred should be offered to the other shareholders at a valuation. This chapter explores the principles of share valuation and the wording which should be inserted in share valuation provisions.

22.2   Share valuation is an art, not a science. The same set of facts given to a number of different valuers will almost be guaranteed to produce as many answers as there are valuers. The valuation process attempts to simulate the actions of buyers and sellers in the marketplace in determining what a third party would be willing to pay for something in particular circumstances. However, no one can know this for certain until a third party actually appears and makes an offer. Although a third party may, when formulating its offer, be guided by commonly accepted general principles of valuation, it may apply them in different ways, may have a different perception of worth from the valuer and will not always act rationally; sometimes a third-party offer seems completely inexplicable. Even a whole stock market can sometimes be based on irrational sentiment, as the dotcom craze of the late 1990s demonstrated.

22.3   At an annual general meeting of a public company in severe financial difficulty the chairman was asked by a shareholder why the company had not obtained a valuation of its surplus head office building. The chairman replied: 'What are we going to do with the valuation when we have got it? Hang it on the wall? I think we must wait until somebody comes along: that is the only valuation I know'. Shareholders agreeing to buy or sell shares at an independent valuation must always bear in mind the reality that an asset is worth only what someone is prepared to pay for it, and the independent valuation process is an attempt to determine this.

2 Valuing shares

22.4   The fundamental principle of share valuation is that value relates to future returns and the risks associated with realising those returns. Purchasers are interested solely in future returns not those realised in the past. Historic returns are relevant only to the extent that they reflect future expectations. This fundamental principle must always be borne in mind when considering the valuation of shares.

22.5   Share valuation is a vast subject; many textbooks have been written on it, which the reader desiring additional information should consult[1]. To discuss the subject in great detail here would be out of place, but the draftsperson of a provision requiring a share valuation does need to have some grasp of the basic principles.

22.6   The aim of a valuation is to arrive at the price at which the shares are to be transferred as at a specific date. Since there is more than one basis of valuation, it is important that the relevant exit provision clearly specifies the basis to be used.

22.7   The term 'value' used alone provides little guidance as to the basis of valuation. Generally the term is qualified by the addition of terms such as 'market', 'fair' or some other qualifier.

22.8   The most common term encountered is 'market value'. The term is defined in certain taxation statutes; however, it has very specific connotations in that context. For commercial purposes, the term is generally defined as 'the price which an asset might reasonably be expected to fetch in a sale on the open market, assuming both buyer and seller are equally willing and informed'.

22.9   Where the market for a particular shareholding is limited, or special factors may influence the value of a holding, such as the ability to convey control to a purchaser, 'fair value' as opposed to market value may be preferable, as explained in para 22.34 below.

1   See, for example, (McKinsey & Company Inc, 7th edn, Wiley, 2020), and Aswath Damodaran, *Valuation Approaches and Metrics* (2007).

22.10   The market value of a share in a company may not necessarily equate to the proportionate part of the market value of the entire company calculated by dividing that value by the number of shares in issue and multiplying that value per share by the number of shares to be sold. Firstly, there may be more than one class of share, with different rights, which will have different values per share, and secondly, the size of the shareholding is relevant. Assuming that there are no special rights conferred upon the minority, a controlling interest, ie an interest of more than 50% will generally be valued as the pro rata share of the value of the company as a whole. The existence of special minority rights will be expected to reduce the valuation in both cases, and the size, dispersion and influence of the other shareholders will also be relevant. If there are numerous small shareholders with no influence, a controlling interest will have more value than if there are fewer shareholders who can be expected to act in concert.

22.11   A minority interest will almost certainly be valued at less than the pro rata share of the value of the company as a whole, and, indeed, the whole basis of its valuation may be different. The extent of any discount will depend upon the actual rights of the minority holder, as set out in the articles of association and any shareholders' agreement, and the involvement and attitudes of the other shareholders.

22.12   There are many methods by which a value for a shareholding may be ascertained and the one selected will depend upon the circumstances surrounding the need for a valuation. The most common methods are:

● earnings;

● cashflow;

● dividend yield;

● net assets;

● cost based methods; and

● turnover.

Earnings

22.13   The earnings basis is most appropriate for valuing the entire issued share capital or a controlling interest where the business carried on by the company is a going concern. The amount of a company's earnings, ie its profit stream, is likely to be the determining factor in deciding what the purchaser of such an interest is prepared to pay. The dividend yield is not relevant, because it can be assumed that the new controller will be able to secure the payment to it of whatever level of dividends it likes, up to the whole amount of the distributable profits. Asset values are not usually relevant because, where the assets are fully employed in the business, their worth is included in the business of which they form a part, and where a company is profitable the market value of its share capital is often considerably greater than the book value of its net assets. A company is therefore not generally to be valued by aggregating the value of its earnings and its tangible assets – to do so would be double counting. Where, however, a company has substantial assets surplus to requirements, the earnings basis of valuation will not include anything for such assets, whereas a purchaser of the entire share capital would be able to secure the disposal of the assets and realise cash for them and it would then be appropriate to add the market value of such assets to the valuation, after deducting the tax which would result from their disposal. A similar argument can be made with respect to liabilities. If a company enjoys reduced or otherwise advantageous debt terms then additional value may arise resulting from the difference between the actual terms of the debt and current market rates.

22.14   The earnings basis of valuation requires the consideration of two variables, the expected level of maintainable earnings and the multiple at which to capitalise those earnings.

22.15   'Earnings' does not necessarily mean the current profits as shown in the accounts. Earnings should be the maintainable earnings or a level of earnings that are likely to arise in the future. It is important therefore to analyse historic earnings to identify trends. If the profits are increasing, a purchaser can be expected to pay more than would be justified if they show no growth. Conversely, if profits are falling, the purchaser will generally pay less. Some early stage companies although loss making may command substantial valuations, reflecting the expectation that profits will arise in the future from developments being undertaken currently or from the exploitation of intellectual property that is close to reaching commercialisation.

22.16   The multiple at which to capitalise maintainable earnings in order to arrive at the price to be paid should reflect the degree of risk that those earnings will or will not be realised and grow. In other words, it should reflect an investors' required rate of return for investing in the capital of the company. The quoted market reflects this in a number of ratios such as EV/EBITDA, EV/EBIT, and the P/E ratio.

22.17   The EV/EBITDA and EV/EBIT ratios are expressions of enterprise value as a function of EBITDA (earnings before interest, taxes, depreciation and amortisation) and EBIT (earnings before interest and taxes). Enterprise value reflects the value of the business of the company before any consideration of funding, or how the company is financed. It also does not reflect the value of surplus or redundant assets and liabilities. To arrive at the value of equity, net debt/net cash at market value is deducted/added.

22.18   The P/E ratio (price/earnings) reflects the value of the equity of the company expressed as a function of after tax earnings. It is an expression of the value of equity directly, ie no adjustment is needed for net cash/net debt.

22.19   The circumstances of the company and the industry in which it operates will determine which of these ratios is more appropriate to use. Therein lies the skill of the valuer.

22.20   A starting point for the determination of an appropriate multiple may be the P/E ratio for quoted companies with similar operations or operating in the same sector as the company being valued.

22.21   The P/E ratio is simply the price of the shares divided by the earnings per share. It produces the number of 'years purchase' of the earnings that the market has determined to be the value of the shares. So if the P/E ratio is ten, the purchaser of those shares is paying a price equal to ten years of present earnings. If the earnings stay the same, the purchaser will make a return of 10% per annum if all earnings are distributed. If the P/E ratio is 20, the return drops to 5%; if it is five it rises to 20%. The P/E ratio can be expressed in a number of ways. It can be based on the last available published accounts either annual or quarterly or trend earnings over a period, usually reflecting an economic cycle.

22.22   The use of quoted P/E ratios without detailed analysis of the company being valued and the quoted companies selected for comparison may produce a highly misleading result. It must be remembered that the earnings used as the denominator in the P/E ratio are after tax earnings. These earnings are after taking into account debt financing costs and non-cash items such as depreciation and amortisation. No two companies have the same financing structure. Adjustments may therefore need to be made to quoted company ratios, or alternatively multiples that eliminate the impact of funding costs and non-cash expenses such as EV/EBITDA or EV/EBIT should be considered.

22.23   Companies in the same sector may have very different P/E ratios; a company that is perceived as growing very quickly may have a very high ratio, and one that is not growing a low P/E ratio. The valuer will have to examine the future prospects of the company to be valued before deciding upon the appropriate P/E ratio – he cannot simply take an average based on quoted company multiples. Secondly, the valuer may consider it appropriate to discount the P/E value derived from quoted shares, especially where the company concerned is small or unquoted, in recognition of the fact that a company with slender resources, lack of diversity or poor liquidity in its shares would be likely to command a lower valuation than a listed company. Thirdly, however, the P/E ratio, so discounted, may undervalue the company in that, whilst a buyer of shares on the stock market is acquiring them purely for investment purposes and the stakes traded are all minority ones conferring no control over the underlying assets, a trade buyer can be expected to pay a premium for control. Such control premiums are often seen when a takeover bid is launched for a quoted company and the bidder pays substantially more than the market price of the company's shares prior to the bid in order to succeed. Fourthly, in view of short-term fluctuations in the share price, the P/E ratio may temporarily bear no relation to real values at all. This may be particularly true at the current time. Stock markets are influenced by events going far beyond the values of the underlying companies. When market confidence is high, shares may trade on P/E ratios which are sometimes beyond rational justification; when confidence is lost, the market may fall suddenly and P/E ratios drop to bargain basement levels. Although such market fluctuations are influenced by external events that a valuer should certainly take into account, markets tend to exaggerate both good and bad news and move disproportionately.

22.24   Subject to market forces, a trade buyer will tend to value a company by reference to the return on the capital invested which will be secured by control of it. Examination of the prices actually paid for companies in similar sectors is therefore likely to be a much more reliable guide than studying quoted P/E ratios based on prices of small parcels of shares, although the control premiums paid in public bids are a valuable guide where the company being valued is large. However, detailed knowledge or information regarding such transactions may not be readily available. The trade buyer's perception of the value of a company will be influenced by a number of factors including perceived synergies, market dynamics and the impact the acquisition will have on the market, including the impact on competitors and the rate of return on its current operations. Buyers will want the acquisition to be earnings accretive not dilutive. A premium may be paid if the market share or power of the purchaser will be significantly increased as a result of the acquisition or significant cost or revenue synergies can be realised. Corporate ambition may also play a part in determining price, as will the likely reaction of any institutional shareholders of a quoted buyer.

Cashflow

22.25   This method of valuation is appropriate where the buyer will be able to achieve control over the cashflows generated by the business. The likely future net cashflows are determined, and then each is discounted over the period between the purchase and their anticipated receipt by an appropriate amount to reflect the purchaser's required rate of return and any uncertainty over the availability of the cashflow, to arrive at the 'present value' of the cashflows, which is the price to be paid. Cash flows are usually divided into two elements. The first element is the discrete cash flows expected to be generated over a defined period, usually for five to ten years, or until the company reaches a steady state. The cash flows at the end of this discrete period do not stop. After this period the company is assumed under a going concern scenario to continue into the future in perpetuity and a terminal value is estimated using either a constant growth or an exit multiple based model. This method recognises that value relates to future expectations and it is the method which most closely follows the investment theory of returns. It is widely used to value a variety of businesses and it is particularly suitable where the future cashflows are highly predictable, or where the asset or venture being valued has a limited future life. It can also be applied in valuing businesses that are in financial difficulty or that are in the throes of being restructured. This method has many advantages over other methods, as it is most closely related to the principle that value relates to future expectations and the risks associated with those expectations not being realised. However, it can be difficult to apply in situations involving less sophisticated enterprises where the availability of forecast data may be limited.

Dividend yield

22.26   Dividend yield is an appropriate measure in valuing a minority holding where the shareholder does not have the ability to influence or control the strategic direction of the company or its dividend policy. The shareholder's only realistic expectation of a return lies in the stream of future dividends and the present value of any expected sale of all of the shares in the company. This only applies in situations where there is a consistent record of dividend payments. Where a private company is paying no or very low dividends, it may result in the conclusion that a minority shareholding is virtually worthless. However, this would be the wrong conclusion where the minority does have substantial minority protection and is able through its share rights or through provisions in the shareholders' agreement to secure a return. In such a case, the rights of the shareholder as to income and capital will be the determining factor. Where the minority holder has substantial influence in relation to the affairs of the company through special provisions in the articles or shareholders' agreement, the dividend yield basis of valuation will not be appropriate and the shares would be more likely to be valued as the appropriate proportion of the market value of the whole company, but appropriately discounted to reflect the differences between the rights attaching to a control stake and the rights attaching to the minority stake; a valuation by reference to a quoted P/E ratio will already reflect the discount.

Net assets

22.27   A net assets basis may be appropriate for asset holding companies, be they property holding companies or cash shells, and for trading companies that are unprofitable and have no expectation of becoming profitable. A property holding company or one whose only income is derived from investments is likely to be valued on a net assets basis. Even here the value of the assets may be a function of earnings; if a property is leased out, its value is likely to be determined as a function of its annual rental income; but an unoccupied property will be valued by reference to its value on the market with vacant possession. Intellectual property which has been fully licensed is likely to be valued on the basis of the stream of royalties relating to the property discounted to present value.

22.28   Where the company is not only unprofitable but not viable as a going concern a break up basis of valuation is likely to be appropriate. This assumes that the assets will be sold in a forced sale, or in an orderly liquidation and that all liabilities will be discharged. The resulting valuation is generally significantly lower than that derived applying other valuation methodologies. It is unlikely that this basis of valuation will be appropriate in relation to share sale provisions in the articles or a shareholders' agreement, since once matters have reached this stage liquidation is more likely.

22.29   Where a company is insolvent, its shares are generally considered to be worthless, but this is an oversimplification, since an insolvent company may still have an excellent future if it can receive an injection of fresh capital from a purchaser. The value of an insolvent company can pose particular difficulties for the valuer because it is difficult to presuppose that a buyer willing to put in the necessary funds is evident or will emerge.

22.30   The net assets basis requires the deduction of all known liabilities of the company, usually determined by reference to the latest available balance sheet. However, whether the taxation liability which would arise if the company sold all its assets should be deducted is often contentious. In the case of a company whose profits are derived from asset sales, such as a property development company, a deduction is appropriate, but in the case of a trading company which would be unlikely to sell its fixed assets in the short term, either no deduction or one discounted to reflect the likelihood of a sale would be appropriate.

Cost-based methods

22.31   Where a purchaser is making the acquisition to move into a new business or to expand an existing business, it may be prepared to pay an amount not exceeding the start up or expansion costs which it would incur if it started from scratch rather than acquiring the business being valued. This may apply even if the business to be acquired is not yet cash generative, on the basis that it might take some time for the purchaser to build up a similar business from scratch.

Turnover

22.32   A valuation based on the turnover of the company to be acquired may be appropriate where a company is in its early stages and has built up an appreciable business but is not yet profitable, or has not yet reached maximum profitability, perhaps because it has not yet achieved the necessary economy of scale or fully amortised its development costs. A buyer in the same business which has achieved economy of scale (or can achieve it by means of the purchase), or any buyer which will not have to fund any further development costs may be prepared to pay a price based on the profits which it might expect to make from the turnover of the company to be acquired. The buyer's required rate of return on that profit will then determine the price.

22.33   The attraction of turnover multiples lies in three areas. Unlike earnings or net assets that can be negative and therefore not meaningful as a valuation base, turnover multiples can be applied even to troubled or fledgling firms. Secondly, unlike earnings and net assets, which can be heavily dependent on accounting judgments and conventions with respect to items such as depreciation and amortisation, research and development and inventory, revenue may be more difficult to manipulate. Lastly, turnover multiples are more stable than earnings multiples and can provide a more realisable valuation base, turnover being less sensitive to economic change than earnings. Once again, however, finding appropriate comparables from which to draw revenue multiple data may be very difficult.

Fair value

22.34   A valuation at market value may not necessarily produce a fair result, particularly for minority shareholders whose shares are likely to be valued at far below the percentage of the total market value of the company which equates to their percentage shareholdings. Opting for fair value instead may produce a more acceptable result, at least for large- and medium-sized percentage holdings.

22.35   There is no generally respected definition of fair value. As a concept it embodies the notion of fairness and equity to both buyer and seller that market value does not provide.

22.36   Instead of trying to determine the price which a theoretical external purchaser would be willing to pay for the shares, a valuer asked to determine a fair value can give effect to the reality that the market for the shares is in practice restricted to the existing shareholders. The concept of 'fair value' will try to do justice as between them, recognising that the seller has not been able to canvass the market to find the highest price and the buyer can only buy the shares from the seller. Fair value should also recognise the realistic expectations of the selling shareholder. In the case of a small uninfluential holding which does not confer control on the purchaser or change the relative balance of power between the shareholders, the realistic expectation of return is by way of a dividend. Therefore a valuer may look to a dividend yield valuation approach as best reflecting fair value, which will probably not differ very much from the market value. However, where there are substantial non-controlling stakes, as in many joint ventures, fair value could result in the stake being worth appreciably more, especially where the stake, when combined with another, would result in the buyer achieving control. In this situation, the buyer might be willing to pay a very substantial premium for the stake, but the valuer will, in trying to be fair to both parties, probably allocate the premium between them to reflect what the seller is giving up and what the buyer is receiving. This might still result in the seller receiving a higher sum than would result if its shares were valued pro rata to the total market value of the company.

Example:

A, B and C are shareholders in a company. Their holdings are, A: 40%, B: 40% and C: 20%. C serves a transfer notice. The articles provide for a fair valuation of C's shares. In case of competition, C's shares will be allocated pro rata.

The valuer decides that the market value of the entire share capital is £1m. The valuer correctly perceives that both A and B will be able to increase their stakes to 50% if they each buy half of C's shares.

The valuer decides that on a market value basis the value of the various stakes is as follows:

50% £450,000

40% £260,000

20% £85,000

If A buys half of C's shares, the value of A's holding rises from £260,000 to £450,000, an increase of £190,000. The position for B is the same, so that the total value of C's shares to A and B is £380,000, as against their value to C of £85,000, or their value as a pro rata proportion of the total value of the company, which is £200,000. The value created is £295,000, being the difference between the value of the stake to C and its value to A and B. The valuer must now apportion the value created between A, B and C. He might decide for example to give one-half to C and one-half to A and B.

Therefore C receives £85,000 plus one-half of £295,000, ie £232,500 which represents slightly more than the pro rata value of £200,000. Can this be considered fair? It all depends on the circumstances. A and B should both be satisfied, the respective value of their holdings has increased from £260,000 to £450,000, a total of £190,000 at a cost to each of £116,250 (50% of £232,500). This represents an instant return of 63.4%. C is undoubtedly happy, having received a premium of £32,500 (16.25%) over the pro-rata value of a 20% holding. Despite the apparent win-win situation portrayed above, the result may not necessarily be considered fair by all valuers.

Suppose the figures in this example were rather different, and A has 50%, B has 40% and C has 10%. Here the valuer will see that by buying its pro rata proportion of C's stake, A can obtain control but B can only increase its holding to 44.4%. This presents him with a tricky problem, because if he values the shares so as to award a control premium, this price may be attractive for A but a bad deal for B, who will not significantly increase the value of its stake. Nevertheless, B has the option of not seeking to acquire the shares, and A could then, if it wished, acquire the whole of C's stake, so the valuer might well decide to reflect the control premium in his valuation.

The valuer decides that the value of the stake to C is only £33,000 against its pro rata value of £100,000, but its value to A is £150,000. The value added is thus £117,000. If the valuer splits the added value in half, this would give a value for C's stake of £91,500, a little below its pro rata value. This would seem fair in view of the advantages to A of acquiring control. B may also feel that this is a reasonable price.

22.37   In the example, the valuation on a 'fair value' basis has equated roughly to the pro rata proportion of the market value of the entire company, but this is by no means always the case. Firstly, where the stake to be valued is small, and when being offered for sale will not materially increase the influence or voting power available to the purchaser, the starting point may not necessarily be the market value of the entire company, but a 'dividend yield' basis of valuation. Secondly, even where the starting point is the market value of the entire company, the valuer may well make certain adjustments. For example, if the majority shareholder has taken out excessive directors' remuneration, it may be fair to add the excessive element back in arriving at the value of a minority stake; such an adjustment would not usually be made in the case of a market valuation, since the minority holder might well not be able to do anything about rectifying the unfairness. Where the minority holder acquired its stake at a discount reflecting its minority status, it would not be fair to allow that shareholder to force the others to pay a price for its shares which contained a proportion of a control premium. However, where the company is a 'quasi-partnership' in which all the shareholders have an equal right to participate in the management, a pro rata proportion of the entire market value may well be appropriate.

22.38   Fair value allows very considerable discretion to the valuer. In the above example, not all valuers would have allocated the premium in the same way, so that although it may produce higher valuations for minority shareholders there is an element of uncertainty, which is even greater than for market value. Nevertheless, it may appeal to shareholders in a family company, and may be acceptable to corporate joint venturers.

Market value on pro rata basis

22.39   Most institutional and many other shareholders will not be satisfied with either market value or fair value, especially if they are minority shareholders. They will wish to realise a proportion of the total market value of the company which is the same proportion of their shareholding, especially if they have paid the same price per share for their stakes, irrespective of the relative sizes of their holdings. To achieve this they will need to specify that the valuer must first determine the market value of the whole company and then value the shares at the proportion of that value which is the same proportion that those shares represent of the entire capital. To simply provide that the shares are to be valued 'without any deduction to reflect any minority interests' will not necessarily produce this result. To provide that the valuer must assume that the entire issued share capital is being sold is nearer the mark, but there seems no substitute for specifying clearly that a pro rata value is required. A majority shareholder will normally prefer shares to be valued on a 'market value' basis without further qualification, or may be happy with fair value. Fair value is generally more appropriate to companies without institutional involvement, particularly family companies.

3 The drafting of valuation clauses

22.40   There are really two conclusions to be drawn from the above analysis. Firstly, the draftsperson should be clear on the basis of valuation to be used and should express the choice in unambiguous language the valuer can understand. Secondly, specifying the method of valuation in greater detail should be avoided, since it will only hamper the valuer in his determination.

22.41   Expressions such as 'full value', 'open market value', 'fair market value' or 'arm's-length value' or conditions such as 'between a willing buyer and a willing seller' should be avoided as they do not provide any additional guidance to the valuer and only serve to cause unnecessary confusion.

22.42   Except in very special cases, specific directions concerning the basis to be applied and the multiples to be used are best avoided. For example, a clause directing the valuer to apply a specific P/E or EV/EBITDA ratio will inevitably result in an inappropriate valuation. As previously discussed value changes with time and what may seem a reasonable valuation ratio to apply when an agreement is drafted may be totally unreasonable when the actual valuation is required. A formula approach does not recognise this and very careful consideration needs to be given before this type of direction is written into the valuation clause.

22.43 A typical valuation clause will appoint the auditors to act as the valuers. The auditors may be highly suitable in that they have very detailed knowledge of the company gained through the audit of its accounts, but they may be constrained by a perceived conflict of interest from taking the appointment. Provision for an alternative can be made by allowing the parties or the directors to appoint such expert as they may in their absolute discretion select. If the parties cannot agree, it can be provided that the President for the time being of the Institute of Chartered Accountants in England and Wales or some other impartial and competent body will appoint the valuer.

22.44 The clause will invariably provide that the valuer shall act as an expert and not as an arbitrator, and that his decision shall be final and binding, except in the case of manifest error. Even in the absence of this wording, a determination can be challenged on the grounds of manifest error. For guidance on what constitutes a 'manifest error' see, for example, *Regent Holdings Inc v Alliance*[2]. Valuing the wrong property, or making a fundamental error of fact, would be likely to be a manifest error. Apart from manifest error, 'final and binding' wording is generally effective to exclude the courts from inquiring into the valuation. It was held in *Nikko Hotels (UK) Ltd v MEPC*[3] that, unless it can be shown that the expert has not performed his task, his decision is binding and conclusive, so that if he answers the right questions in the wrong way the decision is still binding. However, in *Mercury v Director General of Telecommunications*[4], Lord Slynn commented that where an expert has made a determination on the basis of an incorrect interpretation of the contract, his decision can be reviewed. This has thrown the law into a state of some confusion, since the process of valuation almost inevitably requires the expert to interpret the contract. However, it is suggested that the two lines of cases that have followed these decisions[5] are not irreconcilable; if the expert fails to interpret the contract correctly he has answered the wrong question rather than answering the right question in the wrong way. If the parties wish to exclude the courts from interpreting the contract, they should word it so as to expressly include matters of interpretation within the terms of reference of the expert.

---

2   23 July 2000. Lawtel C7 200 133, [1999] All ER (D) 860.
3   [1991] 28 EG 86.
4   [1996] 1 WLR 48.
5   See eg *Veba Oil Supply v Petrotrade* [2001] EWCA Civ 1832; *Bouygues UK Ltd v Dahl Jensen UK Ltd* [2001] 1 All ER (Comm) 1041 (following *Nikko*) and *National Grid Company v M25 Group Ltd* (following *Mercury*).

22.45   The valuer will not generally provide any reasons for his valuation, so that it will be difficult to challenge. The reason for this is simple. The parties to most agreements resort to a valuation only when they have not been able to settle the issue of valuation among themselves. Therefore the role of the valuer is to bring finality and produce a final and binding figure, not to precipitate further debate and discussion. Providing reasons or engaging in discussions with either party, however well-intentioned, is to be avoided.

22.46   The clause should make it clear who pays the expert's fees and expenses – in the case of a pre-emption article, practice differs as to whether the company or the transferee should pay, but it is more common for the company to do so. Where the expert is brought in to rule on a dispute between the parties as to the correct valuation under a provision outside the articles, he might be given the ability to decide which of the parties should pay or whether they should both contribute. He will then have the ability to load the fees onto the party who in his view has been the most unreasonable, but this may cause the impartiality of the expert to be questioned and is a situation to be generally avoided.

22.47   In the case of a pre-emption article, a requirement for valuation normally arises each time a transfer is presented for registration, but where a fairly large number of transfers is expected, such as where there is a large number of employee shareholders, there is sometimes a provision that the fair value shall be certified annually and will apply for all transfers presented during the following year. This has the merit that intending transferors know in advance what the transfer price will be and may also save expense. It may cause difficulties if the financial position of the company deteriorates significantly during the year.

22.48   Where there is more than one class of shares it can generally be left to the valuer to decide the values to be attached to each class, but where proportionate market value is required (itself an artificial concept) a direction may be given as to how the value is to be apportioned between the classes. Where all classes are either ordinary shares or immediately convertible into ordinary shares, one solution is to treat the convertible shares as already converted, and to apportion the value as if all the shares were ordinary shares. Another solution might be to apportion the value between the classes on the basis that only those conversion rights which have actually been exercised are treated as exercised and as if the total value of the company represented the proceeds of a winding up, so that the value would first go to those shares ranking in priority on a liquidation. These two concepts are somewhat in conflict; where the company is thriving it may be reasonable to assume conversion, but where the financial position of the company is such that a shareholder would be likely to receive more if he did not convert, it would not be reasonable to do so. One is driven to the conclusion that this aspect is generally best left to the valuer. Where the different classes are all non-convertible, the liquidation apportionment may be acceptable.

22.49   Finally it should be noted that a variant of the foregoing is to provide that the parties to a sale in a joint venture company effectively decide the price themselves. Each party has to set out the price at which it wishes to buy or sell (as the case may be) the shares in question. The auditors (or some other third party) is then instructed to choose which of the two prices most closely represents the fair value of the shares being sold and that price then becomes binding. The 'advantage' of such an approach is that the parties have a significant part to play in the determination of value and each party is more likely to set a 'realistic' estimate of fair value lest it is rejected in favour of the counterparty's price. A separate issue is valuation of shares and assets by HMRC for tax purposes, in relation to which see https://www.gov.uk/government/collections/shares-and-assets-valuation-for-tax-purposes#4.

Chapter 23

Dispute resolution

Summary

This chapter discusses in brief terms the different methods of dispute resolution which the parties might adopt in the context of the joint venture or shareholders' agreement, and the issues which parties should consider in choosing dispute resolution procedures. The methods discussed include litigation, arbitration, expert determination and alternative dispute resolution ('ADR'). The chapter discusses the advantages and disadvantages of each, and gives guidance on the appropriate provisions for insertion into the joint venture or shareholders' agreement to make the chosen process effective. This chapter is international.

1 Introduction

23.1   Parties would not enter transactions if they did not expect them to succeed. As they do not foresee disputes, dispute resolution clauses can be treated as an afterthought when agreements are negotiated. They should not be. When a disagreement arises, a process which is ill suited to resolving that particular argument can be slow, impractical, costly, embarrassing, and can make a pragmatic, commercial solution to the dispute in question harder rather than easier to achieve.

23.2   In any transaction, therefore, parties and their advisers should think carefully about the disputes which might occur in the context of that transaction. They can do two things:

- *Reduce the possibility that disputes will occur.* Clear, careful understanding of the nature and extent of the parties' respective rights and obligations in all of the circumstances contemplated by the agreement enables tighter drafting and minimises the scope for later disagreement. Considering the different situations which might occur, and recording agreement as to what should happen in those scenarios, closes off what would otherwise be room for argument. In other words, the most effective dispute resolution mechanism is often pre-emptive.

- *Identify the best routes for resolving disputes that cannot be avoided.* The possibility of disputes can never be eliminated completely. However, the range of potential disputes differs from one transaction to the next, and can be diverse even in a single transaction. The text below sets out considerations which will assist in pre-selecting the appropriate mechanism, or mechanisms, for a transaction.

2   Considerations

23.3   Begin by considering *what types of dispute might arise*. There are three broad types to consider:

- *Legal disputes*: over the parties' obligations to, and rights against, each other and the business; the interpretation of the agreement between them; the extent of any rights and obligations which exist independently of their written agreement; and the consequences of an alleged breach of their rights and obligations.

- *Technical disputes*: for example, over the quantification of amounts payable into or out of the business, or between the parties; whether contractual tests or criteria have been satisfied. Chapter 13, on deadlock, has already considered various means of settling disagreements internally.

- *Strategic or business disputes*: for instance, concerning the balance of power between the parties, and their say in strategic decisions; the extent of the parties' day-to-day role, and their involvement in key areas of the business; or how the parties are responsible for the overall direction of the business, and whose will prevails in what circumstances.

23.4   Next, consider the *circumstances in which such disputes might arise*. Again, there are three broad categories:

- *Ongoing disputes*: in which the parties are (or ought to be) able to carry on in business together, provided that a specific disagreement (which may be small, or substantial) can be resolved clearly and cleanly.

- *Break-up disputes*: where the disagreement means that the parties cannot continue to run the business together – though the business may still be viable, and the parties may continue doing other business with each other, for instance on different projects, or as customers.

- *Post-termination disputes*: where the transaction has come to an end (amicably or acrimoniously), but the parties may still owe obligations to each other, for instance where there is a dispute over the mechanics for winding up the venture and dealing with its assets and liabilities, or under non-compete clauses.

23.5   The *legal framework of the transaction* is an important element in identifying potential disputes:

- Most agreements will include a clause selecting the governing law of the contract. This is aimed at controlling the interpretation of the document, the nature of the parties' rights and obligations under the contract, and the remedies which they will have for any breach.

- In purely domestic transactions (where the parties, the company and its operations are all located in one country, and the courts of that country are also selected to determine any dispute), it may be easiest to choose the law of that country to govern the transaction.

- However, it is not uncommon to choose one of the leading systems of national law, irrespective of whether the transaction has any connection with that country. By bringing the parties under an established and reliable legal framework, with a well-developed system of laws suitable to commercial transactions, this can give the parties the greatest possible clarity as to their rights and obligations. It is particularly prudent to take this approach if the transaction has cross-border elements, or the local law of the business is not sufficiently adaptable to the complexities of a joint venture or shareholders' agreement.

- Although an 'entire agreement' clause is generally included as standard, parties may nonetheless be subject to non-contractual obligations. For instance, tortious claims may arise out of their statements or conduct towards each other. Equitable obligations may result from the nature of their relationship with each other: for instance, some joint ventures (large as well as small) amount to 'quasi-partnerships', with the parties obliged to operate the business for their mutual benefit and to preserve the trust and confidence between themselves. Among EU member states other than Denmark, the Rome II Convention now allows contractual parties also to select a national law of their choice to govern non-contractual obligations connected with that contract.

- To the extent that the parties do not select a governing law, rules of general law (including the post-Brexit position regarding choice of law) will operate to determine the law applicable in respect of claims between them. This may be a different law in respect of different disputes. For that reason, it is generally advisable to select expressly a single governing law.

- Although choice of law clauses are respected in most jurisdictions, national courts will not uphold the chosen law insofar as doing so would conflict with public policy or with local 'mandatory rules'. Local legal advice should therefore be taken in all relevant jurisdictions.

- The parties may also be subject to statutory claims. For instance, assuming the business is operated through a company, the law of incorporation will govern all matters concerning the constitution and powers of the company. National company law may therefore provide for claims, such as misfeasance on the part of directors or unfair prejudice on the part of shareholders, in addition to the parties' contractual and tortious obligations.

3   Options

23.6   With an eye to the circumstances in which the parties may fall into dispute, and the nature of those potential disputes, as set out above, consider then the range of processes available for resolving disputes. The principal options are described below.

Mediation

23.7   A non-binding process where an independent third party, usually either a senior lawyer or an expert in the relevant commercial field, and often an experienced specialist mediator, meets with the parties, both together and individually. The mediator discusses with the parties, in private, their respective positions and room for manoeuvre. The mediator's goal is to facilitate an amicable resolution between the parties, and it is worth noting that even where a mediation itself is unsuccessful, it very often moves the parties sufficiently close to settlement that an agreement is reached privately thereafter. Mediators will often look to explore 'creative' solutions, of a sort which parties can agree between themselves, but a court cannot order, and which can help preserve the commercial relationship between the parties.

23.8   In England, mediation is strongly encouraged by the courts. Although an alternative dispute resolution clause is an 'agreement to agree', and so unenforceable in English law, a judge can stay proceedings to allow time for mediation to take place. Furthermore, although a mediation itself is private and what is said there cannot be referred to in proceedings, a party which unreasonably refuses to mediate at all can find itself penalised in terms of its liability for the other side's costs, or its ability to recover its own costs.

23.9   The timing of a mediation can be important. It should not necessarily be held as soon as a dispute arises. It may be more effective when proceedings have commenced, and each party has set out its case (and had its mind concentrated by its lawyers' fees).

Early neutral evaluation

23.10   Like mediation, early neutral evaluation ('ENE') is a non-binding form of alternative dispute resolution ('ADR'). Here, a third party does not seek to probe the parties and push them towards settlement, but reviews the dispute between them and offers them a confidential view as to the merits of their legal position. This can assist the parties in assessing the strengths and weaknesses of their own and each other's positions, and considering what settlement terms might be preferable to the costs and risks of a full-blown dispute.

Expert determination

23.11   Here, an expert in a relevant field makes a binding decision on a specific point referred to them, such as the quantification of amounts or values which are relevant in determining the parties' obligations under their agreement, but which cannot be agreed between them.

Arbitration

23.12   Essentially a private (and privately funded) substitute for the courts, arbitration provides a similar process to litigation. An arbitrator, or panel of three arbitrators, usually lawyers though sometimes experts in a relevant field, determine all the issues (legal or factual) between the parties, in accordance with the relevant laws, and on the same basis as a court would do, though with a somewhat different procedure. The process is confidential, unlike court proceedings in most countries, but the tribunal's award is binding just as a judgment would be (indeed, often more so, since it allows little or no scope for appeal), and is enforceable through the courts. In most major arbitration venues, an arbitral award cannot be challenged on the merits, but only on limited procedural and jurisdictional grounds. In England, although the Arbitration Act 1996 provides for an appeal on a point of law in narrowly defined circumstances, that right may be excluded in the agreement itself.

Litigation

23.13   If the parties cannot resolve a dispute between themselves, and their contract makes no provision for it to be resolved by other means, they will need to resort to the courts. However, litigation tends to be expensive, and often public. Furthermore, as noted below, there may be difficulty in enforcing judgments outside the jurisdiction in which they are given.

4   Making choices

23.14   When selecting dispute resolution mechanisms, take the following points into account.

Jurisdictions

23.15   There are obvious practical advantages in agreeing to submit to the courts of a particular jurisdiction. Parties can pick a court system which they trust. They can reduce, or eliminate, the possibility of having to litigate the same dispute at the same time in different forums, and with it the risk of conflicting judgments.

23.16   Any agreement under which litigation is possible should therefore contain a jurisdiction clause, identifying the courts in which that litigation may take place. Such a clause may be:

- exclusive;

- non-exclusive; or

- exclusive for one party but not the others.

23.17   Under an exclusive clause, proceedings must be brought in the courts of the chosen jurisdiction. If a party seeks to bring proceedings anywhere else, the courts in question (assuming they uphold the choice of jurisdiction) will decline to hear those proceedings. This is generally the appropriate form of clause in a joint venture or shareholders' agreement.

23.18   Under a non-exclusive clause, the parties have the option of proceeding in the nominated jurisdiction, but may proceed in another if its courts will accept jurisdiction. For this reason, non-exclusive jurisdiction clauses are usually not appropriate in the context of shareholders' agreements. Under the last type of clause, one party must proceed in the nominated jurisdiction but the other has the option to proceed elsewhere. This one-sided arrangement is difficult to negotiate and is unlikely to be seen in a shareholders' agreement.

23.19   England is one of the main international centres for dispute resolution. Its courts are internationally respected. The United Kingdom's position since 1 January 2021, due to the ending of the post-Brexit transitional period, has become a little more complicated and in early 2021 the EU proposed that the UK's application to join the Lugano Convention not be approved, but this is likely to be resolved and the UK remains a party to bilateral agreements for the recognition of judgments within most Commonwealth jurisdictions. In practical terms, this has meant at least until 31 December 2020 (when the post-Brexit transitional period ended) UK judgments can generally be enforced without difficulty in the courts of most European Union countries. The same applies to Commonwealth countries. The courts of many other countries will also, in practice, often enforce UK judgments. If a foreign judgment is to be enforced in England and the judgment is entitled to recognition, the English courts have effective enforcement procedures. On 1 January 2021 the UK joined the Hague Convention in its own right.

23.20   Ensure that the choice of jurisdiction will be upheld. A problem which often arises, even within Europe, for English shareholders is that foreign systems of law may be less generous than English law in treating a set of standard terms and conditions (which may include a jurisdiction agreement) as having been incorporated into a contract. States which are not parties to the Brussels Regulation or Lugano Convention, and one state which is – Luxembourg – may require that a jurisdiction agreement to which one of their nationals is a party should be the subject of additional formalities. In the USA, a jurisdiction clause may be impeached on the grounds of 'fraud or overreaching'. Local legal advice should, where appropriate, be taken on these points. In 2020 the EU opposed the UK joining the Lugano Convention. It is best to take detailed legal advice on the post-Brexit choice of jurisdiction legal issue.

23.21   Even if the English courts do not have jurisdiction, they do have power to grant interim relief, including, for instance, freezing injunctions in aid of foreign court proceedings under the Civil Jurisdiction and Judgments Act 1982, s 25.

23.22   The country or countries chosen, though, should be appropriate to the parties and the law under dispute. The most obvious choice of jurisdiction is the country in which the joint venture company is incorporated. If the agreement designates the courts of one country and the governing law of another, the courts in question will need to receive evidence as to the content of the law which they are asked to apply. This complicates proceedings, and is inherently less reliable than asking a court to apply its own system of law. However, the difficulties are markedly less substantial where the two systems are similar, for instance between England and other common law jurisdictions.

Enforceability

23.23   With cross-border litigation, there is the risk that a claimant will succeed in obtaining judgment in one country, but then find that it that will not be enforced by the courts of other countries where the defendant has assets. Consider, then, where the parties have assets, and whether the courts of those countries will enforce judgments given by courts in the chosen jurisdictions.

23.24   Various bilateral and multilateral conventions facilitate the enforcement of judgments given in one country through the courts of other countries, particularly across the EU and the Commonwealth. None of these arrangements is as comprehensive as the 1958 New York Convention for the enforcement of arbitration awards.

23.25   Arbitral awards may need to be given effect by a court before they can be enforced; they will never bind third parties. However, under the New York Convention (http://www.newyorkconvention.org/), arbitral awards are enforceable in the courts of all the countries which have adopted the Convention: now numbering 168 (in 2021). Moreover, local courts often have the power to make their own orders in aid of arbitration, in their own or other jurisdictions: for instance, courts in the UK have such powers under the Arbitration Act 1996. So for US/UK agreements, including the NY Convention in the disputes clause can be wise to ensure enforcement in both jurisdictions.

23.26   Although expert determination is a binding process, and courts should generally enforce an expert's decision, the law in this regard is less settled than in respect of arbitration, where there is minimal scope to challenge an arbitrator's award. Furthermore, there is no equivalent of the New York Convention, and hence no system by which expert determinations obtained in one jurisdiction can easily be enforced in another.

Expertise

23.27   Some courts are more experienced in dealing with substantial commercial disputes, and more likely to approach such disputes from a practical, commercial perspective. Alternatively, an arbitration clause can make provision for the tribunal to include arbitrators from a commercial or technical background as well as, or instead of, lawyers. This can give the parties the technical benefits of an expert determination, but coupled with the procedural robustness and enforceability of an arbitration.

23.28   Furthermore, in an international dispute, where a three-person arbitral tribunal is chosen, any possibility of national bias can be minimised by the appointment of a chairman whose nationality is different from that of any of the parties.

Accessibility and efficiency

23.29   Mediation and other forms of ADR are relatively cheap, although they tend to lead to compromise solutions in which both sides give something. Expert determination can be quick and inexpensive, but its scope is necessarily narrow and its outcome inflexible. Litigation and arbitration can be costly; the costs of the latter include the fees of the arbitrators themselves, who are often eminent individuals, and the administrative costs of the process, in addition to legal fees.

23.30   Both litigation and arbitration can be slow and time consuming processes, to a greater or lesser degree depending on the jurisdiction chosen for litigation, or the procedure chosen for arbitration. With litigation, proceedings are easier to commence, and pursue, in some countries than in others. Some judicial systems are a great deal slower than others.

23.31   In arbitration, the procedure is less formal and can be varied to suit the parties – they may, for example, choose the language of the arbitration. By choosing the 'seat' of the arbitration, they select the national procedural law which will apply. The 'seat', the physical venue of the hearing, and the language of the arbitration may all be different, enabling greater flexibility in the process.

23.32   Arbitration can also raise procedural difficulties, however. There is usually no procedure for consolidating a dispute covered by an arbitration clause with a dispute not so covered or dealing with multi-party issues. Furthermore, there are considerable opportunities for delay, especially when a three-person arbitral tribunal is to be appointed. There may be arguments about the composition of the tribunal and its terms of reference. Getting the arbitrators together in one place may be a problem, and a disaffected arbitrator may stall the proceedings by refusing to co-operate.

23.33   Expert determination procedure is also flexible and informal: generally, the expert chooses the procedure, tailored to the particular dispute and agreed with the parties. There are usually no hearings, nor any formal presentation of evidence. The expert will present his findings in the form of a short determination of the dispute, usually without giving any reasons for it. He can only be sued if he can be proved to have been negligent, but he will invariably exclude such liability in his terms of reference. The absence of reasons in the determination usually makes it very difficult to challenge it in the courts.

23.34   However, when a procedural point (on disclosure of documents, for example) arises in the course of an expert determination, it may (if the expert's terms of reference are silent on the point) have to be resolved by the court, rather than by the expert.

Publicity

23.35   In common law jurisdictions, civil proceedings are generally public. In some civil law jurisdictions, that is not the case. Arbitration proceedings are private and confidential. So too are expert determinations, though that confidentiality may be lost if litigation ensues. Consider the likely business risks of bad publicity in choosing between processes.

5   Contractual provisions and service providers

23.36   Where a process other than litigation is chosen, it should be *clearly defined* in the agreement. In particular, it may be appropriate to specify an appropriate independent institution to oversee the procedure.

Arbitration

23.37   The parties may organise the arbitration themselves under an ad hoc arbitration clause, but it is more usual, in agreements where a dispute is likely to involve considerable sums of money, to provide for arbitration under the auspices of one of the major institutions, which include:

● the International Chamber of Commerce ('ICC');

● the London Court of International Arbitration ('LCIA');

● the International Centre for Dispute Resolution ('ICDR'), a branch of the American Arbitration Association;

● the China International and Economic and Trade Arbitration Commission ('CIETAC');

● the World Intellectual Property Organisation ('WIPO').

Contact details for these institutions are set out in Table 4 at the end of this chapter.

23.38   The advantages of institutional arbitration are that the providers will generally:

● support the arbitration by dealing with administrative matters;

● provide rules for the conduct of the arbitration which cover the most likely difficulties; and

● advise on the appointment of the arbitrators and nominate suitable people.

23.39   If institutional arbitration is selected, the agreement should contain the model arbitration clause of the selected institution (available from the relevant institution). In addition, the clause should specify the seat of the arbitration and the number of arbitrators. It may also be helpful to specify that the venue of the arbitration may be different from its seat (see para 23.31 above); to specify the language of the proceedings and to stipulate that the arbitrators must have certain qualifications. The seat should be in a state which is a signatory to the New York Convention, so that the award may be enforced abroad. Additionally, there should be no local laws which may adversely affect the conduct of the arbitration by preventing the recovery of costs or interest, or providing that any types of commercial dispute may not be referred to arbitration. If a particular location is to be designated as the venue for the arbitration, it should be somewhere which is likely to be convenient for the parties and for witnesses, and where adequate administrative resources will be available.

23.40   A panel of three arbitrators is usually preferable for a large international dispute. Generally, each party will appoint one arbitrator and the selected appointees will appoint the chairman or umpire. For smaller disputes, a single arbitrator is often preferable. It is also advisable to choose experienced arbitrators, since an inexperienced tribunal may not be able to deal effectively with delaying tactics.

23.41   Ad hoc arbitration can be less expensive than institutional arbitration and more suitable for smaller disputes, but it has the disadvantage that the arbitrators are not backed up by the resources of a major institution. Ad hoc arbitrations are also more likely to give rise to challenges.

23.42   Although a very simple arbitration clause may be effective for an ad hoc arbitration, it is best to draft such a clause carefully, using, in international transactions, the UNCITRAL Arbitration Rules with appropriate modifications. The clause should specify the venue and the mode of appointment of the arbitral tribunal.

Expert determination

23.43   The drafting of an expert determination clause in relation to the valuation of shares is discussed in Chapter 22, and the same principles should be followed in drafting a clause for any other type of expert determination. The qualifications to be held by the expert (eg accountant) should be specified, and it is important that the parties agree to provide the expert with all the information which he reasonably considers necessary to make his determination. The general rule that an expert's decision cannot be challenged in the courts is also discussed in Chapter 22 (para 22.44).

23.44   The expert will normally be appointed by the parties, but if they cannot agree it is usual for the expert determination clause to specify that he shall be appointed (if the expert is to be appointed within England) at the instance of any party by the president for the time being of the appropriate professional body. For an accountant the professional body will usually be the Institute of Chartered Accountants in England and Wales; for a valuer of real property, plant or other physical assets (but not shares) it will usually be the Royal Institution of Chartered Surveyors. For a solicitor it will usually be The Law Society of England and Wales.

23.45   As noted above, there is (by contrast with arbitration) no established international framework for the enforcement of experts' decisions. Parties who wish to have the speed and convenience of an expert determination, but also to ensure cross-border enforceability, should consider a tailored clause which brings an expert determination process within the framework of arbitration law (in England, the Arbitration Act 1996). This will require some, though by no means necessarily dramatic, trade off in terms of procedural informality.

Alternative dispute resolution

23.46   Unlike any of the methods of dispute resolution discussed above, alternative dispute resolution ('ADR') does not necessarily lead to a binding resolution of the dispute. The function of ADR is usually to assist the parties to reach a negotiated settlement. If they do so, the settlement agreement will bind them, but if they do not, the dispute may need to be resolved by another method.

23.47   Leading providers of ADR services in the United Kingdom include:

● the Centre for Dispute Resolution ('CEDR');

● the International Chamber of Commerce ('ICC'); and

● the London Court of International Arbitration ('LCIA').

Contact details are set out in Table 5 at the end of this chapter.

23.48   In the English Commercial Court, one of the judges may offer his services as an 'early neutral evaluator' of the dispute.

23.49   A clause may be included in a joint venture or shareholders' agreement requiring an ADR procedure to be followed before court or arbitration procedures are commenced. Such a clause may encourage the parties to settle. On the other hand, it may merely delay proceedings which are inevitable. For this reason, ADR clauses are still quite uncommon.

23.50   The wording of an ADR clause should not prevent legal proceedings from being issued if a limitation period will expire in the meantime, or if proceedings to obtain urgent relief are required, such as an injunction.

Combinations

23.51   A transaction may be susceptible to technical disputes of the sort suitable for expert determination, but also to broader legal disputes beyond those an expert could reasonably be expected to deal with.

23.52   It is perfectly possible to provide that an expert will make binding decisions on the former but have no role in relation to the latter. This enables the parties to adopt a proportionate, cost-effective approach to each type of dispute.

23.53   Care needs to be taken, however, in drawing clear dividing lines between the scope of the different processes. Ideally, an expert ought not to be asked to determine questions of law, nor to give a narrow determination which overlaps with a legitimate broader legal dispute until that broader dispute has been properly resolved.

Table 4
Arbitration contact details

1. International Chamber of Commerce (ICC)

Website: https://iccwbo.org/

Secretariat of the International Court of Arbitration of the International Chamber of Commerce:

Address: 33–43 avenue du Président Wilson
                  75116 Paris,
                  France

Tel: +33 1 49 53 29 05

Fax: +33 1 86 26 67 51

Email: arb@iccwbo.org

2. London Court of International Arbitration (LCIA)

Website: http://www.lcia.org/

Address: LCIA
                  70 Fleet Street
                  London
                  EC4Y 1EU

Tel: +44 (0)20 7936 6200

Fax: +44 (0)20 7936 6211

Email: casework@lcia.org

3. The World Intellectual Property Organization (WIPO)

Website: http://www.wipo.int/portal/en/index.html

WIPO Arbitration and Mediation Center:

Address: WIPO, 34, chemin des Colombettes
                  CH-1211 Geneva 20
                  Switzerland

Tel: +41 22 338 9111

Fax: +41 22 733 5428

4. American Arbitration Association (AAA)

Website: https://www.adr.org/

Corporate headquarters:

Address: 120 Broadway, Floor 21
                  New York, NY 10271

International Center for Dispute Resolution:

Address: 120 Broadway, Floor 21
                  New York, NY 10271

Tel: +1-212-716-5800

5. China International and Economic and Trade Arbitration Commission ('CIETAC')

Website: http://www.cietac.org

Address: 6/F,CCOIC Building, 2 Huapichang Hutong, Xicheng District,
                  Beijing
                  P.C.100035

Tel: 010-82217788,64646688

Fax: 010-82217766,64643500

Email: info@cietac.org

Table 5
ADR contact details

1. Centre for Effective Dispute Resolution

Website: http://www.cedr.com

Address: Centre for Effective Dispute Resolution
                  International Dispute Resolution Centre
                  70 Fleet Street
                  London
                  EC4Y 1EU

Tel: +44(0)20 7536 6000

Email: info@cedr.com

2. International Chamber of Commerce (ICC)

Website: http://www.iccwbo.org/

ICC Dispute Resolution Services – ADR:

Address: 33-43 avenue du Président Wilson
                  75116 Paris
                  France

Tel: +33 1 49 53 29 03

Fax: +33 1 86 26 67 49

Email: mediation@iccwbo.org

3. London Court of International Arbitration (LCIA)

Website: http://www.lcia.org/

Address: LCIA
                70 Fleet Street
                London
                EC4Y 1EU

Tel: +44 (0) 20 7936 6200

Fax: +44 (0) 20 7936 6211

Email: casework@lcia.org

Part C

Joint ventures and shareholders' agreements in practice

Chapter 24

Establishing and documenting a UK corporate joint venture

Summary

This chapter deals with the procedure for implementing and documenting a UK corporate joint venture, detailing the steps required to be taken and the documents required, together with the normal content of the heads of terms, shareholders' agreement and articles of association.

1 The implementation process

24.1   This chapter draws together the various threads discussed in the previous chapters and illustrates how a typical UK corporate joint venture would be documented and implemented.

24.2   The flowchart below illustrates the steps involved in implementing a typical UK corporate joint venture. This should not be read in a prescriptive way, because every joint venture is to some extent unique, and various legal and commercial considerations may cause the steps to be carried out in a different order from that shown. Some ventures will have special features which involve matters not featured in the chart. Conversely, some of the matters featured in the chart may not arise. However, the general procedure will be broadly the same in most cases.

24.3   Table 6 at the end of this chapter sets out a non-exhaustive list of the documents which might be required for a corporate joint venture, not all of which will be required in every case.

Flowchart 8 – steps in implementing a UK corporate joint venture

ABC plc has agreed to enter into a joint venture with XYZ plc in relation to their respective electronics businesses. ABC plc is an established manufacturer of electronics equipment and XYZ plc has developed a new product which it has not yet put into full production. The rationale for the

Flowchart 8
Steps in the establishment of a joint venture

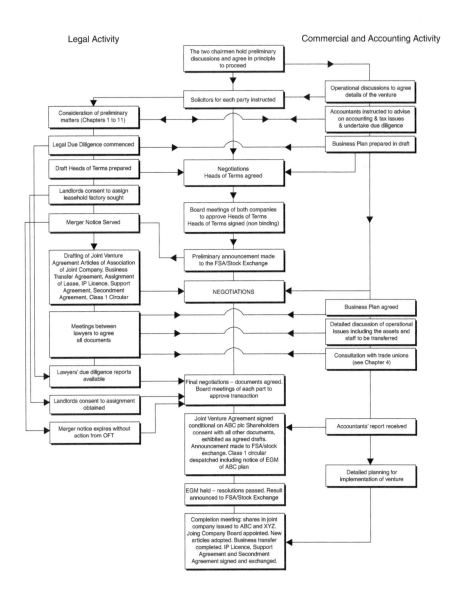

venture for ABC plc is that it will be able to manufacture the new product using spare capacity at one of its factories and in due course the new product will replace the current products made there, which are becoming life expired. As far as XYZ plc is concerned it would cost it more to start a business from scratch and it will obtain the benefit of ABC plc's existing customer base, manufacturing expertise and reputation in the trade. A new company is to be formed held as to 60% by ABC plc and 40% by XYZ plc into which ABC plc will inject the leased factory together with the business currently carried on there. XYZ plc will grant to the joint company a licence to use the intellectual property and know-how relating to the new product and will provide managerial, technical and marketing support services. ABC plc will provide one of its senior executives to act as the managing director of the joint company under a secondment agreement. The transaction is Class 1 for ABC plc, which is a listed company. The turnover of the existing business exceeds £70m, so the transaction is a qualifying merger.

2 Heads of terms

24.4   Heads of terms which, subject to para 24.5, will almost invariably be non-binding legally (other than in limited areas such as confidentiality mentioned below), are by no means essential, but a joint venture is a transaction in which they may be found particularly useful. Where a transaction is very simple, heads of terms often serve no real function other than to delay the preparation and agreement of the detailed documents, but a full set of joint venture documentation can be very long and complicated, especially when all the ancillary documents listed in the second and third columns of the table are added, and there is a distinct danger of the parties becoming unable to 'see the wood for the trees'. In such a case the prior preparation, agreement and signing of some non-binding heads of terms will help to focus the parties and their advisers on the essential features of the transaction, and any subsequent attempt to introduce terms inconsistent with the heads into the detailed documents can be dealt with appropriately. The heads of terms should be drafted in clear, non-technical language, and a format consisting of short paragraphs or bullet points is to be recommended. In order to ensure that the non-binding parts of the heads are not legally binding, appropriate wording will need to be included to make this clear. In English law, the hallowed words 'subject to contract' will be used, but when negotiating cross-border joint ventures it is advisable to take legal advice in the jurisdictions of the other parties in order to ensure that the heads, or any part of them, will not be unintentionally legally binding. Indeed, those negotiating a joint venture with participants in a civil law jurisdiction may run the risk of liability for failure to negotiate in good faith, and liability may also attach if negotiations are broken off without good reason. Appropriate local legal advice should be sought at the outset.

24.5   Heads of terms will not, normally, be entirely legally non-binding. During the course of discussions, each party will reveal to the other(s) a considerable amount of confidential information and it will be usual to include in the heads binding confidentiality provisions whereby each party receiving such information agrees to keep it confidential and not to make use of it for its own purposes (although it is not uncommon to see this already covered in a confidentiality agreement signed at the outset of discussions on a possible joint venture, ie well before heads of terms are reached). There will invariably be an exemption to cover disclosures required by law and for matters which fall into the public domain otherwise than by the fault of the party receiving the information etc. Confidentiality undertakings should survive the termination of the heads of terms, so as to survive if the joint venture is never entered into. It was generally the practice for their duration to be unlimited, but it is now more general for them to last for two or three years after the termination of the heads of terms, although a longer or unlimited duration period may be appropriate for information with a longer commercial life (eg a secret formula). Confidentiality provisions to the like effect will be included in the shareholders' agreement, which will supersede those in the heads of terms when the shareholders' agreement is entered into.

24.6   Another legally binding term which will almost invariably be included is an obligation not to make any public announcement about the transaction (whether that would involve the release of confidential information or not), without the consent of the other parties and their approval of the content of the announcement. An exemption is normally included to cover any announcement required by the Listing Rules or by any regulatory authority, but is usually made subject to an obligation to attempt to agree the wording before the announcement is made.

24.7   There may also be legally binding undertakings on the parties not to solicit the services of the employees of the other parties, with a view to ensuring that if the venture is never implemented none of them can then seek to achieve a similar result through the back door.

24.8   If one or more of the parties have alternative partners for the proposed joint venture, the heads of terms may contain binding exclusivity provisions, whereby one or more of the parties agrees not to initiate negotiations with any alternative party for a certain period so as to allow time for the finalisation of the agreement with the preferred party, without interference from negotiations with an alternative party. However, especially in the case of a party which is a public company, negotiations initiated by an alternative party will usually not be excluded. Always ensure the Heads of Terms very clearly state which clauses if any are legally binding and which are not.

3 Shareholders' agreement

24.9   Generally the shareholders' agreement will:

• define any conditions to which completion of the joint venture is subject, such as any regulatory consents (see para 11.1ff) or any competition clearances (see Chapters 9 and 10) or the approval in general meeting of the shareholders of any of the parties (see para 11.28ff). The parties should strive to satisfy any conditions prior to signing the agreement; it is generally best to apply for any consents or clearances in advance, but sometimes this will not be desirable, as with shareholders' consent, where the circular sent to the shareholders must contain particulars of the negotiated agreement. The agreement will normally provide that the parties will use all reasonable endeavours to satisfy the conditions, but if any of them are not satisfied by a certain date (the 'drop dead' date) the agreement will lapse and cease to have effect, without liability on the part of any of the parties, except for any liability flowing from the failure to use all reasonable endeavours to satisfy the conditions;

• provide for the subscription for shares by the parties in the joint venture company, after the party currently having control of it has reorganised its share capital as required and/or caused it to adopt new articles of association in agreed form (since even though the company is new, having been established for the purpose, one of the venturers will have the beneficial ownership of the subscribers' share or shares);

• provide for the appointment to the board of directors of the directors chosen by each party in accordance with the arrangements for board representation set out in the agreement or attached as class rights in the new articles of association (see para 16.2ff). There may also be provisions for appointment of the chairman and for the establishment of the management structure, such as delegation to a management board of matters of day-to-day management. Where the right to appoint directors is a class right contained in the articles of association, the appointments will be effected by means of the machinery set out in the articles, but as an aide memoire the shareholders' agreement will often include reference to the carrying out of the required procedure at the completion meeting and will often specify the names of the original appointees for each party;

• provide for the appointment of auditors, bankers and company secretary (if required), and any necessary change in the registered office and accounting reference date;

• set out any obligations of the parties to provide for loan finance, (see para 6.8ff), guarantees (see para 6.48ff), transfer assets into the joint company (see para 3.5ff), grant licences or intellectual property (see para 3.10ff), or provide support services (see para 3.15ff) with agreed drafts of each such agreement being attached;

- set out the dividend policy (see para 14.31);

- provide for the production of an annual business plan (see para 1.63);

- contain positive obligations as to the conduct of the business (see para 14.34);

- contain obligations to procure that the joint venture company provides information such as management accounts and cashflow forecasts to the shareholders as agreed by them (see para 14.32);

- contain a positive undertaking by each shareholder signing the agreement to use all reasonable endeavours to develop the business of the joint venture company to the best advantage, followed (if appropriate) by covenants not to compete with it (see paras 10.51ff and 14.35);

- contain confidentiality provisions (see para 16.33ff and 24.5); not only as to the information imparted in the negotiations but also as to confidential information about the joint venture company or the other parties which any party may acquire during the course of the venture;

- in appropriate cases, provide for the making of consortium or group relief claims (see para 7.39ff), including provisions for payment for such consortium or group relief, together with undertakings from each shareholder under which they agree to regulate their affairs so as to preserve the ability to claim consortium or group relief. Provisions for VAT grouping may also be seen, together with an indemnity from the group parent in respect of the VAT liabilities of its members other than the joint venture company (see para 7.30ff);

- provide that no shareholder shall be entitled to sell, transfer, charge, encumber or grant options over its shares otherwise than in accordance with the articles of association (see Chapter 19); in a joint venture with only two or three parties there may be an absolute obligation on each party not to dispose of its shares at all without the consent of the others, except on termination, or perhaps after the expiry of a fixed period;

- if it is not a deadlock company (see Chapter 13), contain undertakings under which the shareholders agree to procure that the joint venture company will not carry out certain transactions without the approval of all or a defined proportion of the shareholders (see Chapter 15);

- if it is a deadlock joint venture company, provide for deadlock resolution (see para 13.10ff);

- set out the events which will allow the agreement to be terminated and their consequences (see Chapter 17);

- contain some form of termination event or exit mechanism (if one is not otherwise contained in it) to ensure that it does not last indefinitely (which is not usually what the parties would expect to be bound for);

- contain procuring obligations by each shareholder to exercise its voting and other rights in relation to the company to ensure compliance with the agreement (see para 14.45ff), contain undertakings by each shareholder to comply with the articles of association (see para 14.83), and state that if there is a conflict between the agreement and the articles of association, the agreement shall prevail, but only for as long as it remains in force; but that this is not to be regarded as an alteration to the articles of association (see para 24.19);

- contain provisions disenfranchising directors from voting where there is a conflict of interest between the joint venture company and their appointor (see paras 3.18 and 16.30);

- provide for the service of notices;

- specify the law which is to apply to the agreement (see para 23.5ff), perhaps contain provisions for non-binding ADR (see para 23.46ff), but will contain submissions by the parties to the jurisdiction of the courts of a specified country (see para 23.15ff) and, if a party is abroad, provide for it to appoint an agent upon whom proceedings may be served in the UK;

- instead of a jurisdiction clause, provide for arbitration (see para 23.37ff).

24.10   An important drafting consideration in relation to the shareholders' agreement is whether the joint venture company should be made a party to it. This issue was discussed at para 14.54ff above in relation to the decision in *Russell v Northern Bank*[1], and in the past there were sometimes worries under the previous Companies Act 1985, s 151 in relation to the company being a party (see para 14.58). Consideration should also be given by the parties to the potential risk, in the event of the joint venture company becoming insolvent, of its liquidator seeking to enforce against the shareholders any obligations that they may have given in favour of the company under the shareholders' agreement (see para 24.11). It is usually possible to avoid making the joint venture company a party to the agreement itself (although it will need to be party to ancillary documents such as business transfer agreements, IP licences, employment contracts, support agreements and so on) by the shareholders agreeing to join in procuring that the joint venture company shall do everything necessary to carry the agreement into effect. However, it may be thought desirable for such company to receive the benefit of non-competition covenants or warranties and indemnities, in which case

---

1   [1992] BCLC 431, CA.

it will normally be found more effective and simpler for the company to become a party rather than relying on other methods of passing the benefit to the company, such as relying on the Contracts (Rights of Third Parties) Act 1999, or creating a trust or agency in favour of the company, both of which require careful thought and some additional drafting before they are likely to be fully effective. It may also be necessary to join the joint venture company as a party in order to impose obligations upon it which the parties desire to keep out of the articles for confidentiality reasons and which are not conveniently contained in a separate agreement. It may be desirable for the joint venture company to give undertakings as to the conduct of the affairs of its subsidiaries (see para 14.83). However, if the joint venture company is to be a party, it should be excluded from all provisions under which the shareholders agree to regulate its affairs in a particular way, so as not to infringe the principle in *Russell*, and the severance clause suggested in para 14.55 should be employed. Consideration should also be given to the other issues stated above. It appears to be normal practice in US and international shareholders' agreements for the company to be made a party.

24.11   It is suggested that undertakings by the shareholders to do positive acts for the benefit of the company, such as, for example, granting it a licence (or advancing it a loan), may preferably be expressed as undertakings entered into between the shareholders, without the company having the benefit of them. This is because the shareholders will probably not wish the company or its liquidator or administrator to be able to sue them for breach of the undertakings. It may be argued that the company is the creature of the shareholders, who order its affairs and, generally, the company should not therefore have the ability to sue for failure to order its affairs in the way the shareholders have decided. If the company is a party, one might, for example, have the possibility of its liquidator or administrator suing the joint venturers for breach of an undertaking to advance money to the company, in circumstances where it has manifestly failed to achieve its intended objective and no joint venturer wishes to put up any more money. Once the loan has been advanced or other obligations complied with by means of a document to which the company is a party, the company should have the right to enforce it (subject to board or, if required, shareholder approval for the institution of proceedings). The shareholders may prefer that failure of a shareholder to comply with its obligations, or to do so on the agreed terms, should be a matter to be dealt with between the shareholders, who should be able to resolve it without the intervention of the company; they may after all wish to alter their agreement so that the obligations of the individual shareholders are on different or new terms.

24.12   It follows from the above that if the company is not a party to the agreement, it should not have any right to enforce the agreement under the Contracts (Rights of Third Parties) Act 1999, and appropriate exclusion wording should be included.

4 Articles of association

24.13   The articles of association will generally deal with the following matters which are not covered by, or are normally dealt with by variations to, the Model Articles:

- where there is more than one class of shares the articles will set out the rights attaching to each class, including any entrenched rights to appoint directors the parties desire to attach to each class (see para 16.1ff), and the articles will include a modification of rights provision (see para 14.63);

- where minority vetoes are to be attached as class rights, these will be set out (see Chapter 15);

- the articles will deal with the composition of the board, and provide for the ability to appoint and remove directors (where there are to be directors additional to those appointed under class rights);

- the articles will define the quorum required for board and general meetings (see paras 13.6 and 16.6) and whether or not the chairman has a casting vote (see paras 13.4 and 16.6);

- the articles will provide for share transfers, often including a pre-emption provision (see Chapter 19);

- where pre-emption provisions are not included, the directors will normally have an absolute discretion as to whether to register a share transfer without giving reasons;

- the articles will deal with the procedure for issue of new shares, and may exclude statutory pre-emption rights, and may or may not substitute alternative provisions. The issue of new shares may be the subject of a class consent (see para 15.11ff);

- the articles will generally modify the Model Articles to allow a director to vote on any matter in which he is interested (see paras 16.14 and 16.18), although care needs to be given to ensure that directors are not able to vote on matters where there is a conflict between the company and the party appointing them.

Should the articles refer to the shareholders' agreement?

24.14   A drafting question which affects articles of association is whether it is appropriate for them to refer specifically to the shareholders' agreement.

24.15   As already mentioned in para 14.82, as a general principle the articles should be drafted so as to be self-standing, on the basis that, unless action is expressly taken to the contrary, they will survive the termination of the shareholders' agreement. Indeed, where there is only one holder of a particular class of shares, the best practice is to assume there may in the future be more than one holder, just in case that shareholder transfers part of its holding, or more shares of that class are issued later. Since the articles should be self-standing, it is therefore best not to refer to the shareholders' agreement.

24.16   In practice, this often proves difficult or impossible. In a complicated joint venture arrangement the articles may be very difficult to draft without cross-references to the shareholders' agreement, but a little ingenuity may avoid the need to do so. For example, it is not uncommon to provide in articles of association that the directors must refuse to register a transfer of shares unless the transferee, if not already bound, has first signed a deed adhering to the shareholders' agreement. However, such a cross-reference to the shareholders' agreement could be avoided if the directors have a discretion to refuse to register a share transfer and the shareholders' agreement provides that the appointors of the directors must procure them to exercise that discretion, so that no share transfer is to be registered unless a deed of adherence has been entered into and a share transfer is always registered where the terms of any pre-emption article have been complied with and a deed of adherence has been obtained. An improvement on this would be to provide in the articles that the directors are not able to register a transfer without a class consent from all classes of shares and to provide in the shareholders' agreement that all shareholders are bound to give their consent to registering a transfer where the terms of any pre-emption article have been complied with and a deed of adherence has been obtained and are otherwise bound to withhold their consent.

24.17   One other reason for avoiding the mention of the shareholders' agreement in the articles of association is that, if it is mentioned, then, arguably, the shareholders' agreement ought then to be filed at Companies House along with the articles, because the articles cannot be fully interpreted without reference to the agreement. This would mean that confidential provisions in the agreement would become publicly available. In practice, most practitioners have in the past ignored this requirement and Companies House has not normally pointed out the omission.

24.18   There have, however, been some instances where Companies House has refused to register articles where they cross-refer to a shareholders' agreement, even where the agreement is sent in for filing with the articles. This does not yet appear to be official Companies Registry policy and their approach is not consistent, but should it become official policy it will mean a change in the current practice of many practitioners. It may be that the view of Companies House is that articles which cross-refer to another document did not meet the requirements of the Companies Act 1985, s 7(5) (repealed by the Companies Act 2006) which required them to be divided into paragraphs numbered consecutively.

24.19   It should also be mentioned that it has been argued that all shareholders' agreements should be filed at Companies House by virtue of the old CA 1985, s 380(4)(d), which required the filing of all resolutions and agreements agreed to by all the members or some class of shareholders, but in practice practitioners generally ignored the point. In any case, it appears that this provision was directed at written resolutions signed by all shareholders, or all of them holding a class of shares, which are signed as an alternative to passing a resolution at a general or class meeting, rather than agreements between shareholders to exercise their rights as shareholders in a particular way. However, a shareholders' agreement might be held to amend the articles. It was held in *Cane v Jones*[2] that even an informal agreement between the members was sufficient to alter the articles, even though a special resolution had not been passed. It was after that case that the word 'agreements' was added into the previous (now repealed) s 380(4)(d). With effect from 1 October 2007, s 380(4)(d) has been repealed and replaced by CA 2006, s 29(1)(c) and (d), which are virtually identical. It is in order to negate this possibility, and arguably avoid the argument that filing of the shareholders' agreement is required, that a clause is often inserted into the shareholders' agreement expressly declaring that its effect is not to amend the articles. The clause usually goes on to declare that, in the case of a conflict between the shareholders' agreement and the articles, the former will prevail and the parties are expressed to be obliged to take all such steps, as shareholders, to give effect to this (eg by resolution). It will assist in establishing the intention that the shareholders' agreement and the articles are to be separate documents if the conflict provision only has effect for so long as the shareholders' agreement remains in force.

5   Other documents

24.20   Many joint ventures will involve a series of transactions being undertaken by the parties either as a preliminary step to setting up the joint venture (eg. a pre-transaction reorganisation) or as part of their contractual obligations upon formation. The latter will often be set out in the shareholders' (or joint venture) agreement. However, in the former case, it may be appropriate for the parties (and possibly the proposed joint venture company) to enter into a formation agreement which will set out the steps to be taken culminating with the execution of the shareholders' agreement and the documents to be entered into pursuant to it. In this way each party can be satisfied that, before starting the initial step(s) it has to undertake,

---

2   [1981] 1 All ER 533.

the other party/parties will be bound to carry out the later step(s) and all will be bound to enter into the shareholders' agreement. It will also provide evidence for tax and accounting purposes that particular transactions took place in a particular order.

Table 6
Documents required for a typical UK corporate joint venture

May be required in all cases	May be required if business undertakings will be transferred	May be required where support is being given
Heads of terms (optional but often useful).	Business transfer agreement.	Support agreements for the provision of services (see Chapter 3).
Joint venture/ shareholders' agreement.	Conveyances and assignments of assets to be transferred as necessary, eg freehold properties, leases, IP.	Secondment agreement (see Chapter 4).
Articles of association for joint company.	New service contracts or employment terms for transferred employees (as necessary) (see Chapter 4).	Letters to the seconded employees (see Chapter 4).
Resolutions of joint venture company to reorganise capital and adopt new articles.	Pensions documentation (as necessary) (see Chapter 4).	IP Licences (see Chapter 3).
Board and (possibly) general meeting resolutions of the parties to approve the joint venture. Announcements to Stock Exchange/FCA and press (if required).	Share sale agreement (if the share capital of a subsidiary is being transferred) together with completion board minutes of the transferred company, and stock transfer forms.	Marketing and distribution agreements (if necessary).
Class 1 and/or related party circular (if required).	Leases of premises – if leases will be granted instead of transferring them.	
Completion board minutes for joint venture company.		
Letters of application for shares.		

May be required in all cases	May be required if business undertakings will be transferred	May be required where support is being given
Loan agreements between one or more parties and the joint venture company (if required).		
Agreements for external finance (if required).		
Merger notice (if required – see Chapter 10).		
Commercial agreements with third parties (as required).		

Chapter 25

Due diligence, warranties and indemnities

Summary

This chapter sets out the considerations relating to due diligence, warranties and indemnities, and discusses what will generally be required in different circumstances. Warranties about assets to be injected into the joint venture, the joint venturers themselves and the joint venture company are considered. The importance of the warranties being available to the joint venturers rather than, or in addition to, the joint venture company is discussed. Guidance is given on the drafting of indemnities or covenants to pay, and the chapter ends with a discussion concerning remedies for breaches of warranty and alternatives to indemnity payments. This chapter is written from a UK standpoint and assumes the relevant documents are governed by English law. However, many of the points made will be capable of general application.

1 Introduction

25.1   Due diligence, warranties and indemnities can be an important consideration in a joint venture, but much depends on the circumstances of the transaction. In a case where well-established public companies who know each other well are establishing a new joint company to carry on a completely new business using technology with which both parties are familiar, the subject will hardly arise at all. On the other hand, where the proposed joint venture company already trades, one or more existing businesses are to be injected into the joint venture company, or one or more of the joint venturers are not well known to the others and are private companies or individuals with very little information publicly available about them, warranties and indemnities may become important.

2 Due diligence

25.2   The amount of due diligence to be carried out and who is to conduct it should be established at an early stage. The procedures will not really differ from those in other transactions and will typically be divided between the accountants and solicitors to the parties and the parties' own managements, with the latter concentrating especially on commercial matters. Care should be taken to avoid duplication between them. In addition external solicitors need to be careful that their clients are sure who is undertaking due diligence so that responsibilities are carefully laid out and divided between professionals involved in the transaction and indeed the client.

Ensure no breaches occur during due diligence of the Data Protection Act 2018 and UKGDPR (which is an amended version of the EU General Data Protection Regulation which has applied in the UK since 1 January 2021). The UK Information Commissioner's Office has guidance for those involved with acquisitions to ensure compliance with data protection legislation during due diligence exercises. The December 2020 version is at https://ico.org. uk/for-organisations/data-sharing-a-code-of-practice/due-diligence/. The annex to this chapter gives the extract from the guidance relating to mergers and acquisitions and due diligence. Non-disclosure agreements should also be put in place to protect all confidential information whether it be personal data about 'living individuals' (ie covered by data protection law) or not.

25.3   Due diligence is a time-consuming process and is best started as soon as possible. Since for a typical joint venture the agreement of the heads of terms can take some time, it will be best to start the due diligence process before these are signed, if the parties are willing to allow this, although a binding confidentiality agreement should be signed before work begins. There is of course the risk that the work will be wasted if the deal does not proceed, but this is invariably a risk with all due diligence since the parties do not normally become legally bound until the formal agreement is signed.

25.4   Where a business or a major asset is to be transferred to the joint venture company, or the joint venture company has already traded, a full due diligence process will normally be indicated and it may well be desirable to commission investigating accountants to prepare a full report, backed up with a solicitor's investigation into such matters as major contracts, litigation, employment liabilities, title to assets and regulatory compliance. If there is a final salary occupational pension scheme, actuaries may be instructed to advise on the state of its funding.

25.5   Where the joint venture is to be established to develop or market some new technology, with which other parties to the venture are unfamiliar, it will usually be appropriate to instruct an independent expert to conduct an evaluation of the technology. Those having the intellectual property in the technology may be very unwilling to allow this, fearing that secrets relating to it will escape into the public domain, but such an evaluation may be essential in order to avoid the other parties making a very expensive mistake. For example, it may be found that there is some flaw which will hamper the manufacture of the products, or that the technology will not result in products which conform to the standards and regulations applying in the countries in which they are to be marketed.

3 Warranties

25.6   Where a business or a major asset is to be transferred into the joint venture company, or the joint venture company is already trading, warranties should be given by the party injecting the assets, or business, or which owns the company, in favour of the other joint venturers and, possibly, the joint venture company. These will generally not be as detailed as those which would be taken by a buyer of a 100% interest. Many warranties taken on the purchase of such an interest are designed to obtain for such a buyer the information which it needs to run the business after completion, rather than with a view to suing the sellers for loss flowing from the warranties proving to be untrue. Where the venturers receiving the warranties will have less than 100% of the share capital and will not solely be responsible for managing the business, such 'informational' warranties are generally unnecessary and warranties should be restricted to matters which are likely to affect the financial performance of their investment. For example, a warranty that the books and records of the company contain true, complete and accurate information and include the names and addresses of all suppliers and customers and all special terms to which they are entitled arguably goes too far, and should be replaced by a warranty that the books and records fairly reflect the financial position of the company. Detailed warranties about matters such as the collectability of book debts, stock levels and fixed assets will usually be found unnecessary if they are covered by a general accounts warranty. The smaller the stake an investor is taking, the fewer and more generalised will be the warranties it may expect to receive.

25.7   Although the joint venture company may receive the benefit of warranties in respect of assets and businesses transferred to it, it will always be more important that the investors should receive them, so it is desirable that all the warranties should appear in the subscription or shareholders' agreement, rather than in a contract or conveyance for the transfer itself, to which only the seller and the company are parties. The investors in the company need the warranties so that they can recover the depletion in the value of their shares which flows from the breach of warranty; any depletion in the worth of the company's net assets does not necessarily relate directly to the value of the company's shares, and in any case a minority shareholder may not be able to procure that the company sues the seller and, if it does, any proceeds go to the company and not the investors.

25.8   Special provisions may need to be made concerning the measure of damages. The normal contractual measure of damages for breach of a warranty in a share acquisition is the difference between the market value of the shares acquired as they are and what their market value would have been had the warranty been true. Where a party is purchasing or subscribing for a minority interest, the consideration it pays is usually that proportion of the market value of the whole company which corresponds to the proportion of its share capital which that party is acquiring, or is that proportion of the monies being subscribed which corresponds to its proportion of the share capital after the subscription. The difficulty with this is that a minority interest is normally valued at a discount, which may result in the party concerned not being adequately compensated for any breach of warranty. For example, if party A pays £10m for a 25% stake in a company which was thought to be worth, or would be worth following the completion of the joint venture agreement, £40m, but due to a breach of warranty is in fact worth £30m, party A would expect to receive damages of £2.5m. If, however, it was shown that the true market value of A's stake could never have been more than £5m, and in the light of the breach of warranty is worth £3.75m, the measure of damages would be only £1.25m. To prevent this result there should be an express provision that, for the purposes of assessing damages, the shares being acquired are taken to have a market value equal to the proportion of the market value of the entire company which corresponds to the proportion of its share capital which is being acquired. The shares should not necessarily be deemed to have a value, assuming the warranties are true, equal to the price paid, since this would deprive the acquirer of any loss of bargain resulting from the shares being worth more. In the example, had the shares party A was acquiring been worth, assuming all the warranties were true, and on a proportionate basis, £12m (ie the whole company was worth £48m) but in the light of the breach were worth £9m, party A would be able to claim £3m, and not £1m only. The warrantors may of course insist that damages should be based on the £10m actually paid for the shares, although this could be a poorer deal than basing the damages on the value of the minority interest; if this was £6m, assuming all the warranties were true, and £4.5m in the light of the breach, the damages should be £1.5m.

25.9   There is generally no purpose at all in an established company providing warranties about its own affairs to subscribers for its own shares. Not only do such warranties run up against the difficulties referred to in para 14.55 (although a shareholder suing for breach of a warranty would be suing otherwise than as a member and may be able to recover), but to sue the company under the warranties would only be likely to further reduce the net worth of the company and adversely affect the value of the claimant's shares. The warranties about the company should be given by the existing owners of its share capital, but the company will often give them also, on a joint and several basis, so that the recipient of the warranties has a choice over whether to sue the company or not. However, if this course is adopted, it is important to remember that if the warranting shareholders are sued they have a right of contribution from the company, which may thereby be liable for a portion of the claim. If this is not desired, the right of contribution will need to be expressly excluded.

25.10   If a public company is to provide warranties and indemnities to an acquirer of its shares, financial assistance becomes a consideration. The view is generally taken that warranties do not amount to financial assistance, as long as the directors reasonably believe that the warranties are true. The rationale is that they are 'other financial assistance' within CA 2006, s 677(1)(d) and there would be no depletion of the net assets if the warranties are true. In relation to indemnities the view is generally taken that they are financial assistance, since an indemnity comes within s 677(1)(b)(i) and therefore cannot be given, even if it does not involve any depletion of net assets. Warranties are, therefore, much more effective than indemnities, especially if the warranties contain a '£ for £' clause. Note that if a public company gives an indemnity in respect of its own neglect or default, this is not financial assistance. There is no provision in the CA 2006 for a public company to 'whitewash' any financial assistance. Note also that the prohibition on a private company giving financial assistance for the acquisition of its own shares or of its private holding company (under CA 1985, s 151) was repealed on 1 October 2008. However, the prohibition on financial assistance continues to apply when the shares being acquired are in a public company, even if the company giving the assistance is private. If a private company gives an indemnity to its shareholders and the liability is recognised, the company must still have sufficient distributable reserves to cover the payment to ensure that it does not amount to an unlawful reduction of capital.

25.11   Where the joint venture company is a company which has never traded, detailed warranties concerning it are unnecessary. The joint venturer which controls the company initially (usually merely because its solicitors incorporated the joint venture company and their client is beneficially entitled to the subscribers' shares) should give warranties to the effect that the company has never traded, has no assets or liabilities other than in respect of its share capital, and has entered into no transactions of any kind whatsoever. The company itself will not provide any warranties.

25.12   It will quite often be appropriate for joint venturers to provide warranties about themselves to the others, the purpose of which is to provide assurances about their financial standing and confirmation that they have no skeletons which may later emerge and impact adversely on the joint venture. For example, a private company would be likely to be asked to provide warranties as to its last accounts, major disputes and litigation, regulatory compliance, product liabilities (particularly if not covered by insurance), current solvency, and such other attributes as are important to the particular joint venture, such as the possession of particular licences or governmental consents, the availability of government grants, or the ownership of intellectual property which will be used or licensed for the purposes of the joint venture.

25.13   Individual joint venturers might be expected to sign and complete a questionnaire in the form generally required by sponsors to a company about to be floated, giving details of their past careers and to warrant its accuracy. It is particularly important to try to establish whether any such individuals have past criminal convictions, or have been successfully sued for fraud, or whether they are now, or have been, bankrupt or disqualified to act as a director. Further due diligence on these matters could be appropriate. Directors of a corporate joint venture who are to play key roles in the venture might possibly be put through the same procedure, unless their pasts are well known.

25.14   The negotiation of warranties can be especially difficult in relation to cross-border joint ventures, particularly where one or more of the parties is in a civil law jurisdiction. In many such jurisdictions the approach to warranties is different, in that the law imposes on a seller a duty to make a certain amount of disclosure, whereas in most common law jurisdictions, including England, the principle of 'caveat emptor' or 'buyer beware' generally applies. This difference of approach may result in overseas warrantors objecting to being requested to provide detailed warranties to parties in a common law jurisdiction who are negotiating an agreement to be governed by a civil law, not realising that duties of disclosure will apply irrespective of the express warranties given by them, and to parties in a civil law jurisdiction negotiating an agreement to be governed by English law, or the law of another common law jurisdiction, failing to request warranties they ought to have asked for, believing that they were effectively implied.

25.15   In *Sycamore Bidco Limited v Breslin and Dawson*[1] the court examined the distinction between warranties and representations. Had the claimant been able to show a provision were a misrepresentation then the damages award would have been £16.75 million. Instead it was found only to be a warranty and the sum was reduced to £6.75 million. .The buyer, Sycamore, purchased the entire share capital of Breslin and Dawson. After the sale had gone through, Sycamore alleged that they had found errors in Breslin and Dawson's audited accounts which had the result – they said – of their paying more for Breslin and Dawson than the company was worth.

25.16   The audited accounts were the subject of a number of express warranties contained in the Share Purchase Agreement ('SPA') which were given by Breslin and Dawson. Sycamore sued for breach of warranty. The breach of warranty claim was for £6.75 million. Sycamore also sued for damages for misrepresentation, alleging that it had been misled into entering the SPA on the basis of the misrepresentations as to the accounts. They argued that if they had known the true position of the accounts they never would have proceeded to purchase. They did not succeed in recovering

---

1   [2012] EWHC 3443 [Ch].

the higher amount. The court held that there had been breaches of the express warranties which related to the audited accounts. However it went on to hold that the warranties were only warranties and not representations. The reasoning was based on a representation being pre-contract and a warranty being part of the contract. The court found that not only was the distinction a legal one, but the distinction was also made clear in the drafting of the SPA itself, which set out differences between warranties and representations. For example, throughout the SPA, warranties were clearly and at all times described as warranties and not described as representations. Those drafting therefore should consider using terms such as 'warrant and represent' rather than simply 'warrant'.

Notification of claims

25.17   Consideration should also be given to the notification of warranty claims. In *Teoco UK Ltd v Aircom Jersey 4 Ltd*[2] the Court of Appeal, upholding the decision of the court below, looked at the construction of share purchase agreements, in particular notification of warranty claims. It was held that the sellers were not liable for certain breach of warranty claims for unpaid tax liabilities as the buyer had not complied with the contractual requirements in the SPA – that the purchaser must give the sellers written notice of a claim setting out reasonable detail of the claim (including the grounds on which it was based and the purchaser's good faith estimate of the amount of the claim, detailing the purchaser's calculations of the loss, liability for damages alleged) as soon as reasonably practicable after it became aware that it had such a claim. The purchaser purported to rely on two letters it had written to the sellers in order to show it had given valid notification.

25.18   Notification supposedly made was held not to be sufficient – there was no reference to the claims clause in the SPA in the letter. A second letter did set out the tax exposure and contained calculations – it did not identify which warranties had been breached and did not say if it were claiming for breach of warranty or under the tax indemnity. So it was held that no notification of the claim had been made and that the buyer had failed to notify as soon as reasonably practicable under the SPA. Jennifer McGuire of LK Shields writing about the case at https://www.lkshields.ie/news-insights/publication/warranty-claims-purchasers-notification said:

> 'This is another case illustrating how easily a Purchaser's rights to pursue a warranty claim can fail by not strictly complying with the notice of claims provisions contained in a share purchase agreement. The Court said that the underlying commercial purpose of contractual notices in

---

2   [2018] EWCA Civ 23, CA.

this area is one of commercial certainty and proper compliance with contractual notice requirements is not a technical or trivial matter.

The focus while negotiating and drafting exclusion clauses in a share purchase agreement is often on the period for serving the notice but this case demonstrates that the parties should bear in mind the importance of what the agreement provides for in terms of form and content of the notice. Purchasers should ensure there is no doubt as to what exactly the clause requires for a purported notice to comply with such clause as the courts will look for strict compliance.'

25.19   In *Towergate Financial Ltd v Hopkinson*[3] the High Court held that an indemnity claim could not be pursued under the sale and purchase agreement concerned because the claimant had not notified the other party of the claim 'as soon as possible' and in any event prior to a long stop date, such requirement being part of the SPA. The court referred to *AIG v Farday*[4] which was a case which had considered the words 'as soon as possible'.

In *Towergate* the court was swayed by the fact the claimant had notified its insurers time and again about the claim but not the other party until much later. Insurers were notified in February 2014 and in March, April, October and December 2014 that there was a potential claim (and the insurance contract required claims to be notified 'as soon as practicable'). However the claimant did not notify the other party against whom the claim was made until as late as July 2015. They were held to be out of time.

25.20   In *Stobart Group Ltd v William Stobart*[5] the Court of Appeal again was called on to consider claims under an SPA, this time under tax provisions therein. It held that the purported notice of claim is to be construed objectively. The case highlighted the consequences of failing to serve a valid notice in such cases. The court followed the basis for construction of unilateral notices in *Mannai Investment Co Ltd v Eagle Star Life Assurance Co Ltd*[6], which had stated:

'The construction of the notices must be approached objectively. The issue is how a reasonable recipient would have understood the notices. And in considering this question, the notices must be construed taking into account the relevant objective contextual scene.'

The consequences in *Stobart* were severe as the claim could not be brought. A lot of work and consideration and in some cases seeking a second opinion may be necessary before serving notices of warranty and indemnity claims to avoid adverse decisions such as this in practice.

---

3   [2020] EWHC 984 (Comm).
4   [2007] Lloyd's Rep IR 267.
5   [2019] EWCA Civ 1376.
6   [1997] AC 749.

In *Dodika Ltd v United Luck Group Holdings Ltd*[7] inadequate notice was given in a US\$1bn transaction in relation to warranty claim with the effect that the buyer had to release US\$50m which had been held in escrow simply because notice had not been given correctly. The notice did not give enough detail of the matters leading to the warranty claim and this mattered even though in reality both parties already knew what the claims were and full details of them. The use of the phrase 'giving rise to' meant there was a requirement in the notice to set out the factual reasons why a pre-completion tax liability had or might accrue.

4 Indemnities

25.21 As with a conventional corporate acquisition, indemnities may be appropriate where the joint venture company is already trading, or a subsidiary of one of the joint venturers is to be acquired by the joint venture company.

25.22 In a corporate acquisition a tax indemnity is usually taken from the sellers, although these days, in view of the possibility that the proceeds of an indemnity in favour of a company may be taxable in the hands of the company, the indemnity is in favour of the purchaser and is really a covenant to pay rather than an indemnity per se. A similar covenant can be considered for the benefit of the joint venturers other than the seller or existing owners of the company, with the difference that, since none of them is acquiring 100% of the shares of the joint venture company, the covenants in favour of each of them should be limited to the percentage of the tax payable by the relevant company which is the same as their respective percentage holdings in the joint venture company. There is in fact no reason why tax should be treated differently from any other liability, and the joint venturers could arguably be perfectly well protected by warranties as to the tax liabilities of the relevant company, but the joint venturers may, in line with the practice in corporate acquisitions, wish to take them.

25.23 Environmental indemnities (or covenants to pay) are another type of indemnity which is quite often taken from the sellers in a corporate acquisition, and such an indemnity might be appropriate where it is possible that the relevant company has undiscovered environmental liabilities, or known liabilities of an uncertain amount, which may impact upon the joint venture. The considerations regarding the structuring of such indemnities are the same as for tax indemnities. If such liabilities are known or suspected, the due diligence procedure should include an investigation into them, usually by independent consultants. Where an indemnity is given by a public

---

7   [2020] EWHC 2101 (Comm).

company in connection with the purchase or subscription of its shares, financial assistance implications arise – see para 25.10.

5 Remedies other than damages or indemnity payments

25.24   Although most practitioners and their clients will think first of monetary compensation for a breach of warranty, this may not be the most appropriate remedy. The breach may be so fundamental that the party in receipt of the warranty may well prefer not to proceed or continue with the joint venture at all. In the event of a serious breach of warranty being discovered before completion of a subscription for new shares, the contract to do so could generally be rescinded (subject to the terms of the agreement), but after completion this right will usually be excluded, since it will be difficult or impossible to restore the parties to their original positions, having regard to the various steps which each party may have taken to implement the joint venture agreement.

25.25   It may therefore be desirable to make a serious breach of warranty a ground for terminating the joint venture agreement, which will set out the consequences of such termination (see Chapter 17). For example, the party in breach might be required to purchase the shares of the other parties at a valuation which ignores the consequences of the breach. A less drastic solution is to provide that the shareholding of the party in breach will be 'squeezed down' in some way. It will not be possible to cancel shares which have already been issued, but a provision for some of the shares to be left unissued for a period, so as to allow for an adjustment in their number following a warranty claim, or the compulsory transfer of some of them to the others at a 'compensatory' price might be included. If there are to be subsequent tranches of share subscriptions, the party in breach might be denied its right to subscribe for some of those shares in favour of the other parties, and the subscription price might be adjusted downwards to reflect the consequences of the breach. Squeeze down is not always a good solution, since it involves the 'innocent' parties acquiring a larger stake in an enterprise which may, in consequence of the breach, have a value lower than was thought or is less likely to achieve its intended objectives, and the 'innocent' parties might be given the options of squeeze down, termination or damages. Squeeze down is, however, particularly useful where the warrantor in breach is unlikely to be able to meet any claim for damages. A further option might be to require the party in breach to pay to the company a sum sufficient to restore its financial position to that which would have existed had the warranty been true; however, where the warranty is in favour of the joint venturers, the required amount will probably be taxable in the hands of the company and would have to be 'grossed up' to be fully effective.

25.26   Indemnities could be treated in a similar manner. If a large indemnity payment becomes due, the parties entitled to it could be given the option of termination or a squeeze down instead of taking the indemnity payment.

25.27   Always ensure the SPA deals properly with representations/misrepresentations issues. In *Idemitsu Kosan Co Ltd v Sumitomo Co Corp*[8], the High Court considered that express warranties in a share purchase agreement (SPA) were not capable of founding an action for misrepresentation. This case serves as a reminder of the consequences of a warranty also amounting to a representation and highlights the significance of an entire agreement clause in this context.

Warranty and related claims – case examples

116 CARDAMON LTD V MACALISTER[9]

25.28   In *116 Cardamon Ltd v MacAlister* the court ordered full payment of the purchase price under the SPA where there was held to be a breach of warranty and unusually the claimant (in this case the seller of the business) was able to keep the shares.

PERSIMMON HOMES LTD V HILLIER AND CREED[10]

25.29   In *Persimmon Homes Ltd v Hillier and Creed*, the Court of Appeal upheld a decision that a SPA and disclosure letter should be 'rectified'. The defendant sellers of two property development companies gave an unqualified warranty that the companies owned certain freehold properties. However the properties were owned by another of the defendants' companies which was not part of the transaction. The High Court and Court of Appeal found that the disclosure letter did not reflect the parties' agreement and it and the SPA could be rectified to correct the error.

TRIUMPH V PRIMUS[11]

25.30   In *Triumph v Primus* the court considered another warranty claim dispute with the usual elements including the claimant seeking to argue the claim was not under the warranties (so the time limit for warranty claims could be avoided). Triumph bought shares in three Primus companies for $76.5m. The loss making firms did not do as well as predicted and Triumph sued the seller. The seller claimed the notice had not been properly served but here the court did not agree. Amongst other issues the court looked

---

8   [2016] EWHC 1909 (Comm).
9   [2019] EWHC 1200 (Comm).
10   [2019] EWCA Civ 800.
11   [2019] EWHC 565 (TCC).

at if the disclosure were adequate. The warranties were subject to matters 'fairly and clearly disclosed … (with sufficient detail to identify the nature of the matter disclosed)'. These were slightly unusual words which did not use the more usual 'nature and scope of the matter disclosed' and nor were the words 'fully and fairly disclosed' included. Given the more common wording was not used, this meant that disclosures about the nature of operational failings at the target companies were enough. This was the case even though they did not reveal the full extent of failings nor the impact on the business.

The case is complex and the court allowed one claim and did not allow two others. The buyer originally claimed for breach of eight different warranties.

The court also looked at *Arnold v Britton*[12], *Rainy Sky v Kookmin Bank*[13], *Chartbrook v Persimmon*[14] and *Wood v Capita*[15]. Given the amounts at stake in relation to some acquisitions it is not surprising so many recent warranty disputes have ended up at Court of Appeal and UK Supreme Court level.

For those in practice who may be bringing a claim, or even trying to decide the words to use in drafting the relevant clauses, keeping up to date with the above cases and other case law as it develops from time to time is a very worthwhile exercise.

Annex to Chapter 25

Extract from Information Commissioner's Office's Data Sharing Code of Practice (Dec 2020) as to due diligence for mergers and acquisitions under data protection law[16]

'If a merger or acquisition or other change in organisational structure means that you have to transfer data to a different or additional controller, you must consider data sharing as part of the due diligence you carry out when taking on the organisation and its obligations. This includes establishing the purposes for which the data was originally obtained, your lawful basis for sharing it, and whether these have changed following the merger or acquisition.

---

12   [2015] UKSC 36.
13   [2011] UKSC 50.
14   [2009] UKHL 38.
15   [2017] UKSC 24.
16   See   https://ico.org.uk/for-organisations/guide-to-data-protection/ico-codes-of-practice/data-sharing-a-code-of-practice/due-diligence/ and see https://ico.org.uk/for-organisations/data-sharing-information-hub.

You must comply with the data protection principles, and document your data sharing.

Consider when and how you will inform individual data subjects about what's happening to their data. You must also ensure sound governance, accountability and security.

Introduction

This section is of particular relevance to the private sector. It highlights situations such as mergers and acquisitions, or other changes in organisational structure, where you need to make good data sharing practice a priority.

How does data sharing apply to mergers and acquisitions?

Data sharing considerations may become a priority when a merger or acquisition or other change in organisational structure means that you have to transfer data to a different organisation. For example, as part of a takeover; or on insolvency, data might be sold as an asset to a different legal personality. You must take care if, as a result of the changes, there is a change in the controller of the data, or if the data is being shared with an additional controller. This is the case whether you are the sharing or recipient controller. You might be an insolvency practitioner or other adviser taking the role of controller for the time being, or advising a different controller. You need to:

- ensure that you consider the data sharing as part of the due diligence you carry out;

- follow this data sharing code;

- establish what data you are transferring;

- identify the purposes for which the data was originally obtained;

- establish your lawful basis for sharing the data;

- ensure you comply with the data processing principles – especially lawfulness, fairness and transparency to start with;

- document the data sharing;

- seek technical advice before sharing data where different systems are involved: there is a potential security risk that could result in the loss, corruption or degradation of the data; and

- consider when and how you will inform data subjects about what is happening. Under the UK GDPR you are required to keep individual data subjects informed about certain changes relating to the processing of their data, and they may have a right to object. Please see the guidance on individual rights on the ICO website. The same considerations may apply in reverse to the controller receiving the data.

How do we manage shared data following a merger or restructure or other change of controller?

On a practical level, it can be difficult to manage shared data immediately after a change of this kind, especially if you are using different databases, or you are trying to integrate different systems. It is particularly important in this period to consider the governance and accountability requirements of the UK GDPR. You must:

- check that the data records are accurate and up to date;

- ensure you document what you do with the data;

- adhere to a consistent retention policy for all records; and

- ensure appropriate security is in place.

Relevant provisions in the legislation – see UK GDPR Articles 5, 6, 7 and 21

Relevant provisions in the legislation – see UK GDPR Recitals 39, 40, 42, 43, 50, 69, 70'

[Information Commissioner's Office, *Data sharing: a code of practice, Due diligence when sharing data following mergers and acquisitions*, (Dec 2020) licensed under the Open Government Licence.]

Chapter 26

Considerations relating to joint ventures and shareholders' agreements involving UK tax resident individuals

Summary

This chapter deals with various considerations which will arise in the case of a joint venture or shareholders' agreement which includes individuals' tax resident in the UK. The tax position of individuals as regards dividends, remuneration and loan interest is dealt with and there is a summary of the special tax rules governing close companies. A vast amount of recent change has occurred to the taxation of dividends and companies in addition to corporation tax changes (with a rise to 25% due in 2023 but with a 19% rate for some). These changes have had a big impact on many transactions and their structures. Always take recent legal advice. Even this section updated in 2021 will be out of date quickly. Tax relief for interest paid on loans to acquire shares and partnership interests is dealt with, guidance is then given as to whether individuals would obtain any tax advantages by structuring the venture as a partnership, rather than as a company, and there is a discussion as to whether it is generally preferable to draw money from a company as remuneration rather than dividends. Income tax charges falling upon employee shareholders are dealt with. Consideration is given to investment incentives available through the Enterprise Investment (EIS), Venture Capital Trust (VCT) and Seed Enterprise Investment (SEIS) schemes. Tax considerations on the realisation of an individual's shareholding are then discussed, together with ways of mitigating the tax then arising. Inheritance tax planning is briefly mentioned. Guidance is given on the share transfer provisions usually applying to a company with individual shareholders which allow their shares to be transferred to their relatives and trustees of family trusts. Some issues relating to retirement are then discussed, including compulsory transfers or termination on the retirement of a working shareholder or on death. Methods of facilitating the realisation of the shares of a deceased shareholder are then dealt with.

1   Tax considerations

The taxation of dividends and other distributions received by individuals

26.1   As mentioned in para 1.45, if a UK resident company pays a dividend or other qualifying distribution to another UK company, there is usually no tax consequence for either company.

26.2   The position regarding UK resident individuals is different. There is a tax free dividend allowance of £2,000. Until 6 April 2018 this was £5,000.

26.3   Above this allowance the tax paid depends on the individual's income tax band, as shown. Income tax on dividends may be due at more than one rate if the dividends take the individual into a higher tax band.

Note also that the £2,000 dividend allowance is not a total exemption: it is added to total income and uses up £2,000 of the basic or higher rate bands, so that the rest of the dividends may be chargeable at a higher rate.

Tax band	Tax rate on dividends over £2,000
Basic rate	7.5% (8.75% from 1 April 2022)
Higher rate	32.5% (33.75% from 1 April 2022)
Additional rate	38.1% (39.35% from 1 April 2022)

(The £2000 above used to be £5000 until 6 April 2018.)

The previous system of tax credits for dividends was abolished on 5 April 2016.

26.4   HMRC gives the following guidance at https://www.gov.uk/tax-on-dividends/how-dividends-are-taxed:

'**Working out tax on dividends**

How much tax you pay on dividends above the dividend allowance depends on your Income Tax band.

Tax band	Tax rate on dividends over the allowance
Basic rate	7.5%
Higher rate	32.5%
Additional rate	38.1%

To work out your tax band, add your total dividend income to your other income. You may pay tax at more than one rate.

Example

You get £3,000 in dividends and earn £29,500 in wages in the 2020 to 2021 tax year.

This gives you a total income of £32,500.

You have a Personal Allowance of £12,500. Take this off your total income to leave a taxable income of £20,000.

This is in the basic rate tax band, so you would pay:

- 20% tax on £17,000 of wages

- no tax on £2,000 of dividends, because of the dividend allowance

- 7.5% tax on £1,000 of dividends' [8.75% from 1 April 2022.]

The taxation of other income received by individuals

26.5   If an individual receives remuneration from a company by virtue of his employment, the normal employment income rules will apply, together with the obligation upon the employing company to deduct PAYE and employees' national insurance contributions and pay employers' national insurance contributions.

26.6   Remuneration legitimately received as consultancy fees or as an independent contractor is not taxable as employee income but instead as trading income, with the result that there is no obligation upon any party to deduct PAYE or account for national insurance contributions. However, in practice, an individual who works full time for the company and has no other 'customers' may be taxed under the employment income rules if HMRC regards him as being in reality an employee. The same applies if the individual supplies his full-time services through a separate service company. Note also that FA 2013 s 22 now requires that IR35 applies where the worker is an officer of the customer company. HMRC tightened its rules in this area with effect from 6 April 2000 and has continued to do since. To assist understanding of these new rules HMRC has published guidance on the IR35 rules which is updated regularly[1].

26.7   Since 6 April 2017 public sector bodies in the UK (of which there are at least 100,000) must deduct tax and Class 1 national insurance contributions (NIC) at source when paying personal service companies of individuals (but not when paying unincorporated sole traders). This provision will not affect the tax position of private company joint venture partners although it may affect some joint venture company recipients of state sector clients.

---

1   See https://www.gov.uk/guidance/understanding-off-payroll-working-ir35.

From 1 April 2021 these rules are extended to private sector limited companies where the end-user is either large or medium sized. The IR 35 rules continue to apply where the end-user or client is a small business (broadly, following the Companies Act 2006 definition). However IR35 does not apply to sole traders. Yet even for sole traders if they meet the requirements of tax law for determining that they are truly an employee such as the control exercised over them and the like then they must be taxed as an employee. HMRC has a useful, but not fool proof, tool on its website which can be used to obtain an initial result as to whether someone is employer or not for tax purposes. This is known as 'CEST'. See https://www.gov.uk/guidance/check-employment-status-for-tax.

There is a separate test as to who is a 'worker' for other employment protection purposes. Some individuals who are self employed for tax purposes are workers for employment law purposes.

26.8   If an individual receives loan interest from a company, the company is liable to deduct basic rate income tax at 20% from the interest before paying it over. Any higher rate income tax due from the individual in respect of such interest is assessed on, and recoverable from, the individual under the income tax self-assessment system.

26.9   New rules were brought in in April 2018 for capped interest deductions for companies. The rules cap deductions for 'interest' in a company or group:

- at the *lower* of 30% of EBITDA or the adjusted net group-interest expense (the 'fixed ratio rule'); or

- optionally by election, at tax EBITDA x group ratio. The group ratio being net qualifying interest of the worldwide group/worldwide group EBITDA (the 'group ratio rule')

in both cases subject to a cap of the net qualifying interest of the world-wide group.

There is a £2m de minimis for each group (not company), to reflect the fact that the measure is targeted at large multi-nationals and Base Erosion and Profit Shifting (BEPS).

Those caught by this need to file a 'Corporate Interest Restriction' return. These rules apply to the company, not payments received by a director/shareholder.

See further at https://www.gov.uk/guidance/corporate-interest-restriction-on-deductions-for-groups.

Special provisions relating to close companies

26.10   Broadly speaking, a close company is a company controlled by five or fewer shareholders, or by any number of shareholder directors. If a company is close, special tax rules apply:

- the definition of what constitutes a distribution is extended; and

- there are special provisions concerning loans to 'participators' (see para 26.12).

Currently, there is a single 19% rate of corporation tax. However it was announced that the 19% rate would increase to 25% from April 2023 under the Finance Act 2021 but with lower rates of 19% for some companies (but not close investment holding companies).

See HMRC https://www.gov.uk/hmrc-internal-manuals/company-taxation-manual/ctm60060.

26.11   The definition of a close company is to be found in the Corporation Tax Act 2010 ('CTA 2010'), s 439. There are three tests, subject to various exceptions. A company will be close if:

- it is controlled by five or fewer 'participators';

- it is controlled by its directors; or

- five or fewer participators, or however many participators who are directors, together possess or are entitled to acquire such rights as will on a winding up entitle them to receive the greater part of the assets which are then available for distribution to the participators.

26.12   A 'participator' is any person with a share or interest in the capital or income of a company, and also includes certain loan creditors. The term also includes a person who is entitled to acquire share capital or voting rights or is entitled to secure that present or future income or assets of the company will be applied for his benefit, directly or indirectly. Loan creditors do not include those making bona fide commercial loans or banks making business loans.

26.13   'Control' for this purpose means the exercise, or the ability to exercise, whether immediately or in the future, or the entitlement to acquire, control over the company's affairs. This is not defined, but the section provides some non-exhaustive examples of the rights which are to amount to control:

- ownership of the greater part of the share capital issued or to be issued;

- ability to exercise the greater part of the voting power;

- ownership of such part of the share capital as carries the right to receive the greater part of the income of the company if, ignoring loan creditors' rights, it was all distributed amongst the participators; or

- ownership of the right to receive the greater part of the assets of the company in a winding up or other capital distribution.

26.14   In ascertaining who has control, there are attributed to a person all rights and powers held by their nominees and associates. An 'associate' of a person includes any of his or her relatives (spouse, direct ancestor or issue, or brother or sister), their partner and the trustees of a settlement in which they or any relative is the settlor. If two or more persons together satisfy the test of control, they are together taken to have control. If a participator in a company or any of their associates has control of another company, the powers exercisable by that company in relation to the first are attributed to that participator.

26.15   A non-resident company cannot be a close company (although it may be for certain special tax purposes) and a company is also not close if it is controlled by one or more non-close companies, and it cannot be treated as close except by taking a non-close company as one of the five or fewer participators. A company is also not close if it has a non-close company loan creditor which has control purely because it is entitled to the greater part of the assets on a winding up. Listed or quoted companies cannot be close if, broadly speaking, 35% or more of the voting power is held by the public.

Extended meaning of distribution

26.16   Where a company is close, the definition of a distribution is extended to cover expenses incurred by the company for the benefit of a participator or his associates[2]. This will mean that the participator or the relevant associate becomes liable to income tax on the amount of the deemed distribution, and further that the expenses concerned are not deductible in computing the profits of the close company for corporation tax purposes. The expenses within the scope of these provisions include the provision of living or other accommodation, entertainment, domestic or other services or other benefits and facilities of whatsoever nature. Where these amounts are subject to tax as employment income or benefits, the employment charging rules take precedence.

Without these provisions, there would be the temptation for family and other closely controlled companies not to declare dividends and instead to give out 'freebies' to their shareholders and members of their families which might well escape taxation.

These provisions do not apply, inter alia, to expenses incurred in the provision of living accommodation provided by reason of employment. Where benefits are given to a working participator who is taxed on them under the employment income rules, the extended distribution rules do not apply to the same benefits.

---

2   See CTA 2010, s 1064.

Loans to participators

26.17   Under CTA 2010, s 455, where a close company makes a loan to an individual who is a participator or an associate of a participator[3], which remains outstanding more than nine months after the end of the company's accounting period, it must pay over to HMRC a sum equal to 32.5% of the loan. This is deemed to be a payment of corporation tax. This payment cannot be set off against any liability to corporation tax on profits, but is refunded when the loan is repaid. These provisions are designed to stop shareholders extracting profits from close companies by taking loans, which are neither remuneration nor dividends, and which would therefore otherwise potentially escape taxation, especially if the loans were then released.

If the loan is released or written off, the borrower is treated for tax purposes as if they had received a distribution (ITTOIA 2005, s 415) and the company is denied a tax deduction for the amount written off (CTA 2009, s 321A). However, the company will be able to claim a refund of the tax originally paid under CTA 2010, s 455, by virtue of s 458 (see below).

HMRC's view is that there is also a charge to Class 1 National Insurance when a loan is released. The national insurance can be claimed as a corporation tax deduction.

Where a loan is repaid or released, the company can claim a refund of the corporation tax, under CTA 2010, s 458. The refund must be claimed within four years of the end of the financial year (NB NOT the company's accounting year) in which the release or repayment was made. HMRC forms are online at https://www.gov.uk/government/publications/corporation-tax-reclaim-tax-paid-by-close-companies-on-loans-to-participators-l2p.

There are rules to prevent avoidance by repaying loans on a 'bed and breakfast' basis, such as borrowing from a bank to repay a loan before the tax becomes due, then immediately borrowing the same amount from the company to repay the bank loan (CTA 2010, ss 464B and 464C introduced by FA 2013, Sch 30). There are also rules imposing a similar charge where a close company provides 'benefits' to participators (CTA 2010, s 464A introduced by FA 2013, Sch 30).

If the loan is at a low rate of interest, the borrower may incur a tax liability under ITEPA 2003, Part 3, Chapter 7 rules on benefits in kind (see para 26.19).

26.18   The close company provisions are directed at corporate practices which are in any case somewhat questionable in company law terms and are unlikely to be tolerated in a company which also has corporate or institutional

---

3   For simplicity, this section will refer throughout to a participator, meaning an individual who is a participator or an associate of a participator.

investors, or which has aspirations to achieve a listing. To give out 'freebies' or soft loans is likely to involve breaches of the director's fiduciary duties and loans to directors are in any case generally outlawed unless approved by shareholders under the Companies Act 2006, s 197 ff. The foregoing is only a somewhat simplified summary of some particularly complicated provisions and in case of doubt reference should be made to the statute and to the established works on taxation.

26.19   Loans by a company to individual directors or employees will also be regarded as giving rise to taxable benefits under the taxable cheap loan rules where such a loan carries interest at less than HMRC 'official rate'.

HMRC guidance on where a director/shareholder owes their company money is as follows (https://www.gov.uk/directors-loans/you-owe-your-company-money):

'If you owe your company money

You or your company may have to pay tax if you take a director's loan.

Your personal and company tax responsibilities depend on how the loan is settled. You also need to check if you have extra tax responsibilities if:

● the loan was more than £10,000 (£5,000 in 2013–14)

● you paid your company interest on the loan below the official rate

How the loan is settled	Your company's responsibilities if you're a shareholder and director	Your personal responsibilities when you get a director's loan
You repay the loan within 9 months of the end of your Corporation Tax accounting period	Use form CT600A when you prepare your Company Tax Return to show the amount owed at the end of the accounting period.	No responsibilities
	If the loan was more than £5,000 (and you took another loan of £5,000 or more up to 30 days before or after you repaid it) pay Corporation Tax at 32.5% of the original loan, or 25% if the loan was made before 6 April 2016. After you permanently repay the original loan, you can reclaim the Corporation Tax – but not interest.	
	If the loan was more than £15,000 (and you arranged another loan when you repaid it) pay Corporation Tax at 32.5% of the original loan, or 25% if the loan was made before 6 April 2016. After you permanently repay the original loan, you can reclaim the Corporation Tax – but not interest.	

How the loan is settled	Your company's responsibilities if you're a shareholder and director	Your personal responsibilities when you get a director's loan
You don't repay the loan within 9 months of the end of your Corporation Tax accounting period	Use form CT600A when you prepare your Company Tax Return to show the amount owed at the end of the accounting period.	No responsibilities
	Pay Corporation Tax at 32.5% of the outstanding amount, or 25% if the loan was made before 6 April 2016.	
	Interest on this Corporation Tax will be added until the Corporation Tax is paid or the loan is repaid.	
	You can reclaim the Corporation Tax – but not interest.	
The loan is "written off" or "released" (not repaid)	Deduct Class 1 National Insurance through the company's payroll.	Pay Income Tax on the loan through your Self Assessment tax return

If the loan was more than £10,000 (£5,000 in 2013–14)

If you're a shareholder and director and you owe your company more than £10,000 (£5,000 in 2013 to 2014) at any time in the year, your company must:

- treat the loan as a "benefit in kind"

- deduct Class 1 National Insurance

You must report the loan on your personal Self Assessment tax return. You may have to pay tax on the loan at the official rate of interest.

If you paid interest below the official rate

If you're a shareholder and director, your company must:

- record interest you pay below the official rate as company income

- treat the discounted interest as a "benefit in kind"

You must report the interest on your personal Self Assessment tax return. You may have to pay tax on the difference between the official rate and the rate you paid.

Reclaim Corporation Tax

Your company can reclaim the Corporation Tax it pays on a director's loan that's been repaid, written off or released. You can't reclaim any interest paid on the Corporation Tax.

Claim after the relief is due – this is 9 months and 1 day after the end of the Corporation Tax accounting period when the loan was repaid, written off or released. You won't be repaid before this.

You must claim within 4 years (or 6 years if the loan was repaid on or before 31 March 2010).

Reclaiming within 2 years

If you're reclaiming within 2 years of the end of the accounting period when the loan was taken out, use form CT600A to claim when you prepare a Company Tax Return for that accounting period or amend it online.

Use form L2P with your Company Tax Return instead if either:

- your tax return is for a different accounting period than the one when the loan was taken out

- you're amending your tax return in writing

Tell HMRC how you want the repayment in your Company Tax Return.

Reclaiming after 2 years

If you're reclaiming 2 years or more after the end of the accounting period when the loan was taken out, fill in form L2P and either include it with your latest Company Tax Return or post it separately.

HMRC will repay your company by either:

- using the details you gave in your latest Company Tax Return

- sending a cheque to your company's registered office address.'

26.20   For completeness where the director lends money to the company, HMRC's summary is as follows:

'If you lend your company money

Your company doesn't pay Corporation Tax on money you lend it.

If you charge interest

Interest you charge your company on a loan counts as both:

- a business expense for your company

- personal income for you

You must report the income on your personal Self Assessment tax return.

Your company must:

- pay you the interest less Income Tax at the basic rate of 20%

- report and pay the Income Tax every quarter using form CT61.'

Relief on interest paid on loans incurred by individual joint venturers

26.21   Where an individual needs to borrow to acquire shares in, or make a loan to, a company they may be able to obtain tax relief on the interest paid on the debt. The main conditions to be satisfied are that:

- the company must be a close company (see para 26.9) at the time of the share acquisition or the making of the loan. This means that where a company is being established between one or more individuals and non-close corporates which will have control, the individuals will need to acquire their shares before the corporates acquire theirs – it does not matter whether the company is close when the interest is paid as long as it was close when the shares are acquired. The same will often apply in a venture capital or private equity transaction where the management team may need to acquire their shares ahead of the investing institutions;

- a loan from an individual must be used 'wholly and exclusively' for the purposes of the company's business;

- the company must generally be a trading company at any time interest is paid;

- the individual paying the interest (together with his associates, if any) must own more than 5% of the share capital of the company. Alternatively, he can own any amount of the share capital but must work for 'the greater part of his time' in the 'actual management or conduct' of the company (or its subsidiary); and

- the individual must, in order to obtain the full relief, not recover any capital from the company throughout the period whilst the interest is being paid; such a recovery of capital is treated as a repayment in respect of the loan so as to reduce or extinguish the amount of interest qualifying for relief (see Income Tax Act 2007, s 392).

The interest relief forms part of the relevant deductions that are taken into account under the 'capping' rules (see Income Tax Act, s 24A). This means that the income tax deduction for interest (together with the other relevant amounts) cannot exceed the greater of £50,000 or 25% of the individual's adjusted taxable income.

26.22   Relief is also available in respect of the interest paid by an individual to purchase a share in a partnership, or to make a loan to a partnership for the purposes of its trade.

Company or partnership? Dividends or remuneration?

26.23   A group of individuals seeking to go into business together should consider from a tax point of view whether (all other things being equal) it would be preferable to conduct the business through a partnership rather than a limited company. The protection of limited liability is still available if they form a limited liability partnership, but the protection of limited liability may in any case be illusory in view of the guarantees which lenders usually require individual shareholders or members of an LLP to provide.

26.24   A related question is whether assuming that a company is selected, it would be most advantageous to receive income from it in the form of dividends rather than remuneration.

The following example shows the different tax effects of extracting funds from a business carried on through a partnership and through a company (which pays out profits either by way of dividend or by way of remuneration) assuming all the available income is to be paid out and also assumes the individual has used his basic rate and higher rate bands (up to £150,000) against other income in the same tax year.

Note from 1 April 2023 the standard corporation tax rate is 25% (with a 19% rate for some companies). Furthermore, from April 2022, employer's NIC and employees' NIC each increase by 1.25% (ie 2.5% for both) as part of the Government's 'health and social care' reforms. Similarly, dividend tax also increases by 1.25%. It is best to recalculate as tax rates change each year in an individual case. Nonetheless the tables below help illustrate the issues.

Individual member receives income from LLP

2021/22	£	£
Gross profits		3,000,000
less self-employed income tax (45%)	1,350,000	
		1,650,000
less uncapped Class 4 NIC (2%)	60,000	
Post-tax receipt		**1,590,000**
Effective tax cost		**47%**

Individual shareholder receives dividend from company

Gross profits (year to 31 March 2021)		3,000,000
less corporation tax (19%)	570,000	
leaves distributable profits		2,430,000
Net dividend received	2,430,000	
less dividend income tax(at 38.1%)	925,830	
Post-tax receipt (Gross profit minus corporation tax minus net dividend income tax payable)		**1,504,170**
Effective tax cost		**49.86%**

Individual employee receives salary from company

Gross profits (for year to 31 March 2021)		3,000,000
less salary	2,636,204	
less employer NICs (at 13.8%)	363,796	
Taxable profits		0
Corporation tax		0
Net profit		0
Salary received		2,636,204
less employment income tax (45%)	1,186,292	
less uncapped employee NIC (2%)	52,724	
Post-tax receipt		**1,397,188**
Effective tax cost		**53.42%**

This table represents an oversimplification, as it ignores the individual's personal allowances and assumes all income tax is chargeable at the additional rate.

26.25 This table above shows that where income is to be paid out to individuals, it can be more advantageous to receive dividends from a company, not profit from an LLP. See para 12.7 for more recent changes to taxation of LLPs particularly as regards salaried partners some of whom have taken out loans so as to avoid tax changes as described in paras 12.7–12.9.

26.26 Indeed in 2016 many individuals running limited companies decided to disincorporate and operate as sole traders due to the disadvantageous dividend tax changes. See IT Contracting 'tax hike' webpage to see the increased taxes resulting from the abolition of dividend tax credits and the new regime – http://www.itcontracting.com/calculators/2016-2017-dividend-tax-increase-calculator/. The April 2021 changes to the IR35 rules which only apply to those trading through a limited company also resulted in more individuals who own a one person company deciding to become sole traders instead.

26.27 However, in practice, where profits have reached £3,000,000 a year the shareholders are unlikely to require to receive all the income and may well wish to re-employ it in the business. In such a case the advantage is with a company, at least where the surplus funds are used to finance capital expenditure. However do not assume that this is always the case. The shareholders may wish to draw it all out. Also remember that companies and LLPs must publish accounts. For some investors privacy is paramount and not having to publish accounts as a standard partnership (or sole trader) may for some outweigh the tax advantages.

Suppose, for example, that the shareholders required income of £500,000 a year:

Individual shareholder receives dividend from Company

2020/21	£	£
Gross profits for year to 31 March 2021		3,000,000
less corporation tax (19%)	570,000	
Leaves distributable profits		2,430,000
Net dividend paid	500,000	
Less income tax at 38.1%	190,500	
Post tax position (Gross profit minus corporation tax minus dividend income tax payable)		**2,239,500**
Effective tax cost	**25.35%**	

This advantage derives from the fact that the profits of a company bear corporation tax at a maximum rate of 19% in the example above (but rising to 25% by 2023), whereas a partner bears income tax at a maximum rate of 45% (and marginal rate 2% national insurance contributions) on all the profits of the partnership whether distributed or not; a shareholder in a company pays income tax only on the income he has actually received.

26.28   In practice, individuals whose business will be reliant on external finance, whether in the form of debt or equity, may find that a limited company is the only option. Banks are reluctant to lend to non-professional ordinary partnerships because they cannot create floating charges over their assets, although an LLP can create a floating charge and so may be found to be an acceptable borrower. However, providers of external equity finance are unwilling to become partners in an ordinary partnership, and probably unwilling to become members in an LLP, although this still remains to be seen; it is more difficult to achieve a satisfactory exit from an LLP, which may make them unacceptable.

26.29   In practice, shareholder directors may not want to take all their income by way of dividends since they will often wish to make pension contributions which attract complete relief from income tax, so that they will then require sufficient salary to be able to pay the desired level of contributions. However given the increasingly lower upper pensions cap (£1,073,100 lifetime allowance 2021/22 and frozen at this level until 2025/26), many now have no right to make further contributions to pensions. Even those under the cap are subject to a £40k a year annual cap on contributions (tapering down to £10k for very higher earners and also with reductions where an individual has cashed in their first pension, eg at age 55 (which lowest age to cash in is being raised to age 57 years by 2028)).

26.30   Whether individuals would be better off participating in a company or a partnership or, if a company is chosen, receiving their income by way of dividend or salary, or some combination of the two, will depend on the personal circumstances of the individual. All this requires careful consideration in each case, taking account of the future expectations of the business concerned.

Employment income tax charges on the acquisition of shares

26.31   Assuming a company is the chosen vehicle, individual shareholders who are to work in the company will want to structure their investment in order to ensure, as far as is possible, that no employment income tax charges are incurred in relation to their shareholdings.

26.32   The legislation in this area has changed dramatically as a result of the Finance Act 2003, Sch 22 which amends the provisions of Part 7 of the Income Tax (Earnings and Pensions) Act 2003 ('ITEPA 2003'). The legislation is such that if an individual subscribes or otherwise acquires shares in a company with the intention of working for the company, they will be treated as having acquired the shares by reason of their office or employment, notwithstanding that the employment has not yet commenced at the time of the acquisition.

26.33   Employment income tax charges will usually be disadvantageous. If a gain made on the disposal of the shares attracts income tax rather than capital gains tax, a higher rate tax will apply (20%/40%/45% income tax instead of 20% or 10% capital gains tax) and an individual will be unable to use any available capital gains tax annual tax free exemption amount. Income tax charges could arise during the ownership of the shares at a time when the shareholder may have no available funds out of which to pay them. Employer's and employee's national insurance contributions may be payable (in addition to the employer being obliged to deduct income tax under PAYE) where the shares are readily convertible assets (RCAs). Broadly, in the context of a private (unlisted) company, shares will only be RCAs if they could be realised for cash very quickly (ie there is a market for the shares or the company is about to be sold or they are held in a subsidiary).

26.34   The levying of income tax in relation to shares acquired by employees was briefly touched on at para 5.4ff.

26.35   The first potential charge to income tax arises on the acquisition of shares at an undervalue, where an income tax charge may arise on the difference between the market value of the shares acquired and the price paid for them. The income tax arises irrespective of whether the shares are restricted or convertible – see para 26.37ff for additional income tax changes which may arise in relation to such shares). Where the individual is subscribing for the shares at the very outset of a company's existence, before it has undertaken any operations at all or has agreed to acquire any assets other than the subscription monies for the shares acquired, it is unlikely that it could ever be successfully argued that the company's shares were then worth more than the subscription monies. However, if it is the intention that further assets or operations shall be injected into the company so as to make the shares more valuable than the amount paid for them, an income tax charge may arise. Once the preliminary stage has been passed and an employee or intending employee is to acquire shares in the company, HMRC may need to be satisfied that the price paid for the shares is not below market value if an income tax charge is to be avoided. It may well be advisable to obtain a professional valuation of the shares before they are acquired. In circumstances where a venture capitalist or other institutional investor subscribes alongside individuals (a situation which often arises in the case of a management buy-out) reference should be made to the HMRC British Venture Capital Association Memorandum of Understanding of 25 July 2003 (the 'MOU') which prescribes the tax treatment for common forms of venture capital and private equity investments (see https://www.gov.uk/hmrc-internal-manuals/employment-related-securities/ersm30520).

It is generally recommended for the director/employee to make an ITEPA, s 431 election within 14 days after the shares are acquired. This ensures that any future commercial growth in the shares remains within the beneficial capital gains regime.

26.36   Another potential charge arises where shares are subject to any restrictions (including provisions whereby there can be a transfer, reversion or forfeiture in certain circumstances), and those restrictions depress the market value of the shares. In practice, HMRC tend to regard almost all private company shares as restricted, due to the pre-emption rights that attach to them.

To the extent that the shares cease to be restricted, or a restriction is varied, or the shares are disposed of subject to any restriction, an income tax charge will arise. If the only restriction on the shares is one which provides for their forfeiture in certain circumstances within five years of acquisition, there is a specific statutory exemption from the income tax charge on acquisition. This may be of little practical use if the parties wish the restrictions to continue for the life of the shareholding. If the parties wish to include a restriction whereby an employee shareholder must offer the shares for sale on cessation of his employment with the company (see paras 26.71–26.73), the only way to be sure of avoiding an income tax charge is for the employee to pay market value for the shares determined on the basis that the restriction is ignored (or by making a s 431 election to be taxed on that basis).

26.37   A further potential charge could arise where the shares acquired by the employee are convertible into other shares of greater value than the original shares. The possible imposition of this charge makes it undesirable for employee shareholders to acquire any form of share capital other than non-convertible ordinary shares, but most companies are normally structured like this in any case; it is usually only institutional investors who wish to hold convertible shares.

26.38   If individual shareholders are to receive an equity 'ratchet' (discussed at para 27.25) where the final proportion of the ordinary share capital held by an individual investor is calculated by reference to the value achieved on an exit by means of a flotation or a trade sale (so that the higher this is, the smaller the percentage of the ordinary share capital which is held by the institution), careful structuring will be needed from a tax perspective. Further guidance is given on this subject in the MOU – see para 26.35. Normally, such ratchets are structured so that the institutional investors hold a different class of share from the employee shareholders, and these shares are converted into ordinary shares by reference to a conversion formula which is variable according to the exit valuation. Notwithstanding that there is no conversion of the employees' shares (their interest being enhanced through the dilution of the institutional shareholdings rather than a conversion), an employment income tax charge will operate on the operation of the ratchet, by reference to the increase in value of the employees' shares. Such a charge will only be avoided if the subscription price paid by the employees for their shares represents their maximum stake should the ratchet operate based on the value of the company on subscription for the shares. So, for example, if the employees subscribe for 10% of a company worth, after the subscription, £100,000, but on the ratchet operating in full they would have 15%, they must pay £15,000 for their shares, not £10,000, even though the ratchet may not in fact operate.

26.39   Additional income tax charges could also be levied if the shares acquired have their value artificially increased by more than 10% (the value will be treated as being 'artificially' increased if it is increased by anything done as part of a scheme for the avoidance of income tax or national insurance contributions).

26.40   Should it be impossible to avoid a potential income tax charge, employee shareholders may at least be slightly consoled by the thought that, should they make a loss on the disposal of their shares, they may be able to set the loss against their other income tax liabilities. However, in the case of shares issued after 5 April 1998 this relief is only available in respect of shares in trading companies which meet strict conditions concerning their trading status. The relief is, however, more valuable than a capital loss, since it is available against any income liable to income tax, whereas a capital loss can only be utilised against a capital gain in the same or a subsequent tax year.

26.41   If a potential income tax charge cannot otherwise be avoided, it may be possible to structure the investment so that it meets the conditions for exemption from income tax under the Share Incentive Plan Rules (discussed at para 5.28) or the Enterprise Management Incentive Scheme (discussed at para 5.38), in respect of which the relevant conditions are somewhat less strict than those applying to the HMRC approved share schemes.

26.42   It should be noted that these potential income tax charges do not apply to interests in a partnership, including an LLP (other than where such a partnership is a collective investment scheme for the purposes of the Financial Services and Markets Act 2000). In such cases, the income tax levied on the partnership profits does not come under the employment income provisions, whether or not the partners work in the business, and there can normally only be a charge to capital gains tax on the sale of the partnership interest; this could be a point in favour of structuring a business as a partnership rather than a company. These charges also have no application to an individual who can legitimately provide his services to the company as a consultant or independent contractor and not as an employee. This is because the income derived from such services is taxable as trading income rather than under the employment income provisions.

Enterprise Investment Scheme (EIS)

26.43   A UK-resident individual non-working subscriber for shares in a company will often be subscribing in order to take advantage of the EIS. The EIS allows the individual income tax relief equal to 30% of the amount subscribed for the EIS (currently up to a maximum aggregate amount of £1,000,000 in EIS investment in each tax year (£2m where a least £1m is invested in 'Knowledge Investment Companies')). EIS relief is a 'tax reducer' and therefore the 30% income tax credit is set off against the investor's *income tax liability* (but this cannot not give rise to any repayment of the EIS tax credit).

In many cases, the most important benefit of the EIS is likely to be the complete capital gains exemption on the shareholding (provided the shares are retained for at least three years and there has been no clawback of EIS income tax relief) – see para 26.54.

Furthermore, if the investor has made a capital gain on another asset, and in the period beginning 12 months before and ending three years after the disposal he subscribes for shares attracting EIS relief, then an amount of the chargeable gain equal to the amount of the EIS investment (or if lower the gain) is deferred until a 'chargeable event' occurs in relation to the EIS investment. Usually, this will be the disposal of the shares, such as the company ceasing to be a qualifying trading company, will also trigger the liability to capital gains tax.

Over the years, the EIS tax reliefs have become increasingly targeted at new or immature trading companies and are subject to a numerous detailed conditions. Some of the more important conditions are summarised below:

- The shares must be 'eligible' shares in a qualifying company. They must be new ordinary shares which throughout the three years from their issue carry no present or future preference on a winding up and no present or future preferential right to be redeemed. EIS-eligible shares can only be issued within seven years of the first commercial sale (ten years for knowledge intensive companies).

- The shares must be issued to raise money for the purpose of a qualifying business activity. The money raised by the issue of the shares must be used for that purpose within 24 months of the issue or, if later, within 24 months of the commencement of a qualifying activity.

- The shares must be subscribed and issued for bona fide commercial purposes and not as part of a scheme or arrangement the purpose, or one of the main purposes, of which is the avoidance of tax. Since 2018, investors must also satisfy the 'risk to capital' conditions. Broadly, this means that the investor must carry a significant risk that they could suffer a loss of capital that is greater than their return.

- The individual investor must not be 'connected' with the company during the period commencing upon the incorporation of the company (or two years before the issue of the shares, if that is later) and ending three years after the issue of the shares, ie they must not control the company, or own more than 30% of the issued share capital or voting power.

  Further, neither they nor any of their associates can be an employee or partner of the company, but unpaid directors are specifically not treated as connected simply by being a director. A director is regarded as unpaid if they merely receive the reimbursement of expenses wholly, exclusively and necessarily incurred in the performance of their duties as a director. However, there is an extremely important rule that permits directors to join the company after the EIS issue (provided they were not previously connected with the company or employed by any predecessor to the company's trade) and be paid a 'reasonable' commercial salary/fee.

- The company must carry on a qualifying business, ie it must either be a company carrying on a qualifying trade wholly or mainly in the UK, or engaged in research and development. It must also have a permanent establishment in the UK.

- For the three years after the issue of the shares the company must be a 'qualifying company', ie it must be unquoted, must be a holding company of a qualifying trading group or carry on one or more qualifying trades (although the legislation permits it to carry on non-qualifying activities provided they are non-substantial). Importantly, it must not be controlled by another company.

26.44   A qualifying trade is mainly defined by excluding particular trades. The exclusion list includes dealing in land, commodities, futures, shares, securities and other financial instruments, the provision of legal and accounting services, banking, insurance, leasing, property development and most hotel businesses. The trade must be conducted on a commercial basis with a view to profit.

26.45   Again, this is only a summary of some extremely complicated provisions. It is possible for individuals to invest through a scheme established by a company specialising in such investments who will make the subscription effectively on behalf of its investors and afterwards manage and realise the investment.

See guidance at: https://www.gov.uk/hmrc-internal-manuals/venture-capital-schemes-manual/vcm10000 and https://www.gov.uk/government/publications/enterprise-investment-scheme-income-tax-relief-hs341-self-assessment-helpsheet.

Venture Capital Trusts (VCTs)

26.46   A VCT is a form of investment trust in which investors may obtain indirect investments in a series of unquoted companies which are managed for them by the managers of the trust. Although these might easily be discussed in Chapter 28, it is convenient to deal with them here, because many of the definitions are the same as for the EIS. An HMRC summary of VCTs is at https://www.gov.uk/hmrc-internal-manuals/venture-capital-schemes-manual/vcm50000.

26.47   An individual subscribing for shares in a VCT is entitled to income tax relief of 30% of the amount he or she subscribes, up to a maximum subscription of £200,000 in any tax year provided that the individual's VCT shares are held for at least five years. In contrast to EIS, VCTs are not eligible for chargeable gain deferral relief.

26.48   In order successfully to structure a tax compliant VCT investment the following conditions are necessary:

- The issuing company must be unquoted, ie none of its shares or securities must have been offered to the general public through any stock exchange or the unlisted securities market, but a listing on the Alternative Investment Market is not a bar; there are provisions allowing a VCT to receive and retain shares issued in preparation for a flotation.

- The issuing company must exist only for the purpose of carrying on one or more qualifying trades, or act as the holding company to one or more subsidiaries which carry on such a trade; a 'qualifying trade' is generally defined in the same way as for the EIS.

- The funds subscribed must be employed, or intended to be employed in a qualifying trade carried on by the company or its subsidiary.

- The VCT's investment in the issuing company must not exceed £5m in any one company in any accounting period.

- The value of the assets of the company, immediately prior to the subscription, must not exceed £15m, and immediately afterwards £16m.

For a useful summary of VCTs and EIS above see https://www.gov.uk/government/publications/income-tax-enterprise-investment-scheme-and-venture-capital-trusts/income-tax-enterprise-investment-scheme-and-venture-capital-trusts.

26.49   Again, this is a simplified summary of some very complicated provisions.

Seed Enterprise Investment Scheme (SEIS)

26.50   The Seed Enterprise Investment Scheme (SEIS) helps small new companies and complements the EIS scheme. It is very commonly used where investors are sought for new ventures. It cannot be used by a shareholder with more than 30% of the shares. A very useful summary is at: https://www.rossmartin.co.uk/companies/seis-eis/3284-seis-seed-enterprise-investment-scheme.

TAX RELIEFS AVAILABLE – INCOME TAX RELIEF

26.51   Income tax relief is available to individuals who subscribe for qualifying shares in a company which meets the SEIS requirements, and who have UK tax liability against which to set the relief. Investors need not be UK resident.

The shares must be held for a period of three years from date of issue for relief to be retained. If they are disposed of within that three year period, or if any of the qualifying conditions cease to be met during that period, relief will be withdrawn or reduced.

Income tax relief is available at 50% of the cost of the shares, on a maximum annual investment of £100,000. The relief is given by way of a reduction of tax liability, providing there is sufficient tax liability against which to set it.

Example 1

26.52   Jenny invests £20,000 in the tax year 2020/21 (6 April 2020 to 5 April 2021) in SEIS qualifying shares. The SEIS relief available is £10,000 (£20,000 at 50%). Her tax liability for the year (before SEIS relief) is £15,000, which she can reduce to £5,000 as a result of her investment.

Example 2

26.53   James invests £20,000 in the tax year 2020/21 in SEIS qualifying shares. The relief available is £10,000, as above. His tax liability for the year (before SEIS relief) is £7,500. James can reduce his tax bill to zero as a result of his SEIS investment, but loses the rest of the relief available.

There is a 'carry-back' facility which allows all or part of the cost of shares acquired in one tax year to be treated as though the shares had been acquired in the preceding tax year. The SEIS rate for that earlier year is then applied to the shares, and relief given for the earlier year. This is subject to the overriding limit for relief each year.

TAX RELIEFS AVAILABLE – CAPITAL GAINS DISPOSAL RELIEF

26.54   For those who have received EIS or SEIS income tax relief (which has not subsequently been withdrawn) on the cost of the shares, and the shares are disposed of after they have been held for at least three years, any gain is free from capital gains tax.

26.55   Please note: if no claim to income tax relief is made, then any subsequent disposal of the shares will not qualify for exemption from capital gains tax.

INTERACTION WITH OTHER VENTURE CAPITAL SCHEMES

26.56   The company can follow a share issue under SEIS with further issues of shares under EIS, or investment from a VCT. However, it must have spent at least 70% of the monies raised by the SEIS issue before it can do so.

A company cannot issue shares under the SEIS scheme if it has already had investment from a VCT, or issued shares in respect of which it has provided an EIS compliance statement (EIS1).

Investor requirements

26.57   HMRC summarise SEIS investor eligibility as follows:

'As an investor you may be eligible for tax relief providing:

- You have subscribed for shares which have been issued to you and which at the time of issue were fully paid for. You may subscribe via a nominee.

- You do not have a "substantial interest" in the company, at any time from date of incorporation of the company to the third anniversary of the date of issue of the shares. "Substantial interest" is defined as owning more than 30 per cent of the company's issued share capital, or of its voting rights, or of the rights to its assets in a winding up. Shareholdings of associates are taken into account in arriving at the

30 per cent figure. "Associates" include business partners, trustees of any settlement of which the investor is a settlor or beneficiary, and relatives. Relatives for this purpose are spouses and civil partners, parents and grandparents, children and grandchildren. Brothers and sisters are not counted as associates for SEIS purposes.

- You are not employed by the company at any time during the period from date of issue of the shares, to the third anniversary of that date. For this purpose, you are not treated as employed by the company if you are a director of the company.

- The shares may not be acquired using a loan made available on terms which would not have applied other than in connection with the acquisition of the shares in question.

- The shares must not be issued under any "reciprocal" arrangements, where company owners agree to invest in each other's companies in order to obtain tax relief.'

HMRC guidance is at https://www.gov.uk/guidance/venture-capital-schemes-apply-to-use-the-seed-enterprise-investment-scheme.

Pension contributions, options, etc

26.58 Pension contributions can be tax efficient both for the company and for the individual, because of the tax relief both receive on their respective contributions. Some considerations regarding pension schemes are set out at para 4.39ff. Share options and incentive schemes are likely to feature in the remuneration packages of individual shareholders who work for their company. These will attract income tax liabilities for the shareholder, as discussed earlier in this chapter, unless they fall into one of the categories of approved scheme, as discussed in Chapter 5.

Tax considerations on realisation of shareholdings

26.59 Careful tax planning can often reduce, or even eliminate, the tax payable by an individual on the sale of his shareholding. These paragraphs only provide an introduction to the subject and discuss some of the main methods of tax mitigation.

26.60 One method of reducing or eliminating the taxation arising on a sale is for the individual seller to accept loan notes instead of cash. If these are structured so as to be non-qualifying corporate bonds, no gain will arise on the exchange of the shares for the notes. This beneficial tax treatment is subject to obtaining advance tax clearance under Taxation of Chargeable Gains Act 1992 ('TCGA 1992'), s 138.

However, when the loan notes are redeemed, or otherwise disposed of, this is treated as a disposal of the loan note. Any gain is computed by reference to the original acquisition cost of the shares. Further, should the issuer default on the notes, so that the sum received from the notes is less than the original acquisition cost of the shares, a capital loss will be available to the holder.

This delay in the disposal is useful because by taking notes redeemable at agreed times throughout their life, the noteholder may (subject to HMRC clearance) be able to spread the gain made over several years, so as to take the maximum advantage of the annual exemption, and any capital losses which they may have available to set against the gain. Note, however, that no part of the loan notes must be redeemable within six months of their issue; if they are, HMRC will treat them as cash, and the exchange of the shares for the notes will be treated as a disposal of the shares for capital gains tax purposes.

26.61   This capital gains deferral mechanism should be used with care if the original disposal would otherwise qualify for business asset disposal relief (BADR) (previously called entrepreneurs' relief). The redemption of loan notes will only qualify for BADR if the holder continues to qualify by virtue of their shareholding in the acquiring company. This will generally be rare, unless the seller is (exceptionally) taking a significant shareholding (at least 5%) in the acquirer and continues to work for it or any group company.

However, provided the seller has sufficient BADR capacity (total limit is £1million – see para **26.69**), they can obtain BADR on their loan note by making a special election to tax it at the date of the share disposal. This will lock in the gain and it is not normally possible to unwind the gain if the loan note is not repaid. Consequently, If an election is made to secure BADR, non-qualifying corporate bonds do not offer any tax advantage over qualifying corporate bonds (see para 26.62).

26.62   Should the notes be structured as qualifying corporate bonds, these are exempt from capital gains tax but do not enable a capital loss to be obtained if they become irrecoverable. The individual seller is treated as disposing of their shares for a loan note consideration equal to the relevant sale value. The resulting gain is then held over until the notes are redeemed or otherwise disposed of. This means that no capital loss is available should the issuer default; indeed, the holder will still be treated as having made the 'gain' which arose on the deemed disposal of the shares in the sale.

However, as with non-qualifying corporate bonds, it is is also possible to make an election to tax the qualifying corporate bond loan note at the date of the share sale to secure BADR (see para 26.61). Once again, by making an election, the taxable gain is locked in and this cannot be reversed in the event of a subsequent default on the loan note.

26.63   Put briefly, a qualifying corporate bond is defined by TCGA 1992, s 117(1) as a security the debt on which represents a normal commercial loan, and which is expressed in sterling and in respect of which no provision is made for conversion into or redemption in a currency other than sterling. A 'normal commercial loan' excludes, amongst other things, a debt that gives the creditor the right to acquire additional shares or securities.

26.64   The most common method for structuring loan notes as non-qualifying corporate bonds is to provide the holder with the option of redemption in a foreign currency (with appropriate caps and collars to minimise foreign exchange risk).

26.65   Under TCGA 1992, s 135 the conditions which have to be satisfied to enable a gain to be rolled over into non-qualifying corporate bonds or qualifying loan notes are that:

(a)   the acquiring company acquires more than a 25% interest in the company as a result of the transaction;

(b)   there is a general offer which, if accepted, would give the acquirer control of the company; or

(c)   the acquirer holds or acquires voting control of the company.

Under TCGA 1992, s 137, where the seller has more than 5% of the shares of the company (or 5% of any class) the transaction must be for bona fide commercial purposes and must not form part of a scheme or arrangement of which the main purpose or one of the main purposes is the avoidance of tax. To minimise any tax risk, a pre-transaction clearance should be made to ensure that HMRC is satisfied that the 'commercial purpose/no main tax avoidance' will be satisfied. Applications should be made to:

BAI Clearance
HMRC
BX9 1JL

HMRC recommend that clearance applications are sent by email to reconstructions@hmrc.gov.uk. HMRC's extremely helpful guidance is at https://www.gov.uk/guidance/seeking-clearance-or-approval-for-a-transaction.

26.66   HMRC has 30 days from the date of receipt of the clearance application to grant or refuse the clearance. In practice, a clearance will generally be granted for a share for loan note exchange negotiated on an arm's length basis.

26.67   Where the seller emigrates and is re-classified as non-resident after the completion of the transaction and before the notes are redeemed, the capital gains tax which would normally arise on the redemption would be avoided altogether (subject to any foreign tax liabilities that may arise). However, when asked to grant a clearance, HMRC would be likely to refuse it in the case of a seller who has decided to become non-resident at the time of the application, unless there is a clear commercial justification for the issue of the notes, such as the need for the purchaser to defer the payment of the purchase consideration. Failure to mention intended emigration in the application would be likely to render any clearance obtained void.

Inheritance tax

26.68   A host of other tax planning issues arise in relation to individual shareholders and family controlled companies, which it would be inappropriate to discuss in full in this book. One of the main considerations for an individual shareholder is the mitigation of inheritance tax (IHT) on the value of his shareholding. Much would depend on whether the shares are intended to be retained at death. If IHT 100% Business Property Relief (BPR) is available, the value of the shareholding should be exempt on death. If the company is likely to be sold, then the sale proceeds would be vulnerable to an IHT charge (since they would represent a chargeable asset).

One of the main ways of mitigating potential IHT is to consider appropriate lifetime transfers of shares or cash etc to spouses, children, or other dependants. Other mitigation schemes will involve the transfer of shares etc to family trusts. Inheritance tax savings schemes can have a great impact on the structure of a family controlled company and may, in some cases, involve the reorganisation of its share capital, or other restructuring operations designed to pass the value in its shares to later generations.

2   Transfers to family members and trusts and CGT BADR (entrepreneurs' relief)

26.69   Each individual currently has a £1m lifetime allowance for business asset disposal relief ('BADR', previously called entrepreneurs' relief) purposes (before 11 March 2020 this the relief had a £10m lifetime allowance). The relief charges capital gains tax on the sale of shares at only 10%, compared with the standard 20% CGT rate. So, with the important proviso that it may not always be sensible from a family and commercial point of view, it may be attractive for many family members to own shares so each has and uses their separate £1m allowance (see https://www.gov.uk/capital-gains-tax-businesses#1). Family members would also have to be employed by the company or be an officer of the company to have the benefit of 10% CGT BDAR.

26.70   With a view to preventing any shares transferred to the trustees of family trusts from 'escaping' into non-family hands, it is usually provided that, if the trust ceases to be for the benefit of defined classes of family members, the trustees must give a transfer notice under the pre-emption article. They are also obliged to give one before transferring any shares to a person who is not such a family member.

3 Dealing with resignation, retirement and death

Retirement or resignation of working shareholders

26.71   Where a company is controlled by individuals who all work for the company, whether they are directors or not, the individuals often desire that if any one of them should cease to do so for any reason their shares should become available to the others, since they often consider that a shareholder who has ceased to provide any contribution towards the progress of the company should cease to reap any further capital profit from his shareholding. Quite apart from this, a shareholder who is retiring may wish to sell their shares so that they may invest the proceeds to provide him with a pension.

26.72   Provisions are therefore often seen that provide that an employee shareholder who leaves must immediately serve a transfer notice under the pre-emption article. Exceptions are often made for an employee who retires at an appropriate retirement age, has to cease work through ill-health or injury, or is wrongfully or unfairly dismissed (often referred to as a 'good leaver'), on the basis that it would be unfair to deprive him of further accretions of value in these circumstances.

26.73   Alternatively, where there is a small number of working shareholders holding all, or nearly all, the capital, and the continuance in work of all of them is an important ingredient of success, the resignation of any of them, for whatever reason, may be made a termination event under the shareholders' agreement, so as to trigger one of the realisation mechanisms discussed in Chapter 17 and the succeeding chapters.

Death

26.74   Should an individual shareholder die, whether before or after retirement, his death may also be a termination event, in which case his personal representatives will be in his shoes as regards the termination consequences. It could be provided that termination triggers a put option under which the personal representatives may put the deceased's shares onto the survivors, although they may not be keen to enter into such an option because of the heavy personal liability which will fall upon them. However, it is now becoming increasingly common for such options to be put to the company, which would then be able to purchase the deceased's shares under a company purchase of own shares arrangement (often using the funds from a key man or similar insurance policy) – see para 26.85.

Alternatively, the deceased's personal representatives will normally be obliged to serve a transfer notice. The individual shareholders may wish their shares to be capable of passing to the beneficiaries under their respective wills or intestacies. This can be provided for by allowing a transfer by personal representatives in favour of any person to whom the deceased could have transferred his shares whilst he was alive, without the necessity for serving a transfer notice under the articles. This will normally cover a transfer to the likely beneficiaries under a will or intestacy. Such a transfer may not, however, be in the interests of the continuing shareholders, since there is no guarantee that the beneficiaries will be able to contribute anything to the business. They may therefore prefer to insist that the personal representatives must give a transfer notice or, alternatively, that a transfer can only be made by them in favour of one or more named persons.

26.75   There is often a reluctance to allow personal representatives or trustees to continue as shareholders if it can possibly be avoided. They are not usually able to contribute anything to the business and their prime responsibility is to safeguard the value of the estate. This makes them adverse to risk, which may often mean that they will exercise any minority vetoes that may be available to them so as to oppose any expansion plans or other strategies which they consider too risky. Since there is generally no reward without risk, this can be extremely frustrating for the other shareholders. They also tend to have a bias towards the distribution of profits rather than ploughing them back into the business. Should a company fall into the control of personal representatives or the trustees of family trusts, the situation is often worse; with leadership often lacking, the business may be allowed to drift into decline, and usually the only practical solution is for the surviving shareholders to try to raise the money to buy out the controllers, or for the entire share capital to be sold to a third party.

26.76   The death of a major shareholder often causes a crisis in the affairs of a company. On the one hand, the personal representatives of the deceased will usually be very keen to realise his holding as soon as possible whereas, on the other hand, the surviving shareholders may not have the means to buy the deceased's shares. If the company is able to buy the shares, this could provide a solution. The surviving shareholders may be able to purchase the shares by borrowing the purchase monies, offering security over the assets of the company.

26.77   A better solution is to couple put and call options with life insurance policies. The company and/or each shareholder takes out a policy on their own life for an amount assured equal to the estimated value of their shareholding, and executes a declaration of trust in favour of the other shareholders so that they become entitled to the policy monies and may use them to buy his shares.

26.78   Mutual put and call options are then entered into by the shareholders, which are expressed to be binding upon their personal representatives under which the deceased's personal representatives have the option to require the other shareholders to buy the deceased's shares, and the other shareholders have the option to require the deceased's personal representatives to sell the deceased's shares to them.

26.79   A separate put and call option arrangement is required for each shareholder. In all cases, the price will usually be that agreed between the transferor and the transferees, or in default of agreement will be fixed by valuation.

26.80   It is important that the arrangements consist only of options exercisable after the death, rather than a purchase and sale agreement which takes effect on death. Any binding contract to sell the shares (as opposed to put and call options) would mean that the shares would not qualify for 100% IHT BPR[4]. Also if a joint venture is a partnership not a limited company then the Partnership Act 1890 will apply and it is even more important to have contractual provisions agreed in advance otherwise the heirs of the partner who has died will have a right to demand payment for the share. If there were only two partners and one dies then death results in the dissolution of the partnership.

26.81   For the arrangement to be successful, each shareholder must top up his life policy periodically to keep pace with any increase in the value of his shares, and there should be undertakings by each shareholder to do this (perhaps in accordance with periodical revaluations produced by the auditors). Furthermore, each shareholder must keep their policy in force, pay the premiums and not to do anything which enables the insurers to avoid liability. If their policy becomes void or expires they must also undertake to take out a replacement policy. The other shareholders should have the power to do this on their behalf should they default, and to recover the cost involved from them.

26.82   New shareholders should also be bound into the arrangement by executing a deed of adherence and then taking out the appropriate life policy. The persons required to purchase should not include any previously deceased shareholders or their personal representatives, nor shareholders who have sold all their shares.

26.83   Each shareholder should make a will so that the executors appointed by the will have authority as from death to exercise their option, albeit that completion will have to be delayed until probate has been granted. Since this cannot be obtained without paying the estate's inheritance tax liability, the personal representatives may have to obtain bridging finance to pay the inheritance tax pending the arrival of the sale proceeds on completion.

26.84   If there are pre-emption rights in the articles of association, care must be taken to ensure that they do not conflict with the options, or that

---

4   See Inland Revenue Statement of Practice SP/12/80. See also https://www.gov.uk/business-relief-inheritance-tax.

the parties to the option agreement are bound to procure any pre-emption waivers.

26.85   Another arrangement, which is possibly more tax efficient, is for the company to take out 'key man' insurance on the life of each shareholder and, should death occur, the proceeds of the policy can be used to enable the company to purchase the shares of the deceased. This is only possible for working shareholders. To keep the cost down, the policy should be written so that the proceeds of the policy are for a capital purpose so that they are not treated as a trading receipt. It is also advisable that the company does not claim a deduction for corporation tax in respect of the premiums, and it may be necessary for the policy to include a small endowment element[5]. The new requirement to disclose and register trusts excludes life policies (and pensions) held in trust. See para 7.90 'Tax transparency issues – PSCs, TRS, PSCOC registers and the draft registration of Overseas Entities Bill'.

26.86   To make this arrangement binding on the company, it would have to enter into a contingent purchase contract with each shareholder[6] and, in order that there should not be an immediate disposal, this would have to take the form of mutual put and call options. However, the arrangement suffers from the defect that the company may, notwithstanding the receipt of the policy monies, turn out to have insufficient distributable profits to buy the shares or sufficient resources to make a payment out of capital, in which case the options could not be enforced against it.

TAX RELIEFS AVAILABLE TO COMPANY – BUSINESS ASSETS ROLL-OVER RELIEF

26.87   HMRC summarise the mechanics of business asset roll-over relief (which would generally apply to the company carrying on the business) as follows[7]:

'This applies when you dispose of some types of business asset, which you intend to replace. You may be able to "roll-over" or postpone the payment of any Capital Gains Tax that would normally be due.

Who qualifies?

You can claim the relief if you're trading and you use both the assets sold or disposed of and the new assets in your trade.

For example you may be able to get relief if you sell your butcher's shop and buy a new one.

---

5   See Inland Revenue Press Release 6/9/1978.
6   See para 20.4.
7   See HMRC 'Capital Gains Tax for Businesses, Capital Gains Tax reliefs for business assets' at http://81.144.160.101/cgt/businesses/reliefs.htm.

Conditions you must meet

You must buy the new asset between one year before and three years after the date you disposed of the old asset.

HM Revenue & Customs (HMRC) may extend this time limit in exceptional circumstances.

There are different additional conditions for different types of disposal. For example, land and buildings must be occupied as well as used for your trade.

See the helpsheet below for more on the qualifying conditions and time limits.

Download the latest helpsheet on Business Asset Roll-Over Relief – Helpsheet 290 (PDF 95K)

How the relief works

If you've reinvested all of the proceeds from the sale or disposal in new business assets, you can "roll-over" (or postpone) all the gain. There'll be no tax to pay at that time.

You may still be able to postpone part of the gain if either of the following applies:

- you only reinvested part of the proceeds

- your old asset has only partly been used for your business, for example, you rented out a property for a time and then started using it in your trade

You only work out the tax due when you sell or dispose of the new asset. You then work out the tax due by reducing the cost of the new asset by the amount of the postponed gain.

Example

You bought a freehold office for £45,000 and sell it for £75,000.

You make a gain of £30,000.

You reinvest all of the proceeds in new freehold business premises costing £90,000.

You can postpone the whole of the £30,000 gain made on the sale of the old office, as you have reinvested all of the proceeds.

When you sell the new business premises and work out your Capital Gains Tax bill, you'll treat the cost of the new premises as £60,000 (£90,000 less the £30,000 gain).

Example – proceeds partly reinvested

You bought a freehold office for £50,000 and sold it for £100,000.

You made a gain of £50,000.

The new business premises cost £80,000.

The office was disposed of for £100,000 and you reinvested £80,000. The amount not reinvested is £100,000 - £80,000 = £20,000.

The amount of the gain that you can postpone is restricted.

You deduct the amount not reinvested (£20,000) from the gain (£50,000). You can postpone the difference of £30,000 (£50,000 – £20,000 = £30,000).

When you sell the new office and work out your Capital Gains Tax bill, you'll treat the cost of the new business premises as £50,000 (£80,000 less the £30,000 gain postponed).

Example – assets used partly for business

You bought a freehold shop for £80,000 and sell it for £100,000, reinvesting all of the proceeds in a new asset.

You make a gain of £20,000.

But you've only used the shop in your trade for five years out of the ten years you've owned it. Therefore it only qualifies as a business asset for 50 per cent of the time.

You can only postpone 50 per cent of the gain, so the postponed gain is £10,000 (50 per cent of the £20,000 gain).

You'll need to work out the Capital Gains Tax due on £10,000 (the remaining 50 per cent of the gain).'

Chapter 27

Special considerations for private equity funds, venture capitalists and other equity providers

Summary

This chapter provides a very general guide to the types of transactions entered into by private equity funds, venture capitalists and other equity providers and the necessity for the investment to provide the possibility of an exit through flotation or trade sale. The maximisation of income and the preservation of capital through the use of convertible preference shares is discussed, as are means by which such an investor may seek to motivate management, such as share option schemes, ratchets and the compulsory transfer of shares on leaving. Crowdfunding is also addressed at the end of this chapter.

1 Introduction

27.1   This chapter deals with the considerations which are likely to be particularly important to investors who are providing equity finance to a private company. Some of these considerations are certainly not unique to such transactions, but can also be relevant in a joint venture. For example, a ratchet may be used to incentivise a working individual participant in a joint venture.

27.2   Private equity and venture capital funds have been active during the 2020/2021 Covid-19 (coronavirus) pandemic, although the picture was mixed. Economic circumstances over the decades always have an impact on the amount of investment activity taking place.

27.3   Although the two terms are sometimes used interchangeably, generally speaking the term 'private equity' refers to the entire activity of investing funds in private companies, whereas the term 'venture capital' refers to that part of the activity which involves the financing of start-up and early stage companies with a view to growing them to a size where they can be sold or floated, in contrast to the financing of buy-outs of established companies, which is the main activity of most private equity funds. The funds invested generally consist of money raised privately from institutions and high net worth individuals.

2   General structure and exit routes

Types of transaction

27.4   Most private equity capital providers will only invest in a company where they can envisage that they will be able to sell their investment at a substantial profit, either by way of a trade sale or a flotation within a short period, typically three to five years.

27.5   The desire for a quick exit and the ease with which this may be achieved in favourable equity markets in the case of a large and well established company is why most of the funds available from the industry are directed at management buy-outs ('MBOs') and buy-ins ('MBIs') and public to private transactions, which are only a specialised form of MBO or MBI. In a buy-out, the provider collaborates with the existing management team of a subsidiary which the parent desires to sell and provides the funds for the purchase, usually through a new company formed for the purpose in which both the providers and the management team are shareholders. A buy-in is basically the same transaction, except that the provider is instrumental in providing new management for the acquired subsidiary, in place of the existing management which may have underperformed. A public to private transaction is again basically the same, only here the provider collaborates with the existing management of a publicly quoted company, which is disenchanted with the stock market, to form a new company which makes a takeover bid for the public company. Many large transactions are led by the investing institutions, rather than the management teams, who may be installed only after the buy-out has been completed. The term Institutional Buy-Out ('IBO') is different from the term MBO or MBI for this type of deal – IBO being where outsiders, not the management, buy the company out.

27.6   In order for any of these kinds of buy-out to be successful the target company generally needs to be fully established and already profitable. There is often a substantial debt element in the transaction alongside the equity; the buy-out vehicle borrows money from third parties to fund a large part of the purchase price of the target, which adds considerable leverage to the transaction and enhances the ultimate profit made by the providers and the management team. The private equity funds themselves often invest by means of a combination of shares and high yield debt, often referred to as an 'institutional strip'. The loans are often repaid from the cashflow of the acquired company before realisation of the buy-out vehicle, so that on realisation its entire value is represented by the equity injected into the buy-out vehicle by the provider and the management team. In a favourable market the buy-out vehicles are usually realisable in a few years, often without any exceptional effort by the management team, since they are often attractive to trade buyers or can be floated.

27.7   However, in a more difficult equity market it is often hard to achieve an exit by means of a flotation or a trade sale, which has given rise to the 'secondary buy-out' under which the original private equity investors sell their entire stakes to another private equity fund. The motivation for this on the seller's side is that there is often pressure on a fund to realise investments in order to show their investors a return, and also that funds tend to be structured to have a ten-year life. It is obviously important to be able to show a return if the private equity house is trying to raise money for the establishment of new funds. On the buyer's side there is often pressure on a newly established fund to invest the money it has raised fairly quickly, which is often difficult given the shortage of new propositions of sufficient quality. The sale and purchase of an investee company which has further growth potential and in respect of which the possibility of an ultimate exit by trade sale or flotation is still real can therefore make sense for both parties. Usually a new buy out vehicle is established to acquire the shares of the original vehicle and the management team exchange their shares in the old one for shares in the new. Secondary buyouts may not be popular with the investors in the funds since they often invest in several, and if one of them buys a stake in an investee company from another they have effectively invested to buy their own investment. In the US, institutional investors are beginning to seek limitations on the ability of funds to undertake secondary buyouts, especially as the selling fund will often sell its last few investments at a low price just to enable the fund to be wound up so as to return the funds to the investors. In 2010 secondary buy-outs represented about 36% of all private equity backed exits and were the source of 14% of all buy-out transactions. By 2018 the percentages had increased to 48% and 18%.

27.8   In these large transactions the management team, who are only required to put up a relatively small amount of funds, are always in a minority. The rest of the share capital will be in the hands of a consortium of equity providers. Originally the managers usually subscribed for their shares at a lower price than the private equity fund, and consequently received the possibility of a higher return relative to the sum invested. This is known as 'sweet equity'. Recent tax changes, however, mean that in order to avoid an income tax charge the managers must now pay the same price as the private equity house when they subscribe alongside them in an MBO or MBI (or indeed a premium if the management's shares can benefit from any sort of equity ratchet – see para 27.25 below). This reduces the managers' equity return, and so they often now desire to obtain a portion of the 'institutional strip' offering an additional return in the form of interest on the debt element.

27.9   In contrast to these large deals are the much smaller ones arranged by providers of venture capital equity to start-up, early stage and small- and medium-sized established companies. Here the exit route is still expected to be a trade sale or flotation – usually the former, but the expected period before realisation is likely to be longer. An established company should be profitable and growing, but a start-up or early stage company need only have a product or service with growth prospects so that the company can, with the aid of the finance provided, be developed into a size which makes it attractive to a buyer or to stock market investors. Historically, start-up and early stage investments have been the Cinderella of the UK private equity industry. Few venture capital houses were prepared to invest in start-ups, particularly if they were hi-tech. This changed during the TMT boom, but following the subsequent collapse, financing of start-ups has again become difficult. These smaller transactions are generally structured in exactly the same way as the larger ones, except that there is usually no loan finance, and the management team sometimes holds the majority of the equity or, if not, has a more significant minority interest. The managers will often have subscribed at the inception of the company, and may legitimately expect the private equity house to subscribe at a higher price without the tax disadvantage which arises where there are differential subscription prices in an MBO or MBI, but this will only be possible if there was little or no likelihood of the private equity house subscribing at the time the company was incorporated. Although these smaller transactions are sometimes syndicated, more often only one equity provider is involved initially, although others may be introduced in later rounds of finance. The difficulty of persuading venture capital funds to invest in start-ups has meant that the founders have often had to resort to their families, associates and 'business angels' for the initial investment in order to develop the business to the extent which will interest a venture capital fund; these first rounds of finance are generally referred to as 'friends and family' rounds. There are, however, a small but increasing number of 'incubator' houses providing seed capital to start-ups, or acting as introducers of such finance.

Minority protection and exit machinery

27.10 In both types of transaction minority protections have generally featured heavily, since even where the providers have a majority position, each of them will usually be in a minority. The management team is often not allowed any minority protection. Typically, the minority protections are conferred both as positive and negative rights in the shareholders (or investment) agreement and as class rights in the articles.

Choice of exit

27.11 The choice of exit route cannot be determined in advance, since much depends upon market conditions, but it may be useful to summarise the main advantages and disadvantages (other than price related considerations) of the two main exit routes, trade sale and flotation. Typically the documentation will be structured so as to prepare the ground for an exit by either route.

27.12 The advantages of a trade sale are generally those of simplicity, lower cost and a clean exit, particularly for an equity provider which will by this route escape giving warranties and indemnities. As explained in para 21.38, a flotation often fails to provide a clean exit because of the likely requirement for 'lock-up' agreements. The disadvantages are possible management opposition (they may be unhappy to work with the buyer) and that if a sale is unsuccessful, confidential information released during due diligence may become available to a competitor.

27.13 One advantage of a flotation for the management is that they will usually be able to retain their positions afterwards, and by retaining all or some of their shares they may be able to reap further capital appreciation. The disadvantages of a flotation are the high costs and complexity involved, the risk of failure should the flotation be badly timed and the difficulty of achieving a clean exit. For the equity provider another disadvantage is that, whilst it may be left holding a substantial stake in the floated company which is subject to a 'lock up' agreement, it will lose the special rights and protections for its shareholding built into the investment agreement after completion of the flotation.

27.14 The provisions which investing institutions typically require to be inserted in order to facilitate an exit are dealt with at para 21.41ff, and in addition 'tag along' and 'drag along' provisions will invariably be seen (see para 21.13ff).

3   Maximising the return before exit

27.15 In addition to a profit upon exit, the provider of equity to a profitable company will generally seek an income return as well. This may be in the form of a preference share dividend and the preference shares are likely to be convertible into ordinary shares, so these can be converted shortly before, or on, exit. There is no consistent practice between providers as to the precise composition of the share capital they require and it will vary with the circumstances; there will invariably be some ordinary shares to give them appropriate voting power, but the rest may consist of preference shares or participating preference shares, or some combination of the two. A dividend which is a percentage of the profits earned in each year, rather than a percentage of the nominal value of the share, is quite often seen. Convertible or non-convertible debt is also an alternative, but care needs to be taken to ensure that the return to the investor is deductible in computing the profits of the company for tax purposes, rather than being treated as a distribution.

The management will normally hold only ordinary shares, but may receive the same combination of equity and debt as the equity providers.

27.16   Providers to a start-up or early stage company are not normally concerned about income. They will generally prefer that all profits (as and when they arise) are ploughed back into the expansion of the business. They will nevertheless sometimes take preference shares, but with no preferential dividend, and only a right to priority in the return of capital on a winding up. They will often be redeemable and convertible.

4   Preservation of capital

27.17   Start-ups and early stage companies are often risky investments. Far more fail than succeed. Others become 'living dead' companies which are able to survive, but not to grow. Investors in this type of company are often concerned to get as far ahead as possible in the queue for repayment, should the company fail.

27.18   It is not unknown for such investors to inject secured loan finance into the company, which is convertible into ordinary share capital at exit. If the company should collapse into insolvency they may then at least have the comfort of ranking in priority to the ordinary creditors, although any floating element of the security will rank behind preferential creditors. For a time this was a less serious problem as Crown preference had been abolished by the Enterprise Act 2002, but Crown preference was restored from 1 December 2020 by the Finance Act 2020 with the result that HMRC is again a preferential creditor. This has substantial implications including for directors who may have given a personal guarantee confident it was unlikely to be called upon had HMRC not been a preferred creditor ahead of other debts and now more likely to be exercised.

27.19   However, a large amount of debt in the company looks bad on the balance sheet and may render the company technically insolvent. Furthermore, start-up and early stage companies rarely have any substantial assets which can form the basis of effective security. Resort may therefore be had to shares carrying priority on return of capital. These provide no comfort at all where the company is insolvent, but may enable the investor to recover its investment in a 'living dead' company ahead of the management team who hold the ordinary shares. If such a company is to be sold, the investor will try to arrange the sale so that any proceeds are first paid to the preference shareholders until they have received their capital in the way set out in para 21.42. If the company enters into solvent liquidation, the preference shareholders will automatically get their capital back before the ordinary shares. There will often be a right to convert into ordinary shares, which will be exercised before an exit, in which it appears that a higher value will attach to the ordinary shares than that attached to the preference shares. A middle way is for the investors to take packages consisting of a mixture of shares and convertible loan stock; sometimes subordinated convertible loan stock is used which, although ranking behind all other creditors on a winding up, may be capable of being repaid even where the company would have insufficient distributable profits to redeem redeemable shares.

5 Retaining and motivating management

Introduction

27.20   The management team is vital to the success of any private equity or venture capital investment. The equity provider relies on them entirely to develop the business of the investee company in order to achieve a successful exit. Retaining and motivating the management team is thus a vital matter. Should a successful exit be achieved, the management team members often stand to reap a far higher reward in relation to the money they have invested than will the equity provider, as well as often earning a very generous salary in the meantime. This might be motivation enough, but a particularly valuable executive may have other temptations open to him which may cause him to walk away. In an effort to avoid this, various other techniques are used, which are a combination of the carrot and the stick.

Service agreements

27.21   The traditional way of retaining and motivating an executive was for the company to enter into a service agreement with him. In return for a salary, and appropriately tempting perquisites, the executive would bind himself to serve the company for a fixed period of years, and in addition would enter into a non-compete covenant to run for a period after expiration.

27.22   However, service agreements are in fact not a good way of retaining an executive. Specific performance is not available to enforce a service agreement and although, in theory, should an executive leave before the expiry of his agreement the company could have a substantial claim in damages, such claims have not often been successful. There is usually great difficulty in quantifying the loss flowing from the breach, and most people are eventually replaceable. The company would be bound to mitigate the loss by making every effort to recruit a replacement and there may be arguments as to whether the company could have found a replacement, or found one sooner than it in fact did. A non-compete covenant may provide comfort, but will be no good against an executive who has skills which can be transferred to a non-competing business and, if too widely drawn, it will be in unlawful restraint of trade and the covenant will be unenforceable, so that even a transfer to a competitor may not be effectively restrained. For example, an area restriction is easily avoided if the executive can obtain employment outside the prohibited area. Indeed, in this era of increased globalisation of business, area restraints are fast becoming useless in many sectors. Non-soliciting covenants are difficult to enforce because of the difficulty of proving that a customer was solicited rather than that he gravitated to the executive of his own accord.

27.23 Not only are service agreements often ineffective to retain an executive, they can also become a heavy liability for the company if it finds it necessary to terminate them early, eg because it is dissatisfied with the performance of the executive or the executive has fallen out with the rest of the management team or the equity provider. It is very difficult to prove incompetence, so any such termination is likely to be a wrongful termination, entitling the executive to damages equal to the value, after taxation, of the salary and benefits which would have been received over the unexpired term of the agreement, less deductions in respect of mitigation and other sundry matters. There have been instances in which a small start-up or early stage company has been virtually crippled by such a claim for damages. Furthermore, if the company is in breach of the agreement, non-compete covenants cannot be enforced unless they are re-affirmed as part of the settlement agreement with the dismissed executive.

27.24 The length of the average management team service contract has therefore tended to be reduced, although it may be necessary to offer a longer-term agreement in order to attract a particularly sought-after executive from outside. Instead, management incentives tend to be provided through the provision of share option schemes which are tied to results, so that the better the company's results are, the more options the executives receive and the bigger the profit they are likely to make on realisation. Option schemes are discussed in Chapter 5. Even if such a scheme is too generous to fall within the criteria for HMRC approval (which criteria often fail to provide enough headroom for the company effectively to motivate a key executive), they may well remain very attractive even though there will be an income tax liability for the executive. Options can also be used to incentivise management members who are not amongst the original subscribers for equity, including less senior executives.

Ratchets

27.25 Another, more direct, mechanism is a 'ratchet', under which the proportion of the ordinary share capital held by the management team is increased should the company's value on exit exceed certain parameters, so that some or all of any 'super profit' goes to the management team. Various mechanisms can be used to achieve this, but where the institution has been issued with convertible preference shares the ratchet can be achieved by varying the number of ordinary shares into which the convertible shares may be converted. Reverse ratchets are sometimes seen, whereby the management's proportion of the equity reduces if they fail to generate the required return. Where convertible preference shares are used this often happens naturally, because the institutional investors are unlikely to convert, and therefore retain their preference on return of capital. Sometimes, a ratchet is geared not only to the exit proceeds, but also to the time taken to achieve it – the longer this takes, the smaller the management's stake becomes, thus encouraging them to achieve an exit more quickly. Another type of reverse ratchet adjusts the conversion rate of the convertible preference shares upwards where a subsequent round of equity finance is obtained at a lower effective price per ordinary share than was paid in earlier rounds. This effectively enables the equity provider to second guess its acquisition cost, should it turn out to have agreed to pay too high a price and avoid dilution of its shareholding. This also incentivises management to perform, since their stake will diminish if the reverse ratchet comes into operation. The taxation of ratchets is extremely complicated, and tax advice should always be taken to ensure all parties are aware of the consequences of what they are proposing. Some of the issues are discussed at para 26.35ff.

27.26   In deciding the percentage of the equity which the management team should receive, institutional investors are guided by their required internal rate of return ('IRR') which is generally set at 30% compound per annum. Accordingly, an institution will aim for an IRR of between 25% and 40% per annum, whereas IRRs for management have typically been 100% or more, although this is less easy to achieve under the current tax rules (see para 26.35ff). The IRR is calculated by means of a complicated mathematical formula, but is simply an expression of the amount of money received by an investor over the life of the investment as a percentage of the original investment. For this purpose, both income and capital sums are included in calculating the return.

27.27   As regards the 'stick' element of the 'carrot and stick' incentivisation package, in an MBO or MBI considerable incentivisation often comes from the very cost of the equity stake for which a management team member is required to subscribe. It is quite common for them to be obliged to mortgage their houses in order to borrow the required sum. Failure could therefore have very serious personal financial consequences for them. This, of course, does not apply where an investor is injecting new funds into an existing company in which the management team are already shareholders, although in the case of early stage companies it is certainly not uncommon for them to have provided personal guarantees and/or security to banks in order to raise the necessary start-up money, and therefore they may be subject to similar risk.

Good leavers and bad leavers

27.28   Another element of the 'stick' approach is the tying of a management member's equity stake to his continuing to work for the investee company. A management team member who leaves before a prescribed date, for whatever reason, is normally required to give a transfer notice under the pre-emption provisions of the articles in respect of his entire shareholding and, if he has transferred all or some of his shares to his spouse, another family member or trustees of a family trust, the transferees will also be required to give a transfer notice. Rather than the shares then being available pro rata to the other shareholders, provision is often made for the lead institutional investor to direct that the shares shall be transferred to a particular person, with the idea that the shares may be passed to another management team member, perhaps one who has been recruited in place of the member who is leaving. An alternative is to arrange for the shares to be transferred to trustees of an employee share scheme, who can re-allocate them as desired. Unexercised options will invariably lapse on leaving.

27.29   In regulating the price of the shares subject to such a compulsory transfer, a distinction is made between a 'good leaver' and a 'bad leaver'. A good leaver is one who retires at an appropriate retirement age, dies or has to cease work through illness or injury or, perhaps, has been wrongfully or unfairly dismissed. He will receive a price which is related to the current market value of his shares, as fixed by valuation (see Chapter 22). The bad leaver is one who has resigned prematurely or been dismissed for good cause, who will generally receive the lower of the market value and the sum he originally paid for the shares, so the most he can expect to get is his money back. There is also what might be termed the 'very bad leaver' who has been dismissed for fraudulent or other improper conduct towards the company; he will not even get his money back. The enforceability of these rather draconian bad leaver provisions has never been tested in the courts. They may one day be challenged on the ground, amongst other things, that they amount to a penalty, although it is no doubt arguable as to whether this is likely to be successful.

27.30   It should be mentioned that where an employee shareholder is intended to hold his shares pursuant to an HMRC approved discretionary company share option scheme, originally the Income Tax (Earnings and Pensions) Act 2003, Sch 4, para 19 prevented the approval of the scheme where there were good leaver/bad leaver provisions. This has now been replaced but along similar lines (below). There is no objection to the scheme shares being subject to the requirement of compulsory transfer on leaving, as long as it is on the same terms as those applying to non-employee-held shares – ie normally a sale at market value. However, the initial investments made by the key members of the management team are unlikely to be pursuant to such a scheme; normally one will be established afterwards to motivate less important members of the management team, particularly those recruited after the original funding has been put in place. In 2013 the said para 19 was removed from the legislation. Below is a summary from the relevant HMRC manual of the current position particularly in relation to good and bad leavers (see https://www.gov.uk/hmrc-internal-manuals/employee-tax-advantaged-share-scheme-user-manual/etassum44310):

'Schedule 4 Company Share Option Plan (CSOP): Requirements relating to options: Exercise of options on cessation of employment

Unlike Schedule 3 (SAYE option schemes), Schedule 4 provides no statutory rights of exercise. Paragraph 24 allows for a scheme to provide for exercise on cessation of employment and paragraph 25 in the event of death. FA 2013 introduced Paragraph 25A which allows a scheme to provide for exercise on certain company events (see [HMRC Guidance] ETASSUM44410). It applies to all schemes including those approved before FA 2013 was enacted.

A company will normally consider it appropriate to determine what will happen to an option in the event of an option holder ceasing to be employed.

As tax relief is provided in specific circumstances (good leavers), HMRC practice is for a scheme that provides for exercise on cessation to state what will happen in the good leaver circumstances (see ETASSUM44320, ETASSUM44330, ETASSUM44340 & ETASSUM44350). Stated practice is that there must be a clear right to exercise (or not exercise) in all of these circumstances. It follows that if there is a right to exercise in one or more of these circumstances, then the remaining circumstances not mentioned would have no right to exercise. As the right to exercise (or not exercise) is clearly stated then this is acceptable.

If the scheme rules were only to include a right to exercise on leaving for "any other reason" and this is subject to discretion, this would not be acceptable as the "any other reason" would include good leavers where there needs to be a clear right of exercise. The application of discretion in these circumstances means that that there is no clear right of exercise. The scheme rules would therefore only meet the requirements of Schedule 4 where good leaver circumstances are excluded from the application of discretion.'

6 Online platforms for raising funds

27.31   In addition to the MBOs, outside investment and like described above in this chapter, some UK companies use online platforms to find investors such as Seedrs and Crowdcube. Always check the relevant platform's terms and conditions carefully if this is part of a proposed transaction.

The Financial Conduct Authority provides some advice on its website: see https://www.fca.org.uk/consumers/crowdfunding on this topic which also, for consumer investors, provides a useful indication of the FCA's role and the different kinds of such platforms.

7 Conclusion

27.32   It will be seen that private equity funds and other equity providers use many of the same techniques as are employed in a typical corporate joint venture. The differences between the two are essentially of emphasis only. A joint venture agreement will generally be drafted so as to be even-handed towards each joint venturer, but the equity provider's investment agreement focuses much more upon the needs of the provider and will contain no, or reduced, protection for the other shareholders. The equity providers make greater use of minority protections and they place much more emphasis on an exit by way of sale or flotation.

Chapter 28

International joint ventures

Summary

This chapter deals with tax and other issues relating to international joint ventures from two perspectives: the first part of the chapter is generally written so as to consider the position of a UK-resident company investing in a joint venture being conducted overseas, and the second part of the chapter considers the position of a non-resident investor in a UK joint venture company.

Matters discussed in the first part include the choice of business location, the choice of the vehicle through which to conduct the joint venture and choice of law and the related tax aspects. The second part of the chapter considers the taxation position on the payment by a UK-resident company to a UK non-resident of dividends, loan interest, royalties and payments for goods and services having regard to the usual provisions inserted in double tax treaties. The availability of consortium relief is also considered.

Notice: UK tax legislation is always subject to change and in particular attempts internationally to reduce the ability for companies to lawfully avoid tax mean the latest legal position should always be checked with tax solicitors. Note also that the UK's General Anti-Abuse Rule ('GARR') has an impact on some schemes. See also HMRC Guidance on this at https://www.gov.uk/government/publications/tax-avoidance-general-anti-abuse-rules.

1 Introduction

28.1   It is difficult to give a comprehensive and detailed account of the legal and other considerations involved in every type of international joint venture in a book such as this. Some general guidelines will, however, be given here on the issues which will typically arise, which can form the basis for seeking legal and other advice in the relevant overseas jurisdictions. At the date of this latest edition the UK Government is engaged in considerable and regular changes to tax rules for public policy reasons including overseas collaboration to reduce the risks of companies picking a jurisdiction based on tax rates and to reduce the risk of companies being able to hide their owners. See para 7.90 Tax transparency issues – PSCs, TRS, PSCOC Registers and the draft Registration of Overseas Entities Bill. Always take the very latest tax advice.

28.2 The first part of this chapter is written from the perspective of a UK corporation seeking to establish a joint venture with overseas corporations to conduct business activities overseas. The second part of this chapter considers some UK tax issues which arise where an overseas investor takes shares in a UK company.

2 Overseas joint ventures

The choice of the business location

28.3 Very often the business location will be ordained by the nature of the venture; very rarely will the prospective joint venturers have a completely free hand to choose a business location anywhere in the world. Many purely commercial factors beyond the scope of this book are likely to govern the choice of location. Such factors could include the nearness of the location to the market, the availability of labour with the necessary skills, the convenience of the location relative to suppliers, the general business environment and the desirability of the location as a place to live.

28.4 However, the following is offered as a checklist of the legal and quasi-legal considerations involved in choosing a business location:

Table 7
Considerations in choosing a business location

(1) Government regulation of foreign ownership.

(2) The ability to transfer funds into and out of the jurisdiction – although they are on the wane, some less developed countries still have exchange controls.

(3) The overall liability to taxation, considering national, regional and local taxes on profits, turnover, ownership or occupation of assets, and capital gains, transfer taxes such as stamp duty, and other taxes such as social security contributions payable by employers.

(4) Whether there are any withholding taxes on distributions of profits or loan interest.

(5) Whether the jurisdiction has a double tax treaty with the jurisdictions of each of the joint venturers and if so what its effect will be.

(6) The flexibility of labour laws and whether they involve any obligations such as compensation for dismissal, paid leave of various kinds, minimum wages or maximum hours.

(7)   The laws relating to trade union recognition and representation in the workplace.

(8)   Whether the laws which will affect the general operation of the business are unusually onerous.

(9)   The extent of the welfare system and the extent to which employers are required to contribute towards the cost of it.

(10) The stability of the government and the strength and sophistication of the government agencies regulating and assisting businesses.

(11) The stability of the currency, and the strength of the economy generally, together with the rate of exchange between that currency and those of the jurisdictions of the joint venturers.

(12) The existence of any import and export taxes and restrictions and the availability of free trade or other favourable trading arrangements with other countries.

(13) The availability of grants and other incentives.

(14) The nature and extent of any immigration controls and, in particular, whether it will be possible for nationals of the countries of the joint venturers to live and work in the jurisdiction without unreasonable restrictions.

(15) The extent to which information regarding the venture and its participants has to be made publicly available.

(16) The strength and effectiveness of the legal system, and the extent to which it allows freedom of contract.

(17) The existence of anti-trust and competition restrictions – those applying to the European Union and the UK are discussed in Chapters 9 and 10 respectively, but other jurisdictions will often have such laws.

Choice of vehicle

28.5   All other things being equal, it will often be appropriate to choose a joint venture vehicle which is tax resident in and governed by the law of the same jurisdiction as that in which the principal trading operations are being conducted. The chosen operational jurisdiction can be expected to levy tax on the profits earned in that jurisdiction, irrespective of whether the legal entity earning those profits is tax resident there or not. The jurisdiction in which the entity is tax resident may be expected to levy tax on the profits of the entity wherever earned, so there may be double taxation, although the effect of this may be mitigated or eliminated by a double tax treaty between the two jurisdictions. If one or more of the joint venturers is tax resident in a different jurisdiction from the entity carrying on the venture, a further possible layer of tax liability is added and consideration will be given to tax efficient methods of remitting the profits to the relevant joint venturers.

28.6   However, especially in some less developed countries or in some civil law jurisdictions, it may be found that no form of entity with which the joint venturers can feel comfortable exists.

28.7   The considerations in choosing the vehicle will include:

• the availability of limited liability;

• the possible need for the vehicle to be a separate legal entity from the joint venturers, so that its assets and liabilities do not appear on the balance sheets of any of the joint venturers (see Chapter 8 as to UK accounting considerations);

• the need to trade through an entity which is acceptable to third parties such as lenders and other contracting parties and which has attributes that can be easily understood;

• the need for a structure which the joint venturers can understand and which gives them legal certainty as to their respective participations, rights and duties; and

• the sophistication of the laws of the jurisdiction concerned and the absence of any legal restrictions which will reduce the freedom of contract so as to hamper the aims of the parties.

28.8   The last factor can be a particularly important one since, as mentioned in Chapter 1, there is a contrast between the civil law systems of the continental European countries and their former colonies and the Anglo-American concept of freedom of contract which prevails in most of the rest of the world. In civil law jurisdictions the relevant civil code often imposes legal requirements upon the parties which can be difficult to circumvent in order to attain the desired result. For example some jurisdictions require that all joint venture companies are majority-owned by a national of their own state.

28.9   The sophistication of the lawyers in a jurisdiction may also be a factor. In some less developed countries, and even in continental Europe, some of the more sophisticated features of joint venture documentation which are referred to in this book may be unfamiliar.

28.10   If an entity established or resident in a different jurisdiction to the jurisdiction of operation has to be used, and there is potential for double taxation, there may be some ways of mitigating it. Firstly, the vehicle could be set up in a jurisdiction which levies no taxes on foreign owned corporations incorporated under its laws, ie in a tax haven. This will leave only the taxes of the countries of the joint venturers to be considered and, once the entity has paid tax on its operating profits, any withholding taxes on the outflow of profits from the jurisdiction of operation to the tax haven entity. The use of holding companies incorporated in tax havens is widespread[1].

28.11   Although by no measure a tax haven particularly with corporation tax for most companies rising to 25% in April 2023 the UK does offer a number of advantages for the incorporation of a holding company for a joint venture conducting its operations overseas.

28.12   A UK company that receives a dividend from an overseas company in respect of which it owns more than 10% of the voting rights may claim a credit in respect of UK tax for tax paid on the profits of the overseas company and its subsidiaries. Prior to the Finance Act 2000, if the rate of tax payable by the overseas company or subsidiary exceeded the UK tax payable on the dividend, the UK company could not get relief for all the foreign tax. To compensate for this inefficiency, off-shore mixing companies were established to mix dividends from overseas subsidiaries which had suffered higher tax and dividends from overseas subsidiaries which had suffered lower tax so that the dividends came into the UK at a blended rate. See HMRC guidance at https://www.gov.uk/tax-foreign-income.

The HMRC summary below is useful (see https://www.gov.uk/tax-foreign-income/taxed-twice):

'If you've already paid tax on your foreign income

You can usually claim Foreign Tax Credit Relief when you report your overseas income in your tax return.

How much relief you get depends on the UK's 'double-taxation agreement' with the country your income's from.

You usually still get relief even if there is not an agreement, unless the foreign tax does not correspond to UK Income Tax or Capital Gains Tax.

Contact HM Revenue and Customs (HMRC) or a get professional tax help if you're not sure, or need help with double-taxation relief.

What you'll get back

You may not get back the full amount of foreign tax you paid. You get back less if either:

●   a smaller amount is set by the country's double-taxation agreement

●   the income would have been taxed at a lower rate in the UK

---

1   More information on the tax havens available is given in Milton Grundy *Offshore Business Centres* (8th edn, 2008).

HMRC has guidance on how Foreign Tax Credit Relief is calculated, including the special rules for interest and dividends in "Foreign notes".

You cannot claim this relief if the UK's double-taxation agreement requires you to claim tax back from the country your income was from.'

See also 'HMRC issue briefing: taxing the profits of companies that are not resident in the UK' https://www.gov.uk/government/publications/issue-briefing-taxing-the-profits-of-companies-that-are-not-resident-in-the-uk/hmrc-issue-briefing-taxing-the-profits-of-companies-that-are-not-resident-in-the-uk. It has been taxing foreign companies which operate in the UK that has been much in the press rather than vice versa.

28.13   The Finance Acts 2000 and 2001 introduced provisions to nullify the effects of offshore mixing for UK tax purposes, by limiting credit for tax paid on each component of a mixed dividend to that which would have been allowable if the dividend had been paid directly by the overseas subsidiary to the UK parent (ie limiting the credit to the rate of UK corporation tax at the time the dividend is paid). It also introduced a regime of on-shore dividend pooling, under which certain dividends which represent profits subject to a low rate of tax can be pooled and used to absorb higher foreign tax elsewhere, and of allowing some relief for excess tax on some foreign dividends against other foreign dividends received by the company or elsewhere in the group. Now that Advance Corporation Tax on dividends has been abolished, a UK company can pay a dividend out of foreign income without itself incurring any further liability to UK tax.

28.14   As part of the Government's reform of the taxation of the foreign profits of companies and as announced in the 2008 Pre-Budget Report, the rules relating to taxation of overseas source dividends changed fundamentally in that overseas source dividends now receive the same treatment as UK source dividends and are, in the majority of cases, exempt from UK corporation tax. In particular, dividends received by 'small companies' are exempt provided that the overseas company is resident in a 'qualifying territory' (ie a territory with which the UK has a double tax treaty containing a non-discrimination provision), is not allowed a tax deduction in respect of the dividend outside the UK and does not pay the dividend as part of a 'tax advantage scheme'. Small companies are companies employing fewer than 50 people and having an annual turnover not exceeding €10m and/or a balance sheet total not exceeding €10m. Dividends received by companies other than small companies are exempt provided that no tax deduction is allowed in respect of the dividend outside the UK, the dividend comes within one of the specified exempt classes and the dividend is not withdrawn from such exempt class because of anti-avoidance provisions. The specified exempt classes include a class for dividends paid to a company that controls the company making the distribution ('controls' broadly meaning that the company has the power to secure the affairs of the company making the distribution in accordance with its wishes). It is understood that a company will control a joint venture company for these purposes where it has a 40% interest in the joint venture company and there is another company that has a 40–55% interest in the joint venture company.

As a result of these changes WPP, the advertising agency, moved away from the UK as the changes had such an adverse impact. In 2012 it announced it may move back after the Government announced that profits of foreign subsidiaries will no longer be potentially subject to tax unless an exemption is met. A charge will only arise on the proportion of overseas profits that have been 'artificially diverted' from the UK.

28.15   Secondly, although the parties will probably think instinctively of using a limited liability company, potential double taxation problems may be overcome by using an entity which is fiscally transparent, such as a partnership. The profits of such an entity are treated as the profits of its participants. For example, a Delaware registered limited liability partnership offers separate legal personality and limited liability but is also fiscally transparent. Care must be taken in choosing such fiscally transparent entities, however, because the different jurisdictions of the participants may view them differently for tax purposes, ie the entity may be taxed transparently in the jurisdiction of one of the participants but not of the other. They may also not receive the benefit of certain double tax treaties. In the USA, limited liability companies ('LLCs') may be treated as partnerships for US federal income tax purposes by making an election, or 'checking the box'.

28.16   Thirdly, where the desire to conduct the joint venture through a company conflicts with tax planning considerations, an agency or nominee arrangement might be used, under which the entity in the country of operation trades as the agent or nominee of the joint venturers. The entity makes only a small profit for acting as agent, so that most of the profits accrue to the joint venturers in their own jurisdictions. Those choosing this route will, however, have to be careful of any relevant anti-avoidance provisions.

Choice of law

28.17   Considerations relating to the choice of law have already been dealt with in Chapter 23. Normally, the choice of law to govern the joint venture will be the same as the law of the joint venture entity, but an exception might be made where that entity is in a jurisdiction which is not thought suitable to govern questions relating to the relationship between the joint venturers, among themselves, and they therefore wish that the joint venture agreement (as opposed to the constitution of the entity itself) should be governed by the laws of a more suitable legal jurisdiction.

Other tax planning issues affecting structure or operation

28.18   During the course of a joint venture, money will flow in and out of the joint venture vehicle for various purposes. Such flows will include equity and loan finance from the joint venturers, and interest payments, dividends and royalties from the joint venture vehicle. All such payments need to be analysed to discover the most tax efficient route for paying them, since monies flowing across borders may attract tax more than once, but may alternatively attract relief more than once, so creating the possibility of a tax saving. If payments which are deductible in a high tax jurisdiction can be paid to an entity in a low tax jurisdiction, there is again the potential for tax saving. Payments made by dual resident companies, which are treated as tax resident in more than one jurisdiction, might attract relief twice. Entities which are treated as transparent in one jurisdiction but not in another also afford opportunities for double relief; in one jurisdiction the entity itself is considered to have made the payment and in the other its participants are considered to have done so. It may be attractive to advance loans, the interest on which will generally be deductible for tax purposes, rather than to provide share capital to the joint venture entity. If initial losses are anticipated, a tax transparent entity will enable the owners of the entity to receive the benefit of the losses rather than their being 'locked up' in the jurisdiction of the entity and a dual resident entity may enable the losses to be available in more than one jurisdiction.

28.19   It used to be the case that a non-UK resident company was unable to be the claimant or surrendering company under the UK group relief rules unless it carried on a UK trade through a permanent establishment in the UK. However, following the Marks & Spencer litigation (*Marks & Spencer plc v David Halsey (HM Inspector of Taxes) (Case C-446/03)*[2]), in which the European Court of Justice criticised the UK's group relief rules for being too restrictive, the surrender of losses made by a non-UK resident group company is now allowed in certain limited circumstances. From 6 April 2020 requirements changed so always take the latest advice. For a summary of the position for non-resident landlords (of real property) see https://www.bkl.co.uk/insights/changes-to-taxation-of-non-resident-corporate-landlords-april-2020/.

28.20   The scope for exploiting differences between the tax regimes of different jurisdictions may be constrained by various anti-avoidance laws:

- transfer pricing rules may prevent artificially high or low prices or rates of interest or royalties being paid for goods, services or loans in order to achieve tax savings (see para 7.49ff for information on the UK's transfer pricing regime);

---

2   [2006] Ch 184.

- thin capitalisation rules may limit the deductibility of interest on loans which are deemed to constitute too high a proportion of an entity's capital (see para 6.29ff for information concerning the UK regime);

- legislation may prevent profits being 'rolled up' in an entity in a low tax jurisdiction, by treating those profits as if earned in the jurisdiction in which the owners in the entity are resident (see para 28.24ff for details of the UK's regime);

- capital gains of an entity resident in one jurisdiction may be taxed as the gains of its owners in another jurisdiction (see para 28.28ff for details of the UK's regime); and

- legislation may prevent losses being used twice in different jurisdictions – the so called 'double dip'.

28.21   In the case of dividends paid by a joint venture company, a key question is whether any withholding tax will be required to be deducted by the domestic law of the payer of the dividend. This is a matter which is normally regulated by any available double tax treaty between the payer's jurisdiction and that of the payee. Until 30 December 2020 where dividends were paid from one EU country to another there was no withholding tax under the EC Parent/Subsidiary Directive[3] where the recipient owned more than 10% of the company which paid the dividend. This made it possible to situate a joint venture holding company in any EU country without incurring additional tax costs, although there are anti-avoidance laws in some jurisdictions. This has encouraged competition between EU countries to act as the jurisdiction for the establishment of European headquarters companies. ICAEW provides some guidance on the 2021 position onwards here – https://www.icaew.com/insights/tax-news/2020/dec-2020/prepare-for-withholding-taxes-on-payments-to-and-from-eu-territories-from-1-january-2021.

28.22   Where an entity in one EU jurisdiction makes a payment to another entity in the same or another EU jurisdiction for the provision of goods or services, including fees for the secondment of employees, a liability to VAT may arise. It may be possible to avoid this by grouping both payer and payee together for VAT purposes, even where they are in different EU jurisdictions. However the UK has left the EU so always take up to date legal advice as the position regularly changes.

---

3   (EEC) 90/435. See also EC Council Directive 2003/123/EC which broadens the scope of the EC Parent/Subsidiary Directive. This only applies in the EU so no longer applies to the UK from 1 January 2021 when the post-Brexit transitional period ended.

The UK's rules for taxing overseas profits

28.23   A UK company investing in a joint venture overseas will need to bear in mind the UK rules under which the income and capital profits of non-UK-resident companies can be taxed in the UK. Income and capital profits are dealt with separately.

INCOME

28.24   The profits of a company which is non-resident in the UK for tax purposes may be taxed in the UK if the company is controlled by UK residents. The test of control for these purposes is that contained now in s 1124 of the Corporation Tax Act 2010 (previously in s 840 of ICTA 1988) (see para 17.21). If no single UK resident has control, but two UK residents each have at least 40%, they will each be considered to have control. Broadly speaking, such a 'controlled foreign company' ('CFC') must be subject to a level of taxation on its income of less than three-quarters of the UK rate. Some tax havens have 'designer rate' regimes which enable companies to choose the rate of tax they pay. This facility enables them to pay the minimum tax necessary to avoid being a CFC in their parent's jurisdiction. Where a company is in a designer rate regime, it will be deemed to be a CFC under the CFC legislation.

HMRC summarise the rules as follows (see https://www.gov.uk/guidance/controlled-foreign-company-an-overview):

'The CFC rules are anti-avoidance provisions designed to prevent diversion of UK profits to low tax territories.

If UK profits are diverted to a CFC, those profits are apportioned and charged on a UK corporate interest-holder that holds at least a 25% interest in the CFC.

The regime operates by applying a series of charge gateways to different types of profits to identify any profits diverted from the UK that will then be apportioned and charged on the relevant UK corporate interest-holders.

There are also a number of entity level exemptions to reflect the fact that it's considered that the majority of CFCs are set up for genuine commercial reasons and to reduce the compliance burden in applying the rules.'

28.25   Subject to certain exemptions, the total income profits, computed according to the rules applying to UK corporation tax, of the CFC and any available tax credits are apportioned between all the persons who have an interest in the company, whether UK-resident or not, and a tax charge arises for all UK residents with an interest of 25% or more in the CFC.

28.26   The exemptions are such that the legislation is generally only likely to apply to a company which has been established for tax avoidance purposes; if the company has a genuine business in the overseas low tax jurisdiction (eg operating an hotel) it is likely to be exempt, but it should be noted that if its activities consist of investment business (including the holding of intellectual property), or dealing in goods for delivery to, or from, the UK, or to, or from, connected or associated persons, it may need to satisfy one of the other exemptions. The most important of these exemptions is that the CFC maintains an acceptable distribution policy which means, broadly speaking, that it must distribute 90% of its net profits (calculated according to UK corporation tax rules), less chargeable gains. CFCs in certain countries (the so called 'white list') may be excluded[4]. The white list has two categories – countries which are excluded altogether and countries which are excluded with qualifications. Reference should be made to the Taxation (International and Other Provisions) Act 2010 (TIOPA).

28.27   As part of the Government's reform of the taxation of the foreign profits of companies, the acceptable distribution policy exemption was repealed in the Finance Act 2009 with effect for accounting periods beginning on or after 1 July 2009. The repeal of the acceptable distribution policy exemption is a consequence of the introduction, also as part of the Government's reform of foreign profits taxation, of an exemption from corporation tax on overseas source dividends.

See the guidance at https://www.gov.uk/guidance/controlled-foreign-company-an-overview.

CAPITAL GAINS

28.28   Under the Taxation of Chargeable Gains Act 1992, s 13 the capital gains of a company resident outside the UK may be imputed to its UK shareholders who hold more than 10% of it. These provisions only apply where the company would be 'close' if it were resident in the UK[5] and it has no application to companies controlled by one or more non-close companies. The terms of the capital gains article of any applicable double tax treaty may also prevent a s 13 charge arising.

Transfer pricing

28.29   The UK's transfer pricing regime (which, with effect from 1 April 2004, applies to both UK domestic transactions and cross-border transactions) is likely to limit the extent to which profits can be rolled up outside of the UK.

---

4   See Controlled Foreign Companies (Excluded Countries) Regulations, SI 1998/3081 and see Controlled Foreign Companies (Excluded Territories) Regulations 2012, SI 2012/3024.
5   See para 26.10ff.

28.30   Following the changes introduced by the Finance Act 2004, the transfer pricing regime will be relevant to UK resident joint venturers in a UK joint venture, UK resident joint venturers in a non-UK joint venture, and non-UK resident joint venturers in a UK resident joint venture. This regime is dealt with in para 7.51ff. See also UK guidance from 2016 – https://www.gov.uk/government/publications/taxing-multinationals-transfer-pricing-rules/taxing-multinationals-how-international-transfer-pricing-rules-work.

3   UK corporate joint ventures with non-resident participants

Double tax treaties

28.31   Where a non-resident is taking a shareholding in a UK company, the tax position will be materially affected by the existence of any double tax treaty between the UK and the country of residence of the non-resident. The UK has the world's largest network of double tax treaties, covering in excess of 130 jurisdictions.

28.32   Double tax treaties deal with the difficulty that two or more jurisdictions might seek to tax the same income more than once. Most jurisdictions seek to tax the worldwide income or gains of all persons treated as resident within them and all income arising within the jurisdiction, whether or not the person entitled to the income is resident there. Double tax treaties relieve taxpayers from paying tax on the same income or gains in one of the jurisdictions concerned, or they can apportion the liability to tax between the countries, but detailed reference needs to be made to the tax treaty concerned in order to determine the precise effect of its provisions in particular circumstances.

Taxation of dividends and other distributions

28.33   The tax position of a non-resident shareholder in relation to dividends and other distributions received from a UK resident company will depend upon whether there is a double tax treaty between the two jurisdictions and upon the treaty's terms, but most of the UK's double tax treaties provide that non-resident shareholders are entitled to a refund of the whole or part of the tax credit attributable to the dividend, subject to a withholding element of between 5% and 15% of the dividend. However the Finance Act 2016 made some important changes. It amended the rules in Part 15 of the Income Tax Act 2007 (ITA 2007) on the deduction of income tax from payments of royalties by inserting a new s 917A. It introduced anti-avoidance rules to prevent the abuse of double taxation arrangements to avoid the duty to deduct income tax from royalty payments made to connected persons. See also HMRC 2016 guidance on deduction of income tax at source – royalties: https://www.gov.uk/government/uploads/system/uploads/attachment_data/file/532314/M1070_revised_TN_final.pdf.

28.34   The HMRC Technical Note on the 2016 changes was summarised as follows:

'•   A targeted anti-avoidance rule denying treaty benefits for royalty payments between connected persons where there are "treaty shopping" arrangements in place so that royalties are routed via a conduit company so that the royalties are ultimately paid tax free to a tax haven company;

•   Widening the definition of "royalties" so that the withholding tax obligation covers payments made in respect of intellectual property previously not caught unless they were "annual payments", such as tradenames and trademarks;

•   Providing a statutory definition make clear that payments made in connection with a UK permanent establishment (PE) or "avoided PE" under the diverted profits tax rules will have a UK source (and hence a withholding obligation as a result.'

28.35   A non-resident shareholder in a UK resident company may prefer to make its investment through a UK resident intermediate holding company, if the holding company is able to employ the dividend income from the UK joint company without the need to pay a dividend itself, since there is no tax at all on a dividend paid from one UK resident company to another under the previous rules. Under the new dividend regime above it is best to take legal advice at the time as the rules are complex (see para 28.33ff). From a capital gains taxation standpoint, the foreign investor may be better advised to invest directly into the UK joint venture from a low tax jurisdiction than via either a UK holding company or its own jurisdiction.

Diverted Profits Tax ('DPT')

28.36   Since 2015 the diverted profits tax (DPT) may apply to international transfers. It applies at a rate of 25%. The UK corporation tax rate is 19% (rising to 25% for many companies from April 2023) and the DPT is intended as a penal tax to encourage businesses to restructure relevant arrangements such that profits are not diverted from the UK and instead the arrangements are subject to the lower 19% rate of corporation tax. See guidance at https://www.gov.uk/hmrc-internal-manuals/international-manual/intm489500.

HMRC's guidance says:

'DPT addresses three situations

- a UK company uses entities or transactions that lack economic substance to exploit tax mismatches; or

- a foreign company with a UK-taxable presence (a permanent establishment) uses entities or transactions that lack economic substance to exploit tax mismatches; or

- a person carries on activity in the UK in connection with the supply of goods, services or other property by a foreign company and that activity is designed to ensure that the foreign company does not create a permanent establishment in the UK, and either the main purpose or one of the main purposes of the arrangements put in place is to avoid UK tax, or there are arrangements designed to secure a tax mismatch, such that the total tax derived from UK activities is significantly reduced.

Although in many cases the arrangements put in place to divert profits will involve non-UK companies, DPT may also apply in circumstances where wholly domestic structures are used if a UK tax reduction is secured. The legislation contains some specific exemptions, including for small and medium-sized companies (SMEs), companies with limited UK sales or expenses, and where arrangements give rise to loan relationships only.'

Loan interest

28.37   The Finance Act 2004 implemented into UK law the provisions of the EC Interest and Royalties Directive 2003/49/EC, which member states were obliged to implement by 1 January 2004. This applied to payments made after 31 December 2003 until 31 December 2020 when it ceased to apply when the post-Brexit transition period expired

28.38   Until then the position was as below which has been retained in this edition of the book for reasons of historic interest.

In summary, payments of interest between a company and its 25% associate in another member state are to be made free of UK withholding tax, subject to satisfaction of four conditions:

- the payer must be either a UK company (excluding its foreign permanent establishments) or a UK permanent establishment of an EU company;

- the person beneficially entitled to the income must be an EU company (excluding its UK and extra-EU permanent establishments);

- the payer and that person must be '25% associates'; and

- HMRC must have issued an exemption notice; in the absence of such a notice, the UK payer must deduct tax at the rate stipulated by UK law (currently 20%) unless a double tax treaty provides otherwise.

28.39 Again under the old law, where there was a special relationship within the meaning of art 4(2) of the Directive and the amount of the interest payment exceeds an arm's length amount, the exemption from deduction only applied to the arm's length amount. For companies to whom these provisions do not apply, the position depended upon the existence of a double tax treaty between the two jurisdictions, but without a double tax treaty a UK company paying loan interest to a non-resident would be liable to deduct income tax at the lower rate (20%) and pay it over to HMRC.

28.40 HMRC summarise the current position as follows:

'The EU Interest and Royalties Directive (Council Directive 2003/49/ EC of 3rd June 2003 – "the IRD") ceased to apply to the UK when the Brexit transition period expired on 31 December 2020. The IRD was implemented into UK law by the Finance Act 2004 and later rewritten at sections 757 to 767 Income Tax (Trading and Other Income) Act 2005 (ITTOIA). This legislation applied independently of the IRD and therefore continued to exempt relevant payments of interest and royalties after the end of the Brexit transition period.

Legislation introduced in the Finance Bill 2021 [*now the Finance Act 2021*] will repeal sections 757 to 767 ITTOIA with effect from 1 June 2021. For payments made on or after this date, no exemption from UK withholding taxes on payments of annual interest and royalties arising in the UK made to connected companies in the EU is therefore due under section 758 ITTOIA.

Exemption notices issued under the Exemption From Tax For Certain Interest Payments Regulations 2004 (SI 2004/2622) are also revoked. As a consequence, from 1 June 2021 these notices no longer entitle a company to make payments of interest without the deduction of income tax, even where the date of expiry on existing letters extends beyond 1 June 2021.

Sections 914 to 917 Income Tax Act 2007 (ITA) are also repealed. These sections entitled a company to make payments of royalties without the deduction of income tax if they reasonably believed that the payment was exempt from income tax as a result of section 758 ITTOIA. For payments made on or after 1 June 2021, the repeal of section 758 ITTOIA means that such a belief cannot be reasonably held.

The repeal of section 758 ITTOIA is also protected by an anti-forestalling rule. This rule will deny relief where a payment is made under arrangements where the main purpose, or one of the main purposes, is to secure that section 758 ITTOIA continues to apply to the payment. Such arrangements would include those that accelerate the timing of a payment that would have been made on or after 1 June 2021 in the absence of the arrangements.

The deduction of tax from payments of interest and royalties arising in the UK is also restricted by the UK's network of bilateral double taxation agreements. The UK has a double taxation agreement with every EU Member State and these agreements are not affected by the UK leaving the EU. A summary of the terms of the UK's double taxation agreements can be found in HMRC's Double Taxation Manual.'

(See HMRC March 2021 guidance https://www.gov.uk/government/publications/making-payments-of-interest-or-royalties-to-connected-companies-in-the-eu/making-payments-of-interest-or-royalties-to-connected-companies-in-the-eu.)

28.41   Many double tax treaties permit loan interest to be paid gross to the non-resident. In order for this to be achieved, however, the lender must obtain a certificate from its own tax authority as to its residence for tax purposes. This certificate is then sent to HMRC, which then issues the borrower with a direction allowing it to pay the interest gross. It is not until this direction has been received that gross payment may be made.

Thin capitalisation and excessive loan interest

28.42   Not only may a double tax treaty allow loan interest to be received gross, but loan interest is normally a deductible expense in determining the taxable profits of a UK company. Due to this more favourable tax treatment for loan interest, as compared to dividends, there may be a temptation to increase the loan interest to above a commercial rate or to increase the proportion of debt to equity. Such a practice is known as 'thin capitalisation'.

28.43   The tax laws of many jurisdictions have rules preventing high gearing and excessive interest from being employed to secure a tax advantage. Usually, the excessive interest, or the interest which is the part of the debt regarded as excessive, is non-deductible for tax purposes. Where an overseas country has such thin capitalisation rules, tax issues may arise from the interaction of these rules with those of the double tax treaties of that country.

28.44   With effect from 1 April 2004, thin capitalisation legislation is included as an aspect of the UK transfer pricing rules. The earlier thin capitalisation legislation in ICTA 1988, s 209 was repealed with effect from the same date. HMRC guidance on thin capitalisation is at https://www.gov.uk/hmrc-internal-manuals/international-manual/intm511015.

28.45   The thin capitalisation rules now cover loans between two UK tax resident, connected companies, as well as between UK and non-UK group companies. These rules are discussed at para 6.30ff.

28.46   Where the transaction is a loan by an offshore investor to a UK joint venture company, HMRC operates a pre-transaction clearance procedure. It is advisable to apply for, and obtain, such a clearance, as it gives significantly greater certainty to the tax deductibility of any interest on the loan.

28.47   As part of the Government's reform of the taxation of the foreign profits of companies, the Finance Act 2009 introduced a worldwide debt cap which will apply to interest payable in accounting periods beginning on or after 1 January 2010. The effect of the worldwide debt cap was to restrict the amount of interest on intra-group debt that UK companies within a worldwide group may claim as a deduction against their taxable profits by reference to the group's non-UK external debt financing costs. Broadly, to the extent that the relevant company's interest on intra-group debt exceeds the group's interest on non-UK external debt the excess will be disallowed. The worldwide debt cap was replaced in April 2017 by the 'modified debt cap'. The changes replaced Part 7 of the Taxation (International and Other Provisions) Act 2010 (TIOPA 2010) by insertion of provisions into the TIOPA 2010 by the Finance (No 2) Act 2017. The legislation on corporate interest deduction runs to 160 pages and HMRC guidance about 500 pages so always seek specialist advice on what is a complex topic. For a summary see https://www.mondaq.com/uk/corporate-and-company-law/702662/uk-corporate-interest-restriction-rules-keeping-pace-with-change.

Royalties

28.48   The Finance Act 2004 implemented into UK law the provisions of the EC Interest and Royalties Directive 2003/49/EC, which member states were obliged to implement by 1 January 2004. This applied to payments made after 31 December 2003, but ceased to apply on 31 December 2020 due to Brexit. See 28.33 above however for international royalty payments as there were important changes in 2021. See also 28.40 above for the 2021 new position.

28.49   From 2021 regard must be had to the position under UK double tax treaties. These generally impose a similar regime to that relating to interest. The royalties may be exempted from withholding tax, or withholding tax at a lower rate may be imposed; and the non-resident recipient is then fully liable for any overseas tax. The payer of the royalties must normally comply with HMRC's administrative requirements before it may pay royalties gross. If there is no applicable double tax treaty, income tax at the basic rate of 20% must be deducted from the royalties and paid over to HMRC.

28.50 Section 911 of ITA 2007 sets out optional arrangements, under which companies are allowed to pay royalties overseas and deduct only the reduced rate of tax prescribed by the relevant double taxation agreement without seeking prior clearance from HMRC. The paying company must reasonably believe that, at the time the payment is made, the beneficial owner of the payment is entitled to claim relief in respect of any double taxation arrangements.

28.51 A royalty payment under this optional scheme includes:

● any payment received as a consideration for the use or right to use any copyright, patent, trademark, design, process or function; or

● any proceeds from the sale of all or any part of the patent rights.

28.52 If the payments are subsequently assessed to UK tax (eg where it is ultimately found that the recipient was not entitled to receive the payments gross or under deduction at reduced rate), then the tax rate at which the payments are assessed is that prescribed in any relevant double taxation agreement.

28.53 The UK's transfer pricing régime can also be used to attack excessive royalties, and indeed any payment for goods or services passing between the UK joint company and a non-resident participant.

Payments for goods and services supplied

28.54 As long as the non-resident provider of the goods or services does not trade in the UK through a permanent establishment when providing the goods or services, any income receivable from such provision is not liable to UK tax and the UK company receiving the goods or services may make payment without deducting UK tax. The UK's transfer pricing régime can be used to attack non-arms' length prices for goods and services where the parties are connected within the terms of that legislation.

28.55 Where the parties are not part of the same group for VAT purposes, it will be necessary to identify the nature of the goods and services being supplied, and their place of supply. If as regards goods, title passes outside the UK (previously outside the EU), the vendor should have no exposure or obligations to VAT. For services, normally it is the supplier who must account to the tax authorities for any VAT due on the supply. However, for certain services, this rule is reversed and it is the customer who must account for the VAT due. The relevant services include:

(1) the transfer and assignment of copyrights, patents, licences, trademarks and similar rights;

(2) advertising services;

(3)   services of consultants, engineers, consultancy bureaux, lawyers, accountants and other similar services, data processing and the provision of information;

(4)   agreeing to refrain from pursuing or exercising rights referred to in (1) above;

(5)   banking, financial and other services;

(6)   the supply of staff;

(7)   letting or hiring of goods other than means of transport;

(8)   telecommunication services;

(9)   electronically supplied services, eg web-hosting; and

(10) the procuring of any of the above.

In 2021 the post-Brexit VAT position is complicated. Tax specialist advice should be sought.

Consortium relief

28.56   Consortium relief was discussed at para 7.40ff. The Finance Act 2000 makes it unnecessary for a non-resident shareholder in a UK-resident joint venture company to make its investment through a UK subsidiary in order to ensure the availability of consortium relief. The companies actually claiming the relief, or through which the relief is made available to the other UK companies owned by the non-resident investor group, need not be UK-tax-resident, but need to have a UK taxable trade.

28.57   Following the decision of the ECJ in *Marks & Spencer plc v Halsey* the Finance Act 2006 extended the UK group relief regime so as to allow a non-UK 75% subsidiary to surrender its losses to a UK parent in certain circumstances. Whilst the FA 2006 changes do not affect the consortium rules, a 51% relationship between a parent and a subsidiary falls within the provisions of the EC Treaty on Freedom of Establishment which formed the basis of the *Marks & Spencer* decision. Although the legislation relating to group relief between UK resident companies is not so wide as to catch 51% subsidiaries there is an argument that the denial of consortium relief between a non-UK 51% subsidiary and its UK parent is inconsistent with the ECJ decision. Whether this argument would extend to a 50% subsidiary, as with a 50/50 joint venture, is somewhat more tenuous and would depend upon an interpretation of the Freedom of Establishment rules. See also *Linpac Group Holdings Ltd v HMRC*[6]. From 6 April 2020 there were some changes made in this area – see para 28.19 above.

---

6   [2020] UKFTT 60 (TC).

Part D

Case studies and precedents

Case study 1

Caspian Pipeline Consortium ('CPC')

In international oil or gas field projects, it is more common for international energy companies to form incorporated joint ventures. An interesting example of an international incorporated joint venture is the pipeline project to build a one thousand, five hundred kilometre crude oil pipeline from the giant Tengiz oil field in Kazakhstan to the Black Sea port of Novorossiysk in Russia. The pipeline is commonly known as the Caspian Pipeline Consortium (or 'CPC').

Background

In 1992, three governments: the Government of the Russian Federation ('Russia'), the Government of the Republic of Kazakhstan ('Kazakhstan') and the Government of the Sultanate of Oman ('Oman') signed a pipeline consortium agreement. The agreement confirmed that Russia, Kazakhstan and Oman wished to participate in CPC. CPC would transport crude oil from fields in Western Kazakhstan to terminal facilities in a Black Sea port in Russia. The crude oil would then be further transported from the Black Sea to world markets.

For the rights of way necessary to build the pipeline, the participation of Kazakhstan and Russia in CPC was essential. Oman was able to participate in CPC because of its political connections with Kazakhstan. Oman had provided Kazakhstan with a $100 million loan soon after Kazakhstan became an independent country in the early 1990s.

Russia, Kazakhstan and Oman wanted to conduct CPC's business activities through a limited liability company. They therefore became shareholders in a Bermudan company called the Caspian Pipeline Consortium Limited (or 'CPC Bermuda'). Each of the shareholders owned one-third of CPC Bermuda's issued share capital.

Financial backing for the several billion dollar pipeline project was needed, which the CPC Bermuda shareholders were not able to provide. CPC Bermuda looked to Chevron, the US energy company, to provide the financing. Chevron owned 50% of the Tengiz oil field, the other 50% being owned by a state-owned Kazakh company. The Tengiz field oil reserves had been estimated at between six to nine billion barrels and Chevron needed a pipeline to export its share of Tengiz production to world markets.

The CPC Bermuda shareholders and Chevron participated in negotiations for CPC. The negotiations broke down in 1995 over the financing terms. Russia, Kazakhstan and Oman sought to obtain alternative financing from third parties. Chevron began to talk to other energy companies with a view to forming an alternative consortium to finance CPC.

Almaty Protocol

After extensive discussions, a protocol relating to CPC was signed in Almaty, Kazakhstan in April 1996 (the 'Almaty Protocol'). The signatories to the Almaty Protocol were Russia, Kazakhstan and Oman (being collectively referred to as the 'Founding Members') and a number of international energy companies including Chevron (being collectively referred to as the 'Producer Companies'). The Almaty Protocol provided for the restructuring of CPC Bermuda through an increase in its share capital, the new shares being acquired by the Producer Companies at their option. The Producer Companies would provide financing for the initial construction costs for the pipeline (and its associated facilities).

The main provisions of the Almaty Protocol were:

(A)   Each Producer Company had an option exercisable by a specified time to purchase a specified percentage of CPC Bermuda's share capital. (Collectively, the Producer Companies could not own more than 50% of CPC Bermuda's share capital.)

(B)   The Founding Members would own collectively 50% of CPC Bermuda's share capital.

(C)   The Producer Companies would provide 100% of the financing for CPC's initial construction costs (later estimated to be US$2.2 billion). Each Producer Company would provide funding equal to double its percentage interest participation, eg a 12.5% shareholding would result in that shareholder funding 25% of the initial construction costs of CPC.

(D)   In addition to transporting crude oil from Tengiz, CPC would transport crude oil from other fields in Kazakhstan and from Russian oil fields.

(E)   The pipeline capacity was specified, with each Producer Company and Founding Member being allocated specific pipeline capacity rights.

Negotiations between the Producer Companies and the Founding Members

For the period from April 1996 to December 1996, the Founding Members and the Producer Companies (collectively the 'Transition Committee') negotiated the terms relating to the acquisition of shares in CPC Bermuda and the rights and obligations of all the shareholders.

In addition, there were separate negotiations between the Producer Companies relating to matters which affected the Producer Companies in their capacity as 'funding' shareholders. The Producer Companies (of which there were then ten) had formed what was known as the 'Producer Company Committee' (the 'PCC'). Each Producer Company had one representative on the PCC. Underneath the PCC, there were a number of specialist sub-committees including a Commercial Sub-committee, a Technical Sub-committee, a Tax Sub-committee and a Legal Sub-committee. Each Producer Company had a representative on each sub-committee. The role of the sub-committees was to provide advice and guidance and make recommendations to the PCC.

It was extremely important that the PCC had a mechanism to reach decisions on key project matters so that a unified position could be presented during the negotiations with the Founding Members. This was provided by a voting passmark which meant that no one Producer Company on its own could force a positive vote through the PCC or have a blocking vote.

The negotiations at the PCC level were lengthy, and not only because of the language barriers. Ten energy companies were involved from six countries, each with their own interests to consider and, where possible, protect. This was exacerbated because the Producer Companies were themselves sub-divided into 'Russian Producer Companies' (companies with production or anticipated production in Russia) and 'Kazakh Producer Companies' (companies with production or anticipated production in Kazakhstan).

CPC shareholders' agreement

On 6 December 1996, the Founding Members and the Producer Companies signed an agreement (the 'CPC Shareholders' Agreement') which specified in great detail the terms upon which the Producer Companies were prepared to exercise their option to acquire shares, and the rights and obligations of each of the shareholders.

The CPC Shareholders' Agreement differed from the Almaty Protocol in one important respect: the Producer Companies would not be acquiring shares in CPC Bermuda. The Transition Committee agreed that the Producer Companies would acquire 50% of the issued share capital of two new companies, with the Founding Members acquiring the remaining 50%.

The Tax Sub-committee had advised the PCC that it would not have been tax efficient for the Producer Companies to have acquired shares in CPC Bermuda. The Producer Companies would be providing the financing for the initial construction costs in the form of loans. The US and the Russian Federation had a tax treaty which allowed, amongst other things, for interest on loans to be deducted from a Russian company's taxable profits if at least 30% of the company's share capital was owned directly or indirectly by US companies. The US and Bermuda did not have a tax treaty which provided for interest deductibility on loans to a Bermudan company.

The two new companies to be formed would be a Russian Closed Joint Stock Company, called CPC-R, and a Kazakh Joint Stock Company, called CPC-K. CPC-R with its 30% US ownership could then take advantage of the tax treaty between the US and the Russian Federation. CPC-R and CPC-K would collectively own 100% of CPC. The Producer Companies, as one group, and the Founding Members, as the other group, would each own 50% of CPC-K and CPC-R. (In 2002, there was a change in Russian tax law. CPC-R now receives the benefit of the US–Russia tax treaty without having to show that its US shareholders own 30% of its share capital.)

Conditions precedent

The share acquisition in CPC-R and CPC-K was subject to a number of conditions precedent, including:

(A)   The execution of all the financing agreements for CPC by all the parties. (The value of CPC Bermuda's assets (including existing pipeline assets in Russia and Kazakhstan) formed the basis of a loan from the Founding Members to CPC-R and CPC-K.)

(B)   The receipt of satisfactory decrees supporting CPC from Russia and Kazakhstan.

Share acquisition

The conditions precedent were satisfied on 16 May 1997. The Founding Members and the Producer Companies then became shareholders in CPC-R and CPC-K. CPC Bermuda transferred all its assets (including certain pipeline assets) to CPC-R and to CPC-K. CPC Bermuda is now effectively a dormant company.

CPC-R and CPC-K shareholder arrangements

The CPC Shareholders' Agreement and the charter documents for CPC-R and CPC-K provide a voting structure for all the matters to be determined by the shareholders of CPC-R and CPC-K. Decisions are taken at a 'Shareholders' Committee', which is the successor committee to the Transition Committee.

After the share acquisition, the Producer Companies retained the PCC to discuss and agree on all matters affecting the project which would ultimately be subject to a vote at the Shareholders' Committee. Retaining the PCC was of particular importance during the period when the Producer Companies provided all of the financing for the pipeline's initial construction costs.

Significance of the CPC joint venture

The significance of the CPC-K and CPC-R joint venture was summarised on 16 May 1997 when Mr Anatoly Shatalov, the then Russian Federation's First Deputy Minister of Fuel and Energy made the following statement:

> 'The CPC project is vital to the national interests of Russia because of the critical link it provides to the international marketplace for Russia's oil exports. I believe that the CPC project will become the model for Russian and international oil business to follow in future projects.'

Current status of the CPC project

The initial construction of the CPC pipeline was completed on 28 April 2003. This represents a significant achievement for all the shareholders. The construction costs of the pipeline and its associated facilities were approximately US$2.6 billion.

In 2003, CPC-R and CPC-K transported more than 1.3 million tons of crude oil per month through the pipeline from at least six companies in Kazakhstan. In 1996, it was anticipated that there would be expansions to the CPC pipeline. The existing and anticipated demand for capacity in the CPC pipeline has meant that CPC-R and CPC-K is currently considering the first pipeline expansion. The design for the first expansion and the options to finance the expansion will be reviewed by CPC-R and CPC-K in 2004.

Case study 2

UK property joint venture

Joint ventures are often encountered in the field of property investment or development. Often, a landowner wanting to develop its land will agree to 'joint venture' with a development company so that they each share the cost and risk of development and, in return, the profits.

The following is a typical recent example of a UK property development joint venture in which Simmons & Simmons were involved, and describes some of the major issues which arose. In the interests of client confidentiality the property owner is referred to as 'O' and the developer as 'D'.

Background

O was a large listed public company with surplus land near a city centre. Previously used for industrial purposes, at the commencement of the venture the land was vacant and did not have outline planning permission for any change of use. O recognised the development potential of the land, but did not have the skills or resources to realise such potential by itself. D was a large property developer. It had the experience of spotting and exploiting development opportunities, and approached O offering to act as development manager/adviser to O for a fee or as a co-principal, sharing the cost of funding the development work in return for a share of the development profits. The parties agreed to the latter and decided to form a new limited liability company as their joint venture vehicle ('JVC').

Timing of the land transfer

The first issue was how and when to transfer the land to the JVC. The parties agreed that any increase in value in the land following any successful planning application made by D on behalf of the project should accrue to the JVC. However, to transfer the land immediately to the JVC would have been premature before any outline planning permission had been obtained and would trigger the acceleration of certain costs, particularly stamp duty. The JVC was also not in a position to pay the purchase consideration until after a successful redevelopment had been completed. The parties therefore agreed that O should contract to sell the land to the JVC conditionally upon the grant of outline planning consent. Since the land was going to be developed in pre-agreed phases, the contract provided that completion of the transfer of the legal title from O to the JVC in respect of each phase would only take place simultaneously with the sale of each phase after it had been developed, and to minimise stamp duty the transfer of each phase would be made direct from O to the ultimate end purchasers[1]. The interests of the JVC in the land were safeguarded by registering the JVC's contractual rights as a caution at the Land Registry.

Payment for the purchase price of the land

A related issue was payment by the JVC of the purchase price for the land. The JVC was unable to fund such payment prior to the development and sale. The parties agreed that the land price should be left outstanding as a debt owed to O but secured by the JVC charging its interest in the land itself. It was agreed that such a charge would be released in stages upon the subsequent sale of each developed phase and that the proceeds of each phase as sold would be applied partly towards repaying the loans made by the parties to the JVC for its development funding and partly by way of repayment of the land purchase price (in agreed proportions).

Funding of the development expenses

A second major issue was funding the development expenses. The shareholders' agreement envisaged the JVC being a 50:50 deadlocked joint venture company and that each of the shareholders would fund the JVC's development expenditure in cash out of their own resources up to certain pre-agreed amounts. Although O knew it had the cash resources itself to do this, it was not clear that D could fund its share, since it was relying upon the receipt of cash from other projects in which it was involved, and which were nearing completion. The agreement therefore provided that if either party defaulted in meeting their funding obligations, the other party had the right to make up the other's shortfall itself, but on the basis that such additional financing carried an enhanced rate of return and would be secured as a second charge over the JVC's land interests. Alternatively, if the non-defaulting party chose not to provide the further funding, it could decide instead to terminate the joint venture and either liquidate the JVC or buy out the other party's interest at market value.

---

1   Now that Stamp Duty Land Tax has replaced stamp duty on land transfers, there would no longer be a saving from making a direct transfer.

Development management agreement

A further issue related to the exercise of the JVC's rights under an ancillary contract with D. It was proposed that D would enter into a development management agreement with the JVC under which D would, for a fee, be appointed as development manager in relation to the project, with the JVC having 'step-in' rights in the event of D's default. The problem for O was ensuring that the JVC could effectively exercise those rights, given the fact that the board of the JVC was deadlocked. Although the JVC directors appointed by D had fiduciary duties to the JVC, and indeed should in law recognise their conflict of interest by abstaining on voting for or against any action that the JVC may wish to take to enforce its rights under the ancillary contract with D, it was by no means clear in practice that they would continue that view if later a dispute arose and they came under pressure from D (which was also their employer). Accordingly, O insisted on changing the articles of the JVC and the shareholders' agreement in order to make it clear that where a conflict of interest arose between the JVC and a shareholder, any directors appointed by that shareholder must abstain from voting on any action which the JVC might decide to take in exercising its rights under such an ancillary agreement. Such a provision should be included in every well drafted shareholders' agreement and articles.

Share transfer provisions

Another important issue concerned the share transfer provisions. In order to ensure that D was fully incentivised as development manager, O wanted to ensure that D could not transfer its shareholding until the development was substantially completed. However, D wanted to be able to charge its shareholding as security for finance to meet its share of funding of the JVC's development costs. O initially resisted this (on the basis that it did not want to end up with a receiver as a joint venture partner). However, O subsequently relented on this point when it realised that if D did get into financial difficulties, O might have to face that possibility eventually anyway.

In reality, O would have the option of purchasing D's shares at market value from the receiver if O became insolvent.

Treatment of shareholders' loans

Normally, where a party exits prematurely by transferring its interest to the remaining partner, the remaining partner procures the repayment of any loans made by the outgoing party to the JVC, if necessary making a new loan in replacement. This would have allowed a party to exit early and put at risk the viability of the development, and so it was agreed that any loans that had been made by the outgoing party would only be repaid on the sale of the development. The concern for the outgoing party in such circumstances is to ensure that the remaining party does not procure that the JVC repays its own loans in advance of those made by the outgoing party and to avoid this the parties agreed that all loan repayments would be made pro rata to the amounts advanced. One means of doing this is to issue loan stock including a repayment mechanism that treats all loan stock holders equally.

Termination and realisation

Other than the above, the joint venture was a classic 50:50 joint venture with a 'deadlock' board and shareholding structure. The venture terminated on the sale of the development. The required funds were provided almost entirely as shareholders' loans and the issued share capital was very small by comparison. Interest on the loans was 'rolled up' pending the receipt of the sale proceeds of the development. When these became available they were applied firstly in repayment of the shareholders' loans and accrued interest, and the balance was extracted by way of dividend. The JVC was then liquidated.

Case study 3

International joint venture

Commercial joint ventures can obviously be established for a variety of reasons and purposes. Although most of them follow a particular structure, each one will be unique in the sense that it will have distinct features or aspects that are particular to it.

The following is an example of an international joint venture in which Simmons & Simmons were involved and describes some of the principal issues which arose. In the interests of client confidentiality the aerospace and defence contractor is referred to as 'D' and the application software developer as 'S'.

Background

D was a large aerospace and defence contractor. Amongst other things it supplied logistics systems and services to civil aviation and military customers around the world. S was a software designer and developer which, inter alia, had developed an application software system with particular application in the airline and defence logistics sector. Unfortunately S did not have the marketing network or structure to be able to support the sale of its products to such a specialised and geographically diverse sector. D operated an international defence and airline sales and support business and a large sales network. D and S agreed to establish a joint venture in which they would pool such part of their respective logistics assets and businesses as would be used in the civil aviation and defence markets.

Contributions from the parties

One of the first issues was to decide what contributions the parties needed to make to establish this joint venture company. It was agreed that D would transfer its logistics business systems division, which consisted, effectively, of certain intellectual property rights (including software and a customer database), goodwill, the benefit of certain customer contracts and a number of employees.

S on the other hand had developed a potentially very valuable software applications package to provide logistical solutions in a variety of different markets (including the civil aviation and military markets). Such software package required maintenance and support as well as consultancy and training services to enable customers to use it effectively for their own particular requirements. In addition, both parties had specialist sales personnel whose responsibilities included sales of these particular systems and related maintenance and support services.

Legal structure

The parties decided to incorporate a new private company incorporated in the UK ('Newco'). It would have been possible to establish this outside the UK but most of its proposed employees and operations were based in the UK. In fact, this company was incorporated by D initially as its wholly owned subsidiary. The parent companies then entered into a formation agreement which established the commitment from them to enter into various pre-agreed agreements in a particular order, including the following:

(A) D agreed to hive its logistics systems business including its related employees into Newco as a separate transfer of undertaking. D also agreed to transfer a wholly owned overseas sales subsidiary to Newco. The consideration in each case consisted of shares in Newco.

(B) S then entered into a Licence and Development Agreement with Newco under which it licensed the application software package exclusively to Newco in this particular sector and agreed to provide Newco and its customers with agreed levels of maintenance, support and development services as well as customer training and consultancy services for an agreed period. The consideration for such grant consisted of an initial licence fee consisting of shares in Newco together with further royalty payments in cash based on the sales of the systems packages by Newco.

(C) The parties agreed to enter into secondment agreements with Newco under which certain key personnel who were being retained by the shareholders would agree to provide certain services as secondees to Newco for particular periods of time (until, effectively, employees of Newco could take over those responsibilities).

(D) D and S also agreed to enter into a Shareholders' Agreement under which they regulated their respective rights as shareholders in Newco.

Key issues

(A) The agreed valuation of assets being hived into Newco resulted in a 75/25 shareholder in favour of D. It was agreed, in consequence, that

D should have a board majority reflecting the split but that S should have a number of veto rights by way of minority protection.

(B) The business of Newco needed to be carefully defined given the other continuing businesses of the two shareholders and the need to impose appropriate non-compete restrictions on them and their respective affiliates.

(C) Both parties felt the need to build in further trading obligations on the other to protect and promote the business of Newco. For example, D wanted to ensure S would be obliged to procure that its overseas affiliates would support the business of Newco locally. S feared that D might be tempted to vary Newco's pricing policy in appropriate circumstances, in effect to subsidise other services D might be providing to the same customer. Appropriate contractual undertakings were negotiated to satisfy these concerns.

Termination

Following the establishment of the joint venture the two principal continuing documents were the Licence and Development Agreement and the Shareholders' Agreement. The Licence and Development Agreement was expressed to be for a term of ten years renewable at the option of Newco for further consecutive periods of ten years. Although terminable earlier by either party in the event of the insolvency or breach of the other party, it was expressed not to terminate automatically upon termination of the Shareholders' Agreement.

On the other hand, the Shareholders' Agreement was expressed to terminate:

(1) in the event of deadlock (see below);

(2) at the option of either party if the other was in breach of it or went into liquidation;

(3) D was given the right to terminate the Shareholders' Agreement if S was in breach of the Licence and Development Agreement; and

(4) S was given the right to terminate the Shareholders' Agreement if Newco (controlled by D) was in breach of the Licence and Development Agreement.

Given that this was not a 50/50 company, 'deadlock' was deemed to occur if the minority protection veto was exercised by S and the parties could not pass a resolution relating to the subject of the vetoed matter. In these circumstances, upon either party notifying the other within 60 days that the matter had not been resolved to its satisfaction, each party would have the right to serve a 'deadlock resolution notice' requiring either to buy the other out at a specified price per share (or to sell at such price). The recipient of such notice could then choose whether to buy or sell at that price.

If the Shareholders' Agreement was terminated for any other reason the right to buy was exercisable by the party not in default and at a fair price. For this purpose, the fair price was calculated by the auditors as being the lower of the proportionate fair price (i) before the breach and (ii) after the breach.

Precedent 1

Checklist of issues for consideration when establishing a UK incorporated joint venture company

1 Principal documents

Shareholders' agreement and articles of association.

Note: Other ancillary documents may well be required, but these will vary according to the requirements of each joint venture.

2 Preliminary matters

2.1 What is the status of discussions between the parties to date?

2.2 Is a confidentiality undertaking required from either, both or all the parties or their affiliates?

2.3 Do the parties want to have a period of exclusive negotiation?

2.4 Identify whether there could be any 'roadblocks' to the proposed transaction (eg competition issues, regulatory consents or licences, consents for assignment of material contracts by parties to the joint venture).

2.5 Consider whether a memorandum of understanding or letter of intent is required to reflect the initial intentions of the parties before proceeding further and whether all or some part (eg exclusivity, confidentiality, costs indemnity (if any), approach to resolution of antitrust/merger/regulatory issues) should be legally binding. *Note:* Care should be taken at this stage to ensure that the Memorandum of Understanding/letter of intent does not itself trigger merger control provisions, if this is an issue for the deal.

2.6 Has a business plan been prepared?

2.7 Are any of the parties a publicly quoted company with public announcement obligations or stock exchange requirements for shareholder approval relating to the joint venture?

2.8 If it is an 'international' joint venture – what local law(s) are applicable and what are their effects?

3 Purpose of the joint venture

3.1   What activities will be carried on by the joint venture? Can these be expanded or developed later? What restrictions will be imposed? Are the proposed activities at the joint venture to be defined?

3.2   Where will the business be based? Will the joint venture's operations be affected by geographical limitations?

3.3   What are each party's objectives and are they consistent/complementary or not? Can any conflict in objectives be accommodated/resolved?

4 Parties, choice of law etc

4.1   Who are the parties and will they or their affiliates enter into the joint venture documentation? If the latter, are parental guarantees required?

4.2   Consider the implications if the parties to the shareholders' agreement and the shareholders are different entities. Are all proposed shareholders (now and in the future) to be party to the shareholders' agreement? Consider the implications if this is not the case.

4.3   Will the joint venture company itself be a party to the shareholders' agreement? Consider the implications of *Russell v Northern Bank Development Corpn Ltd* [1992] 3 All ER 161. Consider also, if the joint venture company becomes insolvent, whether its liquidator could enforce any outstanding funding obligations of the parties for the benefit of creditors.

4.4   What will the name of the joint venture be? If it contains a name similar to that of one or more of the parties, what is to happen upon termination/ their withdrawal?

4.5   What forum and method of dispute resolution will be used in relation to disputes arising under the documents? Courts or arbitration? Consider the respective merits of each.

4.6   Consider whether it is appropriate specifically to exclude the rights of persons who are not party to the agreement but benefit under it (eg the company) to enforce it (which, under English law, would otherwise arise by virtue of the Contracts (Rights of Third Parties) Act 1999).

5 Conditions, regulatory and other approvals etc

5.1   Are any tax clearances, licences, regulatory approvals, third party consents or registration formalities required to establish the joint venture and/or to enable the parties to participate in it and/or to enable them to distribute profits/gains as intended?

5.2   Is the proposed joint venture anti-competitive or will it be treated as a merger which requires clearance or approval from any applicable anti-trust, merger or other regulatory body? In particular, are competition authorities' clearances or notifications needed or desirable under, for example, the Enterprise Act 2002, EC Merger Regulation (where it affects EU states, but not the UK since Brexit) or any national anti-trust legislation etc?

5.3   Are there any conditions (whether relating to the foregoing matters or not) needed and are they to be obtained before the joint venture agreement is entered into or afterwards as conditions to completion? What are the obligations of parties to satisfy them? By what date?

5.4   What provisions should be expressed to apply during any conditional period (eg confidentiality, costs etc)?

5.5   Is it possible that the joint venture (particularly if an unincorporated property joint venture) will be regarded as a 'collective investment scheme' for the purposes of the Financial Services and Markets Act 2000? Consider the implications of this.

5.6   Should provision be made for the parties to provide information or assistance in the event of any regulatory inquiry after the joint venture has been set up?

6 Tax considerations

6.1   What is the optimal joint venture structure/form from a tax perspective?

6.2   Where will the joint venture company be resident for tax purposes? How will the profits/gains of the joint venture company be taxed?

6.3   Will any tax clearances be required in connection with the formation and/or continuing operation of the joint venture company?

6.4   Is it important to the parties to be able to surrender tax reliefs between themselves and the joint venture company on an ongoing basis?

6.5   What is the tax treatment of the chosen method of funding of the joint venture company by the parties? For example, will the parties obtain a tax deduction or loss if the financing cannot be paid in whole or in part?

6.6   Are there any restrictions on the capital structure of the joint venture company (eg transfer pricing rules restricting the amount of debt finance)?

6.7   Is any duty payable on the issue of shares by or the transfer of property/ assets to the joint venture company?

6.8   How will contributions to the joint venture company (eg transfers of assets, intellectual property rights, property etc) be taxed, and are any reliefs available?

6.9   How will payments from the joint venture company to the parties be taxed (eg dividends, interest, intellectual property royalties etc)? Can a structure be used to enable profits to be distributed more efficiently? Are there withholding taxes etc?

6.10 Are there going to be any ongoing supplies between the parties and the joint venture company, such that VAT issues may arise? Is it possible or desirable to VAT group the joint venture company with one of the other parties?

6.11 What is the tax impact if the joint venture succeeds? Will the parties be able to structure an exit which will avoid or reduce any capital gains tax charge?

6.12 What is the tax impact, if the joint venture fails? Will the parties obtain a tax deduction or loss if their investment diminishes in value or is lost entirely?

7 Shareholdings

7.1   What are respective parties' shareholding interests in the joint venture company to be? 50:50 (ie two parties and 'deadlocked') or not?

7.2   Is each party to have a separate class of shares? If so, what rights and restrictions are to be attached to them? Will shares of the same class be capable of being held by more than one person?

7.3   Are the shares of any party to be reclassified (and lose any special rights) if acquired by other shareholder(s)?

7.4   Shareholder meetings – quorum, notice, location?

7.5   Voting – simple majority or 'weighted' voting?

8 Protection of any minorities

8.1   Will any minority shareholders be protected against a majority decision at shareholder and/or director level by:

(A) any requirement for unanimity (which gives every party a veto)?

    (B) any requirements for special majorities (ie majorities of more than 50.1% or more or comprising particular (classes of) shareholders or directors which may give certain parties a veto)?

    (C) contractual protection or by class rights attaching to shares?

8.2 Will any such protections extend to all matters for decision or just to some? A non-exhaustive checklist of matters requiring unanimous or special majority approval follows. Do the parties require unanimity or a special majority for:

    (A) the issue of any new shares (other than perhaps pro-rata)?

    (B) any transfer of shares at all or within a specified period?

    (C) the admission of any new shareholder or creation of any new 'equity interest' (including share options, conversion rights etc)?

    (D) the alteration of articles of association (or other constitutional documents), rights attaching to shares or the name of the joint venture company?

    (E) any incurral of loans or other borrowings of the joint venture company (or perhaps only above specified limits)?

    (F) the making of loans, factoring or discounting of book debts?

    (G) creating any security or giving any guarantees or indemnities for the obligations of third parties (except perhaps within certain limits)?

    (H) the approval or implementation of strategic business plans or operating budgets?

    (I) the incurring of capital expenditure commitments (above specified limits or outside particular plans)?

    (J) the acquisition, disposal or leasing of 'material' assets, business or shares – what is 'material'?

    (K) the formation of subsidiaries or joint ventures, profit sharing arrangements etc with third parties?

    (L) any change of business and/or geographical expansion beyond that agreed?

    (M) commencing or settling 'material' litigation – what is 'material' for this purpose?

    (N) any change of accounting policies or appointment/removal of auditors?

    (O) making any claim, disclaimer, surrender, election or consent (of a 'material' nature – to be defined) for tax purposes?

(P) the employment/removal of 'senior' management (how defined?) or the entering into of long-term/high salary service agreements/ employment contracts?

(Q) the entering into of 'material' (how defined?) consultancy and management agreements?

(R) the approval or adoption of share incentive schemes, pension schemes or anything similar?

(S) any material amendment to any agreed ancillary contracts between the joint venture company and any of the parties/shareholders?

(T) the entry by the joint venture company into other 'material' (how defined?) contracts?

(U) any dealings between the joint venture company and any party/ shareholder (other than trading on arm's length terms in the ordinary course of business), eg the provision of management services?

(V) the declaration of dividends or other distributions (subject to implementation of agreed policies), repayments of loans or loan capital, repurchase of shares?

(W) the entering into of 'exclusive' agency or distribution or other agreements?

(X) the entering into of intellectual property licences or other agreements?

(Y) the entering into of any powers of attorney? Any change of cheque signing authorities?

(Z) any winding up of the joint venture company, commencement of administration or any other insolvency process (except where insolvent)?

9 Board of directors

9.1 How many directors can the joint venture company have? How easily is this number increased?

9.2 How are directors to be appointed and removed? In particular, can each shareholder appoint and remove a given number of directors? How are such rights exercised? Will such rights be reduced or curtailed if a party's shareholding is reduced?

9.3 What other appointment and removal mechanism is there? Can or should shareholders 'entrench' their director appointment and removal rights (eg through class rights, where applicable)?

9.4   How is voting conducted at board meetings (simple or special majority, veto, weighted voting/do such mechanisms work under local law)? How can deadlock be ensured in a 50:50 company if unequal numbers of directors turn up?

9.5   Does a Chairman (or other director) have a second or casting vote? Is there automatic retirement by rotation or anything similar? What is the effect of this on a 50:50 company? Can it be excluded?

9.6   Who will determine the appointment/removal of any managing or other executive directors or personnel?

9.7   Administrative matters, eg frequency of meetings, location, quorum, minimum notice, agenda of meetings, alternates? How are these to be dealt with?

9.8   Are the powers of the board to be fettered in some way? What about minority protection (see paragraph 8 above)? Will particular voting arrangements apply to matters specifically reserved to the board and/or to any other matters?

9.9   What happens where any of the parties have a conflict of interest with that of the joint venture company? See paragraph 14.7 below.

9.10 Consider the need for anti-trust guidelines for Board/shareholder meetings.

10   Contributions of the parties to the joint venture

10.1 What have the parties each agreed to provide to the joint venture?

10.2 Are such contributions by way of specific assets or business or perhaps intangible assets? Intellectual property rights or technology transfer? Secondment of employees? Supply or distribution agreements? Provision of accommodation, facilities etc? What else?

10.3 On what terms will the parties contribute to the joint venture? It will usually be necessary to provide all relevant terms in separate 'ancillary' agreements to be entered into between the relevant party and the joint venture company. Outright transfer, lease or licence to the joint venture? For a fixed or indefinite term?

10.4 Contribution of assets or shares etc? The same considerations should apply on behalf of the joint venture company as if it was acquiring such assets or shares from a third party (eg warranties or indemnities, due diligence etc).

10.5 Will tax or stamp duty considerations affect the method of contribution of assets? If so, what is the most effective method of such contribution? Who will bear such costs?

10.6 Is it possible for all contributions of assets etc to be made contemporaneously? If not, should availability of all or specific assets for contribution be a condition precedent to the establishment of the joint venture company and the contribution(s) of other party/ies? If the assets are not paid for immediately, does the contributor(s) of such assets require security for such obligations from the joint venture company (or each other)?

10.7 How will the contributor's assets be valued? How will the value of the assets affect the contributor's funding obligations? How will any adjustments be made for any shortfall or excess in relation to any contributor's proportionate funding obligation? If assets are to be contributed in return for shares, what local legal requirements apply (eg as to valuation)? What are the timing implications?

10.8 Do any parties require third party approval prior to contribution of any assets etc?

10.9 Are any due diligence investigations into assets being contributed required? Will warranties and indemnities be given by the transferors to the joint company and/or other joint venturers?

10.10   Who is advising the joint venture company in relation to these matters? Does the joint venture company need separate legal advice?

10.11   What is the effect if one party subsequently leaves the joint venture company in relation to (i) assets or other rights leased by it to the joint venture company and (ii) contracts entered into by it with the joint venture company? Are these 'ancillary' contracts also to terminate or should they continue independently? (This could have a significant impact on the valuation of a departing shareholder's interest – see paragraph 20 below.) What effect does breach or perhaps termination of any of these 'ancillary' contracts have on continuation of the joint venture so far as the affected shareholder/party is concerned (see paragraph 18.2(D) below)?

10.12   If any ancillary contracts are not on arm's length terms what are the local law/tax implications?

11   Intellectual property

11.1 Are any intellectual property rights to be contracted by the parties to the joint venture company? Should they be licensed or transferred outright?

Are any intellectual property rights to be conferred on the other joint venture party/ies? If so, on what terms?

11.2 Who will own the intellectual property developed by the joint venture company and (if any) by the joint venture parties? What rights will such joint venture parties have to such intellectual property outside the field of exploitation?

11.3 To what extent will the parties have access to, or rights over, confidential information, know-how and other intellectual property rights concerning or accruing or belonging to the joint venture itself? Can such information flow from the joint venture into competing or potentially competing parts of the parties' own businesses? If so, how can this be prevented?

11.4 What will happen to the intellectual property rights on termination of the joint venture generally or if one party leaves but the joint venture continues between the remaining parties? Will any of the parties require a licence of any intellectual property from the other parties following termination of the joint venture? (See paragraph 19.9 below.)

11.5 Do the parties wish to have different methods of dealing with intellectual property rights depending on the exit route used (eg in the event of termination due to the default of one party)?

12   Employment matters

In every case, the parties to a joint venture should consider which of the following employment matters may be relevant:

12.1 Will the parties second employees or transfer their employment to the joint venture? If so, on what terms? Who will bear the employment related liabilities during the employees' employment (eg cost of salaries, benefits and pension obligations etc)? Who will bear the liabilities that arise on the termination of employment/the secondment arrangements?

12.2 Are secondment letters/new service contracts required? Are there particular individuals with key roles and do such individuals require special treatment? What management incentivisation arrangements will apply?

12.3 What are the parties' expectations in respect of their role in the joint venture? Do the parties envisage that all bar one or two of them will be passive investors? The management structure should reflect these expectations.

12.4 Is there a TUPE transfer either at the outset or on the termination of the joint venture?

12.5 Will it be necessary to harmonise employment terms of employees transferred by the parties to the joint venture company? What are the implications of this?

12.6 What pension arrangements will apply? Whose obligation are they? What impact will any termination/dissolution of the joint venture have on these?

12.7 Are there any restrictions on the use of foreign managers or workers? Are work permits required?

12.8 Will there be any redundancies or other dismissals on the formation and/or termination of the joint venture and, if so, what are the associated costs and how will these be borne by the parties?

12.9 What particular issues arise where the relevant employment contracts are or will be governed by a law other than English law?

13   Finance

13.1 In what proportions/amounts and how (if at all) will the parties provide initial finance to the joint venture company? How much will be provided from third party sources (eg banks)?

13.2 How will finance be structured (eg debt or equity or a combination of both)? Consider the advantages and disadvantages of each under the relevant tax and corporate law. Will any debt finance be secured and, if so, on what terms?

13.3 How will further finance for the joint venture company be funded? Will the parties be required to provide further finance to the joint venture company later? If so, who decides when, how much and how it is to be put in? Are such obligations legally enforceable against the parties? Could any 'unwilling' party block such decision-making? What will happen if one of the parties defaults?

13.4 If third party funding is required, what security and/or recourse to the parties themselves will the lender(s) require and/or will the parties commit to?

13.5 What happens on termination to all or any of these financing arrangements either if the joint venture comes to an end entirely or merely as between one party and the rest? See also paragraph 19.7 below.

13.6 What are the terms of the debt financing? When is it repayable? Can one party be repaid before any other?

13.7 Is any future equity to be offered to all parties pro rata to their interests and/or on what terms?

14   Fair dealing

14.1 What legal duties do the parties have to each other and/or the joint venture company by operation of law?

14.2 Are the parties and their affiliates/subsidiaries to be prevented from competing with the joint venture company (a) during or (b) for a period after termination?

14.3 Are the parties to be prevented from soliciting customers/employees from the joint venture company (a) during or (b) for a period after termination?

14.4 Are the parties to have obligations to promote and develop or refer business/opportunities to the joint venture company? If so, on what terms?

14.5 How is a majority party and its affiliates to be prevented from providing services to, trading with or otherwise entering into contracts with the joint venture company which are not on arm's length commercial terms/ at fair value?

14.6 What restrictions exist on the parties from exploiting information gained about each other or the joint venture company for their own benefit (eg know-how, confidential information such as customer lists etc)?

14.7 What mechanisms exist to prevent a party who subsequently has an actual or potential conflict of interest with the joint venture company (eg if it breaches a contract it has with the joint venture company) from using its voting/blocking rights and preventing the joint venture company from freely and independently exercising its rights? Should the other party/parties be granted, effectively, 'step in' rights to enforce/ exercise the joint venture company's rights for it (eg contractually or by disenfranchising of the defaulting party)?

14.8 To what extent is it appropriate to require a party to procure that its affiliates and their respective employees or agents adhere to its joint venture obligations etc?

14.9 Is it possible/desirable to require each party to procure that the directors of the joint venture company appointed by it 'comply' with the shareholders' agreement? What precisely does this amount to (as such obligations are normally expressed to apply to the parties themselves)? What if it causes them to be in breach of their statutory duties?

Presumably, at least, each party should be obliged to procure attendance of its representatives at both board and shareholder meetings to ensure a quorum is present?

14.10   To what extent is it appropriate for the parties to agree to indemnify the joint venture company and/or each other for all liabilities and losses (including consequential losses) arising out of their subsequent breach of any of the obligations undertaken by them? Is any security or guarantee required for such obligations?

14.11   To what extent should the valuation of any party's interest in the joint venture company upon termination/dissolution be adjusted to compensate for losses caused by that or any other party?

15   Business, accounting and financial matters

15.1 How are the proposed activities of the joint venture company to be defined? Are they to be restricted to those specified? Are they to be confined within geographical limits etc?

15.2 What are the parties' objectives? Is the business intended to be primarily a cash generator or is it intended that profits be ploughed back? Is the joint venture entity intended to be sold or floated? Are the parties in agreement about the objectives? Is it necessary to define them?

15.3 Is it clear what constitutes profits/losses of the joint venture (as opposed to that of the parties/affiliates)? For example, it may be necessary to 'equalise' rights of the parties to share in profits if one has already taken out royalties etc from the joint venture company for the contribution of intellectual property rights etc.

15.4 What provisions are needed relating to the maintenance of books and records, access to them by the parties and the supply of management accounts or other financial information on a regular basis to the parties? Whose responsibility is this?

15.5 What provisions are needed for the preparation of annual audited accounts, accounting principles to be applied and the appointment of auditors?

15.6 Is an annual business plan required? Who prepares/agrees it? Who is responsible for implementation? What are the consequences of any departure from it?

15.7 What provisions should apply regarding the distribution of profits/gains of the joint venture? Who is to decide the level of distribution and by reference to what criteria?

16   Transfer of shares

The provisions of the shareholders' agreement and articles must be consistent and between them deal with the following issues:

16.1 Are restrictions on share transfers or pre-emption provisions on share transfers to be included and, if so, on what terms (eg no transfers allowed at all or for a particular initial period)? Or should the joint venture be wound up if any one party wants to leave?

16.2 Price of shares? Third party price or valuation procedure? How should the shares be valued and by whom?

16.3 Are shareholders to have the right to sell shares in the joint venture company to a third party if pre-emption rights are not taken up at all/ in full? To what extent will the identity of any third party purchaser be relevant to arrangements for permitting transfers or the terms of any pre-emptive rights? Are there to be any time limits or minimum prices for such third party transfers to be effective? *Note:* This may have merger control implications in certain jurisdictions, including the UK and EU, which may need to be addressed.

16.4 Should a 'tag along' right be included (ie transferor to use his best endeavours/be required to require third party purchaser to offer to buy the other party's or parties' interest(s) on no less favourable terms)? Should the minority be obliged to accept such an offer ('drag along') or only if a certain percentage of the shareholders wish to do so?

16.5 Freedom to make intra-group transfers without triggering pre-emption rights etc? Or perhaps transfers to family members? (Individuals only) or to group companies?

16.6 Will any new shareholder be required to become a party to the joint venture agreement as a condition of transfer? This would normally be required.

16.7 Are any specific put or call options to be included at the outset? If so, at what price/price formulation? What are the tax consequences of these for the parties/joint venture company?

16.8 If one party ceases to be a shareholder following a transfer of its shares in the joint venture company a number of consequences will follow and need to be dealt with (see paragraph 19 below).

16.9 Does the proposed shareholding structure meet the accounting requirements of the parties? (eg will any party be obliged to consolidate its interest where it was not intended it should do so?)

17   Resolution of disputes

17.1 When does a dispute arise or is deemed to exist between the parties?

(A)   In a 50:50 company, whenever there is 'deadlock' in decision-making or only in certain circumstances? If the latter, in what circumstances?

(B)   In a joint venture company with a minority shareholder, when the minority's right of veto is used once? Or when it is used on more than one occasion in relation to the same (or different) issues?

(C)   In any joint venture company whenever any party cannot agree any issue or on specific matters only?

(D)   Is it confined to disputes of 'fundamental importance' or similar? If so, how is this defined/in whose opinion?

(E)   When a quorum is not present at a board meeting on two or more consecutive occasions?

17.2 Resolution of dispute – continuation of joint venture:

(A)   Chairman's casting vote?

(B)   Independent non-executive directors (if any) of joint venture company (or shareholders) to decide management deadlock?

(C)   Reference to chairmen of parties to agree (ie 'gin and tonic' clause)? What if they can't reach agreement?

(D)   Reference to mediator? What if he cannot broker an agreement?

(E)   Reference to third party? Who appoints? Depends on nature of dispute – who can the parties rely on (and agree) to be appointed to decide a commercial dispute that they themselves cannot resolve? By what criteria will the third party decide? Is he 'qualified' to make 'commercial' decisions? Is this what the parties want? Is his decision to be binding?

17.3 Failure to resolve dispute – termination of joint venture:

Note: These options may have merger control implications in certain jurisdictions, including the UK and EU, which may need to be addressed.

(A)   Right of one party (usually the majority party) to buy shares from the other (usually minority) party? On what terms and with what consequences? (see paragraph 19 below). How is value determined (see paragraph 20 below)? Does decision to buy become binding on purchaser (and seller) before or after price is determined?

(B) Right to require liquidation of joint venture company? (This might be an alternate (or default) option if the selling/electing party is not satisfied with the value attributed to its shares determination or the majority party is not prepared to buy out the minority. It must be clear who can exercise such a right, when, and in what circumstance.)

(C) Right of continuing shareholder to require the joint venture company to purchase the outgoing shareholder's shares/otherwise use its resources to finance the acquisition of the outgoing interest subject to compliance with legal requirements? (This is usually a means of implementing paragraph (A) above to the extent the relevant company law allows.)

(D) 'Texas Shootout' (ie right of parties to offer on highest sealed bid basis for business of joint venture company on liquidation or for the other's shares)?

(E) 'Russian Roulette'? (ie either party can serve notice (the 'Server') offering either to sell to or buy out another shareholder at a given price or on specified terms. The recipient then has the right to accept the offer. Alternatively, if the Server has offered to (a) sell to the recipient, the recipient may require the Server to buy out the recipient or (b) buy out the recipient, the recipient may require the Server to sell to the recipient, at the same price/terms originally offered by the Server.)

Note: These last two options are usually only applicable in 50:50 companies or where the financial resources and interests of the parties are broadly similar.

18   Termination events

18.1 'Automatic' termination:

(A) Upon all shares in the joint venture company being held by one party (following transfers made in accordance with the relevant joint venture documentation)?

(B) Upon flotation or sale by the joint venture company of the whole of the business/its assets?

(C) Upon winding-up of the joint venture company? Or perhaps the other party?

(D) At the end of a fixed period (if any)?

(E) Upon termination of a particular ancillary agreement?

(F) Are there any other circumstances in which termination should automatically occur (eg loss of licence or regulatory approval, destruction of a particular asset etc)?

18.2 'Voluntary' termination:

(A) In the event of a material breach (which is not remedied after notice to do so) of the shareholders' agreement (or perhaps even an ancillary agreement depending on its importance) by another party?

(B) In the event of insolvency (to be defined) of another party?

(C) In the event of a change of 'control' (to be defined) or even management of another party?

(D) In the event of termination of a particular ancillary contract (applicable to that or another party)?

(E) In any other circumstances?

18.3 How are such rights of termination in paragraph 18.2 to be exercised? Within a particular period after the event in question? By any or all remaining parties or specified parties?

18.4 What are the consequences of automatic/voluntary termination? What rights then arise? See paragraph 19 below.

18.5 What is the impact of these termination provisions on any tax grouping or consortium which the parties might want to create? For example, see Inland Revenue Concession (ESC C10) and Statement of Practice (SP3/93).

19   Consequences of termination

Note: Bear in mind that arrangements for transfer of the joint venture business/ shares on termination for transfer may have merger control implications in a number of jurisdictions, including the UK and EU, which may need to be addressed.

19.1 Upon the occurrence of an 'automatic' termination event, what should happen other than winding up of the joint venture company and everything that follows from that?

19.2 Upon the occurrence of a voluntary termination event, one (or more) party/ies has to exercise a right of termination otherwise the agreement continues. Is such party to have the right (at its option) also to (i) require winding up, (ii) to purchase the shares of, or (iii) sell its shares to, the 'defaulting' or 'affected' party to which the termination event applies? Is it appropriate that if a party undergoes a change of control (or similar) that the other party/ies can require it to buy them out (or is it only fair that they should be able to buy it out)? The same needs to be considered in other events (eg insolvency of one party).

19.3 On what terms – price (see paragraph 20 below), payment of outstanding loans, release of guarantees etc of transferring shareholder? Can any right of termination be exercised without also exercising a right of sale/purchase of shares? If so, presumably the parties will be obliged to wind up the joint venture company if such right of sale/purchase is not exercised? If not, what else is to happen?

19.4 Even on a termination it is likely that certain provisions of the shareholders' agreement will need to continue and these will need to be identified (eg confidentiality, post termination restrictions etc).

19.5 If there are more than two parties, if one party leaves the joint venture, then presumably the joint venture agreement terminates as between that party and the others but continues as between the remaining parties. If so, this will need to be stated clearly.

19.6 If one party ceases to be a party to the joint venture agreement, then what is the effect on other ancillary agreements entered into by that party with the joint venture company? Will they terminate automatically? Will they give the joint venture company a right of termination at its option? Will they continue for a period of time? It is important to be clear about the effect of termination on ancillary contracts, as the business of the joint venture company going forward might be dependent upon them and hence their continuation (or termination) might have a considerable impact upon determination of the share valuation mechanism.

19.7 Where the joint venture agreement is terminated with a party by reason of its breach and the remaining party/ies elect to buy it out, should it be released from any guarantees given by it in respect of the joint venture company and/or have its loans repaid at that point (since to do so might be to its advantage and be seen to be rewarding its breach)? It will be necessary to specify precisely what should happen in such an event. An 'innocent' party will presumably be released?

19.8 If on termination the joint venture company is wound up, then presumably any remaining business or assets will be sold off and each party then shares the proceeds according to the size of its interest. Are there any special circumstances requiring a different treatment? Does any party have any rights in respect of particular assets or contracts (eg right to use confidential information, customer lists etc)?

19.9 If the joint venture company's name is similar to that of one of the shareholders and that shareholder ceases to be a party to the joint venture, should the remaining shareholders be obliged to procure a change of name?

20   Share valuation provisions on exit

20.1 If on termination generally or following a deadlock resolution procedure, one or more of the parties is able or required to buy the shares of one or more of the other parties, how are such shares to be valued and is any adjustment to be made if the reason for the sale is because of a breach by one of the parties? Is the electing party required to commit itself to the purchase before the price is determined or only afterwards?

20.2 The method of valuation of shares in a joint venture company needs to be carefully considered: should it be a formula (eg share of net assets of the joint venture company as determined) or be a wider, more discretionary, valuation basis (eg 'fair value' or 'market value'). If market value is chosen, should directions be given that a discount should be made for a minority stake in the joint venture company or should it be an equivalent percentage interest in the market value of the joint venture company taken as a whole?

20.3 Who decides the valuation? Should it be left entirely to a third party expert (eg auditor or independent accountant)? Who appoints in the event of dispute (eg President of Institute of Chartered Accountants for England and Wales or equivalent)? How is the expert to decide – as an expert or an arbitrator? How are his costs in so acting to be borne? Can his decision be challenged or appealed etc, or is it to be final and binding?

20.4 Does the valuer have complete discretion (according to the valuation basis chosen) or does he choose between two valuations presented by the parties themselves (or their own advisers)? The latter mechanism is often used to enable, effectively, the parties themselves to provide a valuation basis that is broadly reasonable to both of them.

21   General

A number of general provisions will usually be needed:

21.1 Resolution of conflict between shareholders' agreement and articles?

21.2 Requirement that any permitted transferee must agree to be bound by the shareholders' agreement?

21.3 Entire agreement and waiver of pre-contract misrepresentations?

21.4 No waivers except express and in writing?

21.5 Any amendments to the agreement to be in writing signed by all parties?

21.6 Confidentiality?

21.7 No public announcements without consent?

21.8 Severability?

21.9 No partnership?

21.10   Costs? Who bears what?

21.11   Time to be of the essence for all or any purposes?

21.12   Notices? What service provisions apply?

21.13   Anything else?

Precedent 2

Heads of agreement

For a two-party joint venture where one party is in the minority.

Note: **This is purely illustrative of the way in which heads should be set out and merely shows a way in which a joint venture of this kind might be structured. It should not be read in a prescriptive way.**

HEADS OF AGREEMENT made between

(1) **[name of party]** of [address] ('X');

(2) **[name of party]** of [address] ('Y');

1. Establishment of joint venture

1.1 The parties agree in principle to establish a joint venture which will [*set out purpose of venture*].

1.2 The joint venture will be carried on by a new company to be formed ('the Company') with the name [ ] in which X will hold [70]% and Y [30]% of the shares.

2. Contributions of each party

2.1 [X shall transfer into the Company its existing [ ] business, comprising its freehold factory at [ ], the plant and machinery in the factory, the existing stocks, the goodwill, the trade name '[ ]' and the benefits of uncompleted orders, together with all necessary moulds and tools for the manufacture of [ ]. The employees of the business will automatically transfer to the Company under TUPE.

2.2 The price of the transfer shall be market value, which is estimated to be £[ ], subject to adjustment according to a valuation to be made by Messrs [ ], at the expense of X.

2.3 Y shall grant to the Company a licence to manufacture and sell [ ], embodying the features contained in the existing patent applications [details] and all the confidential know-how relating thereto belonging to Y. [Set out outline terms, including duration, territory covered, whether exclusive or non-exclusive, royalty rate and ownership of improvements]. Y shall sell to the Company the existing prototypes, the tools, jigs and moulds used to produce them, and all drawings, specifications and other written material relating to the invention for the sum of £[ ]].

2.4   Y shall enter into a support agreement with the Company, under which it will provide design and technical services for the development of the prototype [ ] into a fully workable product. The timescale for this work shall be one year from the completion of the joint venture agreement. Y shall provide the services of at least six fully qualified engineers to undertake the work at a cost to the Company of £[   ] per annum plus VAT.

2.5   X shall provide the services of Mr [ ] to act as managing director of the Company for a period of three years from the completion of the joint venture agreement on a secondment agreement at the cost to the Company of £[   ] per annum plus VAT, but adjustable upwards to reflect the cost to X of future increases in Mr [ ]'s salary and benefits.]

3. Finance

3.1   [The total capital required is estimated to amount to £[   ] calculated as follows:

	£
Cost of acquiring X's existing business	
Cost of acquiring prototypes etc from Y	
Working capital for the first five years, including the cost of the licence, support and secondment agreements	_____ £ _____

3.2   This will be financed as follows:

Share capital, [ ] ordinary shares of £1 each, of which [ ] will be issued to X and [ ] to Y at par	
Loans of £[ ] from X and £[ ] from Y	
Overdraft facility from [ ] Bank plc	
	_____ £ _____

3.3   The loans from X and Y will be in the form of loan stock, repayable at any time at the option of the Company, but otherwise repayable in five equal annual instalments, beginning at the end of the fifth year from issue. The interest rate shall be [   ]% per annum. Interest for the first three years will be rolled up and added to principal, but thereafter be paid quarterly. The loan stock will be subordinated to the bank overdraft and to the claims of all outside creditors.

3.4   X and Y will guarantee the bank overdraft. They will enter into a contribution agreement so that, as between themselves, they will bear [70%] and [30%] of the liability respectively.]

4. Board and business policy of the Company

4.1   The board of the Company will have [five] directors, of which [three] will be appointed by X and [two] by Y. X will appoint the Chairman. The initial board will consist of [ ] who shall be appointed by X and [ ] who shall be appointed by Y.

4.2   [X will endeavour to transfer Mr [ ] from his employment with it to the Company, and he will then act as marketing director of the Company on the terms of a service agreement to be agreed between Mr [ ] and the Company. The current cost of Mr [ ] is £ per annum.]

4.3   [Mr [ ] will initially act as non-executive Chairman of the Company without charge to the Company.]

4.4   Board meetings will be held not less than [ ] times in each year at not less than [ ] days' notice; the quorum for board meeting shall be at least [two] directors, of which at least [one] shall have been appointed by X and at least [one] by Y.

4.5   The parties shall as soon as possible endeavour to agree a business plan for the Company for the first [five] years. The business plan will be reviewed and revised annually with effect from [ ] in each year, and on each review shall be extended for a further year so that each plan shall cover a rolling five-year period. The revised business plans will be prepared by the Company and approved by its board, but before implementation will require the approval of both X and Y.

Each business plan shall cover the following matters:

- cashflow forecast and estimate of working capital required;
- projected profit and loss accounts and balance sheets;
- operating budget, including estimated capital expenditure;
- review of the business;
- summary of business objectives.

5. Minority protection

5.1   The shares held by X will be designated as 'A' shares and those held by Y as 'B' shares. Such shares will be ordinary shares identical in all respects, apart from the entrenched rights to appoint directors set out in paragraph 4.1 and the minority protection rights for the 'B' Shareholders set out in paragraph 5.2.

5.2   None of the actions set out in Schedule 1 to these heads shall be taken without the consent of the 'B' Shareholders [see clause 8 of Precedent 3 for suggestions].

5.3   It is the parties' intention that, subject to circumstances prevailing at the relevant time including, in particular, the working capital requirements of the Company, at least [   ]% of the profits of the Company after taxation which are available for distribution shall be paid to its shareholders as dividends.

5.4   The financial year end of the company will be [ ] and the first financial year will end on [ ]; audited accounts of the Company for each financial year shall be available not later than [ ] in each year for approval by the parties by not later than [ ] in each year, and if required, any appropriate dividend will be declared not later than [ ] in each year, for payment not later than [ ] in each year.

5.5   The accounts of the Company will be audited by [ ].

6. Termination and realisation

6.1   [Subject to early termination as set out in paragraph 6.4] the parties agree to commit themselves to the joint venture for a minimum of ten years from the completion of the joint venture agreement. During this time, neither party will transfer any of their shares, or be entitled to repayment of their loan stocks, or withdraw their guarantees of the bank overdraft.

6.2   Thereafter either party (the 'server') may at any time serve one year's notice on the other that it desires to terminate the joint venture. In that event the other party (the 'recipient') shall have the right, exercisable by notice given within three months after the service of the termination notice, to purchase the server's shares at an agreed price, or failing agreement at a market valuation to be determined by the auditors who shall act as experts and whose decisions shall be final and binding. If the recipient does not exercise such right, the server shall have the right, exercisable within six months after the service of the termination notice, to purchase the recipient's shares on the like terms. The market valuation of the shares shall be the same proportion of the market value of the entire issued share capital as the proportion of the share capital to be sold, and no discount shall be made in respect of Y's minority holding. Completion of such sale and purchase shall take place on the expiry of the termination notice, and if neither party has exercised its right to buy the other's shares the Company shall then be placed in liquidation.

6.3   On completion of any such sale and purchase the seller shall be entitled to repayment of its Loan Stock in full, with all accrued and unpaid interest, and to be released from its guarantees, but the licence from Y shall survive any purchase by X. Any support agreements then being provided by X or Y shall survive for one year after completion of the sale, but will then terminate automatically without compensation.]

6.4   Either party (the server) may serve notice on the other (the recipient) to terminate the joint venture forthwith if:

(A) the recipient is in material breach of the joint venture agreement or of any agreement then subsisting between it and the Company which, if capable of remedy, has not been remedied within [30] days of notice requiring such remedy;

(B) the recipient shall go into liquidation; or

(C) the recipient shall undergo a change of control.

In this event the server shall have the same right to purchase the shares of the recipient as is set out in paragraphs 6.2 and 6.3, but the recipient shall not have the right to purchase the shares of the server. If the server decides not to purchase such shares then the Company shall be placed in liquidation. If the recipient is Y, its minority protections contained in paragraphs 5.2 and Schedule 1 shall come to an end. [On the purchase of its shares the recipient shall be released from its bank guarantees, but the repayment of its Loan Stock and the continuance of its support agreements (if any) shall be at the discretion of the Company, except in the case of liquidation.]

6.5 If either party shall receive an offer for its shares in the Company from a third party, it shall use all reasonable endeavours to extend the offer to the shares held by the other party. It shall not accept the offer unless it is first so extended and the other party also agrees to accept it.

7. Non-competition

Each party will covenant with the other to use all reasonable endeavours to promote and develop the Company's business and not to compete with the Company [anywhere in the world] until such time as it ceases to hold any shares in the Company or in the case of X it ceases to be entitled to appoint a majority of the Board of Directors or in the case of Y it ceases to be entitled to exercise the rights set out in paragraph 5.2.

8. Confidentiality

Each party hereby covenants with the other to keep confidential all confidential information which it may acquire concerning the affairs of the Company and the other party save where disclosure of the information is required by law, or the information is for the time being in the public domain otherwise than by reason of the fault of the disclosing party or is required to be disclosed in any legal proceedings relating to the joint venture. This covenant will continue without limit of time, and notwithstanding that no joint venture agreement is signed. A similar confidentiality covenant will be included in the joint venture agreement.

9. Tax matters

The parties will conduct themselves to ensure that consortium relief is available to the Company. Each party shall be entitled to require that its proportion of any losses suffered by the Company shall be surrendered to it, subject to the payment to the Company of an amount equal to the tax saved. Similarly, each party may surrender its own losses to the Company on payment by the Company of an amount equal to the tax saved by it, but only where the Company can utilise such losses.

10. Warranties

Each party shall provide warranties to the other as may be agreed between their respective solicitors to be appropriate.

11. [Conditions

The joint venture is subject to the following conditions:

(A) approval of the shareholders of X in general meeting;

(B) confirmation that the transaction will not be referred under the Enterprise Act 2002;

(C) agreement as to the pension arrangements to be made for the employees of X who are transferring to the Company;

(D) review by the accountants to the parties of the tax structure of the joint venture, and the agreement of the parties thereto;

(E) all required consultations with trade unions and employee representatives;

(F) satisfactory completion of due diligence; and

(G) agreement of the first business plan.]

12. Timing and next steps

12.1 [The parties will as soon as is practicable negotiate in good faith the detailed terms for the joint venture with a view to all matters being agreed by [date] so that X may convene a meeting of its shareholders to approve the transaction not later than [date]. Completion is intended to take place no later than [date]. The documents relating to the joint venture shall contain such further provisions as X and Y may agree, following advice from their respective advisers.

12.2 Each party will immediately after the signing of these heads commission, at their own expense, such due diligence as they require into the affairs of the other. In the case of Y, this will consist of an accountant's investigation into X's business. In the case of X, this will consist of a technical evaluation of [ ] to be conducted by [ ].

12.3 For the purposes of such due diligence each party shall provide to the other and to its professional advisers such information as the other reasonably requires for the purpose, but subject in each case to the execution of and delivery of a legally binding confidentiality undertaking in the form set out in Schedule 2, which shall be executed immediately after the signature of these heads.]

13. Announcements

13.1 Neither party shall make any announcements to employees, customers or the public concerning the existence of the discussions relating to the proposed joint venture or as to the existence or the terms of these heads, without the consent of the other, save that disclosure may be made to professional advisers and employees whose knowledge and co-operation is required in order to further the negotiations concerning the joint venture.

13.2 Y however recognises that X will be required to make public announcements and despatch a circular to its shareholders in relation to the joint venture as required by the UK Listing Authority and agrees that X may do so, subject to taking all reasonable steps to agree the terms of any such announcement and the contents of any circular with Y prior to publication.

14. Binding effect

14.1 Subject to paragraph 14.2 these heads of agreement are subject to contract and not legally binding in any way.

14.2 Paragraphs 8 and 13 shall be legally binding.

14.3 These heads of agreement and any non-contractual obligations arising from or connected with them shall be governed by English Law and the parties hereby submit to the exclusive jurisdiction of the English Courts.

SCHEDULE 1: (MINORITY PROTECTION RIGHTS)

SCHEDULE 2: (FORM OF CONFIDENTIALTIY AGREEMENT)

SIGNED by [ ]

for and on behalf of X

SIGNED by [ ]

for and on behalf of Y

Precedent 3

Shareholders' agreement

For two or more parties including deadlock provisions for a 50:50 venture, or alternative minority protection rights – this precedent assumes class rights will be contained in the articles in the form of Precedent 4.

THIS AGREEMENT is dated the [ ] day of [ ] 20[   ] and made

BETWEEN:

(1) *PARTY 1*, ('[X]'), a company registered in England and Wales with company number [ ] and having its registered office at [ ];

(2) *PARTY 2*, ('[Y]'), a company registered in England and Wales with company number [ ] and having its registered office at [ ]; and

(3) *PARTY 3*, ('[Z]'), a company registered in England and Wales with company number [ ] and having its registered office at [ ].

BACKGROUND:

(A) [ ] Limited (the '*Company*') is a company limited by shares and incorporated in England with number [ ] under the Companies Act 2006. [Two] shares have been issued and are [fully] paid up, and beneficially owned by [X] and registered in the name of [X] or [its/his] nominees. The present directors of the Company are [ ] and [ ].

[(B)]   The parties propose that the Company should be used as their joint venture vehicle to [*specify proposed business or purpose of the Company*].

[[(C)] Accordingly the parties have agreed to subscribe for shares in the Company, to enter into certain commitments and to regulate the exercise of their rights in relation to the Company in the manner set out in this Agreement.]

THE PARTIES AGREE THAT:

1 Interpretation

1.1   In this Agreement unless the context otherwise requires:

'Agreed Form' *means, in relation to any document, the form agreed by the parties at the date of this Agreement and initialled by or on behalf of the parties for identification.*

'Authority' *means any competent governmental, administrative, supervisory, regulatory, judicial, determinative, disciplinary, enforcement or tax raising body, authority, agency, board, department, court or tribunal of any jurisdiction and whether supranational, national, regional or local.*

'Board' *means the board of directors of the Company or the directors present at a duly convened meeting of the directors of the Company at which a quorum is present.*

'Business Day' *means a day (other than a Saturday or Sunday) on which banks are open for ordinary face to face banking business in London.*

'Business Plan' *means a business plan for the Company and the Subsidiaries prepared and adopted in accordance with clause 9.2.*

'Company' *means [ ] Limited.*

'Consent' *means any approval, consent, ratification, waiver or other authorisation.*

'Control or Controlled' *has the same meaning as in s 840 of the Income and Corporation Taxes Act 1988 and a 'Change of Control', when applied to any party, shall be treated as occurring if any person who controls, or any number of persons who together control, that party at the date of this Agreement (or the date that party becomes bound by this Agreement, if later) subsequently ceases, or together cease, to control it or if any person acquires, or any number of persons, together acquire, control of that party. [17.20]*

'Director' *means a director of the Company.*

'Financial Year' *means any accounting reference period of the Company, of whatever duration.*

'Group Company' *means, in relation to each of the parties, every company or other entity which is for the time being a subsidiary undertaking of that party, any parent undertaking of that party and any subsidiary undertaking of that parent undertaking.*

'Group Member' *has the same meaning as in s 406 of the Income and Corporation Taxes Act 1988.*

['Majority', *in relation to the parties, means such number of them as for the time being are the beneficial owners of shares in the Company together conferring not less than [   ]% of the total number of votes exercisable at a general meeting of the Company.*]

References to a 'party' *and the* 'parties' *are to references to a party or the parties to this Agreement for the time being, interpreted in accordance with clauses 20.3 and 20.4.*

1.2   In this Agreement unless the context otherwise requires:

(A)   words and phrases the definitions of which are contained in or referred to in the Companies Act 2006 shall be construed as having the meanings attributed to them in that act;

(B)   references to, or to any provision of, any treaty, statute, directive, regulation, decision, order, instrument, by-law, or any other law of, or having effect in, any jurisdiction (*'Laws'*) shall be construed also as references to all other Laws made under the Law referred to, and to all such Laws as for the time being amended, re-enacted (with or without amendment), consolidated or replaced or as their application is modified by other Laws from time to time;

(C)   references to clauses and schedules are references to the clauses of, and schedules to, this Agreement and references to this Agreement include the schedules and the Agreed Form documents;

(D)   references to the singular include the plural and vice versa and references to the masculine, the feminine and the neuter include each other such gender;

(E)   *'person'* includes any individual, partnership, body corporate, corporation sole or aggregate, state or agency of a state, and any unincorporated association or organisation, in each case whether or not having separate legal personality;

(F)   *'company'* includes any body corporate; and

(G)   a person shall be treated for the provisions of this Agreement as connected with another person if they would be regarded as connected under s 839 of the Income and Corporation Taxes Act 1988 (subject to the deletion of the words from 'Except' to 'arrangements' in sub-section (4) thereof).

1.3   The headings and sub-headings are inserted for convenience only and do not affect the construction of this Agreement.

2 [Conditions

2.1   [This Agreement is conditional upon the satisfaction of [all] the following conditions:] [set out any conditions] [24.9[1]]

2.2   If all the condition[s] specified in clause 2.1 have not been satisfied [or waived by] on or before [ ] 200[   ] this Agreement shall lapse and the parties shall be released from all their obligations under it and no party shall make any claim against any other in respect of this Agreement or such non-satisfaction, save in respect of any antecedent breach (including any breach of clause 2.3).

---

1   These references in square brackets are to paragraphs in chapters in the book.

2.3   [ ]shall use its reasonable endeavours to procure the satisfaction of the condition[s] specified in clause [ ]. [ ] shall use its reasonable endeavours to procure the satisfaction of the condition[s] specified in clause [ ].]

3 [Establishment of the Joint Venture Company

3.1   Forthwith upon [the execution of this Agreement/within [five] Business Days of the satisfaction of all the conditions specified in clause 2.1]:

(A)   [X] shall procure that [a general meeting of the Company is convened and held at short notice at which the special resolution set out in the Agreed Form marked 'A' is proposed and passed/a written resolution in the Agreed Form marked 'A' is passed], the New Articles of Association referred to in paragraph (2) of the said resolution being those in the Agreed Form marked 'B'; and

(B)   subject to and forthwith upon the resolution referred to in clause 3.1(A) being passed;

(1)   X shall procure that Messrs [ ] and [ ] shall (subject to them respectively consenting to act) be appointed as additional directors of the Company;

(2)   X, Y [and Z] shall subscribe in cash [at par] for new ordinary shares of [£1] each in the Company as follows (and X shall waive any rights of pre-emption it may have in respect of such subscriptions):

Name	Number of Shares	Class of Shares
X	[ ]	'A' Shares
Y	[ ]	'B' Shares
[Z	[ ]	'C' Shares]

and:

(3)   the parties shall procure that a meeting of the Board is held at which the shares specified above shall be allotted and issued to X, Y [and Z] respectively and registered in their names (or in the names of their respective nominees) credited as fully paid against immediate payment of the relevant subscription moneys.

3.2   Forthwith following the due performance of clause 3.1 the parties shall procure that:

(A)   the registered office of the Company is changed to [ ];

(B)   [ ] are appointed as the auditors of the Company;

(C)   the Company's accounting reference date is [changed to] [ ] (so that its first accounting reference period shall run from its date of incorporation to [ ] 20[   ] (both dates inclusive));

    (D)   [ ] Bank plc [ ] branch is appointed as the bankers to the Company; and

    (E)   [ ] is appointed as the Secretary to the Company in place of [ ].]

4 Directors and board meetings [Chapter 16]

4.1   The parties acknowledge that their respective entitlements to appoint and remove Directors are as contained in the new Articles of Association to be adopted pursuant to clause 3.1(A). Any party instigating the removal of a Director that it has appointed will be required to indemnify the Company and every Subsidiary against any claim by that Director for compensation in respect of his removal from office.

4.2   Unless otherwise agreed, the parties shall procure that

    (A)   Board meetings are convened and held at least [4] times a year;

    (B)   each such meeting is convened by a notice sent to all Directors (or their alternates) entitled to receive notice of such meetings not later than [7] Business Days prior to the meeting; and

    (C)   every notice is accompanied by a written agenda specifying the matters to be raised at the meeting together with copies of all papers to be discussed at the meeting. On receiving notification of a meeting of the Board, any Director is entitled to require the inclusion on the agenda of any matter which he would like raised at the meeting provided that he notifies all the other Directors and their alternates of such inclusion not later than [five] Business Days prior to the meeting. [Unless otherwise agreed by the parties in writing in a particular case, no resolution relating to any business may be proposed or passed at any Board meeting unless the nature of the business is specified in the agenda for the relevant meeting.] [16.6]

5 Business of the Company

5.1   The business of the Company shall [unless and until otherwise determined under clause 8.1(A)] be confined to [ ] and all other activities reasonably related thereto.

5.2   [Subject to clause 8.1] the business in clause 5.1 shall be carried on by the Company itself or through branches or subsidiary companies established in [the United Kingdom] or elsewhere and the Company shall establish such premises as the Board may decide.

6 Specific obligations of the parties [Chapter 3]

[Set out any obligations of the parties in relation to the establishment of the joint venture, eg to transfer assets into the company, grant IP licences to it, or enter into support agreements.]

7 Finance for the Company [Chapter 6]

[Finance for the business of the Company shall be provided initially by the cash subscriptions for the shares referred to in clause 3.1(B)(2)] [and thereafter [subject to clause 8] by loans from X, Y [and Z] on such terms as they may agree with the Board and/or by loans from the Company's bankers.]

[Delete, adapt or replace as necessary. There should be clear arrangements in place for the borrowing of sufficient funds to finance the business in accordance with the first business plan. Where the parties are to provide loans, the terms of them should be agreed at the outset in formal loan agreements. Where external finance is to be provided, the terms should ideally be agreed before the joint venture agreement is signed.]

8 Conduct of the Joint Venture [Chapter 15]

[This clause is intended for the protection of one or more minority interests. If it is intended that these minority protection rights should constitute class rights appropriate changes will need to be made to the Articles.]

8.1   Whilst this Agreement remains in force the parties shall procure, in accordance with the provisions of clause 19.2, that except with the consent [of all/a Majority] of them/[*named party*] (but provided that the consent of a party shall not be required at a time when it is the beneficial owner of shares carrying less than [10]% of the total votes exercisable in a general meeting of the Company):

(A)   the general nature of the business of the Company and the Subsidiaries (if any) shall not be changed from that described in clause 5.1;

(B)   no change shall be made in the issued share [or loan capital] of the Company nor shall any option or right to subscribe be granted to any person in respect of any share [or loan capital] of the Company and no securities convertible into such share or loan capital shall be issued or agreed to be issued [save that there shall be permitted a Permitted Share Issue as defined in clause 8.2];

(C)   no alteration shall be made to the Articles of Association of the Company or the rights attaching to any class of shares of the Company;

(D)   no resolution shall be passed for the winding up or administration of the Company nor shall any of the parties present or cause to be presented any petition for the winding up or administration of the Company (unless in either case the Company shall have become unable to pay its debts within the meaning of s 123 of the Insolvency Act 1986).

(E)   no new equity interest in the Company shall be created or conferred upon any person (including any of the parties) including but not limited to any arrangements for sharing income or profits or any other interest [save that there shall be permitted a Permitted Share Issue as defined in clause 8.2];

(F)   the Company shall not and shall agree not to:

(1)   acquire, whether by formation, purchase, subscription or otherwise, any Subsidiary nor effect or permit the disposal, dilution or reduction of its interest, directly or indirectly in any Subsidiary, whether by the sale, allotment or issue of any shares in its capital or securities convertible into such shares otherwise than to its parent company or any reduction in the voting power or other powers of control exercisable in relation to the Subsidiary by its parent;

(2)   sell, transfer, lease, license or in any way dispose of all or a material part of its business, undertaking or assets, whether by a single transaction or series of transactions related or not (otherwise than in the ordinary course of the Company's business);

(3)   borrow any sums [except from the Company's bankers in the ordinary and usual course of business] which when aggregated with the borrowings of all the Subsidiaries exceed £[   ] outstanding at any one time;

(4)   incur in any Financial Year aggregate capital expenditure (including finance leases but excluding operating leases as respectively defined in SSAP21 and clause 8.3) [which when aggregated with such capital expenditure of all the Subsidiaries for that Financial Year is] in excess of [£[   ]/ the aggregate amount provided for capital expenditure in the Business Plan for that Financial Year];

(5)   enter into or vary any operating lease (as defined by SSAP 21), either as lessor or lessee, of any plant, property or equipment of a duration exceeding [   ] years or involving aggregate premium and annual rental payments in excess of £[

(6)   factor or discount any book debts of the Company;

(7)   make any loan or advance or otherwise give credit (other than credit given in the normal course of the Company's business and on normal arm's length commercial terms) to any person except for deposits with its bankers;

(8)   give any guarantee, bond or indemnity in respect of, or to secure the liabilities or obligations of, any person (other than a wholly-owned Subsidiary);

(9)   create or issue any debenture, mortgage, charge or other security over any assets of the Company [(except for the purpose of securing sums borrowed by the Company from its bankers in the ordinary and usual course of business)] [up to the limit allowed by clause 8.1(F)(3)];

(10) acquire any share or loan capital of any body corporate (including that of the Company or any Subsidiary) or enter into any partnership or profit sharing arrangement with any person;

(11) [declare or pay any dividend or other distribution in respect of any share capital of the Company;] [other than a dividend consistent with the terms of clause 9.3];

(12) enter into or make any material change to any contract or transaction with:

(a) any of the parties or any of their respective Group Companies or persons connected with any of them (except as expressly authorised by this Agreement); or

(b) any other persons except on normal arm's length commercial terms;

(13) enter into any agency, distribution or similar agreement which is expressed to confer any element of exclusivity as regards any goods or services the subject thereof or as to the area of the agreement or vary such an agreement to include any such exclusivity;

(14) enter into or vary any licence or other similar agreement relating to intellectual property to be licensed to or by the Company [which is otherwise than in the ordinary course of business];

(15) enter into or make any material change to any contract of employment or for the provision of services by any Director or senior manager of the Company (whatever his title or job description) [including any increase in salary or other benefits other than any increase budgeted for in any approved Business Plan];

(16) enter into any contract of employment with, or for the provision of services to the Company by, any specified individual which cannot be terminated on less than [six] months' notice without payment of compensation (other than statutory compensation) or vary any such contract so that it cannot be so terminated;

(17) introduce or vary any executive or employee stock or share option or incentive scheme or profit sharing or bonus scheme of any nature;

(18) engage any new employee at remuneration in excess of £[   ] per annum (other than as budgeted for in any approved Business Plan), increase the remuneration of any employee so as to exceed or further exceed such figure (other than any increase budgeted for in any approved Business Plan) or dismiss any employee who receives remuneration in excess of such figure [other than for gross misconduct];

(19) enter into or vary any agreement for the provision of consultancy, management or other services by any person which will, or is likely to result in, the Company being managed otherwise than by its Directors, or which involves a consideration exceeding £[   ] per annum;

(20) [change the auditors of the Company or appoint any auditors in place of any who resign or make any significant change in the accounting policies and practices for the time being adopted by the Company or make any change in the accounting reference date of the Company;]

(21) change the names or the scope of the authority of the persons authorised to sign cheques or other financial instruments on behalf of the Company;

(22) [adopt any Business Plan or amend any Business Plan after the approval thereof;]

(G) no act or event shall occur in relation to any Subsidiary which is analogous to or has any substantially similar effect to any of the acts referred to in clauses 8.1(F)(1) to 8.1(F) (22) above (other than clause 8.1(F)(11)) but so that clause 8.1(F)(8) shall permit any Subsidiary to give any guarantee, bond or indemnity in respect of any liabilities of the Company or any other Subsidiary.

8.2   For the purposes of this clause 8.2 a *'Permitted Share Issue'* means an issue by the Company of ordinary shares complying with Article [12.2] of the Company's Articles of Association [*pre-emptive rights on share issues*] [under which such ordinary shares are offered for subscription at [a price per share approved by [all the parties/a Majority of the parties/ [*named party*]/a price per share which is certified by the auditors to the Company as representing the [market consideration/fair value] for the shares offered and in so certifying the auditors shall act as experts and not as arbitrators and the parties shall procure that their fees and expenses are borne by the Company]] provided that no shares shall be issued to a person who is not a party to this Agreement unless clause 20.1 is first complied with in relation to that person.

8.3   In clause 8.1 the expression 'SSAP 21' means the Statement of Standard Accounting Practice No 21 as issued by or on behalf of the Accounting Standards Board as in force at the date of this Agreement.

9 Accounting Matters, Business Plans and Dividend Policy

9.1   The parties shall procure that:

(A) the Company and every Subsidiary maintain accurate and complete accounting and other financial records in accordance with the requirements of all applicable laws and generally accepted accounting practices applicable in the United Kingdom; [14.34]

(B)   [subject to clause 8] the accounting reference periods of the Company and every Subsidiary are consecutive periods of twelve months commencing on [ ] and that they prepare their audited accounts accordingly;

(C)   the Company prepares [monthly] management accounts [and reports] in relation to the Company and each Subsidiary (containing such information as each party reasonably requires) and sends them to each of the parties within [30] days of the end of the [month] concerned; and

(D)   each party and their respective authorised representatives is allowed access at all reasonable times to examine the books and records of the Company and each Subsidiary and to discuss their affairs with their directors and senior management. [14.32]

9.2   The parties shall procure that:

(A)   the Company prepares a business plan for the Company and the Subsidiaries for each Financial Year which includes the following:

  (1)   an estimate of the working capital requirements of the Company and the Subsidiaries incorporated within a cashflow forecast [together with an indication of the amount (if any) which it is considered prudent to retain out of the distributable profits of the previous Financial Year to meet such working capital requirements];

  (2)   a projected profit and loss account;

  (3)   an operating budget (including estimated capital expenditure requirements) and balance sheet forecast;

  (4)   a review of projected business;

  (5)   a summary of business objectives [15.41]; and

  (6)   a financial report which includes an analysis of the results of the Company and the Subsidiaries for the previous Financial Year compared with the business plan for that Financial Year, identifying variations in sales, revenues, costs and other material items; and

(B)   the business plan for the Financial Year ending on [ ] 20[ ] is [in the Agreed Form marked 'E'/will be prepared by [ ] 20[ ]]. Business plans for subsequent Financial Years must be submitted for approval by [[a Majority/all] of the parties/the Board] not later than [60] days before the commencement of the Financial Year to which they relate.

9.3   Subject to circumstances prevailing at the relevant time including, in particular, the working capital requirements of the Company and the Subsidiaries, it is the intention of the parties that the Company shall distribute by way of dividend in respect of each Financial Year [not less than [ ]% of the post tax consolidated profits of the Company and the Subsidiaries for that Financial Year/all of its profits available for distribution, provided that such a dividend is lawful.] Any distribution for a Financial Year must be made within [six months] after the end of the relevant Financial Year.] [14.31]

10 Promotion of the Company's business [10.50ff]

10.1 Each of the parties covenants with each other party to use all reasonable endeavours to promote and develop the business of the Company and any Subsidiaries to the best advantage in accordance with good business practice and the highest ethical standards.

10.2 In this clause 10, 'Restricted Business' means any business which directly or indirectly competes with the business of the Company or any of the Subsidiaries which is described in clause 5.1.

10.3 Each party undertakes with each of the other parties (for the benefit also of each other party's successors in title) that it will not and that it will procure that none of its Group Companies will, either on its own account or in conjunction with or on behalf of any person:

(A) carry on or be engaged, concerned or interested (directly or indirectly and whether as principal, shareholder, director, employee, agent, consultant, partner or otherwise) in carrying on any Restricted Business, other than as a holder for investment purposes only (which shall exclude an interest conferring a management function or any material influence) of any shares, debentures or other participation [and a holding of not more than 10% of any class of shares or debentures shall be deemed to be for such purposes unless the contrary is shown]; or

(B) solicit, canvass or endeavour to entice away any person who is then [or who was within the previous 12 months] an officer, manager, [senior] employee, agent or consultant of the Company or any of the Subsidiaries whether or not that person would commit a breach of contract by reason of leaving service or office; [10.48] or

(C) in connection with any Restricted Business, solicit the custom of, or endeavour to entice away from the Company or any of the Subsidiaries, any person who is then or who was within the previous 12 months a client or customer of the Company or any of the Subsidiaries whether or not that person would commit a breach of contract by reason of transferring business; or

(D) in connection with any Restricted Business, deal with any person who is then or who was within the previous 12 months a client or customer of the Company or any of the Subsidiaries whether or not that person would commit a breach of contract by reason of transferring business; or

(E) in connection with any Restricted Business, endeavour to entice away from the Company or any of the Subsidiaries any person who is then or who was within the previous 12 months a supplier of the Company or any of the Subsidiaries whether or not such person would commit a breach of contract by reason of transferring business.

10.4 The undertakings in clause 10.3 will in each case continue until such time as the party giving them ceases to hold any shares in the Company or to be entitled to exercise any of the rights set out in clause 8 [provided that upon such undertakings ceasing to apply to any party the same undertakings given to that party by the other parties shall also cease to apply].

OR in the case of a 50:50 deadlocked joint venture where clause 8 is not used – The undertakings given in clause 10.3 will in each case continue until such time as the party giving them ceases to hold any shares in the Company or to be entitled to procure the appointment of at least half of the Directors [provided that upon such undertakings ceasing to apply to either party the same undertakings given to it by the other party shall also cease to apply].

10.5 Each party undertakes with each of the other parties (for the benefit also of each other party's successors in title) that it will not and that it will procure that none of its Group Companies will either on its own account or in conjunction with or on behalf of any person at any time after the date of this Agreement, directly or indirectly use or attempt to use in the course of any business any valid trade or service mark, trade name, design or logo (whether registered or not) from time to time owned or lawfully used by the Company or any Subsidiary or any other name, logo, trade or service mark or design which is or might be confusingly similar thereto.

10.6 Each party undertakes to take all such steps as shall from time to time be necessary to ensure that no breach of clause 10.3 or clause 10.4 arises as a result of any action by any of its Group Companies or any employee or agent of such party or of any such Group Company.

10.7 Each of the undertakings in clauses 10.3 and clause 10.4 shall be construed as a separate and independent undertaking and if one or more of the undertakings is held to be void or unenforceable, the validity of the remaining undertakings shall not be affected.

10.8 Each party agrees that each of the restrictions and undertakings contained in clauses 10.3 and 10.4 are reasonable and necessary for the protection of each other party's legitimate interests in the goodwill of the Company and the Subsidiaries, but if any such restriction or undertaking is found to be void or voidable but would be valid and enforceable if some part or parts of the restriction or undertaking were deleted, such restriction or undertaking shall apply with such modification as may be necessary to make it valid and enforceable.

10.9 Without prejudice to clause 10.6 or clause 10.7, if any restriction or undertaking is found by any court or other competent authority to be void or unenforceable the parties shall negotiate in good faith to replace such void or unenforceable restriction or undertaking with a valid provision which, as far as possible, has the same commercial effect as the provision it replaces.

11 Confidentiality and Announcements

11.1 Each of the parties shall at all times use its best endeavours to keep in strictest confidence and not divulge, communicate or disclose to any person or use or exploit for its own purposes or those of any other person any information of a confidential nature made known or acquired by it at any time and relating to the Company, any of the Subsidiaries or any other party without the prior written consent of the other parties, including, without limitation, technical data, know-how, designs, plans, specifications, methods, processes, controls, systems, trade secrets, recipes, formulae, research and development data, product complaint and testing information, lists of customers and suppliers, all other proprietary information relating to development, engineering, manufacturing, marketing, distribution or accounts, financial statements, financial forecasts, budgets, estimates, sales information, other financial information and any other information which is marked as being confidential or would reasonably be expected to be kept confidential, provided that the obligation of confidentiality shall not apply:

(A) to information for the time being in the public domain other than by reason of a breach of this clause 11;

(B) to information that was in the possession of the relevant party prior to the date of this Agreement (or of its becoming a party to this Agreement, if later) where, to the best of that party's knowledge, such information is not in its possession by reason of the breach of any obligation of confidentiality;

(C) to the extent that disclosure is required by Law or by any order made by a court of competent jurisdiction or by a regulatory or other Authority provided that the party subject to such requirement shall, unless prevented by Law, promptly notify the Company or the party concerned that the requirement has arisen in order to allow it to take any available action to prevent such disclosure, but failing such prevention, the notifying party shall use its reasonable endeavours to obtain confidential treatment of the information concerned;

(D) to the disclosure of information to the directors and officers, auditors, bankers, financiers, insurers or professional advisers of a party who have a legitimate use for such information and who are bound by confidentiality obligations;

(E) to the disclosure of information in the course of legal or arbitration proceedings arising out of this Agreement or concerning any matter relating to or in connection with the Company or any Subsidiary or any party;

(F) to the disclosure of information to any person proposing to acquire all or any of the shares of a party in a manner permitted by this Agreement or approved by the other parties and the professional advisers and financiers of such proposed acquirer where the information is disclosed for the purpose of facilitating such acquisition and is legitimately required for such purpose; and

(G) in the case of information relating to the Company or any Subsidiary, to the disclosure of that information to the extent reasonably required for the advancement of the business of the Company or the relevant Subsidiary. [17.63]

11.2 The obligations of each of the parties contained in clause 11.1 shall survive the termination of this Agreement and shall continue without time limit.

11.3 Where any information of a confidential nature is also privileged, the waiver of such privilege is limited to the purposes of this Agreement and does not, and is not intended to, result in any wider waiver of the privilege. Any party in possession of any confidential information of the Company, any Subsidiary, or any other party (a 'privilege holder') shall take all reasonable steps to protect the privilege of the privilege holder therein and shall inform the privilege holder if any step is taken by any other person to obtain any of its privileged confidential information.

11.4 For the purposes of this clause 11 the expression 'party' shall be extended to include all the Group Companies of that party and the employees and agents of that party and of such Group Companies, and each party shall procure compliance accordingly.

11.5 The parties shall each procure that the Company and the Subsidiaries shall use all reasonable endeavours to ensure that the officers, employees and agents of each of them shall observe a similar obligation as that set out in this clause 11 in favour of each of the other parties.

11.6 No party shall be entitled to make or permit or authorise the making of any press release or other public statement or disclosure concerning this Agreement or any transaction contemplated by it or its termination or cessation without the prior written consent of the other parties, except as required by any stock exchange or any regulatory or other Authority, but before any party makes any such release, statement or disclosure it shall [where practical] first supply a copy of it to the other parties and shall incorporate any amendments or additions they may each reasonably require.

12 Tax Matters

12.1 The central management and control of the Company shall be exercised in the United Kingdom and the parties shall use their respective best endeavours to ensure that the Company is treated by all relevant authorities as being resident for taxation purposes in the United Kingdom and not in any other territory.

12.2 In respect of each accounting period of the Company within the meaning of sections 9 and 10 of the Corporation Tax Act 2009, each of the parties may at any time require (in which case [both/all] the parties shall then procure) that some or all of its Relevant Proportion (as defined in clause 12.5) of any trading losses of the Company and other amounts eligible for relief from taxation are surrendered to it (or to such other company which is entitled to receive the same pursuant to s 402 of the Income and Corporation Taxes Act 1988) and the company receiving the surrender is referred to as the *'recipient'*.

12.3 The party requiring a surrender pursuant to clause 12.2 shall procure that the recipient (unless [all] the parties otherwise agree) pays to the Company a sum equal to 100% of the amount by which the recipient's tax liability is reduced as a result of receiving the amount surrendered, as certified by its auditors for the time being. Each payment shall be made on the date when the recipient's final tax liability for the relevant accounting period would have fallen due for payment but for the surrender.

12.4 If any part of any amount surrendered pursuant to clause 12.2 is not allowed to the recipient by way of relief from tax, the parties shall procure that the Company refunds to the recipient forthwith the amount paid by the recipient in respect of that part.

12.5 For the purposes of this clause 12, *'Relevant Proportion'* when applied to a party (or any of its Group Members) means the maximum proportion of the Company's trading losses which is permitted by law to be surrendered to the relevant party or, as appropriate, the maximum proportion of the Company's trading profits against which the relevant party is permitted by law to surrender its losses.

12.6 In respect of each accounting period of the Company (as defined in clause 12.2) each of the parties may require the Company to accept a surrender of trading losses and other amounts eligible for relief from taxation from that party or from any of its Group Members up to the amount of that party's Relevant Proportion of the total trading losses or other amounts eligible for relief from taxation available for surrender by all the parties (or their respective Group Members) to the Company and which are capable of being utilised by the Company.

12.7 The Company shall (unless [all] the parties otherwise agree) pay to the relevant surrendering company 100% of the amount by which the Company's tax liability is reduced as a result of receiving the amount so surrendered as certified by its auditors for the time being and each payment shall be made on the date on which the Company's final tax liability for the accounting period against which relief is to be claimed would otherwise fall due for payment. If any part of the amount so surrendered is not allowed to the Company by way of relief from taxation the relevant party shall procure that the surrendering company refunds to the Company forthwith the amount paid by the Company in respect of that part not allowed.

12.8 The parties shall procure that all consents required by law for the surrender or acceptance of trading losses or other amounts eligible for relief from taxation pursuant to this clause 12 are given by the Company, the appropriate parties or their respective Group Members as may be required, and in each case within the period required by law.

12.9 Any refund to be paid pursuant to clause 12.4 or clause 12.7 shall be paid together with an amount equal to the interest due to HM Revenue & Customs in relation to the tax payable as a result of the disallowance of any amount surrendered. The obligation to pay interest is limited to that amount of interest actually due to HM Revenue & Customs on the assumption that the additional tax and any interest thereon is in fact paid to HM Revenue & Customs within 28 days of the recipient company informing the surrendering company of the amount of the disallowance and the surrendering company in fact paying the recipient company the monies due within the said 28 day period.

12.10   If there is any dispute between the parties as to any matter referred to in this clause 12 (including but not limited to the amount of group relief to be surrendered to or by the Company, the amount of any tax liability saved as the result of any surrender of group relief or the date on which any tax saved would otherwise have fallen due for payment) the matter shall be referred to an independent firm of accountants appointed by agreement between the parties (or failing such agreement, appointed on the application of [either/any] party by the President for the time being of the Institute of Chartered Accountants in England and Wales), which firm shall act as an expert and not as an arbitrator, and whose decision shall be binding on the parties save in the case of manifest error. The fees and expenses of that firm shall be borne by the parties as the firm directs.

12.11   The parties shall execute and do and procure that their respective Group Members execute and do, and jointly with the other parties procure that the Company executes and does, all documents and things as shall be necessary to enable the surrenders contemplated by this clause 12 to take place and for clause 2 to have full effect. [7.39]

13 Value Added Tax

13.1 The parties shall procure that the Company does not apply to HM Revenue & Customs to be a member of a group registration for the purposes of value added tax ('VAT') other than a registration comprising any two or more of the Company and the Subsidiaries. [7.30]

13.2 Where any taxable supply for the purposes of VAT is made under or in connection with this Agreement by one party (or by the Company) to [the other/another] party (or to the Company), the payer shall in addition to any payment required for that supply, on presentation of a VAT invoice, pay any VAT as is chargeable in respect of it.

14 Share transfers etc

14.1 Save as otherwise expressly provided or allowed by this Agreement [no/neither] party shall, whilst it remains a party to this Agreement, sell, transfer, mortgage, charge, encumber, grant options over or otherwise dispose of any legal or beneficial interest in any of the shares in the Company now or subsequently beneficially owned by it except with the prior written consent of [all] the other parties (which may be withheld for any reason or without giving any reason) [or, in the case of a sale of the entire legal and beneficial interest in any such shares, in compliance with the Articles of Association of the Company] but provided that (where applicable) the provisions of clause 20.1 are first complied with.

14.2 [The parties shall procure that the Directors respectively appointed by them exercise their discretion to register or refuse to register a share transfer in favour of a person not a party to this Agreement so that registration is refused where the provisions of clause 20.1 have not been complied with but registration of such a transfer is always allowed where [any consents required by clause 14.1 have been obtained,] on the transfer is in accordance with the Articles of Association of the Company and clause 20.1 has been complied with.] [24.16]

15 Deadlock Resolution [Chapter 13]

[This is intended primarily for a 50:50 deadlock joint venture]

15.1 For the purposes of this clause 15 a 'deadlock' shall be deemed to have occurred if [13.12]:

(A)

    (1) a matter relating to or affecting the Company has been raised at and/or considered by a meeting of the Board or a general meeting;

    (2) no resolution has been passed at such meeting by reason of an equality of votes for and against any resolution proposed relating to any such matter, and

(3)   either party has subsequently notified the other [within [20] Business Days after such Board or general meeting] that the matter has not been resolved to its satisfaction; or

(B)   [a quorum is not present at two successive Board or general meetings duly convened].

15.2   In the event of a deadlock, the matter in respect of which the deadlock has arisen shall be referred to for a decision by the Chairmen of the parties who shall discuss the matter in good faith and attempt to reach a decision on the same. If they shall fail to do so within 30 days of the matter being referred to them, either party (the 'Server') shall be entitled at any time within 90 days of the Board or general meeting referred to in clause 15.1 [or the second of the Board or general meetings referred to in clause 15.1] to serve a notice (a 'Deadlock Resolution Notice') on the other party (the 'Recipient') offering either to sell all (but not some only) of the shares beneficially owned by the Server in the Company to the recipient at a price per share [specified by it/the [fair/market] value determined in accordance with clause 17.3] (the 'Specified Price') or to purchase all (but not some only) of the shares beneficially owned by the Recipient at a price per share equal to the Specified Price. A Deadlock Resolution Notice shall not be capable of being withdrawn without the written consent of the Recipient.

15.3   Within [20] Business Days of the service of a Deadlock Resolution Notice the Recipient shall by notice to the Server (a 'Counter Notice') be entitled to accept the offer contained in the Deadlock Resolution Notice or (if the offer contained in it was to purchase the Recipient's Shares) to elect to purchase all (but not some only) of the shares beneficially owned by the Server in the Company at a price per share equal to the Specified Price or, if the offer contained in the Deadlock Resolution Notice was to sell the Server's Shares to the Recipient, to elect to sell all (but not some only) of the shares beneficially owned by the Recipient in the Company to the Server at a price per share equal to the Specified Price. If no Counter Notice is served by the Recipient on the Server within the said period of [20] Business Days, the Recipient shall be deemed to have accepted the offer contained in the Deadlock Resolution Notice.

15.4   Upon deemed acceptance of the Deadlock Resolution Notice or upon service of the Counter Notice (as applicable) the parties shall become respectively bound to buy or sell accordingly and completion of such sale and purchase shall take place at the registered office of the Company on the [tenth] Business Day after such event (or such other time and place as the parties may agree) and in respect of which the provisions of clauses 17.5 to 17.9 inclusive shall have effect.

16 Termination [Chapter 17]

16.1 This Agreement shall continue in full force and effect until terminated in accordance with the provisions of this clause 16 but no such termination shall affect any provisions of this Agreement expressed to have effect after such termination or any rights which any party may have against any other party subsisting at the time of termination.

16.2 Any one or more of the parties (a 'Terminator') shall be entitled to terminate this Agreement forthwith by notice in writing (a 'Termination Notice') served in accordance with clause 16.3 if any of the events set out in clause 16.4 ('Termination Events') shall occur (but not after 90 days of the relevant Termination Event first coming to the attention of the Terminator).

16.3 A Termination Notice shall be served upon the party which is affected by the relevant Termination Event (the 'Terminatee') [and in the case of a Termination Notice served pursuant to clause 16.4(D) shall also be served on every party who holds or beneficially owns at the time of service any of the shares in the Company previously held or beneficially owned by the individual whose services have ceased (and such parties shall also be 'Terminatees') and such Termination Notice may be served irrespective of whether the relevant individual continues to hold any shares in the capital of the Company whether legally or beneficially or remains a party to this Agreement] and copies of the Termination Notice shall be served on all other parties (if any). [A Termination Notice shall terminate this Agreement as between the Terminatee and any remaining parties but this Agreement shall continue in full force and effect as between such remaining parties, if more than one.]

16.4 The Termination Events are:
   (A)   the Terminatee shall commit any [material] breach of any of its obligations under this Agreement or of any agreement then subsisting between the Terminatee and the Company and shall fail to remedy such breach (if capable of remedy) within 30 days after having been given notice to do so by the Terminator [17.15];
   (B)   [the Terminatee (being a company) shall enter into liquidation whether compulsory or voluntary (except for the purposes of a bona fide reconstruction or amalgamation with the consent of [all] other parties, such consent not to be unreasonably withheld or delayed where there is no underlying insolvency) or the Terminatee shall have an administrator appointed or a receiver, administrative receiver or manager shall be appointed over any part of the assets or undertaking of the Terminatee; [17.24] or]
   (C)   [the Terminatee (being an individual) shall be adjudged bankrupt or shall die or become a patient for the purposes of any statute relating to mental health; [17.24] or]

(D) [as a separate Termination Event in respect of each of such individuals, any of [ ], [ ] and [ ] shall cease to make their substantially full time services available to the Company or any Subsidiary; [26.73] or]

(E) if there shall be a change in the control of the Terminatee.[17.19]

16.5 [Any one or more of the parties (a 'Terminator') may on, or at any time after, [ ] 20[ ] terminate this Agreement by notice in writing to the other parties (also called a 'Termination Notice'). The effect of such a Termination Notice shall be that this Agreement shall continue in full force and effect [as regards all the parties] until such time as any obligation to buy or sell shares in the Company which arises under clause 17 has been duly discharged by full compliance with clause 17 or the Company enters into liquidation whereupon this Agreement shall terminate completely (apart from those of its provisions which are expressed to have effect after such termination or any rights which any party may have against any other party subsisting at the time of termination) [as between the party serving such notice and the remaining parties but this Agreement shall continue in full force and effect as between such remaining parties (if more than one) but not otherwise.] [17.8, 17.27]

16.6 [Subject to clauses 20.1, 20.3 and 20.4 this Agreement shall terminate in respect of any party [(but shall continue as between the other parties if more than one but not otherwise)] if, as a result of a transfer of shares made in accordance with this Agreement that party ceases to be legally and beneficially entitled to any shares in the capital of the Company.]

16.7 This Agreement (apart from those of its provisions which are expressed to have effect after such termination or any rights which any party may have against any other party subsisting at the time of termination) shall terminate forthwith if an effective resolution is passed to wind up the Company or if a liquidator is otherwise appointed.

17 Consequences of notices under [clause 15] and clause 16 [7.40, 17.28]

17.1 A Terminator (whether comprising one or more parties) shall be entitled by its Termination Notice to require the Terminatee either:

(A) in the case of a notice served under clause 16.4(A), 16.4(D), 16.4(E) or 16.5 only, to purchase all (but not some only) of the shares in the Company beneficially owned by the Terminator [and if there shall be more than one Terminatee requiring them to purchase such shares in such proportions as they may agree or (failing which) as near as may be in the same proportions as the proportions of the share capital of the Company which they each hold bear to one another]; or

(B) to sell to the Terminator (and if more than one, equally or in such other proportions as they may agree) all (but not some only) of the shares in the Company beneficially owned by the Terminatee in either case at a price determined in accordance with clause 17.3 [(or in the case of a Termination Notice served under clause 16.4(A) where the Terminator elects the alternative in clause 17.1(B), clause 17.4)].

17.2 Upon the exercise of any right conferred by clause 17.1, the Terminator and the Terminatee shall become bound respectively to sell or purchase on the terms set out in clause 17 in accordance with the alternative chosen by the Terminator in its Termination Notice but subject to the limitations set out in clause 17.1 and subject to receipt of any regulatory approvals that may be required for such transfers of shares in the Company. If, in a valid Termination Notice served under clause [16.4 or 16.5] no such right is exercised by the Terminator, the Terminatee may within 20 Business Days of the service of the Termination Notice serve a counter-notice on the Terminator [(and if more than one, all of them)] requiring the Terminator to sell to [one or more of the] Terminatee[s] [as they may between themselves agree] all (but not some only) of the shares in the Company beneficially owned by the Terminator, in which case the Terminator and the Terminatee shall become bound respectively to sell and purchase such shares on the terms set out in this clause 17. If no right conferred by clause 17.1 is exercised by the Terminator, and, where applicable, no counter-notice is served by the Terminatee, the parties shall procure that the Company is immediately wound up.

17.3 Subject to clause 17.4, the purchase price of the shares to be bought and sold pursuant to clauses 17.1 or 17.2 [or, if applicable, clause 15] shall be the [fair/market] value thereof as agreed between the parties to such sale or purchase or, in default of such agreement within 15 Business Days after the service of the Termination Notice, or the counter-notice served pursuant to clause 17.2 [(or in the case of a sale pursuant to clause 15, within 15 Business Days of the parties becoming bound to buy and sell pursuant to such clause)], such sum as shall be certified by the auditors for the time being of the Company (at the request of any such party) to be the [fair/market] value of such shares on the date of service of the Termination Notice or the counter-notice, [or at the date upon which the parties become so bound] but after reflecting any diminution in value which will occur on the assumption that all agreements, arrangements or understandings which can be terminated on the transferor ceasing to be a shareholder in the Company have terminated.] [In so certifying the market value the auditors are irrevocably instructed to value such shares at such price as represents the same proportion of the market value of the whole issued share capital of the Company as such shares bear to such whole issued share capital (as if there was a sale of the whole of the issued share capital between a willing seller and a willing purchaser), so as not to take into account whether such shares represent a majority or minority interest.] The auditors shall act as experts and not as arbitrators and their decision shall (save in the case of manifest error) be final and binding upon the parties to such sale and purchase for all purposes and the fees and expenses of the auditors shall be borne in equal shares by all of such parties. [Chapter 22]

17.4 In a case where the shares to be bought from a party upon whom a Termination Notice has been served under clause 16.4(A) ('a Defaulting Party'), clause 17.3 shall apply with the modification that the auditors shall determine the purchase price by determining the market value of the whole issued share capital of the Company, both in the light of the breach concerned and on the basis that such breach had not been committed, and if the first of such valuations is lower than the second, the whole amount of the reduction in the value of the whole issued share capital of the Company shall be attributed to the shares of the Defaulting Party, which shall be sold at a price which is the proportion of the second valuation attributable to the shares being sold, minus the whole amount of such reduction but subject to a minimum consideration of £1.] [Upon transferring its shares for such consideration, the Defaulting Party shall cease to have any liability for the relevant breach.] [17.17]

17.5 Completion of the sale and purchase of any shares in the Company pursuant to clauses 17.1 or 17.2 [or, if applicable clause 15] shall take place at the registered office of the Company at [10.00 am] on the [second] Business Day after the price of such shares has been agreed or determined in accordance with clause 17.3 (or, if applicable, clause 17.4) or the last of any necessary regulatory approvals has been obtained, whichever is the later (or at such other time and/or place as the parties to such sale or purchase may agree) and clauses 17.6, 17.7, 17.8 and 17.9 shall then have effect.

17.6 At each completion referred to in clause 17.5:
(A) the seller(s) shall deliver to the buyer(s) transfers for the shares being sold in favour of the buyer(s) or as the buyer(s) may direct (in accordance with their respective entitlements) duly executed by the seller(s) or the other registered holder(s) of such shares together with the share certificates for such shares (or a reasonably acceptable indemnity in lieu thereof); and
(B) subject to the due performance of clause 17.6(A), the buyer(s) shall pay to the seller(s) the full amount of the purchase monies for the shares being sold together with any sums to be paid pursuant to clause 17.8 by delivering to it or them a banker's draft drawn on a London clearing bank (or such other means of payment as is agreed with the seller(s)).

17.7 All shares bought and sold pursuant to clauses 17.1 or 17.2 [or, if applicable, clause 15] shall be sold free of all liens, mortgages, charges, options and all other encumbrances and together with all rights attaching to them as at the date the seller(s) became bound to sell them and attaching to them subsequently, and the seller(s) shall sell the same with full title guarantee [but shall not be otherwise obliged to enter into any guarantees, representations, warranties or indemnities].

17.8 If any party (an *'Outgoing Party'*) shall become bound pursuant to clauses 17.1 or 17.2 [or, if applicable, clause 15] to sell all the shares then beneficially owned by it in the capital of the Company, the party or parties who have become bound to purchase such shares (the 'purchaser' or 'purchasers') shall upon or immediately prior to completion of the sale procure (or, if more than one, shall jointly and severally procure):

(A)   the immediate release of every guarantee and indemnity which has been given by each Outgoing Party or any of its Group Companies in respect of any liabilities or obligations of the Company or any Subsidiary (and pending such release such purchaser or purchasers shall indemnify and keep each Outgoing Party, and its relevant Group Companies fully and effectively indemnified from and against all claims arising thereunder and where there is more than one purchaser their liability under such indemnity shall be joint and several); [17.50] and

(B)   the immediate repayment to the Outgoing Party and each of its Group Companies of all monies it or they have lent to the Company under, or pursuant to clause 7 and then outstanding together with any interest accrued due thereon down to the date of actual payment (as well before as after judgment) [17.49].

[Note: it is for consideration where one party is being bought out because of its breach or insolvency whether the remaining party should also then be required to procure the discharge of its guarantee or replace its financing.]

17.9 Where a party (the *'Outgoing Party'*) has ceased to be the beneficial owner of any shares in the Company at a time when the Company or any Subsidiary is using as its corporate name or as a trade or business name any name which includes any one or more words which are the same or similar to the corporate name of the Outgoing Party or any of its Group Companies or any trade or business name used by any of them, or any distinctive part of any of such names, the other parties shall procure that within 30 days of such cessation all such names including such same or similar words shall be changed to exclude such words. [17.56]

18 Warranties [Chapter 25]

18.1 X warrants to Y [and Z] that immediately prior to the execution of this Agreement:

(A)   the particulars of the Company set out in recital (B) are true and accurate in all respects;

(B)   the Company:

(1)   has not traded;

(2)   has no assets, contracts, employees, indebtedness or any other liabilities whatsoever, whether actual or contingent;

(3)   has not declared any dividends or other distributions;

(4)   has not prepared any accounts; and

(5)   has complied with all relevant requirements of the Companies Act 2006.

19 Articles of Association

19.1   If at any time whilst this Agreement remains in force any of its provisions are found to conflict with the Articles of Association of the Company, the provisions of this Agreement shall prevail. This Agreement shall not, however, have the effect of amending the Articles of Association of the Company, or except as provided by clause 19.4, of requiring their alteration. [24.19]

19.2   In order to ensure the operation of this Agreement irrespective of any conflict as is mentioned in clause 19.1, each of the parties shall join with each other party in exercising all voting and other rights and powers of control as are from time to time respectively available to them under the Articles of Association and otherwise in relation to the Company and their beneficial holdings therein and shall execute and deliver such waivers and shall each take or refrain from taking all other appropriate action within their respective powers so as to procure at all times whilst this Agreement remains in force all its provisions are duly observed and complied with and given full force and effect and all actions required by the parties are carried out promptly.

19.3   Without prejudice to the generality of clause 19.2, each party shall procure that each of its nominees who are shareholders in the Company and (subject to their statutory duties) each of the directors of the Company appointed or deemed to be appointed by it pursuant to clause 4 or under the Articles of Association of the Company, shall execute and do all acts and things and give and confer all powers and authorities as they would have been required to execute, do, give or confer had they been a party to this Agreement and had consented in the same terms as the party for whom they are a nominee (if a shareholder) or which appointed them (if a Director).

19.4   If it shall not be possible to secure the operation of this Agreement as set out in clauses 19.2 and 19.3 by reason of any contrary provision of the Articles of Association of the Company, the parties shall join in exercising all voting and other rights and powers respectively available to them to procure the alteration thereof to the extent necessary to permit the affairs of the Company to be so operated.

19.5 Subject to the preceding provisions of this clause 19, the parties hereby undertake to each other to observe the provisions of the Articles of Association of the Company.

19.6 The undertakings of each party under this clause 19 shall in each case be several so that each party shall only be liable for its own actions or failures to act in accordance with them, and none of them shall be liable for a failure to procure anything required by this clause 19 where such failure is attributable to any action or failure to act by another party, but without prejudice to the liability of such other party.

19.7 Notwithstanding any other provision of this Agreement, should any party [or any other person connected with it] be in dispute with or shall have a conflict of interest with the Company, such party shall, and shall procure any nominee and the director or directors appointed or deemed to be appointed by it shall not do, or omit to do, anything which would or would be likely to prevent the Company from exercising or from deciding whether or not to exercise such rights as it may have against the party in dispute with it, or in respect of the matter in relation to which the conflict of interest arises. [16.30]

20 General

20.1 Each of the parties shall procure that it shall be a condition of the sale, transfer or other disposition of any shares in the Company for the time being legally or beneficially owned by it or of any interest therein in favour of any person (the 'Transferee') who is not a party to this Agreement that the sale, transfer or other disposition (being one which is otherwise permitted under or pursuant to the provisions of clause 14.1) shall not be effected unless and until the Transferee (and any other person who will in consequence of the sale transfer or other disposition have any beneficial interest in the shares concerned) shall have entered into an undertaking with the other parties for the time being to this Agreement who will remain so after the sale, transfer or other disposition, including those who have become party to this Agreement under clause 20.3 but excluding those who have ceased to be bound by this Agreement to the extent set out in clause 20.4, whereby the Transferee agrees to be bound by and to comply with all the provisions of this Agreement binding upon its transferor (other than any which impose a personal obligation upon its transferor which is not also undertaken by each of the other parties and any warranties given by its transferor) and such undertaking shall be in the form (as nearly as circumstances will permit) set out in

Schedule 3. The parties shall also join in procuring that no shares in the Company shall be allotted or issued except upon the condition that the person to whom the shares are to be issued and any person who will, following the issue, have any beneficial interest in the shares issued, shall also enter into such an undertaking, where they are not already bound by this Agreement. [14.76]

20.2 None of the parties may assign the benefit of any provision of this Agreement, or any legal or beneficial interest therein, separately from the shares in the Company beneficially owned by it.

20.3 This agreement shall bind the personal representatives and successors of the parties. The personal representatives of each party who is deceased and all other successors to any party, together with each person entering into an undertaking in the form required by clause 20.1 shall automatically become entitled to the benefit of this Agreement and may enforce the same as if it or they were named in it in place of the party who previously beneficially owned the shares in the Company in which he or they are interested or, in the case of a person becoming a party by reason of an issue of new shares, as if they had been named in this Agreement as an additional party and all references to a 'party' shall be construed accordingly. This clause 20.3 shall be without prejudice to any provisions contained in the Articles of Association of the Company requiring a transfer notice to be given by such personal representatives or successors in respect of any shares in the Company passing to them.

20.4 A party or any successor of a party who ceases to be legally and beneficially entitled to any shares in the Company and who has complied with clause 20.1 and all other applicable provisions of this Agreement relating to the transfer of such shares (including, without limitation, clause 14.1) shall (subject as provided in clause 16.1) cease to be bound by this Agreement with the exception of clauses 10.4, 10.5, 11, 17 (in so far as it remains to be performed), 18, 20.10 and 22, and subject to those exceptions shall cease to be a party to this Agreement and all references to a 'party' shall be construed accordingly. [14.80]

20.5 This Agreement may be amended by an instrument executed by all the parties for the time being, including each person who has become a party under clause 20.3, but excluding any party who has ceased to be bound by this Agreement to the extent referred to in clause 20.4 (or would have so ceased but for a breach of clause 20.1), but no additional liability shall be imposed upon such a party without its consent. [14.79]

20.6 No exercise or failure to exercise or delay in exercising any right, power or remedy vested in any party under, or pursuant to, this Agreement shall constitute a waiver by that party of that or any other right, power or remedy.

20.7 Nothing in this Agreement shall be deemed to constitute a partnership between the parties (or any of them), nor constitute any of them the agent of any of the others or otherwise entitle any party to bind any other for any purpose.

20.8 Each party shall bear its own costs of or in connection with the preparation, negotiation and execution of this Agreement.

20.9 This Agreement (together with the other documents annexed to or referred to in it) constitutes the entire agreement between the parties in relation to its subject matter and supersedes all previous agreements and understandings, whether oral or written, in relation thereto, and no variation of this Agreement shall be effective unless it complies with clause 20.5. Each party acknowledges to each other party that it has not agreed to enter into this Agreement in reliance on any representation, warranty, assurance or commitment not contained in this Agreement or, to the extent that it has, hereby waives and releases all rights and remedies it would otherwise have in respect of the same otherwise than on the grounds of fraud.

20.10   If any provision of this Agreement shall be held to be unlawful, the same shall be deemed to be deleted from this Agreement, but this Agreement shall remain in full force and effect as if the deleted provision had never been contained in it. The parties shall negotiate in good faith as to the terms of a mutually acceptable and satisfactory provision in place of any deleted, and if such terms shall be agreed, this Agreement shall be amended accordingly.

20.11   This Agreement may be executed in any number of counterparts, each of which is signed by one or more of the parties, provided that all the parties have executed at least one counterpart, and such counterparts shall together constitute this Agreement.

20.12   Time shall be of the essence for the purposes of any provision of this Agreement.

21 Notices

21.1 Any notice to be given by any party shall be in writing and shall be deemed to have been duly served if delivered personally or sent by facsimile or e-mail transmission or by pre-paid [first class/recorded delivery] post (or airmail or air courier in the case of an address for service outside the United Kingdom) to the addressee at its address (or number) for the receipt thereof specified below:

X   Postal Address   [   ]
    Facsimile Number   [   ]
    E-mail Address   [   ]
    For the attention of: [   ]

Y	Postal Address	[ ]
	Facsimile Number	[ ]
	E-mail Address	[ ]
	For the attention of:	[ ]
[Z	Postal Address	[ ]
	Facsimile Number	[ ]
	E-mail Address	[ ]
	For the attention of:	[ ]]

or at any other address or number as the party to be served has notified (in accordance with this clause 21.1).

21.2 A notice shall be deemed to have been duly served as follows:

(A) where personally delivered, upon such delivery;

(B) where sent by facsimile, when despatched subject to confirmation of uninterrupted transmission by a transmission report;

(C) where sent by e-mail, where the e-mail leaves the e-mail gateway of the sender;

(D) where sent by pre-paid post to an address in the United Kingdom, 48 hours after posting;

(E) where sent by pre-paid airmail to an address outside the United Kingdom, five days after posting; and

(F) where sent by air courier [2] Business Days after delivery to a representative of the courier.

21.3 In proving the service of any notice it shall be sufficient to prove:

(A) in the case of a notice sent by post that such notice was properly addressed, stamped and placed in the post;

(B) in the case of a notice personally delivered that it was delivered or left at the specified address;

(C) in the case of a notice sent by facsimile that it was duly despatched to the specified number as confirmed by a transmission report;

(D) in the case of a notice sent by e-mail that the e-mail left the e-mail gateway of the server of the notice; and

(E) in the case of a notice sent by air courier that it was delivered to a representative of the courier.

22 Law and jurisdiction [Chapter 23]

22.1 This Agreement and any non-contractual obligations arising from or connected with it shall be governed by English law and this Agreement shall be construed in accordance with English law.

617

22.2 In relation to any legal action or proceedings to enforce this Agreement or arising out of or connection with this Agreement (whether arising out of or in connection with contractual or non-contractual obligations) ('Proceedings') each party irrevocably submits to the [exclusive/non-exclusive] jurisdiction of the English courts and waives any objection to Proceedings in such courts on the grounds of venue or on the grounds that the Proceedings have been brought in an inappropriate forum.

22.3 [*If non-exclusive*] [The submissions in clause 22.2 shall not affect the right of [either/any] party to take Proceedings in any other jurisdiction to the extent permitted by law, nor shall the taking of Proceedings in any jurisdiction preclude any party from taking Proceedings in any other jurisdiction.]

22.4 [[ ] irrevocably appoints [ ] of [ ] as its process agent to receive on its behalf service of process of any proceedings in England. Service upon the process agent shall be good service upon [ ] whether or not it is forwarded to and received by [ ]. If, for any reason, the process agent ceases to be able to act as process agent, or no longer has an address in England, [ ] irrevocably agrees to appoint a substitute process agent with an address in England acceptable to the other parties and to deliver to each of them a copy of the substitute process agent's acceptance. In the event that [ ] fails to appoint a substitute process agent, it shall be effective service for any such party to serve the process upon the last known address in England of the last known process agent for [ ] notified to any such party notwithstanding that such process agent is no longer found at such address or has ceased to act [provided that a copy of the Proceedings is also sent to [ ]'s current registered office or principal place of business wherever situated.]

22.5 [*As an alternative to clause 22.4*] [ ] irrevocably consents to any process in any proceedings anywhere being served in accordance with the provisions of clause 21, relating to the service of notices. Such service shall become effective 30 days after despatch. Nothing contained in this Agreement shall affect the right to serve process in [the manner permitted by clause 22.4 or in] any other manner permitted by law.]

23 Contracts (Rights of Third Parties) Act 1999

No person who is not for the time being a party to this Agreement shall have any right under the Contracts (Rights of Third Parties) Act 1999 to enforce any term of this Agreement. [24.12]

AS WITNESS the hands of the parties or their duly authorised representatives the day and year first above written.

Schedule 3: (form of undertaking from new shareholders)

THIS DEED is dated the [ ] day of [ ] 200[   ] and made

BETWEEN:

(1)   [ ] of [ ] (the 'New Shareholder') and

(2)   THE PERSONS whose names and addresses appear in the Schedule hereto (the 'Existing Shareholders')

BACKGROUND:

(A)   [recite date and parties to the joint venture/shareholders agreement] (the 'Shareholders' Agreement').

(B)   [recite any previous deeds of adherence and any releases from the joint venture/shareholders agreement]

(C)   The New Shareholder has become entitled to [a transfer of/be issued with] [*class*] ordinary shares of £[   ] each in the capital of the Company.

(D)   It is a term of the Shareholders' Agreement that no [transfer/issue] of shares in the Company shall be effected unless the [transferee/the person to whom such shares are to be issued] has first entered into a deed in the form of this deed.

NOW THIS DEED WITNESSES that the New Shareholder covenants with each of the Existing Shareholders that [with effect from the date of this Deed] the New Shareholder will be bound by and will observe and perform every provision of the Shareholders' Agreement [by which [*outgoing party*] was bound in every way as if the New Shareholder has been named in that agreement as a party to it with the exception of clauses [ ] [*Insert here clauses which contain personal obligations or warranties or which it is otherwise inappropriate to apply*].

IN WITNESS whereof the New Shareholder has executed this Deed the day and year first above written.

SCHEDULE: [NAMES AND ADDRESSES OF EXISTING SHAREHOLDERS]

EXECUTED as a deed by the said [   ] [in the presence of/acting by]

SIGNED by [duly authorised for and on behalf of [   ]] in the presence of

SIGNED by [duly authorised for and on behalf of [   ]] in the presence of

SIGNED by [duly authorised for and on behalf of [   ]] in the presence of

Form 'A'

[ ] LIMITED

NOTICE IS HEREBY GIVEN THAT a **GENERAL MEETING** of the above named Company will be held at [ ] on [ ] at [ ].m. to consider and, if thought fit, pass the following resolution which will be proposed as a Special Resolution of the Company:

Special resolution THAT:

(1) Each of the [two] existing ordinary shares of £1 each be and they are hereby converted into and redesignated as 'A' Shares of £1 each having attached thereto the rights and restrictions set out in the New Articles of Association referred to in paragraph (2) of this resolution.

(2) The draft regulations contained in the document submitted to the Meeting and for the purposes of identification initialled by the Chairman thereof be and are hereby approved and adopted as the Articles of Association of the Company in substitution for and to the exclusion of all existing Articles of Association of the Company; [and]

[(3) The name of the Company be changed to [ ].]

DATED this [ ] day of [ ] 20[   ]

By Order of the Board

[Secretary][Director]

Registered Office:

[*address*]

Note: A member is entitled to appoint a proxy to exercise all or any of the member's rights to attend, speak and vote at the meeting. A proxy need not be a member of the Company.

A member may appoint more than one proxy provided each proxy is appointed to exercise rights attached to a different share or shares held by the member.

Consent to short notice

I/We, the undersigned, being [all] [the majority in number of] the Member[s] of the Company having a right to attend and vote at the General Meeting convened to be held on [ ] 20[   ] and [together] holding [all] [at least [90% or 95%] in nominal value] of the shares giving that right HEREBY AGREE that the said Meeting shall be deemed to have been duly called and that the Special Resolution set out in the Notice of the said Meeting may be proposed and passed notwithstanding that shorter notice than that specified in the Companies Act 2006 or the Company's Articles of Association has been given.

DATED [   ] 20[   ]

....

[Member]

....

[Member]

Precedent 4

Articles of Association

With alternative deadlock provisions and minority protection by way of class rights

THE COMPANIES ACT 2006

NEW ARTICLES OF ASSOCIATION

of [ ] LIMITED

(adopted by Special Resolution passed on [ ] 20[   ])

1 Model Articles

1.1 The model articles for private companies limited by shares contained in Schedule 1 to the Companies (Model Articles) Regulations 2008 (the 'Model Articles') [as amended prior to the date of adoption of these Articles] shall, except where the same are excluded or varied by or inconsistent with these Articles, apply to the Company to the exclusion of all other regulations set out in any statute or statutory instrument concerning companies.

1.2 Articles 4, 5, 6(2), 7, 8, 9(1), (3) and (4), 11, [12], [13], 14, 16, 17, 22(1), 26(5), 27(1) and (2), 28, 29, 41(1), 43, 44(2), 46(4), 50, 52 and 53 of the Model Articles shall not apply to the Company.

2 Interpretation

2.1 In these Articles unless the context otherwise requires:

'Address' in relation to electronic communications includes any number or address used for the purposes of such communications;

'A Director', 'B Director' and 'C Director' shall have the meanings given in Articles 8.1, 8.2 and 8.3 respectively;

'alternate' or 'alternate Director' means a person appointed as such pursuant to Article 9;

'Articles" means these Articles of Association in their present form or as from time to time altered;

'Conflict' has the meaning given in Article 7;

'Director' means a director of the Company and includes any person occupying the position of Director, by whatever name called;

'Eligible Director' means a Director who would be entitled to vote on the matter at a meeting of Directors (but excluding any Director whose vote is not to be counted in respect of the particular matter and for these purposes a Director's vote will not be counted in respect of any Conflict which has not been authorised under Article 7.1);

'Interested Director' has the meaning given in Article 7;

'Member' means a member of the Company;

'Permitted Group' means in relation to a company, any wholly-owned subsidiary of that company, any company of which it is a subsidiary (its holding company) and any other subsidiaries of any such holding company;

'Permitted Share Issue' has the meaning given in Article 12.2;

'Subsidiary' means a subsidiary of the Company for the time being as defined in section 1159 of the 2006 Act;

'the 2006 Act' means the Companies Act 2006;

any words or expressions defined in the 2006 Act to the extent in force at the date when these Articles or any part of them are adopted shall (unless otherwise defined in these Articles) bear the same respective meanings in these Articles or such part (as the case may be); and

where for any purpose an ordinary resolution of the Company is required, a special resolution shall also be effective.

3 Delegation of directors' powers

3.1   Subject to these Articles, the Directors may delegate any of the powers which are conferred on them:

(A) to [such person or] any committee consisting of [at least three] Directors one of whom shall be an 'A' Director, one a 'B' Director [and one a 'C' Director];

(B) by such means [(including by power of attorney)];

(C) to such an extent;

(D) in relation to such matters or territories; and

(E) on such terms and conditions as they think fit.

3.2 If the Directors so specify, any such delegation may authorise further delegation of the Directors' powers by any [person or] committee to whom they are delegated.

3.3 The Directors may revoke any delegation in whole or part, or alter its terms and conditions.

4 Proceedings of directors [16.6]

4.1   Questions arising at any meeting of the Directors or of any committee of the Directors shall, unless otherwise determined by all the Members or determined in accordance with Article 4.2, be decided by a majority of votes of the Eligible Directors present (or their alternates) [(except that, subject to there being a quorum at the relevant meeting, should any Eligible 'A' Director not be present at the meeting in person or by his alternate Director (if any) the vote of that Director may be exercised by another 'A' Director present at such meeting in person or by his alternate, and should there be more than one 'A' Director so present, the vote of the most senior by date of appointment shall be accepted to the exclusion of any other 'A' Director. The same provisions shall apply, in the same manner, in respect of Eligible 'B' Directors [and Eligible 'C' Directors]]. [The Chairman shall not have a second or casting vote.] [13.6]

[*These provisions ensure a board composed of 'A' and 'B' Directors only is deadlocked provided at least one 'A' Director and one 'B' Director are Eligible Directors. In other cases their insertion is optional.*]

4.2   A decision of the Directors may also take the form of a resolution in writing, copies of which have been signed by each Eligible Director [or to which each Eligible Director has otherwise indicated agreement in writing].

4.3   Subject to Article 4.4, the quorum necessary for the transaction of the business of the Directors or of any committee of the Directors shall throughout the meeting be [three] Directors of whom one shall be an 'A' Director, one a 'B' Director [and one a 'C' Director]. A person who holds office only as an alternate Director shall, if the Director he has been appointed to represent is not present, be counted in the quorum.

4.4   If there shall be no quorum at any meeting of the Directors within one hour after the time fixed for the meeting, the meeting shall be adjourned to such time (not being earlier than seven days after the date of the original meeting) as the Director or Directors present at the meeting shall determine, or if none, shall be determined by the Secretary. If there shall be no quorum within one hour after the time fixed for the adjourned meeting, the meeting shall be further adjourned as aforesaid. If there shall be no quorum within one hour after the time fixed for the further adjourned meeting the Director or Directors present, whatever their number and their designations shall constitute a quorum.

4.5   Any Director who ceases to be a Director at a Board meeting may continue to be present and to act as a Director and be counted in the quorum until the termination of the Board meeting if no other Director objects and if otherwise a quorum of Directors would not be present.

5 Number of Directors

5.1   The number of Directors shall not be less than [two/three] or more than [   ].

6 Calling a Directors Meeting

6.1   Unless in any particular case such requirement is waived in writing by all (but not some only) of the Directors then in office, not less than [seven] working days prior notice must be given to each Director of any meeting of the Directors or of any committee of Directors convened under or pursuant to these Articles. Notice of any meeting of the Directors may be given by electronic communication. [It shall be necessary to give notice of a meeting to a Director who is absent from the United Kingdom at such address as he shall have notified to the Secretary]. [   ]

6.2   Any Director or Member may, and the Secretary (if any) at the request of any Director or Member shall, call a meeting of the Directors.

7 Directors' Interests and Conflicts

7.1   For the purposes of section 175 of the 2006 Act and generally, the Members (and not the Directors) shall have the power to authorise, by resolution and in accordance with the provisions of these Articles, any matter or situation proposed to them by, or otherwise relating to, a Director which would, if not so authorised, either (i) involve a breach of duty by a Director under section 175 of the 2006 Act to avoid conflicts of interest or (ii) constitute a conflict of interest in relation to a transaction or arrangement with the Company (in any such case, 'a Conflict'). [For this purpose, a Director appointed or deemed to be appointed by a Member under or pursuant to Articles 8.1, 8.2 or 8.3 (including any alternate for such a Director) shall be deemed to have (in addition to any other interest he may have personally) the same interests as the Member appointing him.]

7.2   A Director, notwithstanding his office, may be a director or other officer of, employed by, or otherwise interested (including by the holding of shares) in, the Member who appointed him as a Director of the Company, or any other member of such Member's Permitted Group, and no authorisation under Article 7.1 shall be necessary by reason of any such interest alone.

7.3   Any A Director, B Director [or C Director] shall be entitled from time to time to disclose to the holders of the A Shares or (as the case may be) the holders of the B Shares [or the C Shares] such information concerning the business and affairs of the Company as he shall at his discretion see fit, subject only to the condition that if there be more than one A shareholder or B [or C] shareholder, the Director concerned shall ensure that each of the shareholders of the same class receives the same information on an equal footing.

7.4 A Director is not required, by reason of being a Director (or because of the fiduciary relationship established by reason of being a Director), to account to the Company for any remuneration, profit or other benefit which he derives from or in connection with a relationship involving a Conflict which has been authorised by the Members in accordance with these Articles (subject in each case to any terms and conditions attaching to that authorisation and provided that all material information concerning that remuneration, profit or other benefit was disclosed to the Members before such authorisation was given) and no contract shall be liable to be avoided on such grounds.

7.5 Subject to sections 177(5) and 177(6) of the 2006 Act, a Director who is in any way, whether directly or indirectly, interested in a proposed transaction or arrangement with the Company shall declare the nature and extent of his interest to the other Directors before the Company enters into the transaction or arrangement in accordance with the 2006 Act.

7.6 Subject to sections 182(5) and 182(6) of the 2006 Act, a Director who is in any way, whether directly or indirectly, interested in a transaction or arrangement that has been entered into by the Company shall declare the nature and extent of his interest to the other Directors as soon as is reasonably practicable in accordance with the 2006 Act, unless the interest has already been declared under Article 7.5.

7.7 Subject, where applicable, to any terms and conditions imposed by the Members in relation to the authorisation of a Conflict under Article 7.1, and provided a Director has declared the nature and extent of his interest in accordance with the requirements of the Companies Acts, a Director who is in any way, whether directly or indirectly, interested in an existing or proposed transaction or arrangement with the Company:

(A) may be a party to, or otherwise interested in, any transaction or arrangement with the Company, or in which the Company is otherwise (directly or indirectly) interested;

(B) shall be an Eligible Director for the purposes of any proposed decision of the Directors (or committee of Directors) in respect of such transaction or arrangement or proposed transaction or arrangement in which he is interested;

(C) shall be entitled to vote at a meeting of Directors (or of a committee of Directors) or participate in any decision taken by written resolution of all Eligible Directors, in respect of such transaction or arrangement or proposed transaction or arrangement in which he is interested;

[(D) may act by himself or his firm in a professional capacity for the Company (otherwise than as auditor) and he or his firm shall be entitled to remuneration for professional services as if he were not a Director;]

(E)   may be a Director or other officer of, or employed by, or a party to a transaction or arrangement with, or otherwise interested in, any body corporate in which the Company is otherwise (directly or indirectly) interested; and

(F)   shall not, save as he may otherwise agree and subject as provided in Article 7.4, be accountable to the Company for any benefit which he (or a person connected with him (as defined in section 252 of the 2006 Act)) derives from any such contract, transaction or arrangement or from any such office or employment or from any interest in any such body corporate and no such contract, transaction or arrangement shall be liable to be avoided on the grounds of any such interest or benefit nor shall the receipt of any such remuneration or other benefit constitute a breach of his duty under section 176 of the 2006 Act.

8 Appointment and removal of directors

8.1   The Members who for the time being hold a majority in nominal value of the issued 'A' shares from time to time shall be entitled to appoint [   ] Director[s] holding office at any one time, to remove any Director so appointed and to appoint another Director in place of any Director so appointed who for any reason ceases to be a Director. [For this purpose Messrs [ ] and [ ] (existing Directors of the Company) shall be deemed to have been appointed under this Article 8.1.] Any persons so appointed or deemed to be so appointed under this Article 8.1 are called 'A' Directors.

8.2   The Members who for the time being hold a majority in nominal value of the issued 'B' shares from time to time shall be entitled to appoint [Director[s] holding office at any one time, to remove any Director so appointed and to appoint another Director in place of any Director so appointed who for any reason ceases to be a Director. [For this purpose Messrs [ ] and [ ] (existing Directors of the Company) shall be deemed to have been appointed under this Article 8.2.] Any persons so appointed or deemed to be so appointed under this Article 8.2 are called 'B' Directors.

[If there are only 'A' & 'B' shares, and an equal number of directors can be appointed by each class and no other directors can be appointed, the board is deadlocked]

8.3   [The Members who for the time being hold a majority in nominal value of the issued 'C' shares from time to time shall be entitled to appoint

[   ] Director[s] holding office at any one time, to remove any Director so appointed and to appoint another Director in place of any Director so appointed who for any reason ceases to be a Director. [For this purpose Messrs [ ] and [ ] (existing Directors of the Company) shall be deemed to have been appointed under this Article 8.3.] Any persons so appointed or deemed to be so appointed under this Article 8.3 are called 'C' Directors.]

8.4   Any appointment or removal under this Article 8 shall be by notice in writing lodged at the registered office of the Company or delivered to a duly constituted meeting of the Directors of the Company and signed under the hand or hands of the holder or holders of a majority in nominal value of the issued shares of the class effecting the same. Any such appointment or removal shall take effect as at the time of such lodgement or delivery or at such later time as shall be specified in the notice. In the case of a corporation such notice may be signed by or on its behalf by a director or secretary of the corporation or by its duly appointed attorney or duly authorised representative. [16.2]

8.5   No Director shall be required to retire or vacate his office or be ineligible for reappointment as a Director, nor shall any person be ineligible for appointment as a Director, by reason of his having attained any particular age.

8.6   In addition to the provisions of Article 18 of the Model Articles, the office of a Director shall be vacated if:

(A)   being a Director appointed or deemed to be appointed under this Article 8 he is removed from office under the provisions of this Article; [or]

(B)   [if being a Director appointed under this Article 8 the Member or the Members entitled to appoint him shall cease to be so entitled.]

9 Alternate directors

9.1   Any Director (other than an alternate Director) may appoint any person willing to act [16.5] to be an alternate Director to exercise the appointor's powers and responsibilities in relation to the taking of decisions by the Directors in the absence of the alternate's appointor. The appointor may remove from office an alternate Director appointed by him. For the purposes of these Articles, an alternate Director appointed by an 'A' Director shall be deemed to be an 'A' Director, an alternate Director appointed by a 'B' Director shall be deemed to be a 'B' Director [and an alternate Director appointed by a 'C' Director shall be deemed to be a 'C' Director]. A person can be appointed an alternate Director by more than one Director provided all such appointors represent the same class of shares but not otherwise. Any appointment or removal of an alternate must be effected by notice in writing to the Company signed by the appointor or in any other manner approved by the Directors.

9.2 An alternate Director has the same rights in relation to any Directors' meeting or Directors' written resolution, as the alternate's appointor.

9.3 Except as these Articles specify otherwise, alternate Directors:

(A) are deemed for all purposes to be Directors;
(B) are liable for their own acts and omissions;
(C) are subject to the same restrictions as their appointors; and
(D) are not deemed to be agents of or for their appointors.

9.4 An alternate Director may be paid expenses as if he were a Director but shall not be entitled to receive from the Company any fee in his capacity as an alternate Director except only such part (if any) of the remuneration otherwise payable to the Director appointing him as such Director may by notice in writing to the Company from time to time direct. [An alternate Director who is absent from the United Kingdom shall be entitled to receive notice of all meetings of the Directors and of all meetings of committees of Directors of which his appointor is a member at such address as he shall have notified to the Secretary. Such notice may be given by electronic communication.]

9.5 Every person acting as an alternate Director shall have one vote for each Director for whom he acts as alternate (in addition to his own vote if he is also a Director) but he shall count as only one 'A' Director or one 'B' Director or one 'C' Director (as appropriate) for the purpose of determining whether a quorum is present. The signature of an alternate Director to any resolution in writing of the Directors or of a committee of the Directors shall, unless notice of his appointment provides to the contrary, be as effective as the signature of his appointor.

9.6 An alternate Director's appointment as an alternate terminates:

(A) when the alternate's appointor revokes the appointment by notice to the Company in writing specifying when it is to terminate;

(B) on the occurrence in relation to the alternate of any event which, if it occurred in relation to the alternate's appointor, would result in the termination of the appointor's appointment as a Director;

(C) on the death of the alternate's appointor;

(D) when the alternate's appointor's appointment as Director terminates.

10 Directors' gratuities and pensions

10.1 The Directors on behalf of the Company may exercise all the powers of the Company to grant pensions, annuities, gratuities and superannuation or other allowances and benefits in favour of any person including any Director or former Director or the relations, connections or dependants of any Director or former Director. A Director or former Director shall not be accountable to the Company or the Members for any benefit of any kind conferred under or pursuant to this Article and the receipt of any such benefit shall not disqualify any person from being or becoming a Director of the Company.

11 Share capital

11.1 The share capital of the Company at the date of the adoption of these Articles is £[   ] divided into:

[ ] 'A' ordinary shares of £1 each ('the 'A' shares')

[ ] 'B' ordinary shares of £1 each ('the 'B' shares')

[[ ] 'C' ordinary shares of £1 each ('the 'C' shares')]

11.2 The 'A' shares, the 'B' shares [and the 'C' shares] shall each constitute different classes of shares for the purposes of the 2006 Act but save as otherwise provided in these Articles shall rank pari passu in all respects.

11.3 [Subject to these Articles] the Company may from time to time by special resolution increase, subdivide, consolidate or redenominate its share capital in accordance with the 2006 Act.

12 Variation of rights

12.1 The rights for the time being respectively attached to any 'A' shares, 'B' shares [and/or 'C' shares] for the time being in issue may from time to time (whether or not the Company is being wound up) be varied or abrogated with the consent in writing of the holders of not less than three-quarters in nominal value of the issued shares of the relevant class or with the sanction of a special resolution passed at a separate general meeting of the holders of the shares of the class. To each such separate general meeting all the provisions of these Articles as to general meetings of the Company shall apply (with necessary modifications), but so that the necessary quorum shall be one holder of the relevant class present in person or by proxy and holding or representing not less than one-third in nominal value of the issued shares of the relevant class, that every holder of shares of the class shall be entitled on a poll to one vote for every such share held by him and that any holder of shares of the class present in person or by proxy or (being a corporation) by a duly authorised representative may demand a poll. For the purpose of this Article one holder present in person or by proxy or (being a corporation) by a duly authorised representative may constitute a meeting.

[Article 12.2 is for the protection of minority interests]

12.2 [The special rights attached to the 'A' Shares, the 'B' Shares [and the 'C' Shares] shall, with the intent that this Article 12.2 shall create rights attaching to each such class of share for the purposes of section 630 of the 2006 Act, be deemed to be varied by any of the following actions, and the prior consent or sanction of the holders of [each of] the 'A' Shares, 'B' Shares [and 'C' Shares] (given in accordance with Article 12.1) shall be required for every such action and the Company shall not permit any of them to be carried out or agreed to be carried out without such consent or sanction (including, where necessary through the exercise of its voting rights and other powers of control over the Subsidiaries) [provided that no such consent or sanction shall be required from the holders of any such class of shares where the aggregate of the votes attaching to the shares of such class represents less than [10]% of the total votes exercisable at a general meeting of the Company]. The said actions are:

(A)   the convening of a meeting of the Company for the purpose of considering a resolution for, or the passing of a resolution for, or any other action being taken to implement, any alteration, increase, reduction, sub-division or consolidation of the issued share capital of the Company, or any purchase or redemption of shares by the Company, or the grant of any right to require the allotment or issue of any shares of the Company [other than a Permitted Share Issue];

(B)   the convening of any meeting of the Company for the purpose of considering a resolution, or the passing of a resolution, to amend or replace these Articles, or any variation of the rights attached to any class of shares of the Company;

(C)   the convening of a meeting of the Company for the purpose of considering a resolution, or the passing of a resolution, or the presentation by the Company of a petition, for the winding up or administration of the Company, unless it is then unable to pay its debts within the meaning of s 123 of the Insolvency Act 1986;

[(D) the convening of a meeting of the Company for the purpose of considering a resolution, or the passing of a resolution, to approve a Conflict under Article 7.1;]

(E)   [*Add any others as required – see clause 8 of the shareholder's agreement for examples*] [Chapter 15].

For the purposes of this Article 12.2 a Permitted Share Issue means an issue of ordinary shares complying with Article [13.4] under which such ordinary shares are offered for subscription at [a price per share approved by [special resolution/in writing by Members holding shares carrying at least [   ]% of the votes exercisable at a general meeting of the Company][a price per share which is certified by the auditors to the Company as representing the [market/fair value] for the shares so offered and in so certifying the auditors shall act as experts and not arbitrators and their fees and expenses shall be borne by the Company.] [Chapter 22]

12.3 No person dealing with the Company or any Subsidiary shall by reason of the provisions of Article 12.2 be concerned to see or enquire whether the requisite class consent for any relevant action has been obtained and no such action shall (as between the Company and any such person) be invalid or ineffectual unless such person had at the time of such action actual knowledge or notice that any such class consent had not been validly obtained.

13 Power of directors to allot shares

13.1 For the purposes of section 551 of the 2006 Act but subject to the provisions of these Articles, the Directors are generally and unconditionally authorised to exercise all powers of the Company to allot shares or grant rights to subscribe for or to convert any security into shares in the Company (together 'Shares') with such rights or restrictions as they may determine, up to an aggregate nominal amount of £[   ]. This authority shall expire five years from the date on which the resolution adopting these Articles is passed but may be previously revoked or varied by the Company in general meeting and may from time to time be renewed by the Company in general meeting for a further period not exceeding five years. The Company may make any offer or agreement before the expiry of this authority that would or might require Shares to be allotted after this authority has expired and the Directors may allot Shares in pursuance of any such offer or agreement as if this authority had not expired.

13.2 Article 13.1 shall not apply to redeemable shares, which shall be governed by the provisions of Article 22(2) of the Model Articles.

13.3 [Sections 561 and 562 (1)–(5) (inclusive) of the 2006 Act shall not apply].

13.4 [Subject to any class consents required by Article 12.2] any shares shall, before they are issued, be offered to the Members in proportion, as nearly as the circumstances admit, to the numbers of existing ordinary shares held by them (of whatever class) [unless the Company shall by special resolution otherwise direct]. Such offer shall be made by notice specifying the number of shares offered and specifying a time (not being less than 14 days from the making of the offer) within which the offer, if not accepted, shall be deemed to have been declined (the 'primary offer'). Each primary offer shall include an invitation in favour of those who accept all the shares offered to them to apply on the same terms and within the same time for any additional shares which will be available if any Members do not accept all the shares offered to them by the primary offer ('excess shares'). After the close of such primary offer the Directors shall allocate the shares applied for amongst the Members on the basis that those who have applied for no more than the shares offered to them in the primary offer shall receive all the shares applied for by them, and the excess shares shall be allocated on the basis that should there be more shares applied for than are available, they shall be allocated to the Members applying for them in the same proportions as their holdings of ordinary shares (of whatever class) bear to one another but so that no Member shall be obliged to subscribe for more shares than the number he applied for but otherwise each Member applying for any excess shares shall receive all the shares he applied for. Upon being notified of such allocation the Members applying for the shares allocated to them shall be bound to subscribe for the same in accordance with the terms of the primary offer. Any shares deemed to be declined pursuant to the primary offer, or for which Members allocated them fail to subscribe, any fractions of a share incapable of being allocated under the offer [and any shares released from this Article 13.4 by special resolution] shall be under the control of the Directors as set out in Article 13.1, provided that in the case of shares declined as aforesaid, such shares shall not be disposed of on terms which are more favourable to the subscribers therefor than the terms upon which they were offered to the Members. Ordinary shares issued under this Article 13.4 to Members holding 'A' Shares shall be 'A' Shares, those issued to Members holding 'B' Shares shall be 'B' Shares [and those issued to Members holding 'C' Shares shall be 'C' Shares]. [Where immediately prior to an issue of shares under this Article 13.4 a Member holds ordinary shares of more than one class, the ordinary shares issued to him shall be divided into the same classes as those previously held by him in the same proportions as the numbers of the shares of each class held by him bear to one another.] [Where ordinary shares are issued under this Article 13.4 to a person who was not previously a Member, such shares shall be of the same class as they would have been had the Member to whom they were originally offered accepted such shares.] [15.11ff]

13.5 [The rights conferred upon the holders of any shares or class of shares shall not, unless otherwise expressly provided in the rights attaching to, or the terms of issue of, such shares, be deemed to be altered by the creation or issue of further shares ranking pari passu therewith.]

14 Transfer of shares

14.1 [[Unless the provisions of Article 14.2 are first complied with] save with the prior consent in writing of all the other Members of the Company for the time being, no Member shall be entitled to transfer any shares in the Company.] [or] [[Unless the provisions of Article 14.2 are first complied with] no transfer of any share shall be made or registered without the previous sanction of the Directors who may in their absolute and unfettered discretion, refuse to give such sanction. If the Directors do refuse to sanction a transfer of shares, they shall, as soon as practicable and in any event within two months after the date on which the transfer is lodged with the Company, send the transferee notice of the refusal together with reasons for the refusal.]

14.2 Every Member (and every person entitled to a share or shares in consequence of the death or bankruptcy of a Member or by operation of law) who intends to transfer or otherwise dispose of shares of any class of the Company or any legal or beneficial interest therein (the *'proposing transferor'*) shall, before so doing or agreeing so to do, inform the Company of his intention by giving it notice in writing (the *'transfer notice'*). The transfer notice shall constitute the Company the proposing transferor's agent empowered to sell the shares referred to in the notice (together with all rights then attached to them) at the prescribed price (defined in Article 14.3) to any Member in the manner set out below and shall not be revocable except with the unanimous agreement of the Directors. [19.12]

14.3 If, not more than fourteen days after the date on which the transfer notice was given (or deemed to have been given) the proposing transferor and the Directors shall have agreed in writing a price per share as representing the [fair/market] value of the shares, or as being acceptable to the proposing transferor [and not more than the [fair/market] value of the shares], then that price shall be the prescribed price. In the absence of any agreement having been reached within that period of fourteen days the Directors shall forthwith request the auditors for the time being of the Company to determine and certify in writing to the Company the sum per share considered by them to be the [fair/market] value as at the date on which the transfer notice was given (or deemed to have been given) and the sum per share so determined and certified shall be the prescribed price. [In so certifying the [fair/market] value, the auditors are irrevocably instructed to value the shares concerned at the same proportion of the market value of the whole issued share capital of the Company as the proportion which such shares bear to such whole issued share capital and on the basis all restrictions on transferring the shares contained in these Articles are ignored] and on the basis that all agreements, arrangements and understandings which can be terminated on the transfer of such shares being effected have terminated. The auditors shall act at the cost and expense of the proposed transferor as experts and not as arbitrators and their determination shall be final and binding for all purposes (save in respect of manifest error). [Chapter 22]

14.4 Within seven days of the prescribed price being so agreed or determined and fixed all shares included in the transfer notice shall be offered for purchase at the prescribed price by notice in writing given by the Company to all Members holding shares of whatever class in the Company (other than the Member to whose shares the transfer notice relates). Such offer shall be on the basis that in the case of competition for them the shares so offered shall (in accordance with, but subject to, Article 14.5) be sold to acceptors holding shares of the same class as the shares being offered, in proportion (as nearly as may without involving fractions or increasing the number sold to any Member beyond that applied for by him) to their existing holdings of shares of the same class and in the event of Members holding shares of the same class not taking all the shares so offered, then the shares so offered but not so sold shall be sold to the Members holding shares of any other class and in the case of competition on a similar basis and in the same manner as aforesaid. Any such offer shall specify a period (being not less than twenty-one days and not more than forty-two days) within which it must be accepted or will lapse. [19.2]

14.5 If Members (*'purchasers'*) shall within the said period of the offer agree to purchase the shares concerned or any of them the Company shall forthwith give notice in writing to the proposing transferor and to the purchasers and upon payment of the prescribed price the proposing transferor shall be bound to transfer the shares to the respective purchasers accordingly with full title guarantee, [free from all liens, charges and encumbrances and other equities and with all rights then attaching thereto and becoming attached thereafter]. Every such notice shall state the name and address of each purchaser and the number and class of shares agreed to be purchased by him and the purchase shall be completed at a place and time to be appointed by the Directors not being less than seven days nor more than thirty days after the date of the notice except that if the transfer notice shall state that the proposing transferor is not willing to transfer part only of the shares the subject of the notice, the foregoing provisions of this Article 14.5 shall not apply unless the Company shall have found purchasers for all of such shares and (unless as aforesaid) any offer referred to in Article 14.4 shall be deemed to have lapsed without having been validly accepted. [19.10]

14.6 If a proposing transferor shall fail or refuse to transfer any shares to a purchaser the Directors may authorise some person to execute the necessary transfer and may deliver it on his behalf and the Company may receive the purchase money in trust for the proposing transferor (which it shall pay into a separate bank account in the Company's name) and cause the purchaser to be registered as the holder of such shares. The receipt of the Company for the purchase money shall be a good discharge to the purchaser (who shall not be bound to see to the application of it) and after the purchaser has been registered in purported exercise of these powers the validity of the proceedings shall not be questioned by any person. [19.15]

14.7 [If at the expiry of the period for acceptance of the offer referred to in Article 14.4, Members of the Company shall not have agreed to purchase all the shares so offered, the Company shall forthwith give notice in writing of that fact to the proposing transferor and [(subject to the previous sanction of the Directors, such sanction not to be unreasonably withheld)] he shall then be at liberty within three months after the giving of such notice to transfer those shares which Members shall not have so agreed to purchase to any person on a bona fide sale at any price not being less than the prescribed price provided that:

(A) if the transfer notice shall state that the proposing transferor is not willing to transfer part only of the shares the subject of the transfer notice he shall not be entitled to transfer any of the shares unless in aggregate the whole of the shares are so transferred; and

(B) the Directors may require to be satisfied that the shares are being transferred in pursuance of a bona fide sale for the consideration stated in the instrument of transfer without any deduction, rebate or allowance whatsoever being given to the purchaser and if not so satisfied may refuse to register the instrument of transfer.]

14.8 [If a Member, or other person entitled to transfer a share, at any time attempts to deal with or dispose of a share or any legal or beneficial interest in it otherwise than in accordance with the foregoing provisions of this Article, he shall be deemed immediately prior to such attempt to have served a transfer notice on the Company in respect of the share and the provisions of this Article shall thereupon apply to the share. Any such transfer notice shall be deemed to have been served on the date on which the Directors shall receive actual notice of such attempt.] [19.7]

14.9 [The executors or administrators or other personal representatives (if any) of any deceased Member or the trustee in bankruptcy of a bankrupt Member shall be bound at the expiry of two months from the date of his death or bankruptcy (as applicable), to give a transfer notice in respect of all the shares registered in the name of the deceased Member at the date of his death or bankruptcy, or such of them as still remain so registered, and if he or they fail to give such transfer notice within fourteen days after the expiry of such period of two months or should there be no such executors, administrators, trustee in bankruptcy or other personal representative at the expiry of such period of two months, a transfer notice shall be deemed to have been given (on the basis that there is no requirement that all but not some only of the shares the subject of the notice must be sold to existing Members) and the provisions of this Article 14 shall have effect accordingly.] [26.76]

14.10   [If any Member (being a corporation) shall enter into liquidation (compulsorily or voluntarily) or have an administrator appointed or have a receiver, administrative receiver or similar official appointed of the whole or any part of its assets, its liquidator, administrator, receiver, administrative receiver or other similar official, shall be bound forthwith to give to the Company a transfer notice in respect of all the shares registered in the name of the Member, and in default of a transfer notice being given within thirty days of such event, its liquidator, administrator, receiver, administrative receiver or other similar official shall be deemed to have given such notice at the expiration of that period of thirty days (on the basis that there is no requirement that all but not some only of the shares the subject of the notice must be sold to existing Members) and the provisions of this Article 14 shall apply accordingly.] [17.24ff]

14.11   For the purpose of ensuring that a transfer of shares is duly authorised under this Article and that no circumstances have arisen whereby a transfer notice is required to be served, the Directors may from time to time require any Member or past Member or the personal representatives, trustee in bankruptcy, receiver, administrative receiver, liquidator, administrator or similar officer of any Member or any person named as a transferee in any instrument of transfer lodged for registration, to provide them with such information and evidence as the Directors may reasonably think fit regarding any matter which they consider relevant to establish whether such transfer is duly authorised or whether any circumstances have arisen whereby a transfer notice is required to be served. Failing such information being furnished to the reasonable satisfaction of the Directors within a reasonable time after it has been requested, or if in the reasonable opinion of the Directors any such information or evidence is false in any material respect, the Directors may refuse to register the relevant transfer and/or declare by notice in writing to the relevant Member, personal representatives, trustees in bankruptcy, receiver, administrative receiver or administrator or similar officer that a transfer notice shall be deemed to have been given in respect of any relevant shares. [19.7]

15 Purchase of own shares

15.1 Except with the consent in writing of and in the manner authorised by [all the Members/any class consents required by Article 12.2], the powers conferred by section 690 of the 2006 Act shall not be exercised.

16 Proceedings at general meetings

16.1 Any Member or Director may convene a general meeting in addition to the ability of the Directors to do so.

16.2 No business other than the appointment of the chairman of the meeting shall be transacted at any general meeting unless a quorum of Members is present at the time when the meeting proceeds to business. In default of a quorum within one hour after the time appointed for the meeting or if during a meeting a quorum ceases to be present, the chairman of the meeting must adjourn the meeting to such time (not being earlier than seven days from the date of the original meeting) and place as the chairman of the meeting may determine. If there is no quorum at the adjourned meeting within one hour after the time appointed for the meeting, the meeting shall again be adjourned as aforesaid. If there shall be no quorum at the further adjourned meeting within one hour after the time appointed for the meeting the Member or Members present, whatever their number and the class or classes of shares held by them, shall constitute a quorum.

16.3   Subject to Article 16.2 the quorum at any general meeting (and at any adjourned general meeting) shall be [three] Members present in person or by proxy or, being a corporation, by a duly authorised representative, of whom one shall be a holder of 'A' shares, one a holder of 'B' shares [and one a holder of 'C' shares.]

16.4   At any general meeting a poll may be demanded by any Member present in person or by proxy or, being a corporation, by a duly authorised representative.

16.5   In the case of an equality of votes whether on a show of hands or on a poll, the Chairman of the meeting at which the show of hands takes place or at which the poll is demanded shall not have a second or casting vote. [13.4]

17 Votes of members

17.1   Subject to the Companies Acts and to any rights or restrictions for the time being attached to any class or classes of shares (including, without limit, the provisions of Articles [17.2, 17.3 and 17.4]), on a show of hands every Member present in person or by proxy or (being a corporation) by a duly authorised representative shall have one vote, and on a poll every Member present in person or by proxy or (being a corporation) by a duly authorised representative shall have one vote for each share of which he is the holder.

17.2   Upon any resolution for the removal from office of any Director appointed or deemed to be appointed under the provisions of Article 8.1 by the holders of the 'A' shares, no 'B' share [or 'C' share] shall confer upon the holder any right to vote either on a poll or a show of hands or otherwise.

17.3   Upon any resolution for the removal from office of any Director appointed or deemed to be appointed under the provisions of Article 8.2 by the holders of the 'B' shares, no 'A' share [or 'C' share] shall confer upon the holder any right to vote either on a poll or a show of hands or otherwise.

17.4 [Upon any resolution for the removal from office of any Director appointed or deemed to be appointed under the provisions of Article 8.3 by the holders of the 'C' shares, no 'A' share or 'B' share shall confer upon the holder any right to vote either on a poll or a show of hands or otherwise.] [16.4]

17.5 The appointment of a proxy and the power of attorney or other authority (if any) under which it is signed, or a notarially certified copy of such power or authority, shall in the case of an appointment in writing, be deposited at the registered office of the Company (or at such other place in the United Kingdom as is specified for that purpose in the notice of meeting or any instrument of proxy sent by the Company in relation to the meeting) [not less than [one] hour] before the time for holding the meeting or adjourned meeting at which the person named in the appointment proposes to vote, or handed to the Chairman of the meeting or adjourned meeting before the commencement of such meeting or, in the case of an appointment contained in an electronic communication, where an address in the United Kingdom has been specified in:

(A) the notice convening the meeting; or

(B) any instrument of proxy sent out by the Company in relation to the meeting; or

(C) any invitation contained in an electronic communication to appoint a proxy issued by the Company in relation to the meeting it shall be received at such address not less than [one hour] before the time for holding the meeting or adjourned meeting at which the person named in the appointment proposes to vote. In default, the appointment shall not be treated as valid.

18 Notices

18.1 Any notice or other document (including a share certificate or other document of title) may be served on or delivered to any Member by the Company either personally or by sending it through the post in a prepaid letter addressed to that Member at his registered address as appearing in the Register of Members (whether or not that address is within the United Kingdom) and sent by first class post (or in the case of an address outside the United Kingdom by airmail) or by delivering it to or leaving it at such registered address, addressed as aforesaid, or (except for a share certificate or other document of title) by giving it by electronic communication to an address notified to the Company by the Member for that purpose. In the case of joint holders of a share, service or delivery of any notice or other document on or to one of the joint holders shall for all purposes be deemed a sufficient service on or delivery to all the joint holders. Any notice or other document served or delivered in accordance with these Articles shall be deemed duly served or delivered notwithstanding that the Member is then dead or bankrupt or otherwise under any legal disability or incapacity and whether or not the Company had notice thereof. [Any such notice or other document sent by first-class post shall be deemed to have been served or delivered 48 hours after it was put in the post (or in the case of a notice or other document sent by airmail five days after posting), and in proving such service or delivery it shall be sufficient to prove that the notice or document was properly addressed, prepaid and put in the post.] Any such notice or other document sent by an electronic communication shall be deemed to have been served [48 hours] after it was sent and proof that it was sent in accordance with guidance issued by the Institute of Chartered Secretaries and Administrators shall be conclusive evidence that the notice was given or document sent. In calculating a period of hours for the purposes of this Article [no account shall be taken of any part of a day that is not a working day] [any part of a day that is not a working day shall be taken into account].

18.2 Notice of every general meeting shall be given in any manner authorised by or under these Articles to all Members other than such as, under the provisions of these Articles or the terms of issue of the shares they hold, are not entitled to receive such notices from the Company, provided that any Member may in writing waive notice of any meeting either prospectively or retrospectively and if he shall do so it shall be no objection to the validity of such meeting that notice was not given to him.

19 Indemnity

19.1 Subject to Article 19.2, a relevant Director, secretary, or other officer (excluding any auditor) of the Company, or an associated company may be indemnified out of the Company's assets against:

(A) any liability incurred by such a person in connection with any negligence, default, breach of duty or breach of trust in relation to the company or an associated company;

(B) any liability incurred by such a person in connection with the activities of the Company or an associated company in its capacity as a trustee of an occupational pension scheme (as defined in section 235(6) of the 2006 Act);

(C) any other liability incurred by such a person as an officer of the Company or an associated company.

19.2 This Article does not authorise any indemnity which would be prohibited or rendered void by any provision of the Companies Acts or by any other provision of law.

19.3 In this Article:

    (A) companies are associated if one is a Subsidiary of the other or both are Subsidiaries of the same body corporate; and

    (B) a 'relevant Director' means any Director, alternate Director or former director of the Company or an associated company.

20 Insurance

20.1 The Directors may decide to purchase and maintain insurance, at the expense of the Company, for the benefit of any relevant Director, secretary or other officer (excluding any auditor) in respect of any relevant loss.

20.2 In this Article:

    (A) a 'relevant Director' means any Director, alternate director or former director of the Company or an associated company;

    (B) a 'relevant loss' means any loss or liability which has been or may be incurred by a relevant Director, secretary or other officer (excluding any auditor) in connection with that person's duties or powers in relation to the Company, any associated company or any pension fund or employees' share scheme of the Company or associated company; and

    (C) companies are associated if one is a Subsidiary of the other or both are Subsidiaries of the same body corporate.

Precedent 5

International joint venture agreement

This precedent is offered as an agreement which would be suitable for use where the joint venture company is incorporated outside the UK whether or not one or more of the parties are other than UK nationals, and where the parties wish English Law to govern the agreement. The agreement is drafted so as to avoid citing statutes and referring to technical legal terms. Care will need to be taken to ensure the agreement does not conflict with the constitution of the Company where it could not in fact be altered as contemplated by clause 16.

The agreement might be adapted to be governed by other than English law, but only after careful review by a lawyer in the jurisdiction concerned.

THIS AGREEMENT is dated the [ ] day of [ ] 20[   ] and made

BETWEEN:

(1) **PARTY 1** ('[X]') a company incorporated under the laws of [ ] whose principal place of business is at [ ];

(2) **PARTY 2** ('[Y]') a company incorporated under the laws of [ ] whose principal place of business is at [ ]; and

(3) **PARTY 3** ('[Z]') a company incorporated under the laws of [ ] whose principal place of business is at [ ].

BACKGROUND:

(A) [ ] (the 'Company') is a company with limited liability incorporated or existing in [ ], of which [two] shares have been issued and are [fully] paid up, and beneficially owned by [X] and registered in the name of [X] or [its/his] nominees. The present directors of the Company are [ ] and [ ].

OR

The parties wish to incorporate a company with limited liability in [*jurisdiction*] with the name

[ ] [*set out proposed capital structure*].

(B) The parties propose that the Company should be used as their joint venture vehicle to [*specify proposed business or purpose of the Company*].

(C) Accordingly the parties have agreed to subscribe for shares in the Company, to enter into certain commitments and to regulate the exercise of their rights in relation to the Company in the manner set out in this Agreement.

THE PARTIES AGREE THAT:

1 Interpretation

1.1   The definitions and rules of interpretation in Schedule 1 apply to this Agreement.

2 [Conditional Agreement [24.9]

2.1   This Agreement is conditional upon the satisfaction or waiver (if applicable) of [all the] following condition[s]:

(A)   [the passing at a duly convened and held general meeting of [ ] of a resolution in the Agreed Form marked '[ ]' to approve the entry by [ ] into this Agreement]; and
(B)   [the conditions specified in Schedule 2];
(C)   [any others, eg the obtaining of any other required consent(s), the entry into of an agreement vital to the venture].

2.2   If all the condition[s] specified in clause 2.1 shall not have been satisfied [or waived by [ ]] on or before [ ] [ ] 20[ ] this Agreement shall lapse and the parties shall be released from all their obligations under it and no party shall be entitled to make any claim against any other in respect or arising out of this Agreement or such non-satisfaction and lapse, save in respect of any antecedent breach (including any breach of clause 2.3).

2.3   [ ] shall use its reasonable endeavours to procure the satisfaction of the condition[s] specified in clause 2.1 [[ ] shall use its reasonable endeavours to procure the satisfaction of the condition[s] specified in clause 2.1[ ]].]

3 Warranties and Representations [Chapter 25]

[3.1 only applicable if the Company already exists]

3.2   X warrants to Y [and Z] that immediately prior to the execution of this Agreement:

(A)   the particulars of the Company set out in recital (A) above are true and accurate in all respects;
(B)   the Company has been duly incorporated as a limited liability company under the laws of [ ] and has the necessary corporate power to carry on its business as described in this Agreement; and

(C)   the Company:

(1)   has not traded;
(2)   has no assets, contracts, employees, indebtedness or any other liabilities whatsoever whether actual or contingent;

      (3)   has not declared any dividends or other distributions;

      (4)   has not prepared any accounts; and

      (5)   has complied with all relevant requirements of all laws relating to companies applying in the jurisdiction of its incorporation.

3.3   Except as may have been fairly disclosed [in writing] to the [other party/ each of the other parties] prior to the date of this Agreement, each party severally warrants and represents to [the other party/each of the other parties] as follows:

   (A)   that it (and each of its Affiliates who enter into any agreement or arrangement to be entered into by it under or in connection with this Agreement) is a corporation duly organised or incorporated under the laws of the jurisdiction of its organisation or incorporation and has full power and authority and has obtained all necessary corporate authority and consents of other persons and Authorities to enter into and perform its obligations under this Agreement and such other agreements and arrangements;

   (B)   that this Agreement and each of such other agreements and arrangements has been or will be duly and validly executed and delivered by it and/or its Affiliates and all the obligations contained therein are legal, valid and enforceable in accordance with their terms; and

   (C)   that the signing, delivery and performance by each of them of this Agreement and each other such agreement or arrangement will not:

      (1)   result in a breach of, or constitute a default under, or give rise to any right of termination, cancellation or acceleration under any agreement or arrangement to which it (or any of its Affiliates) is a party or by which any of them are bound or under their respective constitutional documents; or

      (2)   result in the breach of any law or any judgment, decision or order of any Authority to which it is a party or by which it is bound.

4 Legal Opinions

4.1   Immediately prior to execution of this Agreement, each party shall deliver to [each of] the other part[y][ies] an opinion as to its capacity to enter into this Agreement, that its entry into this Agreement has been duly authorised and that this Agreement is binding on it in accordance with its terms. In each case, such opinion shall be given to the other part[y][ies] by a lawyer reasonably acceptable to [that/those] party[y] [ies], and such opinions shall be the respective Agreed Forms marked '[ ]' and '[ ]' [and '[ ]'].

5 Establishment of the Joint Company

5.1   Forthwith upon [the execution of this Agreement/within [seven] days of the satisfaction of all the conditions specified in clause 2.1]:

(A)   [X] shall exercise its voting rights in respect of its Shares to cause the Company to adopt [*constitutional documents*] in the form set out in the Agreed Form marked '[ ]';

(B)   subject to and forthwith upon compliance with the preceding provisions of this clause 5.1:

(1)   X shall procure that (at the request of Y) Messrs [ ] and [ ] and (at the request of Z) Messrs [ ] and [ ] shall (subject to each of them respectively consenting to act) be appointed as additional Directors of the Company;

(2)   X, Y [and Z] shall subscribe in cash [at par] for new Shares as follows (and X shall waive any rights of pre-emption which it may have in respect of such subscriptions);

Name	Number of Shares
X	[ ]
Y	[ ]
[Z	[ ]]

and

(3)   [the parties shall procure that a meeting of the Directors is held at which the Shares specified above shall be allotted and issued to X and Y [and Z] respectively and registered in their respective names (or in the names of their respective nominees) credited as fully paid against immediate payment of the relevant subscription moneys.]

[OR for use where the Company is not yet incorporated]

(C)   Forthwith upon [the execution of this Agreement/within [seven] days of the satisfaction of all the conditions specified in clause 2.1] the parties agree to forthwith incorporate the Company in accordance with the laws of [*jurisdiction*] under the name [ ] [Limited] (or such other lawfully permissible name as the parties shall agree upon) with a share capital consisting of [   ] [Ordinary Shares] [of [   ] each par value] and with [*constitutional documents*] in the Agreed Form marked '[ ]'.

(D)   The parties each agree to execute such documents and take such steps as may be necessary to incorporate the Company on the terms set out in clause (A) [and each party shall bear [   ]% [*or if unequal specify percentages*] of all reasonable costs and expenses borne by all of them in relation to the formation of the Company and each will account to the other[s] accordingly.]

(E)   Immediately upon the incorporation of the Company:

(1)   XY [and Z] shall subscribe in cash [at par] for new Shares as follows:

Name	Number of Shares
X	[ ]
Y	[ ]
[Z	[ ]]

(2)   the parties shall procure the appointment to [the board of Directors] of the Company of [ ] (nominated by X) [ ] (nominated by Y) and [[ ] (nominated by Z)]; and

(3)   [the parties shall procure that a meeting of the Directors is held at which the Shares specified above shall be allotted and issued to X and Y [and Z] respectively and registered in their respective names (or in the names of their respective nominees) credited as fully paid against immediate payment of the relevant subscription monies.]

5.2   Immediately following the due performance of clause 5.1 the parties shall procure that:

(A)   the [registered/principal office] of the Company shall be [changed to] [ ];

(B)   [ ] shall be appointed the auditors of the Company;

(C)   the date to which the Company prepares its audited accounts shall be [changed to] [ ] (so that its first accounting period shall run from its date of incorporation to [   ] [ ] 20[   ] (both dates inclusive));

(D)   [ ] Bank [ ] branch shall be appointed the bankers to the Company; and

(E)   [[ ] shall be appointed [the Secretary] to the Company [in place of] [ ].]

6 Directors and Board meetings [Chapter 16]

6.1   At all times whilst this Agreement remains in force and subject to the provisions of clause 6.4 the parties shall procure that the Board shall consist of [not less than [ ] and] not more than [ ] Directors and that (subject as otherwise expressly provided in this Agreement) each of the parties shall be entitled to appoint Directors (and remove any Director which it has appointed) so that the number of Directors appointed by it and holding office at any one time shall not exceed the number respectively specified below:

X   [ ] Directors;

Y   [ ] Directors; and

[Z   [ ] Directors].

[For these purposes [ ] and [ ], who are existing Directors at the date of this Agreement, shall be deemed to have been appointed by X.]

6.2   Save as otherwise expressly provided in this Agreement, a party wishing to appoint or remove a Director in accordance with the provisions of this clause shall serve a notice upon the other parties specifying the Director to be appointed or removed and the parties shall then become bound to procure the appointment or removal of the Director so specified within 14 days. A party requesting the removal of a Director shall be required to indemnify the Company and every Subsidiary against any claim by such Director for compensation in respect of his removal from office.

6.3   [Except as provided in clause 6.4,] no party shall exercise the voting rights attaching to its Shares or take any other action to remove a Director appointed at the request of any other party except where such removal is requested by that party [or the removal is for Cause.]

6.4

(A)   If a party entitled to appoint Directors under this Agreement ceases for any reason at any time to be the beneficial owner of Shares conferring at least [   ]% of the voting rights ordinarily attaching to all the Shares then in issue the entitlement of that party to appoint and remove Directors shall be modified as follows:

(1)   where its beneficial holding is of Shares conferring less than [   ]% of such voting rights but at least [   ]% thereof, the number of Directors entitled to be appointed by it and holding office at any one time shall not exceed [   ]; and

(2)   where its beneficial holding is of Shares conferring less than [   ]% of such voting rights its right to appoint and remove Directors shall cease.

(B)   [Where the provisions of clause 6.4(A) have become applicable in relation to any party (the 'Appointor') the parties shall immediately procure the removal from office of all, or an appropriate number of, the Directors appointed by the Appointor as shall be necessary to ensure that the number of such Directors remaining in office is reduced to the number allowed by clause 6.4(A). The Directors to be removed shall be those specified in a notice served by their Appointor, but if the Appointor shall fail or delay in serving such a notice the other parties shall be entitled to designate the Directors to be removed and may procure their removal. Such removal shall be without prejudice to the right of the Appointor to request the removal of any of its remaining Directors and request the appointment in substitution of any Director removed under this clause 6.4(B) provided that the limit set out in clause 6.4(A) is not thereby exceeded.]

[adapt as necessary – it may be necessary to deal with each party's reduced entitlement separately]

6.5   Nothing in this Agreement shall prevent the removal of a Director for Cause but any such removal shall not prevent the party who requested the appointment of that Director to request the appointment of a replacement Director pursuant to this clause 6, to the extent that it is still then so entitled.

6.6   Unless otherwise agreed by the parties, meetings of the Board shall take place at such locations and at such time or times as may be designated by the Chairman (or any [two] other Directors) but not less frequently than once every three months. Any of the parties may also convene a meeting of the Board at any time.

6.7   Unless otherwise agreed by the parties, at least 14 days' prior written notice of a meeting of the Board shall be given to all Directors and their alternates or proxies together with a written agenda specifying the matters to be raised at the meeting together with copies of all papers to be laid before the meeting. Upon receiving notification of a meeting of the Board, any Director shall be entitled to require the inclusion on the agenda of any matter that he would like raised at the meeting provided that he notifies all the other Directors and their alternates of such inclusion not later than seven days prior to the meeting. [16.6]

6.8   The following provisions shall apply in relation to the conduct of meetings:

(A)   No business shall be transacted at a Board meeting unless a quorum is present. The quorum for a Board meeting shall be [one of/all the] Director[s] appointed at the instance of each party [or such lesser number of them as will, assuming all the Directors present vote, enable the Directors who are present and appointed at the request of each party in each case to exercise the same proportion of the votes available at the meeting as the Directors appointed at the request of that party would be able to exercise at a meeting at which all the Directors appointed at the request of all the parties were present] who are present in person or by proxy or alternate, or by means of a conference telephone call. In the event that no quorum is so present at a meeting of the Directors within half an hour after the time appointed for the meeting then the same shall stand adjourned to the day which is seven days after the day for which the meeting was convened at the same time and place and the quorum for such adjourned meeting shall be any [two] Directors present in person or by proxy or alternate or by means of a conference telephone call.

(B) Each Director shall have the right, by written notice to the Company (addressed to the Company Secretary (or equivalent officer) and delivered to the Company's registered office or principal place of business for the time being), to appoint any person (including another Director) as his alternate or proxy to attend and vote in place of such director at any meeting of the Directors held during the period of his appointment, and to remove any alternate or proxy so appointed. Such appointment may be for a specific meeting or for a specified period or may continue indefinitely until revoked. No such alternate or proxy shall be entitled to attend a meeting of the Directors unless the notice appointing him has been received by the Company before the commencement of the meeting. If the Director who has appointed such an alternate or proxy shall cease to be a Director for any reason, such appointment shall cease to be effective immediately on such cessation. An alternate or proxy shall be entitled to exercise the vote of the Director who appointed him and if more than one Director has appointed him to act at the same time, the votes of all such appointors in addition to his own vote if the appointee is himself a Director.

(C) The Chairman of the Board shall be appointed by a majority of the Directors. [The Chairman shall not be entitled to any second or casting vote.]

(D) Subject as otherwise expressly provided in this Agreement, resolutions proposed at a meeting of the Board shall be passed upon receiving the affirmative vote of a majority of the Directors (or their alternates or proxies) present at the meeting in person, by alternate or proxy or by conference telephone call and voting thereat. Each Director shall have one vote.

7 Shareholders' Meetings

7.1 Meetings of the shareholders of the Company shall be convened by the Board as required by the laws governing the Company and otherwise in order to propose a resolution which relates to a matter outside the authority of the Board as provided by such laws. Such a meeting may also be convened by any of the parties or any Director. Unless otherwise agreed by all the Directors, at least 21 days prior written notice of any meeting of the shareholders of the Company shall be given to all such shareholders.

7.2   Each shareholder of the Company shall attend meetings of the shareholders of the Company by its authorised representative, appointed by it in writing, who may be any person, including a Director. Such appointment may be delivered to the Company at its registered office or principal place of business for the time being and addressed to the Company Secretary (or equivalent officer) at any time prior to the meeting or delivered at the meeting itself.

7.3   No business may be transacted at any meeting of the shareholders of the Company unless a quorum is present at such meeting. [Two/three] shareholders, each of whom is for the time being a party to this Agreement, represented by their authorised representatives who are present in person or by a conference telephone call shall be such a quorum. If no quorum shall be present at a meeting of the shareholders within half an hour after the time appointed for the meeting, the same shall stand adjourned to the day which is seven days after the date appointed for such meeting at the same time and place and the quorum for the adjourned meeting shall be one shareholder which is a party to this Agreement whose authorised representative is present in person.

7.4   Subject as otherwise expressly provided in this Agreement and to any higher majority which may be required by the laws governing the Company or by its [constitution], a resolution of the shareholders of the Company shall be passed on receiving a majority of the votes exercised at the meeting and subject to any contrary provision in the [constitution] of the Company, each shareholder shall be entitled to one vote for each Share of which it is the holder.

8 Specific obligations of the parties [Chapter 3]

[*Set out any obligations of the parties in relation to the establishment of the joint venture, eg to transfer assets into the company, grant IP licences to it, or enter into support agreements etc*]

9 Finance for the Company [Chapter 6]

9.1   Finance for the business of the Company shall be provided initially by the cash subscriptions for the Shares referred to in clause 5 [and thereafter [subject to clause 10] by loans from X and Y [and Z] on such terms as they may agree with the Board and/or by loans from the Company's bankers].

[*Delete, adapt or replace as necessary. There should be clear arrangements in place for the borrowing/injection of sufficient funds to finance the business in accordance with the first business plan. Where the parties are to provide loans the terms of them should be agreed at the outset in formal loan agreements. Where external finance is to be provided the terms should ideally be agreed before the joint venture agreement is signed – the shareholders should not be asked to commit or guarantee finance without some form of cap or other limitations.]*

9.2   [Any further finance shall only be provided in a manner which will not result in the Company being thinly capitalised so as to result in any interest payable in respect of such finance not being allowable as a deduction in computing the profits of the Company for the purposes of any taxation laws to which it is for the time being subject.]

10 Conduct of the Joint Venture

10.1 The parties shall procure that the Company and every Subsidiary shall:

(A)   comply with all applicable laws of the countries of their incorporation, organisation and operation;

(B)   do or cause to be done all things necessary to obtain and maintain in force all authorisations from Authorities which may at any time be required under the laws of the countries of their incorporation, organisation or operation to enable them to conduct their respective businesses in accordance with the terms of this Agreement and any decisions of the parties or the Directors taken pursuant thereto;

(C)   pay all taxes, assessments and other governmental charges of any kind imposed on or in respect of their respective incomes, gains, businesses or assets of and in respect of taxes or other amounts which they are required by law to withhold from amounts paid by them to their employees or any other person before any penalty or interest accrues on the amount payable and before any lien on the property of any of them exists as a result of non-payment, provided that nothing shall require the Company or any Subsidiary to pay or withhold any amount if it is diligently contesting its alleged obligation to do so in good faith through appropriate proceedings and is maintaining appropriate reserves or other provisions in respect of the contested amount as may be required under applicable accounting policies.

10.2 Each party shall promptly notify the other[s] and the Company as soon as it or any Director appointed by it becomes aware of:

(A)   the occurrence of any event that constitutes a default or event of default in respect of any indebtedness of the Company or any Subsidiary; and

(B)   any litigation or investigation, enquiry, order or other proceeding by any Authority pending against the Company or any Subsidiary or any other event affecting the Company of any Subsidiary which affects materially and adversely the assets, liabilities, business, operations, profitability or prospects of the Company and any Subsidiaries taken as a whole.

[clause 10.3 is for the protection of minority interests]

10.3 Whilst this Agreement remains in force the parties shall procure that, except with the consent [of all/a Majority] of them/[named party] (but provided that the consent of a party shall not be required at a time when it is the beneficial owner of Shares carrying less than [10]% of the total votes ordinarily exercisable in a shareholders' meeting of the Company) [Chapter 15]:

(A) the general nature of the business of the Company and the Subsidiaries (if any) shall not be changed from that described in clause 12.1;

(B) no change shall be made in the issued share [or loan capital] of the Company nor shall any option or right to subscribe be granted to any person in respect of any share [or loan capital] of the Company and no securities convertible into such share or loan capital shall be issued or agreed to be issued [save that there shall be permitted a Permitted Share Issue];

(C) no alteration shall be made in the by-laws, articles of association or other equivalent constitutional documents of the Company or the rights attaching to any class of shares of the Company;

(D) no resolution shall be passed for the winding up of the Company nor shall any of the parties take any action for the winding up of the Company or for any procedure terminating or restricting the ability of the Board to manage the business and affairs of the Company or subjecting it to the control or supervision of any court (unless in either case the Company shall have become liable to be wound up or subject to any such procedure by reason of its insolvency);

(E) no new equity interest in the Company shall be created or conferred upon any person (including any of the parties) including but not limited to any arrangements for sharing income or profits of any other interest [save that there shall be permitted a Permitted Share Issue];

(F) the Company shall not and shall not agree to:

(1) acquire, whether by formation, purchase, subscription or otherwise, any Subsidiary nor effect or permit the disposal, dilution or reduction of its interest, directly or indirectly, in any Subsidiary, whether by the sale, allotment or issue of any shares in its capital or securities convertible into such shares

otherwise than to its parent company or any reduction in the voting power or other powers of control exercisable in relation to the Subsidiary by its parent;

(2) sell, transfer, lease, license or in any way dispose of all or a material part of its business, undertaking or assets, whether by a single transaction or series of transactions related or not (otherwise than in the ordinary course of the Company's business);

(3) borrow any sums [except from the Company's bankers in the ordinary and usual course of business] which when aggregated with the borrowings of all the Subsidiaries exceed [ ] outstanding at any one time;

(4) incur in any Financial Year aggregate capital expenditure (including finance leases but excluding operating leases [which when aggregated with the capital expenditure of all the Subsidiaries for that Financial Year is] in excess of [[ ]/ the aggregate amount provided for capital expenditure in the Business Plan for that Financial Year];

(5) enter into or vary any operating lease, either as lessor or lessee, of any plant, property or equipment of a duration exceeding [ ] years or involving aggregate premium and annual rental payments in excess of [ ];

(6) factor or discount any book debts of the Company;

(7) make any loan or advance or otherwise give credit (other than credit given in the normal course of the Company's business and on normal arm's length commercial terms) to any person except for deposits with its bankers;

(8) give any guarantee, bond or indemnity in respect of or to secure the liabilities or obligations of any person (other than its wholly-owned Subsidiary);

(9) create or issue any debenture, mortgage, charge or other security over any assets of the Company [(except for the purpose of securing sums borrowed by the Company from its bankers in the ordinary and usual course of business)] [up to the limit allowed by clause 10.3(F)(3)];

(10) acquire any share or loan capital of the body corporate (including that of the Company or any Subsidiary) or enter into any partnership or profit sharing arrangement with any person;

(11) [declare or pay any dividend or other distribution in respect of any share capital of the Company [other than a dividend consistent with the terms of clause 11.3];]

(12) enter into or make any material change to any contract or transaction with:

    (a) any of the parties or any of their respective Affiliates or persons connected with any of them (except as expressly authorised by this Agreement); or

    (b) any other persons except on normal arm's length commercial terms;

(13) enter into any agency, distribution or similar agreement which is expressed to confer any element of exclusivity as regards any goods or services the subject thereof or as to the geographical area of the agreement or vary such an agreement to include any such exclusivity;

(14) enter into or vary any licence or other similar agreement relating to intellectual property to be licensed to or by the Company [which is otherwise than in the ordinary course of business];

(15) enter into or make any material change to any contract of employment or for the provision of services by any director or senior manager of the Company (whatever his title or job description) [including any increase in salary (other than any increase budgeted for in any approved Business Plan)];

(16) enter into any contract of employment with, or for the provision of services to, the Company by any specified individual which cannot be terminated on less than [six] months' notice without payment of compensation (other than statutory compensation) or vary any such contract so that it cannot be so terminated;

(17) introduce or vary any executive or employee stock or share option or incentive scheme or profit sharing or bonus scheme of any nature;

(18) engage any new employee at remuneration in excess of [ ] per annum, increase the remuneration of any employee so as to exceed such figure (other than in each case as budgeted for in any approved Business Plan) or dismiss any employee who receives remuneration in excess of [ ] per annum [other than for gross misconduct];

(19) enter into or vary any agreement for the provision of consultancy, management or other services by any person which will, or is likely to, result in the Company being managed otherwise than by its Directors, or which involves a consideration exceeding [ ] per annum;

(20) [change the auditors of the Company or appoint any auditors in place of any who resign or make any significant change in the accounting policies or practices for the time being adopted by the Company or make any change in the accounting date of the Company;]

(21) change the names or the scope of the authority of the persons authorised to sign cheques or other financial instruments on behalf of the Company;

(22) [adopt any Business Plan or amend any Business Plan after the adoption thereof;]

(G) no act or event shall occur in relation to any Subsidiary which is analogous to or has any substantially similar effect to any of the acts or events referred to in clause 10.3(F)(1) to 10.3(F)(22) (other than clause 10.3(F)(8)) [but so that clause 10.3(F)(8) shall permit any wholly owned Subsidiary to give any guarantee, bond or indemnity in respect of any liabilities of the Company or any other wholly owned Subsidiary.]

10.4 For the purpose of this clause 10 a 'Permitted Share Issue' means one which satisfies the following requirements:

(A) the Shares proposed to be issued by the Company are [ordinary] shares ranking pari passu in all respects with the existing [ordinary] shares;

(B) the Shares proposed to be issued are offered by the Company to all the shareholders of the Company in proportion, as nearly as the circumstances permit, to the numbers of existing Shares held by them;

(C) the Shares are offered for subscription at a price per Share which is [approved by [*named party*]/all the parties/a Majority of the parties/certified by the auditors to the Company] to represent the [market consideration/fair value] for the Shares offered. In so certifying the auditors of the Company shall act as experts and not as arbitrators and the parties shall procure that their fees and expenses shall be borne by the Company;

(D) such offer ('the Primary Offer') is made by notice given to each shareholder specifying the Shares offered and specifying a time (being not less than 14 days from the making of the Primary Offer) within which the Primary Offer, if not accepted, shall be deemed to have been declined;

(E) the Primary Offer shall include an invitation in favour of those who accept all the Shares offered to them by the Primary Offer to apply on the same terms and within the same time for any Shares in addition to those offered to them which will be available if any parties do not accept all the Shares offered to them by the Primary Offer ('Excess Shares');

(F)   after the close of the Primary Offer the Board shall allocate the Shares applied for amongst the Shareholders on the basis that those who have applied for no more than the Shares offered to them in the Primary Offer shall receive all the Shares applied for by them and the Excess Shares shall be allocated on the basis that should there be more Shares applied for than are available, they shall be allocated to the Shareholders applying for them in the same proportions as their holdings of existing Shares bear to one another but so that no Shareholder shall be obliged to subscribe for more Shares than the number it applied for; and

(G)   any Shares not taken up in the Primary Offer may be offered by the Board to any other person and (unless otherwise agreed by [all the parties]) at no less a sum per share than they were offered to the Shareholders, provided that no Shares shall be issued to a person who is not a party unless clause 18.1 is first complied with in relation to that person.

11 Accounting Matters, Business Plans, Dividend Policy and Tax

11.1   The parties shall procure that:

(A)   the Company and every Subsidiary shall maintain accurate and complete accounting and other financial records in accordance with the requirements of all applicable laws and [International/ United States/United Kingdom] generally accepted accounting practices; [14.34]

(B)   [subject to clause 10] the accounting periods of the Company and every Subsidiary shall be consecutive periods of twelve months commencing on [ ] [ ] 20[ ] and they shall prepare audited accounts complying with the foregoing accounting principles accordingly [in addition to any such accounts which they may be required to prepare under any laws to which they are subject];

(C)   the Company shall prepare [monthly] management accounts [and reports] in relation to the Company and each Subsidiary containing such information as each party shall reasonably require and which shall be despatched by the Company to each of the parties within [30] days of the end of the [month] concerned; and

(D)   each party and their respective professional representatives authorised by them shall be allowed access at all reasonable times on prior written notice to examine the books and records of the

Company and each Subsidiary and to discuss their affairs with their directors and senior management. [14.32]

11.2

(A) The parties shall procure that the Company shall prepare a business plan for the Company and the Subsidiaries for each Financial Year which shall include the following:

(1) an estimate of the working capital requirements of the Company and the Subsidiaries incorporated within a cashflow statement [together with an indication of the amount (if any) which it is considered prudent to retain out of the distributable profits of the previous Financial Year to meet such working capital requirements];

(2) a projected profit and loss account;

(3) an operating budget (including estimated capital expenditure requirements) and balance sheet forecast;

(4) a review of projected business;

(5) a summary of business objectives [15.41]; and

(6) a financial report which includes an analysis of the results of the Company and the Subsidiaries for the previous Financial Year compared with the business plan for that Financial Year, identifying variations in sales, revenues, costs, and other material items.

(B) The first such business plan for the Financial Year ending [ ] [ ] 20[ ] shall be [in the Agreed Form marked '[ ]'/prepared by [ ] [ ] 20[ ]]. Business plans for subsequent Financial Years shall be submitted for approval by [[a Majority/all] of the parties/the Board] not later than [60] days before the commencement of the Financial Year to which they relate.

11.3 [Subject to circumstances prevailing at the relevant time including, in particular, the working capital requirements of the Company and the Subsidiaries, it is the intention of the parties that the Company shall distribute by way of dividend in respect of each Financial Year, provided that such dividend is lawful, [not less than [ ]% of the post tax consolidated profits of the Company and the Subsidiaries for that Financial Year/all of its profits available for distribution.] Any distribution for a Financial Year shall be made within [six months] after the end of that Financial Year.]

11.4 [*Insert here any specific provisions re utilisation of tax losses and reliefs between parties – if applicable*]

12 Nature and Promotion of the Company's business

12.1 The business of the Company shall unless otherwise determined by agreement between the parties be confined to [ ].

12.2 Such business shall be carried on by the Company itself or through branches or subsidiary companies established in such jurisdictions as the Board may decide and the Company shall establish such premises as the Board may decide.

12.3 Each of the parties covenants with [the/each] other party to use all reasonable endeavours to promote and develop the business of the Company and any Subsidiaries to the best advantage in accordance with good business practice and the highest ethical standards. [14.35]

12.4 In this clause 12 'Restricted Business' means any business which directly or indirectly competes with the business of the Company, or any of the Subsidiaries as carried on from time to time within [area].

12.5 Each party undertakes with each of the other parties (for the benefit also of each other party's successors in title) that it will not, and that it will procure that none of its Affiliates will, either on its own account or in conjunction with or on behalf of any other person, firm or company, for the period commencing on the date of the subscriptions for Shares in accordance with clause 5.1 and ending at the expiration of a period of [two] years after it ceases to be bound by this Agreement to the extent set out in clause 18.4:

(A) carry on or be engaged, concerned or interested (directly or indirectly and whether as a principal, shareholder, director, employee, agent, consultant, partner or otherwise) in carrying on any Restricted Business except as the holder of not more than 5% of the shares carrying unrestricted voting rights in any company whose shares are listed in or dealt in on any public investment exchange; or

(B) solicit or endeavour to entice away from the Company or any Subsidiary any person who is then [or was within the previous 12 months] an officer, manager, senior employee or consultant of the Company or any Subsidiary and became such prior to such party ceasing to be bound as aforesaid, whether or not such person would commit a breach of contract by reason of leaving service or office; or

(C) in connection with any Restricted Business, solicit the custom of or endeavour to entice away from the Company or any Subsidiary any person who is then, or was within the previous 12 months, a client or customer of the Company or any Subsidiary, whether or not such person would commit a breach of contract by reason of transferring business, but excluding any person who becomes such a client or customer after such party has ceased to be bound as aforesaid; or

(D) in connection with any Restricted Business, deal with any person who is then, was within the previous 12 months, a client or customer of the Company or any Subsidiary, whether or not such person would commit a breach of contract by reason of transferring business, but excluding any person who becomes such a client or customer after such party has ceased to be bound as aforesaid; or

(E) in connection with any Restricted Business endeavour to entice away from the Company or any Subsidiary any person who is then, or was within the previous 12 months, a supplier of the Company or any Subsidiary, whether or not such person would commit a breach of contract by reason of transferring business, but excluding any person who becomes such a supplier after such party has ceased to be bound as aforesaid.

OR

[alternative clauses 12.4 and 12.5 for use where the joint venture is subject to EU Competition Law or competition law modelled on EU Competition Law]

12.6 In this clause 12, 'Restricted Business' means any business which directly or indirectly competes with the business of the Company or any of the Subsidiaries which is described in the first Business Plan adopted under clause 11.2.

12.7 Each party undertakes with each of the other parties (for the benefit also of each other party's successors in title) that it will not, and that it will procure that none of its [Affiliates/Subsidiaries] will, either on its own account or in conjunction with or on behalf of any person, firm or company:

(A) carry on or be engaged, concerned or interested (directly or indirectly and whether as principal, shareholder, director, employee, agent, consultant, partner or otherwise) in carrying on any Restricted Business, other than as a holder for investment purposes only (which shall exclude an interest conferring a management function or any material influence) of any shares, debentures or other participation [and a holding of not more than 10% of any class of shares or debentures shall be deemed to be for such purposes unless the contrary is shown]; or

(B) solicit or endeavour to entice away any person who is then [or who was within the previous 12 months] an officer, manager, [senior] employee, agent or consultant of the Company or any Subsidiary whether or not such person would commit a breach of contract by reason of leaving service or office; or

(C) in connection with any Restricted Business, solicit the custom of or endeavour to entice away from the Company or any Subsidiary

659

any person who is then or who was within the previous 12 months a client or customer of the Company or any of the Subsidiaries whether or not such person would commit a breach of contract by reason of transferring business; or

(D) in connection with any Restricted Business, deal with any person who is then or who was within the previous 12 months a client or customer of the Company or any Subsidiary whether or not such person would commit a breach of contract by reason of transferring business; or

(E) in connection with any Restricted Business, endeavour to entice away from the Company or any of the Subsidiaries any person who is then or who was within the previous 12 months a supplier of the Company or any Subsidiary whether or not such person would commit a breach of contract by reason of transferring business;

and such undertakings given by each party to the others shall in each case continue until such time as the party giving them ceases to hold any Shares or to be entitled to exercise any of the rights set out in clause 10.3 [provided that upon such undertakings ceasing to apply to any party the like undertakings given to that party by the other parties shall also cease to apply].

OR in the case of a 50:50 deadlocked joint venture where clause 10.3 is not used – and such undertakings given by each party to the other shall in each case continue until such time as the party giving them ceases to hold any Shares or to be entitled to procure the appointment of at least half of the Directors [provided that upon such undertakings ceasing to apply to either party the like undertakings given to it by the other party shall also cease to apply].

12.8 Each party undertakes with each of the others (for the benefit also of each other party's successors in title) that it will not and that it will procure that none of its [Affiliates/Subsidiaries] will either on its own account or in conjunction with or on behalf of any person, firm or company at any time after the date of this Agreement, directly or indirectly use or attempt to use in the course of any business any valid trade or service mark, trade name, design or logo (whether registered or not) from time to time owned or lawfully used by the Company or any Subsidiary or any other name, logo, trade or service mark or design which is or might be confusingly similar thereto.

12.9 Each party undertakes to take all such steps as shall from time to time be necessary to ensure that no breach of clause 12.5 or clause 12.6 arises as a result of any action by any of its [Affiliates/Subsidiaries] or any employee or agent of such party or of any such [Affiliates/Subsidiaries].

12.10   Each of the undertakings in clauses 12.5 and 12.6 shall be construed as a separate and independent undertaking and if one or more of the undertakings is held to be void or unenforceable, the validity of the remaining undertakings shall not be affected.

12.11   Each party agrees that each of the restrictions and undertakings contained in clauses 12.5 and 12.6 is reasonable and necessary for the protection of each other party's legitimate interests in the goodwill of the Company and the Subsidiaries, but if any such restriction or undertaking shall be found to be void or voidable but would be valid and enforceable if some part or parts of the restriction or undertaking were deleted, such restriction or undertaking shall apply with such modifications as may be necessary to make it valid and enforceable.

12.12   Without prejudice to clause 12.9, if any restriction or undertaking is found by any court or other competent authority to be void or unenforceable the parties shall negotiate in good faith to replace such void or unenforceable restriction or undertaking with a valid provision which, as far as possible, has the same commercial effect as that which it replaces.

13 Confidentiality and Announcements

13.1 Each of the parties shall at all times use its best endeavours to keep in strictest confidence and not divulge, communicate or disclose to any person or use or exploit for its own purposes or those of any other person any information of a confidential nature made known or acquired by it at any time and relating to the Company, any of the Subsidiaries or any other party without the prior written consent of the other parties, including, without limitation, technical data, know-how, designs, plans, specifications, methods, processes, controls, systems, trade secrets, recipes, formulae, research and development data, product complaint and testing information, lists of customers and suppliers, all other proprietary information relating to development, engineering, manufacturing, marketing, distribution or accounts, financial statements, financial forecasts, budgets, estimates, sales information, other financial information and any other information which is marked as being confidential or would reasonably be expected to be kept confidential, provided that the obligation of confidentiality shall not apply:

(A)   to information for the time being in the public domain other than by reason of a breach of this clause 13;

(B)   to information that was in the possession of the relevant party prior to the date of this Agreement (or of its becoming a party to this Agreement, if later) where, to the best of that party's knowledge, such information is not in its possession by reason of the breach of any obligation of confidentiality;

661

(C)   to the extent that disclosure is required by law or by any order made by a court of competent jurisdiction or by a regulatory or other Authority provided that the party subject to such requirement shall, unless prevented by law, promptly notify the Company or the party concerned that the requirement has arisen in order to allow it to take any available action to prevent such disclosure, but failing such prevention, the notifying party shall use its reasonable endeavours to obtain confidential treatment of the information concerned;

(D)   to the disclosure of information to the directors and officers, auditors, bankers, financiers, insurers or professional advisers of a party who have a legitimate use for such information and who are bound by confidentiality obligations;

(E)   to the disclosure of information in the course of legal or arbitration proceedings arising out of this Agreement or concerning any matter relating to or in connection with the Company or any Subsidiary or any party;

(F)   to the disclosure of information to any person proposing to acquire all or any of the shares of a party in a manner permitted by this Agreement or approved by the other parties and the professional advisers and financiers of such proposed acquirer where the information is disclosed for the purpose of facilitating such acquisition and is legitimately required for such purpose; and

(G)   in the case of information relating to the Company or any Subsidiary, to the disclosure of that information to the extent reasonably required for the advancement of the business of the Company or the relevant Subsidiary. [17.63]

13.2   The obligations of each of the parties contained in clause 13.1 shall survive the termination of this Agreement and shall continue without time limit.

13.3   Where any information of a confidential nature is also privileged, the waiver of such privilege is limited to the purposes of this Agreement and does not, and is not intended to, result in any wider waiver of the privilege. Any party in possession of any confidential information of the Company, any Subsidiary, or any other party (a 'privilege holder') shall take all reasonable steps to protect the privilege of the privilege holder therein and shall inform the privilege holder promptly in writing if any step is taken by any other person to obtain any of its privileged confidential information.

13.4   For the purposes of this clause 13 the expression 'party' shall be extended to include all the Affiliates of that party and the employees, officers and agents of that party and of such Affiliates, and each party shall procure compliance accordingly.

13.5 The parties shall each procure that the Company and the Subsidiaries shall use all reasonable endeavours to ensure that the officers, employees and agents of each of them shall observe a similar obligation as that set out in this clause 13 in favour of each of the other parties.

13.6 No party shall be entitled to make or permit or authorise the making of any press release or other public statement or disclosure concerning this Agreement or any transaction contemplated by it or its termination or cessation without the prior written consent of the other parties, except as required by any stock exchange, any other regulatory or other authority, but before any party makes any such release, statement or disclosure it shall [where practical] first supply a copy of it to the other parties and shall incorporate any amendments or additions they may each reasonably require.

14 Share Transfers and Deadlock Resolution

14.1 Save as otherwise expressly provided or allowed by this Agreement no party shall, whilst it remains a party to this Agreement, sell, transfer, mortgage, charge, encumber, grant options over or otherwise dispose of any legal or beneficial interest in any of the Shares now or subsequently beneficially owned by it except with the prior written consent of each of the other parties (which may be withheld for any reason or without giving any reason) and in accordance with the constitution of the Company but provided that (where applicable) the provisions of clause 18.1 are first complied with.

[*Note: it may be appropriate to allow a party to transfer its shares after a particular period and/or subject to pre-emption provisions in favour of existing shareholders. Alternatively if to do so would confer Control on a new third party perhaps a tag-along/drag-along mechanism would be appropriate.*

14.2 [Chapter 13]

(A) For the purposes of this clause 14.2 a 'deadlock' shall arise if [13.11]:

(1) a resolution to approve a particular transaction [(being one of those specified in clause 10.3 or any other transaction requiring the approval of all or a majority of the parties)] has been proposed at a meeting of the Board or of the shareholders of the Company but has not been passed due to the failure to achieve the required majority or unanimity and one of the parties shall give notice to [the other party/ all the other parties] referring to this clause 14.2 requiring that the transaction shall be considered again at a special meeting of the Board or the shareholders of the Company (which for this purpose shall be convened by the said notice

which shall specify a date, time and place for the meeting, not being earlier than seven days after service of the notice) and at such meeting either unanimity or such required majority in favour of a resolution to approve the transaction is again not achieved or there is no quorum at the meeting within one hour after the time appointed for it; or

(2) if one party shall give notice to the [other party/each of the other parties], referring to this clause 14.2 that a deadlock shall exist if a quorum is not achieved at the reconvening of a meeting of the Board or the shareholders of the Company which has been adjourned for want of a quorum and a quorum is again not achieved at the reconvened meeting.

(B) If a deadlock shall occur the following provisions shall apply:

(1) the matter in respect of which the deadlock has arisen shall be referred for decision by the Chairmen of each of the parties who shall discuss the matter in good faith and attempt to reach a decision thereon on behalf of the parties;

(2) if they fail to do so within 30 days of the matter being referred to them, any party or parties who voted with the majority on the resolution referred to in clause 14.2(A)(1) or any party which was present at any meeting at which no quorum was present referred to in clause 14.2(A)(1) or clause 14.2(A)(2) (individually or, if more than one, together the 'Server') shall be entitled, no later than 90 days after the deadlock has arisen, to serve upon the Directors and each of the other parties a 'Deadlock Resolution Notice' requiring either:

(a) that the Company be wound up; or

(b) that the party or parties named in the Deadlock Resolution Notice (the 'Sellers') being persons who voted with the minority [or abstained] on the resolution referred to in clause 14.2(A)(1) or were not present at any meeting at which a quorum was not present referred to in clause 14.2(A) (1) or 14.2(A)(2) be required to sell all (but not some only of) its or their Shares to the Server (and if there shall be more than one Server in such proportions as they shall specify in the Deadlock Resolution Notice). The service of a Deadlock Resolution Notice shall preclude any other party from serving another such notice which arises out of the same subject matter or the same circumstances which enabled the first such notice to be served until the first such notice has been implemented or withdrawn by the Server;

(3)   upon service of a Deadlock Resolution Notice:

    (a)   if the notice requires the Company to be wound up the parties shall forthwith procure that the Company is wound up; or

    (b)   if the notice requires the Sellers to sell their shares to the Server the Sellers and the Server shall be bound to sell and buy respectively and the purchase price shall be determined in accordance with the provisions of clause 15.3 and completion of such sale(s) and purchase(s) shall take place in accordance with the provisions of clauses 16.5 to 16.9 inclusive.

15 Termination [Chapter 17]

15.1 This Agreement shall continue in full force and effect unless and until terminated in accordance with the provisions of this clause 15 but no such termination shall affect any provisions of this Agreement expressed to have effect after such termination or any rights which any party may have against any other party subsisting at the time of termination.

15.2 Any one or more of the parties (a 'Terminator') shall be entitled to terminate this Agreement forthwith by notice in writing (a 'Termination Notice') served [either (i)] in accordance with clause 15.3 if any of the events set out in clause 15.4 ('Termination Events') shall occur (but not after 90 days of the relevant Termination Event first coming to the attention of the Terminator) [and/or (ii) under clause 15.5].

15.3 A Termination Notice shall be served upon the party which is affected by the relevant Termination Event (the 'Terminatee') [and in the case of a Termination Notice served pursuant to clause 15.4(D) shall also be served on every party who holds or beneficially owns at the time of service any of the Shares previously held or beneficially owned by the individual whose services have ceased (and such parties shall also be 'Terminatees')] and such Termination Notice may be served irrespective of whether the relevant individual continues to hold any Shares whether legally or beneficially or remains a party to this Agreement]. Copies of the Termination Notice shall be served on all other parties (if any) but failure to do so shall not invalidate the Termination Notice. [A Termination Notice shall terminate this Agreement as between the Terminatee and any remaining parties but this Agreement shall continue in full force and effect as between such remaining parties, if more than one.]

15.4 The Termination Events are:

    (A)   if the Terminatee shall commit any [material] breach of any of its obligations under this Agreement or of any agreement then subsisting between the Terminatee and the Company and shall fail to remedy such breach (if capable of remedy) within 30 days after having been given notice to do so by the Terminator [17.15];

(B) if [the Terminatee (being a company) shall enter into liquidation whether compulsory or voluntary (except for the purposes of a bona fide reconstruction or amalgamation with the consent of [all] other parties, such consent not to be unreasonably withheld or delayed where there is no underlying insolvency) or the Terminatee shall become subject to any insolvency procedure; or]

(C) if [the Terminatee (being an individual) shall become bankrupt or shall die or become subject to any law relating to mental health [17.24]; or]

(D) [as a separate Termination Event in respect of each of such individuals, if any of [ ], [ ] and [ ] shall be lawfully dismissed or otherwise cease to make their substantially full time services available to the Company or any Subsidiary [26.73]; or]

(E) if there shall be a change in the Control of the Terminatee [17.19]; or

(F) [specify any other events].

15.5 Any of the parties may on, or at any time after, [ ] [ ]20[   ] terminate this Agreement by notice in writing to each of the other parties [17.8] in which case this Agreement shall continue in full force and effect until any obligation to buy or sell shares which arises under clause 15 has been duly discharged [17.27].]

15.6 This Agreement shall terminate if, as a result of a transfer of Shares lawfully made in accordance with this Agreement, only one party is legally and beneficially entitled to any Shares.

15.7 This Agreement shall terminate forthwith if the Company enters into liquidation.

16 Consequences of Termination Notices [17.28]

16.1 A Terminator (whether comprising one or more parties) shall be entitled by its Termination Notice to require the Terminatee either:

(A) in the case of a notice served under clause 15.4(A), 15.4(D), 15.4(E) [and 15.5] only, to purchase all (but not some only) of the Shares [beneficially] owned by the Terminator [and if there shall be more than one Terminatee requiring them to purchase such shares in such proportions as they may agree or (failing which) as near as may be in the same proportions as the proportions of the share capital of the Company which they each hold bear to one another]; or

(B)   [(except in the case of termination under clause 15.4(B) or 15.4(C))] to sell to the Terminator (and if more than one, equally or in such other proportions as they may agree) all (but not some only) of the Shares beneficially owned by the Terminatee

in either case at a price in [*currency*] determined in accordance with the provisions of clause 16.3, or if applicable clause 16.4.

16.2   The following provisions shall apply:

(A)   Upon the exercise of any right conferred by clause 16.4, the Terminator and the Terminatee shall become bound respectively to sell or purchase such Shares on the terms set out in this clause 16 in accordance with the alternative chosen by the Terminator in its Termination Notice.

(B)   If, in a valid Termination Notice [served in relation to a Termination Event specified in clause 15.4] no right conferred by clause 16.1 is exercised by the Terminator, the Terminatee may within 30 days of the service of the Termination Notice serve a counter-notice on the Terminator [(and if more than one, all of them)] requiring the Terminator to sell to [one or more of the Terminatee[s] [as they may between themselves agree] all (but not some only) of the Shares beneficially owned by the Terminator, in which case the Terminator and the Terminatee shall become bound respectively to sell and purchase such Shares on the terms set out in this clause 16.

(C)   If no right conferred by clause 16.1 is exercised by the Terminator, and, where applicable, no counter-notice is served by the Terminatee [or a notice is served under clause 15.5] (unless the parties otherwise agree) the parties shall procure that the Company is immediately wound up.

16.3   Subject to clause 16.4, the purchase price of the Shares to be bought and sold pursuant to the foregoing provisions of this clause [or, if applicable, clause 14.2] shall be the [fair] value thereof as agreed between the parties to such sale or purchase or, in default of such agreement within 21 days after the service of the Termination Notice (or the counter-notice if applicable) [(or in the case of a sale pursuant to clause 14.2, within 21 days of the parties becoming bound to buy and sell pursuant to such clause)], such sum as shall be certified by the auditors for the time being of the Company (at the request of any such party) to be the [fair] value of such Shares on the date of service of the Termination Notice or the counter-notice [or at the date upon which the parties become so bound]. [In so certifying the auditors are irrevocably instructed to value such Shares at such price as represents the same proportion of the market value of the whole issued share capital of the Company as such Shares bear to such whole issued share capital, so as not to take into account whether such Shares represent a majority or minority interest and on the basis that all agreements, arrangements and understandings which can be terminated on the transfer of such Shares being effected have terminated.] The auditors shall act as experts and not as arbitrators and their decision shall (save in the case of manifest error) be final and binding upon the parties to such sale and purchase for all purposes and the fees and expenses of the auditors shall be borne in equal shares by all of such parties. [Chapter 22]

16.4 [In a case where Shares are to be bought from a party upon whom a Termination Notice has been served under clause 15.4(A) ('a Defaulting Party') clause 16.3 shall apply with the modification that the auditors shall determine the purchase price by determining the market value of the whole issued share capital of the Company, both in the light of the breach concerned and on the basis that such breach had not been committed, and if the first of such valuations is lower than the second, the whole amount of the reduction in the value of the whole issued share capital of the Company shall be attributed to the Shares of the Defaulting Party, which shall be sold at a price which is the proportion of the second valuation attributable to the Shares being sold, minus the whole amount of such reduction but subject to a minimum consideration of [*one unit of currency*].] [Upon transferring its Shares for such consideration, the Defaulting Party shall cease to have any liability for the relevant breach.] [17.17]

16.5 Completion of the sale and purchase of any Shares pursuant to the provisions of this clause 16 [or, if applicable clause 14] shall take place at the principal place of business of the Company at [10.00 am] on the [tenth] day (not being a day upon which business is not normally conducted in the jurisdiction of completion) after the price of such Shares has been agreed or determined (or at such other time and/or place as the parties to such sale or purchase may agree) and the following provisions of this clause 16 shall then have effect.

16.6 At each completion referred to in the clause 16.5:

(A) the seller(s) shall deliver to the buyer(s) such documents and do such other acts and things as are required to transfer the whole title in the Shares being sold to the buyer(s) or as it or they may direct, such documents being duly executed by the seller(s) or the other registered holder(s) of such Shares together with the share certificates or other documents of title for such shares (or a reasonably acceptable indemnity in lieu thereof); and

(B) subject to the due performance by the seller(s) of the obligations in clause 16.6(A) the buyer(s) shall pay to the seller(s) the full amount of the purchase monies for the shares being sold together with any other sums to be paid pursuant to this clause 16 by delivering to it cleared funds by such means of payment as is agreed with the seller(s).

16.7 All Shares bought and sold pursuant to this clause 16 [or, if applicable, clause 14] shall be sold free and clear of all liens, charges, pledges, options and all other encumbrances and together with all rights attaching to them as at the date the seller(s) became bound to sell them and attaching to them subsequently [and with full title guarantee] [but the seller(s) shall not be obliged to provide any further representations, warranties or indemnities.]

16.8 If any party (an 'Outgoing Party') shall become bound pursuant to the preceding provisions of this clause 16 [or, if applicable, clause 14] to sell all the Shares then [beneficially] owned by it in the capital of the Company, the party or parties who have become bound to purchase such Shares (the 'Purchaser' or 'Purchasers') shall [unless termination arises by reason of a material breach of this Agreement by the Outgoing Party under clause 15.4(A)] upon or immediately prior to completion of the sale procure (or if more than one, shall jointly and severally procure):

(A)   the immediate release of every guarantee and indemnity which has been given by each Outgoing Party or any of its Affiliates in respect of any liabilities or obligations of the Company or any Subsidiary (and pending such release such Purchaser or Purchasers shall indemnify and keep each Outgoing Party, and its relevant Affiliates, fully and effectively indemnified from and against all claims arising thereunder and where there is more than one Purchaser their liability shall be joint and several) [17.50]; and

(B)   the immediate repayment to the Outgoing Party and any of its Affiliates of all monies it or they have lent to the Company or any Subsidiary under or pursuant to the provisions of this Agreement and then outstanding together with any interest accrued due thereon down to the date of actual payment (as well before as after judgment). [17.49]

16.9 Where the Outgoing Party has ceased to be the beneficial owner of any Shares at a time when the Company or any Subsidiary is using as its corporate name or as a trade or business name any name which includes any one or more words which are the same or similar to the corporate name of the Outgoing Party or any of its Affiliates or any trade or business name used by any of them, or any distinctive part of any of such names, the other parties or remaining party shall procure that within 30 days of such cessation all such names including such same or similar words shall be changed to exclude such words. [17.56]

17 Constitution and Supremacy

17.1 If at any time whilst this Agreement remains in force any of its provisions are found to conflict with the bye-laws, articles of association or other constitutional documents of the Company, the provisions of this

Agreement shall prevail in accordance with the provisions of this clause 17. This Agreement shall not, however, have the effect of amending such constitutional documents or, except as set out in clause 17.4, requiring their alteration. [24.19]

17.2 In order to ensure the operation of this Agreement irrespective of any conflict as is mentioned in clause 17.1, each party shall join with each other party in exercising all voting and other rights and powers of control as are from time to time respectively available to them under the relevant constitutional documents and otherwise in relation to the Company and their Shares and shall execute and deliver such waivers and shall each take or refrain from taking all other appropriate action within their respective powers so as to procure at all times whilst this Agreement remains in force all its provisions are duly observed and complied with and given full force and effect and all actions required by the parties are carried out promptly.

17.3 Without prejudice to the generality of clause 17.2, each party shall procure that each of its nominees who are shareholders in the Company and (subject to any statutory duties) each of the Directors appointed or deemed to be appointed by it pursuant to clause 6 (or under the constitutional documents of the Company) shall execute and do all acts and things and give and confer all powers and authorities as they would have been required to execute, do, give or confer had they been a party to this Agreement and had consented in the same terms as the party for whom they are a nominee (if a shareholder) or which appointed them (if a Director).

17.4 If it shall not be possible to secure the operation of this Agreement as set out in this clause 17 by reason of any contrary provision of the constitutional documents of the Company, the parties shall join in exercising all voting and other rights and powers respectively available to them to procure the alteration thereof to the extent necessary to permit the affairs of the Company to be so operated.

17.5 Subject to the preceding provisions of this clause 17, the parties hereby undertake to each other to observe the provisions of the constitutional documents of the Company.

17.6 The undertakings of each party under this clause 17 shall in each case be several so that each party shall only be liable for its own actions or failures to act in accordance with them, and none of them shall be liable for a failure to procure anything required by this clause where such failure is attributable to any action or failure to act by another party, but without prejudice to the liability of such other party.

17.7 Notwithstanding any other provision of this Agreement should any party or any person connected with it be in dispute with or shall have a conflict of interest with the Company, such party shall, and shall procure any nominee and the Director or Directors appointed or deemed to be appointed by it shall, not do or omit to do anything which would or would be likely to prevent the Company from exercising or from deciding whether or not to exercise such rights as it may have against the person in dispute with it, or in respect of the matter in relation to which the conflict of interest arises.

18 General

18.1 Each of the parties shall procure that it shall be a condition of the sale, transfer or other disposition of any Shares for the time being legally or beneficially owned by it or of any interest therein in favour of any other person (a 'Transferee') who is not a party to this Agreement that the sale, transfer or other disposition (being one which is otherwise permitted under or pursuant to any of the provisions of this Agreement) shall not be effected unless and until the Transferee (and any other person who in consequence of the sale transfer or other disposition will have any beneficial interest in the Shares concerned) shall have entered into an undertaking with the other parties for the time being to this Agreement who will remain so after the sale, transfer or other disposition. Under that undertaking the Transferee agrees to be bound by and to comply with all the provisions of this Agreement binding upon its transferor (other than any which impose a personal obligation upon its transferor which is not also undertaken by each of the other parties and any warranties given by its transferor) and such undertaking shall be in the form (as nearly as circumstances will permit) set out in Schedule 3. The parties shall also join in procuring that no Shares shall be allotted or issued except upon the condition that the person to whom the Shares are to be issued and any person who will, following the issue, have any beneficial interest in the Shares issued, shall also enter into such an undertaking, where they are not already bound by this Agreement. [14.76]

18.2 None of the parties may assign the benefit of any provision of this Agreement, or any legal or beneficial interest therein, separately from the Shares beneficially owned by it.

18.3 This Agreement shall bind the personal representatives and successors of the parties. The personal representatives of each party who is deceased and all other successors to any party, together with each person entering into an undertaking in the form required by clause 18.1, shall automatically become entitled to the benefit of this Agreement and may enforce the same as if it or they were named in it in place of the party who previously beneficially owned the Shares in which he or they are interested or, in the case of a person becoming a party by reason of an issue of new Shares, as if they had been named in this Agreement as an additional party and all references to a 'party' shall be construed accordingly but without prejudice to any provisions contained in the constitutional documents of the Company requiring such personal representatives or successors to offer for sale any Shares passing to them.

18.4 A party or any successor of a party who ceases to be legally and beneficially entitled to any Shares and who has complied with clause 18.1 and all other applicable provisions of this Agreement relating to the transfer of such Shares shall (subject as otherwise expressly provided in this Agreement) cease to be bound by this Agreement with the exceptions of clauses 3, [12.4, 12.5, 12.6, 12.7], 13, 18.10, and 20], and subject to those exceptions shall cease to be a party to this Agreement and all references to a 'party' shall be construed accordingly. [14.80]

18.5 This Agreement may be amended by an instrument executed by all the parties for the time being (which shall for this purpose exclude any party who has ceased to be legally and beneficially entitled to any Shares whether or not it has complied with clause 18.1) but no additional liability shall be imposed upon such a party without its consent. [14.79]

18.6 No exercise or failure to exercise or delay in exercising any right, power or remedy vested in any party under, or pursuant to, this Agreement shall constitute a waiver by that party of that or any other right, power or remedy.

18.7 Nothing in this Agreement shall be deemed to constitute a partnership between the parties (or any of them), nor constitute any of them the agent of any of the others or otherwise entitle any party to bind any of the others for any purpose.

18.8 Each party shall bear its own costs of or in connection with the preparation, negotiation and execution of this Agreement.

18.9 This Agreement (together with the other documents attached to or referred to in it) constitutes the entire agreement between the parties in relation to its subject matter and supersedes all previous agreements and understandings, whether oral or written, in relation thereto. Each party acknowledges to each other party that it has not agreed to enter into this Agreement in reliance on any representation, warranty, assurance or commitment not contained in this Agreement or, to the extent that it has, hereby waives and releases all rights and remedies that it would otherwise have in respect of the same otherwise than on grounds of fraud.

18.10 If any provision of this Agreement shall be held to be unlawful, the same shall be deemed to be deleted from this Agreement, but this Agreement shall remain in full force and effect as if the deleted provision had never been contained in it. The parties shall negotiate in good faith as to the terms of a mutually acceptable and satisfactory provision in place of any deleted, and if such terms shall be agreed, this Agreement shall be amended accordingly.

18.11 This Agreement may be executed in any number of counterparts, each of which is signed by one or more of the parties, provided that each of the parties has executed at least one counterpart, and such counterparts shall together constitute this Agreement.

18.12 Time shall be of the essence for the purposes of any provision of this Agreement.

18.13 No person who is not for the time being a party to this Agreement shall have any right to enforce any term of this Agreement. [24.12]

18.14 If this Agreement is translated into any language other than English, the English language text shall prevail.

19 Notices

19.1 Any notice to be given by any party to another party shall be in writing [in the [ ] language] and shall be deemed to have been duly served if delivered personally or sent by facsimile or e-mail transmission or by pre-paid [recorded delivery] post (or prepaid airmail or air courier in the case of an address for service outside the country from which service is made) to the addressee at its address (or number) for the receipt thereof specified below:

X	Postal Address	[	]
	Facsimile Number	[	]
	E-mail Address	[	]
	For the attention of:	[	]
Y	Postal Address	[	]
	Facsimile Number	[	]
	E-mail Address	[	]
	For the attention of:	[	]
[Z	Postal Address	[	]
	Facsimile Number	[	]
	E-mail Address	[	]
	For the attention of:	[	]]

or at any other address or number as the party to be served has notified (in accordance with this clause 19.1).

19.2 A notice shall be deemed to have been duly served as follows:

(A) where personally delivered, upon such delivery;

(B) where sent by facsimile, when despatched subject to confirmation of uninterrupted transmission by a transmission report;

(C) where sent by e-mail, when the e-mail leaves the e-mail gateway of the sender;

(D) where sent by pre-paid [recorded delivery] post to an address in the country from which service is made, [48] hours after posting;

   (E) where sent by prepaid airmail to an address outside the country from which service is made, [five] days after posting; and

   (F) where sent by air courier [2] business days after delivery to a representative of the courier.

19.3 In proving the service of any notice it shall be sufficient to prove:

   (A) in the case of a notice sent by post that such notice was properly addressed, stamped and placed in the post;

   (B) in the case of a notice personally delivered that it was delivered or left at the specified address;

   (C) in the case of a notice sent by facsimile that it was duly despatched to the specified number as confirmed by a transmission report;

   (D) in the case of a notice sent by e-mail that the e-mail left the e-mail gateway of the server of the notice; and

   (E) in the case of a notice sent by air courier that it was delivered to a representative of the courier.

20 Governing Law and Dispute Resolution [Chapter 23]

20.1 This Agreement and any non-contractual obligations arising from or connected with it shall be governed by [English law] and this Agreement shall be construed in all respects in accordance with [English law].

20.2 In relation to any legal action or proceedings to enforce this Agreement or arising out of or in connection with this Agreement, whether arising out of or in connection with contractual or non-contractual obligations, (in this clause 20.2 'Proceedings') each of the parties irrevocably submits to the [exclusive/non-exclusive] jurisdiction of the [English] courts and waives any objection to Proceedings in such courts on the grounds of venue or on the grounds that the Proceedings have been brought in an inappropriate forum. [*Where non-exclusive*] These submissions shall not affect the right of any party to take Proceedings in any other jurisdiction to the extent permitted by law, nor shall the taking of Proceedings in any jurisdiction preclude any party from taking Proceedings in any other jurisdiction.

   OR

20.3

   (A) Any dispute arising out of or in connection with this Agreement, including any question regarding the existence, scope, validity or termination of this Agreement or this clause 20.2 (and including any tortious or statutory claims) shall be referred to and finally resolved under [the Rules of the London Court of International

Arbitration/the Arbitration Rules of the International Chamber of Commerce], which Rules are deemed to be incorporated by reference into this clause 20.2 [save that notwithstanding anything in those Rules, the parties preserve their right to appeal or refer to the English courts on questions of law].

(B)   The number of arbitrators shall be [1]/[3].

(C)   The place of the arbitration shall be [London, England].

(D)   The arbitration proceedings shall be conducted in the [English] language and the award shall be in [English].

(E)   The parties agree that information concerning or arising out of any arbitration, including information concerning any arbitration award, shall be treated as confidential and not disclosed to any person other than a party without the prior consent in writing of all of the parties unless any of the circumstances specified in clause 13.1 applies or the disclosure is to a person intended to be called as a witness in the arbitration by the party disclosing the information, for the purpose of preparing the witness statement of such witness, provided that in any such case a written confidentiality undertaking in a form equivalent to that contained in this clause 20.2(E) has first been obtained from such person. The restrictions contained in this clause 20.2(E) shall survive the termination of this Agreement and shall continue without limit of time.

20.4   [*only include if arbitration is not selected*] Party B [*Foreign party*] irrevocably appoints [ ] of [ ] as its process agent to receive on its behalf service of process in any Proceedings in [*chosen jurisdiction*]. Service upon the process agent shall be good service upon Party B whether or not it is forwarded to and received by Party B. If, for any reason, the process agent ceases to be able to act as process agent or no longer has an address in [*chosen jurisdiction*], Party B irrevocably agrees to appoint a substitute process agent with an address in [*chosen jurisdiction*] acceptable to the other parties and to deliver to each of the other parties a copy of the substitute process agent's acceptance of that appointment within 30 days. In the event that Party B fails to appoint a substitute process agent, it shall be effective service for any other party to serve process upon Party B upon the last known address in [chosen jurisdiction] of the last known process agent for Party B notified to the other parties notwithstanding that such process agent is no longer found at such address or has ceased to act.

OR

Party B [*Foreign party*] irrevocably consents to process in any Proceedings anywhere being served in accordance with the provisions of this

Agreement relating to the service of notices. Such service shall become effective 30 days after dispatch. Nothing contained in this Agreement shall affect the right to serve process in any other manner permitted by law.]

AS WITNESS the hands of the parties or their duly authorised representatives the day and year first above written.

Schedule 1: construction of certain references

1   In this Agreement unless the context otherwise requires:

(A)   *'Agreed Form'* means, in relation to any document, the form agreed by, and initialled by or on behalf of, the parties for identification;

(B)   *'Authority'* means any competent governmental, administrative, supervisory, regulatory, judicial, determinative, disciplinary, enforcement or tax raising body, authority, agency, board, department, court or tribunal of any jurisdiction and whether supranational, national, regional or local;

(C)   *'Affiliate'* means, in relation to any party, any person which Controls or is Controlled by that party or which is Controlled by any person which Controls that party;

(D)   *'Appointor'* shall bear the meaning specified in clause 6.4(B);

(E)   *'Board'* means the Board of Directors of the Company or the Directors present at a duly convened meeting of the Directors at which a quorum is or is deemed to be present and *'Director'* means a director [*or other governing officer*] of the Company;

(F)   *'Business Plan'* means a business plan for the Company and the Subsidiaries prepared and adopted in accordance with clause 11.2;

(G)   [*'Cause'* means the wilful and/or persistent failure by a Director to substantially perform his duties as a Director, the engaging by a Director in conduct which is materially injurious to the Company or any Subsidiary or the Director's conviction of a crime involving violence, theft, fraud or dishonesty;]

(H)   *'Company'* shall bear the meaning set out in recital (A) above;

(I)   *'Consent'* means any approval, consent, ratification, waiver or other authorisation;

(J)   *'Financial Year'* means any accounting period of the Company, of whatever duration;

(K)   [*'Majority'*, in relation to the parties, means such number of them as for the time being are the beneficial owners of Shares together conferring not less than [   ]% of the total number of votes ordinarily exercisable at a shareholders' meeting of the Company;]

(L) 'Shares' means shares in the Company [which currently consist of [ordinary shares of [ ] each];]

(M) ['Subsidiary' means a company for the time being Controlled by the Company;]

(N) the headings and sub-headings are inserted in this Agreement for convenience only and shall not affect the construction of this Agreement;

(O) references to a 'party' and the 'parties' shall be references to a party or the parties to this Agreement for the time being;

(P) references to 'person' include any individual, partnership, body corporate, corporation sole or aggregate, state or agency of a state, and any unincorporated association or organisation, in each case whether or not having separate legal personality and also the successors in title and permitted assigns of any person;

(Q) references to 'Control' mean the possession, directly or indirectly, of the right or power to direct or cause the direction of the management policies of a person either by contract or through ownership of shares or securities carrying a majority of the votes ordinarily exercisable by the holders of all such shares or securities or through the ability to appoint the majority of the directors or other governing officers of a person or through ownership of shares or other securities which carry the right to receive the greater part of the income of such person (if all its income were to be distributed) or the right to receive the greater part of the assets of such person (if all its net assets were to be distributed) or howsoever otherwise and 'Controlled' shall be construed accordingly. A 'change of Control' when applied to any party shall be deemed to have occurred if any person or persons who Control such party at the date of the execution of this Agreement (or the date such party becomes bound by this Agreement if later) subsequently cease to Control it or if any person or persons acting together subsequently acquire Control of it; [17.20]

(R) references to 'law' or 'laws' mean and include a reference to every treaty, statute, directive, regulation, decision, order, instrument, by-law, or any other law (statutory or otherwise) of, or having effect in, any jurisdiction as for the time being amended, re-enacted (with or without amendment), consolidated or replaced or as their application is modified by other laws from time to time;

(S) references to clauses and schedules are references to the clauses of and schedules to this Agreement, references to sub-clauses are to sub-clauses of the clause in which the reference appears and references to this Agreement include the schedules and the Agreed Form documents;

(T) references to the singular shall include the plural and vice versa and references to the masculine, the feminine and the neuter shall include each other such gender;

(U) references to *'company'* include any body corporate wherever and under whatever laws incorporated or existing;

(V) any reference to any document, instrument or agreement (i) shall include all its exhibits, schedules and other attachments, (ii) shall include all documents, instruments or agreements issued or executed in replacement thereof, and (iii) shall mean such document, instrument or agreement or replacement or predecessor thereto as amended, modified and supplemented from time to time and in effect at any time;

(W) references to a 'day' mean a calendar day;

(X) general words shall not be given a restrictive meaning because they are followed by words which are particular examples of the acts, matters or things covered by the general words and words introduced by the word 'other' shall not be given a restrictive meaning because they are preceded by words referring to a particular class of acts, matters or things and the word 'including' shall be construed without limitation;

(Y) a person shall be treated as 'connected' with a party to this Agreement if it is that party's Affiliate or is a director of any such Affiliate or is entitled to exercise more than 30% of the aggregate voting rights normally exercisable at a shareholders' meeting by all the shareholders of any such Affiliate;

(Z) accounting terms shall be construed in accordance with [International/United States/United Kingdom] generally accepted accounting practices;

(AA) wherever in this Agreement any sum of money is expressed in any particular currency this shall, where the context so admits or requires, include an equivalent sum of money in any other relevant currency ascertained by reference to the spot rate of [*name of bank*] applying in London for the conversion of any such currency into the other as at the date of this Agreement or, for the purposes of any particular clause, as at the date upon which the relevant liability of the Company or any Subsidiary is, or is proposed to be, incurred. The foregoing shall not apply to any sum which is payable by the terms of this Agreement by one party to another, which shall be payable in the currency specified in this Agreement, but in determining the amount of any such payment, any amount relevant to that determination which is expressed in another currency shall be converted into the currency of payment at the aforesaid spot rate applying as at the due date of payment, save that for the purpose of any certificate required under this Agreement the auditors may employ such conversion date and rate as they may determine to be appropriate; and

(BB) [references to any provision or requirement of English law and to any English legal term for any action, remedy, method of judicial proceeding, legal document, legal status, court, official, or any legal concept or thing shall in respect of any jurisdiction other than England be deemed to include that which most nearly approximates in that jurisdiction to the English legal provision, requirement or term.]

Schedule 2: competition conditions (chapters 10 & 11) (use either 1 or 2 as appropriate)

1   To the extent that the establishment of the joint venture contemplated by this Agreement constitutes a concentration with a Community dimension within the scope of Council Regulation (EC) 139/2004 (the 'ECMR'):

(A)   the Commission of the European Communities (the 'European Commission') adopting a decision under ECMR, art 6(1)(b) in terms [reasonably] satisfactory to each of the parties declaring such joint venture to be compatible with the common market; or

(B)   such joint venture being deemed to have been declared compatible with the common market pursuant to ECMR, art 10(6);

(C)   in the event that a request is made under ECMR, art 9(2) by a European Union state, the European Commission indicating, in terms [reasonably] satisfactory to each of the parties, that it does not intend to refer such joint venture or any aspect of it to the competent authorities of such state in accordance with ECMR, art 9 and no such referral being deemed to have been made pursuant to ECMR, art 9(5).

2   To the extent that the establishment of the joint venture contemplated by this Agreement constitutes a relevant merger situation within the meaning of s 23 of the Enterprise Act 2002:

(A)   the Competition and Markets Authority/Office of Fair Trading having indicated in terms [reasonably] satisfactory to each of the parties that it does not intend in the exercise of its powers under the Enterprise Act 2002 to refer the joint venture contemplated by this Agreement or any aspect of it to further scrutiny by the CMA/the Competition Commission; or

(B) where a Merger Notice has been submitted pursuant to the Enterprise Act 2002 (Merger Pre-notification) Regulations 2003, the period for consideration of the Merger Notice and any extension thereof having expired without the Merger Notice having been rejected or withdrawn or the Office of Fair Trading having issued a notice pursuant to s 97(7) of the Enterprise Act 2002 or the matters covered by such Merger Notice or any of them having been referred to the CMA/Competition Commission by the Office of Fair Trading;

[and in either such case, the period during which an application to the Competition Appeal Tribunal under s 120 of the Enterprise Act 2002 for review of any decision (within the meaning of that section) by the CMA/Office of Fair Trading in connection with a reference or possible reference of the joint venture contemplated by this Agreement or any aspect of it to the CMA/Competition Commission having expired without an application for review having been made;]

3   The waiting period under the applicable anti-trust or competition laws in any other affected jurisdictions expiring, and all material related Consents, licences, registrations, or declarations of, or filings with, any Authority in any such jurisdictions required to be obtained or made prior to the share subscription pursuant to clause 2.3 having been obtained or made on a basis [reasonably] satisfactory to the parties.

[Note: the conditions do not cover the public interest intervention process [10.31]]

Schedule 3: form of undertaking from new shareholders

THIS DEED is dated the [ ] day of [ ] 20[   ] and made

BETWEEN:

(1) [ ] of [ ] (the 'New Shareholder') and

(2) THE PERSONS whose names and addresses appear in the Schedule hereto (the 'Existing Shareholders')

BACKGROUND:

(A) [recite date and parties to the joint venture/shareholders agreement] (the 'Shareholders' Agreement').

(B)   [recite any previous deeds of adherence and any releases from the joint venture/shareholders agreement]

(C)   The New Shareholder has become entitled to [a transfer of/be issued with] [class] ordinary shares of £[   ] each in the capital of the Company.

(D)   It is a term of the Shareholders' Agreement that no [transfer/issue] of shares in the Company shall be effected unless the [transferee/the person to whom such shares are to be issued] shall have first entered into a deed in the form of this Deed.

NOW THIS DEED WITNESSES that the New Shareholder covenants with each of the Existing Shareholders that [with effect from the date of this Deed] the New Shareholder will be bound by and will observe and perform every provision of the Shareholders' Agreement [by which [*outgoing party*] was bound in every way as if the New Shareholder was a party thereto but subject to the exception of clauses [ ] [ ] thereof [*Insert here clauses which contain personal obligations or warranties*]

IN WITNESS whereof the New Shareholder has executed this Deed the day and year first above written.

THE SCHEDULE [insert names and addresses of existing shareholders]

Executed as a Deed by the said [   ] in the presence of [   ] acting by [   ]

SIGNED by
[duly authorised for and on behalf of [   ]]
in the presence of

SIGNED by
[duly authorised for and on behalf of [   ]]
 in the presence of

SIGNED by
[duly authorised for and on behalf of [   ]]
in the presence of

Precedent 6

Support agreement

Agreement by one joint venturer to provide management or other services to the joint venture company

THIS AGREEMENT is dated the [ ] day of [ ] 20[   ] and made

BETWEEN:

(1) **PARTY 1** ('X Co') registered in England and Wales as company number and having its registered office at [ ]; and

(2) **PARTY 2** ('JV Co') registered in England and Wales as company number and having its registered office at [ ]

WHEREAS:

(A) JV Co has been formed as a joint venture vehicle to undertake the business of [ ].

(B) X Co is the holder of [ ] shares in JV Co having subscribed for the same pursuant to [*set out description, date and parties to the Joint Venture Agreement*].

(C) X Co has, pursuant to clause 4 of the Agreement referred in recital (B), agreed to enter into this Agreement to provide [*brief description of services*] to JV Co on the terms set out below.

NOW IT IS HEREBY AGREED as follows:

1 Interpretation

1.1   In this Agreement unless the context otherwise requires:

'Effective Date' means [ ]

'Joint Venture Agreement' means the agreement referred to in Recital (B).

'Services' means the services to be performed by X Co for JV Co upon the terms of this Agreement, a detailed description of which is set out in the Appendix hereto as amended from time to time.

1.2   References to *'party'* or *'parties'* shall be construed as references to a party or parties to this Agreement.

1.3   References to *'persons'* and *'parties'* shall include bodies corporate and unincorporated associations and partnerships.

1.4   References to statutory provisions shall be construed as references to those provisions as amended or re-enacted or as their application is modified by other provisions from time to time and shall include references to any provisions of which they are re-enactments (whether with or without modification).

1.5   References to clauses are to clauses of this Agreement. References to this Agreement include the schedules, and the Appendix hereto.

1.6   The headings are inserted for convenience only and shall not affect the construction of this Agreement.

2 Duration

Subject as provided in clauses 10 and 11, this Agreement shall commence on the Effective Date and continue unless and until terminated by either party giving to the other not less than [   ] months' notice in writing expiring on or at any time after the [   ] anniversary of the Effective Date [*effect on joint venture agreement to be considered*].

3 Provision of the services

X Co shall provide the services to JV Co at the times and at the places, in the manner and in accordance with the terms set out in schedule 1.

4 Charges

JV Co shall pay charges for the Services in the amounts and at the times set out in schedule 1. Such charges and all other amounts payable under this Agreement shall be exclusive of any Value Added Tax chargeable thereon, which shall be paid by JV Co in addition to such charges and other amounts, subject to the provision to it of appropriate tax invoices.

5 Independent contractor

In performing the services and carrying out its obligations under this Agreement, X Co shall act as an independent contractor and not the agent of JV Co, and neither X Co nor any of its directors, employees or agents shall have any authority to negotiate or enter into contracts on behalf of or otherwise to bind JV Co (except where authorised expressly in writing).

6 Standard of work

In performing the Services X Co shall use reasonable care and skill to perform the Services in accordance with the description given in the Appendix hereto, and comply with the terms set out in schedule 1 and with generally accepted standards of good practice. The said obligations shall replace all conditions and warranties which would otherwise be implied herein by statute, common law or otherwise (including, without limitation, the Supply of Goods and Services Act 1982) all of which are hereby expressly excluded.

7 Intellectual property and confidential information

7.1   To the extent that in the provision of the Services X Co makes use of any inventions, discoveries, processes, confidential information, designs or other works to which X Co has any industrial or intellectual property rights, X Co hereby grants, so far as such grant does not conflict with any obligation owed by X Co to any other person, to JV Co a non-exclusive royalty free licence to use the same in relation to any products or services in any way derived from the provision of the Services, [*within JV Co's area of interest to be defined*] with full power for JV Co to assign such licence and to grant sub-licences subject to JV Co, and such assignees and sub-licensees, if any, undertaking to X Co to maintain as confidential any confidential information of X Co licensed hereunder. [3.12, 3.22].

7.2   X Co undertakes to JV Co that it will not in the provision of the Services knowingly infringe any patents, copyrights or any other intellectual or industrial property rights of any third party [in any part of the world] and that X Co will indemnify and keep indemnified JV Co in respect of all liabilities, costs, claims, demands and expenses (including legal fees and expenses) which JV Co may incur or sustain to any third party as a result of the breach by X Co of the foregoing undertaking.

7.3   X Co shall not during this Agreement or at any time thereafter, use or disclose to any person (other than as authorised by JV Co or as required in the provision of the Services) any trade secrets or other information which is for the time being confidential relating to the business of JV Co or any of its subsidiaries or to its clients, customers and other persons with whom JV Co or any of its subsidiaries has business dealings being information which is marked confidential or which JV Co shall have notified X Co is to be kept confidential or which to the knowledge of X Co has been obtained by JV Co or any of its subsidiaries from another person on terms that JV Co or such subsidiary is to keep it confidential, and X Co shall ensure that any persons to whom its obligations are sub-contracted by virtue of clause 12.1 are either contractually bound to X Co to observe the same obligation or are aware of their obligations under common law and X Co will take all reasonable steps to enforce such contractual requirements and/or obligations at common law provided that nothing in this obligation shall extend to information or knowledge which is for the time being in the public domain (otherwise than by reason of its wrongful disclosure) or which is required to be disclosed by law) or which X Co can demonstrate was lawfully in its possession prior to [*date discussions on the agreement commenced*] and was not received by it under any obligation of confidentiality. [3.22]

7.4   X Co may disclose confidential information which would otherwise be subject to clause 7.3 if but only to the extent that it can demonstrate that:

7.4.1 such disclosure is required by law or by any securities exchange or regulatory or governmental body having jurisdiction over it, wherever situated (and including the Financial Conduct Authority, the London Stock Exchange, the Panel on Takeovers and Mergers and the Serious Fraud Office), and whether or not the requirement has the force of law;

7.4.2 the confidential information was lawfully in its possession prior to its disclosure by the JV Co (as evidenced by written records) and had not been obtained from the JV Co;

7.4.3 the confidential information has come into the public domain other than through its fault or the fault of any person to whom the confidential information has been disclosed in accordance with clause 7.5;

provided that any such disclosure shall not be made without prior [notice to *(or)* consultation with] the party from whom the confidential information was obtained.

7.5   X Co may for the purposes contemplated by this agreement disclose confidential information to the following persons or any of them[, provided that a written confidentiality undertaking in a form equivalent to clause 7.3 has been obtained from such person]:

7.5.1 its professional advisers, auditors, bankers and insurers, acting as such; and

7.5.2 its directors, officers [and] senior employees[, and sub-contractors].

7.6   In fulfilling its obligations under this clause 7, X Co shall only be required to use the same degree of care to prevent unauthorised disclosure of confidential information as it would use to prevent the disclosure of confidential information relating to itself.

7.7   For the purposes of the obligations of confidentiality contained in this clause 7, references to X Co shall include X Co's Subsidiaries and Holding Company and any Subsidiaries of that Holding Company and any other company controlled by X Co and the employees or agents of X Co or its Subsidiary, Holding Company or controlled companies.]

8 Health and safety

8.1   *'Health and Safety Requirements'* means in respect of JV Co and X Co all of their obligations under the Health and Safety at Work etc Act 1974, all relevant statutory provisions (as defined in that Act) and all other obligations imposed by statute and common law relating to health and safety.

8.2   Where the provision of Services requires employees or sub-contractors or agents of X Co to work on the premises of JV Co then:

(A)   JV Co shall ensure that its premises and safety procedures and all plant and equipment which is used by such employees sub-contractors or agents or with which they may come into contact or to which they may be exposed complies with all Health and Safety Requirements; and

(B)   X Co shall ensure that all its employees, sub-contractors and agents from time to time working on the provision of the Services are properly trained in all relevant Health and Safety Requirements for the safety of themselves and others and are issued with all equipment for their personal safety as required by law or which it is best practice to provide and that all plant and equipment brought by any such employee, sub-contractor or agent onto JV Co's premises complies with all Health and Safety Requirements and will not be a danger to them or to others.

8.3   The parties shall each indemnify and keep indemnified the other in respect of all liabilities, costs, claims, demands, expenses, fines and other penalties (including legal fees and expenses) which the other may incur or sustain and which in any way relate to or arise from the breach by the indemnifying party of any of its obligations under clause 8.2. [3.22]

9 Limitation of liability

9.1   [In respect of those of the Services which are of a managerial or advisory nature (as identified in the Appendix) X Co shall not be liable to JV Co for any loss suffered or liability incurred by JV Co arising out of any act, omission or error of judgment [(whether or not negligent)] which may be committed by X Co or by any of its employees, agents or subcontractors in the course of the provision of those Services except where such loss or liability arises from the [negligence] dishonesty or wilful default of X Co or of any of such employees, agents or subcontractors.] [3.22]

9.2   X Co shall not be liable to JV Co in respect of any indirect or consequential loss, including loss of anticipated profits, goodwill or reputation, howsoever caused which is suffered by JV Co [other than by reason of a claim by another person for which X Co is liable to indemnify JV Co under clauses 7 or 8].

9.3   [Consider overall cap on X Co's liability and/or a scale of agreed liquidated damages in respect of direct losses arising from X Co's breach of contract.] [Note that the availability of insurance is an important factor in determining the approach of the courts to liability.] [   ].

9.4   Nothing in this clause 9 or elsewhere in this Agreement shall exclude, restrict or limit the liability of either party for death or personal injury caused by that party's negligence or for fraud.

10 Force majeure

10.1 *'Force Majeure'* means any circumstances not foreseeable at the date of this Agreement and not within the reasonable control of X Co, including, without limitation, strikes, lockouts, other industrial action, shortages of raw materials or components, natural disaster including fire, flood, earthquake, volcanic activity, disease or pandemic; any destruction, temporary or permanent breakdown, malfunction or damage of or to any premises, plant, equipment (including computer systems) or materials; any breach of contract, default or insolvency by any person other than X Co or a company in the same group as X Co, or an employee or officer of X Co or that other company [or/but excluding] an agent or sub-contractor of X Co]; any action taken by a governmental or public authority of any kind including [not granting a consent, exemption, approval or clearance or] imposing an embargo, export or import restriction, rationing, quota or other restriction or prohibition; civil commotion or disorder, riot, invasion, war, threat of or preparation for war; unavoidable accident, fire, explosion, storm, flood, earthquake, subsidence, epidemic or other natural physical disaster.

10.2 If and to the extent that the provision of the Services is prevented or delayed by Force Majeure, X Co shall promptly notify JV Co, specifying the nature, extent, effect and likely duration of the Force Majeure, and X Co shall then be relieved of any liability for failure to perform or for delay in performing the Services but shall nevertheless use all reasonable endeavours to minimise the effect of the Force Majeure on the performance of the Services and to resume full performance thereof and shall make such alternative arrangements for doing so which may be practicable without incurring material additional expense provided that as a result of such Force Majeure the Services are not fully supplied for more than [   ] months, JV Co may terminate this Agreement forthwith by notice to X Co. [During such time as X Co is relieved of its obligations to perform the Services, JV Co shall likewise be relieved of liability to pay for the Services save in so far as they are actually provided.] [   ].

11 Termination

11.1 Either party may terminate this Agreement forthwith by notice to the other if the other shall have committed a material breach of this Agreement which is incapable of remedy or (if so capable) is not remedied within 30 days of the party committing the breach having been served with notice by the other party, specifying the breach and requiring its remedy.

[Consider termination on insolvency – it may be thought inappropriate for X Co to have the right to terminate on JV Co's insolvency because termination is likely to prejudice any realisation available to X Co or a rescue of JV Co. Any provision allowing for termination for insolvency must comply with the insolvency provisions in the Enterprise Act 2002.]

11.2 [This Agreement shall automatically terminate without any necessity for notice should [the Joint Venture Agreement be terminated for any reason/X Co cease to be the beneficial owner of any shares in JV Co.]]

[*Consider grace period to enable the other joint venturers to make other arrangements.*] [3.21].

11.3 Termination of this Agreement shall be without prejudice to any rights or claims which either party may have against the other which are subsisting at the time of termination and all provisions of this Agreement which are expressed to have effect after termination shall continue in force accordingly including clauses 7, 8, 9, and 14.

[*Consider generally whether and if so how the termination of this Agreement should impact on the Joint Venture Agreement.*]

12 General

12.1 X Co may subcontract any of its obligations under this Agreement [to persons approved by JV Co] [such approval not to be unreasonably withheld or delayed] but shall ensure that the provisions of clause 7.3 are complied with in relation to every such sub-contractor. This Agreement shall be binding upon the parties and their successors and permitted assigns but neither of the parties may assign any of their respective rights and obligations under this Agreement without the prior written consent of the other [save that JV Co may assign its rights and obligations hereunder to any purchaser of the whole or any part of the undertaking of JV Co, and if so requested by JV Co, X Co shall enter into a novation of this Agreement with any such purchaser whereby JV Co is released from this Agreement and the purchaser substituted as a party for JV Co with effect from the effective date of the novation].

12.2 No exercise or failure to exercise or delay in exercising any right power or remedy vested in either party shall constitute a waiver by that party of that or any other right power or remedy.

12.3 Nothing in this Agreement shall be deemed to constitute a partnership between the parties nor constitute either party the agent of the other or otherwise entitle either party to have authority to bind the other party for any purpose.

12.4 This Agreement together with any documents referred to in it, constitutes the entire agreement between the parties in relation to its subject matter and extinguishes any prior agreements or understandings whether oral or written with respect to it and no variation of this Agreement shall be effective unless reduced to writing and signed by or on behalf of a duly authorised representative of each of the parties. Each party acknowledges that it has not been induced to enter into this Agreement by any representation or warranty other than those (if any) contained in this Agreement, or to the extent that it has, agrees that having negotiated and freely entered into this Agreement, it shall have no remedy in respect of any such representation or warranty except in the case of fraud. Each party acknowledges that its legal advisers have explained to it the effect of this clause 12.4.

12.5 In the event that any term, condition or provision of this Agreement is held to be a violation of any applicable law, statute or regulation the same shall be deemed to be deleted from this Agreement and shall be of no force and effect and this Agreement shall remain in full force and effect as if such term, condition or provision had not originally been contained in this Agreement. Notwithstanding the foregoing, in the event of any such deletion the parties agree to negotiate in good faith in order to agree the terms of a mutually acceptable and satisfactorily alternative provision in place of the provision so deleted.

12.6 Any time, date or period mentioned in this Agreement shall be of the essence.

12.7 If either party shall default in the payment when due of any sum payable by it under this Agreement its liability shall be increased to include interest on such sum from the due date until the date of actual payment (both before and after judgment) at that annual rate which is [8] percentage points above the base rate of [*Named Bank*] from time to time in effect during such period. All such interest shall be calculated on the actual number of days elapsed over a 365 day year [and compounded at [quarterly] rests].

12.8 No person who is not a party to this Agreement shall have any right to enforce any term of this Agreement.

13 Notices

13.1 Any notice to be given by either party to the other shall be in writing and shall be deemed to be duly served if delivered personally or sent by fax or electronic mail or by pre-paid [first class/recorded delivery] post (or air mail or air courier in the case of an address for service outside the United Kingdom) to the addressee at its address (or number) for the receipt thereof specified below:

X Co	Postal Address	[	]
	Fax Number	[	]
	E-mail Address	[	]
	For the attention of:	[	]
JV Co	Postal Address	[	]
	Fax Number	[	]
	E-mail Address	[	]
	For the attention of:	[	]

or at any other address or number as the party to be served has notified in accordance with this clause 13.1.

13.2 A notice shall be deemed to have been duly served as follows:

(A) where personally delivered, upon such delivery;

(B) where sent by fax, at the time of transmission, when despatched, subject to confirmation of uninterrupted transmission by a transmission report;

(C) where sent by electronic mail, when the electronic mail leaves the gateway of the server;

(D) where sent by pre-paid post to an address in the United Kingdom 48 hours after posting;

(E) where sent by pre-paid airmail to an address outside the United Kingdom, five days after posting; and

(F) where sent by air courier [2] business days after delivery to a representative of the courier.

13.3 In proving service of any notice it shall be sufficient to prove:

(A) in the case of a notice sent by post that such notice was properly addressed, stamped and placed in the post;

(B) in the case of a notice personally delivered that it was delivered or left at the specified address;

(C) in the case of a notice sent by fax that it was duly despatched to the specified number as confirmed by a transmission report;

(D) in the case of a notice sent by electronic mail, that the electronic mail left the gateway of the server of the notice; and

(E) in the case of a notice sent by air courier that it was delivered to a representative of the air courier.

14 Law and jurisdiction [Chapter 23]

14.1 Any contractual or non-contractual obligations arising from or connected with this Agreement shall be governed by English Law and this Agreement shall be construed in all respects in accordance with English law.

14.2 In relation to any legal action or proceedings to enforce this Agreement or arising out of or in connection with this Agreement (whether arising out of or in connection with contractual or non-contractual obligations) ('Proceedings'), each of the parties irrevocably submits to the exclusive jurisdiction of the English courts and waives any objection to Proceedings in such courts on the grounds of venue or on the grounds that the Proceedings have been brought in an inappropriate forum.

14.3 [irrevocably consents to any process in any proceedings anywhere being served in accordance with the provisions of this Agreement relating to the service of notices. Such service shall become effective 30 days after despatch. Nothing herein contained shall affect the right to serve process in any other manner permitted by law.]

AS WITNESS the hands of the duly authorised representatives of the parties the day and year first above written.

Schedule 1

(Detail the terms on which the services are to be provided and the charges to be made for them – clauses 3 and 4).

Appendix

(*Description of Service*)

Precedent 7

Limited Liability Partnership deed

(Suitable for a joint venture between corporates for commercial purposes)

THIS LIMITED LIABILITY PARTNERSHIP DEED is dated the [ ] day of [ ] 20[ ] and made

BETWEEN:

PARTY 1 ['X'], registered in England and Wales as company number [ ] and having its registered office at [ ];

PARTY 2 ['Y'], registered in England and Wales as company number [ ] and having its registered office at [ ];

PARTY 3 ['Z'], registered in England and Wales as company number [ ] and having its registered office at [ ]; and

[ ] LLP [the *'Partnership'*], registered in England and Wales with partnership number [ ] and having its registered office at [ ].

BACKGROUND:

(A) The Partnership was incorporated on [ ] 20[ ].

(B) X, Y and Z were the Members of the Partnership on its incorporation and X and Y were specified as the designated Members of the Partnership on such incorporation.

(C) The registered office of the Partnership on incorporation was [and remains] [ ].

(D) The parties to this Deed wish to enter into it to govern the operation of the Partnership and their respective rights and duties in relation thereto.

THE PARTIES agree that:

1 Interpretation

1.1 Save where the context otherwise requires in this Deed the following words and expressions shall have the meanings respectively assigned to them below:

'the Act' means the Limited Liability Partnerships Act 2000.

'Board' means the board of the Partnership constituted in accordance with clause 12.

'Business' means the business of the Partnership as described in clause 4.

'Business Day' means a day (other than a Saturday or Sunday) upon which banks are open for ordinary face to face banking business in London.

'Capital Contribution Account' means the Capital Contribution Account established for each Member pursuant to clause 9.

'Deed of Adherence' means a deed substantially in the form contained in Schedule 1 pursuant to which a Further Member agrees to become a Member on the terms specified therein.

'Designated Members' means such Members, being not less than two in number, as shall be specified by the Board as designated members for the purposes of the Act.

'Distribution Account' means the Distribution Account established for each Member pursuant to clause 9.

'Further Member' means any person who enters into a Deed of Adherence pursuant to clause 14.

'Group Company' means in relation to a body corporate every subsidiary undertaking and parent undertaking for the time being of that body corporate and every subsidiary undertaking for the time being of any such parent undertaking.

'Law' and *'Laws'* includes all applicable legislation, statutes, directives, regulations, judgments, decisions, decrees, orders, instruments, by-laws and other legislative measures or decisions having the force of law and rules of common law, customary law and equity and all civil or other codes and all other laws of, or having effect in, any applicable jurisdiction from time to time and whether before or after the date of this Deed.

'Members' means the Members of the Partnership for the time being.

'Outgoing Member' means a Member who ceases to be a Member pursuant to clause 19.

'Regulations' means the Limited Liability Partnerships Regulations 2001 together with any successor regulations.

'Subsidiary' means a subsidiary undertaking of the Partnership.

1.2   In this Deed where the context admits:

    (A)   words and phrases the definitions of which are contained or referred to in the Act or the Companies Act 2006 or as the latter is amended in relation to limited liability partnerships by the Regulations shall have the respective meanings thereby attributed to them;

(B) every reference to a statutory provision or other Law shall be construed also as a reference to all other Laws made under the Law referred to and to all such Laws as amended, re-enacted, consolidated or replaced or as their application or interpretation is affected by other Laws from time to time;

(C) references to clauses and schedules are references to clauses of and schedules to this Deed, references to paragraphs are, unless otherwise stated, references to the paragraphs of the schedule in which the reference appears and references to this Deed include the schedules thereto, and

(D) references to the singular shall include the plural and vice versa and references to the masculine, the feminine and the neuter shall include each other such gender.

2 Designated Members

2.1 Any Member who is a Designated Member may cease to be such by giving notice to the Partnership to that effect, such notice to take effect immediately or, if later, at such date specified in the notice, provided that if there would be only one Designated Member then remaining, such notice shall not take effect until such time as the Board shall have specified a replacement Designated Member.

2.2 The Designated Members shall be responsible for ensuring compliance with all registration and other requirements of the Act and the Regulations.

3 Office

The registered office and principal place of business of the Partnership shall each be at such place or places as the Board may designate from time to time.

4 Business

The business of the Partnership shall be [ ] or such other business as is for the time being approved under clause 12.9(B).

5 Name

5.1 The Business shall be carried on under the name of '[ ] LLP' (the 'Name') or such other name as the Board may from time to time determine.

5.2 Each of the Members acknowledges that all proprietary and other rights in the Name are vested exclusively in the Partnership and agrees that no Member shall use the Name or any name which may be substituted therefor or which is so similar to any such name that it is likely to be confused with it for any purpose other than for the purposes of the Business whilst he is a Member or at any time after ceasing to be a Member without the consent of the Board.

6 Duration

Each of the Members acknowledges and agrees that the Partnership commenced on the date of its incorporation and that it shall continue unless and until terminated in accordance with clause 20, only one member remains entitled to any interest in the Partnership or the Partnership is wound up.

7 Capital and Loan contributions

7.1 The initial capital contributions of each of the Members at the date of this Deed to the Partnership shall be as set out in the second column of schedule 2 against the name of each Member in the first column of schedule 2, and each Member shall forthwith pay such sum in cash to the Partnership. Any Further Members shall each contribute upon admission to the Partnership such sum to its capital (if any) as shall be determined by the Board (subject to approval under clause 12.9(A)) and as shall be specified in the Deed of Adherence executed by that Further Member and schedule 2 shall then be amended to reflect each such contribution.

7.2 No Member shall be entitled to interest on the amount of any capital contributions made by him pursuant to this clause 7 [unless otherwise agreed between the Member concerned and the Board].

7.3 Any Member may contribute further capital to the Partnership by agreement with the Board [subject to approval under clause 12.9(C)] and schedule 2 shall then be amended to reflect every such contribution.

7.4 Any further funding which may be required by the Partnership in addition to the funds raised through capital contributions may be provided by way of loans from banks and other financial institutions on such terms as may be negotiated by the Board [subject, where applicable, to approval under clause 12.9(G)], on the basis that unless the Board [with such approval] shall otherwise agree, no such lender or prospective lender shall be allowed to obtain any interest (direct or indirect) in the assets of the Partnership (other than by way of security) as a condition of such borrowings. Loan contributions may also be made to the Partnership by any or all the Members on such terms as to repayment, interest and otherwise as may be agreed between the Board and the Member making the loan contribution but subject to the same approval.

7.5 Repayment of all loans and loan contributions made to the Partnership shall be discharged out of the assets of the Partnership.

8 Profit allocations

8.1 The profits or losses [including any capital profits or losses] of the Partnership in respect of each of its Accounting Reference Periods shall be allocated amongst the Members and any Further Members entitled to participate in the same in the proportions set out against the respective names of such Members in the third column of schedule 2, provided that the allocation to a Further Member in respect of the Accounting Reference Period in which he becomes a Member shall be reduced in proportion to such part of the Accounting Reference Period during which he was a Member.

8.2   The Board shall procure that accounts are drawn up in respect of each Accounting Reference Period of the Partnership in accordance with the provisions of the Act, the Regulations and this clause 8 and subject thereto in accordance with accounting practices generally accepted in the United Kingdom. Such accounts shall in each case comprise a profit and loss account in respect of such Accounting Reference Period and a balance sheet as at the end of that Accounting Reference Period (the 'Partnership Accounts') and the Board shall procure that the Partnership Accounts in respect of each Accounting Reference Period shall be audited in accordance with the requirements of the Act.

8.3   Following the end of each Accounting Reference Period the Board shall, by reference to the Partnership Accounts drawn up in respect of that Accounting Reference Period, determine the allocations of any profits amongst the Members in accordance with clause 8.1 and shall determine what proportion of any such profits that have been so allocated may be withdrawn by such Members. In deciding what proportion of any profits may be withdrawn, the Board shall make appropriate allowance (to the extent that allowance has not already been made) as the Board determines in good faith to be required to meet anticipated and foreseen liabilities and expenditure of the Partnership and to be sufficient to cover other contingencies in accordance with general principles of prudent management.

9 Members' accounts and distributions

9.1   Each Member shall have a Capital Contribution Account and a Distribution Account.

9.2   The capital contributions of each Member shall be credited to that Member's Capital Contribution Account.

9.3   The profits (or losses) allocated to the Members in respect of each Accounting Reference Period of the Partnership shall be credited (or debited as the case may be) to the Distribution Accounts of the Members.

9.4   Each Member shall be permitted (after taking into account by way of deduction any advance drawings by or to that Member in accordance with clause 9.5) to withdraw amounts standing to the credit of its Distribution Account at the end of any Accounting Reference Period (less any amounts which are determined not to be withdrawn under clause 8.3) provided that such withdrawals shall be limited to [50]% of the amount of such credit to be withdrawn within 30 days after the end of each Accounting Reference Period and as to the balance within 30 days after the approval by the Members of the audited accounts of the Partnership in respect of that Accounting Reference Period.

9.5 Subject in all respects to the Board being satisfied that the level of profits anticipated in respect of any Accounting Reference Period will be sufficient, the Board shall have the discretion to allow Members to make drawings in advance of the end of an Accounting Reference Period in anticipation of their profit entitlements for such Accounting Reference Period.

9.6 To the extent that any Member withdraws an amount from its Distribution Account pursuant to clause 9.5 such that in a particular Accounting Reference Period it withdraws an amount greater than the profits or losses allocated to it by virtue of clause 9.3 and 9.4 for the same Accounting Reference Period, the Member shall be liable to pay an amount equal to such excess to the Partnership, such payment to be made within [   ] months after the start of the following Accounting Reference Period.

9.7 Save as may be required by clause 9.6, no Member shall have any obligation to pay back to the Partnership any profits of the Partnership standing to the credit of the Distribution Account of that Member, otherwise than as required by Law.

10 Return of Capital Contributions

10.1 Subject to clause 10.2, no Member shall have the right, directly or indirectly, to withdraw or receive back any part of the amount standing to the credit of its Capital Contribution Account except upon liquidation of the Partnership to the extent allowed by clause 20.

10.2 [Where the Board determines (taking into account the working capital requirements of the Partnership) that all the Members (other than any Further Member whose initial capital contribution results in a reduction of the capital required from the other Members) may withdraw a pro rata proportion of their respective capital contributions each of the Members shall be entitled to make such a withdrawal accordingly.]

10.3 In no event shall any Member be entitled to withdraw or receive back property other than cash.

11 Accounting Reference Period

The first Accounting Reference Period of the Partnership shall begin on the date of its incorporation and shall end on [ ] 20[   ] and, thereafter the Accounting Reference Periods of the Partnership shall be periods of twelve months which shall begin on [ ] in each year and end on [ ] in the following year but subject to any change made pursuant to clause 12.9(V).

12 Management of the Partnership

12.1 Subject to the provisions of this Deed and any applicable Laws, and subject to any matter which may from time to time be delegated by the Board to any of its members, the Board shall have exclusive responsibility for the management and control of the Business and the affairs of the Partnership and shall have the power and authority to do all things necessary to carry out the purpose of the Partnership and shall carry on and manage the same with the assistance from time to time of agents and employees of the Partnership as they shall deem necessary. The Members (otherwise than in their capacity as members of the Board) shall have no right or authority to act for the Partnership or to take any part in the management thereof or to vote on matters relating thereto other than as provided in any Law applicable thereto or as set out in this Deed. In the event that any such Law shall require a meeting of the Members, such meeting shall be convened by the Board and the provisions of schedule 3 shall apply thereto.

12.2 Each Member shall have the right by the service of notice to the Partnership signed by the appointor, to appoint the number of persons holding office at any one time specified against its name in the fifth column of schedule 2 to be members of the Board and by a like notice to remove any member of the Board which it has appointed. Such notice shall have effect immediately upon such service.

12.3 Any member of the Board shall be entitled to appoint any person as his alternate to attend, speak and vote at any meeting of the Board instead of him and to do any other act or thing which his appointor is permitted or required to do by virtue of him being a member of the Board, and the appointor may at any time remove such appointee and appoint another in his place. If an alternate shall himself be a member of the Board he shall be entitled to his own votes at a meeting of the Board in addition to those of his appointor. The appointment or removal of an alternate shall be effected by the service on the Partnership of a notice signed by the appointor and shall have effect immediately upon such service.

12.4 The Board shall meet as and when determined by its Chairman, but not fewer than four times in each calendar year. At least five clear Business Days written notice must be given to each member of the Board of all Board meetings, except if there are exceptional circumstances and a majority of the members of the Board agree to shorter notice. Any member of the Board may convene a Board meeting by giving notice as specified in this clause 12.4 and in clause 12.5. [ ] shall be the Chairman of the Board and shall chair its meetings for as long as he is a member of the Board. If [ ] or any subsequent Chairman of the Board is not present within ten minutes after the time specified for the start of the meeting, the Board members present may appoint one of their number to act as chairman of that meeting. Should [ ] or any subsequent Chairman of the Board cease to be a member of the Board, the Board may appoint one of their number to be Chairman in his place.

12.5 Every notice of a Board meeting shall specify a reasonably detailed agenda and be accompanied by any relevant papers.

12.6 The quorum for Board meetings shall be [ ] members of the Board [consisting of at least [one] member of the Board appointed by each Member] or their alternates present in person or by means of communication equipment complying with clause 12.8 at the time when the relevant business is transacted. If a quorum is not present within half an hour after the time appointed for the meeting, or ceases to be present during the meeting, the members of the Board who are present shall adjourn the meeting to such place and time as they may specify, being three Business Days after the original date. Notice of the adjourned meeting, complying with clauses 12.4 and 12.5, shall be given by those who adjourned the meeting. The quorum for any such adjourned Board meeting shall be such members of the Board or their alternates who shall be present, regardless of their number [or the identity of their appointors].

12.7 Each member of the Board entitled to attend and vote at any Board meeting shall be entitled to [one] vote. Save as required by Law, at any meeting of the Board decisions shall be taken by a simple majority of votes. The Chairman shall [not] be entitled to a second or casting vote. A resolution in writing signed by all members of the Board shall be as valid and effective as a resolution passed at such a meeting and may consist of several identical documents provided that each member of the Board has signed at least one of them.

12.8 All or any members of the Board may participate in a meeting of the Board by means of any communication equipment which allows all persons participating in the meeting to hear and address each other such person simultaneously. A person so participating shall be deemed to be present in person at the meeting and shall be entitled to be counted towards the quorum and to vote. Such a meeting shall be deemed to take place where the largest group of those participating is assembled or, if there is no largest group, where the Chairman of the meeting then is.

12.9 The Members shall join in procuring by all means available to them that, notwithstanding the provisions of clause 12.1, the Partnership shall not take, or agree to take, any of the following actions without the prior written consent of Members who are for the time being entitled to at least [three-quarters] of the votes exercisable at a general meeting of the Members and the Board shall have no authority to procure or allow the Partnership to take any of such actions without such consent namely:

(A) the admission of a Further Member;

(B) the making of any change in the general nature of the business of the Partnership from that described in clause 4;

(C) the contribution of any further capital to the Partnership by a Member;

(D) the entry into by the Partnership of any partnership or joint venture or any other arrangement for the sharing of income or profits with any person;

(E) the acquisition whether by formation, purchase, subscription or otherwise of any Subsidiary or the disposal, dilution or reduction of the interest of the Partnership, directly or indirectly in any Subsidiary, whether by the sale, allotment or issue of any Shares in its capital or securities convertible into such Shares otherwise than to its parent company or the Partnership, or any reduction in the voting power or other powers of control exercisable in relation to the Subsidiary by its parent company or the Partnership;

(F) the sale, transfer, lease, licence or other disposal of all or a material part of the business of the Partnership, or its undertaking or assets, whether by a single transaction or series of transactions related or not (otherwise than in the ordinary course of the business of the Partnership);

(G) the borrowing by the Partnership of any sums [except from the bankers of the Partnership in the ordinary and usual course of business] which when aggregated with the borrowings of all the Subsidiaries exceed £[   ] outstanding at any one time;

(H) the incurring in any Accounting Reference Period of the Partnership of aggregate capital expenditure (including finance leases but excluding operating leases as respectively defined by SSAP 21 [which when aggregated with such capital expenditure of all the Subsidiaries for that Accounting Reference Period is] in excess of [£[   ]/the aggregate amount provided for capital expenditure in the Business Plan for that Accounting Reference Period];

(I) the entry into or the variation of any operating lease (as defined by SSAP 21), either as lessor or lessee of any plant, property or equipment of a duration exceeding [   ] years or involving aggregate premium and annual rental payments in excess of £[   ];

(J) the factoring or discounting of any book debts of the Partnership;

(K)   the making of any loan or advance or the giving of credit by other means (other than credit given in the normal course of the Partnership's business on normal arm's length commercial terms) to any person except for deposits with the Partnership's bankers;

(L)   the giving of any guarantee, bond or indemnity in respect of or to secure the liabilities or obligations of any person (other than a wholly-owned Subsidiary);

(M)   the creation or issue of any debenture, mortgage, charge or other security over any assets of the Partnership [(except for the purpose of securing sums borrowed by the Partnership from its bankers in the ordinary and usual course of its business)] [up to the limit allowed by clause 12.9(G)];

(N)   the acquisition of any share or loan capital of any body corporate (including that of any Subsidiary);

(O)   the entry into or the making of any material change to any contract or transaction with:

   (1)   any of the Members or any of their respective Group Companies or persons connected with any of them (except as expressly authorised by this Deed); or

   (2)   any other persons except on normal arm's length commercial terms;

(P)   the entry into any agency, distribution or similar agreement which is expressed to confer any element of exclusivity as regards any goods or services the subject thereof or as to the area of the agreement or the variation of such an agreement to include any such exclusivity;

(Q)   the entry into or variation of any licence or similar agreement relating to intellectual property to be licensed to or by the Partnership [which is otherwise than in the ordinary course of business];

(R)   the entry into or the making of any material change to any contract of employment or for the provision of services by any member of the Board or any senior manager of the Partnership (whatever his title or job description) [including any increase in salary or other benefits other than any increase budgeted for in any approved Business Plan];

(S)   the entry into any contract of employment with, or for the provision of services to the Partnership by any specified individual which cannot be terminated on less than [six] months' notice without payment of compensation (other than statutory compensation) or the variation of any such contract so that it cannot be so terminated;

(T) the engagement by the Partnership of any new employee at remuneration in excess of £[ ] per annum (other than as budgeted for in any approved Business Plan), the increase of the remuneration of any employee of the Partnership so as to exceed or further exceed such figure (other than any increase budgeted for in any approved Business Plan) or the dismissal of any employee of the Partnership who receives remuneration in excess of such figure [other than for gross misconduct];

(U) the entry into or variation of any agreement for the provision of consultancy, management or other services by any person which will, or is likely to result in, the business of the Partnership being managed otherwise than by the Board, or which involves a consideration exceeding £[ ] per annum;

(V) [any change in the auditors of the Partnership or the appointment of any such auditors in place of any who resign, the making of or any significant change in the accounting policies and practices for the time being adopted by the Partnership or the making of any change to the accounting reference date of the Partnership];

(W) the making of any change in the names of or the scope of the authority of the persons authorised to sign cheques or other financial instruments on behalf of the Partnership;

(X) [the adoption of any Business Plan or amendment of any Business Plan after the approval thereof];

and the Members shall also join in procuring that without such consent as aforesaid no act or event shall occur in relation to any Subsidiary which is analogous to or has any substantially similar effect to any of those referred to in clauses 12.9(A) to 12.9(X) above (other than clause 12.9(C)) but so that clause 12.9(L) shall permit any Subsidiary to give any guarantee, bond or indemnity in respect of the liabilities of the Partnership or any other Subsidiary without such consent.

The expression 'SSAP 21' means the Statement of Standard Accounting Practice No 21 as issued by or on behalf of the Accounting Standards Board as in force on the date of this Deed.

12.10 None of the members of the Board shall be liable, responsible for or accountable in damages or otherwise to the Partnership or any of the other Members or their successors or assigns, except by reason of acts or omissions due to his bad faith, recklessness, [gross] negligence or wilful default or any [material] breach of this Deed.

12.11 Every Member shall be liable to account to the Partnership for any benefit derived by him, without the consent of the Board, from any transaction concerning the Partnership or from any use by it of the property, name or business connection of the Partnership.

12.12   The Board may delegate any of its powers or discretions to committees of its number. In so far as any such power or discretion is validly delegated to a committee, any reference in this Deed to the exercise by the Board of any power or discretion so delegated shall be read and construed as if it was a reference to the exercise thereof by such committee. [Every committee shall consist of [ ] members, and shall include [one] member who is appointed a member of the Board by each Member]. Every committee shall in the exercise of its powers or discretions so delegated conform to any regulations which may from time to time be imposed by the Board. The meetings and proceedings of every such committee consisting of two or more persons shall be governed mutatis mutandis by the provisions of this Deed regulating the meeting and proceedings of the Board.

12.13   The Board shall procure that:

(A)   the Partnership and every Subsidiary shall maintain accurate and complete accounting and other financial records in accordance with the requirements of all applicable Laws and generally accepted accounting practices applicable in the United Kingdom;

(B)   the Partnership shall prepare [monthly] management accounts [and reports] in relation to the Partnership and every Subsidiary [containing such information as each Member shall reasonably require] and which shall be despatched by the Partnership to each Member within [30] days of the end of the [month] concerned; and

(C)   each Member and their respective authorised representatives shall be allowed access at all reasonable times to examine the books and records of the Partnership and each Subsidiary and to discuss their affairs with the Members of the Board, the directors of each Subsidiary and the senior management of the Partnership and each Subsidiary.

12.14

(A)   The Board shall prepare a business plan for the Partnership and its Subsidiaries for each Accounting Reference Period which shall include the following:

(1)   an estimate of the working capital requirements of the Partnership and the Subsidiaries incorporated within a cashflow forecast [together with an indication of the amount (if any) which it is considered prudent to retain out of the

profits of the previous Accounting Reference Period to meet such working capital requirements];

(2)   a projected profit and loss account;

(3)   an operating budget (including estimated capital expenditure requirements) and balance sheet forecast;

(4)   a review of projected business;

(5)   a summary of business objectives; and

(6)   a financial report which includes an analysis of the results of the Partnership and the Subsidiaries for the previous Accounting Reference Period compared with the business plan for that Accounting Reference Period identifying variations in sales, revenues, costs and other material items.

(B)   The first such business plan for the Accounting Reference Period ending on [ ] 200[ ] shall be [in the Agreed Form marked [' ']/ prepared by [ ] 200[ ]. Business plans for each subsequent Accounting Reference Period shall be submitted for approval by [the Members in accordance with clause 12.9(X)/the Board] not later than [60] days before the commencement of the Accounting Reference Period to which they relate.

13 Assignment of Member's Interests

13.1 No Member may sell, assign, transfer, exchange, pledge, encumber, grant options over or otherwise dispose of his legal or beneficial interest in the Partnership or any part thereof, or enter into any agreement or arrangement to do any of the foregoing unless the same is required by the terms of this Deed or Members who are for the time being entitled to at least [three-quarters] of the votes exercisable at a general meeting of the Members shall consent thereto in writing.

13.2 Clause 13.1 shall not apply to any proposed transfer of any legal or beneficial interests in the Partnership to a prospective transferee (the *'Offeror'*) who would following such transfer and any other transfers resulting from acceptances of a Qualifying Offer (as defined in this clause 13.2), either alone or in conjunction with persons acting in concert with him (as such term is defined by the City Code on Takeovers and Mergers), become entitled to a direct or indirect beneficial interest in the Partnership having attached thereto at least [75]% of the voting rights for the time being exercisable at a general meeting of the Members provided that all of the conditions set out in clause 13.3 are satisfied and an offer meeting all such conditions is hereinafter referred to as a *'Qualifying Offer'*.

13.3 The conditions for a Qualifying Offer are:

(A) the Offeror makes a bona fide offer (the *'Offer'*) on arm's length terms in writing to all of the Members to acquire all of their interests in the Partnership (other than any interest held by the Offeror and such persons acting in concert with the Offeror);

(B) the consideration set out in the Offer is in cash (or such other form as the Board shall [unanimously] approve) and the Offer is made to all of the Members on the terms that each shall receive the same percentage of the aggregate consideration as his percentage entitlement to share in the profits of the Partnership;

(C) the Offer is open for acceptance in England for at least 21 days and copies of all the documents required to be executed by the Members in order to accept the offer have been made available to them for that period; and

(D) the Offeror completes the purchase of all the interests in the Partnership in respect of which the Offer is accepted at the same time.

13.4 If a Qualifying Offer shall be accepted by Members entitled at such time to not less than [75]% of the voting rights exercisable at a general meeting of the Members, then the Partnership shall give written notice to all the other Members of that fact, who shall all thereupon become bound to accept the Qualifying Offer and to transfer their interests in the Partnership to the Offeror (or its nominee) on the same terms as are set out in the Qualifying Offer. If any Member shall not, within five Business Days of being requested to do so, execute and deliver such documentation as may reasonably be required by the Offeror in order to transfer his interests in the Partnership, then the Partnership shall appoint a person to execute such documentation and complete the sale of that Member's interests in accordance with the terms of the Qualifying Offer. The consideration for such sale shall be held on trust by the Partnership for each non-accepting Member and upon completion of the relevant documentation the validity of the proceedings shall not be questioned by any person.

14 Further Members

Each Further Member shall execute a Deed of Adherence and be a Member upon the terms of this Deed as from the date specified in such Deed of Adherence.

15 Restrictive covenants

15.1 Save as expressly set out in this Deed, no Member shall owe any duty or obligation to any other Member in respect of its membership of the Partnership [and in particular (but without limitation) each Member shall be entitled to vote its interest howsoever it wishes].

15.2 Each of the Members covenants with each other Member to use all reasonable endeavours to promote and develop the Business to the best advantage in accordance with good business practice and the highest ethical standards.

15.3 In this clause 15, 'Restricted Business' means any business which directly or indirectly competes with the Business as described in the first Business Plan adopted under clause 12.14.

15.4 Each Member undertakes with each of the other Members (for the benefit also of each other Member's successors in title) that it will not and that it will procure that none of its Group Companies will, either on its own account or in conjunction with or on behalf of any person, firm or company, for the period commencing on the incorporation of the Partnership or the date of his admission as a Partner, where later, and ending on the date on which such party ceases to hold any interest in the Partnership [or to have the ability to exercise the rights set out in clause 12.9]:

(A) carry on or be engaged, concerned or interested (directly or indirectly and whether as principal, shareholder, director, employee, agent, consultant, partner or otherwise) in carrying on any Restricted Business, other than as a holder for investment purposes only (which shall exclude an interest conferring a management function or any material influence) of any shares, debentures or other participation [and a holding of not more than 10% of any class of shares or debentures shall be deemed to be for such purposes unless the contrary is shown]; or

(B) solicit, canvass or endeavour to entice away any person who is then [or who was within the previous 12 months] an officer, manager, [senior] employee, agent or consultant of the Partnership or any of the Subsidiaries whether or not such person would commit a breach of contract by reason of leaving service or office; or

(C) in connection with any Restricted Business, solicit the custom of or endeavour to entice away from the Partnership or any of the Subsidiaries any person who is then or who was within the previous 12 months a client or customer of the Partnership or any of the Subsidiaries whether or not such person would commit a breach of contract by reason of transferring business; or

(D) in connection with any Restricted Business, deal with any person who is then or who was within the previous 12 months a client or customer of the Partnership or any of the Subsidiaries whether or not such person would commit a breach of contract by reason of transferring business; or

(E) in connection with any Restricted Business, endeavour to entice away from the Partnership or any of the Subsidiaries any person who is then or who was within the previous 12 months a supplier of the Partnership or any of the Subsidiaries whether or not such person would commit a breach of contract by reason of transferring business.

15.5 Each Member undertakes with each of the others (for the benefit also of each other Member's successors in title) that it will not and that it will procure that none of its Group Companies will either on its own account or in conjunction with or on behalf of any person, firm or company at any time after the date of this Agreement, directly or indirectly use or attempt to use in the course of any business any valid trade or service mark, trade name, design or logo (whether registered or not) from time to time owned or lawfully used by the Partnership or any Subsidiary or any other name, logo, trade or service mark or design which is or might be confusingly similar thereto.

15.6 Each Member undertakes to take all such steps as shall from time to time be necessary to ensure that no breach of clause 15.3 or clause 15.4 arises as a result of any action by any of its Group Companies or any employee or agent of such party or of any such Group Company.

15.7 Each of the undertakings in clause 15.3 and clause 15.4 shall be construed as a separate and independent undertaking and if one or more of the undertakings is held to be void or unenforceable, the validity of the remaining undertakings shall not be affected.

15.8 Each Member agrees that each of the restrictions and undertakings contained in clauses 15.3 and 15.4 are reasonable and necessary for the protection of each other Member's legitimate interests in the goodwill of the Partnership and the Subsidiaries, but if any such restriction or undertaking shall be found to be void or voidable but would be valid and enforceable if some part or parts of the restriction or undertaking were deleted, such restriction or undertaking shall apply with such modification as may be necessary to make it valid and enforceable.

15.9 Without prejudice to clause 15.6 or clause 15.7, if any restriction or undertaking is found by any court or other competent authority to be void or unenforceable the Members shall negotiate in good faith to replace such void or unenforceable restriction or undertaking with a valid provision which, as far as possible, has the same commercial effect as that which it replaces.

16 Indemnification

Each Member and its officers, directors, and employees and each person, if any, who controls (and for this purpose *'control'* shall bear the meaning ascribed thereto in s 840 of the Income and Corporation Taxes Act 1988) a Member (for the purposes of this clause 16 the *'indemnified party'*) shall be entitled to be indemnified from and out of the assets of the Partnership from and against any loss, liability, damage, cost, or expense (including legal fees and expenses incurred in defence of any demands, claims, or legal proceedings) actually and reasonably incurred arising from actions or omissions concerning the Business or activities undertaken by or on behalf of the Partnership (otherwise than due to the bad faith, recklessness, [gross] negligence or wilful default of the indemnified party, or due to the indemnified party not having acted in good faith in the reasonable belief that its actions were in, or not opposed to, the best interests of the Partnership). All rights to indemnification and payment of legal fees and expenses shall not be affected by the winding up of the Partnership.

17 Confidentiality and announcements

17.1 Each of the Members shall at all times use its best endeavours to keep in strictest confidence and not divulge, communicate or disclose to any person or use or exploit for its own purposes or those of any other person any information of a confidential nature made known or acquired by it at any time and relating to the Partnership, any of the Subsidiaries or any other Member without the prior written consent of the other Members, including, without limitation, technical data, know-how, designs, plans, specifications, methods, processes, controls, systems, trade secrets, recipes, formulae, research and development data, product complaint and testing information, lists of customers and suppliers, all other proprietary information relating to development, engineering, manufacturing, marketing, distribution or accounts, financial statements, financial forecasts, budgets, estimates, sales information, other financial information and any other information which is marked as being confidential or would reasonably be expected to be kept confidential, provided that the obligation of confidentiality shall not apply:

(A) to information for the time being in the public domain other than by reason of a breach of this clause 17;

(B) to information that was in the possession of the relevant Member prior to [ ] [ ] 200[   ] [*date negotiations commenced on the Deed*] (or on its becoming a party to this Deed; if later) where, to the best of that Member's knowledge, such information is not in its possession by reason of the breach of any obligation of confidentiality;

(C) to the extent that disclosure is required by Law or by any order made by a court of competent jurisdiction or by a regulatory or other authority provided that the Member subject to such requirement shall, unless prevented by Law, promptly notify the Board or the Member concerned that the requirement has arisen in order to allow it to take any available action to prevent such disclosure, but failing such prevention, the notifying Member shall use its reasonable endeavours to obtain confidential treatment of the information concerned;

(D) to the disclosure of information to the directors and officers, auditors, bankers, financiers, insurers or professional advisers of a Member who have a legitimate use for such information and who are bound by confidentiality obligations;

(E) to the disclosure of information in the course of legal or arbitration proceedings arising out of this Deed or concerning any matter relating to or in connection with the Partnership or any Subsidiary or any Member;

(F) to the disclosure of information to any person proposing to acquire all or any of the interests of a Member in the Partnership in a manner permitted by this Deed or approved by the other Members and the professional advisers and financiers of such proposed acquirer where the information is disclosed for the purpose of facilitating such acquisition and is legitimately required for such purpose; and

(G) in the case of information relating to the Partnership or any Subsidiary, to the disclosure of that information to the extent reasonably required for the advancement of the business of the Partnership or the relevant Subsidiary.

17.2 The obligations of each of the Members contained in clause 17.1 shall survive the termination of this Deed and shall continue without time limit.

17.3 Where any information of a confidential nature is also privileged, the waiver of such privilege is limited to the purposes of this Deed and does not, and is not intended to, result in any wider waiver of the privilege. Any Member in possession of any confidential information of the Partnership, any Subsidiary, or any other Member (a 'privilege holder') shall take all reasonable steps to protect the privilege of the privilege holder therein and shall inform the privilege holder if any step is taken by any other person to obtain any of its privileged confidential information.

17.4 For the purposes of this clause 17 the expression 'Member' shall be extended to include all the Group Companies of that Member and the employees and agents of that Member and of such Group Companies, and each Member shall procure compliance accordingly.

17.5 The parties shall each procure that the Partnership and the Subsidiaries shall use all reasonable endeavours to ensure that the officers, employees and agents of each of them shall observe a similar obligation as that set out in this clause 17 in favour of each of the Members.

17.6 No Member shall be entitled to make or permit or authorise the making of any press release or other public statement or disclosure concerning this Deed or any transaction contemplated by it or its termination or cessation without the prior written consent of the other Members, except as required by any stock exchange any other regulatory or other authority, but before any Member makes any such release, statement or disclosure it shall [where practical] first supply a copy of it to the other Members and shall incorporate any amendments or additions they may each reasonably require.

18 Termination

18.1 Any one or more of the Members (a 'Terminator') shall be entitled to terminate the membership of another Member by notice in writing (a 'Termination Notice') served in accordance with clause 21 if any of the events set out in clause 18.4 ('Termination Events') shall occur (but not after 90 days of the relevant Termination Event first coming to the attention of the Terminator).

18.2 A Termination Notice shall be served upon the Member which is affected by the relevant Termination Event (the 'Terminatee') and copies of the Termination Notice shall be served on all other Members (if any).

18.3 The Termination Events are:

(A)   the Terminatee shall commit any [material] breach of any of its obligations under this Deed or of any agreement then subsisting between the Terminatee and the Partnership or any Subsidiary and shall fail to remedy such breach (if capable of remedy) within 30 days after having been given notice to do so by the Terminator;

(B)   [the Terminatee (being a company) shall enter into liquidation whether compulsory or voluntary (except for the purposes of a bona fide reconstruction or amalgamation with the consent of [all] other Members, such consent not to be unreasonably withheld or delayed where there is no underlying insolvency) or the Terminatee shall have an administrator appointed or a receiver, administrative receiver or manager shall be appointed over any part of the assets or undertaking of the Terminatee; or]

(C)   [the Terminatee (being an individual) shall be adjudged bankrupt or shall die or become a patient for the purposes of any statute relating to mental health; or]

(D)   [as a separate Termination Event in respect of each of such individuals, any of [ ], [ ] and [ ] shall cease to make their substantially full time services available to the Partnership or any Subsidiary; or]

(E)   there shall be a change in the control of the Terminatee.

18.4 [Any one or more of the members (a 'Terminator') may on, or at any time after, [ ] 20[ ] terminate its membership by giving [ ] months' notice in writing to the other parties (also called a 'Termination Notice').

19 Consequences of termination

19.1 A Terminator (whether comprising one or more Members) shall be entitled by its Termination Notice to require the Terminatee either:

(A)   In the case of a notice served under clause 18.3(A), 18.3(D), 18.3(E) or 18.4 only, to purchase the entire interest of the Terminator in the Partnership [and if there shall be more than one Terminatee requiring them to purchase such interest in such proportions as they may agree or (failing which) as near as may be in the same proportions as the proportions of the capital of the Partnership which they have each then contributed bear to one another]; or

(B)   [(except in the case of termination under clause 18.3(B) and 18.3(C)] to sell to the Terminator (and if more than one, equally or in such other proportions as they may agree) the entire interest in the Partnership of the Terminatee

in either case at a price determined in accordance with clause 19.3 [(or in the case of a Termination Notice served under clause 18.3(A) where the Terminator elects the alternative in clause 19.1(B), clause 19.4)].

19.2 Upon the exercise of any right conferred by clause 19.1 the Terminator and the Terminatee shall become bound respectively to sell or purchase on the terms set out in this clause 19 in accordance with the alternative chosen by the Terminator in its Termination Notice but subject to the limitations set out in clause 19.1 and subject to receipt of any regulatory approvals that may be required for such transfers of interests in the Partnership. If, in a valid Termination Notice served under clause 19.1 no such right is exercised by the Terminator, the Terminatee may within 20 Business Days of the service of the Termination Notice serve a counter-notice on the Terminator [(and if more than one, all of them)] requiring the Terminator to sell to [one or more of the] Terminatee[s] [as they may between themselves agree] the entire interest of the Terminator in the Partnership, in which case the Terminator and the Terminatee shall become bound respectively to sell and purchase such interest on the terms set out in this clause 19. If no right conferred by clause 19.1 is exercised by the Terminator, and, where applicable, no counter-notice is served by the Terminatee, the Members shall procure that the Partnership is immediately wound up.

19.3 Subject to clause 19.4, the purchase price of the interest to be bought and sold pursuant to clauses 19.1 or 19.2 shall be the [fair/market] value thereof as agreed between the Members who are party to such sale or purchase or, in default of such agreement within 15 Business Days after the service of the Termination Notice, or the counter-notice served pursuant to clause 19.2, such sum as shall be certified by the auditors for the time being of the Partnership (at the request of any such Member) to be the [fair/market] value of such interest on the date of service of the Termination Notice or the counter-notice on the basis that all agreements, arrangements and understandings which can be terminated on the relevant Member ceasing to be a Member have terminated. The auditors shall act as experts and not as arbitrators and their decision shall (save in the case of manifest error) be final and binding upon the Members who are party to such sale and purchase for all purposes and the fees and expenses of the auditors shall be borne in equal shares by all of such Members.

19.4 In a case where the interest is to be bought from a Member upon whom a Termination Notice has been served under clause 18.3(A) ('a Defaulting Member') clause 19.3 shall apply with the modification that the auditors shall determine the purchase price by determining the market value of the entire undertaking and assets of the Partnership, both in the light of the breach concerned and on the basis that such breach had not been committed, and if the first of such valuations is lower than the second, the whole amount of the reduction in the value of the undertaking and assets of the Partnership shall be attributed to the interest in the Partnership of the Defaulting Member, which shall be sold at a price which is the proportion of the second valuation attributable to the interest being sold, minus the whole amount of such reduction but subject to a minimum consideration of £1.] [Upon transferring its interest for such consideration, the Defaulting Member shall cease to have any liability for the relevant breach.]

19.5 Completion of the sale and purchase of an interest in the Partnership pursuant to clause 19.1 or 19.2 shall take place at the registered office of the Partnership at [10.00 am] on the [second] Business Day after the price of such interest has been agreed or determined in accordance with clause 19.3 (or, if applicable, clause 19.4) or the last of any necessary regulatory approvals has been obtained, whichever is the later (or at such other time and/or place as the parties to such sale or purchase may agree) and clauses 19.6, 19.7 and 19.8 shall then have effect.

19.6 At each completion referred to in clause 19.5:

(A) the seller(s) shall deliver to the buyer(s) one or more assignments of the relevant interest in the Partnership in such form as the buyer(s) may reasonably require in favour of the buyer(s) or as the buyer(s) may direct (in accordance with their respective entitlements) duly executed by the seller(s) together with a duly signed Form LLP288b.

(B)   subject to the due performance of clause 19.6(A), the buyer(s) shall pay to the seller(s) the full amount of the purchase moneys for the interest being sold together with any sums to be paid pursuant to clause 19.8 by delivering to it or them a banker's draft drawn on a London clearing bank (or such other means of payment as is agreed with the seller(s)).

19.7 All interests bought and sold pursuant to clauses 19.1 or 19.2 shall be sold free of all liens, mortgages, charges, options and all other encumbrances and together with all rights attaching to them as at the date the seller(s) became bound to sell them and attaching to them subsequently, and the seller(s) shall sell the same with full title guarantee [but shall not be otherwise obliged to enter into any guarantees, representations, warranties or indemnities].

19.8 If any Member shall become bound pursuant to clause 19.1 or 19.2 to sell its entire interest in the Partnership (a 'Departing Member'), Member or Members who have become bound to purchase such interest (the 'purchaser' or 'purchasers') shall upon or immediately prior to completion of the sale procure (or if more than one, shall jointly and severally procure):

(A)   the immediate release of every guarantee and indemnity which has been given by each Departing Member or any of its Group Companies in respect of any liabilities or obligations of the Partnership or any Subsidiary (and pending such release such purchaser or purchasers shall indemnify and keep each Departing Member, and its relevant Group Companies fully and effectively indemnified from and against all claims arising thereunder and where there is more than one purchaser their liability under such indemnity shall be joint and several); and

(B)   the immediate repayment to the Departing Member and each of its Group Companies of all monies it or they have lent to the Partnership under, or pursuant to clause 7 and then outstanding together with any interest accrued due thereon down to the date of actual payment (as well before as after judgment).

19.9 Where a Departing Member has ceased to own any interest in the Partnership at a time when the Partnership or any Subsidiary is using as its corporate name or as a trade or business name any name which includes any one or more words which are the same or similar to the corporate name of the Departing Party or any of its Group Companies or any trade or business name used by any of them, or any distinctive part of any of such names the other Members shall procure that within 30 days of such cessation all such names including such same or similar words shall be changed to exclude such words.

19.10   Upon completion taking place in accordance with clause 19.6, the Departing Member shall become an Outgoing Member and shall no longer be a Member of the Partnership and shall have no right to vote or participate in the management or affairs of the Partnership or participate in the profits or losses of the Partnership.

19.11   Save as required by law, no Member shall have any personal liability for the debts or obligations or losses or liabilities of the Partnership beyond the amount of the ordinary capital contributions made by such Member to the Partnership from time to time in accordance with the provisions of Clauses 7.1 or 7.3. If the Partnership is wound up, no Member or former Member shall be liable to contribute further to the assets of the Partnership [other than to clear any negative balance on its Distribution Account in accordance with the provisions of this Agreement]. For the avoidance of doubt no Member has agreed with the other Members or with the Partnership that he will, in the event of any dissolution or winding up of the Partnership, contribute in any way to the assets of the Partnership in accordance with section 74 of the Insolvency Act 1986 as amended by the Act and the Regulations.

19.12   Upon a Member becoming an Outgoing Member, this Deed shall continue in full force and effect as between the remaining Members.

20 Winding up

20.1 Where the dissolution or liquidation of the Partnership is conducted as a members' voluntary winding-up in accordance with the provisions of the Insolvency Act 1986 (as amended by the Regulations) then:

(A)   the Members shall be entitled to be allocated such profits of the Partnership for the period from the commencement of the Accounting Reference Period in which the resolution for voluntary winding-up was passed to the date such resolution was passed to which they would have been entitled in accordance with clause 8 in calculating the entitlement of each Member);

(B)   the assets of the Partnership remaining after payment of its liabilities and any entitlement under clause 20.1(A) shall be applied in returning to the Members the amounts standing to the credit of their Capital Contribution Accounts and in the event that there are insufficient assets to return such amounts in full then the available assets shall be applied pro rata as between the Members in proportion to the amount standing to the credit of their respective Capital Contribution Accounts; and

(C)   the assets of the Partnership remaining after payment of its liabilities and any entitlements under clause 20.1(A) and 20.1(B) shall be distributed amongst the Members in the proportions in which they would be allocated profits in accordance with clause 8.

20.2   In the case of any other dissolution or liquidation of the Partnership the assets (if any) of the Partnership remaining after payment of its liabilities shall be distributed:

(A)   firstly in returning to the Members the amounts standing to the Capital Contribution Accounts and in the event that there are insufficient assets to return such amounts in full then the available assets shall be applied pro rata as between the Members in proportion to the amounts standing to the credit of their Capital Contribution Accounts; and

(B)   the remainder (if any) shall be distributed amongst the Members in the proportions in which they would be allocated profits of the Partnership in accordance with clause 8.

20.3   This Deed shall terminate forthwith if an effective resolution is passed to wind up the Partnership or if a liquidator is otherwise appointed, save in respect of any provisions contained herein which expressly survive the winding up of the Partnership (including for the avoidance of doubt, but without limitation, this clause 20).

21 Notices

21.1   Any notice to be given by any Member shall be in writing and shall be deemed to have been duly served if delivered personally or sent by facsimile or e-mail transmission or by pre-paid [first class/recorded delivery] post (or airmail or air courier in the case of an address for service outside the United Kingdom) to the addressee at its address (or number) for the receipt thereof specified below:

X	Postal Address	[ ]
	Facsimile Number	[ ]
	E-mail Address	[ ]
	For the attention of:	[ ]
Y	Postal Address	[ ]
	Facsimile Number	[ ]
	E-mail Address	[ ]
	For the attention of:	[ ]
[Z	Postal Address	[ ]
	Facsimile Number	[ ]
	E-mail Address	[ ]
	For the attention of:	[ ]]

or at any other address or number as the Member to be served has notified (in accordance with this clause 21.1).

21.2 A notice shall be deemed to have been duly served as follows:

    (A) where personally delivered, upon such delivery;

    (B) where sent by facsimile, when despatched subject to confirmation of uninterrupted transmission by a transmission report;

    (C) where sent by e-mail, where the e-mail leaves the e-mail gateway of the sender;

    (D) where sent by pre-paid post to an address in the United Kingdom, 48 hours after posting;

    (E) where sent by pre-paid airmail to an address outside the United Kingdom, five days after posting; and

    (F) where sent by air courier [2] Business Days after delivery to a representative of the courier.

21.3 In proving the service of any notice it shall be sufficient to prove:

    (A) in the case of a notice sent by post that such notice was properly addressed, stamped and placed in the post;

    (B) in the case of a notice personally delivered that it was delivered or left at the specified address;

    (C) in the case of a notice sent by facsimile that it was duly despatched to the specified number as confirmed by a transmission report;

    (D) in the case of a notice sent by e-mail that the e-mail left the e-mail gateway of the server of the notice; and

    (E) in the case of a notice sent by air courier that it was delivered to a representative of the courier.

22 Miscellaneous

22.1 This Deed constitutes the entire agreement between the Members and there are no other written or verbal agreements or representations with respect to the subject matter hereof.

22.2 This Deed shall enure for the benefit of the successors of the parties but shall not be assignable.

22.3 Each of the Members acknowledges and agrees that he has not entered into this Deed in reliance upon any representation, warranty or undertaking of any other Member or of the Partnership which is not expressly set out or referred to in this Deed.

22.4 If any provision of this Deed shall be held to be illegal, void, invalid or unenforceable under the Laws of any jurisdiction, the legality, validity and enforceability of the remainder of this Deed in that jurisdiction shall not be affected, and the legality, validity and enforceability of the whole of this Deed in any other jurisdiction shall not be affected.

22.5 No failure on the part of any Member to exercise, and no delay on its part in exercising, any right or remedy under this Deed shall operate as a waiver thereof, nor shall any single or partial exercise of any right or remedy preclude any other or further exercise thereof or the exercise of any other right or remedy. The rights and remedies provided in this Deed are cumulative and not exclusive of any rights or remedies provided by Law.

22.6 This Deed may be executed in one or more counterparts each of which shall be deemed an original, but all of which shall constitute one and the same document.

22.7 The Members each intend this Deed to be a deed and agree to execute and deliver it as a deed.

22.8 None of the default provisions set out in Regulations 7 and 8 of the Regulations (or any other such provision as is mentioned in section 5(1)(b) of the Act or as shall replace Regulations 7 and 8 which have substantially similar effect) shall apply to the Partnership or the mutual rights and duties of the Members.

23 Law and jurisdiction

23.1 This Deed and any non-contractual obligations arising from or connected with it shall be governed by English law and the Deed shall be construed in all respects in accordance with English law.

23.2 In relation to any legal action or proceedings to enforce this Deed or arising out of or in connection with it, whether arising out of or in connection with contractual or non-contractual obligations, (*'Proceedings'*) each Member irrevocably submits to the [exclusive/non-exclusive] jurisdiction of the English courts and waives any objection to Proceedings in such courts on the grounds of venue or on the grounds that the Proceedings have been brought in an inappropriate forum.

23.3 [*If non-exclusive*] [The submissions in clause 23.2 shall not affect the right of any Member to take Proceedings in any other jurisdiction to the extent permitted by law, nor shall the taking of Proceedings in any jurisdiction preclude any Member from taking Proceedings in any other jurisdiction.]

23.4 [ ] irrevocably appoints [ ] of [ ] as its process agent to receive on its behalf service of process of any proceedings in England. Service upon the process agent shall be good service upon [ ] whether or not it is forwarded to and received by [ ]. If, for any reason, the process agent ceases to be able to act as process agent, or no longer has an address in England, [ ] irrevocably agrees to appoint a substitute process agent with an address in England acceptable to the other parties and to deliver to each of them a copy of the substitute process agent's acceptance. In the event that [ ] fails to appoint a substitute process agent, it shall be effective service for any such party to serve the process upon the last known address in England of the last known process agent for [ ] notified to any such party notwithstanding that such process agent is no longer found at such address or has ceased to act [provided that a copy of the Proceedings is also sent to [ ]'s current registered office or principal place of business wherever situated.]

23.5   [*As an alternative to clause 23.4*] [ ] irrevocably consents to any process in any proceedings anywhere being served in accordance with the provisions of clause 21, relating to the service of notices. Such service shall become effective 30 days after despatch. Nothing contained in this Agreement shall affect the right to serve process in [the manner permitted by clause 23.4 or in] any other matter permitted by law.]

24 Contracts (Rights of Third Parties) Act 1999

No person who is not for the time being a party to this Deed shall have any right under the Contracts (Rights of Third Parties) Act 1999 to enforce any term of this Deed.

25 Unfair prejudice

The rights contained in s 994(1) of the Companies Act 2006 shall be excluded [for the period of 100 years from the date of incorporation of the Partnership].

IN WITNESS whereof the Members have executed this Deed as a deed the day and year first above written.

Schedule 1: draft form of deed of adherence

THIS DEED is made the [ ] day of [ ] 20[   ]

BETWEEN:

(1)   [ ], (the 'LLP'), a limited liability partnership incorporated in England and Wales under no [ ] and having its registered office at [ ]; and
(2)   [ ], (the 'Further Member'), of [ ], and in favour of [ ], [ ] and [ ] being the existing members of the LLP.

BACKGROUND:

(A)   By a Limited Liability Partnership Deed (the *'LLP Deed'*) dated [ ] [ ] 20[   ], the Members (as defined therein) agreed to regulate their relations as Members of the LLP.
(B)   The LLP is entering into this Deed for the benefit, and on behalf, of the Members of the LLP.
(C)   By Deed(s) dated [ ] [ ] 20[   ] [and [ ] [ ] 20[   ]] and made in substantially identical form to this Deed, [name(s) of prior Further Member(s)] became parties to the LLP Deed.]

IT IS HEREBY AGREED as follows:

1 Interpretation

Save where the context otherwise requires, the words and expressions used in this Deed shall have the meanings respectively assigned to them in the LLP Deed.

2 Adherence to Partnership

2.1   The Further Member covenants with the Members for the time being to observe and perform the terms and conditions of the LLP Deed on terms that the Further Member shall become a Further Member under the LLP Deed with effect from [   ].

2.2   The Further Member shall contribute £[   ] to the Partnership in cash forthwith upon the execution of this Deed pursuant to clause 7 of the LLP Deed.

2.3   This Deed shall be supplemental to and read together with the LLP Deed.

2.4   For the purposes of clause 21 of the LLP Deed, the address of the Further Member shall be [ ] subject to notification of a change of address by the Further Member to other Members in accordance with that clause.

2.5   The Further Member acknowledges and agrees that with effect from the date of this Deed the table set out in the schedule to this LLP Deed shall replace and supersede schedule 2 of the LLP Deed as in force immediately prior to the execution of this Deed. [The Further Member further acknowledges and agrees that his allocation of profits in accordance with the Agreement in respect of the Accounting Reference Period in which he becomes a Member (if any) shall be reduced pro rata to only reflect the part of such Accounting Reference Period during which he was a Member.]

IN WITNESS WHEREOF the parties have executed this Deed the day and year first above written.

The Schedule

[*Executed as a deed*]

Schedule 2: capital contributions, profit allocations, voting rights and rights to appoint board members

(1)	(2)	(3)	(4)	(5)
Name of Member	Capital contribution	Percentage of profit to which entitled	Number of votes exercisable in a meeting of the Members	Number of Board Members

Schedule 3: meetings of members

1   The Board or any of the Members may convene a meeting of the Members as and when it or he believes it to be necessary in accordance with the requirements of the Act, the Regulations or any other statutory provision applicable to the Partnership.

2   Not less than 14 clear days written notice of any meeting of the Members shall be given to all those entitled to attend and vote at such meeting, save that a meeting of the Members may be called at shorter notice than that specified in this paragraph 2 where a majority of the Members entitled to attend and vote at such meeting agree in writing that such meeting may take place at short notice.

3   The notice of a Members' meeting shall:

   (A)   specify the date, place and time of the meeting; and

   (B)   include an agenda indicating in general terms the business to be conducted.

4   Meetings of the Members shall be chaired by the Chairman of the Board or, in his absence, such Member as shall be appointed for the purpose by those present at the meeting.

5   The quorum for Members' meetings shall be [two] Members present in person or by communication equipment complying with paragraph 8 at the time when the relevant business is transacted. If a quorum is not present within half an hour of the time appointed for the meeting or ceases to be present, the Member(s) present shall adjourn the meeting to a specified place and time three Business Days after the original date. Notice of the adjourned meeting shall be given by those persons who adjourned the meeting. The quorum for any such adjourned Members' meeting shall be such Members as shall be present.

6   Any corporation which is a Member may by resolution of its directors or other governing body authorise such person as it thinks fit to act as its representative at any meeting of the Members and the person so authorised shall be entitled to exercise the same powers on behalf of the corporation which he represents as that corporation could exercise if it were an individual Member.

7   The accidental omission to give notice of any meeting of the Members to, or the non-receipt of any notice by, any Member entitled to receive notice shall not invalidate the proceedings of that meeting.

8   All or any of the Members may participate in a meeting of the Members by means of any communication equipment which allows all persons participating in the meeting to hear each other and to address all of

the other participants simultaneously. A person so participating shall be deemed to be present in person at the meeting and shall be entitled to be counted towards the quorum and to vote. Such a meeting shall be deemed to take place where the largest group of those participating is assembled or, if there is no such group, where the chairman of the meeting then is.

9   All Members entitled to attend and vote at any Members' meeting shall be entitled to the number of votes set opposite their names in the fourth column of schedule 2 and votes shall not be cast on the basis of a show of hands. Save as required by Law, at any meeting of the Members a decision may be taken by a simple majority.

10   A written resolution signed by or on behalf of each Member who would have been entitled to vote upon it had it been proposed at a meeting of the Members at which he was present shall be as valid and effectual as a resolution passed at a meeting of the Members duly convened and held and may consist of several documents in the like form each signed by one or more of such Members. In the case of a corporation, a written resolution may be signed on its behalf by a director or the secretary thereof or by its duly authorised representative.

11   Any Member who is at any time within any of the circumstances prescribed by s 7(1) of the Act shall have no entitlement to attend any meeting of the Members or have any vote at any such meeting and any reference to a resolution requiring to be signed by Members shall be deemed to exclude reference to signature by any such Member.

Index

Downloadable precedents

The precedents for this edition are available to download electronically from https://bloomsburyprofessionallaw.com/jointventures6.

They are password-protected and the password is 5MDH76.

They can be downloaded individually or in totality.

If you have any problems downloading the precedents or have any questions, please contact Bloomsbury Professional customer services on 01444 416119 or by email at customerservices@bloomsburyprofessional.com.

For a Licence agreement relating to the use of this Data, please see overleaf at p 752.

Licence agreement